# Frommer's

POSTCARDS FROM

# London 2005

W9-CZH-442

*Spanning the Thames River since 1894, the Tower Bridge is one of London's most photographed sights. You can ascend the towers for a panoramic view of the area. See chapter 7. © Wolfgang Kaehler Photography.*

*Enjoy the atmosphere, food, and drink at the many historic watering holes featured in The Best of London's Pubs: The World's Greatest Pub Crawl in chapter 9. Pubs and their fare are also described in chapter 6.* © Dave Bartruff Photography.

*Buckingham Palace, home of the Queen and site of the Changing of the Guard. See chapter 7.* © Chris Warren/International Stock.

*Big Ben, the world's most famous timepiece, is housed in the clock tower of the Houses of Parliament. The name "Big Ben" refers to the largest bell in the chime, which weighs almost 14 tons. See chapter 7.* © Andrea Pistolesi Photography.

*Hyde Park, with adjoining Kensington Gardens, is one of London's "green lungs," covering 615 acres, with velvety lawns, a lake for boating, and the famous Speakers Corner. See chapter 7. © Robert Holmes Photography.*

*A full English breakfast is a complete meal, with eggs, bread, meat, cereal, and plenty of coffee, tea, and juice to wash it all down. In chapter 5, we've noted which hotels include a full English or continental breakfast in their room rate. © Dave Bartruff Photography.*

*Theatergoers can watch plays performed as they were in Shakespeare's day at the Globe Theatre, a modern reconstruction of the original. See chapter 9.* © Kelly/Mooney Photography.

*The Yeoman Warders, "Beefeaters," keep watch at the Tower of London, where famous prisoners such as Anne Boleyn, Lady Jane Grey, and Sir Thomas More lost their lives. See chapter 7.* © Catherine Karnow Photography.

When Londoners speak of "the City," they mean the original square mile that's become the British version of Wall Street. © Lisl Dennis/The Image Bank.

Portobello Market was once known only for its produce (above), but is now a magnet for collectors of virtually anything, especially antiques (see facing page). See chapter 8.
© Jan Butchofsky-Houser/Houserstock, Inc. Photography; facing page © Kelly/Mooney Photography.

*Westminster Abbey, where English rulers have been crowned for a thousand years. See chapter 7.* © Kelly/Mooney Photography.

# Frommer's®

# London

## 2005

### by Darwin Porter & Danforth Prince

Here's what the critics say about Frommer's:

"Amazingly easy to use. Very portable, very complete."

*—Booklist*

"For the detail-demanding traveler."

*—Journal Star*

"Hotel information is close to encyclopedic."

*—Des Moines Sunday Register*

"Frommer's Guides have a way of giving you a real feel for a place."
*—Knight Ridder Newspapers*

WILEY

Wiley Publishing, Inc.

## About the Authors

As a team of veteran travel writers, **Darwin Porter** and **Danforth Prince** have produced numerous titles for Frommer's, including best-selling guides to Italy, France, the Caribbean, England, and Germany. Porter, a former bureau chief of *The Miami Herald,* is also a Hollywood biographer, his most recent releases entitled *The Secret Life of Humphrey Bogart* and *Katharine the Great,* the latter a close-up of the private life of the late Katharine Hepburn. Prince was formerly employed by the Paris bureau of the *New York Times,* and is today the president of Blood Moon Productions and other media-related firms.

Published by:

## Wiley Publishing, Inc.

111 River St.
Hoboken, NJ 07030-5774

ISBN 0-7645-6894-9

Editor: Christina Summers
Production Editor: Donna Wright
Cartographer: Nick Trotter
Photo Editor: Richard Fox
Production by Wiley Indianapolis Composition Services

Front cover photo: Hats and hatmaker at Lock's
Back cover photo: Houses of Parliament

For information on our other products and services or to obtain technical support, please contact our Customer Care Department within the U.S. at 800/762-2974, outside the U.S. at 317/572-3993 or fax 317/572-4002.

Wiley also publishes its books in a variety of electronic formats. Some content that appears in print may not be available in electronic formats.

Manufactured in the United States of America

5   4   3   2   1

# Contents

# List of Maps

## An Invitation to the Reader

In researching this book, we discovered many wonderful places—hotels, restaurants, shops, and more. We're sure you'll find others. Please tell us about them, so we can share the information with your fellow travelers in upcoming editions. If you were disappointed with a recommendation, we'd love to know that, too. Please write to:

*Frommer's London* 2005
Wiley Publishing, Inc. • 111 River St. • Hoboken, NJ 07030-5774

## An Additional Note

Please be advised that travel information is subject to change at any time—and this is especially true of prices. We therefore suggest that you write or call ahead for confirmation when making your travel plans. The authors, editors, and publisher cannot be held responsible for the experiences of readers while traveling. Your safety is important to us, however, so we encourage you to stay alert and be aware of your surroundings. Keep a close eye on cameras, purses, and wallets, all favorite targets of thieves and pickpockets.

## Other Great Guides for Your Trip:

*Frommer's Irreverent London*

*Frommer's Memorable Walks in London*

*The Unofficial Guide to London*

*London For Dummies*

*Suzy Gershman's Born to Shop London*

*Frommer's Best Day Trips from London:
25 Great Escapes by Train Bus or Car*

## Frommer's Star Ratings, Icons & Abbreviations

Every hotel, restaurant, and attraction listing in this guide has been ranked for quality, value, service, amenities, and special features using a **star-rating system.** In country, state, and regional guides, we also rate towns and regions to help you narrow down your choices and budget your time accordingly. Hotels and restaurants are rated on a scale of zero (recommended) to three stars (exceptional). Attractions, shopping, nightlife, towns, and regions are rated according to the following scale: zero stars (recommended), one star (highly recommended), two stars (very highly recommended), and three stars (must-see).

In addition to the star-rating system, we also use **seven feature icons** that point you to the great deals, in-the-know advice, and unique experiences that separate travelers from tourists. Throughout the book, look for:

| | |
|---|---|
| **Finds** | Special finds—those places only insiders know about |
| **Fun Fact** | Fun facts—details that make travelers more informed and their trips more fun |
| **Kids** | Best bets for kids and advice for the whole family |
| **Moments** | Special moments—those experiences that memories are made of |
| **Overrated** | Places or experiences not worth your time or money |
| **Tips** | Insider tips—great ways to save time and money |
| **Value** | Great values—where to get the best deals |

The following **abbreviations** are used for credit cards:

| | | | | | |
|---|---|---|---|---|---|
| AE | American Express | DISC | Discover | V | Visa |
| DC | Diners Club | MC | MasterCard | | |

## Frommers.com

Now that you have the guidebook to a great trip, visit our website at **www.frommers.com** for travel information on more than 3,000 destinations. With features updated regularly, we give you instant access to the most current trip-planning information available. At Frommers.com, you'll also find the best prices on airfares, accommodations, and car rentals—and you can even book travel online through our travel booking partners. At Frommers.com, you'll also find the following:

- Online updates to our most popular guidebooks
- Vacation sweepstakes and contest giveaways
- Newsletter highlighting the hottest travel trends
- Online travel message boards with featured travel discussions

# What's New in London

London is the most volatile and ever-changing city in Europe. "The scene" is constantly shifting. Here are some of the latest developments:

**ACCOMMODATIONS** For those frugal travelers, a new discovery is the **Ashburn Hotel,** 111 Cromwell Rd., SW7 (© **020/7370-3321**), in the Royal Borough of Kensington. Within walking distance of such major attractions as Kensington Palace (former home of Princess Di), it is old-fashioned yet comfortably up-to-date. And in pricey London, its charges are most affordable.

**St. George Hotel,** 49 Gloucester Place, W1 (© **020/7486-8586**), has been recently restored and is now offering visitors an affordable yet central choice a short walk from Oxford and Baker streets. Furnishings are of a high quality, and the comfort is first rate.

**DINING** A forever swank address in Knightsbridge, **The Berkeley,** Wilton Place, SW1 (© **020/7950-5490**), is experiencing rebirth with the opening of not one, but two, world-class restaurants. Hailed as London's greatest chef today, Gordon Ramsay is the guiding force behind the less grand and somewhat whimsical Boxwood Café. For more formal and elegant dining—and more expensive—Marcus Wareing, hailed as one of the rising new chefs of England, operates the Pétrus.

Visitors to "The City," the business district of London, are flocking to a new and fashionable brasserie and brewery, **Pacific Oriental,** 1 Bishops Gate, EC2 (© **020/7621-9988**), serving a Pacific Rim cuisine. Its location is only a 10-minute walk from Liverpool Street. Market-fresh produce combined with the restaurant's own brew make this an ideal choice to feast on Asian cuisine, mainly Thai-influenced.

Garnering the most publicity in 2003 was a restaurant called **Fifteen,** 15 Westland Place, N1 (© **020/7251-1515**), serving British and Continental cuisine. Jamie Oliver, author of *The Naked Chef,* caused a media blitz when he opened his place—touted on the Food Network. He takes what he calls "disadvantaged" youths and turns them into chefs almost overnight. Far from culinary disasters, London's food critics continue to heap high praise on the viands dished up here.

As fashionable London pushes into the East End, **Eyre Brothers,** 70 Leonard St., EC16 (© **020/7613-5346**), is all the rage in trendy Shoreditch. The cuisine, surprisingly, is Portuguese. The chef is inspired by frequent visits to Portugal itself, and many of the dishes were also based on recipes from former Portuguese colonies in Africa.

Long a London dining legend, the **Savoy Restaurant,** in the Savoy Hotel, the Strand, WC2 (© **020/7592-1600**), has made a comeback with a brightened decor and a modern menu of alluring taste, created by Marcus Wareing, one of the country's premier chefs. The modern British cuisine served here has never been better, and once again, celebrities, among others, are making "supper at the Savoy" a hot ticket.

The once staid restaurant at the Savoy's competitor, the Connaught Hotel, has also made a comeback. **Menu,** 16 Carlos Place, W1 (℃ **020/ 7592-1222**), is under the domain of a female chef, Angela Hartnett, and she has breathed new life and exciting tastes into the revised menu here. The dining room is also considerably brightened under Nina Campbell's decorating.

In chic Knightsbridge, Britain's wonder chef, Marco Pierre White, has taken over the once famous **Drones,** 1 Pont St., SW1 (℃ **020/7259-6166**). The place had gone stale, but not any more. The Continental cuisine served here is light, sophisticated, and delicately prepared. A trendy crowd, often celebrities, is showing up at the doorstep.

The best for last. The hottest new dining ticket in London today is **Sketch,** 9 Conduit St., W1 (℃ **0870/ 777-4488**), a sensation ever since it was inaugurated in 2003. Food, art, and music are artfully harmonized in the various venues open to you here. Wear your most fashionable young attire and be prepared for "a happening."

**EXPLORING Tate Britain,** Milbank SW1 (℃ **020/7887-8000**), and the **Tate Modern,** Bankside SE1 (℃ **020/7887-8008**), on opposite sides of the Thames River, are now linked by a "Tate to Tate boat" (℃ **020/7887-8888**), taking art lovers from one stellar museum to the other. Long the residence of the late Queen Mother, **Clarence House,** Stable Yard Gate, SW1 (℃ **020/7766-7303**), has now opened its doors to the public. The John Nash–designed mansion has been restored and is now the official residence of the Prince of Wales.

In 2003, nine more underground **Cabinet War Rooms,** Clive Steps, SW1 (℃ **020/7930-6961**), were restored and opened to the public for the first time. Churchill, his family, and key staff members rode out some of the worst of World War II's Nazi blitzkrieg in these bunkerlike rooms. Newly opened are Churchill's kitchen and dining room and Mrs. Churchill's bedroom.

London's newest museum is the **Fashion & Textile Museum,** 83 Bermondsey St., SE1 (℃ **020/7403- 0222**), on the south bank of the Thames River. A Mexican architect took a warehouse and converted it into this vibrant museum, the first of its kind in the United Kingdom devoted to textiles and contemporary fashion. It's all here, including some of the more daring apparel from London of the "Swinging Sixties."

**SHOPPING** New outlets selling top-quality merchandise keep opening in London. One of the finest of these is **Emmet,** 380 King's Rd. SW3 (℃ **020/ 7351-7529**), selling one of the best selections of shirts in town. Shirt styles are sold in limited editions of about two dozen each. One of the most delightful discoveries is **The Couverture Shop,** 310 King's Rd., SW3 (℃ **020/7795-1200**), which is like an emporium of the unexpected, placing an emphasis on "bedroom must-haves."

# 1

# The Best of London

The British capital is more eclectic and electric than it's been in years. *Newsweek* hailed London as a "hip compromise between the nonstop newness of Los Angeles and the aspic-preserved beauty of Paris—sharpened to New York's edge." *Wine Spectator* proclaims more modestly: "The sun is shining brighter in London these days."

The sounds of Brit-pop and techno pour out of Victorian pubs; experimental theater is popping up on stages built for Shakespeare's plays; upstart chefs are reinventing the bland dishes that British mums have made for generations; and Brits are even running the couture houses of Dior and Givenchy. In food, fashion, film, music, and just about everything else, London, as it moves deeper into the 21st century, stands at the cutting edge again, just as it did in the 1960s.

If this sea of change worries you more than it appeals to you, rest assured that traditional London survives, basically intact under the veneer of hip. This ancient city has withstood a thousand years of invasion, from the Normans to the Blitz, so a few hipsters aren't going to change anything fundamental. From high tea at Brown's to the Changing of the Guard at Buckingham Palace, the city still abounds with the culture and charm of days gone by.

Discovering London and making it your own can be a bit of a challenge, especially if you have limited time. Even in the 18th century, Daniel Defoe found London "stretched out in buildings, straggling, confused, out of all shape, uncompact and unequal; neither long nor broad, round nor square." The actual City of London proper is 1 square mile (2.6 sq. km) of very expensive real estate around the Bank of England. All of the gargantuan rest of the city is made up of separate villages, boroughs, and corporations—each with its own mayor and administration. Together, however, they add up to a mammoth metropolis.

Luckily, whether you're looking for Dickens's house or hot designer Vivienne Westwood's flagship store, only the heart of London's huge territory need concern you. The core of London is one of the most fascinating places on earth. With every step, you'll feel the tremendous influence this city once exerted over global culture when it had an empire on which the sun never set.

London is a mass of contradictions. On the one hand, it's a decidedly royal city, studded with palaces, court gardens, coats of arms, and other regal paraphernalia, yet it's also the home of the world's second-oldest parliamentary democracy. (Iceland was the first.)

Today, London has grown less English and more international. The gent with the bowler hat has long gone out of fashion; today's Londoner might have a turban, a Mohawk, or even a baseball cap. It's becoming easier to find a café au lait and a croissant than a scone and a cup of tea. The city is home to thousands of immigrants and refugees, both rich and poor, from all reaches of the world.

# Central London

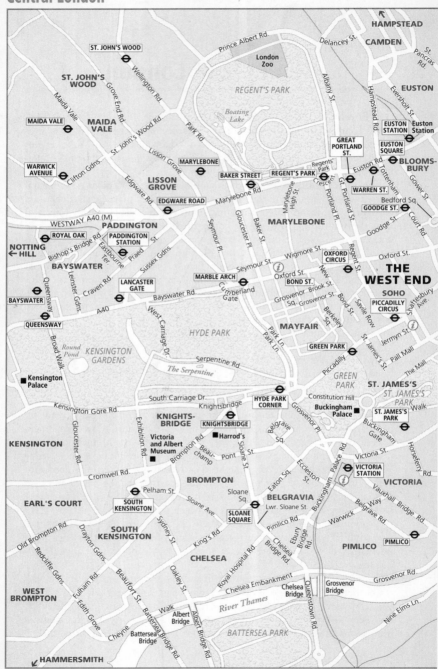

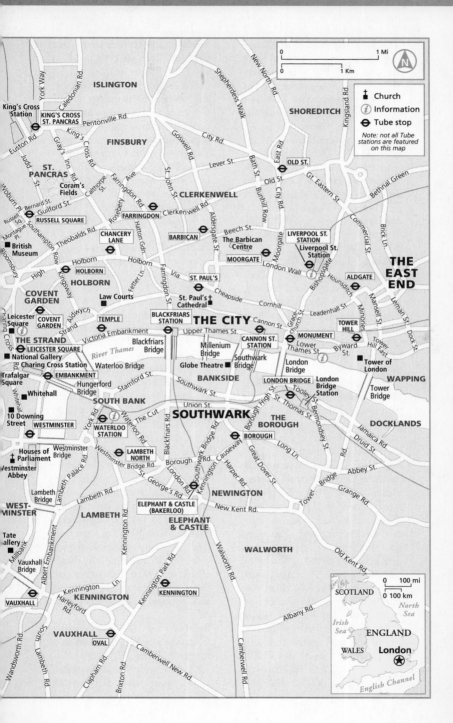

## 1 Frommer's Favorite London Experiences

- **Watching the Sunset at Waterloo Bridge:** This is the ideal place for watching the sun set over Westminster. You can see the last rays of light bounce off the dome of St. Paul's and the spires in the East End. See chapter 4.

- **Enjoying a Traditional Afternoon Tea:** At The Ritz hotel, the tea ritual carries on as it did in Britain's heyday. You could invite the queen of England herself here for a "cuppa." The pomp and circumstance of the British Empire live on here—only the Empire is missing. See p. 107.

- **Cruising London's Waterways:** In addition to the Thames, London has an antique canal system, with towpath walks, bridges, and wharves. Replaced by the railroad as the prime means of transportation, the canal system remained forgotten until it was rediscovered by a new generation. Now undergoing a process of urban renewal, the old system has been restored, with bridges painted and repaired, and paths cleaned up, for you to enjoy. See "River Cruises Along the Thames," in chapter 7.

- **Spending Sunday Morning at Speakers Corner:** At the northeast corner of Hyde Park, a British tradition carries on. Speakers sound off on any subject, and "in-your-face" hecklers are part of the fun. You might hear anything from denunciations of the monarchy to anti-gay rhetoric. Anyone can get up and speak. The only rules: You can't blaspheme, be obscene, or incite a riot. The tradition began in 1855—before the legal right to assembly was guaranteed in 1872—when a mob of 150,000 gathered to attack a proposed Sunday Trading Bill. See p. 253.

- **Studying the Turners at the Tate Britain:** When he died in 1851, J. M. W. Turner bequeathed his collection of 19,000 watercolors and some 300 paintings to the people of Britain. He wanted his finished works, about 100 paintings, displayed under one roof. Today, you see not only the paintings, but glimpses of Turner's beloved Thames through the museum's windows. The artist lived and died on the river's banks and painted its many changing moods. See p. 216.

- **Strolling Through Covent Garden:** George Bernard Shaw got his inspiration for *Pygmalion* here, where the Cockney lass who inspired the character of Eliza Doolittle sold violets to wealthy opera-goers. The old market, with its cauliflower peddlers and butchers in blood-soaked aprons, is long gone. What's left is London's best example of urban renewal and one of its hippest shopping districts. In the footsteps of Chippendale and Dickens, you can discover colorful street stalls, boutiques, and shops selling one-of-a-kind items, and enjoy some of the city's best sidewalk entertainment. There's an antiques market on Monday and a crafts market Tuesday through Saturday. See p. 292 for market details. When you're parched, there are plenty of pubs to quench your thirst, including the **Nag's Head** (p. 312), an Edwardian pub that'll serve you a draft Guinness and a plate of pork cooked in cider.

- **Rowing on the Serpentine:** When the weather's right, we head to Hyde Park's 17-hectare (42-acre) man-made lake dating from 1730, whose name derives from its winding, snakelike shape. At the Boathouse, you can rent boats by the hour. It's an idyllic way to spend a sunny afternoon. Renoir must have agreed; he depicted the custom on canvas. See p. 253.

- **Making a Brass Rubbing:** Take home some costumed ladies and knights in armor from England's age of chivalry. Make your very own brass rubbing in the crypt of St. Martin-in-the-Fields in Trafalgar Square; the staff there will be happy to show you how. See p. 229.

- **Getting to Know North London on a Sunday:** Begin by looking for some smart fashion at **Camden Market** (p. 293), a Sunday event on Camden High Street where stallholders hawk designer jewelry and clothing. Next, walk up to Hampstead Heath off Well Walk and take the right fork, which leads to an open field with a panoramic view of London. Cap your jaunt with a visit to the **Freud Museum** (p. 258), open on Sunday until 5pm. See "Attractions on the Outskirts," in chapter 7, for more information on North London.

- **Dining at Rules:** Rules, at 35 Maiden Lane, WC2, was established as an oyster bar in 1798; it may be the oldest restaurant in London. Long a venue for the theatrical elite and literary beau monde, it still serves the same dishes that delighted Edward VII and his mistress, Lillie Langtry, who began their meals with champagne and oysters upstairs. Charles Dickens had a regular table. Over the years, everyone from William Thackeray to Clark Gable has enjoyed Rules' pheasant and grouse. And where else can you get a good purée of parsnips these days? If you're looking for an old-fashioned British dessert, finish off with the treacle sponge or apple suet pudding. See p. 159.

- **Spending an Evening at the Theater:** London is the theatrical capital of the world. The live stage offers a unique combination of variety, accessibility, and economy— and maybe a look at next season's Broadway hit. See "The Play's the Thing: London's Theater Scene," in chapter 9.

- **Crawling the London Pubs:** Americans barhop; Londoners pub-crawl. With some 5,000 pubs within the city limits, you would certainly be crawling if you tried to have a drink in each of them! We have suggested the traditional pubs that we think will make a worthwhile crawl. While making the rounds, you can partake of that quintessentially British fare known as "pub grub," which could be anything from a ploughman's lunch (a hunk of bread, cheese, and a pickle) to shepherd's pie to nouveau British cuisine. Today, in the right places, some of that pub grub tastes better than the fare served in many restaurants. Our favorite crawl gives you a chance to see several London districts. Begin at **Ye Olde Cheshire Cheese** (p. 150), Wine Office Court, 145 Fleet St., EC4, before heading to **Cittie of Yorke** (p. 308), 22–23 High Holborn, WC1. Have a pint in the heart of the West End at the **Red Lion** (p. 313), 2 Duke of York St., SW1. If you're still standing, rush to **Shepherd's Tavern** (p. 313), 50 Hertford St., W1, in Mayfair, before the publican rings the bell for "final call." See our pick of London's best pubs under "The Best of London's Pubs: The World's Greatest Pub Crawl," in chapter 9.

## 2 Best Hotel Bets

London is home to some of the finest hotels in the world (and some of the priciest). Happily, there are good, affordable options as well.

- **Best in the East End:** The first luxury hotel to be built in Holborn, **Renaissance London Chancery Court,** 252 High Holborn, WC1 (© **020/7829-9888**), has become an instant hit. A 1914 landmark building has been stunningly transformed into this citadel of luxury and plush comfort. See p. 93.
- **Best for a Romantic Getaway:** The hip couple of today checks into the **Covent Garden Hotel,** 10 Monmouth St., WC2 (© **020/ 7806-1000**), which has been hailed as 1 of the 25 hottest places to stay in the world. The former hospital is now the epitome of chic and comfort, with rooms that are so elegant and stylish that romance is inevitable. See p. 99.
- **Best Historic Hotel:** Founded by the former manservant to Lord Byron, the stylish **Brown's Hotel,** 30 Albemarle St., W1 (© **020/ 7493-6020**), dates back to Victorian times. It's one of London's most genteel hotels, with its legendary afternoon tea and paneled bar. See p. 103.
- **Best for Business Travelers:** Wheelers and dealers head to **The Langham Hilton,** 1C Portland Place, W1 (© **020/7636-1000**), Hilton's flagship hotel in Europe, which boasts sleek styling and grand public rooms. At times, it seems that all the world's business is conducted from this nerve center. See p. 124.
- **Best Trendy Hotel: St. Martins Lane,** 45 St. Martin's Lane (© **020/7300-5500**), is almost without challenge in this category. Ian Schrager has brought New York cutting-edge style to a 1960s

building in Covent Garden. It's his first hotel outside the U.S., and it's eccentric, irreverent, and whimsical. Would Madonna go anywhere else? See p. 100.
- **Best Lobby for Pretending You're Rich: The Dorchester,** 53 Park Lane, W1 (© **020/7629-8888**), has a long promenade with London's largest floral display and rows of faux-marble columns with ornate gilt capitals. Even if you can't afford to stay at this citadel of luxury, come by for the traditional afternoon tea. See p. 104.
- **Best Quirky Hotel: The Rookery,** 12 Peter's Lane, Cowcross St., EC1 (© **020/7336-0931**), is eccentric but fun, loaded with atmosphere, and lures some of London's most discerning visitors. Its individually decorated rooms offer charm and comfort; the bathrooms retain their Victorian cast-iron fittings. The owners combed London's antiques stores and flea markets to create the decor. See p. 89.
- **Best Grande Dame:** The **Sheraton Park Lane Hotel,** Piccadilly, W1 (© **020/7499-6321**), evokes the grand old days of debutante balls. Suites still have their 1920s styling and Art Deco bathrooms. Parts of *Brideshead Revisited* were filmed here. See p. 105.
- **Best Quintessentially English Hotel: Durrants Hotel,** George Street, W1 (© **020/7935-8131**), established in 1789, is often called "the poor man's Brown's" (see the review of Brown's, p. 103). A soothing retreat, it's been run by the Miller family for a century. They have joined several houses into a unified Georgian hotel. Stay here for charm and comfort, not grand style. See p. 125.
- **Best for Showing Off:** Anouska Hempel's luxurious **Blake's Hotel,** 33 Roland Gardens, SW7

(© 020/7370-6701), is personal-ized, elegant, and fun, with beauti-ful bathrooms in marble, opulent accessories, and a restaurant packed with London glitterati. Wait until after your stay to worry about how much you spent. See p. 122.

- **Best for Thoroughly British Ambience:** In a gas-lit courtyard in back of St. James's Palace, **Dukes Hotel,** 35 St. James's Place, SW1 (© 020/7491-4840), has an unsur-passed dignity. From the bread-and-butter pudding served in the clubby dining room to the impec-cable service, at Dukes there will always be an England. See p. 107.

- **Best Modern Design: The Hempel,** 31–35 Craven Hill Garden Sq., W2 (© 020/7298-9000), might be housed in a trio of 1800s row houses, but the ren-ovations by designer Anouska Hempel are purely modern. A grand Italian sense of proportion is balanced with Asian simplicity, and soothing monochromatic tones prevail. See p. 130.

- **Best Re-creation of an English Country House:** Tim and Kit Kemp are hoteliers with charm, taste, and sophistication. They combined two Georgian town houses into the **Dorset Square Hotel,** 39–40 Dorset Sq., NW1 (© 020/7723-7874), creating an English country house in the heart of the city. Gilt-framed paintings, antiques, tapestry cushions, and marble bathrooms make you feel warm, cozy, and refined. See p. 125.

- **Best Service: 22 Jermyn Street,** 22 Jermyn St., SW1 (© 020/7734-2353), does more for its guests than any other hotel in London. The owner has outfitted a room on the sixth floor with a superbly equipped computer cen-ter, which guests are free to use. He also informs you of the hottest

and newest restaurants, along with old favorites, the best shopping, and even what's hot in theater. The staff won't deny any reasonable request—they even grant some unreasonable ones. See p. 108.

- **Best Location:** Creaky, quirky **Fielding Hotel,** 4 Broad Court, Bow Street, WC2 (© 020/7836-8305), is hardly London's finest hotel, but oh, the location! It's in an alleyway in the center of Covent Garden, in the heart of the excitement of London, almost opposite the Royal Opera House, with pubs, shops, markets, restau-rants, even street entertainment, right outside your door. Stay here, and London is at your fingertips. See p. 101.

- **Best Health Club & Pool: The Savoy,** the Strand, WC2 (© 020/7836-4343), has a health club and large swimming pool atop the historic Savoy Theatre, overlook-ing the heart of London. It's the best gym in central London; the views make it extra special. There's a massage room, plus state-of-the-art health and beauty treatments. See p. 100.

- **Best Boutique Hotel: The Beau-fort,** 33 Beaufort Gardens, SW3 (© 020/7584-5252), is a gem that's sure to charm. Personal serv-ice and tranquillity combine for a winning choice, a private but not snobbish place 200 yards from the famed Harrods Department Store. Even longtime patrons of Clar-idge's and The Dorchester have deserted those bastions of luxury to check into The Beaufort. See p. 115.

- **Best Small Hotel:** Housed in three historic homes on Soho Square, **Hazlitt's 1718,** 6 Frith St., W1 (© 020/7434-1771), was a fashionable address 2 centuries ago—and is again today. One of London's best small hotels, it's a favorite with artists, actors, media people, and models. Many bedrooms boast four-poster beds. See p. 103.

• **Best Moderately Priced Hotel:** In the heart of Bloomsbury, you can find cozy charm at the attractively priced **Morgan Hotel,** 24 Bloomsbury St., WC1 (✆ **020/ 7636-3735**), which occupies a row of 1790s Georgian houses. Warmth and hospitality await you in accommodations overlooking the British Museum. See p. 113.

• **Best Inexpensive Hotel:** In this price category, it's hard to be chic, but **The Pavilion Hotel,** 34–36 Sussex Gardens, W2 (✆ **020/ 7262-0905**), manages to do it. Known for its bedrooms' wacky themes, this theatrical and slightly outrageous hotel attracts models and music-industry folks. Rooms range in decor from "Oriental Bordello" to "Honky-Tonk Afro." See p. 132.

• **Best for Families Who Don't Want to Break the Bank: The Colonnade Town House,** 2 Warrington Crescent, W9 (✆ **020/7286-1052**), stands in the canal-laced Little Venice section. This family-friendly hotel lets children under 12 stay free in their parents' room. The staff can also arrange babysitting. This residential area of London is safe at night, with tree-lined avenues leading down to a canal. It's got a real neighborhood feel to it. See p. 135.

• **Best B&B:** For 2 years in a row (2001 and 2002), **Aster House,** 3 Sumner Place, SW7 (✆ **020/ 7581-5888**), has won the London Tourism Award for the city's best B&B. A friendly, inviting, welcoming place, it's safely tucked away on a tree-lined street in the heart of South Kensington. See p. 118.

• **Best for Value:** In the Royal Borough of Kensington, **Ashburn Hotel,** 111 Cromwell Rd., SW7 (✆ **020/7370-3321**), is cozy and old-fashioned, yet comfortably up-to-date. For such a convenient location, close to Kensington Palace, it is a most affordable choice. See p. 120.

## 3 Best Dining Bets

London's restaurant scene is booming. What follows is a sampling of the city's best restaurants, in enough categories for us to name our favorites:

• **Best Chef of the Year:** London's hottest chef is now installed at the city's most prestigious hotel, at **Gordon Ramsay at Claridge's,** Brook Street, W1 (✆ **020/7499-0099**). Ramsay's modern European menu delights the senses. See p. 172.

• **Best Newcomer:** The author of *The Naked Chef,* Jamie Oliver, is creating a media blitz with the opening of **Fifteen,** 15 Westland Place, N1 (✆ **020/7251-1515**), which has been featured on the *Food Network.* He takes disadvantaged young people, trains them

to be skilled chefs, and Fifteen's cuisine has won the praise of some of London's toughest food critics. See p. 151.

• **Best Place for a Business Lunch:** Impress your clients by taking them to **Poons in the City,** 2 Minster Pavement, Minster Court, Mincing Lane, EC3 (✆ **020/7626-0126**). This famous Chinese restaurant is outfitted with furniture and accessories from China, and the menu is wide-ranging. After a taste of the finely chopped wind-dried meats or the crispy aromatic duck, it'll be a snap to seal the deal. See p. 149.

• **Best Spot for a Celebration:** There's no spot in all of London that's more fun than **Quaglino's,**

16 Bury St., SW1 (✆ **020/7930-6767**), which serves up Continental cuisine. On some nights, as many as 800 diners show up at Sir Terence Conran's gargantuan Mayfair eatery. It's the best place in London to celebrate almost any occasion—and the food's good, too. There's live jazz on Friday and Saturday nights. See p. 179.

- **Best Wine List:** The renowned wine list at the **Tate Gallery Restaurant,** in the Tate Gallery, Millbank, SW1 (✆ **020/7887-8825**), reads like a "who's who" of famous French châteaux. Plus, the Tate offers the city's best bargains on fine wines; management keeps the markups between 40% and 65%, instead of the 100% to 200% that most restaurants add per bottle. See p. 180.

- **Best for Value:** Called the market leader in cafe salons, **Veronica's,** 3 Hereford Rd., W2 (✆ **020/7229-5079**), serves not only some of the best traditional British fare, but also some of the most affordable. Many of the chef's recipes are based on medieval or Tudor culinary secrets, and some even go back to the days of the conquering Romans. See p. 196.

- **Best Modern British Cuisine:** In a former smokehouse just north of Smithfield Market, **St. John,** 26 St. John St., EC1 (✆ **020/7251-0848**), serves a modern interpretation of British cuisine like none other in town. The chefs here believe in using offal (those parts of the animal that are usually discarded)—after all, why use just parts of the animal when you can use it all? Although some diners are a bit squeamish at first, they're usually hooked once they get past the first bite. Book ahead of time. See p. 150.

- **Best Traditional British Cuisine:** There is no restaurant in London

that's quite as British as **Simpson's-in-the-Strand,** 100 the Strand, WC2 (✆ **020/7836-9112**), which has been serving the finest English roast beef since 1828. Henry VIII, were he to return, would surely pause for a feast here. This place is such a British institution that you'll think they invented roast saddle of mutton. See p. 159.

- **Best for Kids:** The owner, the Earl of Bradford, feeds you well and affordably at **Porter's English Restaurant,** 17 Henrietta St., WC2 (✆ **020/7836-6466**). Kids of all ages dig Lady Bradford's once secretly guarded recipe for banana-and-ginger pudding, along with the most classic English pies served in Central London, including such old-fashioned favorites as lamb and apricot; and ham, leek, and cheese. See p. 160.

- **Best Continental Cuisine: Le Gavroche,** 43 Upper Brook St., W1 (✆ **020/7408-0881**), was one of the first London restaurants to serve the modern French approach to cuisine, and it's lost none of its appeal. If you want to know why, order *pigeonneau de Bresse en vessie aux deux celeris:* The whole bird is presented at your table, enclosed in a pig's bladder; the pigeon is removed, and then carved and served on a bed of braised fennel and celery. Trust us—it's fabulous. See p. 172.

- **Best Indian Cuisine:** London's finest Indian food is served at **Cafe Spice Namaste,** in a landmark Victorian hall near Tower Bridge, 16 Prescot St., E1 (✆ **020/7488-9242**). You'll be tantalized by an array of spicy southern and northern Indian dishes. We like the cuisine's Portuguese influence; the chef, Cyrus Todiwala, is from Goa (a Portuguese territory absorbed by India), where he learned many of his culinary secrets. See p. 147.

- **Best Italian Cuisine:** At **Zafferano,** 15 Lowndes St., SW1 (© **020/ 7235-5800**), master chefs prepare delectable cuisine with ingredients that conjure up the Mediterranean shores. The most refined palates of Knightsbridge come to this chic, rustic trattoria for refined dishes like pheasant and black-truffle ravioli with rosemary. See p. 184.
- **Best Innovative Cuisine:** Irish chef Richard Corrigan brings sophisticated modern British cuisine to **Lindsay House,** 21 Romilly St., W1 (© **020/7439- 0450**). The menu depends on what looks good at the daily market combined with the chef's inspiration for the day. When you sample his breast of wood pigeon with foie gras and pumpkin chutney, you'll want to kidnap him for your kitchen. See p. 165.
- **Best View:** From the terrace of **The Bridge,** 1 Paul's Walk, EC4 (© **020/7236-0000**), next to the Millennium Bridge, the panoramic view encompasses a vista of the Thames that stretches from Shakespeare's Globe Theatre to the Tate Modern. The modern British cooking is good, too. See p. 146.
- **Best for Spotting Celebrities: Archipelago,** 110 Whitfield St., W1 (© **020/7383-3346**), is small and intimate, a cozy retreat for Hugh Hefner and the other celebs in London. Media headliner Michael Von Hruschka runs this Thai and French restaurant with whimsy and many precious touches, such as a drink list inserted in an ostrich eggshell. But the cuisine doesn't depend on gimmicks. It's first-rate both in ingredients and preparation. See p. 155.
- **Best Seafood: Back to Basics,** 21A Foley St., W1 (© **020/7436- 2181**), is no fish-and-chips joint.

Stefan Plaumer's Fitzrovia bistro serves some of the freshest seafood in town. You name it: broiled, grilled, baked, or poached; anything except fried—and the chefs will cook the fish to your specifications. An array of delicacies from the sea awaits you here, from plump, tasty mussels to sea bass given an extra zing with chili oil. See p. 158.

- **Best Wine-Bar Food: Cork & Bottle Wine Bar,** 44–46 Cranbourn St., WC2 (© **020/7734- 7807**), serves the best wine-bar food in London. The raised ham-and-cheese pie alone is worth the trek across town—it's hardly your typical quiche. Also try the Mediterranean prawns with garlic and asparagus, or the lamb in ale. The wine selection is superb, with a strong emphasis on selections from Australia. See p. 163.
- **Best Cantonese Cuisine: Fung Shing,** 15 Lisle St., WC2 (© **020/ 7437-1539**), is a culinary landmark, serving the finest Cantonese cuisine in London, both traditional and innovative. The seasonal specials are the way to go. Stewed duck with yam, tender ostrich in yellow-bean sauce, and a delectable whole sea bass are some of the delicious treats. See p. 161.
- **Best Late-Night Dining: Atlantic Bar & Grill,** 20 Glasshouse St., W1 (© **020/7734-4888**), is a Titanic restaurant installed in a former Art Deco ballroom off Piccadilly Circus. Modern British cuisine, with an emphasis on organic and homegrown products, is served in a cosmopolitan atmosphere until 3am Monday through Saturday. See p. 166.
- **Best Japanese Cuisine:** Robert De Niro and his gang have generated much excitement about **Nobu,** in the Metropolitan Hotel, 19 Old Park Lane, W1 (© **020/7447-4747**).

The sushi chefs create gastronomic pyrotechnics with their raw dishes. See p. 173.

- **Best Trendy Restaurant:** Following chic and trendy London as it moves east to Shoreditch, **Les Trois Garçons,** 1 Club Row, E1 (© 020/7613-1924), attracts fashionable young London after dark. In an amusingly kitschy setting, it is known for its first-rate French cuisine. See p. 151.

- **Best for People-Watching:** The decades come and go, but **The Ivy,** 1 West St., WC2 (© 020/7836-4751), remains a favorite of theatrical luminaries. Noel Coward and Vivien Leigh have given up their tables to the likes of Nicole Kidman and Nicholas Cage. The modern British and international cuisine remains as reliable as ever. See p. 162.

- **Best Afternoon Tea:** The most fashionable place in London to order afternoon tea is the **Ritz Palm Court,** in The Ritz hotel, Piccadilly, W1 (© 020/7493-8181). If you're a woman, dress as if you were the late Queen Mother. Men would do well to dress as Noel Coward in 1937. You've got to make those reservations, though, way, way in advance. See p. 200.

- **Best Pretheater Dining:** Opposite the Ambassador Theatre, **The Ivy,** 1 West St., WC2 (© 020/7836-4751), is popular for both pre- and après-theater dining. The brasserie-style food reflects English and modern Continental influences. Try favorites such as potted shrimp or tripe and onions, or imaginative dishes like butternut pumpkin salad or wild-mushroom risotto. See p. 162.

- **Best Picnic Fare:** For a picnic fit for a queen, go to **Fortnum & Mason,** 181 Piccadilly, W1 (© 020/7734-8040), the world's most famous grocery store. You'll find an array of foodstuffs to take away to your favorite park. See p. 276.

## 4 The Best Pubs

- **Fox and Anchor,** 115 Charterhouse St., EC1 (© 020/7253-5075), is a favorite among early-morning pub crawlers and club trawlers who fancy a pint and a bite to start (or end) the day. The array of breakfast goodies is "gut-busting"—everything from black pudding to fried bread and baked beans. After the "full house" breakfast here (including at least eight breakfast items, such as sausage or black pudding), you won't be ready to eat again until the following morning. See p. 149.

- **Grenadier,** 18 Wilton Row, SW1 (© 020/7235-3074), was the favorite of the Duke of Wellington's officers, who downed many a pint here on leave from fighting Napoleon's troops. It's a traditional pub with the aura of 19th-century England pervading, thanks to the portrait of the Duke of Wellington hanging over the fireplace, the wooden stools and benches, and the pewter-topped bar counter. See p. 309.

- **The Cow,** 89 Westbourne Park Rd., W2 (© 020/7221-0021), attracts patrons who haven't been in an English pub for years. Leading the revolution in upgrading pub cuisine, The Cow manages to secure the biggest and juiciest oysters in town. Ox tongue poached in milk? Don't knock it 'til you've tried it. See p. 196.

- **Red Lion,** 2 Duke of York St., SW1 (© 020/7321-0782), is where you'd take Oscar Wilde if he should miraculously reappear. The writer would feel that nothing had changed in London since his departure. As you gaze upon the Belle Epoque decorations, you'll think Victoria is still on the throne. See p. 313.

- **Salisbury,** 90 St. Martin's Lane, WC2 (© **020/7836-5863**), decked out in Art Deco, is the ideal spot for a pint in the theater district. Regrettably, Lord Olivier isn't around anymore, but you just might spot a young actor who will be the Olivier of 2010. See p. 313.

- **Nag's Head,** 53 Kinnerton St., SW1 (© **020/7235-1135**), is where you go to escape tourists and hang with the locals. This quaint discovery is one of the most unspoiled pubs in London. Only minutes from Harrods, it's intimate and traditional, like something you'd encounter in a country village in Devon. See p. 312.

## 5 Best for Kids

- **Sightseeing:** London is filled with attractions that appeal to young and old—take **Madame Tussaud's** wax museum (p. 247), that all-time favorite. There's more: everything from the **London's Transport Museum** (p.247) to the **National Army Museum** (p. 248), and, of course, the **Natural History Museum** (p. 248). A cruise along the Thames (see "River Cruises Along the Thames," in chapter 7) is a great way to spend an afternoon, as is a trip to the **London Zoo** (p. 268).

- **Trips Out of London:** Board a riverboat for a **cruise to Greenwich** (p. 260), with its **National Maritime Museum** and other amusements. Part of the fun is getting there. In Greenwich you'll find many attractions, including the **Old Royal Observatory.** See "Greenwich," under "Attractions on the Outskirts," in chapter 7.

- **Royal London:** No kid wants to leave London without a visit to the **Tower of London** (p. 219). And of course, children will want to see the **Changing of the Guard** (p. 210). For castles that evoke Disney, take them on a trip to **Windsor Castle** (p. 319) or **Hampton Court Palace** (p. 263).

- **Playgrounds:** London brims with a system of parks, nicknamed "green lungs," including **Regent's Park** with its two boating lakes, one just for children. An afternoon in sprawling **Hampstead Heath** (see "Hampstead," under "Attractions on the Outskirts," in chapter 7) can fill enjoyable hours, as can a stroll through **Kensington Gardens** with its playgrounds. **Battersea Park** has a small children's zoo and adventure playground. For more information on **Regent's Park, Kensington Gardens,** and **Battersea Park,** see "Parks & Gardens," under "More Central London Attractions," in chapter 7.

- **Entertainment:** London has a number of theaters designed for children, notably **Little Angel Theatre,** which hosts regular visiting puppeteers. The minimum age is 3. See p. 265.

# 2

# A Traveler's Guide to London's Art & Architecture

*by Reid Bramblett*

**N**o one artist, period, or museum defines London's art and architecture; rather, the city builds upon the work of artists and craftsmen from its earliest days to the thriving, sometimes shocking art scene today, which could shape the look and view of the city in the future. You can see the art of London in medieval illuminated manuscripts, Thomas Gainsborough portraits, and Damien Hirst's pickled cows and sharks; its architecture from Roman walls and Norman castles to baroque St. Paul's Cathedral and towering postmodern skyscrapers. Let us illuminate some of the art and architecture that surrounds you in this graceful, exciting city.

## 1 Art 101

### CELTIC & MEDIEVAL (CA. 800 B.C.–16TH CENTURY)

The Celts, mixed with Scandinavian and Dutch tribes, ruled England until the Romans established rule in A.D. 43. Celtic art survived the Roman conquest and Dark Ages Christianity mainly as carved swirls and decorations on the "Celtic Crosses" in medieval cemeteries. During the Dark and Middle Ages, colorful Celtic images and illustrations decorated "illuminated manuscripts" copied by monks. Plenty of these have ended up in London's libraries and museums.

Important examples and artists of this period include:

- **Wilton Diptych,** National Gallery. The first truly British painting was crafted in the late 1390s for Richard II by an unknown artist who mixed Italian and Northern European influences.
- **Lindisfarne Gospels,** British Library. One of Europe's greatest illuminated manuscripts from the 7th century.
- **Matthew Paris** (d. 1259). A Benedictine monk who illuminated his own writings, Paris was the St. Albans Abbey chronicler. Examples of his work are now in the British Library and Cambridge's Corpus Christi College.

### THE RENAISSANCE & BAROQUE (16TH–18TH CENTURIES)

While the Renaissance was more of a Southern European movement, London's museums contain the works of many important old masters from Italy and Germany. Renaissance means "rebirth"; in this case, the renewed use of classical styles and forms. Artists strove for greater naturalism, using newly developed techniques such as linear perspective to achieve new heights of realism. A few foreign Renaissance artists did come to English courts and had an influence on some local artists; however, significant Brits didn't emerge until the baroque period.

The baroque mixes a kind of super-realism based on using peasants as models and an exaggerated use of light and dark, called chiaroscuro, with compositional complexity and explosions of dynamic fury, movement, color, and figures.

Significant artists of this period include:

- **Pietro Torrigiano** (1472–1528). An Italian sculptor, Pietro fled from Florence after breaking the nose of his classmate, Michelangelo. In London, he crafted tombs for the Tudors in Westminster Abbey, including Henry VII and Elizabeth of York. The Victoria and Albert Museum preserves Pietro's terra-cotta bust of Henry VII.
- **Hans Holbein the Younger** (1497–1543). A German Renaissance master of penetrating portraits, Holbein the Younger cataloged many significant figures in 16th-century Europe. You'll find examples in the National Gallery, the National Portrait Gallery, and Windsor Castle.
- **Anton Van Dyck** (1599–1641). This Belgian painted royal portraits in the baroque style for Charles I and other Stuarts, setting the tone for British portraiture for the next few centuries and gaining a knighthood. You'll find his works in the National Portrait Gallery, the National Gallery, the Wallace Collection, and Wilton House, with more in Oxford's Ashmolean Museum.
- **William Hogarth** (1697–1764). Influenced by Flemish masters, Hogarth painted and engraved scenes of everyday life. His serial works, such as *The Rake's Progress* (in Sir John Soane's Museum), were popular morality tales presented as a sort of early version of a comic strip. Seek out his other works in the National Gallery and the Tate Britain, and Cambridge's Fitzwilliam Museum.
- **Sir Joshua Reynolds** (1723–92). A staunch traditionalist and fussy baroque painter, Reynolds was the first president of London's Royal Academy of Arts. Reynolds spent much of his career casting his noble patrons as ancient gods in portrait compositions cribbed from old masters. Many of his works are in the National Gallery, the Tate Britain, the Wallace Collection, the Dulwich Picture Gallery, and in Oxford's Cathedral Hall.
- **Thomas Gainsborough** (1727–88). Although Gainsborough was a classical/ baroque portraitist like Reynolds, he could be more original. When not immortalizing noble patrons such as Jonathan Buttell (better known as "Blue Boy"), he painted quite a collection of landscapes for himself. His works grace the National Gallery and the National Portrait Gallery, Cambridge's Fitzwilliam Museum, Oxford's Cathedral Hall and Ashmolean Museum, and Gainsborough's House, a museum and gallery in his birthplace in Suffolk.

## THE ROMANTICS (LATE 18TH–19TH CENTURIES)

The Romantics idealized the Romantic tales of chivalry; had a deep respect for nature, human rights, and the nobility of peasantry; and were suspicious of progress. Their paintings tended to be heroic, historic, dramatic, and beautiful. They were inspired by critic and art theorist **John Ruskin** (1819–1900), who was among the first to praise pre-Renaissance painting and Gothic architecture.

Significant artists of this period include:

- **William Blake** (1757–1827). Romantic archetype, Blake snubbed the Royal Academy of Arts to do his own engraving, prints, illustrations, poetry, and painting. He believed in divine inspiration, but it was the vengeful Old Testament God he channeled; his works were filled with melodrama, muscular figures, and sweeping lines. See his work at the Tate Britain.
- **John Constable** (1776–1837). A little obsessed with clouds, Constable was a great British landscapist whose scenes (especially those of happy, agrarian peasants) got more idealized with each passing year—while his compositions

and brushwork became freer. You'll find his best stuff in the National Gallery and the Victoria and Albert Museum.

- **J. M. W. Turner** (1775–1851). Turner, called by some "The First Impressionist," was a prolific artist whose mood-laden, freely brushed watercolor landscapes influenced Monet. London and the Thames River were frequent subjects. He bequeathed his collection of some 19,000 watercolors and 300 paintings to the people of Britain. The Tate Britain's Clores Gallery displays the largest number of Turner's works, and others grace the National Gallery and Cambridge's Fitzwilliam Museum.
- **Pre-Raphaelites** (1848–70). This "Brotherhood" declared art had gone all wrong with Raphael (1483–1520) and set about to emulate the 15th-century Italian painters who preceded him—though their symbolically imbued, sweetly idealized, hyper-realistic work actually looks nothing like it. They loved depicting scenes from Romantic poetry and Shakespeare as well as the Bible. There were seven founders and many followers, the most important of whom were Dante Rossetti, William Hunt, and John Millais; you can see work by all three at the Tate Britain and Oxford's Ashmolean Museum.

## THE 20TH CENTURY

The only artistic movement or era the Brits can claim a major stake in is contemporary art, with many young British artists bursting onto the international gallery scene just before and after World War II. The 20th century, if anything, showed the greatest artists searching for a unique, individual expression rather than adherence to a particular school.

Important artists of this period include:

- **Henry Moore** (1898–1986). A sculptor, Moore saw himself as a sort of reincarnation of Michelangelo. He mined his marble from the same quarries as the Renaissance master and let the stone itself dictate the flowing, abstract, surrealistic figures carved from it. Moore did several public commissions (*Knife Edge* [1967] at Abingdon St. Gardens underground garage; *The Arch* [1979] on the east bank of the Longwater in Kensington Gardens), and started working in bronze after the 1950s. His sculptures also grace the Tate Modern and Cambridge's Fitzwilliam Museum and Clare College.
- **Ben Nicholson** (1894–1982). The most famous of Britain's abstract artists, Nicholson is known for his low-relief abstract paintings using layered cardboard and minimalist colors (his most famous are just white). His work is in the Tate Modern and Cambridge's Fitzwilliam Museum.
- **Francis Bacon** (1909–92). A dark, brooding expressionist, Bacon used formats such as the triptych, which were usually reserved for religious subjects, to show man's foibles. Examples of his work are in the Tate Modern, including *Triptych August 1972* (1972).
- **Lucien Freud** (b. 1922). Freud's portraits and nudes live in a depressing world of thick paint, fluid lines, and harsh light. The grandson of psychiatrist Sigmund Freud, this artist has pieces at the Tate Modern, including *Girl With a White Dog* (1950–51) and *Standing in Rags* (1988–89).
- **David Hockney** (b. 1937). Hockney employs a less pop-arty style than American Andy Warhol—though Hockney does reference modern technologies and culture—and is much more playful with artistic traditions. The Tate Modern is the place to see his creations, including *Mr. and Mrs. Clark and Percy* (1970–71).

- **Damien Hirst** (b. 1965). The guy who pickles cows, Hirst is a celebrity/ artist whose work sets out to shock. He's a winner of Britain's Turner Prize, and his work is prominent in the collection of Charles Saatchi (whose Saatchi Gallery in London displays his holdings) and was featured in "Sensation," the exhibition that traveled to New York City where it prompted protest, vandalism, and the formation of a decency commission.

## 2 Architecture 101

While each architectural era in London has its own distinctive features, there are some elements, floor plans, and terms common to many.

From the Romanesque period on, most **churches** consist either of a single wide **aisle** or a wide central **nave** flanked by two narrow, less tall aisles. The aisles are separated from the nave by a row of **columns,** or square stacks of masonry called **piers,** connected by **arches.** Sometimes—especially in the medieval Norman and Gothic eras—there is a second level to the nave, above these arches (and hence above the low roof over the aisles) punctuated by windows, called a **clerestory.** Often, between the arches and clerestory windows there is a small passageway inside the wall called the **triforium,** open on the nave side via a series of small arches.

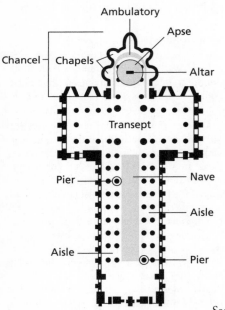

*Church Floor Plan*

This main nave/aisle assemblage is usually crossed by a perpendicular corridor called a **transept** near the far, east end of the church, so that the floor plan looks like a **Latin Cross.** The shorter, east arm of the nave is called the **chancel;** it often houses the stalls of the **choir** and the **altar.** Some churches use a **rood screen** (so called because it supports a *rood,* the Saxon word for *crucifixion*) to separate the nave from the chancel. If the far end of the chancel is rounded off, it is called an **apse.** An **ambulatory** is a corridor outside the altar and choir area, separating it from the ring of smaller chapels radiating off the chancel and apse.

Some churches, especially after the Renaissance when mathematical proportion became important, were built on a **Greek Cross** plan, each axis the same length, like a giant **+**.

It's worth pointing out that very few buildings (especially churches) were built in only one style. They often took centuries to complete, during which time tastes would change and plans would be altered.

## NORMAN (1066–1200)

Aside from a smattering of ancient sites—**pre-classical** stone circles at Stonehenge and Avebury, and **Roman** ruins such as the Bath spa and Hadrian's Wall—the oldest surviving architectural style in England dates to when the 1066 Norman Conquest brought the Romanesque era to Britain, where it flourished as the **Norman style.**

Churches were large, with a wide nave and aisles to fit the masses that came to hear Mass and worship at the altars of various saints. But to support the weight of all that masonry, the walls had to be thick and solid (pierced only by a few small windows) and resting on huge piers, which gives Norman churches a dark, somber, mysterious feeling.

Some of the features of this style include:

- **Rounded arches.** These load-bearing architectural devices allowed the architects to open up wide naves and spaces, channeling the weight of the stone walls and ceiling across the curve of the arch and down into the ground via the columns or pilasters.
- **Thick walls.**
- **Infrequent and small windows.**
- **Huge piers.** These are square stacks of masonry.
- **Chevrons.** These zigzagging decorations often surround a doorway or wrap around a column.

**White Tower,** London (Gundulf, 1078), William the Conqueror's first building in Britain, is the central keep of the Tower of London. The tower's fortress-thick walls and rounded archways provide a textbook example of a Norman-era castle. **St. John's Chapel,** located in the White Tower, is one of the few remaining Norman churches in England.

*White Tower*

## GOTHIC (1150–1550)

The French Gothic style invaded England in the late 12th century, trading rounded arches for pointy ones—an engineering discovery that freed architects from the thick walls of Norman structures and allowed ceilings to soar, walls to thin, and windows to proliferate.

Instead of dark, somber, relatively unadorned Norman interiors that forced the eyes of the faithful toward the altar, the Gothic interior enticed the churchgoers' gazes upward to high ceilings filled with light. While the priests conducted Mass in Latin, the peasants could "read" the Bible stories in the stained-glass windows.

The squat exteriors of the Norman churches were replaced by graceful buttresses and soaring spires, which rose from town centers.

The Gothic style made comebacks in the 17th century as **Laudian Gothic** in some Oxford and Cambridge buildings, in the 18th century as **rococo** or **Strawberry Hill Gotick,** and in the 19th century as **Victorian Gothic Revival,** discussed below.

The Gothic proper in Britain can be divided into three periods or styles: **Early English** (1150–1300), **Decorated** (1250–1370), and **Perpendicular** (1350–1550). Although each has identifiable features, they all include:

- **Pointed arches.** The most significant development of the Gothic era was the discovery that pointed arches could carry far more weight than rounded ones.
- **Ribbed vaulting.** In Gothic buildings, the square patch of ceiling between four columns arches up to a point in the center, creating four sail shapes. This is called a **crossvault.** The "X" separating these four sails is often reinforced with ridges called **ribbing.** As the Gothic progressed, the spaces between the structural ribbing became more decorative, often filled with **tracery** (delicate and lacelike carved stone). In the Perpendicular style, **fan vaulting** (cone-shaped concave vaults springing from the same point) was often used.

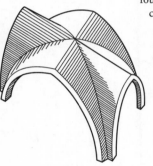

*Ribbed Vaulting*

- **Flying buttresses.** These freestanding exterior pillars connected by graceful, thin arms of stone help channel the weight of the building and its roof out and down into the ground.
- **Plate tracery.** The tip of a window, or the tips of two side-by-side windows, is often filled with a flat plate of stone pierced by a **light** (tiny window), which is either round or in a **trefoil** (3 round petals, like a clover) or **quatrefoil** (4 petals) shape.
- **Stained glass.** The multitude and size of Gothic windows allowed them to be filled with Bible stories and symbolism writ in the colorful patterns of stained glass. The use of stained glass was more common in the later Gothic periods.

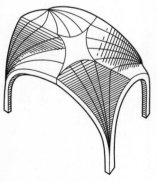

*Fan Vaulting*

- **Rose windows.** These huge, circular windows, often the centerpieces of facades, are filled with elegant tracery and "petals" of stained glass.
- **Spires.** These pinnacles seem to defy gravity and reach toward Heaven itself.
- **Gargoyles.** These are drain spouts disguised as wide-mouthed creatures or human heads.
- **Choir screen.** Serving as the inner wall of the ambulatory and the outer wall of the choir section, the choir screen is often decorated with carvings or tombs.

Among England's towering Gothic achievements, **Salisbury Cathedral** (1220–65) is almost unique for the speed with which it was built and the uniformity of its architecture. **King's College Chapel** (1446–1515) at Cambridge has England's most magnificent fan vaulting, along with some fine stained glass. At Windsor are two great examples, the **College Chapel** at Eton College (the stained glass is modern, and the fan vaulting painstakingly redone in 1957, but the 15th-century murals are original), and the **St. George's Chapel** in Windsor Castle (a gorgeous nave vault with fan vaulting in the aisles and carved choir stalls).

## RENAISSANCE (1550–1650)

While Italy and even France were experimenting with the Renaissance ideals of proportion, classical inspiration, and mathematical precision to create unified, balanced structures, England was trundling along with the late **Tudor Gothic** Perpendicular style (the Tudor use of red brick became a major feature of later Gothic revivals) in places such as Hampton Court Palace.

It wasn't until the Elizabethan era that the Brits turned to the **Renaissance** style sweeping the Continent. Architect **Inigo Jones** (1573–1652), England's greatest Renaissance architect, brought back from his travel in Italy a fevered imagination full of the exactingly classical theories of **Palladianism,** as developed by **Andrea Palladio** (1508–80). Although Jones applied what he'd learned to several English structures, most English architects at this time tempered the Renaissance style with a heavy dose of Gothic-like elements.

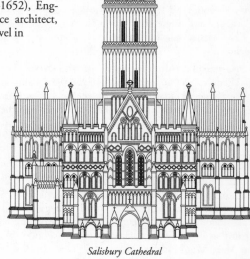

*Salisbury Cathedral*

Little specifically identifies Renaissance buildings, except:

- **A sense of proportion.**
- **A reliance on symmetry.**
- **The use of classical orders.** This idea specifies three different column types: Corinthian, Ionic, and Doric.

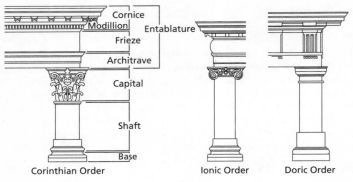

*Classical Orders*

Noteworthy structures in this style by Inigo Jones include the **Queen's House,** Greenwich (1616–18 and 1629–35); the **Queen's Chapel,** St. James's Palace (1623–25), and the **Banqueting House,** Whitehall (1619–22), both in London; and the state rooms of Wiltshire's **Wilton House** (1603), where Shakespeare performed and D-Day was planned. Recently, **Shakespeare's Globe Theatre** dusted off one of Jones's never-realized plans and used it to construct the new indoor theater.

## BAROQUE (1650–1750)

England's greatest architect was **Sir Christopher Wren** (1632–1723), a scientist and member of Parliament who got the job of rebuilding London after the Great Fire of 1666. He designed 53 replacement churches alone, plus the new St. Paul's Cathedral and numerous other projects.

The identifiable features of the baroque as practiced by Wren and others include:

- **Classical architecture rewritten with curves.** The baroque is similar to the Renaissance; however, many of the right angles and ruler-straight lines are exchanged for curves of complex geometry and an interplay of concave and convex surfaces. The overall effect is to lighten the appearance of structures and to add some movement of line.
- **Complex decoration.** Unlike the sometimes severe and austere designs of Renaissance and other classically inspired styles, the baroque was often playful and apt to festoon structures with decorations to liven things up.

**St. Paul's Cathedral,** London (1676–1710), is the crowning achievement both of the English baroque and of Christopher Wren himself. The city's other main Wren attraction is **Royal Naval College,** Greenwich (1696).

A student of Wren, **Nicholas Hawksmoor** practiced a baroque more fanciful than that of his teacher. Hawksmoor left London several churches, including **St. Mary Woolnoth** (1716–24); **St. George's,** Bloomsbury (1716–30); **Christ Church,** Spitalfields (1714–29); and **St. Anne's,** Limehouse (1714–30).

## NEOCLASSICAL & GREEK REVIVAL (1714–1837)

Many 18th-century architects cared little for the baroque, and during the Georgian era (1714–1830) a restrained, simple neoclassicism reigned, balanced between a resurgence of the precepts of Palladianism (see "Renaissance," above) and an even more distilled vision of classical theory called Greek Revival.

Buildings in these styles may be distinguished by:

- **Mathematical proportion, symmetry, and classical orders.** These classical ideals first rediscovered during the Renaissance are the hallmark of every classically styled era.
- **Crescents and circuses.** The Georgians were famous for these seamless, curving rows of identical stone town houses with tall windows, each one simple yet elegant inside.
- **Open double-arm staircases.** This feature was a favorite of the neo-Palladians.

*Crescent*

**The chapel in Greenwich Hospital** (1779–88) is a fine example of the style, courtesy of the most textbook of Greek Revivalists, James "Athenian" Stuart. The greatest site by Greek Revivalist John Soane is his own idiosyncratic house at **No. 13 Lincoln's Inn Fields** (1812–13), now Sir John Soane's Museum (other Soane buildings include the **Dulwich Picture Gallery** and the facade of the **Bank of England** in Bartholomew Lane). Another example of this style is the **British Museum** (Robert and Sidney Smirke, 1823).

## VICTORIAN GOTHIC REVIVAL (1750–1900)

While neoclassicists were reinterpreting the classical age, the Romantic movement swept up many others with rosy visions of the past. Their imaginary and fairytale version of the Middle Ages led to such creative developments as the Pre-Raphaelite painters (see "The Romantics," above) and Gothic Revival architects, who really got a head of steam under their movement during the eclectic Victorian era.

Buildings in the Victorian Gothic Revival style can be distinguished by:

- **Mishmash of Gothic features.** Look at the Gothic features described earlier, and then imagine going on a shopping spree through them at random. How to tell the copycats from the original? Victorian buildings are much younger, so they tend to be in better shape. They're also often much larger than original Gothic buildings.
- **Eclecticism.** Few Victorians bothered with getting all the formal details of a particular Gothic era right (London's Houses of Parliament comes closest). They just wanted to make sure the overall effect was pointy with pinnacled turrets, busy with decorations, and medieval.
- **Grand scale.** These buildings tend to be very large. This was usually accomplished by using Gothic only on the surface, with Industrial Age engineering underneath.

Charles Barry designed the British seat of government, the **Palace of Westminster** (Houses of Parliament) (1835–52), in a Gothic idiom that sticks pretty

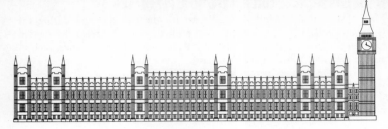

*Palace of Westminster*

faithfully to the old Perpendicular period's style. His clock tower, usually called "Big Ben" after its biggest bell, has become an icon of London.

The massive pinnacled and redbrick Victorian mansion, **St. Pancras Station** (George Gilbert Scott, 1867), makes for a quirky entrance to the Industrial Age phenomenon of rail travel. (And, while purely industrial and not Gothic, the station's steel-and-glass train shed was an engineering marvel, the widest in the world at its time.) The **Albert Memorial** (George Gilbert Scott, 1863–72), a massive Gothic canopy by the same architect, was commissioned by Queen Victoria in memory of her husband. Like St. Pancras, the **Natural History Museum** (Alfred Waterhouse, 1873–81) is another delightful marriage of imposing neo-Gothic clothing hiding an Industrial Age steel-and-iron framework.

## THE 20TH CENTURY

For the first half of the 20th century, London was too busy expanding into suburbs (in an architecturally uninteresting way) and fighting world wars to pay much attention to architecture. After the Blitz, much of central London had to be rebuilt, but most of the new buildings that went up in the City held to a functional school of architecture aptly named **Brutalism.** It wasn't until the late 1970s and 1980s that **postmodern** architecture gave British architects a bold, new direction.

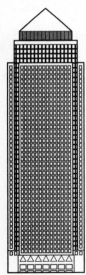

Identifiable features of postmodern architecture in London include:

- **The skyscraper motif.** Glass and steel as high as you can stack it.
- **A reliance on historic details.** Like the Victorians, postmodernists also recycled elements from architectural history, from classical to exotic.

The **Lloyd's Building** (1978–86) is *the* British postmodern masterpiece by architect Richard Rogers, who had a hand in the design of Paris's funky Centre Pompidou. Britain's tallest building, **Canary Wharf Tower** (César Pelli, 1986), is the centerpiece of the early 1990s Canary Wharf office complex and commercial development. **Charing Cross** (Terry Farrell, 1991) capped the famous old train station with an enormous postmodern office-and-shopping complex in glass and pale stone.

*Canary Wharf Tower*

# 3

# Planning Your Trip to London

This chapter tackles the hows of your trip to London—those issues required to get your trip together and get on the road, whether you're a frequent traveler or a first-timer.

## 1 Visitor Information

Visit Britain maintains a website at **www.visitbritain.com**. You can also get information from **Visit Britain** offices. There's one in the **United States,** at 551 Fifth Ave., 7th Floor, New York, NY 10176-0799 (© **800/ 462-2748** or 212/986-2266; fax 212/ 986-1188). In **Australia,** the office is at Level 16, Gateway, 1 Macquarie Place, Sydney, NSW 2000 (© **02/ 9377-4400;** fax 02/9377-4499). In **New Zealand,** go to the Fay Rich-white Building, 17th Floor, 151 Queen St., Auckland 1 (© **09/303-1446;** fax 09/377-6965). For a full information packet on London, write to **Visit London Tourist Board,** Glen House, Stag Place, Victoria, SW1E 5LT (© **020/7932-2000**). You can call the recorded-message service, **Londonline** (© **090/6866-3344**), 24 hours a day for information once you're in Britain (the number cannot be dialed outside Britain). Various topics are listed; calls cost 60p ($1) per minute.

*Time Out,* the most up-to-date magazine for what's happening in London, is online at **www.timeout. com/london**. You can pick up a print copy at any international newsstand.

To book accommodations with a credit card (MasterCard or Visa), call **Visit London Booking Office** at © **020/7604-2890,** or fax them at 020/7372-2068. They're available Monday to Friday from 9am to 6pm (London time). There is a £5 ($9.25) fee for booking.

**WHAT'S ON THE WEB?** The most useful site was created by a very knowledgeable source, the Visit Britain itself, and U.S. visitors are its target audience. A wealth of information is available at **www.visitbritain. com**, which lets you order brochures online, provides trip-planning hints, and even grants prompt answers to e-mail questions. This site covers all of Great Britain. Visit London, the official visitor organization for the city, offers even more specific information about the city on its website, **www.visitlondon.com**. The site has recently been overhauled, giving users the opportunity to organize their trip online by booking discounted rail tickets, accommodations, restaurants, and a London Pass that offers free or reduced entry into more than 50 London attractions. The Visit London website includes comprehensive information on what's new in town, as well as more specific sections including Kids Love London, Gay London, and London by Night. Go to **www.baa. com** for a guide and terminal maps for Heathrow, Gatwick, Stansted, and other London-area airports, including flight arrival times, duty-free shops, airport restaurants, and info on getting

## Destination: London—Red Alert Checklist

- Citizens of EU countries can cross into Britain for as long as they wish with an identity card. Citizens of other countries must have a passport.
- If you purchased traveler's checks, have you recorded the check numbers and stored that document separately from the checks?
- Did you pack your camera and an extra set of camera batteries, and purchase enough film?
- Do you have a safe, accessible place to store money?
- Did you bring ID cards that may entitle you to discounts, such as AAA and AARP cards, student IDs, and so forth?
- Did you bring emergency drug prescriptions and extra glasses and/or contact lenses?
- Do you have your credit card PIN?
- If you have an E-ticket, do you have documentation (a printout with the confirmation number)?
- Did you leave a copy of your itinerary with someone at home?
- Did you check to see if any travel advisories have been issued by the **U.S. State Department** (http://travel.state.gov/travel_warnings.html)?
- Do you have the address and phone number of your country's embassy with you?

from the airports to downtown London. Getting around London can be confusing, so you might want to visit **www.londontransport.co.uk** for up-to-the-minute info. For the latest details on London's theater scene, consult **www.officiallondontheatre.co.uk** or **www.londontheatre.co.uk**. At **www.multimap.com**, you can access detailed street maps of the whole United Kingdom—just key in the location or even just the postal code, and a map of the area with the location circled will appear. For directions to specific places in London, consult **www.streetmap.co.uk**.

## 2 Entry Requirements & Customs

### ENTRY REQUIREMENTS

Citizens of the United States, Canada, Australia, New Zealand, and South Africa require a passport to enter the United Kingdom, but not a visa. Irish citizens and citizens of European Union countries need only an identity card. The maximum stay for non-European Union visitors is 6 months. Some Customs officials request proof that you have the means to leave the country (usually a round-trip ticket) and means of support while you're in Britain (someone in the U.K. will have to vouch that they are supporting you, or you may be asked to show documents that indicate that you have an income). If you're planning to fly on from the United Kingdom to a country that requires a visa, it's wise to secure the visa before you leave home.

Your valid driver's license and at least 1 year's experience is required to drive personal or rented cars. You must be 25 or over to rent a car.

For information on how to get a passport, go to the Fast Facts section of chapter 4 (p. 83)—the websites listed provide downloadable passport applications as well as the current fees for processing passport applications. For an up-to-date country-by-country listing of passport requirements around the world, go to the "Foreign Entry Requirements" Web page of the U.S. State Department at **http:// travel.state.gov/foreignentryreqs/ americansabroad.html**.

## CUSTOMS REGULATIONS
### WHAT YOU CAN BRING INTO LONDON
**For Non-E.U. Nationals 18 Plus** You can bring in, duty-free, 200 cigarettes, 100 cigarillos, 50 cigars, or 250 grams of smoking tobacco. The amount allowed for each of these goods is doubled if you live outside Europe.

You can also bring in 2 liters of wine and either 1 liter of alcohol over 22 proof or 2 liters of wine under 22 proof. In addition, you can bring in 60cc (2.03 oz.) of perfume, a quarter liter (250ml) of eau de toilette, 500 grams (1 lb.) of coffee, and 200 grams (½ lb.) of tea. Visitors 15 and over may also bring in other goods totaling £145 ($268); the allowance for those 14 and under is £72.50 ($134). (Customs officials tend to be lenient about general merchandise, realizing the limits are unrealistically low.)

You can't bring your pet straight to England. Six months' quarantine is required before it is allowed in. An illegally imported animal may be destroyed.

**For E.U. Citizens** Visitors from fellow European Union countries can bring into Britain any amount of goods as long as the goods are intended for their personal use—not for resale.

The current policy for bringing pets into the U.K. from the E.U. is under review. Right now, animals or pets of any kind are forbidden from entering without a long quarantine period.

### WHAT YOU CAN BRING HOME
**For U.S. Citizens** If you've been out of the country for 48 hours or more, you can bring $800 worth of goods (per person) back into the United States without paying a duty. On the next $1,000 worth of goods you pay a flat 4%. Beyond that, it works on an item-by-item basis. There are a few restrictions on amounts: 1 liter of alcohol (you must be over 21), 200 cigarettes, and 100 cigars. Antiques over 100 years old and works of art are exempt from the $400 limit, as is anything you mail home. Once per day, you can mail yourself $200 worth of goods duty-free; mark the package "For Personal Use." You can also mail $200 worth of goods per person per day to other people; label each package "Unsolicited Gift." Any package must state a description of the contents and their values on the exterior. You can't mail alcohol, perfume (it contains alcohol), or tobacco products.

For more details on regulations, check out the **U.S. Customs Service** website at **www.customs.gov** or

---

*Tips* **Passport Savvy**

Allow plenty of time before your trip to apply for a passport; processing normally takes 3 weeks but can take longer during busy periods (especially spring). When traveling, safeguard your passport in an inconspicuous, inaccessible place like a money belt, and keep a copy of the critical pages with your passport number in a separate place. If you lose your passport, visit the nearest consulate of your native country as soon as possible for a replacement.

contact the Customs office at P.O. Box 7407, Washington, DC 20044 (© 202/354-1000) to request the free "Know Before You Go" pamphlet.

To prevent the spread of diseases, you can't bring in any plants, fruits, vegetables, meats, or other foodstuffs. This includes cured meats like salami. You may bring in the following: bakery goods, all but the softest cheeses (the rule is vague, but if the cheese is at all spreadable, don't risk confiscation), candies, roasted coffee beans and dried tea, fish (packaged salmon is okay), seeds for veggies and flowers (but not for trees), and mushrooms. Check out the USDA's website at www.aphis.usda.gov for more details.

**For Canadian Citizens**   For a clear summary of **Canadian** rules, write for the booklet *I Declare,* issued by the **Canada Customs and Revenue Agency,** 333 Dunsmuir St., Vancouver, BC V6B 5R4 Canada (© 800/461-9999), or check out the website at www.ccra-adrc.gc.ca. Canada allows its citizens a C$750 exemption if you're gone for 7 days or longer (only C$200 if you're gone between 48 hr. and 7 days), and you're allowed to bring back, duty-free, 200 cigarettes, 50 cigars, and 1.5 liters of wine *or* 1.14 liters of liquor *or* 8.5 liters of beer or ale. In addition, you're allowed to mail gifts to Canada at the rate of C$60 a day, provided they're unsolicited and aren't alcohol or tobacco (write "Unsolicited Gift, Under $60 Value" on the package).

**For Australian Citizens**   The duty-free allowance in Australia is A$400 or, for those under 18, A$200. Upon returning to Australia, citizens can bring in 250 cigarettes or 250 grams of loose tobacco, and 1.125 liters of alcohol. A helpful brochure, available from Australian consulates or Customs offices, is *"Know Before You Go."* For more information, contact **Australian Customs Services,** GPO Box 8, Sydney NSW 2001, Australia (© 02/6275-6666 within Australia; 1300/363-263); or log onto www.customs.gov.au.

**For New Zealand Citizens**   The duty-free allowance for New Zealand is NZ$700. Citizens over 17 can bring back 200 cigarettes or 50 cigars or 250 grams of tobacco (or a mix of all 3 if their combined weight does not exceed 250g); plus 4.5 liters of wine or beer, plus 1.125 liters of liquor. Most questions are answered in the free "Advice to Travellers" pamphlet available at New Zealand consulates and Customs offices. For more information, contact **New Zealand Customs,** The Customhouse, 17–21 Whitmore St., Box 2218, Wellington, New Zealand (© 1800/428-786-60 www.customs.govt.nz).

## 3 Money

### POUNDS & PENCE

Britain's decimal monetary system is based on the pound (£), which is made up of 100 pence (written as "p"). Pounds are also called "quid" by Britons. There are £1 and £2 coins, as

---

**Tips   Make Sure Your PIN Works**

Make sure that the PINs on your bank cards and credit cards will work in Britain. You'll need a **four-digit code** (six digits won't work), so if you have a six-digit code you'll have to get a new PIN from your bank before your trip. If you're unsure about this, contact Cirrus or PLUS (see below). Be sure to check the daily withdrawal limit at the same time.

## Foreign Currencies vs. the U.S. Dollar

Conversion ratios between the U.S. dollar and other currencies fluctuate, and their differences could affect the relative costs of your holiday. The figures reflected in the currency chart below were valid at the time of this writing, but they might not be valid by the time of your departure. This chart would be useful for conversions of small amounts of money, but if you're planning on any major transactions, check for more updated rates prior to making any serious commitments.

**The U.S. Dollar and the Euro**   One U.S. dollar was worth approximately 1.15 euros at the time of this writing. (Inversely stated, that means that 1 euro was worth approximately 87 U.S. cents.)

**The British pound, the U.S. Dollar, and the Euro**   At press time, one pound equaled approximately $1.85 U.S. or approximately 1.50 euros.

**The Canadian dollar, the U.S. dollar, and the Euro**   At press time, one Canadian dollar equaled approximately 74 U.S. cents or approximately 60 eurocents.

| US$ | UK£ | C$ | Euro€ | US$ | UK£ | C$ | Euro€ |
|-----|------|-------|-------|-------|--------|----------|----------|
| 1 | .55 | 1.35 | 1.15 | 75 | 40.54 | 101.25 | 86.25 |
| 2 | 1.08 | 2.70 | 2.30 | 100 | 54.05 | 135.00 | 115.00 |
| 3 | 1.62 | 4.05 | 3.45 | 125 | 67.57 | 168.00 | 143.75 |
| 4 | 2.16 | 5.40 | 4.60 | 150 | 81.08 | 202.50 | 172.50 |
| 5 | 2.70 | 6.75 | 5.75 | 175 | 94.59 | 236.25 | 201.25 |
| 6 | 3.60 | 8.10 | 6.90 | 200 | 120.00 | 270.00 | 230.00 |
| 7 | 4.20 | 9.45 | 8.05 | 225 | 135.00 | 303.75 | 258.75 |
| 8 | 4.80 | 10.80 | 9.20 | 250 | 150.00 | 337.50 | 287.50 |
| 9 | 5.40 | 12.15 | 10.35 | 275 | 165.00 | 371.25 | 316.25 |
| 10 | 6.00 | 13.50 | 11.50 | 300 | 180.00 | 405.00 | 345.00 |
| 15 | 9.00 | 20.25 | 17.25 | 350 | 210.00 | 472.50 | 402.50 |
| 20 | 12.00 | 27.00 | 23.00 | 400 | 240.00 | 540.00 | 460.00 |
| 25 | 15.00 | 33.75 | 28.75 | 500 | 300.00 | 675.00 | 575.00 |
| 50 | 30.00 | 87.50 | 57.50 | 1,000 | 600.00 | 1,350.00 | 1,150.00 |

well as coins of 50p, 20p, 10p, 5p, 2p, and 1p. Banknotes come in denominations of £5, £10, £20, and £50.

As a general guideline, the price conversions in this book have been computed at the rate of £1 = $1.85 (U.S.). Bear in mind, however, that exchange rates fluctuate daily.

## ATMS

ATMs are easily found throughout London. ATMs are also connected to the major networks at airports such as Heathrow and Gatwick. You'll usually get a better exchange rate by withdrawing money at an ATM (currency exchange booths take a huge commission or give an unfavorable rate, or both), but your bank may charge a fee for using a foreign ATM. You may also need a different PIN to use overseas ATMs. Call your bank to check and get a new PIN if needed before you go.

The most popular ATM networks are **Cirrus** (© 800/424-7787; www.mastercard.com) and **PLUS**

| What Things Cost in London | UK£ | US$* | C$** |
|---|---|---|---|
| Taxi from Heathrow to Central London | 40 | 74 | 100 |
| Underground from Heathrow to Central London | 5.40 | 9.99 | 13.50 |
| Local Telephone Call | 20p | 37¢ | 50¢ |
| Double Room at The Dorchester (very expensive) | 385 | 712.25 | 962.50 |
| Double Room at the Hallam Hotel (moderate) | 100 | 185 | 250 |
| Double Room at Boston Court (inexpensive) | 69 | 127.65 | 172.50 |
| Lunch for one at The Ivy (expensive) | 25 | 46.25 | 62.50 |
| Lunch for one at Ye Olde Cheshire Cheese (moderate) | 20 | 37 | 50 |
| Dinner for one, without wine, at Bibendum, The Oyster Bar (expensive) | 38 | 70.30 | 95 |
| Dinner for one, without wine, at Porter's English Restaurant (moderate) | 22 | 40.70 | 55 |
| Dinner for one, without wine, at Cork & Bottle Wine Bar (inexpensive) | 14 | 25.90 | 35 |
| Pint of beer | 2.50 | 4.63 | 6.25 |
| Coca-Cola | 1.80 | 3.33 | 4.50 |
| Cup of coffee | 1.60 | 2.96 | 4 |
| Roll of ASA 100 Color film, 36 exposures | 7.50 | 13.88 | 18.75 |
| Admission to British Museum | Free | Free | Free |
| Movie ticket | 6–10 | 11.10–18.50 | 15–25 |
| Theatre ticket | 18–70 | 33.30–129.5 | 45–175 |

\* Assuming a £ to US$ conversion rate of £1=US$1.85
\*\* Assuming a £ to CD$ conversion rate of £1=C$2.50

(© 800/843-7587; www.visa.com); check the back of your ATM card to see which network your bank belongs to. You can use the 800 numbers in the U.S. (also on your card) to locate ATMs in your destination or ask your bank for a list of overseas ATMs. You can find the locations of ATMs on www.visa.com and www.mastercard.com.

## TRAVELER'S CHECKS

These days, traveler's checks are less necessary because most English cities and towns, especially London, have 24-hour ATMs, allowing you to withdraw small amounts of cash as needed. But if you prefer the security of the tried and true, you might want to stick with traveler's checks—provided that

---

**Tips**  **Emergency Cash—The Fastest Way**

If you need emergency cash over the weekend when all the banks and American Express offices are closed, you can have money wired to you from **Western Union** (℃ **800/325-6000;** www.westernunion.com). You must present valid ID to pick up the cash at the Western Union office. However, in most countries, you can pick up a money transfer even if you don't have valid identification, as long as you can answer an identifying test question provided by the sender. Be sure to let the sender know in advance that you don't have ID. If you need to use a test question instead of ID, the sender must take cash to his or her local Western Union office, rather than transfer the money over the phone or online.

---

you don't mind showing an ID every time you want to cash a check.

Exchange rates are more favorable at your destination. Nevertheless, it's often helpful to exchange at least some money before going abroad (standing in line at the exchange bureau in the London airport could make you miss the next bus leaving for downtown after a long flight). Check with any of your local American Express or Thomas Cook offices or major banks. Or, order pounds in advance from the following: **American Express** (℃ **800/ 221-7282;** www.americanexpress. com), **Thomas Cook** (℃ **800/223-7373;** www.thomascook.com), or **Visa** (℃ **800/732-1322**).

It's best to exchange currency or traveler's checks at a bank, not a hotel or shop. Currency and traveler's checks (which garner a better exchange rate than cash) can be changed at all principal airports and at some travel agencies, such as American Express and Thomas Cook. Note the rates and ask about commission fees; it can sometimes pay to shop around and ask.

Keep a record of your traveler's checks' serial numbers—separate from the checks, of course—so you're ensured a refund in an emergency.

## CREDIT CARDS

Credit cards are a safe way to carry money and they provide a convenient record of all your expenses. You can also withdraw cash advances from your credit cards at any bank (although you'll pay interest on the advance the moment you receive the cash, and you won't get frequent-flier miles on an airline credit card). At most banks you can get a cash advance at the ATM with your PIN. If you don't have a PIN, call your credit card company and ask for one. It usually takes 5 to 7 business days, but some banks provide the number over the phone if you pass a security clearance.

---

## 4  When to Go

### CLIMATE

Charles Dudley Warner once said that the trouble with the weather is that everybody talks about it but nobody does anything about it. Well, Londoners talk about weather more than anyone, but they have also done something about it: Air-pollution control has resulted in the virtual disappearance of the pea-soup fogs that once blanketed the city.

A typical London-area weather forecast for a summer day predicts "scattered clouds with sunny periods and showers, possibly heavy at times." Summer temperatures seldom rise above 78°F (25°C), nor do they drop below 35°F (2°C) in winter. London,

---

**Tips    Best Weather in London**

If balmy weather is your dream, the month of July is as warm as it gets in London. Temperatures range from the 50s (teens Celsius) in the morning, rising to the low 70s (20s Celsius) in the afternoon. But it still rains 1 day in 5. For some "real weather," with wind, storms, rain, and all the works, visit during the other months.

---

being in one of the mildest parts of the country, can be very pleasant in the spring and fall. Yes, it rains, but you'll rarely get a true downpour. Rains are heaviest in November, when the city averages 2½ inches.

The British consider chilliness wholesome and usually try to keep room temperatures about 10° below the American comfort level, so bring sweaters year-round if you tend to get cold.

**London's Average Daytime Temperature & Rainfall**

|                | Jan | Feb | Mar | Apr | May  | June | July | Aug  | Sept | Oct  | Nov | Dec |
|----------------|-----|-----|-----|-----|------|------|------|------|------|------|-----|-----|
| Temp. (°F)     | 40  | 40  | 44  | 49  | 55   | 61   | 64   | 64   | 59   | 52   | 46  | 42  |
| Temp. (°C)     | 4.4 | 4.4 | 6.7 | 9.4 | 12.8 | 16.1 | 17.8 | 17.8 | 15.0 | 11.1 | 7.8 | 5.6 |
| Rainfall (in.) | 2.1 | 1.6 | 1.5 | 1.5 | 1.8  | 1.8  | 2.2  | 2.3  | 1.9  | 2.2  | 2.5 | 1.9 |

## CURRENT WEATHER CONDITIONS

In the United States, you can dial ℂ **1/900-WEATHER** and then press the first four letters of the desired foreign city—in this case, LOND for London—for the time of day in that city, plus current temperatures, weather conditions, and forecasts. The cost is 95¢ per minute. Another good way to check conditions is at the Weather Channel's website: **www.weather.com**. In London, you can listen to BBC One–TV for the weather.

## HOLIDAYS

In England, public holidays include New Year's Day, Good Friday, Easter Monday, May Day (1st Mon in May), spring and summer bank holidays (last Mon in May and Aug, respectively), Christmas Day, and Boxing Day (Dec 26).

# LONDON CALENDAR OF EVENTS

## January

**January Sales.** Most shops offer good reductions at this time. Many sales start as early as late December to beat the post-Christmas slump. Truly voracious shoppers camp overnight outside Harrods so that they have first pickings.

**London Parade.** Bands, floats, and carriages contribute to the merriment as the parade wends its way from Parliament Square to Berkeley Square in Mayfair. January 1. Procession starts around noon.

**Schroders London Boat Show,** ExCel, Docklands, E16 XL. The largest boat show in Europe. Call ℂ **01784/223627;** www.boatshows.co.uk for details. Early January.

**Charles I Commemoration.** This is the anniversary of the execution of King Charles I "in the name of freedom and democracy."

Hundreds of cavaliers march through central London in 17th-century dress, and prayers are said at the Banqueting House in Whitehall. Free. Call ✆ **0207/930-4179** for details. Last Sunday in January.

## February

**Chinese New Year.** The famous Lion Dancers appear in Soho. Free. Either in late January or early February (based on the lunar calendar). Call ✆ **0891/505490** for schedule and event details.

**Great Spitalfields Pancake Race,** Old Spitalfields Market, Brushfield Street, E1. Teams of four run in relays, tossing pancakes. To join in, call ✆ **020/7375-0441** or visit www.alternativearts.co.uk. At noon on Shrove Tuesday (last day before Lent).

## March

**St. David's Day,** Chelsea Barracks. A member of the Royal Family presents the Welsh Guards with the principality's national emblem, a leek. Call ✆ **020/7414-3291** for more information. March 1 (or the nearest Sun).

**Oranges and Lemons Service,** at St. Clement Danes, the Strand, WC2. As a reminder of the nursery rhyme "Bells of St. Clements," children are presented with the fruits during the church service, and the church bells ring out the rhyme (part of which is "Oranges and Lemons, Say the bells of St. Clements") at 9am, noon, 3pm, and 6pm; call ✆ **020/7242-8282** for information. Third week of March.

**Westminster Abbey on Holy Week Tuesday;** call ✆ **020/7654-4900** for information. Free. Late March or early April.

## April

**Easter Parade.** Floats, marching bands, and a full day of Easter Sunday activities enliven Battersea Park. Free. Easter Sunday.

**Harness Horse Parade.** A morning parade of heavy-working horses in superb gleaming brass harnesses and plumes, at Battersea Park. Call ✆ **01737/646-132.** Easter Monday.

**Boat Race, Putney to Mortlake.** Oxford and Cambridge Universities eights battle upstream with awesome power. Park yourself at one of the Thames-side pubs along the route to see the action. Early April; check *Time Out* for exact dates and times.

**Flora London Marathon.** Thirty thousand competitors run from Greenwich Park to Buckingham Palace. Call ✆ **020/7902-0189** or visit www.london-marathon.co.uk for more information or to register for the marathon. Mid- to late April.

**The Queen's Birthday.** The queen's birthday is celebrated with 21-gun salutes in Hyde Park, and by troops in parade dress on Tower Hill at noon. April 21.

**National Gardens Scheme.** More than 3,000 private gardens in London are open to the public on set days, and tea is sometimes served. Pick up the NGS guidebook for £8 ($15) from most bookstores, or contact the National Gardens Scheme Charitable Trust, Hatchlands Park, East Clandon, Guildford, Surrey GU4 7RT (✆ **01483/211-535;** www.ngs.org.uk). Late April to early May.

## May

**May Fayre and Puppet Festival,** Covent Garden. There is a procession of puppets, puppeteers, and a brass band at 10am; a service at St. Paul's on Bedford Street at 10:30am; then Punch and Judy shows until 6pm at the site where British diarist Pepys watched them in 1662. Everything is free. Call

© **020/7375-0441** for details. Second Sunday in May.

**The Royal Windsor Horse Show,** Home Park, Windsor Castle. You might spot a royal at this multiday horse-racing and horse-showing event. Call © **01753/860-633** or visit www.royal-windsor-horse-show.co.uk for more details. Mid-May.

**Glyndebourne Festival Opera Season,** Sussex. The Glyndebourne Festival presents opera performances in a beautiful setting, with champagne picnics before and between the shows. Since the completion of the Glyndebourne opera house, one of the world's best, tickets are a bit easier to come by. Call © **1273/812-321** or visit www.glyndebourne.com for a schedule and to purchase tickets. The season runs from mid-May to late August.

**Chelsea Flower Show,** Chelsea Royal Hospital. This show exhibits the best of British gardening, with displays of plants and flowers from all seasons. The show runs from 8am to 8pm; tickets are £29 ($54). On the last day, the show runs from 8am to 5:30pm, and tickets are £31 ($57). Tickets must be purchased in advance; they are available through the Royal Horticultural Society (© **020/7828-4125;** www.rhs.org.uk). Call © **0870/906-3781** for information. Three days in May.

**June**

**Trooping the Colour,** Horse Guards Parade, Whitehall. The official birthday of the queen (as opposed to her actual birthday, which is Apr 21) is held on a designated date in June. Seated in a carriage, the monarch inspects her regiments and takes their salute as they parade their colors. It's a quintessentially British event, with exquisite pageantry and pomp. Tickets for the parade and for two

reviews, held on preceding Saturdays, are allocated by ballot. Those interested in attending must apply for tickets between January 1 and the end of February, enclosing a stamped, self-addressed envelope or International Reply Coupon—exact dates and ticket prices are supplied later. The drawing is held in mid-March, and successful applicants *only* are informed in April. For details, and to apply for tickets, write to **HQ Household Division,** Horse Guards, Whitehall, London SW1X 6AA, enclosing a self-addressed envelope and International Reply Coupon (available at any post office). Call © **020/741-2479** for more information.

**Vodafone Derby Stakes,** Epsom Downs Racecourse, Epsom, Surrey. These famous horse races constitute the best-known event on the British horseracing calendar. It's also a chance for men to wear top hats and women, including the queen, to put on silly millinery creations. Grandstand tickets range from £19 to £27 ($35–$50). Call © **1372/470-047** or visit www.epsomderby.co.uk for more information and to buy tickets. The "darby" (as it's pronounced) is run the first week in June.

**Royal Academy's Summer Exhibition,** Burlington House in Piccadilly Circus, W1. The Royal Academy, founded in 1768 with Sir Joshua Reynolds as president and Thomas Gainsborough as a member, has sponsored summer exhibitions of living painters' work for some 2 centuries. Visitors can browse and purchase art. Call © **020/7439-7438** or visit www.royalacademy.org.uk for details. Early June to mid-August.

**Grosvenor House Art and Antique Fair,** Le Méridien Grosvenor House, 86–90 Park Lane, W1 3AA. This is a very prestigious antiques fair featuring the world's leading dealers and more than £400 million worth of fine art and antiques. Call ℂ **020/7495-8743** or visit www. grosvenor-antiquesfair.co.uk for more information. Second week of June.

**Royal Ascot Week,** Ascot, Berkshire, SL5 7JN. Ascot Racecourse is open year-round for guided tours, events, exhibitions, and conferences. There are 25 race days throughout the year, with the feature race meetings being the Royal Meeting in June, Diamond Day in late July (p. 36), and the Festival at Ascot in late September (p. 36). For Royal Ascot week, which runs from mid- to late June, everyone (including the queen) shows up in their finery to watch 24 races over 4 days. For further information and tickets, call ℂ **1344/622-211** or visit www.ascot.co.uk. Tickets should be purchased in advance. Mid- to late June.

**Lawn Tennis Championships,** Wimbledon, Southwest London. Ever since players in flannels and bonnets took to the grass courts at Wimbledon in 1877, this tournament has drawn a socially prominent crowd. You'll still find an excited hush at Centre Court (where the most hotly contested championship matches are held). Savoring strawberries and cream is part of the experience. Tickets for Centre and Number One courts are handed out through a lottery; write to **All England Lawn Tennis Club,** P.O. Box 98, Church Road, Wimbledon, London SW19 5AE (ℂ **020/8944-1066**) between August and December. Include a self-addressed and stamped envelope with your letter. A number of tickets are set aside for visitors from abroad, so you may be able to purchase some in spring for this year's

games; call to inquire. Outside court tickets are available daily, but *be prepared to wait in line.* Call ℂ **020/8971-2473** or visit www. wimbledon.org. Late June to early July.

**City of London Festival.** This is an annual arts celebration held throughout the city. Call ℂ **020/7377-0540** or visit www.colf.org for information about programs and venues. Late June to early July.

**Shakespeare Under the Stars,** Open Air Theatre, Inner Circle, Regent's Park, NW1 4NU. If you want to see *Macbeth, Hamlet,* or *Romeo and Juliet* (or any other Shakespeare play), our advice is to bring a blanket and a bottle of wine to watch the Bard's works performed at the Open Air Theatre. Performances are Monday through Saturday at 8pm; plus Wednesday, Thursday, and Saturday at 2:30pm. Call ℂ **020/7935-5756** or visit www.open-air-theatre.org.uk for more information and to buy tickets. There is an on-site box office, but it's best to purchase tickets in advance. Previews begin in late June and the season lasts until early September.

**July**

**Kenwood Lakeside Concerts,** north side of Hampstead Heath. Fireworks and laser shows enliven the excellent performances at these annual outdoor concerts on Hampstead Heath. Classical music drifts across the lake to the fans every Saturday and Sunday in summer from early July to late August. Call ℂ **020/8348-1286** for a schedule and information and to buy tickets. Tickets are popular, so buy yours in advance (they range from £16 to £24 [$30–$44]). Early July to late August.

**Hampton Court Palace Flower Show,** East Molesey, Surrey. This

5-day international flower show is eclipsing its sister show in Chelsea; here, you can purchase the exhibits on the last day. Call © **0870/906-371** or visit www.rhs.org.uk for exact dates and details. Early to mid-July.

**Diamond Day,** Ascot, Berkshire, SL5 7JN. This is one of the most important horse races on the international racing calendar. The major event of Ascot's summer season, it is a stylish sporting and social occasion where Brits appear in all their finery. More than £1 million ($1,850,000) in prize money is at stake at this horse race, and the world's greatest thoroughbreds are on display here. Tickets must be booked early. For more information, call © **01344/876876.** July 26, 2004.

**The Proms,** Royal Albert Hall. "The Proms"—the annual Henry Wood Promenade Concerts at Royal Albert Hall—attract music aficionados from around the world. Staged daily, the concerts were launched in 1895 and are the principal summer venue for the BBC Symphony Orchestra. Cheering, clapping, banners, balloons, and Union Jacks on parade contribute to the festive summer atmosphere. Call © **020/7589-8212** or visit www.bbc.co.uk/proms for more information and for tickets. Tickets should be bought in advance. Mid-July to mid-September.

**August**

**Notting Hill Carnival,** Notting Hill. This is one of the largest street festivals in Europe, attracting more than a half-million people annually. You'll find live reggae and soul music combined with great Caribbean food. Free. Call © **020/8964-0544;** www.portowebbo.co.uk, for information. Two days in late August (usually the last Sun and Mon).

**September**

**Chelsea Antiques Fair,** This is a gathering of England's best antiques dealers, held at Chelsea Old Town Hall, King's Road, SW3, © **0870/350-2442.** Mid-September.

**Open House.** During this 2-day event, the public has access to buildings of architectural significance that are normally closed. Call © **020/7267-7697** or visit www.londonopenhouse.org for a schedule and further information. Mid-to late September.

**Horse of the Year Show,** NEC Arena, Birmingham. This is the premier equestrian event on the English calendar. Riders fly in from all over to join in this festive event of jumping competitions, parading, and pony showing. For more information, call © **020/8900-9282** or visit www.hoys.co.uk. End of September to early October.

**Raising of the Thames Barrier,** Unity Way, SE18. Once a year, in September, a full test is done on the flood barrier. All 10 of the massive steel gates are raised out of the river for inspection, and you can get a close look at this miracle of modern engineering. Call © **020/8854-1373** for the exact date and time (usually a Sun near the end of Sept).

**The Ascot Festival,** Ascot, Berkshire, SL5 7JN. This is Britain's greatest horse-racing weekend, providing the grand finale to the summer season at Ascot. The 3-day "meeting" combines some of the most valuable racing of the year with other entertainment. A highlight of the festival is the £250,000 ($462,500) Watership Down Stud Sales race restricted to 2-year-old fillies. Other racing highlights include the Queen Elizabeth II

Stakes, with the winning horse crowned champion miler in Europe. To book tickets, call © **01344/876876.** Last weekend in September.

## October

**Opening of Parliament,** House of Lords, Westminster. The monarch opens Parliament in the House of Lords by reading an official speech written by the Prime Minister's office. The queen rides from Buckingham Palace to the House of Lords in a royal coach accompanied by the Yeoman of the Guard and the Household Cavalry. The Strangers' Gallery at the House of Lords is open to spectators on a first-come, first-served basis. Call © **0870/960-3773** or visit www. parliament.uk. Late October to mid-November.

**Judges Service,** Westminster Abbey. The judiciary attends a service in Westminster Abbey to mark the opening of the law term. Afterward, in full regalia—wigs and all—they form a procession and walk to the House of Lords for their "Annual Breakfast." You'll have a great view of the procession from behind the Abbey. First Monday in October at 10am.

**Quit Rents Ceremony,** Royal Courts of Justice, WC2. The City Solicitor pays one of the queen's officials a token rent for properties leased from the kingdom long, long ago. Two fagots of wood, a billhook, and a hatchet pay for land in Shropshire, and 61 nails and six horseshoes pay for a long-gone

forge in the Strand. Call © **020/ 7947-6000** for free tickets. Early October.

## November

**Guy Fawkes Night.** On the anniversary of the Gunpowder Plot, an attempt to blow up King James I and his Parliament, huge bonfires are lit throughout the city and Guy Fawkes, the most famous conspirator, is burned in effigy. Free. Check *Time Out* for locations. November 5th.

**Lord Mayor's Procession and Show,** from the Guildhall to the Royal Courts of Justice, in The City of London. This annual event marks the inauguration of the new lord mayor of The City of London. The queen must ask permission to enter the City—a right jealously guarded by London merchants during the 17th century. You can watch the procession from the street; the show is by invitation only. Call © **020/7332-1754;** www. lordmayorshow.org, for more information. Second week in November.

## December

**Caroling Under the Norwegian Christmas Tree.** There's caroling most evenings beneath the tree in Trafalgar Square. December.

**Harrods After-Christmas Sale,** Knightsbridge. Call © **020/7730-1234** for dates. Late December.

**Watch Night,** St. Paul's Cathedral. A lovely New Year's Eve service takes place at 11:30pm. Call © **020/7236-4128** for information. December 31.

## 5 Travel Insurance

Check your existing insurance policies and credit card coverage before you buy travel insurance. You may already be covered for lost luggage, cancelled tickets, or medical expenses. If your standard insurance doesn't cover travel and you decide that you'd like to purchase additional insurance, first ask your travel agent about a comprehensive package, which may be less expensive. The cost of travel insurance varies widely, depending on the cost and length of your trip, your age and overall health, and the type of trip you're taking.

For information in the U.S., contact one of the following popular insurers:

- **Access America** (© 866/807-3982; www.accessamerica.com)
- **Travel Guard International** (© 800/826-4919; www.travel guard.com)
- **Travel Insured International** (© 800/243-3174; www.travel insured.com)
- **Travelex Insurance Services** (© 888/457-4602; www.travel ex-insurance.com)

For information in Great Britain, contact the following agency:

- **Columbus Direct,** 17 Devonshire Sq., London, EC2M 4SO (© 020/7375-0011; www.columbusdirect.com)

For information in Canada, contact:

- **Travel Guard International** (see contact information above)

**TRIP-CANCELLATION INSUR-ANCE**  Trip-cancellation insurance helps you get your money back if you have to back out of a trip, if you have to go home early, or if your travel supplier goes bankrupt. Allowed reasons for cancellation can range from sickness to natural disasters to the State Department's declaring your destination unsafe for travel. (Insurers usually won't cover vague fears, though, as many travelers discovered who tried to cancel their trips in October 2001 because they were wary of flying.) In this unstable world, trip-cancellation insurance is a good buy if you're getting tickets well in advance—who knows what the state of the world, or of your airline, will be in 9 months? Insurance policy details vary, so read

the fine print—and especially make sure that your airline or cruise line is on the list of carriers covered in case of bankruptcy. For information, contact one of the insurers listed above.

**MEDICAL INSURANCE**  With the exception of certain HMOs and Medicare/Medicaid, your medical insurance should cover medical treatment—even hospital care—overseas. However, most out-of-country hospitals make you pay your bills up front and send you a refund after you've returned home and filed the necessary paperwork. And in a worst-case scenario, there's the high cost of emergency evacuation. If you require additional medical insurance, try **MEDEX International** (© 800/527-0218 or 410/453-6300; www.medex assist.com) or **Travel Assistance International** (© 800/821-2828; www.travelassistance.com; for general information on services, call the company's Worldwide Assistance Services, Inc., at © **800/777-8710**).

## LOST-LUGGAGE INSURANCE

On international flights (including U.S. portions of international trips), lost baggage is reimbursed to approximately $9.07 per pound, with a limit of about $635 per checked bag. If you plan to check items more valuable than the standard liability, see if your valuables are covered by your homeowner's policy, get baggage insurance as part of your comprehensive travel-insurance package, or buy Travel Guard's "BagTrak" product. Be sure to take any valuables or irreplaceable items with you in your carry-on luggage, as many valuables (including books, money, and electronics) aren't covered by airline policies.

If your luggage is lost, immediately file a lost-luggage claim at the airport, detailing the luggage contents. For most airlines, you must report delayed, damaged, or lost baggage within 4 hours of arrival. The airlines are required to deliver luggage, once found, directly to your house or destination free of charge.

## 6 Health & Safety

You'll encounter few health risks while traveling in England. The tap water is safe to drink, the milk is pasteurized, and health services are good. The mad cow disease crisis appears to be over, as does the epidemic of foot-and-mouth disease. Traveling to London doesn't pose any health risk.

### WHAT TO DO IF YOU GET SICK AWAY FROM HOME

If you need an ambulance, call ☎ **999.** If you need a doctor, your hotel can recommend one, or you can contact your embassy or consulate. Outside London, dial ☎ **100** and ask the operator for the local police, who will give you the name, address, and telephone number of a doctor in your area. Also see "Fast Facts: London," in chapter 4. *Note:* U.S. visitors who become ill while they're in England are eligible only for free *emergency* care. For other treatment, including follow-up care, you'll be asked to pay.

In most cases, your existing health plan will provide the coverage you need. But double-check; you may want to buy **travel medical insurance** instead. (See the "Travel Insurance" section earlier in this chapter.) Bring your insurance ID card with you when you travel.

If you suffer from a chronic illness, consult your doctor before your departure. For conditions like epilepsy, diabetes, or heart problems, wear a **MedicAlert Identification Tag** (☎ **800/825-3785;** www.medicalert. org), which will immediately alert doctors to your condition and give them access to your records through MedicAlert's 24-hour hot line.

Pack **prescription medications** in your carry-on luggage and in their original containers, with pharmacy labels—otherwise they won't make it through airport security. Also bring along copies of your prescriptions in case you lose your pills or run out. Carry the generic name of prescription medicines, in case a local pharmacist is unfamiliar with the brand name.

And don't forget to bring along an extra pair of contact lenses or prescription glasses.

Contact the **International Association for Medical Assistance to Travellers (IAMAT)** (☎ **716/754-4883;** www.iamat.org) for tips on travel and health concerns in London or England. In Canada, call ☎ **416-652-0137.** The United States **Centers for Disease Control and Prevention** (☎ **800/311-3435;** www.cdc.gov) provides up-to-date information on necessary vaccines and health hazards by region or country (their booklet, *Health Information for International Travel,* is $25 by mail; on the Internet, it's free).

### STAYING SAFE

Like all big cities, London has its share of crime, but in general it is one of the safer destinations in Europe. Pickpockets are the most major concern. Violent crime is relatively rare, especially in the heart of London, which hasn't seen a Jack the Ripper in a long time. Even so, it is not wise to go walking in parks at night. King's Cross at night can also be a dangerous area, frequented by prostitutes and their clients. In London, take all the precautions a prudent traveler would in going to any city, be it Los Angeles, Paris, or New York. Conceal your wallet or hold onto your purse, and don't flaunt your wealth by displaying jewelry or cash. In these uncertain times, it is always prudent to check the U.S. State Department's travel advisories at http://travel.state.gov.

## 7 Specialized Travel Resources

### TRAVELERS WITH DISABILITIES

Many London hotels, museums, restaurants, and sightseeing attractions have wheelchair ramps. Persons with disabilities are often granted special discounts at attractions and, in some cases, nightclubs. These discounts are called "concessions" in Britain. It always pays to ask. Free information and advice is available from **Holiday Care Service,** Sunley House, 7th Floor, 4 Bedford Park, Croydon, Surrey CR0 2AP (℡ **0845/124-9972;** fax 0845/124-9972; www.holidaycare. org.uk).

Bookstores in London often carry *Access in London,* a publication listing hotels, restaurants, sights, shops, and more for persons with disabilities. It costs £7.95 ($14.70).

The transport system, cinemas, and theaters are still extremely hard for the disabled to negotiate, but **Transport for London** does publish a leaflet called *Access to the Underground,* which gives details on elevators and ramps at individual Underground stations; call ℡ **020/7941-4500** or visit www.londontransport.co.uk. And the **London black cab** is perfectly suited for those in wheelchairs; the roomy interiors have plenty of room for maneuvering.

London's most visible organization for information about access to theaters, cinemas, galleries, museums, and restaurants is **Artsline,** 54 Chalton St., London NW1 1HS (℡ **020/ 7388-2227;** fax 020/7383-2653; www. artsline.org.uk). It offers free information about wheelchair access, theaters with hearing aids, easily wheelchair-accessible tourist attractions and cinemas, and sign language–interpreted tours and theater productions. Artsline will mail information to North America, but it's more helpful to contact them once you arrive in London;

the line is staffed Monday through Friday from 9:30am to 5:30pm.

An organization that cooperates closely with Artsline is **Tripscope,** The Vassall Centre, Gill Avenue, Bristol B516 2QQ (℡ **08457/585-6451** or 0117/939-7782; www.tripscope. uk), which offers advice on travel in Britain and elsewhere for persons with disabilities.

Many travel agencies offer customized tours and itineraries for travelers with disabilities. **Flying Wheels Travel** (℡ **507/451-5005;** www.flying wheelstravel.com) offers escorted tours and cruises that emphasize sports and private tours in minivans with lifts. **Accessible Journeys** (℡ **800/846-4537** or 610/521-0339; www.disability travel.com) caters specifically to slow walkers and wheelchair travelers and their families and friends.

Organizations that offer assistance to disabled travelers include **Moss-Rehab** (www.mossresourcenet.org), which provides a library of accessible-travel resources online; the **Society for Accessible Travel and Hospitality** (℡ **212/447-7284;** www.sath.org; annual membership fees: $45 adults, $30 seniors and students), which offers a wealth of travel resources for all types of disabilities, in addition to informed recommendations on destinations, access guides, travel agents, tour operators, vehicle rentals, and companion services; and the **American Foundation for the Blind** (℡ **800/232-5463;** www.afb.org), which provides information on traveling with Seeing Eye dogs.

For more information specifically targeted to travelers with disabilities, the community website **iCan** (www. icanonline.net/channels/travel/index. cfm) has destination guides and several regular columns on accessible travel. Also check out the quarterly magazine *Emerging Horizons* ($14.95 per year,

$19.95 outside the U.S.; www. emerginghorizons.com); and *Open World Magazine,* published by the Society for Accessible Travel and Hospitality (see above; subscription: $18 per year, $35 outside the U.S.).

## GAY & LESBIAN TRAVELERS

London has one of the most active gay and lesbian scenes in the world; we've recommended a number of the city's best gay clubs, lounges, and bars in chapter 9, "London After Dark."

One of the best places for information on what's hot in London's gay and lesbian scene is **Gay's the Word,** 66 Marchmont St., WC1N 1AB (© 020/7278-7654; www.gaysthe word.co.uk; Tube: Russell Square), London's best gay-oriented bookstore and the largest such store in Britain. The staff is friendly and helpful and will offer advice about the ever-changing gay scene in London. It's open Monday through Saturday from 10am to 6:30pm and Sunday from 2 to 6pm. At Gay's the Word, as well as at other gay-friendly venues, you can find a number of gay publications, many free, including the popular *Boyz* and *Pink Paper* (this one has a good lesbian section). Also check out *9X,* filled with data about all the new clubs and whatever else is hot on the scene.

**The International Gay & Lesbian Travel Association (IGLTA)** (© 800/ 448-8550 or 954/776-2626; www. iglta.org) is the trade association for the gay and lesbian travel industry, and offers an online directory of gay- and lesbian-friendly travel businesses; go to their website and click on "Members."

Many agencies offer tours and travel itineraries specifically for gay and lesbian travelers. **Above and Beyond Tours** (© 800/397-2681; www.above beyondtours.com) is the exclusive gay and lesbian tour operator for United Airlines. **Now, Voyager** (© 800/255-6951; www.nowvoyager.com) is a well-known San Francisco–based gay-owned and -operated travel service.

The following travel guides are available at most travel bookstores and gay and lesbian bookstores (including London's excellent Gay's the Word bookstore, mentioned earlier), or you can order them from **Giovanni's Room** bookstore, 1145 Pine St., Philadelphia, PA 19107 (© 215/ 923-2960; www.giovannisroom.com): *Out and About* (© 800/929-2268 or 415/644-8044; www.outandabout. com), which offers guidebooks and a newsletter 10 times a year packed with solid information on the global gay and lesbian scene; *Spartacus International Gay Guide* and *Odysseus,* both good, annual English-language guidebooks focused on gay men; the *Damron* guides, with separate, annual books for gay men and lesbians; and *Frommer's Gay & Lesbian Europe* features chapters on London and nearby beach resort town Brighton.

## SENIOR TRAVEL

Many discounts are available to seniors. Be advised that in England you sometimes have to be a member of a British seniors association to get discounts. Public-transportation reductions, for example, are available only to holders of British Pension books. However, many attractions do offer discounts for seniors (Britain defines seniors as women 60 or over, and men 65 or over). Even if discounts aren't posted, ask if they're available.

If you're over 60, you're eligible for special 10% discounts on **British Airways** through its Privileged Traveler program. You also qualify for reduced restrictions on Advanced Purchases airline ticket cancellations. Discounts are also granted for British Airways' tours and for intra-Britain air tickets booked in North America. **British Rail** offers seniors discounted rates on first-class rail passes around Britain.

See "By Train," under "Getting There," later in this chapter.

Don't be shy about asking for discounts, but carry some kind of identification that shows your date of birth. Also, mention that you're a senior when you make your hotel reservations. Many hotels offer seniors discounts. In most English cities, women over the age of 60 and men over the age of 65 qualify for reduced admission to theaters, museums, and other attractions.

Members of **AARP** (formerly known as the American Association of Retired Persons), 601 E St. NW, Washington, DC 20049 (✆ **800/424-3410** or 202/434-2277; www.aarp.org), get global discounts on hotels, airfares, and car rentals. AARP offers members a wide range of benefits, including *Modern Maturity* magazine and a monthly newsletter. Anyone over 50 can join.

Many reliable agencies and organizations target the 50-plus market. **Elderhostel** (✆ **877/426-8056**; www.elderhostel.org) arranges study programs for those aged 55 and over (and a spouse or companion of any age) in the U.S. and in more than 80 countries around the world. Most courses last 5 to 7 days in the U.S. (2–4 weeks abroad), and many include airfare, accommodations in university dormitories or modest inns, meals, and tuition. **ElderTreks** (✆ **800/741-7956**; www.eldertreks.com) offers small-group tours to off-the-beaten-path or adventure-travel locations, restricted to travelers 50 and older.

Recommended publications offering travel resources and discounts for seniors include the quarterly magazine *Travel 50 & Beyond* (www.travel50andbeyond.com); *Travel Unlimited: Uncommon Adventures for the Mature Traveler* (Avalon); *101 Tips for Mature Travelers,* available from Grand Circle Travel (✆ **800/221-2610** or 617/350-7500; www.gct.com); *The 50+ Traveler's Guidebook* (St. Martin's Press); and *Unbelievably Good Deals and Great Adventures That You Absolutely Can't Get Unless You're Over 50* (McGraw-Hill).

## FAMILY TRAVEL

For the best places to stay and eat, see "Family-Friendly Hotels," in chapter 5, and "Family-Friendly Restaurants," in chapter 6. For details on sightseeing, check out the section called "Especially for Kids" in chapter 7. On airlines, you must request a special menu for children at least 24 hours in advance. Bring your own baby food; you can ask a flight attendant to warm it.

Arrange ahead of time for such necessities as a crib, bottle warmer, and car seat (in England, small children aren't allowed to ride in the front seat). If you're staying with friends, you can rent baby equipment from **Chelsea Baby Hire,** 108 Dorset Rd., SW19 3HD (✆ **020/8540-8830;** www.chelseababyhire.co.uk). The **London black cab** is a lifesaver for families; the roomy interior allows a stroller to be lifted right into the cab without unstrapping baby.

A recommended babysitting service is **Childminders** (✆ **020/7487-5040;** www.babysitter.co.uk). Babysitters can also be found for you at most hotels. Just ask at the front desk.

Before you go, help your kids to check out London Tourist Board's **Kids Love London** at **www.kidslovelondon.com**, a site created to give kids the lowdown on kid-friendly attractions, events, restaurants, and more. If you have specific questions or want a listing of special events and places to visit with children, call the free **Kidsline** (✆ **020/7487-5040**) Monday through Friday from 4 to 6pm and summer holidays from 9am to 4pm, or **London Tourist Board's** special children's information line (✆ **0891/505490**). The Tourist

Board number is accessible in London at 50p (92¢) per minute. To find out what's on for kids while you're in London, pick up the leaflet *Where to Take Children,* published by the London Tourist Board.

**Familyhostel** (© **800/733-9753;** www.learn.unh.edu/familyhostel) takes the whole family, including kids ages 8 to 15, on moderately priced domestic and international learning vacations. Lectures, field trips, and sightseeing are guided by a team of academics.

You can find good family-oriented vacation advice on the Internet from sites like the **Family Travel Network** (www.familytravelnetwork.com); **Traveling Internationally with Your Kids** (www.travelwithyourkids.com), a comprehensive site offering sound advice for long-distance and international travel with children; and **Family Travel Files** (www.thefamilytravel files.com), which offers an online magazine and a directory of off-the-beaten-path tours and tour operators for families.

*How to Take Great Trips with Your Kids* (The Harvard Common Press) is full of good general advice that can apply to travel anywhere.

## STUDENT TRAVEL

If you're planning to travel outside the U.S., you'd be wise to arm yourself with an **International Student Identity Card (ISIC),** which offers substantial savings on rail passes, plane tickets, and entrance fees. It also provides you with basic health and life insurance and a 24-hour help line. The card is available for $22 from **STA Travel** (© **800/781-4040;** www. statravel.com), the biggest student-travel agency in the world. If you're no longer a student but are still under 26, you can get an **International Youth Travel Card (IYTC)** for the same price from the same people, which entitles you to some discounts (but

not on museum admissions). (*Note:* In 2002, STA Travel bought competitors **Council Travel** and **USIT Campus** after they went bankrupt, so both of these companies are now owned by STA.)

**Travel CUTS** (© **800/667-2887,** 416/614-2887, or 020/7361-4132; www.travelcuts.com) offers similar services for both Canadians and U.S. residents. Irish students should turn to **USIT** (© **01/602-1600;** www. usitnow.ie).

**The International Students House,** 229 Great Portland St., W1W 5PN (© **020/7631-8310;** www.ish. org.uk), lies at the foot of Regent's Park across from the Tube stop for Great Portland Street. It's a beehive of activity, offering discos and film showings. See p. 96 for information on renting rooms here.

**University of London Student Union,** Malet Street, WC1E 7HY (© **020/7664-2000;** www.ulu.lon.ac. uk; Tube: Goodge Street or Russell Square), is the best place to go to learn about student activities in the Greater London area. The Union has a swimming pool, a fitness center, a gymnasium, a general store, a sports shop, a ticket agency, banks, bars, inexpensive restaurants, venues for live events, an office of STA Travel (see above), and many other facilities. It's open Monday through Thursday from 8:30am to 11pm, Friday from 8:30am to 1pm, Saturday from 9am to 2pm, and Sunday from 9:30am to 10:30pm. Bulletin boards at the Union provide a rundown on events, some of which you will be able to attend, although others might be "closed door."

**The Hanging Out Guides** (www. frommers.com/hangingout), published by Frommer's, are the top student travel series for today's students, covering everything from adrenaline sports to the hottest club and music scenes.

## SINGLE TRAVELERS

Many people prefer traveling alone, and for independent travelers, solo journeys offer infinite opportunities to make friends and meet locals. Unfortunately, the travel industry is geared toward couples, and so singles often wind up paying the penalties of traveling alone if they don't know how to avoid them. Single travelers can avoid these supplements, of course, by agreeing to room with other single travelers on the trip. An even better idea is to find a compatible roommate before you go from one of the many roommate-locator agencies.

**Travel Companion Exchange (TCE)** (℡ 631/454-0880; www.travelcompanions.com) is one of the nation's oldest roommate finders for single travelers. Register with them and find a travel mate who will split the cost of the room with you and be around as little, or as often, as you like during the day.

**Travel Buddies Singles Travel Club** (℡ 800/998-9099; www.travelbuddiesworldwide.com), based in Canada, runs small, intimate, single-friendly group trips and will match you with a roommate free of charge and save you the cost of single supplements.

**TravelChums** (℡ 212/787-2621; www.travelchums.com) is an Internet-only travel-companion matching service with elements of an online personals-type site, hosted by the respected New York–based Shaw Guides travel service.

Many reputable tour companies offer singles-only trips. **Singles Travel International** (℡ 877/765-6874; www.singlestravelintl.com) offers singles-only trips to London. **Backroads** (℡ 800/462-2848; www.backroads.com) offers more than 160 active trips to 30 destinations worldwide, including England.

For more information, check out Eleanor Berman's *Traveling Solo: Advice and Ideas for More Than 250 Great Vacations* (Globe Pequot), a guide with advice on traveling alone, whether on your own or on a group tour. (It was updated for 2003.) Or turn to the **Travel Alone and Love It** website (www.travelaloneandloveit.com), designed by former flight attendant Sharon Wingler, the author of the book of the same name. Her site is full of tips for single travelers.

## 8 Planning Your Trip Online

### SURFING FOR AIRFARES

The "big three" online travel agencies, **Expedia.com, Travelocity,** and **Orbitz,** sell most of the air tickets bought on the Internet. (Canadian travelers should try expedia.ca and Travelocity.ca; U.K. residents can go to expedia.co.uk and opodo.co.uk.) Each has different business deals with the airlines and may offer different fares on the same flights, so it's wise to shop around. Expedia and Travelocity will also send you **e-mail notification** when a cheap fare becomes available to your favorite destination. Of the smaller travel agency websites, **Side-Step** (www.sidestep.com) has gotten

the best reviews from Frommer's authors. It's a browser add-on that purports to "search 140 sites at once," but in reality only beats competitors' fares as often as other sites do.

Also remember to check **airline websites,** especially those for low-fare carriers such as Southwest, JetBlue, AirTran, WestJet, or Ryanair, whose fares are often misreported or simply missing from travel agency websites. Even with major airlines, you can often shave a few bucks from a fare by booking directly through the airline and avoiding a travel agency's transaction fee. But you'll get these discounts only by **booking online:** Most airlines now offer online-only fares that even their phone agents know nothing about. For the websites of airlines that fly to and from your destination, see "Getting There," later in this chapter.

Great **last-minute deals** are available through free weekly e-mail services provided directly by the airlines. Most of these are announced on Tuesday or Wednesday and must be purchased online. Most are valid only for travel that weekend, but some (such as Southwest's) can be booked weeks or months in advance. Sign up for weekly e-mail alerts at airline websites or check mega-sites that compile comprehensive lists of last-minute specials, such as **Smarter Living** (http:// smarterliving.com). For last-minute trips, **www.site59.com** in the U.S. and **www.lastminute.com** in Europe often have better deals than the major-label sites.

If you're willing to give up some control over your flight details, use an **opaque fare service** like **Priceline** (www.priceline.com; www.priceline. co.uk for Europeans) or **Hotwire** (www.hotwire.com). Both offer rock-bottom prices in exchange for travel on a "mystery airline" at a mysterious time of day, often with a mysterious change of planes en route. The mystery airlines are all major, well-known carriers—and the possibility of being sent from Philadelphia to Chicago via Tampa is remote; the airlines' routing computers have gotten a lot better than they used to be. But your chances of getting a 6am or 11pm flight are pretty high. Hotwire tells you flight prices before you buy; Priceline usually has better deals than Hotwire, and you no longer have to play their "name our price" game. You also have the option to pick your flights, times, and airlines from a list of low prices they offer. If you're new at this, the helpful folks at **BiddingForTravel** (www.biddingfortravel.com) do a good job of demystifying Priceline's

prices. Priceline and Hotwire are great for flights within North America and between the U.S. and Europe. But for flights to other parts of the world, consolidators will almost always beat their fares.

For much more about airfares and savvy air-travel tips and advice, pick up a copy of *Frommer's Fly Safe, Fly Smart* (Wiley Publishing, Inc.).

## SURFING FOR HOTELS

Shopping online for hotels is much easier in the U.S., Canada, and certain parts of Europe than it is in the rest of the world. If you try to book a Chinese hotel online, for instance, you'll probably overpay. Also, many smaller hotels and B&Bs—especially outside the U.S.—don't show up on websites at all. Of the "big three" sites, **Expedia** may be the best choice, thanks to its long list of special deals. **Travelocity** runs a close second. Hotel specialist sites **hotels.com** and **hoteldiscounts. com** are also reliable. An excellent free program, **TravelAxe** (www.travelaxe. net), can help you search multiple hotel sites at once, even ones you may never have heard of.

Priceline and Hotwire are even better for hotels than for airfares; with both, you're allowed to pick the neighborhood and quality level of your hotel before offering up your money. Priceline's hotel product even covers Europe and Asia, though it's much better at getting five-star lodging for three-star prices than at finding anything at the bottom of the scale. *Note:* Hotwire overrates its hotels by one star—what Hotwire calls a four-star is a three-star anywhere else.

## SURFING FOR RENTAL CARS

For booking rental cars online, the best deals are usually found at rental-car company websites, although all the major online travel agencies also offer rental-car reservations services. Priceline and Hotwire work well for rental cars, too; the only "mystery" is which major rental company you get, and for most travelers the difference between Hertz, Avis, and Budget is negligible.

## 9 The 21st-Century Traveler

### INTERNET ACCESS AWAY FROM HOME

Travelers have any number of ways to check their e-mail and access the Internet on the road. Of course, using your own laptop—or even a PDA (personal digital assistant) or electronic organizer with a modem—gives you the most flexibility. But even if you don't have a computer, you can still access your e-mail and even your office computer from cybercafes.

### WITHOUT YOUR OWN COMPUTER

It's hard nowadays to find a city that *doesn't* have a few cybercafes. Although there's no definitive directory for cybercafes—these are independent businesses, after all—three places to start looking are at **www.cybercaptive. com**, **www.netcafeguide.com**, and **www.cybercafe.com**.

Aside from formal cybercafes, most **youth hostels** nowadays have at least one computer on which you can access the Internet. And most **public libraries** across the world offer Internet access free or for a small charge. Avoid **hotel business centers,** which often charge exorbitant rates.

Most major airports now have **Internet kiosks** scattered throughout their gates. These kiosks, which you'll also see in shopping malls, hotel lobbies, and tourist information offices around the world, give you basic Web access for a per-minute fee that's usually higher than cybercafe prices. The kiosks' clunkiness and high price means they should be avoided whenever possible.

To retrieve your e-mail, ask your **Internet Service Provider (ISP)** if it has a Web-based interface tied to your existing e-mail account. If your ISP doesn't have such an interface, you can use the free **mail2web** service (www. mail2web.com) to view (but not reply to) your home e-mail. For more flexibility, you may want to open a free, Web-based e-mail account with **Yahoo! Mail** (http://mail.yahoo.com). (Microsoft's Hotmail is another popular option, but Hotmail has severe spam problems.) Your home ISP may be able to forward your e-mail to the Web-based account automatically.

If you need to access files on your office computer, look into a service called **GoToMyPC** (www.gotomypc. com). The service provides a Web-based interface for you to access and manipulate a distant PC from anywhere—even a cybercafe—provided your "target" PC is on and has an always-on connection to the Internet (such as with Road Runner cable). The service offers top-quality security, but if you're worried about hackers, use your own laptop rather than a cybercafe to access the GoToMyPC system.

### WITH YOUR OWN COMPUTER

Major Internet Service Providers (ISPs) have **local access numbers** around the world, allowing you to go online by simply placing a local call. Check your ISP's website or call its toll-free number and ask how you can use your current account away from home, and how much it will cost.

If you're traveling outside the reach of your ISP, the **iPass** network has dial-up numbers in most of the world's countries. You'll have to sign up with an iPass provider, who will then tell you how to set up your computer for your destination(s). For a list of iPass providers, go to www. ipass.com and click on "Reseller Locator." Under "Select a Country" pick the country that you're coming from, and under "Who is this service for?" pick "Individual." One solid provider is **i2roam** (www.i2roam. com; © **866/811-6209** or 920/233-5863).

Wherever you go, bring a **connection kit** of the right power and phone adapters, a spare phone cord, and a spare Ethernet network cable. British current is 240 volts, AC, so you'll need a converter or transformer for U.S.-made electrical appliances, as well as an adapter that allows the plug to match British outlets. Some (but not all) hotels supply them for guests. If you've forgotten one, you can buy a transformer/adapter at most branches of **Boots the Chemist.**

Most business-class hotels throughout the world offer dataports for laptop modems, and a few thousand hotels in the U.S. and Europe now offer high-speed Internet access using an Ethernet network cable. You'll have to bring your own cables either way, so **call your hotel in advance** to find out what the options are.

Community-minded individuals have also set up **free wireless networks** in major cities around the world. These networks are spotty, but you get what you (don't) pay for. Each network has a home page explaining how to set up your computer for its particular system; start your explorations at www.personaltelco.net/index.cgi/WirelessCommunities.

## USING A CELLPHONE IN LONDON

The three letters that define much of the world's **wireless capabilities** are GSM (Global System for Mobiles), a big, seamless network that makes for easy cross-border cellphone use throughout Europe and dozens of other countries worldwide. In the U.S., T-Mobile, AT&T Wireless, and Cingular use this quasi-universal system; in Canada, Microcell and some Rogers customers are GSM, and all Europeans and most Australians use GSM.

If your cellphone is on a GSM system, and you have a world-capable phone such as many (but not all) Sony, Ericsson, Motorola, or Samsung models, you can make and receive calls across civilized areas on much of the globe, from Andorra to Uganda. Just call your wireless operator and ask for "international roaming" to be activated on your account. Unfortunately, per-minute charges can be high—usually $1 to $1.50 in Western Europe.

World-phone owners can bring down their per-minute charges with a bit of trickery. Call up your cellular operator and say you'll be going abroad for several months and want to "unlock" your phone to use it with a local provider. Usually, they'll oblige. Then, in your destination country, pick up a cheap, prepaid phone chip at a mobile phone store and slip it into your phone. (Show your phone to the salesperson, as not all phones work on all networks.) You'll get a local phone number in your destination country—and much, much lower calling rates.

Otherwise, **renting** a phone is a good idea. While you can rent a phone from any number of overseas sites, including kiosks at airports and at car-rental agencies, we suggest renting the phone before you leave home. That way you can give loved ones your new number, make sure the phone works, and take the phone wherever you go—especially helpful when you rent overseas, where phone-rental agencies bill in local currency and may not let you take the phone to another country.

Phone rental isn't cheap. You'll usually pay $40 to $50 per week, plus airtime fees of at least a dollar a minute. If you're traveling to Europe, though, local rental companies often offer free incoming calls within their home country, which can save you big bucks. The bottom line: Shop around.

## Online Traveler's Toolbox

Veteran travelers usually carry some essential items to make their trips easier. Following is a selection of online tools to bookmark and use.

- To find out what's on in London, check out **www.visitbritain.com** or **www.timeout.co.uk**.
- **Visa ATM Locator** (www.visa.com), for locations of PLUS ATMs worldwide, or **MasterCard ATM Locator** (www.mastercard.com), for locations of Cirrus ATMs worldwide.
- **Intellicast** (www.intellicast.com) and **Weather.com** (www.weather. com). Gives weather forecasts for cities around the world.
- **Mapquest** (www.mapquest.com). This best of the mapping sites lets you choose a specific address or destination, and in seconds it will return a map and detailed directions.
- **Universal Currency Converter** (www.xe.com). See what your dollar or pound is worth in more than 100 other countries.
- **Travel Warnings** (http://travel.state.gov/travel_warnings.html, www.fco.gov.uk/travel, www.voyage.gc.ca, and www.dfat.gov.au/consular/advice). These sites report on places where health concerns or unrest might threaten American, British, Canadian, and Australian travelers. Generally, U.S. warnings are the most paranoid; Australian warnings are the most relaxed.

Two good wireless rental companies are **InTouch Global** (© 800/872-7626; www.intouchglobal.com) and **Roadpost** (© 888/290-1616 or 905/272-5665; www.roadpost.com). Give them your itinerary and they'll tell you what wireless products you need. InTouch will also, for free, advise you on whether your existing phone will work overseas; simply call © **703/222-7161** between 9am and 4pm EST, or go to http://intouchglobal.com/travel.htm.

If you have not arranged to rent a cellphone before you depart, your best deal in London is through **Rent-A-Mobile** (© 0870/011-9892), which, among other locations, will deliver your phone to you at Heathrow Airport Terminal 2, Gatwick South

Terminal, or your hotel in London. If you're renting a car, perhaps to tour England after a visit to London, you can also arrange cellphone rental through your car-rental company. The phone rentals from **Auto Europe** (© 888/223-5555 in the U.S. or © 0800-89-9893 in Britain) are especially recommended.

For trips of more than a few weeks spent in one country, **buying a phone** becomes economically attractive, as many nations have cheap, no-questions-asked prepaid phone systems. Stop by a local cellphone shop and get the cheapest package; you'll probably pay less than $100 for a phone and a starter calling card. Local calls may be as low as 10¢ per minute, and in many countries incoming calls are free.

## 10 Getting There

### BY PLANE

Don't worry about which airport, Heathrow versus Gatwick, to fly into

unless you are extremely pressed for time. Heathrow is closer to central London than Gatwick, but there is fast train service from both of the airports to the West End (see "Getting into Town from the Airport," below). **High season** on most airlines' routes to London is usually from June to the beginning of September. This is the most expensive and most crowded time to travel. **Shoulder season** is from April to May, early September to October, and December 15 to 24. **Low season** is from November 1 to December 14 and December 25 to March 31.

**FROM THE UNITED STATES** **American Airlines** (✆ **800/433-7300;** www.aa.com) offers daily nonstop flights to London's Heathrow Airport from eight U.S. gateways: New York's JFK (nine times daily), Chicago's O'Hare (once a day), Boston's Logan (once daily), Miami International (twice daily), Los Angeles International (two to three times daily), Newark and LaGuardia (three times daily), and Dallas (once daily).

**British Airways** (✆ **800/247-9297;** www.britishairways.com) offers mostly nonstop flights from 21 U.S. cities to Heathrow and Gatwick. With more add-on options than any other airline, British Airways can make a visit to Britain cheaper than you might expect. Of particular interest are the "Value Plus," "London on the Town," and "Europe Escorted" packages that include airfare and discounted accommodations throughout Britain.

**Continental Airlines** (✆ **800/231-0856;** www.continental.com) flies daily to Gatwick Airport from Newark, Houston, and Cleveland.

Depending on the day and season, **Delta Air Lines** (✆ **800/221-1212;** www.delta.com) runs either one or two daily nonstop flights between Atlanta and Gatwick. Delta also offers nonstop daily service from Cincinnati.

Although **Air India** (✆ **800/223-7776** or 212/407-1300) doesn't immediately come to mind when you think of flying from the U.S. to London, it's a viable option and is competitively priced. Air India (www.airindia.com) offers daily flights from New York's JFK and three flights a week—Tuesday, Friday, and Sunday—from Chicago to London's Heathrow Airport.

**Northwest Airlines** (✆ **800/225-2525;** www.nwa.com) flies nonstop from Minneapolis and Detroit to Gatwick.

**United Airlines** (✆ **800/241-6522;** www.united.com) flies nonstop from New York's JFK and Chicago's O'Hare to Heathrow two or three times a day, depending on the season. United also offers nonstop service three times a day from Dulles Airport, near Washington, D.C., to London's Gatwick, plus once-a-day service to Heathrow from Newark, Los Angeles, San Francisco, and Boston.

**Virgin Atlantic Airways** (✆ **800/862-8621;** www.virgin-atlantic.com) flies daily to either Gatwick or Heathrow from Boston, Newark, New York's JFK, Los Angeles, San Francisco, Washington, D.C.'s Dulles, Miami, Orlando, and Las Vegas.

**FROM CANADA** For travelers departing from Canada, **Air Canada** (✆ **888/247-2262** in the U.S. or

---

**Tips  Airport Taxes**

You pay a departure tax of £12 ($22) for flights within Britain and the European Union; and £24 ($44) for flights to the U.S. and other countries. Your airline ticket may or may not include this tax. Ask in advance to avoid a surprise at the gate.

800/268-7240 in Canada; www.air canada.com) flies daily to London Heathrow nonstop from Vancouver, Montreal, and Toronto. There are also frequent direct flights from Calgary and Ottawa.

**FROM AUSTRALIA** Qantas (© 800/227-4500 or 612/13-13-13; www.qantas.com) flies from both Sydney and Melbourne daily. **British Airways** (© 800/247-9297; www.british airways.com) has five to seven flights weekly from Sydney and Melbourne. Both airlines have a stop in Singapore.

**FROM SOUTH AFRICA** South African Airways (© 011/978-1762; www.flysaa.com) schedules two daily flights from Johannesburg and two daily flights from Cape Town. From Johannesburg, both **British Airways** (© 0845/773-377; www.british airways.com) and **Virgin Atlantic Airways** (© 011/340-3400; www. virgin-atlantic.com) have daily flights to Heathrow. British Airways flies five times weekly from Cape Town.

## GETTING INTO TOWN FROM THE AIRPORT

**LONDON HEATHROW AIRPORT** Located west of London in Hounslow (© 0870/000-0123 for flight information), Heathrow is one of the world's busiest airports. It has four terminals, each relatively self-contained. Terminal 4 handles the long-haul and transatlantic operations of British Airways. Most transatlantic flights on U.S.–based airlines arrive at Terminal 3. Terminals 1 and 2 receive the intra-European flights of several European airlines.

It takes 35 to 40 minutes by the Underground (Tube) and costs £5.40 ($10) to make the 24km (15-mile) trip from Heathrow to the center of London. A taxi is likely to cost from £40 to £55 ($74–$102). For more information about Tube or bus connections, call © 020/7222-1234.

The British Airport Authority now operates **Heathrow Express** (© 0845/ 600-1515 or 877/677-1066; www. heathrowexpress.com), a 100-mph train service running every 15 minutes daily from 5:10am until 11:40pm between Heathrow and Paddington Station in the center of London. Trips cost £13 ($24) each way in economy class, rising to £21 ($39) in first class. Children under 15 go for free (when accompanied by an adult). You can save £1 ($1.85) by booking online or by phone. The trip takes 15 minutes each way between Paddington and Terminals 1, 2, and 3, 23 minutes from Terminal 4. The trains have special areas for wheelchairs. From Paddington, passengers can connect to other trains and the Underground, or they can hail a taxi. You can buy tickets on the train or at self-service machines at Heathrow Airport (also available from travel agents).

**GATWICK AIRPORT** While Heathrow still dominates, more and more scheduled flights land at relatively remote **Gatwick** (© 0870/002-468 for flight information), located some 40km (25 miles) south of London in West Sussex but only a 30-minute train ride away. From Gatwick, the fastest way to get to London is via the **Gatwick Express trains** (© 0845/850-1530; www. gatwickexpress.co.uk), which leave for Victoria Station in London every 30 minutes during the day and every hour at night. The one-way charge is £11 ($20) Express Class for adults, £18 ($33) for First Class, half price for children 5 to 15, free for children under 5. There are also Airbus **buses** from Gatwick to Victoria Coach Station (which is adjacent to Victoria Rail Station) operated by **National Express** (© 0870/580-8080; www. nationalexpress.com), approximately every hour from 4:15am to 9:15pm; the round-trip fare is £14 ($25) per

---

**Tips**  **Getting from One London Airport to the Other**

Some visitors will need to transfer from one airport to the other. One bus company offers these transfers. **Speedlink** (© **08705/747-777**; www.speed link.co.uk) buses leave from both terminals at Gatwick and Terminals 1, 3, and 4 at Heathrow. Trip time is about an hour, with a one-way fare costing £17.50 ($32).

---

person, and the trip takes approximately 1½ hours. A **taxi** from Gatwick to central London usually costs £50–£105 ($93–$194). However, you must negotiate a fare with the driver before you enter the cab; the meter doesn't apply because Gatwick lies outside the Metropolitan Police District. For further transportation information, call © **020/7222-1234.**

**LONDON STANSTED AIRPORT**
Located some 80km (50 miles) northeast of London's West End, **Stansted,** in Essex (© **0870/000-0303**), handles mostly flights to and from the European continent. From Stansted, your best bet to central London is the **Stansted Express train** (© **0845/ 8500-150;** www.stanstedexpress.com) to Liverpool Street Station, which runs every 15 minutes from 8am to 4:30pm, and every 30 minutes in the early mornings, evening weekdays, and weekends. It costs £14 ($26) for a standard ticket and £20 ($37) for first class, and takes 45 minutes.

By bus, you can take the **A6 Airbus** (**www.gobycoach.com**), which runs regular departures 24 hours a day to both Victoria rail and coach stations, and costs £7 ($13). If you prefer the relative privacy of a taxi, you'll pay dearly for the privilege. For a ride to London's West End, they'll charge you from £50 ($93) for up to four passengers and from £110 ($204) for five or six passengers. Expect the ride to take around 75 minutes during normal traffic conditions, but beware of Friday afternoons when dense traffic may double your travel time. Our advice: Stick to the Express.

**LONDON CITY AIRPORT**
Located just 5km (3 miles) east of the bustling business community of Canary Wharf and 9.5km (6 miles) east of the City, **London City Airport** (© **020/7646-0000**) is served by 14 airlines (Air Wales, British Airways, Cirrus Airlines, Fly Be, Luxair, Jet Magic, KLM, CityJet, OLT, Lufthansa, Scot Airways, Swiss International Airlines, and VLM) that fly from 18 cities in western Europe and Scandinavia. A blue-and-white bus charges £6 ($11) each way to take you from the airport to the Liverpool Street Station, where you can connect with rail or Underground transportation to almost any destination. The bus runs daily every 10 minutes during the hours the airport is open (approximately 6:55am–9:20pm, closed on Sat at 1:15pm, Sun 11am–9:20pm).

A shuttle bus can take you to Canary Wharf, where trains from the Dockland Line Railway make frequent 10-minute runs to the heart of London's financial district, known as "the City." Here, passengers can catch the Underground from the Bank Tube stop.

In addition, London Transport bus no. 473 goes from the City Airport to East London, where you can board any Underground at the Plaistow Tube stop.

**GETTING THROUGH U.S. AIRPORTS**
With the federalization of airport security, security procedures at U.S. airports are more stable and consistent than ever. Generally, you'll be fine if you arrive at the airport **1 hour** before

a domestic flight and **2 hours** before an international flight; if you show up late, tell an airline employee and she'll probably whisk you to the front of the line.

Bring a **current, government-issued photo ID** such as a driver's license or passport, and if you've got an e-ticket, print out the **official confirmation page;** you'll need to show your confirmation at the security checkpoint and your ID at the ticket counter or the gate. For international travel to London, obviously, passports are required of all passengers. (Children under 18 do not need photo IDs for domestic flights, but the adults checking in with them need them.)

Security lines are getting shorter than they were during 2001 and 2002, but some doozies remain. If you have trouble standing for long periods of time, tell an airline employee; the airline will provide a wheelchair. Speed up security by **not wearing metal objects** such as big belt buckles or clanky earrings. If you've got metallic body parts, a note from your doctor can prevent a long chat with security screeners. Keep in mind that only **ticketed passengers** are allowed past security, except for folks escorting disabled passengers or children.

Federalization has stabilized **what you can carry on** and **what you can't.** The general rule is that sharp things are out, nail clippers are okay, and food and beverages must be passed through the X-ray machine—but that security screeners can't make you drink from your coffee cup. The Transportation Security Administration (TSA) has issued a list of restricted items; check its website (www.tsa.gov/public/index. jsp) for details. Bring food in your carry-on rather than checking it, as explosive-detection machines used on checked luggage have been known to mistake food (especially chocolate, for some reason) for bombs. Travelers in the U.S. are allowed one carry-on bag, plus a "personal item" such as a purse, briefcase, or laptop bag. Carry-on hoarders can stuff all sorts of things into a laptop bag; as long as it has a laptop in it, it's still considered a personal item. In 2003, the TSA began phasing out **gate check-in** at all U.S. airports. Passengers with e-tickets and without checked bags can still beat the ticket-counter lines by using **electronic kiosks** or even **online check-in.** Ask your airline which alternatives are available, and if you're using a kiosk, bring the credit card you used to book the ticket. If you're checking bags, you will still be able to use most airlines' kiosks; again, call your airline for up-to-date information. **Curbside check-in** is also a good way to avoid lines, although a few airlines still ban curbside check-in entirely; call before you go.

At press time, the TSA is also recommending that you **not lock your checked luggage** so screeners can search it by hand if necessary. The agency says to use plastic "zip ties" instead, which can be bought at hardware stores and can be easily cut off.

## FLYING FOR LESS: TIPS FOR GETTING THE BEST AIRFARE

Passengers sharing the same airplane cabin rarely pay the same fare. Travelers who need to purchase tickets at the last minute, change their itinerary at a moment's notice, or fly one-way often get stuck paying the premium rate. Here are some ways to keep your airfare costs down.

- Passengers who can book their ticket **long in advance,** who can **stay over Saturday night,** or who **fly midweek** or **at less-trafficked hours** will pay a fraction of the full fare. If your schedule is flexible, say so, and ask if you can secure a cheaper fare by changing your flight plans.

- You can also save on airfares by keeping an eye out in local newspapers for **promotional specials** or **fare wars,** when airlines lower prices on their most popular routes. You rarely see fare wars offered for peak travel times, but if you can travel in the off-months, you may snag a bargain.
- Search **the Internet** for cheap fares (see "Planning Your Trip Online," earlier in this chapter).
- Try to book a ticket **in its country of origin.** For instance, if you're planning a one-way flight from Johannesburg to Bombay, a South Africa–based travel agent will probably have the lowest fares. For multileg trips, book in the country of the first leg; for example, book New York–London–Amsterdam–Rome–New York in the U.S.
- **Consolidators,** also known as bucket shops, are great sources for international tickets, although they usually can't beat the Internet on fares within North America. Start by looking in Sunday newspaper travel sections; U.S. travelers should focus on the *New York Times, Los Angeles Times,* and *Miami Herald.* For less-developed destinations, small travel agents who cater to immigrant communities in large cities often have the best deals. *Beware:* Bucket shop tickets are usually nonrefundable or rigged with stiff cancellation penalties, often as high as 50% to 75% of the ticket price, and some put you on charter airlines with questionable safety records.

The best specialist in arranging travel to London and England is the **London Travel Center** (© 800/FLY-TDAY in the U.S.). This agency can handle all your travel needs between the United States and Britain, including airfare, hotels, car rentals, rail passes, and travel insurance.

Several reliable consolidators are worldwide and available on the Net. **STA Travel** is now the world's leader in student travel, thanks to its purchase of Council Travel. It also offers good fares for travelers of all ages. **Flights.com** (© 201/541-3867; www.flights. com) started in Europe and has excellent fares worldwide, but particularly to that continent. It also has "local" websites in 12 countries. **FlyCheap** (© 800/ FLY-CHEAP; www.1800flcheap. com) is owned by package-holiday monolith MyTravel and so has especially good access to fares for sunny destinations. **Air Tickets Direct** (© 800/778-3447; www. airticketsdirect.com) is based in Montreal and leverages the currently weak Canadian dollar for low fares; it'll also book trips to places that U.S. travel agents won't touch, such as Cuba.

- Join **frequent-flier clubs.** Accrue enough miles and you'll be rewarded with free flights and elite status. It's free, and you'll get the best choice of seats, faster response to phone inquiries, and more prompt service if your luggage is stolen, if your flight is canceled or delayed, or if you want to change your seat. You don't need to fly to build frequent-flier miles— **frequent-flier credit cards** can provide thousands of miles for doing your everyday shopping.
- For many more tips about air travel, including a rundown of the major frequent-flier credit cards, pick up a copy of *Frommer's Fly Safe, Fly Smart* (Wiley Publishing, Inc.).

## LONG-HAUL FLIGHTS: HOW TO STAY COMFORTABLE

- Emergency-exit seats and bulkhead seats typically have the most legroom. Emergency-exit seats are usually held back to be assigned the day of a flight (to ensure that the seat is filled by someone able-bodied); it's worth getting to the ticket counter early to snag one of these spots for a long flight. Keep in mind that bulkheads are where airlines often put baby bassinets, so you may be sitting next to an infant.

- To have two seats for yourself, try for an aisle seat in a center section toward the back of coach. If you're traveling with a companion, book an aisle and a window seat. Middle seats are usually booked last, so it's possible you'll end up with three seats to yourselves.
- Get up, walk around, and stretch every 60 to 90 minutes to keep your blood flowing. This helps avoid deep-vein thrombosis, or "economy-class syndrome," a rare and deadly condition that can be caused by sitting in cramped conditions for too long.
- Drink water before, during, and after your flight to combat the lack of humidity in airplane cabins—which can be drier than the Sahara. Bring a bottle of water on board. Avoid alcohol, which will dehydrate you.
- If you're flying with kids, don't forget to carry on toys and books for entertainment, and pacifiers and chewing gum to help them relieve ear-pressure buildup during ascent and descent. Let each child pack his or her own backpack with favorite toys.

## BY CAR
If you plan to take a rented car across or under the Channel, check with the rental company about license and insurance requirements before you leave.

### FERRIES FROM THE CONTINENT
There are many "drive-on, drive-off" car-ferry services across the Channel.

The most popular ports in France for Channel crossings are Boulogne and Calais, where you can board Stena ferries or hovercraft taking you to the English ports of Dover and Folkestone. For details, see "Hovercraft & Seacats," under "By Boat," below.

### LE SHUTTLE
The Chunnel accommodates not only trains, but also passenger cars, charter buses, taxis, and motorcycles. Le Shuttle, a half-mile-long train carrying motor vehicles under the English Channel (© **08705/353-535;** www.eurotunnel.com), connects Calais, France, with Folkestone, England, and vice versa. It operates 24 hours a day, 365 days a year, running every 15 minutes during peak travel times and at least once an hour at night.

With Le Shuttle, gone are weather-related delays, seasickness, and a need for reservations. Before boarding Le Shuttle, you stop at a tollbooth to pay, and then pass through Immigration for both countries at one time. During the ride, you travel in bright, air-conditioned carriages, remaining inside your car or stepping outside to stretch your legs. An hour later, when you reach England, you drive off toward London. The cost of Le Shuttle varies according to the season and the day of the week. Count on at least £223 ($413) per car for a round-trip ticket.

Stores selling duty-free goods, restaurants, and service stations are available to travelers on both sides of the Channel. A bilingual staff is on hand to assist travelers at both the British and French terminals.

Hertz offers **Le Swap,** a service for passengers taking Le Shuttle. At Calais, you can switch cars for one with the steering wheel on the opposite side, depending on which country you're heading for.

## BY TRAIN
### VIA THE CHUNNEL FROM THE CONTINENT

Since 1994, when the Channel Tunnel opened, the *Eurostar Express* train has been operating twice-daily passenger service between London and both Paris and Brussels. The $15-billion tunnel, one of the great engineering feats of all time, is the first link between Britain and the Continent since the Ice Age.

Rail Europe (© 800/848-7245; www.raileurope.com) sells tickets on the *Eurostar* for direct train service between Paris or Brussels and London. A round-trip fare between Paris and London, for example, costs £312 ($577) for first class, or £223 ($413) in second class. You can reduce that rate further, to £94 ($174), with a second-class, 14-day advance-purchase (nonrefundable) round-trip fare. In London, make reservations for *Eurostar* at © 0870/530-0003, or 800/EUROSTAR in the U.S. (www.eurostar.com). *Eurostar* trains arrive and depart from London's Waterloo Station, Paris's Gare du Nord, and Brussels's Central Station.

### BRITRAIL TRAVEL PASSES

If you're traveling beyond London anywhere in the United Kingdom, consider purchasing a **BritRail Classic Pass.** These passes allow you to travel for a consecutive number of days for a flat rate. In first class, adults pay $279 for 4 days, $405 for 8 days, $599 for 15 days, $765 for 22 days, and $909 for 1 month. In second class, fares are $189 for 4 days, $269 for 8 days, $399 for 15 days, $509 for 22 days, and $605 for 1 month. Senior citizens (60 and over) qualify for discounts in first-class travel: It's $237 for 4 days, $344 for 8 days, $509 for 15 days, $650 for 22 days, and $773 for 1 month. Passengers under 26 qualify for a **Youth Pass:** $142 for 4 days, $202 for 8 days, $285 for 15 days, $382 for 22 days,

and $454 for 1 month. One child (5–15) can travel free with each adult or senior pass by requesting the BritRail Family Pass. Additional children pay half the regular adult fare.

A more versatile pass is the **BritRail FlexiPass,** which allows you to travel whenever you want during a 2-month period of time. In first class it costs $349 for 4 days, $515 for 8 days, and $775 for 15 days of travel. Second class costs $239 for 4 days, $345 for 8 days, and $519 for 15 days of travel.

BritRail Passes allow unlimited travel in England, Scotland, and Wales on any British Rail scheduled train over the whole of the network during the validity of the pass without restrictions. **BritRail Euro Consecutive Pass** is ideal if you plan to hop on and off the train. A typical fare for 8 days of travel costs $405 in first class, $269 in standard class. The more versatile pass is **BritRail Euro FlexiPass,** which allows you to travel wherever you want. It costs $519 for 8 days of travel in first class or $349 in standard class. Discounts are granted to seniors, and children (ages 5–15) pay half the adult fare. For the **BritRail Family Pass,** you can purchase any adult or senior BritRail Pass, which allows one child (ages 5–15) to travel for free according to the same limitations as the adult fare.

A new BritRail Pass for travel in England only, the **BritRail England Pass,** is sold at a price 20% lower than regular BritRail Passes, and covers rail travel throughout the U.K. (England, Scotland, Wales, and Northern Ireland). Starting at $149 U.S. for 4 consecutive days of travel in standard class, the BritRail England Pass is also offered for 8, 15, or 22 consecutive days, or 1 month, or as a Flexipass (days may be consecutive or nonconsecutive) for 4, 8, or 15 days within a 2-month period. It is also available in first class, starting at $279 U.S. and at discounted prices for seniors (60 and over) in first class and youth (under 26) in standard class. As with other BritRail Passes, one child (5–15) may travel free when accompanied by an adult or senior purchasing a BritRail England Pass and requesting the Family Pass.

To call BritRail in the United States, dial © **866/BRITRAIL** or 877/677-1066. The fax is 877/477-1066. You can purchase tickets and passes on the Web at **www.britrail. net**. For hotels, trip planning, promotions, and vacation packages through BritRail, visit www.britainsecrets.com.

The **BritRail Days Out from London Pass** is best suited for visitors wishing to make day trips to places like Oxford and Cambridge. There's no need to hassle with lines to purchase tickets; you can go directly to your train and board. The cost for 2 days within an 8-day period is $89 for adults and $31 for children in first class, or $59 for adults and $21 for children in second class.

Travelers who arrive from France by boat (see "By Boat," below) and pick up a British Rail train at Dover, arrive at **Victoria Station,** in the center of London. Those journeying south by rail from Edinburgh arrive at **King's Cross Station.**

## BY BUS
If you're traveling to London from elsewhere in the United Kingdom, consider purchasing a **Britexpress Card,** which entitles you to a 30% discount on National Express (England and Wales) and Caledonian Express (Scotland) buses. Contact a travel agent for details.

Bus connections to Britain from the Continent, using the Euro-tunnel (Chunnel) or ferry services, are generally not very comfortable, although some lines are more convenient than others. One line with a relatively good reputation is **Eurolines,** 52 Grosvenor Gardens, SW1W OAU (© **0870/808080;** www.eurolines.co. uk). They book passage on buses traveling two times a day between London and Paris (9 hr.); three times a day from Amsterdam (12 hr.); three times a week from Munich (24 hr.); and three times a week from Stockholm (44 hr.). On longer routes, which use alternating drivers, the bus proceeds almost without interruption, taking only occasional breaks for meals.

## BY BOAT
### CROSSING THE ATLANTIC
The **Cunard Line,** 6100 Blue Lagoon Dr., Suite 400, Miami, FL 33126 (© **800/7-CUNARD;** www.cunard line.com), boasts that its newly launched flagship, *Queen Mary 2,* is the only five-star-plus luxury ocean liner providing regular transatlantic service—some 15 voyages a year between April and December. QM2 is the world's largest, longest, tallest, grandest ocean liner ever, setting sail from Southampton on her maiden voyage on January 12, 2004. Carrying 2,620 passengers, the ship cost a staggering $800 million. Athletes find not just a good gym but a virtual playing field, and hedonists can enjoy a world-class spa. There's even a planetarium—it's a veritable city at sea. Many passengers appreciate the cruise's graceful introduction to British mores, as well as the absolute lack of jet lag.

Fares vary, based on the season and the cabin grade. The average 6-day crossing begins at $1,869 per person and can go up to as high as $27,499 per person for one of the standard outside suites. All prices are double occupancy; a fee of $275 port and handling charges is included in these rates. Many packages are offered, which include inexpensive airfare from your home city to the point of departure, plus a return flight to your home city from London on British Airways.

## CAR & PASSENGER FERRIES

**P&O Ferries** (© **0870/520-2020;** www.poferries.com) operates car and passenger ferries between Dover (England) and Calais (France) only. Trip time is 75 minutes at a cost of £97 ($179) one-way for a car and driver, or £6 ($11) for a foot passenger round-trip. Once you arrive in Dover, you can pick up a BritRail train to London (see "By Train," above). Traveling from Portsmouth (England) to Cherbourg (France), depending on the vessel, this trip can take from 2 hours and 45 minutes up to 5 hours. One-way car passage costs £118 ($218) for up to two adults and two children. One-way foot passengers pay £20 ($37).

## HOVERCRAFT & SEACATS

Traveling by hovercraft or Seacat offers a speedy journey from the Continent to Britain, and vice versa. **HoverSpeed** operates at least six daily 35-minute hovercraft crossings, as well as slightly longer crossings via Seacat (a catamaran propelled by jet engines; these go four times daily and take about 50 min.), between Boulogne and Folkestone. A hovercraft trip is definitely fun, as the vessel is technically "flying" over the water. Seacats also travel from the mainland of Britain to the Isle of Wight, Belfast, and the Isle of Man. For reservations and information, call **HoverSpeed** at © **0870/524-0241** (www.hoverspeed.com). For foot passengers, a typical adult fare, round-trip with a 5-day return policy, is £26 ($48). Children pay half fare.

## 11 Packages for the Independent Traveler

Before you start your search for the lowest airfare, you may want to consider booking your flight as part of a travel package. Package tours are not the same thing as escorted tours. Package tours are simply a way to buy the airfare, accommodations, and other elements of your trip (such as car rentals, airport transfers, and sometimes even activities) at the same time and often at discounted prices—kind of like one-stop shopping. Packages are sold in bulk to tour operators—who resell them to the public at a cost that usually undercuts standard rates.

One good source of package deals is the airlines themselves. Most major airlines offer air/land packages, including **American Airlines Vacations** (© 800/321-2121; www.aavacations. com), **Delta Vacations** (© 800/221-6666; www.deltavacations.com), **Continental Airlines Vacations** (© 800/301-3800; www.coolvacations.com), **United Vacations** (© 888/854-3899; www.unitedvacations.com), **US Airways Vacations** (© 800/455-0123;

www.usairwaysvacations.com), and **Virgin Atlantic Airways** (© 800/862-8621; www.virgin-atlantic.com). Several big **online travel agencies**— Expedia, Travelocity, Orbitz, Site59, and Lastminute.com—also do a brisk business in packages. If you're unsure about the pedigree of a smaller packager, check with the Better Business Bureau in the city where the company is based, or go online at www.bbb.org. If a packager won't tell you where it's based, don't fly with it.

**British Airways** (© **800/369-8722;** www.britishairways.com/holiday) offers the most diversified packages in all price ranges. BA books not only the government-rated 4-star hotels, but also the more moderate 2-star hotels (the latter charging moderate tariffs). BA is also a pioneer in student/youth specials.

If you're seeking cut-rate package deals, try **Liberty Travel** (© **888/271-1584;** www.libertytravel.com) and **British Travel International** (© **800/327-6071;** www.britishtravel.com).

Travel packages are also listed in the travel section of your local Sunday newspaper. Or check ads in the national travel magazines such as *Arthur Frommer's Budget Travel Magazine, Travel & Leisure, National Geographic Traveler,* and *Condé Nast Traveler.*

Package tours can vary by leaps and bounds. Some offer a better class of hotels than others. Some offer the same hotels for lower prices. Some offer flights on scheduled airlines, while others book charters. Some limit your choice of accommodations and travel days. You are often required to make a large payment upfront. On the plus side, packages can save you money, offering group prices but allowing for independent travel. Some even let you add on a few guided excursions or escorted day trips (also at prices lower than if you booked them yourself) without booking an entirely escorted tour.

Before you invest in a package tour, get some answers. Ask about the **accommodations choices** and prices for each. Then look up the hotels' reviews in a Frommer's guide and check their rates for your specific dates of travel online. You'll also want to find out what **type of room** you get. If you need a certain type of room, ask for it; don't take whatever is thrown your way. Request a nonsmoking room, a quiet room, a room with a view, or whatever you fancy.

Finally, look for **hidden expenses.** Ask whether airport departure fees and taxes, for example, are included in the total cost.

## 12 Escorted General-Interest Tours

Escorted tours are structured group tours with a group leader. The price usually includes everything from airfare to hotels, meals, tours, admission costs, and local transportation.

The two largest tour operators conducting escorted tours of Europe are **Globus/Cosmos** (© 800/338-7092; www.globusandcosmos.com) and **Trafalgar** (© 800/854-0103; www.trafalgartours.com). Both of these companies have first-class tours that run about $100 a day and budget tours for about $75 a day. The differences are mainly in hotel location and the number of activities. There's little difference in the companies' services (though Globus/Cosmos is slightly more of a budget choice than the upmarket Trafalgar), so choose your tour based on the itinerary and preferred date of departure. Brochures are available at travel agencies, and all tours must be booked through travel agents.

Many people derive a certain ease and security from escorted trips. Escorted tours—whether by bus, motor coach, train, or boat—let travelers sit back and enjoy their trip without having to spend lots of time behind the wheel. All the little details are taken care of; you know your costs upfront; and there are few surprises. Escorted tours can take you to the maximum number of sights in the minimum amount of time with the least amount of hassle—you don't have to sweat over the plotting and planning of a vacation schedule. Escorted tours are particularly convenient for people with limited mobility.

On the downside, an escorted tour often requires a big deposit upfront, and lodging and dining choices are predetermined. As part of a cloud of tourists, you'll get little opportunity for serendipitous interactions with locals. The tours can be jam-packed with activities, leaving little room for individual sightseeing, whim, or adventure—plus they also often focus only on the heavily touristed sites, so you miss out on the lesser-known gems.

Before you invest in an escorted tour, ask about the **cancellation policy:** Is a deposit required? Can they cancel the trip if they don't get enough people? Do you get a refund if they cancel? If *you* cancel? How late can you cancel if you are unable to go? When do you pay in full? ***Note:*** If you choose an escorted tour, think strongly about purchasing trip-cancellation insurance, especially if the tour operator asks you to pay upfront. See the section on "Travel Insurance," earlier in this chapter.

You'll also want to get a complete **schedule** of the trip to find out how much sightseeing is planned each day and whether enough time has been allotted for relaxing or wandering solo.

The **size** of the group is also important to know upfront. Generally, the smaller the group, the more flexible the itinerary, and the less time you'll spend waiting for people to get on and off the bus. Find out the **demographics** of the group as well. What is the age range? What is the gender breakdown? Is this mostly a trip for couples or singles?

Discuss what is included in the **price.** You may have to pay for transportation to and from the airport. A box lunch may be included in an excursion, but drinks might cost extra. Tips may not be included. Find out if you will be charged if you decide to opt out of certain activities or meals.

Before you invest in a escorted tour, get some answers. Ask about the **accommodations choices** and prices for each. Then look up the hotels' reviews in a Frommer's guide and check their rates for your specific dates of travel online. You'll also want to find out what **type of room** you get. If you need a certain type of room, ask for it; don't take whatever is thrown your way. Request a nonsmoking room, a quiet room, a room with a view, or whatever you fancy.

Finally, if you plan to travel alone, you'll need to know if a **single supplement** will be charged and if the company can match you up with a roommate.

## 13 Recommended Books

### GENERAL HISTORY

Anthony Sampson's *The Changing Anatomy of Britain* (Hodder & Stoughton, 1982) still gives great insight into the idiosyncrasies of English society. *London Perceived* (Harcourt, Reissue Edition, 1985), by novelist and literary critic V. S. Pritchett, is a witty portrait of the city—its history, art, literature, and life. Virginia Woolf's *The London Scene: Five Essays* (Random House, 1982), a literary gem, brilliantly depicts 1930s London. *In Search of London* (DaCapo Press, 2002), by H. V. Morton, is filled with anecdotal history and is well worth reading even though it was written in the 1950s.

In *London: The Biography of a City* (Viking Press, 1983), popular historian Christopher Hibbert paints a lively portrait of the city. For 17th-century history, you can't beat the *Diary of Samuel Pepys (1660–69)* (University of California Press, 1971), and for the flavor of the 18th century, try Daniel Defoe's *Tour Thro' London About the Year 1725* (Ayer Co. Pub., 1970). Winston Churchill's *History of the English-Speaking Peoples* (Greenwich House, 1983) is a four-volume tour de force, while his *The Gathering Storm* (Mariner Books Reissue Edition, 1986) captures London and Europe on the brink of World War II.

*Americans in London* (Olivia & Hill Press, 1986), by Brian N. Morton, is a street-by-street guide to the clubs, homes, and favorite pubs of more than 250 illustrous Americans (Mark Twain, Joseph Kennedy, Dwight Eisenhower, and Sylvia Plath among them) who made London their temporary home.

*Children of the Sun* (Basic Books, 1976), by Martin Green, depicts the decadent post–World War I period in Britain and the lives of such people as Randolph Churchill, Rupert Brooke, Edward VIII (the then Prince of Wales), and Christopher Isherwood.

George Williams's *Guide to Literary London* (Batsford, 1989) charts a series of literary tours through London, from Chelsea to Bloomsbury. Peter Gibson's *The Capital Companion* (HarperCollins, 1986), containing more than 1,200 alphabetical entries, is filled with facts and anecdotes about the streets of London and their inhabitants.

*Bloomsbury at Home,* by Pamela Todd (Harry N. Abrams, 2000), brings alive the famous literati crowd, the Bloomsbury group, who embodied the Arts and Letters society in London at the turn of the 20th century.

Sarah Valente Kettler and Carole Trimble have written the *Amateur Historian's Guide to Medieval and Tudor London* (Capital Books, Inc., 2001), which is one of the best compendiums of these two important areas. It focuses on the sometimes offbeat aspects of London's charm.

A unique walking tour for London, *Our Sisters' London: Feminist Walking Tours,* by Katherine Sturtevant (Chicago Review Press, 1990), hits the trail of some of the most illustrious (or notorious) women who called London home.

## ARCHITECTURE

*The Architect's Guide to London* (Butterworth Architecture, 1990), by Renzo Salvadori, documents 100 landmark buildings with history, descriptions, photographs, and maps. *Nairn's London* (Penguin, 1988) is Ian Nairn's stimulating, opinionated discourse on London's buildings. Donald Olsen's *The City as a Work of Art:*

*London, Paris, and Vienna* (Yale University Press, 1986) is a well-illustrated text tracing the evolution of these great cities. *London One: The Cities of London and Westminster* (Viking Press, 1984) and *London Two: South* (Penguin, 1999) are labors of love by well-known architectural writers Bridget Cherry and Nikolaus Pevsner. *Looking Up In London* (Wiley, 2003), by Jane and Helen Peyton, guides readers to architectural gems above eye-level all over central London. The book is filled with stunning photographs and fascinating facts.

In one of the best overviews of its kind, Ann Saunders tackles *The Art and Architecture of London: An Illustrated Guide* (HarperCollins, 1984). The book is particularly articulate about the City of London, its medieval core and modern-day financial district, but it covers all neighborhoods well.

The fascinating story of the re-creation of London's most famous theater is told in *Shakespeare's Globe Rebuilt,* edited by J. R. Mulryne (Cambridge University Press, 1997). Theater buffs especially will appreciate this keen insight into the Elizabethan stage.

## FICTION & BIOGRAPHY

Peter Ackroyd's *London: The Biography* (Nan A. Talese/Doubleday, 2001) is a biography of London, warts and all, perhaps the most entertaining in years. It makes a lot of unknowable London knowable. It's somewhat of a tour de force.

*The Queen: 50 Years—A Celebration* (HarperCollins, 2002) is a well-written and beautifully illustrated book tracing the 50-year reign of Queen Elizabeth II by her former press secretary Ronald Allison.

A good feel for English life, both urban and rural, has been created by some of the country's leading exponents of mystery and suspense fiction. Agatha Christie, P. D. James, Dorothy Sayers, and Ruth Rendell are just a few of the familiar authors. Of course, the great London mystery character is Sir Arthur Conan Doyle's Sherlock Holmes.

Master storyteller Charles Dickens re-creates Victorian London in such books as *Oliver Twist* (Tor Books, 1998), *David Copperfield* (Penguin, 1997), *Great Expectations* (Penguin, 2003), and his earlier, satirical *Sketches by Boz* (Oxford, 1987).

Edwardian London and the 1920s and 1930s are wonderfully captured in any of Evelyn Waugh's social satires and comedies. Any work from the Bloomsbury Group will also prove enlightening—Virginia Woolf's *Mrs. Dalloway* (Harvest Books, 1990), for example, which peers behind the surface of the London scene. For a portrait of wartime London, there's Elizabeth Bowen's *Heat of the Day* (Anchor Books, 2002).

For an American slant on London and on England, Henry James's *The Awkward Age* (Penguin, 1987) dissects the social order of the English upper class when a young woman finds herself impossibly spoiled for the marriage market by her contact with her mother's "fast set."

Colin MacInnes's novels *City of Spades* and *Absolute Beginners* (Farrar, Straus & Giroux, 1969) focus on more-recent social problems. Among contemporary writers, Margaret Drabble and Iris Murdoch are both challenging.

No "man about town" in London became more famous than Shakespeare, and the Bard's life and the English Renaissance are illuminated in Dennis Kay's *Shakespeare: His Life, Work, and Era* (Morrow, 1992). Another interesting portrait emerges in *Shakespeare, the Latter Years,* by Russell Fraser (Columbia University Press, 1992).

An equally famous man about London was Sir Winston Churchill (1874–1965). The latest engaging study emerges in *Churchill: A Life* by Martin Gilbert (Holt, 1992).

Richard Ellmann's *Oscar Wilde* (Vintage Books, 1988) is a masterpiece, bringing the Victorian era and such personalities as Lillie Langtry, Gilbert and Sullivan, and Henry James to light. More recently, *The Lives of John Lennon* by Albert Goldman (A Cappella Books, 2001) traces the life of the most famous of all 1960s musicians.

The British Tourist Authority has produced *A Movie Map of Britain,* available at local visitor centers, pinpointing London locales used in various films.

# 4

# Getting to Know London

England's largest city is like a great wheel, with Piccadilly Circus at its hub and dozens of communities branching out from it. Since London is such a large conglomeration of neighborhoods and areas, each with its own personality, first-time visitors are sometimes intimidated until they get the hang of it. Many visitors spend all their time in the West End, where most of the attractions are, with a visit to the City (London's financial district) to see the Tower of London.

This chapter provides a brief orientation to the city's neighborhoods and tells you how to get around London by public transport or on foot. In addition, the "Fast Facts" section helps you find everything from babysitters to camera-repair shops.

## 1 Orientation

### ARRIVING

For information on getting into London from the various airports, see "Getting into Town from the Airport" on p. 50.

### BY TRAIN

Each of London's train stations is connected to the city's vast bus and Underground network, and each has phones, restaurants, pubs, luggage storage areas, and London Regional Transport Information Centres.

If you're coming from France, the fastest way to get to London is by the **Hover-Speed** connection between Calais and Dover (see "Hovercraft & Seacats," under "By Boat," in chapter 3), where you can get a BritRail train into London. For one-stop travel, you can take the Chunnel train direct from Paris to Waterloo Station in London.

### BY CAR

Once you arrive on the English side of the channel, the M20 takes you directly into London. *Remember to drive on the left.* Two roadways encircle London: the A406 and A205 form the inner beltway; the M25 rings the city farther out. Determine which part of the city you want to enter and follow signposts.

We suggest you confine driving in London to the bare minimum, which means arriving and parking. Because of parking problems and heavy traffic, getting around London by car is not a viable option. Once there, leave your car in a garage and rely on public transportation or taxis. Before arrival in London, call your hotel and inquire if it has a garage (and what the charges are), or ask the staff to give you the name and address of a garage nearby.

### VISITOR INFORMATION

The **British Travel Centre,** Rex House, 1 Regent St., Haymarket, London SW1 Y4XT (Tube: Piccadilly Circus), caters to walk-in visitors with information about all parts of Britain. There's no telephone service; you must go in person and there is often a wait in a lengthy line. On the premises you'll find a British

Rail ticket office, travel and theater ticket agencies, a hotel-booking service, a bookshop, and a souvenir shop. It's open Monday through Friday from 9am to 6:30pm, Saturday and Sunday from 10am to 4pm, with extended hours on Saturday from June to September.

London Tourist Board's **Visit London,** 1 Warwick Row, London, SW1 E5ER (© **020/7932-2000;** Tube: Victoria Station), can help you with almost anything. The center deals chiefly with accommodations in all price categories and can handle most travelers' questions. It also arranges ticket sales for tours, and theater reservations, and offers a wide selection of books and souvenirs. From Easter to October, the center is open daily from 8am to 7pm; from November to Easter, it's open Monday through Saturday from 8am to 6pm and Sunday from 9am to 4pm.

## CITY LAYOUT
### AN OVERVIEW OF LONDON

While **Central London** doesn't formally define itself, most Londoners today would probably accept the Underground's Circle Line as a fair boundary.

**"The City"** (the financial district) is where London began; it's the original square mile that the Romans called *Londinium,* and it still exists as its own self-governing entity. Rich in historical, architectural, and social interest, the City is one of the world's great financial areas. Even though the City is jeweled with historic sights, it empties out in the evenings and on weekends, and there are lots of better places to stay if you are looking for a hopping nightlife scene.

**The West End,** where most of London's main attractions are found, is unofficially bounded by the Thames to the south, Farringdon Road/Street to the east, Marylebone Road/Euston Road to the north, and Hyde Park and Victoria Station to the west. Most visitors will spend their time in the West End, whether at Buckingham Palace, the British Museum, or the shops and theaters of Soho. You'll find the greatest concentration of hotels and restaurants in the West End. Despite attempts to extend central London's nocturnal life to the south side of the Thames(notably the ambitious South Bank Arts Centre—London's energy fades when it crosses the river. Still, the new urban development of Docklands, the tourist attraction of the new Globe Theatre, and some up-and-coming residential neighborhoods are infusing energy into the area across the river.

Farther west are the upscale neighborhoods of Belgravia, Kensington, Knightsbridge, Chelsea, Paddington and Bayswater, Earl's Court, and Notting Hill. This is also prime hotel and restaurant territory. To the east of the City is the **East End,** which forms the eastern boundary of **Inner London** (Notting Hill and Earl's Court roughly form the western boundary). Inner London is surrounded, like a donut, by the sprawling hinterland of **Outer London.**

## FINDING YOUR WAY AROUND

It's not easy to find an address in London, as the city's streets—both names and house numbers—follow no pattern whatsoever. London is checkered with innumerable squares, mews, closes, and terraces that jut into, cross, overlap, or otherwise interrupt whatever street you're trying to follow. And house numbers run in odds and evens, clockwise and counterclockwise—when they exist at all. Many establishments, such as the Four Seasons Hotel and Langan's Brasserie, don't have numbers, even though the building right next door is numbered. Just ask if you're having trouble finding something. Throughout this book, street addresses are followed by designations like SW1 and EC1, which are postal areas. The original post office was at St. Martin-le-Grand in the City, so the postal districts are related to where they lie geographically from there. Victoria is SW1 since it's the first area southwest of St. Martin-le-Grand; Covent Garden is west (west central), so its postal area is WC1 or WC2; Liverpool Street is east central of St. Martin-le-Grand, so its postal area is EC1.

If you plan to explore London in any depth, you'll need a detailed street map with an index. No Londoner is ever without a *London A to Z*, the ultimate street-by-street reference guide, available at bookstores and newsstands. There's even a *Mini A to Z*, which all but the most myopic will find easier to carry around.

## LONDON'S NEIGHBORHOODS IN BRIEF

### The City & Environs

**The City** When Londoners speak of "the City" (EC2, EC3), they mean the original square mile that's now the British version of Wall Street. The buildings of this district are known all over the world: the Bank of England, the London Stock Exchange, and famed insurance company Lloyd's of London. The City was the original site of *Londinium,* the first settlement of the Roman conquerors. Despite its age, the City doesn't easily reveal its past. Although it retains some of its medieval character, much of the City has been swept away by the Great Fire of 1666, the bombs of 1940, the IRA bombs of the 1990s, and the zeal of modern developers. Landmarks include Sir Christopher Wren's masterpiece, **St. Paul's Cathedral,** which stood virtually alone in the surrounding rubble after the Blitz. Some 2,000 years of history unfold at the City's **Museum of London** and at the **Barbican Centre,** opened by Queen Elizabeth in 1982.

Following the Strand eastward from Trafalgar Square, you'll come to Fleet Street. In the 19th century, this corner of London became the most concentrated newspaper district in the world. William Caxton printed the first book in English here, and the *Daily Consort,* the first daily newspaper printed in England, was launched at Ludgate Circus in 1702. In recent times, however, most London tabloids have abandoned Fleet Street for the Docklands across the river. Where the Strand becomes Fleet Street stands Temple Bar, where the actual City of London begins. The Tower of London looms at the eastern fringe of the City, shrouded in legend, blood, and history, and permanently besieged by battalions of visitors.

The average visitor will venture into the City during the day to sample its attractions or to lunch at pubs such as **Ye Olde Cheshire Cheese,** then return to the West End for evening amusement. As a hotel district, the City wasn't even on the map until recent times. The opening of the **Great Eastern Hotel** has brought a lot of business clients who prefer to stay here to avoid the traffic jams involved in getting into and out of the City. Stay in the City if you would prefer a hotel in a place like New York's Wall Street instead of a midtown address. If you can't afford the Great Eastern, consider the cheaper **Rookery** in newly fashionable Smithfield. The City lures hotel guests who prefer its quirky, quiet, offbeat flavor at night, when it's part ghost town, part movie set. There is some nightlife here, including pubs and restaurants. It's fun to wander the area when all the crowds are gone, pondering the thought that you're walking the same streets that Samuel Johnson trod so long ago.

The City of London still prefers to function on its own, separate from the rest of London. It maintains its own **Information Centre** at St. Paul's Churchyard, EC4 (✆ **020/7332-1456**), which is open Monday through Friday from 9:30am to 5pm and Saturday from 9:30am to 12:30pm.

**The East End** Traditionally, this was one of London's poorest districts, nearly bombed out of existence during World War II. In the words of one commentator at the time, Hitler created "instant urban renewal" here. The East End extends east from the City Walls, encompassing Stepney, Bow, Poplar, West Ham, Canning Town, and other districts. The East End is the home of the Cockney. To be a true Cockney, it's said that you must be born within the sound of the Bow Bells of **St. Mary-le-Bow** church, an old church rebuilt by Sir Christopher Wren in 1670.

These days, many immigrants to London make their homes in the East End. London is pushing eastward, and the East End might even become fashionable, somewhat like the Lower East Side of New York. But that day isn't quite here, and except for the Docklands area (see below), much of the East End doesn't concern the average visitor. Attractions that you may want to visit if you are in the area include St. Clements Danes church, the Temple of Mithras, and Sir Christopher Wren's Monument to the Great Fire of 1666.

**Docklands** In 1981, the London Docklands Development Corporation (LDDC) was formed to redevelop Wapping, the Isle of Dogs, the Royal Docks, and Surrey Docks, in the most ambitious scheme of its kind in Europe. The area is bordered roughly by Tower Bridge to the west and London City Airport and the Royal Docks to the east. Many businesses have moved here; Thames-side warehouses have been converted to Manhattan-style lofts; and museums, entertainment complexes, shops, and an ever-growing list of restaurants have popped up at this 21st-century river city in the making.

**Canary Wharf,** on the Isle of Dogs, is the heart of Docklands. This 28-hectare (69-acre) site is dominated by a 240m-high (787-ft.) tower, which is the tallest building in the United Kingdom, and was designed by Cesar Pelli. The Piazza of the tower is lined with shops and restaurants. On the south side of the river at Surrey Docks, Sir Terence Conran has converted the Victorian warehouses of Butler's Wharf into offices, workshops, houses, shops, and restaurants. Butler's Wharf is also home to the **Design Museum.** Chances are you'll venture here for sights and restaurants, not for lodging, unless you've got business in the area. The area is fun during the day, and you'll find some of London's finest restaurants here, offering good food and a change of pace from the West End—this is postmillennium London, whereas the West End is the essence of traditional. See our recommendations in chapter 6, "Where to Dine." To get to Docklands, take the Underground to Tower Hill and pick up the **Docklands Light Railway** (✆ **020/ 7222-1234**), which operates Monday to Saturday from 5:30am to 12:30am, from 7:30am to 11:30pm Sunday.

**South Bank** Although not officially a district, this is where you'll find the **South Bank Arts Centre,** the largest arts center in Western Europe and still growing. Reached by Waterloo Bridge (or on foot by Hungerford Bridge), it lies across the Thames from the Victoria Embankment. Culture buffs flock to its galleries and halls, which encompass the **National Theatre, Queen Elizabeth Hall, Royal Festival Hall,** and the **Hayward Gallery.** The center also houses the National Film Theatre and the Museum of the Moving Image (MOMI).

Although its day as a top hotel district in London may come in a decade or so (since there's no room left in the West End), that hasn't happened yet. The South Bank is a destination for daytime adventures or for evening cultural attractions. You may want to dine here during a day's and evening's exploration of the area. See our recommendations in chapter 6, "Where to Dine."

Nearby are such neighborhoods as Elephant and Castle, and Southwark, home to **Southwark Cathedral.** To get here, take the Tube to Waterloo Station.

**Clerkenwell** This neighborhood, north and a bit west of the City, was the site of London's first hospital and is the home of several early churches. **St. Bartholomew-the-Great,** built in 1123, still stands as London's oldest church and the best example of large-scale Norman building in the city. In the 18th century, Clerkenwell declined into a muck-filled cattle yard, home to cheap gin distilleries. During a 19th-century revival, John Stuart Mill's London Patriotic Club moved here in 1872 and William Morris's socialist press called Clerkenwell home in the 1890s— Lenin worked here editing *Iskra.* The neighborhood again fell into disrepair, but has recently been reinvented by the moneyed and groovy. A handful of hot restaurants and clubs have sprung up, and art galleries line St. John's Square and the border of Clerkenwell Green.

Lest you think that the whole area has become trendy, know that trucks still rumble into **Smithfield Market** throughout the night, unloading thousands of beef carcasses. Farringdon is Clerkenwell's central Tube stop.

No one ever accused Clerkenwell of being a hotel district. But it is increasingly known for containing some of London's better restaurants, which have been pushed out of the West End because of high rents. See our recommendations in chapter 6, "Where to Dine."

## West End Neighborhoods

**Bloomsbury** This district, a world within itself, is bound roughly by Euston Road to the north, Gower Street to the west, and Clerkenwell to the east. It is, among other things, the academic heart of London. You'll find the **University of London,** several other colleges, and many **bookstores** here. Writers like Virginia Woolf, who lived in the area (it figured in her novel *Jacob's Room*), have fanned the neighborhood's reputation as a place devoted to liberal thinking, arts, and "sexual frankness." The novelist and her husband, Leonard, were unofficial leaders of a group of artists and writers known as "the Bloomsbury Group." However, despite its student population, Bloomsbury is a fairly staid neighborhood. The heart of Bloomsbury is **Russell Square,** whose outlying streets are lined with moderately priced to expensive hotels and B&Bs. It's a noisy but central place to stay. Most visitors come to visit the **British Museum,** one of the world's greatest repositories of treasures from around the globe. The **British Telecom Tower** (1964) on Cleveland Street is a familiar landmark.

Of all the areas described so far, this is the only one that could be called a hotel district. Hotel prices have risen dramatically in the past decade, but are nowhere near the levels of those in Mayfair and St. James's. In price, Bloomsbury's hotels are comparable to what you'll find in Marylebone to the west. But Bloomsbury is more convenient than Marylebone. At its southern doorstep lie the restaurants and nightclubs of Soho, the theater district, and the markets of Covent Garden. If you stay here, it's a 10-minute Tube ride to the heart of the action of the West End.

At the western edge of Bloomsbury you'll find **Fitzrovia,** bounded by Great Portland, Oxford, and Gower streets, and reached by the Goodge Street Tube. Goodge Street, with its many shops and pubs, forms the heart of the village. Fitzrovia was once the stamping ground for writers and artists like Ezra Pound, Wyndham Lewis, and George Orwell, among others. The bottom end of Fitzrovia is a virtual extension of Soho, with a cluster of Greek restaurants.

**Holborn** The old borough of Holborn (*Ho*-burn), which abuts the City southeast of Bloomsbury, encompasses the heart of legal London—this is where you'll find the city's barristers, solicitors, and law clerks. Still Dickensian in spirit, the area preserves the Victorian author's literary footsteps in the two Inns of Court (where law students perform their apprenticeships and where barristers' chambers are located), featured in *David Copperfield,* and the Bleeding Heart Yard of *Little Dorrit* fame. **The Old Bailey** courthouse, where judges and lawyers still wear old-fashioned wigs, has stood for English justice through the years—Fagin went to the gallows from this site in *Oliver Twist.* Everything in Holborn is steeped in history. For example, as you're downing a half-pint of bitter at the

**Viaduct Tavern,** 126 Newgate St. (Tube: St. Paul's), you can reflect on the fact that the pub was built over the notorious Newgate Prison. You might come here for some sightseeing, perhaps quenching your thirst in a historic pub.

**Covent Garden & the Strand** The flower, fruit, and "veg" market is long gone (since 1970), but memories of Professor Higgins and his "squashed cabbage leaf," Eliza Doolittle, linger on. **Covent Garden** contains the city's liveliest group of restaurants, pubs, and cafes outside Soho, as well as some of the city's hippest shops. The restored marketplace here, with its glass and iron roofs, has been called a magnificent example of urban recycling. London's **theater district** begins in Covent Garden and spills over into Leicester Square and Soho. Inigo Jones's **St. Paul's Covent Garden** is known as the actors' church; over the years, it has attracted everybody from Ellen Terry to Vivien Leigh. The **Theatre Royal Drury Lane** was where Charles II's mistress Nell Gwynne made her debut in 1665, and was also where Irish actress Dorothea Jordan caught the eye of the Duke of Clarence, later William IV. The **Strand** forms the southern border of Covent Garden. It's packed with theaters, shops, first-class hotels, and restaurants. Old pubs, **Dr. Johnson's House,** and tearooms fragrant with brewing Twinings English tea evoke memories of the rich heyday of this district as the center of London's activity. The Strand runs parallel to the Thames River, and to walk it is to follow in the footsteps of Charles Lamb, Mark Twain, Henry Fielding, James Boswell, William Thackeray, and Sir Walter Raleigh, among others. The Strand's **Savoy Theatre** helped make Gilbert and Sullivan household names.

You'll probably come here for theater or dining rather than for a hotel room. Covent Garden has few hotels (although the ones that do exist are very nice). We recommend the best ones (beginning on p. 99). Expect to spend a lot for the privilege of staying in such a central zone. The Strand, of course, has always been known for its swank Savoy Hotel.

**Piccadilly Circus & Leicester Square** Piccadilly Circus, with its statue of Eros, is the heart and soul of London. The circus isn't Times Square yet, but its traffic, neon, and jostling crowds might indeed make "circus" an apt word to describe this place. Piccadilly, which was the western road out of London, was named for the "picadil," a ruffled collar created by Robert Baker, a 17th-century tailor. If you want grandeur, retreat to the Regency promenade of exclusive shops, the **Burlington Arcade,** designed in 1819. The English gentry—tired of being mud-splashed by horses and carriages along Piccadilly—came here to do their shopping. Some 35 shops, offering a treasure trove of expensive goodies, await you. A bit more tawdry is **Leicester Square,** a hub of theaters, restaurants, movie palaces, and nightlife. Leicester Square is London's equivalent of New York's Times Square. The square changed forever in the Victorian era, when four towering entertainment halls were opened. In time, the old entertainment palaces changed from stage to screen; today, three of them still show films. In another sign of the times, the old Café de Paris is no longer a chic cabaret—now it's a disco.

There are a few hotels here, although they're invariably expensive. Stay here if you'd want a hotel in Times Square in New York. It's convenient for those who want to be at the center of the action. The downside is noise, congestion, and pollution.

**Soho** A nightclubber's paradise, Soho is a confusing grid of streets crammed with restaurants. It's a great place to visit, but you probably won't want to stay there (there aren't many hotels, anyway). These densely packed streets in the heart of the West End are famous for their cosmopolitan mix of people and trades. A decade ago, much was heard about the decline of Soho with the influx of sex shops; even the pub where Dylan Thomas used to drink himself into oblivion became a sex cinema. Since then, non-sex-oriented businesses have returned, and fashionable restaurants and shops prosper. Soho is now the heart of London's expanding gay scene.

Soho starts at Piccadilly Circus and spreads out, more or less bordered by Regent Street to the west, Oxford Street to the north, Charing Cross Road to the east, and the **theaters along Shaftesbury Avenue** to the south. Carnaby Street, a block from Regent Street, was the center of the universe in the Swinging '60s, but is now a schlocky tourist trap. Across Shaftesbury Avenue is London's **Chinatown,** centered on Gerrard Street. It's small, authentic, and packed with good restaurants. **Soho's** heart—featuring great delicatessens, butchers, fish stores, and wine merchants—is farther north, on Brewer, Old Compton, and Berwick streets (Berwick St. features a wonderful open-air fresh-food market). To the north of Old Compton Street, Dean, Frith, and Greek streets have fine restaurants, pubs, and clubs. The British movie industry is centered in Wardour Street. The average visitor comes to Soho to dine because many of its restaurants are convenient to the theater district. Most travelers don't stay in Soho, but a certain action-oriented visitor prefers the *joie de vivre* of the neighborhood as compared to staid Bloomsbury or swank Mayfair. Does this sound like you? Check out Soho's accommodations starting on p. 102.

**Marylebone**  West of Bloomsbury and Fitzrovia, Marylebone extends north from Marble Arch, at the eastern edge of Hyde Park. Most first-time visitors head here to explore **Madame Tussaud's** waxworks or walk along **Baker Street** in the footsteps of Sherlock Holmes. The streets form a near-perfect grid, with the major ones running north–south between Regent's Park and Oxford Street. Architect Robert Adam laid out **Portland Place,** one of the most characteristic squares in London, from 1776 to 1780. At **Cavendish Square,** Mrs. Horatio Nelson waited for the return of Admiral Nelson. Marylebone Lane and High Street retain a bit of small-town atmosphere, but this is otherwise a rather anonymous area. Dickens wrote nearly a dozen books while he resided here. At **Regent's Park,** you can visit Queen Mary's Gardens or, in summer, see Shakespeare performed in an open-air theater. **Marylebone** has emerged as a major "bedroom" district for London, competing with Bloomsbury to its east. It's not as convenient as Bloomsbury, but the hub of the West End's action is virtually at your doorstep if you lodge here, northwest of Piccadilly Circus and facing Mayfair to the south. Once known only for its town houses turned into B&Bs, the district now offers accommodations in all price ranges, catering to everyone from rock stars to frugal family travelers.

**Mayfair**  Bounded by Piccadilly, Hyde Park, and Oxford and Regent streets, this is the most elegant, fashionable section of London, filled with luxury hotels, Georgian town houses, and swank shops. The area is sandwiched between Piccadilly Circus and Hyde Park. It's convenient to London's best shopping and close to the West End theaters, yet (a bit snobbily) removed from the peddlers and commerce of Covent Garden and Soho.

**Grosvenor Square** (pronounced *Grov*-nor) is nicknamed "Little America" because it's home to the American Embassy and a statue of Franklin D. Roosevelt. **Berkeley Square** (*Bark*-ley) was made famous by the song "A Nightingale Sang in Berkeley Square." You'll want to dip into this exclusive section at least once. One of the curiosities of Mayfair is **Shepherd Market,** a village of pubs, two-story inns, restaurants, and book and food stalls, nestled within Mayfair's grandness. The hotels of Mayfair, especially those along Park Lane, are the most expensive and grand in London. This is the place if you're seeking sophisticated, albeit expensive, accommodations that are close to the **Bond Street** shops, boutiques, and art galleries. Also, if "address" is important to you, and you're willing to pay for a good one, Mayfair has a bed waiting for you.

**St. James's**  Often called "Royal London," St. James's basks in its associations with everybody from the "merrie monarch" Charles II to Elizabeth II, who lives at its most famous address, **Buckingham Palace.** The neighborhood begins at **Piccadilly Circus** and moves southwest, incorporating **Pall Mall, The Mall, St. James's Park,** and **Green Park.** It's "frightfully convenient," as the English say; within its confines are American Express and many of London's leading department stores. This is the neighborhood where English gentlemen seek haven at that male-only bastion of English tradition, the gentlemen's club, where poker is played, drinks are consumed, and pipes are smoked (St. James's Club is one of the most prestigious of these clubs). Be sure to stop in at **Fortnum & Mason,** 181 Piccadilly, the world's most luxurious grocery store. Launched in 1788, the store sent hams to the Duke of Wellington's army and baskets of tinned goodies to Florence Nightingale in the Crimea. Hotels in this neighborhood tend to be expensive, but if the queen should summon you to Buckingham Palace, you won't have far to go.

**Westminster** Westminster has been the seat of the British government since the days of Edward the Confessor (1042–66). Dominated by the **Houses of Parliament** and **Westminster Abbey,** the area runs along the Thames to the east of St. James's Park. **Trafalgar Square,** one of the city's major landmarks, is located at the area's northern end and remains a testament to England's victory over Napoleon in 1805. The square is home to the landmark National Gallery, which is filled with glorious paintings. Whitehall is the main thoroughfare, linking Trafalgar Square with **Parliament Square.** You can visit Churchill's Cabinet War Rooms and walk down **Downing Street** to see **Number 10,** home to Britain's prime minister. No visit is complete without a call at **Westminster Abbey,** one of the greatest Gothic churches in the world. It has witnessed a parade of English history, beginning when William the Conqueror was crowned here on Christmas Day 1066.

Westminster also encompasses **Victoria,** an area that takes its name from bustling Victoria Station, "the gateway to the Continent." Many B&Bs and hotels have sprouted up here because of the neighborhood's proximity to the rail station. Victoria is cheap and convenient if you don't mind the noise and crowds.

Welfare recipients occupy many hotels along Belgrave Road. If you've arrived without a hotel reservation, you'll find the pickings better on the streets off Belgrave Road. Your best bet is to walk along Ebury Street, east of Victoria Station and Buckingham Palace Road. Here you'll find some of the best moderately priced lodgings in central London. Since you're near Victoria Station, the area is convenient for day trips to Oxford, Windsor, or Canterbury.

## Beyond the West End

**Knightsbridge** One of London's most fashionable neighborhoods, Knightsbridge is a top residential, hotel, and shopping district just south of Hyde Park. **Harrods** on Brompton Road is its chief attraction. Founded in 1901, Harrods has been called "the Notre Dame of department stores." Right nearby, **Beauchamp Place** (*Bee*-cham) is one of London's most fashionable shopping streets, a Regency-era, boutique-lined street with a scattering of restaurants. Most hotels here are deluxe or first class.

Knightsbridge is one of the most convenient areas of London; ideally located if you want to head east to the theater district or the Mayfair shops, or west to Chelsea or Kensington's restaurants and attractions. Knightsbridge is also a swank address, with many fine hotels, although none are at the level of the palaces of Mayfair.

**Belgravia** South of Knightsbridge, this area has long been an aristocratic quarter of London, rivaling Mayfair in grandeur. Although it reached its pinnacle of prestige during the reign of Queen Victoria, the duke and duchess of Westminster still live at **Eaton Square,** and Belgravia remains a hot area for chic hotels. The neighborhood's centerpiece is **Belgrave Square.** When town houses were built from 1825 to 1835, aristocrats followed—the duke of Connaught, the earl of Essex, and even Queen Victoria's mother.

Belgravia is a tranquil district. If you lodge here, no one will ever accuse you of staying on the "wrong side of the tracks." The neighborhood is convenient to the little restaurants and pubs of Chelsea, which is located to Belgravia's immediate west. Victoria Station is located to its immediate east, so Belgravia is convenient if you're planning to take day trips from London.

**Chelsea** This stylish Thames-side district lies south and to the west of Belgravia. It begins at **Sloane Square,** with **Gilbert Ledward's Venus fountain** playing watery music. The area has always been a favorite of writers and artists, including Oscar Wilde (who was arrested here), George Eliot, James Whistler, J. M. W. Turner, Henry James, and Thomas Carlyle (whose former home can be visited). Mick Jagger and Margaret Thatcher (not together) have been more recent residents, and the late Princess Diana and her "Sloane Rangers" (a term used to describe posh women, derived from Chelsea's Sloane Square) of the 1980s gave the area even more recognition. There are some swank hotels here and a scattering of modestly priced ones. The main drawback to Chelsea is inaccessibility. Except for Sloane Square, there's a dearth of Tube stops, and unless you like to take a lot of buses or expensive taxis, you may find getting around a chore.

Chelsea's major boulevard is **King's Road,** where Mary Quant launched the miniskirt in the 1960s and where the English punk look began. King's Road runs the length of Chelsea; it's at its liveliest on Saturday. The outrageous fashions of the King's Road boutiques aren't typical of otherwise upmarket Chelsea, an elegant village filled with town houses and little mews dwellings which only successful stockbrokers and solicitors can afford to occupy. On the Chelsea/Fulham border is **Chelsea Harbour,** a luxury development of apartments and restaurants with a marina. You can spot its tall tower from far away; the golden ball on top moves up and down to indicate the tide level.

**Kensington** This Royal Borough (W8) lies west of Kensington Gardens and Hyde Park and is traversed by two of London's major shopping streets, **Kensington High Street** and **Kensington Church Street.** Since 1689, when asthmatic William III fled Whitehall Palace for Nottingham House (where the air was fresher), the district has enjoyed royal associations. In time, Nottingham House became Kensington Palace, and the royals grabbed a chunk of Hyde Park to plant their roses. Queen Victoria was born here. Kensington Palace, or "KP," as the royals say, was home to the late Princess Margaret (who had 20 rooms with a view), and is still home to Prince and Princess Michael of Kent, and the duke and duchess of Gloucester. Kensington Gardens is now open to the public, ever since George II decreed that "respectably dressed" people would be permitted in on Saturday—providing that no servants, soldiers, or sailors came (as you might imagine, that rule is long gone). During the reign of William III, Kensington

Square developed, attracting artists and writers. Thackeray wrote *Vanity Fair* while living here. With all those royal associations, Kensington is a fashionable neighborhood. If you're a frugal traveler, head for South Kensington (see below) for moderately priced hotels and B&Bs. Southeast of Kensington Gardens and Earl's Court, primarily residential **South Kensington** is often called "museumland" because it's dominated by a complex of museums and colleges, including the **Natural History Museum,** the **Victoria and Albert Museum,** and the **Science Museum;** nearby is **Royal Albert Hall.** South Kensington boasts some fashionable restaurants and town-house hotels. One of the neighborhood's curiosities is the **Albert Memorial,** completed in 1872 by Sir George Gilbert Scott; for sheer excess, this Victorian monument is unequaled in the world.

A hotel room in Kensington is a prestigious address. But as Princess Margaret may have told you, you're at the far stretch of the West End, lying some 20 minutes by Tube from the heart of the theater district. As for South Kensington, it was once considered the "boondocks," although with the boundaries of the West End expanding, the neighborhood is much closer to the action than it has ever been before.

**Earl's Court** Earl's Court lies below Kensington, bordering the western half of Chelsea. For decades a staid residential district, drawing genteel ladies wearing pince-nez glasses, Earl's Court now attracts a younger crowd (often gay), particularly at night, to its pubs, wine bars, and coffeehouses. It's a popular base for budget travelers thanks to its wealth of B&Bs and budget hotels and its convenient access to central

London: A 15-minute Tube ride takes you into the heart of Piccadilly.

**West Brompton** Once regarded as a hinterland, this neighborhood is seen today as an extension of central London. It lies directly south of Earl's Court (take the Tube to West Brompton) and southeast of West Kensington. Its focal point is the sprawling **Brompton Cemetery,** a flower-filled "green lung" (park) and burial place of such famous names as Frederick Leyland, the Pre-Raphaelite patron, who died in 1892. It has many good restaurants, pubs, and taverns, as well as some budget hotels.

**Paddington & Bayswater Paddington** radiates out from Paddington Station, north of Hyde Park and Kensington Gardens. It's one of the major B&B centers in London, attracting budget travelers who fill the lodgings in Sussex Gardens and Norfolk Square. After the first railway was introduced in London in 1836, a circle of sprawling railway terminals, including Paddington Station (which was built in 1838), spurred the growth of this middle-class area. Just south of Paddington, north of Hyde Park, and abutting more fashionable Notting Hill to the west is **Bayswater,** also filled with a large number of B&Bs that attract budget travelers. Inspired by Marylebone and elegant Mayfair, a relatively prosperous set of Victorian merchants built terrace houses around spacious squares in this area.

Paddington and Bayswater are a sort of "in-between" area of London. If you've come to London to see the attractions in the east, including the British Museum, the Tower of London, and the theater district, you'll find yourself commuting a lot. Stay here for

*Tips* **London Fights Gridlock with Pounds**

In a desperate move to ease traffic, gridlocked London has begun charging cars £5 ($9.25) to enter the most congested parts of Central London. The charge is in effect from 7am to 6:30pm Monday through Friday. A network of some 700 video cameras records license plates of vehicles moving into the zone. Traffic fees, at least according to the mayor (who rides the Tube), are expected to cut car usage by 10% to 15%.

How to pay? Londoners can pay online, over the phone, or at specially installed machines at newspaper shops, petrol stations, and food stores. Before renting a car to drive into Central London (not recommended), check with your rental company about how the charges will apply to you.

moderately priced lodgings (there are expensive hotels, too) and for convenience to transportation. Rapidly gentrifying, this area ranges from seedy to swank.

On the other (north) side of Westway/Marylebone Road are **Maida Vale** and **St. John's Wood,** two villages that have been absorbed by central London. Maida Vale lies west of **Regent's Park,** north of Paddington, and next to the more prestigious St. John's Wood (home to the Beatles' Abbey Road Studios). The area is very sports-oriented; if you take the Tube to Maida Vale, you'll find Paddington Recreation Ground, plus a smaller "green lung" called Paddington Bowling and Sports Club. The area is also home to some of the BBC studios.

**Notting Hill** Increasingly fashionable Notting Hill is bounded on the east by Bayswater and on the south by Kensington. Hemmed in on the north by Westway and on the west by the Shepherd's Bush ramp leading to the M40, it has many turn-of-the-century mansions and small houses sitting on quiet, leafy streets, plus a growing number of hot restaurants and clubs. Gentrified in recent years, it's becoming an extension of central London. Hotels are few, but increasingly chic.

Even more remote than Paddington and Bayswater, Notting Hill lies at least another 10 minutes west of those districts. In spite of that, many young professional visitors to London wouldn't stay anywhere else.

In the northern half of Notting Hill is the hip neighborhood known as **Notting Hill Gate,** home to Portobello Road, which boasts one of London's most famous street markets. The area Tube stops are Notting Hill Gate, Holland Park, and Ladbroke Grove.

Nearby **Holland Park,** an expensive residential neighborhood, promotes itself as "10 minutes by Tube from practically anywhere," a bit of an exaggeration.

**Shepherd's Bush** To the immediate west of Notting Hill Gate, this increasingly fashionable area is attracting a slew of artists and photographers, and in their wake a number of trendy new hangouts. Old milk-bottling factories are being turned into chic dives, and so on. The area is close to more-upscale districts such as Holland Park and Notting Hill Gate. The main BBC national office is in Shepherd's Bush, and, yes, that is Kate Moss rushing along Goldhawk Road.

**Farther Afield**

**Greenwich** To the southeast of London, this suburb, which

# Greater London Area

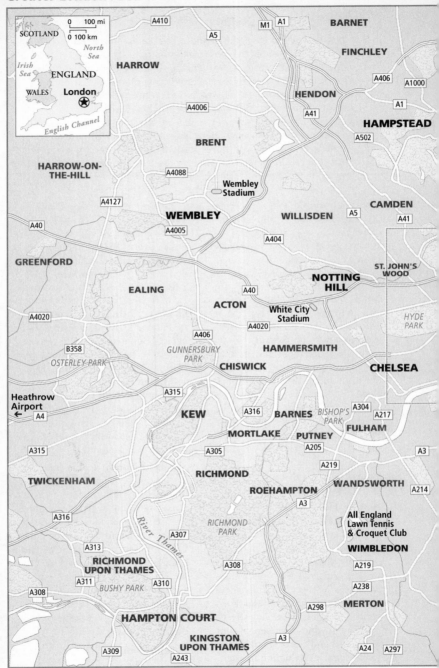

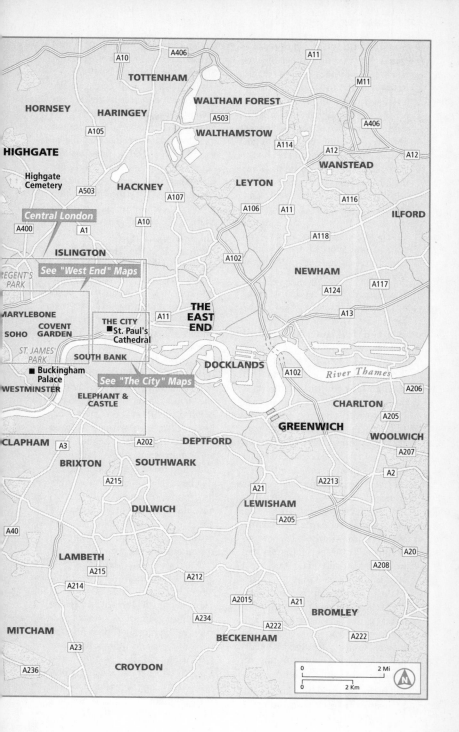

contains the prime meridian— "zero" for the reckoning of terrestrial longitudes—enjoyed its heyday under the Tudors. Henry VIII and both of his daughters, Mary I and Elizabeth I, were born here. Greenwich Palace, Henry's favorite, is long gone, though. Today's visitors come to this lovely port village for nautical sights along the Thames, including visits to the 1869 tea clipper, *Cutty Sark,* and the tiny *Gipsy Moth IV,* a 16m (52-ft.) ketch in which Sir Francis Chichester sailed solo around the world from 1966 to 1967. Other attractions include the **National Maritime Museum.**

**Hampstead** This residential suburb of north London, beloved by Keats and Hogarth, is a favorite excursion destination for Londoners. Everybody from Sigmund Freud and D. H. Lawrence to Anna Pavlova and John Le Carré has lived here, and it's still one of the most desirable districts in the Greater London area. It has very few hotels, and, of course, is quite far from central London. Nonetheless, it's an attractive residential area and many visitors appreciate its bucolic charms. Staying here is rather like going to a hotel in Westchester when you visit New York City. Hampstead's centerpiece is Hampstead Heath, nearly 320 hectares (790 acres) of rolling meadows and woodland; it maintains its rural atmosphere even though it's surrounded by cityscapes on all sides. The hilltop village of Hampstead is filled with cafes, tearooms, and restaurants, and there are pubs galore, some with historic pedigrees. Take the Northern Line to Hampstead Heath station.

**Highgate** Along with Hampstead, Highgate in north London is another choice residential area, particularly on or near **Pond Square** and along Hampstead High Street. Once celebrated for its "sweet salutarie airs," Highgate has long been a desirable place for Londoners to live; locals still flock to its taverns and pubs for "exercise and harmless merriment" as they did in the old days. Today, most visitors come to see moody **Highgate Cemetery,** London's most famous burial ground. It's the final resting place of such famous figures as Karl Marx and George Eliot.

**Hammersmith** Sitting on the north bank of the Thames, just to the west of Kensington, Hammersmith will fool you at first into thinking it's an industrial park, thanks to the stretch of factories between Putney and Hammersmith bridges. Actually, the area is predominantly residential. Its most attractive feature is its waterfront, filled with boathouses, small businesses, some very good restaurants, and artists' studios. Beyond Hammersmith Bridge, the neighborhood blossoms with balconied 18th-century homes behind lime and catalpa trees, more boathouses, and old pubs that spill out onto the riverbank as soon as warm weather hits. Some of London's best chefs have fled the heart of the West End and its ridiculous rents to open quality dining rooms here. For our recommendations, see p. 198.

Nearby is the delightful old village of **Barnes,** with its iron-work-decorated Barnes Terrace. **Hammersmith Terrace,** a favorite stamping ground of artists, adds color to the neighborhood. Another stretch of gracious homes lies along **Chiswick Mall,** curling into Church Street. This area deftly imitates an English village before thrusting you back into teeming London along Great West Road.

## 2 Getting Around

## BY PUBLIC TRANSPORTATION

The London Underground and the city's buses operate on the same system of six fare zones. The fare zones radiate out in rings from the central zone 1, which is where most visitors spend the majority of their time. Zone 1 covers the area from Liverpool Street in the east to Notting Hill in the west, and from Waterloo in the south to Baker Street, Euston, and King's Cross in the north. To travel beyond zone 1, you need a multizone ticket. Note that all single one-way, round-trip, and 1-day pass tickets are valid only on the day of purchase. Tube and bus maps should be available at any Underground station. You can download them before you travel from the excellent **London Transport (LT)** website: www.tfl.gov.uk/tfl. (You can also send away for a map by writing to **London Transport,** Travel Information Service, 42–50 Victoria St., London SW1H 0TL.) There are also **LT Information Centres** at several major Tube stations: Euston, King's Cross, Oxford Circus, St. James's Park, Liverpool Street Station, and Piccadilly Circus, as well as in the British Rail stations at Euston and Victoria and in each of the terminals at Heathrow Airport. Most of them are open daily (some close Sun) from at least 9am to 5pm. A 24-hour public-transportation information service is also available at ✆ **020/7222-1234.**

**TRAVEL DISCOUNTS**   If you plan to use public transportation a lot, investigate the range of fare discounts available. **Travelcards** offer unlimited use of buses, Underground, and British Rail services in Greater London for any period ranging from a day to a year. Travelcards are available from Underground ticket offices, LT Information Centres, main post offices in the London area, and some newsstands. You need to bring a passport-size photo to purchase a Travelcard; you can take a photo at any of the instant photo booths in London's train stations. Children under age 5 generally travel free on the Tube and buses.

The **1-Day Travelcard** allows you to go anywhere throughout Greater London. For travel anywhere within zones 1 and 2, the cost is £5.30 ($9.80) for adults or £2.60 ($4.80) for children 5 to 15. The **Off-Peak 1-Day Travelcard,** which isn't valid until after 9:30am on weekdays (or on night buses), is even cheaper. For two zones, the cost is £4.30 ($7.95) for adults and £2 ($3.70) for children 5 to 15.

**Weekend Travelcards** are valid for 1 weekend, plus the Monday if it's a national holiday. They're not valid on night buses; travel anywhere within zones 1 and 2 all weekend costs £6.40 ($12) for adults or £2 ($3.70) for kids 5 to 15.

**1-Week Travelcards** cost adults £17 ($31) and children £7 ($13) for travel in zones 1 and 2.

The 1-day **Family Travelcard** allows as many journeys as you want on the Tube, buses (excluding night buses) displaying the London Transport bus sign, and even the Docklands Light Railway or any rail service within the travel zones designated on your ticket. The family card is valid Monday through Friday after 9:30am and all day on weekends and public holidays. It's available for families as small as two (one adult and one child) to as large as six (two adults and four children). Cost is £2.80 ($5.20) per adult and 80p ($1.50) per child.

You can also buy **Carnet** tickets, a booklet of 10 single Underground tickets valid for 12 months from the issue date. Carnet tickets are valid for travel only in zone 1 (Central London) and cost £15 ($28) for adults and £5 ($9.25) for children (up to 15). A book of Carnet tickets saves you £5 ($9.25) over the cost of 10 separate single tickets.

> **Tips   Don't Leave Home Without It**
>
> For another option for public transportation in London, make sure you buy a **London Visitor Travelcard** before you leave home. This card, which allows unlimited transport within all six zones of Greater London's Underground (as far as Heathrow) and bus network, as well as some discounts on London attractions, isn't available in the U.K. You don't even need a passport picture. A pass good for 3 consecutive days of travel is $35 for adults, $16 for children 5 to 15; for 4 consecutive days of travel, it's $46 for adults, $19 for children; and for 7 consecutive days of travel, it's $69 for adults, $29 for children. Contact **BritRail Travel International**, 44 S. Broadway, White Plains, NY 10601 (© **800/677-8585**, or 800/555-2748 in Canada; www.raileurope.com). It will take up to 2 to 3 business days for the card to reach you at home.

## THE UNDERGROUND

The Underground, or Tube, is the fastest and easiest way to get around. All Tube stations are clearly marked with a red circle and blue crossbar. Routes are conveniently color-coded.

If you have British coins, you can get your ticket at a vending machine. Otherwise, buy it at the ticket office. You can transfer as many times as you like as long as you stay in the Underground. The flat fare for one trip within the Central zone is £2 ($3.70). Trips from the Central zone to destinations in the suburbs range from £2.20 to £3.80 ($4.05–$7) in most cases. It's also possible to purchase weekly passes (see "Travel Discounts" above), going for £17 ($31) for adults or £7 ($13) for children in the Central zone, £38.30 ($71) for adults or £16.50 ($31) for children for all six zones.

Slide your ticket into the slot at the gate, and pick it up as it comes through on the other side and hold on to it—it must be presented when you exit the station at your destination. If you're caught without a valid ticket, you'll be fined £10 ($19) on the spot. If you owe extra money, you'll be asked to pay the difference by the attendant at the exit. The Tube runs roughly from 5am to 11:30pm. After that you must take a taxi or night bus to your destination. For information on the London Tube system, call the **London Underground** at © **020/7222-1234,** but expect to stay on hold for a good while before a live person comes on the line. Information is also available on **www.london transport.co.uk**.

The long-running saga known as the Jubilee Line Extension is beginning to reach completion. This line, which once ended at Charing Cross, has been extended eastward to serve the growing suburbs of the southeast and the Docklands area. This east–west axis helps ease traffic on some of London's most hardpressed underground lines. The line also makes it much easier to reach Greenwich.

## BY BUS

The first thing you learn about London buses is that nobody just boards them. You "queue up"—that is, form a single-file line at the bus stop.

The comparably priced bus system is almost as good as the Underground and gives you better views of the city. To find out about current routes, pick up a free bus map at one of London Transport's Travel Information Centres, listed above.

The map is available in person only, not by mail. You can also obtain a map at **www.londontransport.co.uk/buses**.

As with the Underground, fares vary according to distance traveled. Generally, bus fares are £1 ($1.85), slightly less than Tube fares. If you want your stop called out, simply ask the conductor or driver. To speed up bus travel, passengers have to purchase tickets before boarding. Drivers no longer collect fares on board. Some 300 road-side ticket machines serve stops in central London—in other words, it's "pay as you board." You'll need the exact fare, however, as ticket machines don't make change. It will still be possible to pay on the double-decker red buses that continue to serve 20 of the 60 major bus routes in London, although in time these may be phased out.

Buses generally run 24 hours a day. A few night buses have special routes, running once an hour or so; most pass through Trafalgar Square. Keep in mind that night buses are often so crowded (especially on weekends) that they are unable to pick up passengers after a few stops. You may find yourself waiting a long time. Consider taking a taxi. Call the 24-hour **hot line** ((C) **020/7222-1234**) for schedule and fare information.

## BY TAXI

London cabs are among the most comfortable and best-designed in the world. You can pick one up either by heading for a cab rank or by hailing one in the street (the taxi is available if the yellow taxi sign on the roof is lit); once it has stopped for you, a taxi is obliged to take you anywhere you want to go within 9.5km (6 miles) of the pickup point, provided it's within the metropolitan area. To **call a cab,** phone (C) **020/7272-0272** or 020/7253-5000.

The meter starts at £3.80 ($7.05), with increments of £3.40 ($6.30) per mile thereafter, based on distance or time. Each additional passenger is charged 40p (75¢). Passengers pay 10p (20¢) for each piece of luggage in the driver's compartment and any other item more than .6m (2 ft.) long. Surcharges are imposed after 8pm and on weekends and public holidays. All these tariffs include VAT. Fares usually increase annually. It's recommended that you tip 10% to 15% of the fare.

If you call for a cab, the meter starts running when the taxi receives instructions from the dispatcher, so you could find that the meter already reads a few pounds more than the initial drop of £3.60 ($6.70) when you step inside.

**Minicabs** are also available, and they're often useful when regular taxis are scarce or when the Tube stops running. These cabs are meterless, so you must negotiate the fare in advance. Unlike regular cabs, minicabs are forbidden by law to cruise for fares. They operate from sidewalk kiosks, such as those around Leicester Square. If you need to call one, try **Brunswick Chauffeurs/Abbey Cars** ((C) **020/8969-2555**) in west London; **London Cabs, Ltd.** ((C) **020/8778-3000**) in east London; or **Newname Minicars** ((C) **020/8472-1400**) in south London. Minicab kiosks can be found near many Tube or BritRail stops, especially in outlying areas.

If you have a complaint about taxi service or if you leave something in a cab, contact the **Public Carriage Office,** 15 Penton St., N1 9PU (Tube: Angel Station). If it's a complaint, you must have the cab number, which is displayed in the passenger compartment. Call (C) **020/7918-2000** with complaints.

Cab sharing is permitted in London, as British law allows cabbies to carry two to five persons. Taxis accepting such riders display a notice on yellow plastic, with the words "Shared Taxi." Each of two riders sharing is charged 65% of the fare a lone passenger would be charged. Three persons pay 55%, four pay 45%, and five (the seating capacity of all new London cabs) pay 40% of the single-passenger fare.

## BY CAR

Don't drive in congested London. It is easy to get around without a car, traffic and parking are nightmares, and—to top it all off—you'd have to drive from what you normally consider the passenger seat on the wrong side of the road. It all adds up to a big headache.

## BY BICYCLE

One of the most popular bike-rental shops is **On Your Bike,** 52–54 Tooley St., London Bridge, SE1 (© **020/7378-6669;** Tube: London Bridge), open Monday through Friday from 8am to 7pm, and Saturday from 10am to 6pm, Sunday 11am to 5pm. The first-class mountain bikes, with high seats and low-slung handlebars, cost £12 ($22) per day, £25 ($46) per weekend, or £60 ($111) per week, and require a £200 ($370) deposit on a credit card.

---

### FAST FACTS: **London**

*American Express* The main Amex office is at 30–31 Haymarket, SW1 (© **020/7484-9600;** Tube: Piccadilly Circus). Full services are available Monday to Saturday from 9am to 6pm. On Sundays from 10am to 5pm, only the foreign-exchange bureau is open.

*Area Codes* London now has only one area code: **020.** Within the city limits, you don't need to dial it; use only the eight-digit number. If you're calling London from home before your trip, the country code for England is **44.** It must precede the London area code. When you're calling London from outside Britain, drop the "0" in front of the local area code.

*Babysitters* If your hotel can't recommend a sitter, call **Childminders,** 6 Nottingham St. (© **020/7935-2049;** www.babysitter.co.uk). The rates are £6.80 ($13) per hour during the day and £5.20 to £6.40 ($9.60–$12) per hour at night, with a 4-hour minimum. Hotel guests pay a £10 ($19) booking fee each time they use a sitter. You must also pay reasonable transportation costs.

*Business Hours* Banks are usually open Monday through Friday from 9:30am to 3:30pm. Business offices are open Monday through Friday from 9am to 5pm; the lunch break lasts an hour, but most places stay open during that time. Pubs and bars stay open from 11am to 11pm Monday through Saturday and from noon to 10:30pm on Sunday. Stores generally open at 9am and close at 5:30pm, staying open until 7pm on Wednesday or Thursday. Most central shops close on Saturday around 1pm. In a recent change, some stores are now open for 6 hours on Sunday, usually from 11am to 5pm.

*Camera Repair* **Sendean,** Shop 2, 9–12 St. Anne's Court, W1V (© **020/ 7439-8418**), gives free estimates and does quick work. It's open weekdays from 10am to 6pm and accepts MasterCard and Visa.

*Climate* See "When to Go," in chapter 3.

*Currency* See "Money," in chapter 3.

*Dentists* For dental emergencies, call **Eastman Dental Hospital** (© 020/7915-1000; Tube: King's Cross or Chancery Lane).

*Doctors* Call © **999** in a medical emergency. Some hotels have physicians on call for emergencies. For nonemergencies, try **Medical Express,** 117A Harley St., W1 (© **020/7499-1991;** Tube: Regent's Park). A private British clinic, it's not part of the free British medical establishment. For filling the British equivalent of a U.S. prescription, there's sometimes a surcharge of £20 ($37) on top of the cost of the medications. The clinic is open Monday through Friday from 9am to 5:30pm and Saturday from 9:30am to 2pm.

*Documents* See "Entry Requirements & Customs," in chapter 3.

*Drugstores* In Britain they're called chemists. Every police station has a list of emergency chemists (dial 0 and ask the operator for the local police). One of the most centrally located, keeping long hours, is **Bliss the Chemist,** 5 Marble Arch, W1 (© **020/7723-6116;** Tube: Marble Arch), open daily from 9am to midnight. Every London neighborhood has a branch of **Boots the Chemist,** Britain's leading pharmacy, which is also open until midnight.

*Electricity* British current is 240 volts, AC, so you'll need a converter or transformer for U.S.-made electrical appliances, as well as an adapter that allows the plug to match British outlets. Some (but not all) hotels supply them for guests. If you've forgotten one, you can buy a transformer/adapter at most branches of **Boots the Chemist.**

*Embassies & High Commissions* The **U.S. Embassy** is at 24 Grosvenor Sq., W1 (© **020/7499-9000;** Tube: Bond St.). Hours are Monday through Friday from 8:30am to 5:30pm. However, for passport and visa information, go to the **U.S. Passport and Citizenship Unit,** 55–56 Upper Brook St., London, W1 (© **020/7499-9000,** ext. 2563 or 2564; Tube: Marble Arch or Bond St.). Passport and Citizenship Unit hours are Monday through Friday from 8:30 to 11:30am and Monday and Friday from 2 to 4pm.

The **Canadian High Commission,** MacDonald House, 38 Grosvenor Sq., W1 (© **020/7258-6600;** Tube: Bond St.), handles visas for Canada. Hours are Monday through Friday from 8am to 4pm; 8 to 11am for immigration services.

The **Australian High Commission** is at Australia House, the Strand, WC2 (© **020/7379-4334;** Tube: Charing Cross or Aldwych). Hours are Monday through Friday from 9am to 5:20pm; 9 to 11am for immigration services; passports 9:30am to 3:30pm.

The **New Zealand High Commission** is at New Zealand House, 80 Haymarket at Pall Mall, SW1 (© **020/7930-8422;** Tube: Charing Cross or Piccadilly Circus). Hours are Monday through Friday from 10am to 4pm.

The **Irish Embassy** is at 17 Grosvenor Place, SW1 (© **020/7235-2171;** Tube: Hyde Park Corner). Hours are Monday through Friday from 9:30am to 1pm and 2 to 5pm.

*Emergencies* For police, fire, or an ambulance, dial © **999.**

*Eyeglass Repair* **David Clulow** has 10 offices in Central London; the one in Soho, 70 Old Compton St., W1 (© **020/7287-1128**), can handle most repairs and fills eyeglass prescriptions.

*Holidays* See "When to Go," in chapter 3.

*Hospitals* The following offer emergency care in London, 24 hours a day, with the first treatment free under the National Health Service: **Royal Free Hospital,** Pond Street (✆ **020/7794-0500;** Tube: Belsize Park), and **University College Hospital,** Grafton Way (✆ **020/7387-9300;** Tube: Warren St.). Many other London hospitals also have accident and emergency departments.

*Hot Lines* If you're in some sort of legal emergency, call **Release** (✆ **020/7729-9904**), open from 10am to 5:30pm. The **Rape Crisis Line** (✆ **0845/1232-324**) accepts calls after 6pm. **Samaritans,** 46 Marshall St. (✆ **020/7734-2800**), maintains a crisis hot line that helps with all kinds of trouble, even threatened suicides. From 9am to 9pm daily, a live attendant is on duty to handle emergencies; the rest of the time, a series of recorded messages tells callers other phone numbers and addresses where they can turn to for help. **Alcoholics Anonymous** (✆ **020/7833-0022**) answers its hot line daily from 10am to 10pm. The **AIDS** 24-hour hot line is ✆ **0800/567-123.**

*Legal Aid* In every case where legal aid is required by a foreign national within Britain, the British Tourist Authority advises visitors to contact their embassy.

*Liquor Laws* No alcohol is served to anyone under 18. Children under 16 aren't allowed in pubs, except in certain rooms, and then only when accompanied by a parent or guardian. Pubs are open Monday through Saturday from 11am to 11pm and Sunday from noon to 10:30pm. Restaurants are allowed to serve liquor during the same hours as pubs; however, only people eating a meal on the premises can be served. You can buy beer, wine, and liquor in supermarkets, liquor stores (called off-licenses), and many local grocery stores during any hour that pubs are open. In hotels, liquor may be served from 11am to 11pm to both residents and nonresidents; after 11pm, only residents may be served. Any nightclub that charges admission is allowed to serve alcohol until 3am or so. Don't drink and drive; penalties are stiff.

*Lost & Found* Be sure to tell all of your credit-card companies the minute you discover your wallet has been lost or stolen, and file a report at the nearest police precinct. Your credit card company or insurer may require a police report number or record of the loss. Most credit card companies have an emergency toll-free number to call if your card is lost or stolen; they may be able to wire you a cash advance immediately or deliver an emergency credit card in a day or two. Visa's U.S. emergency number is ✆ **800/847-2911** or 410/581-9994. American Express cardholders and traveler's check holders should call ✆ **800/221-7282.** MasterCard holders should call ✆ **800/307-7309** or 636/722-7111. For other credit cards, call the toll-free number directory at ✆ **800/555-1212.**

In Britain, for Amex issues call ✆ **0208/551-1111;** for Visa and MasterCard issues, call ✆ **0870/242-4240.**

If you need emergency cash over the weekend when all banks and American Express offices are closed, you can have money wired to you via **Western Union** (✆ **800/325-6000;** www.westernunion.com).

Identity theft and fraud are potential complications of losing your wallet, especially if you've lost your driver's license along with your cash and credit cards. Notify the major credit-reporting bureaus immediately;

placing a fraud alert on your records may protect you against liability for criminal activity. The three major U.S. credit-reporting agencies are **Equifax** (📞 **888/766-0008**; www.equifax.com), **Experian** (📞 **888/397-3742**; www.experian.com), and **TransUnion** (📞 **800/680-7289**; www.transunion. com). Finally, if you've lost all forms of photo ID, call your airline and explain the situation; they might allow you to board the plane if you have a copy of your passport or birth certificate and a copy of the police report you've filed.

*Mail*   An airmail letter to North America costs 47p (87¢) for 10 grams; postcards require a 42p (77¢) stamp; letters generally take 7 to 10 days to arrive from the United States. See "Post Offices," below, for locations.

*Maps*   See "Finding Your Way Around," under "Orientation," earlier in this chapter.

*Money*   See "Money," in chapter 3.

*Newspapers & Magazines*   The Times, Daily Telegraph, Daily Mail, and *Guardian* are dailies carrying the latest news. The *International Herald Tribune,* published in Paris, and an international edition of *USA Today,* beamed via satellite, are available daily (*USA Today* will be printed as a newsletter). Copies of *Time* and *Newsweek* are sold at most newsstands. Magazines such as *Time Out, City Limits,* and *Where* contain useful information about the latest happenings in London.

*Passports*   **For Residents of the United States:** Whether you're applying in person or by mail, you can download passport applications from the U.S. State Department website at **travel.state.gov**. For general information, call the **National Passport Agency** (📞 **202/647-0518**). To find your regional passport office, either check the U.S. State Department website or call the **National Passport Information Center** (📞 **877/487-2778**), Monday to Friday 8am to 8pm. Automated phone information is available 24 hours a day.

**For Residents of Canada:** Passport applications are available at travel agencies throughout Canada or from the central **Passport Office,** Place du Centre, 200 Promenade du Portage, commercial Level 2, Gatineau, Quebec (📞 **800/567-6868**; www.dfait-maeci.gc.ca/passport).

**For Residents of Ireland:** You can apply for a 10-year passport at the **Passport Office,** Setanta Centre, Molesworth Street, Dublin 2 (📞 **01/671-1633**; www.irlgov.ie/iveagh). Those under age 18 and over 65 must apply for a €12 3-year or 10-year passport. You can also apply at 1A South Mall, Cork (📞 **021/494-4700**), or at most main post offices.

**For Residents of Australia:** You can pick up an application from your local post office or any branch of Passports Australia, but you must schedule an interview at the passport office to present your application materials. Call the **Australian Passport Information Service** at 📞 **131-232,** or visit the government website at www.passports.gov.au.

**For Residents of New Zealand:** You can pick up a passport application at any New Zealand Passports Office or download it from their website. Contact the **Passports Office** at 📞 **0800/225-050** in New Zealand or 04/474-8100, or log onto www.passports.govt.nz.

*Police*   In an emergency, dial 📞 **999** (no coins required).

*Post Offices* The **main post office** is at 24–28 William IV St. (© **020/ 7484-9307**; Tube: Charing Cross). It operates as three separate businesses: inland and international postal service and banking (Mon–Fri 8:30am– 6:30pm and Sat 9am–5:30pm); philatelic postage-stamp sales (Mon–Fri 8:30am–6:30pm and Sat 9am–5:30pm) for collectors; and the post shop, selling greeting cards and stationery (Mon–Sat 8:30am–6:30pm). Other post offices and post-office branches are open Monday to Friday from 9am to 5:30pm and Saturday from 9am to 12:30pm. Many post-office branches and some main post offices close for an hour at lunchtime.

*Radio* There are 24-hour radio channels operating throughout the United Kingdom, including London. They offer mostly pop music and chat shows at night. Some "pirate" stations add more spice. So-called legal FM stations are **BBC1** (104.8); **BBC2** (89.1); **BBC3** (between 90 and 92); and the classical station, **BBC4** (95). There is also the **BBC Greater London Radio** (94.9) station, with lots of rock, plus **LBC Crown** (97.3), with news and reports of "what's on" in London. Pop/rock U.S.–style is heard on **Capital FM** (95.8); if you like jazz, reggae, or salsa, tune in to **Choice FM** (96.9). **Jazz FM** (102.2) offers jazz, blues, and big-band music.

*Restrooms* They're marked by PUBLIC TOILETS signs in streets, parks, and Tube stations; many are automatically sterilized after each use. The English often call toilets "loos." You'll also find well-maintained lavatories in all larger public buildings, such as museums and art galleries, large department stores, and railway stations. It's not really acceptable to use the lavatories in hotels, restaurants, and pubs if you're not a customer, but we can't say that we always stick to this rule. Public lavatories are usually free, but you may need a small coin to get in or to use a proper washroom.

*Safety* See section 6, "Health & Safety," in chapter 3.

*Smoking* Most U.S. cigarette brands are available in London. Smoking is forbidden in the Underground (on the cars and the platforms) and on buses, and it's increasingly frowned upon in many other places. But London still isn't a particularly friendly place for the nonsmoker. Most restaurants have nonsmoking tables, but they're usually separated from the smoking section by only a little bit of space. Nonsmoking rooms are available in the bigger hotels. Some of the smaller hotels claim to have nonsmoking rooms, but we've often found that this means the room is smoke-free only during our visit; if you're bothered by the odor, ask to be shown another room.

*Taxes* There is a 17.5% national **value-added tax (VAT)** added to all hotel and restaurant bills and included in the price of many items you purchase. It can be refunded if you shop at stores that participate in Global Refund Tax-Free Shopping (signs are posted in the window). See the "How to Get Your VAT Refund" box in chapter 8.

You also pay a departure tax of £10 ($19) for flights within Britain and the European Union; it's £20 ($37) for flights to the U.S. and other countries. Your airline ticket may or may not include this tax. Ask in advance to avoid a surprise at the gate.

To encourage energy conservation, the British government levies a 25% tax on gasoline (petrol). If you've read our warnings about driving in London, this will be of no importance to you whatsoever.

*Taxis* See "Getting Around," earlier in this chapter.

*Telephone* **To call London:** If you're calling London from the United States:

1. Dial the international access code: 011.
2. Dial the country code 44.
3. Dial the city code 20 and then the number. (London's official city code is 020, but you will dial 20 because you always have to omit the zero from the area code when calling London from outside of England.) So the whole number you'd dial would be 011-44-20-0000-0000.

**To make international calls:** To make international calls from London, first dial 00 and then the country code (U.S. or Canada, 1; U.K., 44; Ireland, 353; Australia, 61; New Zealand, 64). Next you dial the area code and number. For example, if you wanted to call the British Embassy in Washington, D.C., you would dial 00-1-202-588-7800.

Or call through one of the following long-distance access codes: **AT&T USA Direct** (*✆* **0800/890-011**), **Canada Direct** (*✆* **0800/890-016**), **Australia** (*✆* **0800/890-061**), or **New Zealand** (*✆* **0800/890-064**). Common country codes are **U.S. and Canada,** 1; **Australia,** 61; **New Zealand,** 64; **South Africa,** 27.

**For directory assistance:** Dial *✆* **118212** for a full range of services; for the rest of Britain, dial *✆* **118118**. See also "Area Codes," above.

**For operator assistance:** If you need operator assistance in making a call, dial *✆* **100** if you're trying to make an international call and *✆* **192** if you want to call a number in England.

**Toll-free numbers:** Numbers beginning with 0800 within London are toll-free, but calling a 1-800 number in the U.S. from England is not toll-free. In fact, it costs the same as an overseas call.

**To call within London:** Dial the local seven- or eight-digit number.

**To call within Britain (outside of London):** Phone numbers outside the major cities consist of an exchange code plus telephone number. To dial the number, you need to dial the exchange code first. Information sheets on call-box walls give the codes in most instances. If your code isn't there, call the operator by dialing *✆* **100.**

There are three types of public pay phones: those taking only coins, those accepting only phonecards (called Cardphones), and those taking both phonecards and credit cards. At coin-operated phones, insert your coins before dialing. The minimum charge is 10p (19¢).

Phone cards are available in four values £2 ($3.70), £5 ($9.25), £10 ($19), and £20 ($37)—and are reusable until the total value has expired. Cards can be purchased from newsstands and post offices. You can also use credit cards—Access (MasterCard), Visa, American Express, and Diners Club—at credit-call pay phones, commonly found at airports and large railway stations.

*Time Zone* England follows Greenwich Mean Time (5 hr. ahead of Eastern Standard Time). Most of the year, Britain is 5 hours ahead of the time observed on the East Coast of the United States. When it's noon in New York, it's 5pm in London. Because the U.S. and Britain observe Daylight Savings Time at slightly different times of year, there's a brief period (about a week) in the spring when London is 6 hours ahead of New York.

*Tipping* In restaurants, service charges in the 15% to 20% range are usually added to the bill. Sometimes this is clearly marked; at other times, it isn't. When in doubt, ask. If service isn't included, it's customary to add 15% to the bill. Sommeliers get about £1.95 ($3.60) per bottle of wine served. You can leave small change if the service is good. There's no tipping in pubs. In cocktail bars, the server usually gets about 75p ($1.40) per round of drinks.

Hotels, like restaurants, often add a service charge of 10% to 15% to most bills. In smaller B&Bs, the tip isn't likely to be included. Therefore, tip people who performed special services, such as for the person who served you breakfast. If several persons have served you in a B&B, many guests ask that 10% or 15% be added to the bill and divided among the staff. Tip chambermaids £1 ($1.85) per day for cleaning up (more if you've made their job extra difficult).

It's standard to tip taxi drivers 10% to 15% of the fare, although a tip for a taxi driver should never be less than 30p (55¢), even for a short run. Barbers and hairdressers expect 10% to 15%. Tour guides expect £3 ($5.55), although it's not mandatory. Theater ushers don't expect tips.

*Transit Information* See "Getting Around," earlier in this chapter. For more information on travel on London's Tube and bus system, call ℂ 020/7222-1234, 24 hours a day.

*Water* London's water is safe to drink. Tap water is free in restaurants, so be sure to ask for it if you don't want to pay for bottled water.

*Weather* Call ℂ 020/7939-9946 for current weather information, but chances are the line will be busy. You can also tune into 1152 AM (The Voice of London) for weather reports.

# 5

# Where to Stay

The good news is that more than 10,000 hotel rooms have opened in London post-millennium, relieving the overcrowding that existed at peak travel months. The downside is that most of these hotels are in districts far from the city center and are of the no-frills budget-chain variety.

Some hoteliers have decided to adapt former public or institutional buildings rather than start from scratch. The imposing County Hall building in the S1 district now boasts two chains: a luxurious Marriott and a leaner, meaner Travel Inn. Another trend is a shift away from the West End to such respectable sections as Greenwich (now a virtual suburb of London), Docklands, and even the City (London's financial district).

With all the vast improvements and upgrades made at the turn of the 21st century, chances are you'll like your room. What you won't like is the price. Even if a hotel remains scruffy, London hoteliers have little embarrassment about jacking up prices. Hotels in all categories remain overpriced.

London boasts some of the most famous hotels in the world—temples of luxury like Claridge's and The Dorchester and more recent rivals like the Four Seasons. The problem is that there are too many of these high-priced hotels (and now there are many budget options) and not enough moderately priced options.

Even at the luxury level, you might be surprised at what you don't get. Many of the stately Victorian and Edwardian gems are so steeped in tradition that they lack many modern conveniences that are standard in other luxury hotels around the world. Some have modernized with a vengeance, but others retain amenities from the Boer War era. London does have some cutting-edge, chintz-free hotels that seem to have been flown in straight from Los Angeles—complete with high-end sound systems and gadget-filled marble bathrooms. However, these cutting-edge hotels are not necessarily superior; though they're streamlined and convenient, they frequently lack the personal service and spaciousness that characterize the grand old hotels.

Since the late 1990s, new boutique hotels have been generating lots of excitement. With their charm, intimacy, and attention to detail, they're an attractive alternative to the larger, stuffier establishments. The "boutiquing" of the hotel scene continues postmillennium. The city offers more personally run and privately operated hotels than ever. We've surveyed the best of them, concentrating on the reasonably priced choices.

If you're looking for budget options, don't despair. London has some good-value places in the lower price ranges, and we've included the best of these. An affordable option is a bed-and-breakfast. At their best, B&Bs are clean, comfortable, and friendly. Good B&Bs are in short supply, so don't reserve a room at one without a recommendation you can trust. The following reliable services will recommend and arrange a B&B room for you: **London Bed & Breakfast Association** (© **800/852-2632**

---

*Tips* **Upstairs, Downstairs**

Elevators are called "lifts." Some of them are just as Victorian as the edifices in which they operate. They are, however, regularly inspected and completely safe. Many hotels (and especially B&Bs) lack even these rudimentary elevators, making them inaccessible for individuals with disabilities. If you have mobility issues, call ahead and make sure there isn't a steep, narrow staircase between the lobby and your guest room.

---

in the U.S., fax 020/8749-7084; fax from U.S. 619/531-1686). **The London Bed and Breakfast Agency Limited** (② 020/7586-2768; fax 020/7586-6567; www.londonbb.com) is another reputable agency that can provide inexpensive accommodations in selected private homes for £22 to £44 ($41–$81) per person per night, based on double occupancy (although some accommodations will cost a lot more). **London B&B** (② 800/872-2632** in the U.S.; fax 619/531-1686; www.londonbandb.com) offers B&B accommodations in private family residences or unhosted apartments. Homes are inspected for quality and comfort, amenities, and convenience.

You can almost always get a room at a deluxe hotel if you're willing to pay the price. But during certain peak periods, including the high season (roughly Apr–Oct) and during certain trade shows, seasonal events, and royal occasions, rooms in all kinds of hotels might be snatched up early. Book ahead. If you arrive without a reservation, begin your search for a room as early in the day as possible. If you arrive late at night, you might have to take what you can get, often at a much higher price than you'd like.

The vast majority of the hotels and B&Bs listed below offer nonsmoking rooms—just ask for one when you book.

**A NOTE ABOUT PRICES** Unless otherwise noted, published prices are rack rates for rooms with a private bathroom. Many include breakfast (usually continental) and a 10% to 15% service charge. The British government also imposes a VAT (value-added tax) that adds 17.5% to your bill. This is not included in the prices quoted in the guide. Always ask for a better rate, particularly at the first-class and deluxe hotels (B&Bs generally charge a fixed rate). Parking rates are per night.

**RATE REGULATIONS** All hotels, motels, inns, and guesthouses in Britain with four bedrooms or more (including self-catering accommodations) must display notices listing minimum and maximum overnight charges in a prominent place in the reception area or at the entrance, and prices must include any service charge and may include VAT, and it must be made clear whether these items are included; if VAT isn't included, then it must be shown separately. If meals are included, this must be stated. If prices aren't standard for all rooms, then only the lowest and highest prices need be given.

---

## 1 In & Around the City

There are precious few hotels within the confines of the City (the financial district). If you plan to do a lot of business or sightseeing in the City, and you're not very interested in shopping, theater, and nightlife, then the location might be perfect for you. (For a map showing the location of the following hotels as well as restaurants in the City, see "Where to Stay and Dine in & Around 'the City,'" in chapter 6.)

## VERY EXPENSIVE

**Great Eastern Hotel** ⭐⭐    Terrence Conran's monolithic hotel is one of only three hotels in London's financial district. One London writer claimed that the financial district was "nosebleed territory" for visitors to London, saying: "Just try meeting someone for a drink who lives in fashionable Chelsea." Back in 1884, the Great Eastern sprouted up next to the Liverpool Street Station. The hotel lies at the doorstep of two increasingly trendy London "villages," Shoreditch and Hoxton, with their explosive arts scenes. The building was the creation of Charles Barry, better known for his Houses of Parliament. The hotel was a tired and dreary relic when it closed in 1997. Today, it is abloom outside in all its Victorian glory, with a stained-glass dome and roof towers; but inside it is sleek and modern. Jacob Jacobsen's chrome-plated architect's lamps (those goose-necked ones you find in offices) light up the interior. In the bedrooms, the upholstery comes in traditional fabrics such as houndstooth and herringbone. Full bathrooms are state of the art, and the beds offer grand comfort. In terms of the theater, Great Eastern would be Broadway, and The Rookery (see below) would be a play in New York's West Greenwich Village.

Liverpool St., London EC2M 7QN. ⓒ 020/7618-5000. Fax 020/7618-5001. www.great-eastern-hotel.co.uk. 267 units. £265–£495 ($490–$916) double. AE, DC, MC, V. Tube: Liverpool St. Station. **Amenities:** 4 restaurants, 4 bars; health club; concierge; tour desk; business center; 24-hr. room service; laundry service/dry cleaning; rooms for those w/limited mobility; nonsmoking rooms. *In room:* A/C, TV/VCR, dataport, minibar, safe.

**Threadneedles** ⭐⭐ *Finds*    This was the first luxury hotel to be built in the City, home to many of London's major financial institutions. In 1856, the building housing the hotel was constructed as a bank, with solid oak doors and marble columns. The conversion to its latest role is successful. Contemporary comforts are found in the midsize to spacious bedrooms and suites. The limestone bathrooms contain shower/tub combinations, and there are such elegant touches as Egyptian-cotton and duck-down duvets on the beds. This luxury boutique hotel lies near the Bank of England, called "The Old Lady of Threadneedle Street"—hence, the name of the hotel.

5 Threadneedle St., London EC2R 8AY. ⓒ 020/7657-8080. Fax 020/7657-8100. www.theetongroup.com. 70 units. £175–£230 ($324–$426) double; £300–£376 ($555–$696) suite. AE, DC, MC, V. Tube: Bank. **Amenities:** Restaurant; bar; 24-hr. room service; babysitting; laundry service; same-day dry cleaning; 1 room for those w/limited mobility; nonsmoking rooms. *In room:* A/C, TV/VCR, CD player, dataport, minibar, hair dryer, trouser press, safe.

## EXPENSIVE

**The Rookery** ⭐ *Finds*    This quirky hotel lies in newly fashionable Smithfield, just east of Farringdon Road. The only remaining Georgian houses in Peter's Lane form a delightful small hotel that's a short walk from the attractions of the Square Mile. The brainchild of Peter McKay and Douglas Blain, who gave the world the trendy Hazlitt's in Soho, The Rookery has been restored with its period features relatively intact—even the coal-fired bread ovens still survive in the basement, a former bakery. The decorators spent thousands of hours combing auction rooms, antiques shops, and flea markets for funky yet elegant pictures, furniture, beds, and carpets to create maximum atmosphere. Regardless of where the bed is from, each is fitted with a superb mattress and fine bed linen. Each room is different and full of character. The Rook's Nest, for example, is on two levels with a 12m (39-ft.) ceiling, boasting a panoramic view across London's rooftops from St. Paul's to

# Guide to London Hotel Maps

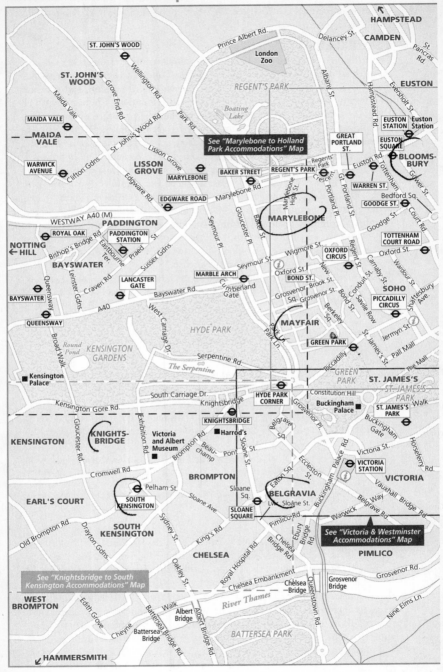

HAMPSTEAD

CAMDEN

St. Pancras Rd.

EUSTON

Prince Albert Rd.

Delancey St.

London Zoo

Albany St.

Hampstead Rd.

Eversholt St.

ST. JOHN'S WOOD

ST. JOHN'S WOOD

Wellington Rd.

Grove End Rd.

Park Rd.

REGENT'S PARK

Boating Lake

EUSTON STATION

Euston Station

MAIDA VALE

Maida Vale

St. John's Wood Rd.

Lisson Grove

GREAT PORTLAND ST.

EUSTON SQUARE

WARREN ST.

BLOOMS-BURY

MAIDA VALE

Clifton Gdns.

Edgware Rd.

See "Marylebone to Holland Park Accommodations" Map

Regents' Park Crescent

Euston Rd.

Gt. Portland St.

Tottenham Ct. Rd.

Gower St.

WARWICK AVENUE

LISSON GROVE

BAKER STREET

REGENT'S PARK

Portland Pl.

Bedford Sq.

GOODGE ST.

MARYLEBONE

EDGWARE ROAD

Marylebone Rd.

Marylebone High St.

Goodge St.

Court Rd.

WESTWAY A40 (M)

Gloucester Pl.

Baker St.

MARYLEBONE

TOTTENHAM COURT ROAD

PADDINGTON

ROYAL OAK

Bishop's Bridge Rd.

Eastbourne Ter.

Praed St.

Seymour Pl.

Wigmore St.

Regent St.

New Bond St.

Oxford St.

Carnaby St.

Wardour St.

PADDINGTON STATION

Sussex Gdns.

OXFORD CIRCUS

SOHO

NOTTING HILL

BAYSWATER

Craven Rd.

LANCASTER GATE

Seymour St.

MARBLE ARCH

Oxford St.

BOND ST.

Brook St.

Bond St.

Savile Row

PICCADILLY CIRCUS

Leinster Gdns.

A40

Bayswater Rd.

Cumberland Gate

Grosvenor Sq.

Grosvenor St.

Berkeley Sq.

Shaftesbury Ave.

BAYSWATER

Queensway

West Carriage Dr.

HYDE PARK

MAYFAIR

Jermyn St.

Pall Mall

QUEENSWAY

Broad Walk

Round Pond

KENSINGTON GARDENS

Serpentine Rd.

Park Ln.

GREEN PARK

Piccadilly

St. James's St.

The Mall

Kensington Palace

The Serpentine

GREEN PARK

ST. JAMES'S

ST. JAMES'S PARK Walk

Kensington Gore Rd.

South Carriage Dr.

Knightsbridge

HYDE PARK CORNER

Constitution Hill

Buckingham Palace

ST. JAMES'S PARK

Buckingham Gate

KNIGHTSBRIDGE

Exhibition Rd.

KNIGHTSBRIDGE

Belgrave Sq.

Grosvenor Pl.

Horseferry Rd.

KENSINGTON

Gloucester Rd.

Victoria and Albert Museum

Harrod's

Brompton Rd.

Beauchamp Pl.

Sloane St.

Eccleston St.

Victoria St.

VICTORIA STATION

Cromwell Rd.

Pont St.

Eaton Sq.

Buckingham Palace Rd.

Vauxhall Bridge Rd.

VICTORIA

EARL'S COURT

Pelham St.

SOUTH KENSINGTON

BROMPTON

Sloane Ave.

Sloane Sq.

BELGRAVIA

Lwr. Sloane St.

Belgrave Rd.

SOUTH KENSINGTON

Sydney St.

King's Rd.

SLOANE SQUARE

Pimlico Rd.

Ebury Bridge

Warwick Way

See "Victoria & Westminster Accommodations" Map

Old Brompton Rd.

Drayton Gdns.

CHELSEA

Royal Hospital Rd.

Chelsea Bridge Rd.

PIMLICO

Grosvenor Rd.

WEST BROMPTON

Oakley St.

Chelsea Embankment

Chelsea Bridge

Queenstown Rd.

Grosvenor Bridge

Nine Elms Ln.

Edith Grove

Battersea Walk

Albert Bridge

Albert Bridge Rd.

River Thames

Cheyne

Battersea Bridge

Battersea Bridge Rd.

BATTERSEA PARK

HAMMERSMITH

See "Knightsbridge to South Kensington Accommodations" Map

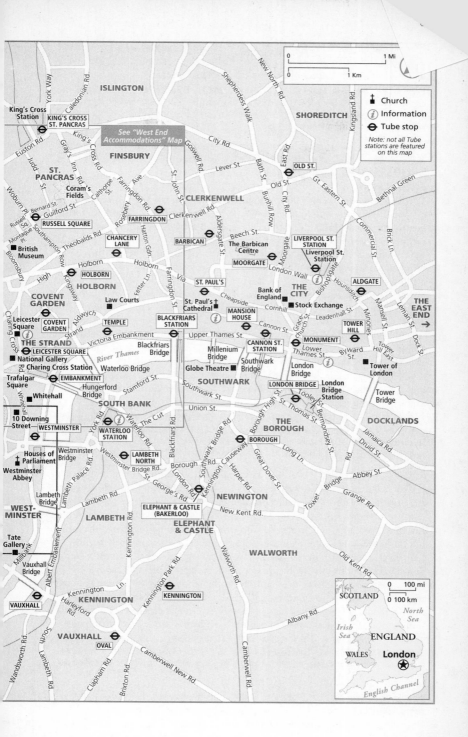

the Old Bailey. The bathrooms with shower/tub combinations are a special treat, with Victorian cast-iron fittings and polished copper pipe work. A garden (very unusual in the City district of London) is an added bonus.

12 Peter's Lane, Cowcross St., London EC1M 6DS. (C) 020/7336-0931. Fax 020/7336-0932. www.rookeryhotel. com. 33 units. £225–£295 ($416–$546) double; £495 ($916) suite. AE, DC, MC, V. Tube: Farringdon. **Amenities:** Limited room service (7am–11pm); laundry service; same-day dry cleaning; nonsmoking rooms. *In room:* TV/ VCR, dataport, minibar, hair dryer, safe.

## 2 The West End

# BLOOMSBURY
## EXPENSIVE

**The Academy Hotel** 🌴     The Academy is in the heart of London's publishing district. If you look out your window, you see where Virginia Woolf and other literary members of the Bloomsbury Group passed by every day. Many original architectural details were preserved when these three 1776 Georgian row houses were joined. The hotel was substantially upgraded in the 1990s, with a bathroom added to every bedroom (whether there was space or not). Fourteen have a shower/tub combination; the rest have showers only. The beds, so they say, were built to "American specifications." True or not, they promise you a restful night's sleep. Grace notes include glass panels, colonnades, and intricate plaster-work on the facade. With overstuffed armchairs and half-canopied beds, rooms sometimes evoke English country-house living, but that of the poorer relations. Guests who have been here before always request rooms opening on the garden in back and not those in front with ducted fresh air, though the front units have double-glazing to cut down on the noise. The theater district and Covent Garden are within walking distance. *Warning:* If you have a problem with stairs, know that no elevators rise to the four floors.

21 Gower St., London WC1E 6HG. (C) 020/7631-4115. Fax 020/7636-3442. www.etontownhouse.com. 49 units. £163–£189 ($302–$350) double; £215 ($398) suite. AE, DC, MC, V. Tube: Tottenham Court Rd., Goodge St., or Russell Sq. **Amenities:** Bar; limited room service; laundry service; same-day dry cleaning; nonsmoking rooms. *In room:* A/C, TV, dataport, minibar, hair dryer, iron/ironing board, safe, beverage maker, trouser press.

**Blooms Town House Hotel** 🌴     This restored 18th-century town house has a pedigree: It stands in what were formerly the grounds of Montague House (now the British Museum). It has had a distinguished, if eccentric, list of former occupants: everybody from Richard Penn (the Whig member of Parliament from Liverpool) to Dr. John Cumming, who firmly believed he'd witness the end of the world (on long winter nights, his ghostly presence has supposedly been spotted). Even though it's in the heart of London, the house has a country-home atmosphere, complete with fireplace, period art, and copies of *Country Life* in the magazine rack. Guests take morning coffee in a walled garden overlooking the British Museum. In summer, light meals are served. The small- to medium-size bedrooms are individually designed with traditional elegance, in beautifully muted tones, and the shower/tub combination bathrooms are well maintained.

7 Montague St., London WC1B 5BP. (C) 020/7323-1717. Fax 020/7636-6498. www.bloomshotel.com. 26 units. £175–£192 ($324–$355) double. Extra person £40 ($74). AE, DC, MC, V. Tube: Russell Sq. **Amenities:** 24-hr. room service; courtesy car; laundry service/dry cleaning; nonsmoking rooms. *In room:* TV, minibar, coffeemaker, hair dryer, trouser press.

**The Montague on the Gardens** 🌴🌴     This member of the deluxe Red Carnation Hotel Group—others include The Rubens at the Palace (p. 109) and The Milestone (p. 120)—offers a winning combination of plush accommodations and exceptional service. The location is right across the street from the British Museum, and a short walk from the West End and the shopping on Oxford and Bond streets. One staff member aptly describes the Montague as a "country house hotel in the heart of London." The public rooms are meticulously (if not minimally) decorated in various woods, light fabrics, and antiques, conjuring the atmosphere of an expensive manor home.

Guest rooms are individually sized and decorated; most aren't huge, but all are cozy and spotless. The beds are most comfortable; some are four-posters and most sport half-canopies. Bilevel deluxe king rooms feature pullout couches and would be classified as suites in many other hotels. Rooms overlooking the garden offer the best views and are quiet, although guaranteeing one for your stay will cost you a bit more. *Note:* Always ask about discount rates when you book; the hotel usually offers a number of promotions throughout the year.

15 Montague St., London WC1B 5BJ. ℂ 877/955-1515 in the U.S. and Canada, or 020/7637-1001. Fax 020/ 7637-2516. www.redcarnationhotels.com. 104 units. £140–£238 ($259–$440) double; £245–£495 ($453– $916) suite. AE, DC, MC, V. Tube: Russell Sq. **Amenities:** Restaurant; 4 lounges; bar; health club; steam room; sauna; business center; 24-hr. room service; laundry service; dry cleaning; rooms for those w/limited mobility; nonsmoking rooms. *In room:* A/C, TV w/pay movies, fax (in some rooms), dataport, tea/coffeemaker, hair dryer, iron/ironing board, safe.

**Myhotel** ★ *Finds*   Creating shock waves among staid Bloomsbury hoteliers, Myhotel is a London row house on the outside with an Asian *moderne*-style interior. It is designed according to feng shui principles—the ancient Chinese art of placement that analyzes the flow of energy in a space. The rooms have mirrors, but they're positioned so you don't see yourself when you first wake up—feng shui rule no. 1 (probably a good rule, feng shui or no feng shui). Rooms are havens of comfort, taste, and tranquillity. Excellent sleep-inducing beds are found in all rooms, along with a small bathroom with a tub. Tipping is discouraged, and each guest is assigned a personal assistant responsible for that guest's happiness. Aimed at today's young, hip traveler, Myhotel lies within a short walk of Covent Garden and the British Museum.

11–13 Bayley St., Bedford Sq., London WC1B 3HD. ℂ 020/7667-6000. Fax 020/7667-6001. www.myhotels. co.uk. 78 units. £185–£250 ($342–$463) double; from £330 ($611) suite. AE, DC, MC, V. Tube: Tottenham Court Rd. **Amenities:** Restaurant; bar; exercise room; spa; car at discounted rate; 24-hr. room service; massage; babysitting; laundry service; same-day dry cleaning; nonsmoking rooms. *In room:* A/C, TV w/pay movies, dataport, hair dryer, safe, beverage maker, trouser press (in some).

**Renaissance London Chancery Court** ★★★   The *London Times* may have gotten carried away with the hype, proclaiming this "one of the most exciting hotels in the world," but this landmark 1914 building in the financial district has been stunningly transformed into a government-rated five-star hotel, retaining the grandeur of the past but boasting all the comforts and conveniences of today. The surprise hit of 2003, this is a seven-floor Edwardian monument with a marble staircase. The building has been used as a backdrop for such films as *Howard's End* and *The Saint* because filmmakers were drawn to its soaring archways and classical central courtyard. The interior of the hotel encases you in womblike luxury. The glamorous and exceedingly comfortable rooms are all furnished with fine linens and decorated in different hues of cream, red, and blue. The bathrooms are about the most spacious in London, clad in Italian marble with lavish shower/tub combinations. The best accommodations are on the sixth floor, opening onto a cozy interior courtyard hidden from the busy world outside.

252 High Holborn, WC1V 7EN. ℂ 800/468-3571 in the U.S. or Canada, or 020/7829-9888. Fax 020/7829-9889. www.renaissancehotels.com. 356 units. £180–£240 ($333–$444) double; £285–£465 ($527–$860) suite.

# Where to Stay in the West End

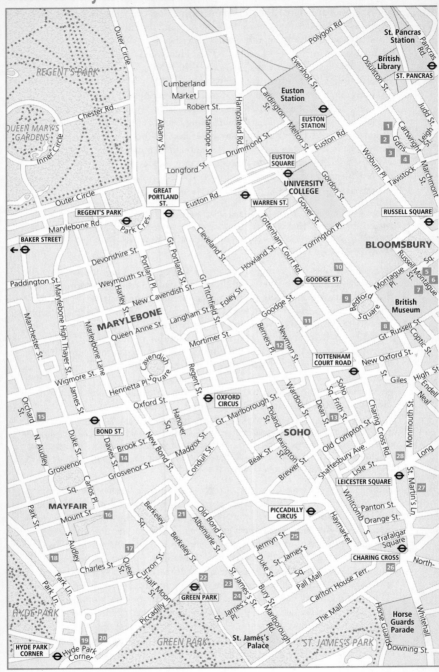

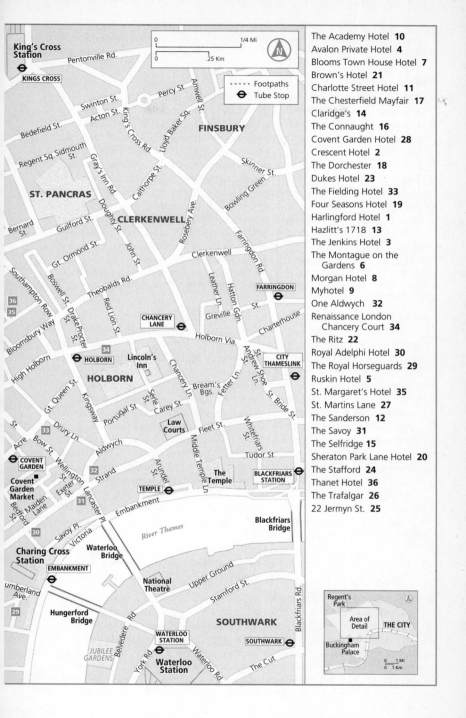

The Academy Hotel **10**
Avalon Private Hotel **4**
Blooms Town House Hotel **7**
Brown's Hotel **21**
Charlotte Street Hotel **11**
The Chesterfield Mayfair **17**
Claridge's **14**
The Connaught **16**
Covent Garden Hotel **28**
Crescent Hotel **2**
The Dorchester **18**
Dukes Hotel **23**
The Fielding Hotel **33**
Four Seasons Hotel **19**
Harlingford Hotel **1**
Hazlitt's 1718 **13**
The Jenkins Hotel **3**
The Montague on the Gardens **6**
Morgan Hotel **8**
Myhotel **9**
One Aldwych **32**
Renaissance London Chancery Court **34**
The Ritz **22**
Royal Adelphi Hotel **30**
The Royal Horseguards **29**
Ruskin Hotel **5**
St. Margaret's Hotel **35**
St. Martins Lane **27**
The Sanderson **12**
The Savoy **31**
The Selfridge **15**
Sheraton Park Lane Hotel **20**
The Stafford **24**
Thanet Hotel **36**
The Trafalgar **26**
22 Jermyn St. **25**

AE, DC, MC, V. Tube: Holborn. **Amenities:** 2 restaurants; 2 bars; cocktail lounge; luxurious spa; business center; 24-hr. room service; massage; babysitting; sauna; laundry service/dry cleaning; nonsmoking rooms; rooms for those w/limited mobility. *In room:* A/C, TV w/pay movies, dataport, kitchenette, minibar, coffeemaker, hair dryer, iron, safe.

## MODERATE

**Harlingford Hotel** *(Value)*    This hotel is comprised of three town houses built in the 1820s and joined together around 1900 with a bewildering array of staircases and meandering hallways. Set in the heart of Bloomsbury, it's run by a management that seems genuinely concerned about the welfare of its guests, unlike the management at many of the neighboring hotel rivals. (They even distribute little mincemeat pies to their guests during the Christmas holidays.) Double-glazed windows cut down on the street noise, and all the bedrooms are comfortable and inviting. Shower-only bathrooms are small, however, since the house wasn't originally designed for them. The most comfortable rooms are on the second and third levels, but expect to climb some steep English stairs (there's no elevator). Avoid the rooms on ground level, as they are darker and have less security. You'll have use of the tennis courts in Cartwright Gardens.

61–63 Cartwright Gardens, London WC1H 9EL. ℂ 020/7387-1551. Fax 020/7387-4616. www.harlingfordhotel. com. 44 units. £95 ($175) double; £105 ($194) triple; £110 ($204) quad. Rates include English breakfast. AE, DC, MC, V. Tube: Russell Sq., King's Cross, or Euston. **Amenities:** Use of tennis courts in Cartwright Gardens. *In room:* TV, coffeemaker, hair dryer.

## INEXPENSIVE

**Avalon Private Hotel**    A bit of a comedown after the Harlingford (see above), this hotel is easier on the purse. One guidebook from Victoria's day claimed that the Bloomsbury neighborhood attracted "medical and other students of both sexes and several nationalities, American folk passing through London, literary persons 'up' for a week or two's reading in the British Museum, and Bohemians pure and simple." The same might be said for today's patrons of this hotel, which was built in 1807 as two Georgian houses in residential Cartwright Gardens. Guests have use of a semiprivate garden across the street with tennis courts. Top-floor rooms, often filled with students, are reached via steep stairs, but bedrooms on the lower levels have easier access. A professional decorator recently added many Victorian-inspired touches to the hotel, in addition to new carpeting, making it more inviting. The bedrooms were also recently renewed with new linens and fresh curtains. Private bathrooms with showers are extremely small. Most guests in rooms without bathrooms have to use the corridor bathrooms (four bedrooms to a bathroom), which are generally adequate and well maintained.

---

*Value* **Cheap Lodging for Students**

**The International Students House,** 229 Great Portland St., W1W 5PN (ℂ 020/7631-8310; www.ish.org.uk), offers blandly furnished, institutional rooms for £33 ($61) single, £25 to £27 ($46–$49) per person double, £20 ($37) per person triple, and £18 ($33) per person in a four-person mixed room. A £10 ($19) key deposit is charged. Laundry facilities are available. Facilities include laundry machines, a bar, an Internet cafe, a fitness center, and sunbeds. Reserve way in advance, because these rooms go very quickly. For more information on the International Student House, see p. 43.

---

46–47 Cartwright Gardens, London WC1H 9EL. ☎ **020/7387-2366.** Fax 020/7387-5810. www.avalonhotel. co.uk. 27 units (5 with shower). £59 ($109) double without shower, £79 ($146) double with shower; £69 ($128) triple without shower, £89 ($165) triple with shower; £79 ($146) quad without shower, £99 ($183) quad with shower. Rates include English breakfast. AE, DC, MC, V. Tube: Russell Sq., King's Cross, or Euston. **Amenities:** Use of tennis courts in Cartwright Gardens; coin-op washers and dryers; same-day dry cleaning; nonsmoking rooms. *In room:* TV, dataport, coffeemaker, safe.

**Crescent Hotel**    Although Ruskin and Shelley no longer pass by, the Crescent still stands in the heart of academic London. The private square is owned by the City Guild of Skinners (who are furriers, as you might have guessed) and guarded by the University of London, whose student residential halls are across the street. You have access to the gardens and private tennis courts belonging to the City Guild of Skinners. The hotel owners view Crescent as an extension of their home and welcome you to its comfortably elegant Georgian surroundings, which date from 1810. Some guests have been returning for 4 decades. Bedrooms range from small singles with shared bathrooms to more spacious twin and double rooms with private showers. All have extras such as alarm clocks. Twins and doubles have private plumbing, with tiny bathrooms. Many rooms are singles, ranging in price from £46 to £83 ($85–$154), depending on the plumbing.

49–50 Cartwright Gardens, London WC1H 9EL. ☎ **020/7387-1515.** Fax 020/7383-2054. www.crescenthotel oflondon.com. 27 units, 18 with bathroom (some with shower only, some with tub and shower). £89 ($165) double with bathroom. Rates include English breakfast. MC, V. Tube: Russell Sq., King's Cross, or Euston. **Amenities:** Use of tennis courts in Cartwright Gardens; babysitting. *In room:* TV, coffeemaker.

**The Jenkins Hotel** ★ *Value*    Followers of the Agatha Christie TV series *Poirot* will recognize this Cartwright Gardens residence—it was featured in the series. The antiques are gone and the rooms are small, but some of the original charm of the Georgian house remains—enough so that the London *Mail on Sunday* proclaimed it one of the "10 best hotel values" in the city. All the rooms have been redecorated in traditional Georgian style, and many have been completely refurbished with new beds and upholstery. All but one room has a private bathroom. Most have shower-only bathrooms. The location is great, near the British Museum, theaters, and antiquarian bookshops. There are some drawbacks: no lift and no reception or sitting room. But this is a place where you can settle in and feel at home.

45 Cartwright Gardens, London WC1H 9EH. ☎ **020/7387-2067.** Fax 020/7383-3139. www.jenkinshotel. demon.co.uk. 13 units. £85 ($157) double; £105 ($194) triple. Rates include English breakfast. MC, V. Tube: Russell Sq., King's Cross, or Euston. **Amenities:** Use of washer/dryer; all nonsmoking rooms. *In room:* TV, dataport, minibar, fridge, coffeemaker, hair dryer, iron, safe.

**Morgan Hotel**    Located in a row of Georgian houses, each built in the 1790s, this hotel is easily recognizable by its gold-tipped iron fence railings. The flower boxes outside preview the warmth and hospitality inside. The family management does all the work themselves, and they have such a devoted following that it's hard to get a reservation in summer. Several rooms, each individually designed, overlook the British Museum. Even if things are a bit cramped and the stairs are rather steep, the rooms are pleasant and the atmosphere congenial. The carpeted bedrooms, refurbished in 2003, have big beds (by British standards), dressing tables with mirrors, ample wardrobe space, and batik bedspreads. Eleven of the rooms have air-conditioning. The suites are worth the extra money if you can afford it. They're furnished tastefully with polished dark English pieces, framed English prints, and decorator fabrics, all with spacious bathrooms equipped with showers. Suites also have irons and kitchenettes.

24 Bloomsbury St., London WC1B 3QJ. ℂ **020/7636-3735.** Fax 020/7636-3045. 21 units. £98 ($181) double; £140 ($259) triple; £180 ($333) suite. Rates include English breakfast. MC, V. Tube: Russell Sq. or Tottenham Court Rd. **Amenities:** Nonsmoking rooms. *In room:* TV, kitchenette in suites, hair dryer, iron in suites, safe.

**Ruskin Hotel**   Although the hotel is named for author John Ruskin, the ghosts of other literary legends who lived nearby haunt you: Mary Shelley plotting her novel, *Frankenstein,* and James Barrie fantasizing about *Peter Pan.* This hotel has been managed for 2 decades by a hard-working family and enjoys a repeat clientele. Management keeps the place spic-and-span, though you shouldn't expect a decorator's flair. The furnishings, though well polished, are a bit worn. Double-glazing in the front blots out the noise, but we prefer the cozily old-fashioned chambers in the rear, as they open onto a park. Sorry, no elevator. The greenery in the cellar-level breakfast room provides a nice touch, and the breakfast is big enough to fortify you for a full day at the British Museum next door. *Insider's Tip:* Although the private bathrooms are ridiculously small, the shared bathrooms in the hall are generous and well maintained; all have shower units.

23–24 Montague St., London WC1B 5BH. ℂ **020/7636-7388.** Fax 020/7323-1662. 32 units, 6 with bathroom. £67 ($124) double without bathroom, £84 ($155) double with bathroom. Rates include English breakfast. AE, DC, MC, V. Tube: Russell Sq. or Tottenham Court Rd. *In room:* Coffeemaker, hair dryer.

**St. Margaret's Hotel**   As you trudge along Bedford Place in the footsteps of Hogarth, Yeats, and Dickens, you'll come across this hotel, composed of four interconnected Georgian town houses. Furnishings are a mismatched medley, a bit tattered here and there, but endurable and fine nevertheless. All is forgiven on a spring day when you look out back onto the duke of Bedford's private gardens in full bloom. Rooms are fairly large, except for a cramped single here or there. Many still retain their original fireplaces, which is how the rooms were once heated. Families should ask for no. 53, with a glassed-in garden along the back. A single guest who doesn't mind sharing a shower-only bathroom will find ample space in no. 24. Guests have use of two lounges, one with a TV.

26 Bedford Place, London WC1B 5JH. ℂ **020/7636-4277.** Fax 020/7323-3066. www.stmargaretshotel.co.uk. 64 units, 16 with bathroom (5 with shower). £64 ($117) double without shower, £95 ($176) double with shower; £98 ($181) double with shower and bathroom. Rates include English breakfast. MC, V. Tube: Holborn or Russell Sq. **Amenities:** Laundry service; same-day dry cleaning; nonsmoking rooms. *In room:* TV (VCR on request), dataport.

**Thanet Hotel**   Most of the myriad hotels around Russell Square become almost indistinguishable at some point, but the Thanet stands out. It no longer charges the same rates it did when it appeared in *England on $5 a Day,* but it's still a winning choice, and an affordable option close to the British Museum, the theater district, and Covent Garden. It's a landmark-status building on a quiet Georgian terrace between Russell and Bloomsbury squares. Although it has been restored many times, many original features remain. For the most part, the Orchard family (third-generation hoteliers) offers small, adequately furnished rooms. However, scattered throughout the hotel are some unacceptable bedrooms. One guest reported that the foot of her lumpy bed was higher than the head. Try to see the room before accepting it. This place is always full, so it must be doing something right, and indeed many of the bedrooms are fine. It depends largely on which rooms were most recently renovated—ask for those. All units are equipped with shower-only bathrooms that are very small but neatly maintained. Washbasins in the bathrooms must have been designed for Tiny Tim.

## Kids   Family-Friendly Hotels

Although the bulk of their clients are business travelers, the major hotel chains are also geared to family fun. Look for special summer packages at most hotel chains between June and August. Some of the most generous offers come from the **Travelodge** (© **800/435-4542** in the U.S.) and **Hilton International** (© **800/445-8667** in the U.S.) chains. For best results, call the 800 number and ask about family packages. Here are some other family-friendly spots:

**The Colonnade Town House** (p. 135)   Located in the canal-laced Little Venice section of London, this hotel lets children under 12 stay free in their parents' room. This residential area is safe, with tree-lined avenues leading down to a canal. With its shops, cafes, and restaurants, Little Venice has a real neighborhood feel to it. The staff can arrange babysitting.

**Hart House Hotel** (p. 128)   This small, family-run B&B is right in the center of the West End, near Hyde Park. Many of its rooms are triples. If you need even more room, special family suites, with connecting rooms, can be arranged.

**James House/Cartref House** (p. 113)   This is one of London's finest B&Bs. Some of the large accommodations have bunk beds that make them ideal for families.

**The Vicarage Hotel** (p. 123)   This is one of the most family-friendly hotels in the general area of Kensington and Notting Hill Gate. A Victorian town house, it offers many bedrooms that are large enough to accommodate four, all at an affordable price.

---

8 Bedford Place, London WC1B 5JA. © **020/7636-2869.** Fax 020/7323-6676. www.thanethotel.co.uk. 16 units. £96 ($178) double; £105 ($194) triple; £116 ($215) quad. Rates include English breakfast. AE, MC, V. Tube: Holborn or Russell Sq. **Amenities:** All nonsmoking rooms. *In room:* TV, dataport, coffeemaker, hair dryer.

## COVENT GARDEN & THE STRAND
### VERY EXPENSIVE

**Covent Garden Hotel** ★★★   This former hospital building lay neglected for years until it was reconfigured in 1996 by hot hoteliers Tim and Kit Kemp—whose flair for interior design is legendary—into one of London's most charming boutique hotels in one of the West End's hippest shopping neighborhoods. *Travel and Leisure* called this hotel 1 of the 25 hottest places to stay in the *world.* It remains so. Behind a bottle-green facade reminiscent of a 19th-century storefront, the hotel has a welcoming lobby outfitted with elaborate inlaid furniture and elegant draperies, plus two charming restaurants. Upstairs, accessible via a dramatic stone staircase, soundproof bedrooms are furnished in English style with Asian fabrics, many adorned with hand-embroidered designs. The hotel has a decorative trademark—each room has a clothier's mannequin, a female form draped in the fabric that decorates that particular room. Each room comes with luxurious amenities including full marble bathrooms with double vanities and deep soaking tubs. Some guests prefer the attic rooms with their sloping ceilings and small arched windows.

10 Monmouth St., London WC2H 9HB. © 800/553-6674 in the U.S., or 020/7806-1000. Fax 020/7806-1100. www.firmdale.com. 58 units. £245–£295 ($453–$546) double; £350–£795 ($648–$1,471) suite. AE, MC, V. Tube: Covent Garden or Leicester Sq. **Amenities:** Restaurant; bar; small exercise room; concierge; tour desk; business services; 24-hr. room service; massage; babysitting; laundry service; same-day dry cleaning; video library; nonsmoking rooms. *In room:* A/C, TV/VCR, dataport, minibar, hair dryer, safe.

**One Aldwych** ★★ Just east of Covent Garden, this government-rated five-star hotel occupies the classic-looking 1907 building that served as headquarters for the now defunct *Morning Post.* Before its conversion in 1998, all but a fraction of its interior was gutted and replaced with an artfully simple layout. Although a first-rate hostelry in every way, it lacks the cutting-edge chic of the Covent Garden Hotel (see above). The bedrooms are sumptuous, decorated with elegant linens and rich colors and accessorized with raw-silk curtains, deluxe furnishings, and electrical outlets that can handle both North American and European electrical currents. Bathrooms boast full tubs and showers, plus luxurious toiletries.

1 Aldwych, London WC2B 4RH. © 800/745-8883 or 020/7300-1000. Fax 020/7300-1001. www.onealdwych. co.uk. 105 units. £283–£355 ($524–$657) double; from £515 ($953) suite. AE, DC, MC, V. Parking £35 ($65). Tube: Temple. **Amenities:** 2 restaurants; 2 bars; indoor heated pool; state-of-the-art health club; spa; sauna; concierge; tour desk; courtesy car; 24-hr. room service; massage; babysitting; laundry service; same-day dry cleaning; rooms for those w/limited mobility; nonsmoking rooms. *In room:* A/C, TV/VCR w/pay movies, CD player, dataport, minibar, hair dryer, safe.

**The Savoy** ★★★ Although not as swank as The Dorchester, this London landmark is the premier hotel in the Strand/Covent Garden area. Richard D'Oyly Carte built it in 1889 as an annex to his nearby Savoy Theatre, where many Gilbert and Sullivan operettas were staged. Each room is individually decorated with color-coordinated accessories, solid and comfortable furniture, large closets, and an eclectic blend of antiques, such as gilt mirrors, Queen Anne chairs, and Victorian sofas. Forty-eight units have their own sitting rooms. The handmade beds—real luxury models—have top-of-the-line crisp linen fabrics and other lavish appointments. Some bathrooms have tubs, but most have a shower/tub. Bathrooms are spacious, with deluxe toiletries. The suites overlooking the river are the most sought after, and for good reason—the vistas are the best in London. *Tip:* Ask for one of the newer rooms, with a view of the river, in what was formerly a storage space. They are among the best in the hotel, with views of the Thames and Parliament.

The Strand, London WC2R 0EU. © 800/63-SAVOY in the U.S., or 020/7836-4343. Fax 020/7240-6040. www. the-savoy.co.uk. 263 units. £345–£425 ($638–$786) double; from £465 ($860) suite. AE, DC, MC, V. Parking £34 ($63). Tube: Charing Cross or Covent Garden. **Amenities:** 3 restaurants (including the celebrated Savoy Grill and the River Restaurant, which overlooks the Thames); 2 bars; city's best health club; spa; business center; sauna; 24-hr. room service; laundry service/dry cleaning; nonsmoking rooms; rooms for those w/limited mobility. *In room:* A/C, TV/VCR, dataport, minibar, hair dryer, safe.

**St. Martins Lane** ★★★ "Eccentric and irreverent, with a sense of humor," is how Ian Schrager describes his cutting-edge Covent Garden hotel, which he transformed from a 1960s office building into a chic enclave. This was the first hotel that Schrager designed outside the United States, after a string of successes from New York to West Hollywood. The mix of hip design and a sense of cool have been imported across the pond. Whimsical touches abound. For example, a string of daisies replaces DO NOT DISTURB signs. Rooms are all white, but you can use the full-spectrum lighting to make them any color. Floor-to-ceiling glass windows in every room offer a panoramic view of London, and down comforters and soft pillows ensure a good night's sleep. Some rooms are nonsmoking. Bathrooms are spacious and state-of-the-art, with deluxe toiletries.

45 St. Martins Lane, London WC2N 4HX. (C) **020/7300-5500.** Fax 020/7300-5501. www.ianschragerhotels. com. 204 units. £235–£325 ($435–$601) double; from £1,400 ($2,590) suite. AE, DC, MC, V. Tube: Covent Garden or Leicester Sq. **Amenities:** Restaurant; bar; state-of-the-art health club; spa services from nearby spa on request; courtesy car; business center; 24-hr. room service; babysitting; laundry service; same-day dry cleaning; nonsmoking rooms; rooms for those w/limited mobility. *In room:* A/C, TV/VCR, dataport, minibar, hair dryer, safe.

## MODERATE

**The Fielding Hotel** ★ *Finds*    One of London's more eccentric hotels, the Fielding is cramped, quirky, and quaint, and an enduring favorite. Luring media types, the hotel is named after novelist Henry Fielding of *Tom Jones* fame, who lived in Broad Court. It lies on a pedestrian street still lined with 19th-century gas lamps. The Royal Opera House is across the street, and the pubs, shops, and restaurants of lively Covent Garden are just beyond the front door. Rooms are small but charmingly old-fashioned and traditional. Some units are redecorated or at least "touched up" every year, though floors dip and sway, and the furnishings and fabrics, though clean, have known better times. The bathrooms, some with antiquated plumbing, are equipped with showers. But with a location like this, in the heart of London, the Fielding keeps guests coming back; in fact, many love the hotel's rickety charm. Children under 13 are not welcome.

4 Broad Court, Bow St., London WC2B 5QZ. (C) **020/7836-8305.** Fax 020/7497-0064. www.the-fielding-hotel. co.uk. 24 units. £100–£115 ($185–$213) double; £130 ($241) suite. AE, DC, MC, V. Tube: Covent Garden. **Amenities:** Bar; laundry service; nonsmoking rooms. *In room:* TV, dataport, coffeemaker.

## INEXPENSIVE

**Royal Adelphi Hotel**    If you care most about being in a central location, consider the Royal Adelphi. Close to Covent Garden, the theater district, and Trafalgar Square, it's an unorthodox choice away from the typical B&B stamping grounds. London has far better B&Bs, but not in this part of town. Although the bedrooms call to mind London's swinging 1960s heyday, accommodations are decently maintained and comfortable, with good beds. Plumbing, however, is a bit creaky, and the lack of air-conditioning can make London feel like summer in the Australian outback during the city's few hot days.

21 Villiers St., London WC2N 6ND. (C) **020/7930-8764.** Fax 020/7930-8735. www.royaladelphi.co.uk. 47 units, 34 with bathroom. £70 ($130) double without bathroom, £92 ($170) double with bathroom. AE, DC, MC, V. Tube: Charing Cross or Embankment. *In room:* TV, coffeemaker, hair dryer.

# TRAFALGAR SQUARE
## EXPENSIVE

**The Royal Horseguards** ★    This hotel is owned by Thistle, a popular chain of hotels in Great Britain. This is their flagship hotel in London, close to Parliament, Charing Cross, and Horse Guards, with rooms opening onto the Thames River near Trafalgar Square. This bustling area of London becomes relatively quiet at night. The hotel still maintains some of the atmosphere it once knew during its role as a men's club. MPs still frequent the place, especially the bar, where a light signals them to finish their liquor fast and get back to vote in Parliament. Rooms have been refurbished, and for the most part they are comfortable, although we've found that many of them are too small, especially if you've arrived in London with a lot of luggage. Those accommodations with a river view are the best and the largest. The hotel is geared mainly to business travelers but could be ideal for sightseers as well. Most doubles are at the low end of the price scale.

2 Whitehall Court, London SW1A 2EJ. © 0870/3339-122. Fax 0870/3339-222. www.thistlehotels.com/royal horseguards. 280 units. £134–£329 ($248–$609) double; from £270 ($500) suite. AE, DC, MC, V. Tube: Embankment. Parking: £40 ($74). **Amenities:** Restaurant; bar; exercise room; business center; 24-hr. room service; laundry service; same-day dry cleaning; nonsmoking rooms. *In room:* A/C (in some), TV w/pay movies, dataport, minibar, coffeemaker, hair dryer, iron, safe.

**The Trafalgar** ★★   In the heart of landmark Trafalgar Square, this is Hilton's first boutique hotel in London. The facade of this 19th-century structure was preserved, while the guest rooms inside were refitted to modern standards. Because of the original architecture, many of the rooms are uniquely shaped and sometimes offer split-level layouts. Large windows open onto panoramic views of Trafalgar Square. The decor in the rooms is minimalist, and comfort is combined with simple luxury, including the deluxe tiled bathrooms with shower/tub combinations. The greatest view of London's cityscape is from the Hilton's rooftop garden.

Unusual for London, the bar, **Rockwell,** specializes in bourbon, with more than 100 brands. **Jago** is the hotel's organic-produce restaurant, serving comfort food.

2 Spring Gardens, Trafalgar Sq., London SW1A 2TS. © 800/774-1500 in the U.S., or 020/7870-2900. Fax 020/7870-2911. www.hilton.com. 129 units. £159–£229 ($294–$424) double; from £289 ($535) suite. AE, DC, MC, V. Tube: Charing Cross. **Amenities:** Restaurant; bar; concierge; sauna; courtesy car; business services; 24-hr. room service; laundry service; same-day dry cleaning; nonsmoking rooms; rooms for those w/limited mobility. *In room:* A/C, TV w/pay movies, dataport, minibar, hair dryer, safe, beverage maker.

## SOHO
### VERY EXPENSIVE
**The Sanderson** ★★★   Ian Schrager, the king of New York hip, has brought Tenth Avenue in Manhattan to London. For his latest London hotel, Schrager secured the help of talented partners, Philippe Starck and Andra Andrei, to create an "ethereal, transparent urban spa," in which walls are replaced by glass and sheer layers of curtains. The hotel, located in a former corporate building near Oxford Street, north of Soho, comes with a lush bamboo-filled roof garden, a large courtyard, and spa. That's not all—Alain Ducasse, arguably the world's greatest chef, directs its restaurant. The accommodations are cutting edge. Although the transformation of this building into a hotel has been remarkable, the dreary grid facade of aluminum squares and glass remains. Your bed is likely to be an Italian silverleaf sleigh attended by spidery polished stainless-steel night tables and draped with a fringed pashmina shawl the color of dried lemon verbena.

50 Berners St., London W1P 3AD. © 020/7300-1400. Fax 020/7300-1401. www.ianschragerhotels.com. 150 units. £205–£340 ($379–$629) double; from £400 ($740) suite. Ask about weekend specials. AE, DC, MC, V. Tube: Oxford Circus. **Amenities:** 2 restaurants; 2 bars; health club; spa; business services; 24-hr. room service; in-room massage; babysitting; laundry service; same-day dry cleaning; nonsmoking rooms; rooms for those w/limited mobility. *In room:* A/C, TV w/pay movies, dataport, minibar, hair dryer, safe, beverage maker.

### EXPENSIVE
**Charlotte Street Hotel** ★★ *Finds*   In North Soho, a short walk from the heartbeat of Soho Square, this town house has been luxuriously converted into a high-end hotel that is London chic at its finest, possessing everything from a Los Angeles–style juice bar to a private screening room. The latter has made the hotel a hit with the movie, fashion, and media crowd, many of whom had never ventured to North Soho before. One local told us, "Charlotte Street is for those who'd like to imagine themselves in California." Midsize to spacious bedrooms have fresh, modern, English interiors and everything from two-line phones with

voice mail to dataports and fax outlets. Bathrooms are state of the art, designed in solid granite and oak with twin basins, walk-in showers, and even color TVs. Guests can relax in the elegant drawing room and library with a log-burning fireplace. The decor evokes memories of the Bloomsbury set of Virginia Woolf.

15–17 Charlotte St., London W1P IRJ. Ⓒ 800/553-6674 in the U.S., or 020/7806-2000. Fax 020/7806-2002. www.firmdale.com. 52 units. £220–£310 ($407–$574) double; from £340 ($629) suite. AE, MC, V. Tube: Tottenham Court Rd. **Amenities:** Restaurant and long pewter bar; exercise room; 24-hr. room service; laundry service; same-day dry cleaning; nonsmoking rooms; rooms for those w/limited mobility. In room: A/C, TV/DVD, fax, dataport, minibar, hair dryer, safe.

✝ **Hazlitt's 1718** ★★ (Finds)   This gem, housed in three historic homes on Soho Square, is one of London's best small hotels. Built in 1718, the hotel is named for William Hazlitt, who founded the Unitarian church in Boston and wrote four volumes on the life of his hero, Napoleon.

Hazlitt's is a favorite with artists, actors, and models. It's eclectic and filled with odds and ends picked up around the country at estate auctions. Some find its Georgian decor a bit spartan, but the 2,000 original prints hanging on the walls brighten it considerably. Many bedrooms have four-poster beds, and some bathrooms have their original claw-foot tubs (only two units have a shower). Some of the floors dip and sway, and there's no elevator, but it's all part of the charm. It has just as much character as The Fielding Hotel (see above) but is a lot more comfortable. Some rooms are a bit small, but most are spacious, all with state-of-the-art appointments. Most bathrooms have 19th-century styling but up-to-date plumbing, with oversize tubs and old brass fittings; the showers, however, are mostly hand-held. Accommodations in the back are quieter but perhaps too dark, and only those on the top floor have air-conditioning. Swinging Soho is at your doorstep; the young, hip staff will be happy to direct you to the local hot spots.

6 Frith St., London W1V 5TZ. Ⓒ 020/7434-1771. Fax 020/7439-1524. www.hazlittshotel.com. 23 units. £205–£255 ($379–$472) double; £300 ($555) suite. AE, DC, MC, V. Tube: Leicester Sq. or Tottenham Court Rd. **Amenities:** 24-hr. room service; babysitting; laundry service; same-day dry cleaning; nonsmoking rooms. In room: A/C (some rooms), TV/VCR, dataport, minibar, hair dryer, safe.

# MAYFAIR
## VERY EXPENSIVE

**Brown's Hotel** ★★   Almost every year a hotel sprouts up trying to evoke an English country-house ambience with Chippendale and chintz; this quintessential town-house hotel watches these competitors come and go, and it always comes out on top. Brown's was founded by James Brown, a former manservant to Lord Byron, who knew the tastes of well-bred gentlemen and wanted to create a dignified, clublike place for them. He opened its doors in 1837, the same year Queen Victoria took the throne.

Brown's occupies 14 historic houses just off Berkeley Square and its guest rooms vary considerably in decor, but all show restrained taste in decoration and appointments; even the wash basins are antiques. Accommodations range in size from small to extra spacious; some suites have four-poster beds. Bathrooms come in a variety of sizes, but they are beautifully equipped with robes, luxurious cosmetics, tubs, and showers.

30 Albemarle St., London W1S 4BP. Ⓒ 020/7493-6020. Fax 020/7493-9381. www.brownshotel.com. 118 units. £239–£345 ($442–$638) double; from £403 ($746) suite. AE, DC, MC, V. Off-site parking £40 ($74). Tube: Green Park. **Amenities:** Restaurant; bar; health club; concierge; business center; 24-hr. room service; laundry service; same-day dry cleaning; nonsmoking rooms. In room: A/C, TV/VCR w/pay movies, dataport, minibar, hair dryer, safe.

**Claridge's** ★★★ That once-fading 1812 beauty has experienced a $75 million rebirth, and its staid image has changed. *Dynasty* diva Joan Collins may have staged her latest marriage here, but now Kate Moss is spotted in the hip bar, Elizabeth Hurley strolls through the lobby, and Gordon Ramsay—Britain's most talked about and controversial chef (and also the best)—is loud-mouthing it in the kitchen and swinging sharp knives for the benefit of the cameras. What would Queen Victoria have said about his foul tongue and fiery temper?

If you want to live in the total lap of luxury, at an even tonier address than The Connaught and The Dorchester, make it Claridge's. Though renovations have been extensive, much of the Art Deco style of the 1930s remains. You'll expect Fred Astaire and Ginger Rogers to emerge dancing at any minute. The hotel's strong sense of tradition and old-fashioned "Britishness" are also intact, in spite of the gloss and the hip clientele. Stand anywhere in any of the halls, and you'll find it easy to imagine the duke of Windsor striding through the halls, trailed by his two-timing wife. Afternoon tea at Claridge's remains a quintessentially English tradition. The accommodations here are the most diverse in London, ranging from the costly and stunning Brook Penthouse—complete with a personal butler—to the less-expensive so-called superior queen rooms with queen-size beds. You'll find sumptuous fabrics, exceedingly comfortable beds, elegant linens, chandeliers, and all sorts of modern amenities in the bedrooms. The bathrooms are the most elegant in Britain, with enormous tubs and showerheads the size of frying pans.

Brook St., London W1A 2JQ. ✆ 020/7629-8860. Fax 020/7499-2210. www.the-savoy-group.com/claridges. 197 units. £370–£395 ($685–$731) double; from £515 ($953) suite. AE, DC, MC, V. Parking: £50 ($93). Tube: Bond St. **Amenities:** 3 restaurants; 2 bars; health club; salon; spa; 24-hr. room service; massage; business services; babysitting; laundry service; same-day dry cleaning; nonsmoking rooms; rooms for those w/limited mobility. *In room:* A/C, TV/VCR w/pay movies, fax, dataport, minibar, hair dryer, iron/ironing board, safe, beverage maker.

**The Connaught** ★★★ This elegant hotel, located in the heart of Mayfair, is one of Europe's most prestigious. It is not the most glamorous, nor even the most fashionable in London, but it nonetheless coddles you in comfort and luxury, with a hospitality that's legendary. It has the atmosphere of an English country house—a world of fresh flowers, crystal chandeliers, Wedgwood, and antiques. The hotel guarantees privacy even if you're a film star sex symbol or Barbara Bush (the former president's wife is a fan of The Connaught). Situated near Grosvenor Square, this brick house is like a club, with many repeat guests demanding their favorite rooms. There is something of an aura of aristocratic decay at The Connaught, just as the country gentry like it; whereas The Dorchester (see below) has more flash.

Rooms range from medium to large, and are a world of antiques, chintz, and tasteful details such as gilt-trimmed white paneling. Sumptuous beds are dressed in the finest Irish linens. Marble fireplaces, ornate plasterwork, and oak paneling add to the stately allure of the rooms. The large, old-fashioned bathrooms are still intact and are outfitted with robes and deep tubs.

Carlos Place, London W1K 2AL. ✆ 800/63-SAVOY in the U.S., or 020/7499-7070. Fax 020/7495-3262. www.the-savoy-group.com/connaught. 92 units. £390–£405 ($722–$749) double; £495–£855 ($916–$1,582) suite. AE, DC, DISC, MC, V. Parking £50 ($93). Tube: Green Park. **Amenities:** 2 restaurants; 2 bars; health club; spa services can be arranged in advance; 24-hr. concierge; courtesy car; business services; 24-hr. room service; babysitting; laundry service; same-day dry cleaning; rooms for those w/limited mobility; nonsmoking rooms. *In room:* A/C, TV/VCR w/pay movies, fax, dataport, minibar, hair dryer, iron, safe, CD/DVD player.

**The Dorchester** ★★★ *Finds* One of London's best hotels, it has all the elegance of The Connaught, but without the upper-crust attitude that can verge on snobbery. Few hotels have the time-honored experience of "The Dorch," which has maintained a tradition of fine comfort and cuisine since it opened in 1931.

Breaking from the neoclassical tradition, the most ambitious architects of the era designed a building of reinforced concrete clothed in terrazzo slabs. Within you'll find a 1930s take on Regency motifs: The monumental arrangements of flowers and the elegance of the gilded-cage promenade seem appropriate for a diplomatic reception, yet they convey a kind of comfort in which guests from all over the world feel at ease.

The Dorchester boasts guest rooms outfitted with Irish linen sheets on comfortable beds, plus all the electronic gadgetry you'd expect, and double- and triple-glazed windows to keep out noise, along with plump armchairs, cherry-wood furnishings, and, in many cases, four-poster beds piled high with pillows. The large bathrooms are equally stylish, with mottled Carrara marble and Lalique-style sconces, makeup mirrors and posh toiletries, and deep tubs. The best rooms offer views of Hyde Park.

53 Park Lane, London W1A 2HJ. ℂ **800/727-9820** in the U.S., or 020/7629-8888. Fax 020/7409-0114. www.dorchesterhotel.com. 248 units. £330–£385 ($611–$712) double; from £500 ($925) suite. AE, DC, MC, V. Parking £33 ($61). Tube: Hyde Park Corner or Marble Arch. **Amenities:** 3 restaurants; bar; health club; spa; tour desk; car-rental desk; courtesy car; business services and center; small shopping arcade; 2 salons; 24-hr. room service; babysitting; laundry service; same-day dry cleaning; nonsmoking rooms; rooms for those w/limited mobility. *In room:* A/C, TV/VCR, dataport, minibar, hair dryer, iron, safe.

**Four Seasons Hotel** ⭐⭐    This deluxe hostelry has captured the imagination of glamour-mongers the world over ever since it was inaugurated by Princess Alexandra in 1970. Its clientele includes heads of state, superstars, and top business execs. Sitting tastefully behind a modern facade in one of the most exclusive neighborhoods in the world, it's located opposite its major competitors, the London Hilton and the Inter-Continental, but has better food, better rooms, and more style and refinement than either of its rivals. Even so, it falls just a little bit short of the platinum credentials of The Dorchester and The Connaught (see above), both longer-established. Inside, acres of superbly crafted paneling and opulent but conservative decor create the impression that the hotel is far older than it is.

The guest rooms are large and beautifully outfitted with well-chosen chintz, reproductions, plush upholstery, and dozens of well-concealed electronic extras. Most rooms are medium size, although some are quite large, and all are maintained in perfect condition. There is plenty of desk space, and in many instances tall windows open onto stand-up balconies. Mattresses are of the finest quality, as are bed linens. Bathrooms are ample, with thought-out extras such as deep tubs, robes, and deluxe toiletries.

Hamilton Place, Park Lane, London W1A 1AZ. ℂ **800/819-5053** or 020/7499-0888. Fax 020/7493-1895. www.fourseasons.com. 220 units. £345–£370 ($638–$685) double; £490 ($907) conservatory double; from £620 ($1,147) suite. AE, DC, MC, V. Parking £21 ($39). Tube: Hyde Park Corner. **Amenities:** Restaurant; bar; access to nearby indoor tennis courts; health club; children's center; concierge; tour desk; business services; 24-hr. room service; massage; babysitting; laundry service; same-day dry cleaning; rooms for those w/limited mobility; nonsmoking rooms. *In room:* A/C, TV/VCR w/pay movies, fax, dataport, minibar, hair dryer, safe.

**Sheraton Park Lane Hotel** ⭐⭐    Since 1924, this has been the most traditional of the Park Lane mansions, even more so than The Dorchester. The hotel was sold in 1996 to the Sheraton Corporation, which continues to upgrade it but maintains its quintessential British style. Its Silver Entrance remains an Art Deco marvel that has been used as a backdrop in many films, including the classic BBC miniseries *Brideshead Revisited*.

Overlooking Green Park, the hotel offers luxurious accommodations that are a good deal—well, at least for pricey Park Lane, where anything under $500 a night is a bargain. Many suites have marble fireplaces and original marble bathrooms. The rooms have all benefited from impressive refurbishment. All have double-glazed windows to block out noise. The most tranquil rooms open onto a street in the rear. Rooms opening onto the court are dark. In the more deluxe rooms, you get trouser presses and better views. Bathrooms are generally spacious and well equipped with shower/tub combos; many also have robes.

Piccadilly, London W1J 7BX. © 800/325-3535 in the U.S., or 020/7499-6321. Fax 020/7499-1965. www.starwood.com/sheraton. 307 units. £270–£310 ($500–$574) double; from £429 ($794) suite. AE, DC, MC, V. Parking £35 ($65). Tube: Hyde Park Corner or Green Park. **Amenities:** 2 restaurants; fabled 1920s palm court; bar; health club; concierge; business center; 24-hr. room service, laundry service; same-day dry cleaning; nonsmoking rooms; rooms for those w/limited mobility. *In room:* A/C (in most rooms), TV w/pay movies, dataport, minibar, hair dryer, iron, safe.

## EXPENSIVE

**The Chesterfield Mayfair** ★★   Just a short distance from Berkeley Square, the elegant Chesterfield serves up a traditional English atmosphere and offers a lot more bang for your buck than most hotels in pricey Mayfair. The hotel, once home to the earl of Chesterfield, still sports venerable features that evoke an air of nobility, including richly decorated public rooms featuring woods, antiques, fabrics, and marble. The secluded Library Lounge is a great place to relax, and the glassed-in conservatory is a good spot for tea. The sumptuously decorated restaurant is well regarded, as is the bar, where a pianist plays on most nights. The staff, from the reception clerks to the chambermaids, couldn't be nicer. Many of the hotel's large contingent of repeat guests—mostly Brits and Americans—cite the service here as a big reason for their loyalty.

The guest rooms are generally not huge, but they are dramatically decorated and make excellent use of space—there's a ton of closet and counter space—and feature such unusual amenities as complimentary bottled waters and jellybeans. The spotless marble bathrooms are similarly compact, but are well equipped with bathrobes and heated floors. For a more memorable experience, book one of the themed junior or executive suites, which offer excellent value for Mayfair. You'll get larger amounts of space, upgraded amenities (DVD players and umbrellas, for example), complimentary canapés, and theatrical decorating schemes. Most executive rooms have Jacuzzi tubs or separate tubs and power showers, and some have wholly separate sitting rooms. Some favorites include the Music Suite, with a lace canopy bed and pop-up TV; the Theatre Suite, which features a Jacuzzi and draperies that once hung in the Drury Lane theatre; the exotic African Suite, with its leopard prints, leather sofa, and flat-screen TV; and the lovely Garden Suite, with a latticework headboard and a two-person Jacuzzi bath.

35 Charles St., London W1J 5EB. © 877/955-1515 in the U.S. and Canada, or 020/7491-2622. Fax 020/7491-4793. www.chesterfieldmayfair.com. 110 units. £165–£275 ($305–$509) double; £295–£595 ($546–$1,101) suite. Special packages available. AE, DC, MC, V. Tube: Green Park. **Amenities:** 2 restaurants; bar; concierge; business services; 24-hr. room service; babysitting; laundry service; same-day dry cleaning; nonsmoking rooms. *In room:* A/C, TV w/pay movies, CD player (in suite), dataport, minibar (in suite), coffeemaker, hair dryer, iron/ironing board, safe.

**The Selfridge**   The location, right next door to Selfridge's food hall off Oxford Street, is wonderful, especially for shoppers. In fact, the hotel's seven floors look as if they are part of Selfridge's itself. This mammoth hotel is a member of the Thistle hotel chain and caters to an even mix of business and leisure travelers. Ignore the drab entrance; the hotel brightens considerably in the second floor reception room, with its wingback chairs, antique art, pine-paneled walls, and a rustic bar whose half-timbered decor was brought and installed piece by piece from an English barn that stood in the Middle Ages. The rooms are hardly the finest in this part of town, but they are usually affordable, especially if you snag one of the promotional offerings (our editor once stayed here for £37/$68 a night—a steal!—thanks to an off-season special on Thistle's website). Accommodations are well maintained, nicely decorated, tranquil, and generally spacious, with small bathrooms. Double-glazing on the windows cuts back on noise. *Tip:* Try for a room facing Orchard Street, as these are larger. Also, the best rooms are the premium units on floors 3 to 5.

Orchard St., London W1H 0JS. © 020/7408-2080. Fax 020/7409-2295. www.thistle.co.uk. 294 units. £210–£236 ($389–$437) double; £379–£470 ($710–$870) suite. AE, DC, MC, V. Parking: £38 ($70). Tube: Bond St. **Amenities:** 2 restaurants; bar; 24-hr. room service; baby-sitting; laundry service; same-day dry cleaning. *In room:* TV w/pay movies, dataport (in some), coffeemaker, hair dryer, safe (in some).

## ST. JAMES'S
### VERY EXPENSIVE

**Dukes Hotel** ★★★  Dukes provides elegance without ostentation in what was presumably someone's "Upstairs, Downstairs" town house. Along with its nearest competitors, The Stafford and 22 Jermyn Street, it caters to those looking for charm, style, and tradition in a hotel. It stands in a quiet courtyard off St. James's Street; turn-of-the-last-century gas lamps help put you into the proper mood before entering the front door. Each well-furnished guest room is decorated in the style of a particular English period, ranging from Regency to Edwardian. All rooms are equipped with marble bathrooms containing shower/tub combinations. Even though it's claustrophobically small—it was once described as England's smallest castle—Dukes offers full hotel services.

35 St. James's Place, London SW1A 1NY. © 800/381-4702 in the U.S., or 020/7491-4840. Fax 020/7493-1264. www.dukeshotel.co.uk. 89 units. £225–£260 ($416–$481) double; from £350 ($648) suite. AE, DC, MC, V. Parking £54 ($100). Tube: Green Park. **Amenities:** Restaurant; bar; health club; spa; concierge; tour desk; business services; 24-hr. room service; babysitting; laundry service; same-day dry cleaning; nonsmoking rooms; rooms for those w/limited mobility. *In room:* A/C, TV, dataport, minibar, hair dryer, safe.

**The Ritz** ★★★  Built in French Renaissance style and opened by César Ritz in 1906, this hotel overlooking Green Park is synonymous with luxury. Gold-leafed molding, marble columns, and potted palms abound, and a gold-leafed statue, *La Source*, adorns the fountain of the oval-shaped Palm Court. After a major restoration, the hotel is better than ever: New carpeting and air-conditioning have been installed in the guest rooms, and an overall polishing has recaptured much of The Ritz's original splendor. Still, this Ritz lags far behind the much grander one in Paris (with which it is not affiliated). The Belle Epoque guest rooms, each with its own character, are spacious and comfortable. Many have marble fireplaces, elaborate gilded plasterwork, and a decor of soft pastel hues. A few rooms have their original brass beds and marble fireplaces. Bathrooms are elegantly appointed in either tile or marble and filled with deep tubs with showers, robes, phones, and deluxe toiletries. Corner rooms are grander and more spacious.

150 Piccadilly, London W1J 9BR. © 877/748-9536 in the U.S. or 020/7493-8181. Fax 020/7493-2687. www.theritzlondon.com. 133 units. £310–£405 ($574–$749) double; from £785 ($1,452) suite. Children under 12 stay free in parent's room. AE, DC, MC, V. Parking £54 ($100). Tube: Green Park. **Amenities:** 2 restaurants (including the Palm Court); bar; exercise room; concierge; business services; 2 salons; 24-hr. room service; massage; babysitting; laundry service; same-day dry cleaning; nonsmoking rooms; rooms for those w/limited mobility. *In room:* A/C, TV/VCR w/pay movies, fax, dataport, minibar, hair dryer, safe.

**The Stafford Hotel** ★★★    Famous for its American Bar, its clubby St. James's address, and the warmth of its Edwardian decor, The Stafford is in a cul-de-sac off one of London's most centrally located and busiest neighborhoods. The recently refurbished late-19th-century hotel has retained a country-house atmosphere, with antique charm and modern amenities. The Stafford competes well with Dukes and 22 Jermyn Street for a tasteful, discerning clientele, and seems to maintain a slight edge in attracting an upmarket clientele.

All the guest rooms are individually decorated, reflecting the hotel's origins as a private home. Many singles contain queen-size beds. Some of the deluxe units offer four-posters that will make you feel like Henry VIII. Nearly all the bathrooms are clad in marble with tubs and stall showers, toiletries, and chrome fixtures. A few of the hotel's more modern accommodations, boasting king-size beds, are located in the restored stable mews across the yard. Much has been done to preserve the original style of these rooms, including preservation of the original A-beams on the upper floors. You can bet that no 18th-century horse ever slept with the electronic safes, stereo systems, and quality furnishings (mostly antique reproductions) that these rooms feature. Units on the top floor are small.

16–18 St. James's Place, London SW1A 1NJ. ℭ **800/525-4800** in the U.S., or 020/7493-0111. Fax 020/7493-7121. www.thestaffordhotel.co.uk. 81 units. £225–£250 ($416–$463) double; from £270 ($500) suite. AE, DC, MC, V. Tube: Green Park. **Amenities:** Restaurant; famous American bar; health club privileges nearby; concierge; business services; 24-hr. room service; babysitting; laundry service; same-day dry cleaning; all non-smoking rooms. *In room:* A/C, TV/VCR, fax, dataport, hair dryer, safe.

**22 Jermyn Street** ★★★    This is London's premier town-house hotel, a bastion of elegance and discretion. Set behind a facade of gray stone with neoclassical details, this structure, only 45m (148 ft.) from Piccadilly Circus, was built in 1870 for English gentlemen doing business in London. Since 1915, the Togna family has been in charge. After a radical renovation and reopening in 1990, 22 Jermyn revels in its role as a chic, upscale boutique hotel. It offers an interior filled with greenery, and the kind of art you might find in an elegant private home. The sixth floor features one of the best-equipped computer centers in London, which guests may use for free. This hotel doesn't have the bar or restaurant facilities of The Stafford or Dukes, but its recently refurbished rooms are more richly appointed, done in traditional English style with fresh flowers and chintz. Beds are luxurious and bathrooms are clad in granite and contain deep tubs and showers, luxurious toiletries, and phones. If you like space, ask for one of the studios in the rear. The staff is incredibly helpful.

22 Jermyn St., London SW1Y 6HL. ℭ **800/682-7808** in the U.S., or 020/7734-2353. Fax 020/7734-0750. www.22jermyn.com. 18 units. £210 ($389) double; from £295 ($576) suite. AE, DC, MC, V. Valet parking £35 ($65). Tube: Piccadilly Circus. **Amenities:** Access to nearby health club and spa; concierge; business services; 24-hr. room service; massage; babysitting; laundry service; same-day dry cleaning; nonsmoking rooms. *In room:* TV/VCR w/pay movies, dataport, minibar, hair dryer, safe.

---

*Tips*  **How to Avoid Getting Knocked Up**

If you don't want a rude awakening, remember to hang the DO NOT DISTURB sign on your doorknob (or bolt the door, if that's an option). English hotel service personnel have a disconcerting habit of bursting in simultaneously with their knock. (As you might have deduced, "knocking someone up" doesn't have the same meaning in England as it does in the United States.)

## 3 Westminster & Victoria

### VERY EXPENSIVE

**The Goring** ★★★   For tradition and location, the Goring is our first choice in Westminster. Just behind Buckingham Palace, it lies within easy reach of the royal parks, Victoria Station, Westminster Abbey, and the Houses of Parliament. It also offers the finest personal service of all its nearby competitors.

Built in 1910 by O. R. Goring, this was the first hotel in the world to have central heating and a private bathroom in every room. Today's guest rooms still offer all the comforts, including luxurious refurbished bathrooms with extra-long tubs, red marble walls, dual pedestal basins, bidets, deluxe toiletries, and power showerheads. There is an ongoing refurbishment of all the bedrooms, including frequent replacement of linens. The beds, in fact, are among the most comfortable in London. Queen Anne and Chippendale are usually the decor styles, and the maintenance level is of the highest order. The rooms overlooking the garden are best. The charm of a traditional English country hotel is conjured in the paneled drawing room, where fires crackle in the ornate fireplaces on nippy evenings.

15 Beeston Place, Grosvenor Gardens, London SW1W OJW. © **020/7396-9000.** Fax 020/7834-4393. www. goringhotel.co.uk. 74 units. £255–£340 ($472–$629) double; from £340 ($629) suite. AE, DC, MC, V. Parking £30 ($56). Tube: Victoria. **Amenities:** Grand afternoon tea in the drawing room (a London highlight); classic restaurant; bar; free use of nearby health club; 24-hr. room service; babysitting; laundry service; same-day dry cleaning; nonsmoking rooms; rooms for those w/limited mobility. *In room:* A/C, TV w/pay movies, dataport, hair dryer, safe.

### EXPENSIVE

**41** ★★★ *Finds*   This relatively unknown but well-placed gem is a treasure worth seeking out, especially if you're looking for a touch of class. The property offers the intimate atmosphere of a private club combined with a level of personal service that's impossible to achieve at larger hotels. It's best suited to couples or those traveling alone—especially women, who will be made to feel comfortable. The cordial staff goes the extra mile to fulfill a guest's every wish. The surroundings match the stellar service. Public areas feature an abundance of mahogany, antiques, fresh flowers, and rich fabrics. Read, relax, or watch TV in the library-style lounge, where a complimentary continental breakfast, afternoon snacks, and evening canapés (all included in the room rate) are served each day.

Guest rooms are individually sized, but all feature elegant black-and-white color schemes, magnificent beds with Egyptian-cotton linens, and "AV centers" that offer free Internet access and DVD/CD players. Most rooms have working fireplaces. The spotless marble bathrooms sport separate tubs and power showers (only one room has a shower/tub combo) and feature Penhaligon toiletries. The bilevel junior suites toss in a separate seating area (good for families looking for extra space) and Jacuzzi tubs.

41 Buckingham Palace Rd., London SW1W OPS. © **877/955-1515** in the U.S. or Canada, or 020/7300-0041. Fax 020/7300-0141. www.41hotel.com. 18 units. £200 ($370) double; £400–£500 ($740–$925) suite. Rates include continental breakfast, afternoon snacks, and evening canapés. Extra person £45 ($83). Special Internet packages and discounts available. AE, DC, MC, V. Tube: Victoria. **Amenities:** Lounge; bar; access to nearby health club; concierge; business center; 24-hr. room service; laundry service/dry cleaning; nonsmoking rooms; 1 room for those w/limited mobility. *In room:* A/C, TV, minibar, tea/coffeemaker, hair dryer, iron/ironing board, safe.

**The Rubens at the Palace** ★★ *Value*   The very British Rubens is popular with Americans and Europeans seeking traditional English hospitality combined with the latest in creature comforts. And its location is one of the best in town—directly across the street from Buckingham Palace, only a 2-minute walk from Victoria Station. The public rooms are lavishly decorated with antiques, fabric wall-coverings, and fresh flowers. A pianist plays in the military-style Cavalry Bar, the ideal place for a nightcap, on most evenings.

The size and decor of the guest rooms varies, but all feature grand comfort. Bathrooms vary in size, but almost all have deep tubs. Housed in a private wing, each of the eight "Royal Rooms" is named for an English monarch, and is decorated in the style of that ruler's period, but also features modern luxuries. Some Royal Rooms aren't particularly big. If it's available and your budget allows, we suggest the Henry the Eighth room, a relatively large Tudor fantasy done up in red and gold, with a half-canopy bed fit for a king, and a spacious marble bathroom. *Note:* Always check the hotel's website for specials; the hotel often runs promotions that can make it an attractive value option.

39 Buckingham Palace Rd., London SW1W OPS. ② **877/955-1515** in the U.S. or Canada, or 020/7834-6600. Fax 020/7828-5401. www.redcarnationhotels.com. 172 units. £210–£250 ($389–$463) double; £320–£480 ($592–$888) Royal Room; £230–£260 ($426–$481) suite. AE, DC, MC, V. Tube: Victoria. **Amenities:** 2 restaurants; lounge; bar; access to nearby health club; concierge; tour desk; babysitting; 24-hr. room service; laundry service; same-day dry cleaning; nonsmoking rooms. *In room:* A/C, TV, minibar (in suites), coffeemaker, hair dryer, iron, safe.

**Tophams Belgravia** ⟨*⟩  Tophams came into being in 1937, when five small row houses were interconnected. With its flower-filled window boxes, the place has a bucolic flavor. The petite informal reception rooms are done in flowery chintzes and antiques. All bedrooms are tastefully furnished, and the best are appointed with four-poster beds and private bathrooms equipped with shower/tub combinations. Not all rooms have private bathrooms. The restaurant offers traditional and modern English cooking for lunch and dinner. And the location is ideal, especially if you're planning to cover a lot of ground by Tube or train: It's only a 3-minute walk to Victoria Station.

28 Ebury St., London SW1W 0LU. ② **020/7730-8147.** Fax 020/7823-5966. www.tophams.co.uk. 39 units, 34 with bathroom. £110 ($204) double without bathroom; £130–£170 ($241–$315) double with bathroom; £170 ($315) triple with bathroom. AE, DC, MC, V. Tube: Victoria. **Amenities:** Restaurant; bar; access to nearby health club; 24-hr. room service; babysitting; laundry service; same-day dry cleaning; rooms for those w/limited mobility; nonsmoking rooms. *In room:* TV, dataport, coffeemaker, hair dryer, iron/ironing board.

## MODERATE

**Lime Tree Hotel**  The Wales-born Davies family, longtime veterans of London's B&B business, have transformed a run-down guesthouse into a cost-conscious, cozy hotel for budget travelers. The simply furnished bedrooms are scattered over four floors of a brick town house; each has been recently refitted with new curtains and cupboards. The front rooms have small balconies overlooking Ebury Street; units in the back don't have balconies, but are quieter and feature views over the hotel's small rose garden. The Lime Tree's rooms tend to be larger than other hotel rooms offered at similar prices, and breakfasts are generous. Six rooms come with a shower/tub combo, the rest with shower only. Buckingham Palace, Westminster Abbey, and the Houses of Parliament are within easy reach, as is Harrods. Nearby is the popular Ebury Wine Bar.

135–137 Ebury St., London SW1W 9RA. ② **020/7730-8191.** Fax 020/7730-7865. www.limetreehotel.co.uk. 29 units. £84–£125 ($155–$231) double. Rates include English breakfast. AE, DC, MC, V. No children under 5. Tube: Victoria. **Amenities:** All nonsmoking rooms. *In room:* TV, coffeemaker, hair dryer, safe.

**New England**  A family-run business, going strong for nearly a quarter of a century, this hotel shut down at the millennium for a complete overhaul. Today, it's better than ever and charges an affordable price. Its elegant 19th-century

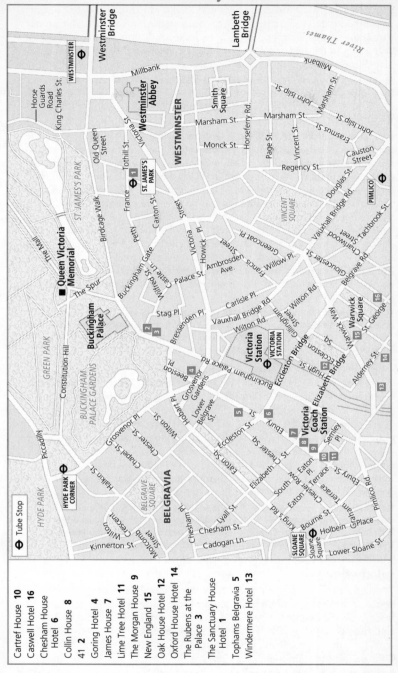

Cartref House 10
Caswell Hotel 16
Chesham House Hotel 6
Collin House 8
41 2
Goring Hotel 4
James House 7
Lime Tree Hotel 11
The Morgan House 9
New England 15
Oak House Hotel 12
Oxford House Hotel 14
The Rubens at the Palace 3
The Sanctuary House Hotel 1
Tophams Belgravia 5
Windermere Hotel 13

exterior conceals a completely bright and modern interior. The hotel is justly proud of its clientele of "repeats." On a corner in the Pimlico area, which forms part of the City of Westminster, the hotel is neat and clean and one of the most welcoming in the area. It's also one of the few hotels in the area with an elevator. All the bathrooms have power showers.

20 Saint George's Dr., London SW1V 4BN. ℂ 020/7834-1595. Fax 020/7834-9000. www.newenglandhotel. com. 25 units. £95–£99 ($176–$183) double; £119 ($220) triple; £139 ($257) quad. Rates include breakfast. AE, MC, V. Tube: Victoria. **Amenities:** Nonsmoking rooms; rooms for those w/limited mobility. *In room:* TV, dataport, hair dryer.

**The Sanctuary House Hotel** ✦    Only in the new London, where hotels are bursting into bloom like daffodils, would you find a hotel so close to Westminster Abbey. And a pub hotel, no less, with rooms on the upper floors above the tavern. The building was converted by Fuller Smith and Turner, a traditional brewery in Britain. Accommodations have a rustic feel, but they have first-rate beds, along with restored bathrooms with shower/tub combinations. Downstairs, a pub/restaurant, part of The Sanctuary, offers old-style British meals that have ignored changing culinary fashions. "We like tradition," one of the perky staff members told us. "Why must everything be trendy? Some people come to England nostalgic for the old. Let others be trendy." Actually, the food is excellent if you appreciate the roast beef, Welsh lamb, and Dover sole that pleased the palates of Churchill and his contemporaries. Naturally, there's always plenty of brew on tap.

33 Tothill St., London SW1H 9LA. ℂ 020/7799-4044. Fax 020/7799-3657. www.fullershotels.com. 34 units. £85–£130 ($157–$241) double. AE, DC, MC, V. Parking £25 ($46). Tube: St. James's Park. **Amenities:** Restaurant; pub; limited room service; laundry service/dry cleaning; nonsmoking rooms; rooms for those w/limited mobility. *In room:* A/C, TV, dataport, coffeemaker, hair dryer, trouser press.

**Windermere Hotel** ✦ *Value*    This award-winning small hotel is an excellent choice near Victoria Station. The Windermere was built in 1857 as a pair of private dwellings on the site of the old Abbot's Lane. The lane linked Westminster Abbey to its abbot's residence—so all the kings of medieval England trod here. A fine example of early Victorian classical design, the hotel has lots of English character. Most rooms have a small bathroom equipped with a shower, and the public bathrooms are adequate and well maintained. Rooms come in a wide range of sizes, some accommodating three or four lodgers. The cheaper ones are somewhat cramped. The ground-floor rooms facing the street tend to be noisy at night, so stay away from those if you're a light sleeper.

142–144 Warwick Way, London SW1V 4JE. ℂ 020/7834-5163. Fax 020/7630-8831. www.windermere-hotel. co.uk. 22 units, 20 with bathroom. £89 ($165) double without bathroom, £109 ($202) double with bathroom; £145 ($268) triple with bathroom; £149 ($276) quad with bathroom. Rates include English breakfast. AE, MC, V. Tube: Victoria. **Amenities:** Restaurant; bar; limited room service; nonsmoking rooms. *In room:* TV, dataport, coffeemaker, hair dryer, safe.

## INEXPENSIVE

**Caswell Hotel**    Thoughtfully run by Mr. and Mrs. Hare, Caswell is on a cul-de-sac, a calm oasis in a busy area. Mozart lived nearby while he completed his first symphony, as did that "notorious couple" of the literati, Harold Nicholson and Victoria Sackville-West. Beyond the chintz-filled lobby, the decor is understated. There are four floors of well-furnished but not spectacular bedrooms. Both the private bathrooms (small units with shower stalls) and the corridor bathrooms are adequate and well maintained. How does the Caswell explain its success? One staff member said, "This year's guest is next year's business."

25 Gloucester St., London SW1V 2DB. ℂ **020/7834-6345.** www.hotellondon.co.uk. 19 units, 8 with bathroom. £58 ($107) double without bathroom; £78 ($144) double with bathroom. Rates include English breakfast. MC, V. Tube: Victoria. *In room:* TV, minibar, hair dryer, safe, beverage maker, no phone.

**Collin House** ⭐   This B&B emerges as a winner on a street lined with the finest Victoria Station–area B&Bs. William IV had just begun his reign when this house was constructed in 1830. Private, shower-only bathrooms have been discreetly installed, and everything works efficiently. For rooms without bathrooms, there are adequate hallway facilities, some of which are shared by only two rooms. Traffic in this area of London is heavy outside, and the front windows are not soundproof, so be warned if you're a light sleeper. Year after year, the owners continually make improvements in the furnishings and carpets. All bedrooms, which vary in size, are comfortably furnished and well maintained. Two rooms are large enough for families. A generous breakfast awaits you each morning in the basement of this nonsmoking facility.

104 Ebury St., London SW1W 9QD. ℂ and fax **020/7730-8031.** www.collinhouse.co.uk. 12 units, 8 with bathroom (shower only). £68 ($126) double without bathroom, £82 ($152) double with bathroom; £95 ($176) triple without bathroom. Rates include English breakfast. MC, V. Tube: Victoria. *In room:* TV, hair dryer available, safe, no phone.

**James House/Cartref House** 🅺🄸🄳🅂   Hailed by many publications, including the *Los Angeles Times,* as one of the top 10 B&B choices in London, James House and Cartref House (across the street from each other) deserve their accolades. Each room is individually designed. Some of the large rooms have bunk beds that make them suitable for families. Clients in rooms with a private shower-only bathroom will find somewhat cramped quarters; corridor bathrooms are adequate and frequently refurbished. The English breakfast is so generous that you might end up skipping lunch. There's no elevator, but guests don't seem to mind. Both houses are nonsmoking. You're just a stone's throw from Buckingham Palace should the queen invite you over for tea. *Warning:* Whether or not you like this hotel will depend on your room assignment. Some accommodations are fine but several rooms (often when the other units are full) are hardly large enough to move around in. This is especially true of some third-floor units. Some "bathrooms" reminded us of those found on small ocean-going freighters. Ask before booking and request a larger room.

108 and 129 Ebury St., London SW1W 9QU. James House ℂ **020/7730-7338;** Cartref House ℂ **020/ 7730-6176.** Fax 020/7730-7338. www.jamesandcartref.co.uk. 19 units, 12 with bathroom. £70 ($130) double without bathroom, £85 ($157) double with bathroom; £135 ($250) quad with bathroom. Rates include English breakfast. AE, MC, V. Tube: Victoria. **Amenities:** All nonsmoking rooms. *In room:* TV, hair dryer, beverage maker, no phone.

**The Morgan House**   This Georgian house is a handy, convenient address, but its rooms are often booked in summer. Morgan's finest feature is a small courtyard open to guests. Many rooms are small to midsize, while others are large enough to house up to four people in reasonable comfort. Guest rooms are individually decorated and have orthopedic mattresses. Hallway bathrooms are well maintained and adequate for guests who don't have their own private facilities. A hearty English breakfast is served in a bright, cheerful room.

120 Ebury St., London SW1W 9QQ. ℂ **020/7730-2384.** Fax 020/7730-8442. www.morganhouse.co.uk. 11 units, 4 with private bathroom. £66 ($122) double without bathroom, £86 ($159) double with bathroom. Rates include English breakfast. MC, V. Tube: Victoria. *In room:* TV, coffeemaker, hair dryer, phone only for receiving calls.

**Oak House Hotel** ⭐ 🄵🄸🄽🄳🅂   This little jewel of a hotel, perhaps the smallest in the area, is a real find, with lots of homespun charm. The Symingtons bring

---

> ( *Tips* Hot & Cold
>
> London hotel rooms aren't kept as warm as in other parts of the world. Bring a sweater if you find yourself chilly at a lower-than-usual room temperature. In summer, rooms without air-conditioning can get quite hot. Don't assume that your hotel, even at the luxury level, has central air; many have only partial air-conditioning or none at all. Call ahead and ask if this is a concern for you.

---

their Scottish hospitality to their home in the Victoria Station area. When Mr. Symington isn't putting on his kilt to do the Scottish war dance, he's out driving a London taxi. Mrs. Symington is here to welcome you to her tidily maintained bedrooms, which are small yet handsomely furnished and appointed. Half of the rooms have double beds; the others contain twins. The closets are small, so you'll have to hang your garments on hooks and store other items on shelves. Shower-only bathrooms are adequate and spotlessly maintained. Rooms may be reserved only for 5 or more consecutive days.

29 Hugh St., London SW1V 1QJ. ② 020/7834-7151. 6 units. £46 ($85) single or double. No credit cards. Tube: Victoria. *In room:* TV, coffeemaker, hair dryer; no phone.

**Oxford House Hotel** *Value* Just a 10-minute walk from Victoria Station, Oxford House is known for value. Since many of its rooms sleep three to four guests, it's a family favorite as well. Yunus and Terry Kader operate this small hotel like the private family home that it is, and the atmosphere is informal. The biggest drawback is the lack of a private bathroom. However, only two bedrooms usually share one shower-only bathroom, so waiting time is minimal. Guests from all over the world converge in the TV lounge. Rooms are midsize and furnished with comfortable, well-chosen pieces, as Mr. Kader is an interior designer. Although it's in a heavily congested area of London, Cambridge Street is not a major thoroughfare, and rooms tend to be tranquil.

92–94 Cambridge St., London SW1V 4QG. ② 020/7834-6467. Fax 020/7834-0225. 17 units, none with private bathroom. £45 ($83) double; £60 ($111) triple; £80 ($148) quad. Rates include English breakfast. AE, MC, V; (5% surcharge). Tube: Victoria. *In room:* No phone.

## 4 Hotels from Knightsbridge to South Kensington

### KNIGHTSBRIDGE
#### VERY EXPENSIVE

**Basil Street Hotel** ⚐ An Edwardian charmer, the Basil is a favorite with travelers whose trips to London wouldn't be complete without a pilgrimage (or two, or three) to Harrods—"just 191 steps away." The Chelsea Flower Show is right nearby as well. Several spacious, comfortable lounges are furnished in an English country-house style befitting the lord of a manor, and are accented with 18th- and 19th-century accessories. There are smaller sitting rooms off the hotel's many corridors. Rooms come in varying shapes and dimensions, reminiscent of the era when hotels housed everyone from grand dukes in large suites, to their valets in small rooms on the upper floors. Nearly all units are traditional in decor. Persons with disabilities should check in elsewhere because the stairs make this hotel an Olympic feat to traverse. Even so, some older clients particularly like this hotel, which calls itself a "Hotel for Those Who Hate Hotels." We love its old-fashioned Edwardian gentility, particularly the antiquated bathrooms with deep tubs that still function perfectly. The best rooms are those overlooking the courtyard, because they are the quietest. Front rooms are subject to the sound of heavy traffic.

8 Basil St., London SW3 1AH. ℂ 020/7581-3311. Fax 020/7581-3693. www.thebasil.com. 80 units. £205 ($379) double; £275 ($509) family room. AE, DC, MC, V. Parking £36 ($67) at 24-hr. lot nearby. Tube: Knightsbridge. **Amenities:** Restaurant; bar; 24-hr. room service; car-rental desk; babysitting; laundry service; same-day dry cleaning; nonsmoking rooms. *In room:* TV, dataport, coffeemaker, hair dryer.

**The Beaufort** ★★　If you'd like to stay at one of London's finest boutique hotels, offering personal service in an elegant, tranquil town-house atmosphere, head here. The Beaufort, only 180m (590 ft.) from Harrods, sits in a cul-de-sac behind two Victorian porticoes and an iron fence. Owner Diana Wallis, a television producer, combined a pair of adjacent houses from the 1870s, ripped out the old decor, and created a graceful and stylish hotel that has the feeling of a private house. You register at a small desk extending off a bay-windowed parlor, and then climb the stairway used by the queen of Sweden during her stay. Each guest room is tasteful and bright, individually decorated in a modern color scheme and adorned with well-chosen paintings by London artists. Rooms come with earphone radios, flowers, and a selection of books. Most bedrooms are exceedingly small, but they're efficiently organized. The most deluxe and spacious rooms are in the front. Those in the back are smaller and darker. Included in the rates are a 24-hour free bar, continental breakfast, and light meals from room service, plus English cream teas each afternoon, and brandy, chocolates, and shortbread in each room. The junior suites offer a personal fax/answering machine, dataport, and use of a mobile phone. Bathrooms are adequate and tidily maintained, with shower/tub combinations.

33 Beaufort Gardens, London SW3 1PP. ℂ 020/7584-5252. Fax 020/7589-2834. www.thebeaufort.co.uk. 28 units. £165–£260 ($305–$481) double; £300 ($555) junior suite. Rates include continental breakfast, bar, light meals, and afternoon tea. AE, DC, MC, V. Tube: Knightsbridge. **Amenities:** Bar; access to nearby health club; junior suites include complimentary limo to or from the airport; 24-hr. room service; babysitting; laundry service; same-day dry cleaning; nonsmoking rooms. *In room:* A/C, TV, dataport, hair dryer, iron/ironing board.

**The Berkeley** ★★★　One of London's most appealing hotels, The Berkeley is housed in a travertine-faced French Regency–inspired building in Knightsbridge near Hyde Park, a premise it has occupied since it was built in 1972. This newer version replaced a hotel, built in the late 19th century, that was frequently visited and widely praised by Noel Coward, and from which were salvaged some of the original architectural embellishments, including what is now the popular Blue Bar. Inside, you'll find an understated environment inspired by Art Deco and French classical precedents, all with a contemporary edge. Adjacent to the small lobby is the newly redesigned Caramel Room where tea, drinks, informal dining, and even a doughnut menu are served. Each of the accommodations offers high-end style, but most elegant of all are the suites, many of which contain elegant paneling and luxurious, marble-and-tile-trimmed baths. The Berkeley offers two world-class restaurants, both of them established by celebrity chefs. They include Marcus Wareing's Petrus, and Gordon Ramsay's somewhat less grand and more whimsical Boxwood Cafe. The rooftop swimming pool with its associations to ancient Rome is one of many highlights within this extraordinary hotel.

Wilton Place, London SW1X 7RL. ℂ 800-63-SAVOY (72869) or 020/7950-5490. Fax 020/7950-5484. www.savoygroup.com or www.the-berkeley.com. 157 units. £279–£395 ($516–$731) double; £490–£3,100 ($907–$5,735) suite. AE, DC, MC, V. Tube: Knightsbridge or Hyde Park Corner. **Amenities:** 2 restaurants; 2 bars; rooftop swimming pool; health club with sauna; spa; 24-hr. room service; babysitting; laundry service/dry cleaning;. *In room:* A/C, TV w/rental movies, dataport, minibar, hair dryer, safe, beverage maker, trouser press, films on demand.

# Where to Stay from Knightsbridge to South Kensington

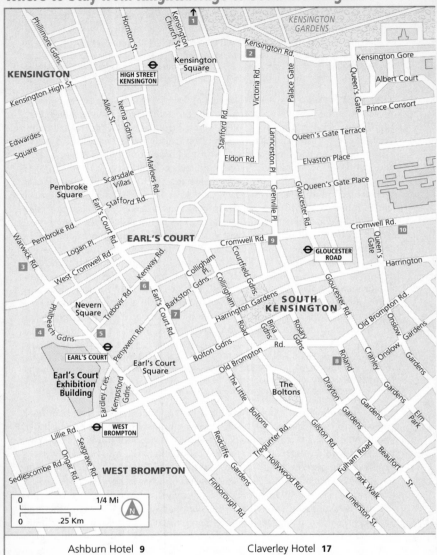

Ashburn Hotel **9**
Aster House **12**
Avonmore Hotel **3**
Basil Street Hotel **21**
The Beaufort **18**
The Berkeley **24**
Blake's Hotel **8**
The Capital Hotel **22**

Claverley Hotel **17**
The Diplomat Hotel **15**
The Gallery **10**
Henley House **7**
Knightsbridge Green Hotel **20**
Knightsbridge Hotel **19**
Mandarin Oriental Hyde Park **23**
Mayflower Hotel **5**

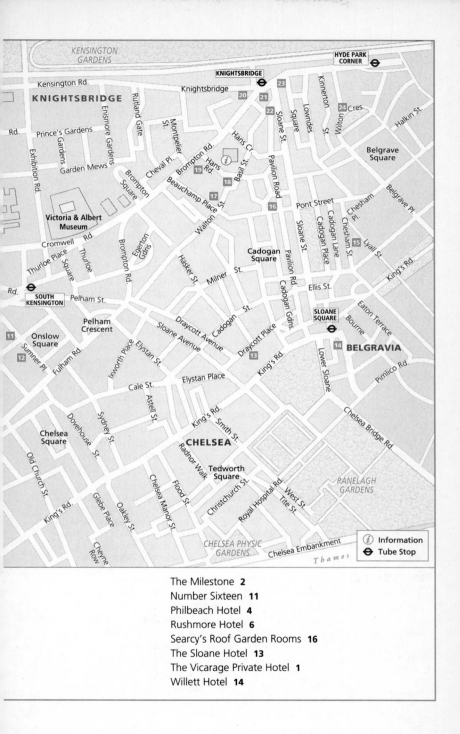

KENSINGTON GARDENS

HYDE PARK CORNER

KNIGHTSBRIDGE

Kensington Rd.

Knightsbridge

**KNIGHTSBRIDGE**

20  21  22  23

24 Cres.

Kinnerton St.

Wilton Cres.

Halkin St.

Rd.

Prince's Gardens

Enismore Gardens

Rutland Gate

Montpelier St.

Lowndes Square

Sloane St.

**Belgrave Square**

Belgrave Pl.

Exhibition Rd.

Gardens

Garden Mews

Cheval Pl.

Brompton Rd.

Hans Rd.

Hans Cr.

Basil St.

Pavilion Road

Chesham Pl.

Chesham St.

Brompton Square

Beauchamp Place

19

18

17

Pont Street

Cadogan Lane

Cadogan Place

Lyall St.

**Victoria & Albert Museum**

Cromwell Rd.

Walton

16

Sloane St.

Cadogan St.

15

Thurloe Place

Thurloe Square

Thurloe

Brompton Rd.

Egerton Gdns

Hasker St.

Milner St.

**Cadogan Square**

Pavilion Rd.

Cadogan Gdns.

Ellis St.

King's Rd.

SOUTH KENSINGTON

Rd.

Pelham St.

**Pelham Crescent**

Draycott Avenue

Cadogan St.

Draycott Place

SLOANE SQUARE

Eaton Terrace

Bourne

11

**Onslow Square**

12 Summer Pl.

Fulham Rd.

Ixworth Place

Elystan St.

Sloane Avenue

13

King's Rd.

14 **BELGRAVIA**

Lower Sloane

Pimlico Rd.

Cale St.

Elystan Place

Astell St.

King's Rd.

Smith St.

Chelsea Bridge Rd.

**Chelsea Square**

Dovehouse St.

Sydney St.

Radnor Walk

**CHELSEA**

**Tedworth Square**

*RANELAGH GARDENS*

Old Church St.

King's Rd.

Glebe Place

Oakley St.

Chelsea Manor St.

Flood St.

Christchurch St.

Royal Hospital Rd.

West St.

Tite St.

Cheyne Row

*CHELSEA PHYSIC GARDENS*

Chelsea Embankment

*Thames*

ⓘ Information

⊖ Tube Stop

**The Capital Hotel** ★★★    We'd be delighted to check in here for the season. Only 45m (148 ft.) from Harrods department store, this family-run town-house hotel is also at the doorstep of the shops of Knightsbridge and the "green lung" of Hyde Park. There are less than 40 bedrooms here, but you get many of the luxuries and services of a mammoth hotel. Warmth, intimacy, and an attention to detail are the hallmarks of this luxurious oasis. Fabled designer Nina Campbell created the spacious bedrooms, furnishing them with sumptuous fabrics, art, and antiques. David Linley, nephew of Her Majesty, also assisted in the design. Bathrooms with tubs and showers are luxurious. The liveried doorman standing outside has welcomed royalty, heads of state, and international celebrities to this hotel. For dining, you don't have far to go. The restaurant, directed by chef Eric Chavot, has already achieved the distinction of two Michelin stars.

22–24 Basil St., London SW3 1AT. © 020/7589-5171. Fax 020/7225-0011. www.capitalhotel.co.uk. 48 units. £250–£325 ($463–$601) double, from £385 ($712) suite. AE, DC, MC, V. Tube: Knightsbridge. Parking £28 ($52) per night. **Amenities:** Restaurant; bar; concierge; 24-hr. room service; babysitting; laundry service; same-day dry cleaning; nonsmoking rooms. *In room:* A/C, TV/VCR, dataport, minibar, hair dryer, safe in most units.

**Mandarin Oriental Hyde Park Hotel** ★★★    Set behind a stately looking late-19th-century brick facade whose style is defined by art historians as "Franco-Flemish," this is one of London's most appealing and historic hotels. It was built in 1889 as a private men's club, then converted into a hotel in 1902. In May 2000, the hotel reopened after a £50 million ($93 million) restoration by its owners, Mandarin Oriental. Today, the hotel occupies an enviable niche, wherein Edwardian grandeur and Asian postmodern chic manage to comfortably coexist. The recent restoration brought lavish amounts of brass, marble, mahogany, and stained glass back to its original turn-of-the-20th-century gloss, and added state-of-the-art infrastructures (many of them invisible) that will help carry this outstanding property deep into the 21st century. The lobby maintains a perpetually tasteful allegiance to pomp and circumstance, complete with a multimillion pound collection of paintings on long-term loan from the National Maritime Museum. Bedrooms are opulent, decorated with pale colors, countless yards of silk and satin, some of the meticulously restored antiques that have been in the hotel since its earliest years, and state-of-the-art tiled bathrooms with tubs big enough for several Sir Winstons at a time.

66 Knightsbridge, London SW1X 7LA. © **800/526-6566** for reservations in the U.S. and Canada, or 020/7235-2000. Fax 020/7235-2001. www.mandarinoriental.com. 200 units. £305–£545 ($564–$1,008) double; from £695 ($1,286) suite. AE, DC, MC, V. Tube: Knightsbridge. **Amenities:** 2 restaurants; bar; health club/exercise area; full-service spa with its own art collection and an emphasis on Asian healing and relaxation techniques; sauna; courtesy car; business center and services; 24-hr. room service; laundry service; same-day dry cleaning; nonsmoking rooms. *In room:* A/C, TV/DVD, dataport, minibar, hair dryer, safe.

## EXPENSIVE

**Aster House** ★★★ *Value*    This is the winner of the 2002 London Tourism Award for best B&B in London. It's just as good now as it was then. Within an easy walk of Kensington Palace, the late Princess Diana's home, and the museums of South Kensington, it is a friendly, inviting, and well-decorated lodging on a tree-lined street. The area surrounding the hotel, Sumner Place, looks like a Hollywood set depicting Victorian London. Aster House guests eat breakfast in a sunlit conservatory and can feed the ducks in the pond outside. Since the B&B is a Victorian building spread across five floors, each unit is unique in size and shape. Rooms range from spacious, with a four-poster bed, to a Lilliputian special with a single bed. Some beds are draped with fabric tents for extra drama, and each room is individually decorated in the style of an English manor-house bedroom. The small bathrooms are beautifully kept with showers ("the best in Europe," wrote one guest) or tubs and showers.

3 Sumner Place, London SW7 3EE. (© **020/7581-5888.** Fax 020/7584-4925. www.asterhouse.com. 14 units. £130–£175 ($241–$324) double. Rates include buffet breakfast. MC, V. Tube: South Kensington. **Amenities:** Laundry service; same-day dry cleaning. *In room:* A/C, TV, dataport, coffeemaker, hair dryer, safe.

**Claverley Hotel** 🌠    Located on a quiet cul-de-sac, this tasteful hotel, one of the neighborhood's very best (and winner of the Spencer Trophy for the Best Bed & Breakfast Hotel in Central London), is just a few blocks from Harrods. It's a small, cozy place accented with Georgian-era accessories. The lounge has the atmosphere of a country house, and complimentary tea, coffee, and biscuits are served all day in the Reading Room. Most rooms have wall-to-wall carpeting and comfortably upholstered armchairs, and each has a tidy bathroom with a shower stall. Recently refurbished rooms have a marble bathroom and "power shower." Rooms are individually decorated, some with four-poster beds.

13–14 Beaufort Gardens, London SW3 1PS. (© **800/747-0398** in the U.S., or 020/7589-8541. Fax 020/7584-3410. www.claverleyhotel.co.uk. 33 units. £120–£190 ($222–$352) double; £190–£215 ($352–$398) junior suite. Rates include English breakfast. AE, DC, MC, V. Parking £3 ($6) per hour on the street. Tube: Knightsbridge. **Amenities:** Same-day dry cleaning; all nonsmoking rooms. *In room:* TV, dataport, hair dryer, safe.

**Knightsbridge Green Hotel** 🌠    Repeat guests from around the world view this dignified 1890s structure as their home away from home. In 1966, when it was converted into a hotel, the developers kept its wide baseboards, cove moldings, high ceilings, and spacious proportions. Even without kitchens, the well-furnished suites come close to apartment-style living. The well-appointed marble bathrooms are deluxe, most with tubs and power showers. Most rooms are spacious, with adequate storage space. Bedrooms are decorated with custom-made colors and are often individualized—one has a romantic sleigh bed. This is a solid choice for lodging, just around the corner from Harrods.

159 Knightsbridge, London SW1X 7PD. (© **020/7584-6274.** Fax 020/7225-1635. www.theKGHotel.co.uk. 28 units. £145 ($268) double; from £170 ($315) suite. AE, DC, MC, V. Tube: Knightsbridge. **Amenities:** Limited room service; laundry service; same-day dry cleaning; all nonsmoking rooms. *In room:* A/C, TV, dataport, hair dryer, safe, beverage maker.

**Knightsbridge Hotel** 🌠🌠 *(Value*    The Knightsbridge Hotel attracts visitors from all over the world seeking a small, comfortable hotel in a high-rent district. It's fabulously located, sandwiched between fashionable Beauchamp Place and Harrods, with many of the city's top theaters and museums close at hand. Built in the early 1800s as a private town house, this place sits on a tranquil, tree-lined square, free from traffic. Two of London's premier hoteliers, Kit and Tim Kemp, who have been celebrated for their upmarket boutique hotels, have gone more affordable with a revamp of this hotel in the heart of the shopping district. All the Kemp "cult classics" are found here including such *luxe* touches as granite-and-oak bathrooms, the Kemps' famed honor bar, and Frette linens. The hotel has become an instant hit. All the beautifully furnished rooms have shower-only private bathrooms clad in marble or tile. Most bedrooms are spacious and furnished with traditional English fabrics. The best rooms are nos. 311 and 312 at the rear, each with a pitched ceiling and a small sitting area.

10 Beaufort Gardens, London SW3 1PT. (© **020/7584-6300.** Fax 020/7584-6355. www.firmdalehotels.com. 44 units. £155–£285 ($287–$527) double; from £335 ($620) suite. Rates include English or continental breakfast. AE, MC, V. Tube: Knightsbridge. **Amenities:** Bar; concierge; courtesy car; 24-hr. room service; babysitting; laundry service; same-day dry cleaning. *In room:* TV w/pay movies (DVD in most rooms), dataport, minibar, hair dryer, safe.

**Searcys Roof Garden Rooms** ★ *Finds*   Searcy's, one of London's best catering firms, operates this recycled surprise: an old pumping station that's been turned into a hotel that's only a hop, skip, and a jump from Harrods and the boutiques of Sloane Street. At this Knightsbridge oasis, you press a buzzer and are admitted to a freight elevator that carries you to the third floor. Upstairs, you'll encounter handsomely furnished rooms with antiques, tasteful fabrics, comfortable beds (some with canopies), and often a sitting alcove. Some of the bathtubs are placed right in the room instead of in a separate unit. Opt, if possible, for room no. 7, 14, or 15. For an extra charge, the staff will bring you a continental breakfast. Check out the rooftop garden.

30 Pavilion Rd., London SW1X 0HJ. ⓒ **020/7584-4921**. Fax 020/7823-8694. 10 units. £140 ($259) double; £160–£190 ($296–$352) apt. AE, DC, MC, V. Tube: Knightsbridge. **Amenities:** Communal kitchen; courtesy car; breakfast-only room service; laundry service/dry cleaning; nonsmoking rooms. *In room:* TV, hair dryer, iron/ironing board.

## KENSINGTON
### VERY EXPENSIVE

**The Milestone** ★★★   This outstanding boutique hotel, conveniently located in a Victorian town house across the street from Kensington Palace, offers modern luxury in an intimate, traditional setting. The Milestone's beautiful public rooms are awash with fresh flowers, dark woods, antique furnishings, and fabric wall coverings, creating the cozy atmosphere of a private manor house. The staff is gracious, and guests aren't just pampered—they're spoiled rotten. There's a small but well-equipped health club, which is a real rarity in London hotels of this size.

Guest rooms and suites are spread over six floors and vary in size and shape (a few rooms are a bit small). They feature a full range of amenities, luxurious beds, and marble bathrooms, some of which have Jacuzzis. All accommodations are individually and creatively decorated, though some are more theme-intensive than others. The masculine Savile Row Room is "papered" in pinstriped material and sports a tailor's dummy and books on men's fashion; the serene Royal Studio has a small balcony and a sleigh bed; and the bilevel Club Suite offers an English library–style lounge, complete with an antique billiards table. You can request a room overlooking the palace and Kensington Gardens, but be advised that these have original leaded windows, which look wonderful but can't be double-glazed, so traffic noise does leak through. Suites come with 24-hour butler service. *Note:* This hotel often offers special deals on its website, so it's possible to stay here for a princely rather than a kingly sum.

1 Kensington Court, London W8 5DL. ⓒ **877/955-1515** in the U.S. and Canada, or 020/7917-1000. Fax 020/7917-1010. www.redcarnationhotels.com. 57 units. £175–£335 ($324–$620) double; £440–£810 ($814–$1,499) suite. AE, DC, MC, V. Tube: High St. Kensington. **Amenities:** 3 restaurants; bar; health club; Jacuzzi; sauna; concierge; 24-hr. room service; babysitting; laundry service; same-day dry cleaning; nonsmoking rooms. *In room:* A/C, TV/VCR w/pay movies, CD/DVD player, fax, dataport, minibar, coffeemaker, hair dryer, iron/ironing board, safe.

### INEXPENSIVE

**Ashburn Hotel** *Value*   In the Royal Borough of Kensington, this discovery lies within walking distance of the major shopping areas and such attractions as Kensington Palace and the Victoria and Albert Museum. The hotel is imbued with an old-fashioned but cozy aura, with comfortably furnished bedrooms. Housekeeping is immaculate, and the welcome is friendly. Rooms come in a wide range of configurations, and can be suitable for many different travelers—singles, twins, doubles, triples, or family accommodations. It's not the most glamorous address in the area, but is known for its good value.

*Travel Tip: He who finds the best hotel deal has more to spend on facials involving knobbly vegetables.*

Hello, the Roaming Gnome here. I've been nabbed from the garden and taken round the world. The people who took me are so terribly clever. They find the best offerings on Travelocity. For very little cha-ching. And that means I get to be pampered and exfoliated till I'm pink as a bunny's doodah.

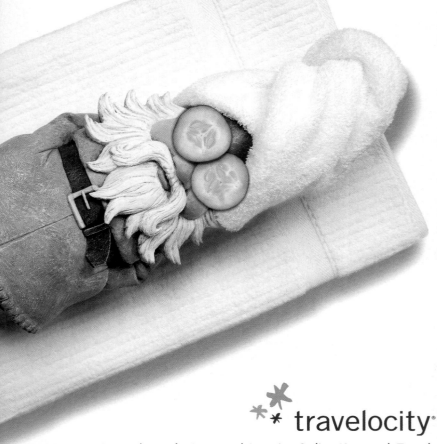

**travelocity**®

**1-888-TRAVELOCITY / travelocity.com / America Online Keyword: Travel**

111 Cromwell Rd., London SW7 4DP. © 020/7370-3321. www.ashburn-hotel.co.uk/prices/asp. 41 units. MC, V. £95 ($176) double; £105 ($194) triple; £115 ($213) quad; £28 ($52) per person in family unit. Tube: Gloucester Rd. **Amenities:** Secretarial services; lounge; Internet in lobby. *In room:* TV, hair dryer, beverage maker.

## BELGRAVIA
### EXPENSIVE

**The Diplomat Hotel** ★ *Finds*    Part of The Diplomat's charm is that it is a small and reasonably priced hotel located in an otherwise prohibitively expensive neighborhood. Only minutes from Harrods Department Store, it was built in 1882 as a private residence by noted architect Thomas Cubbitt. It's very well appointed and was completely overhauled in 2002 and 2003. The registration desk is framed by the sweep of a partially gilded circular staircase; above it, cherubs gaze down from a Regency-era chandelier. The staff is helpful, well mannered, and discreet. The high-ceilinged guest rooms are tastefully done in Victorian style. You get good—not grand—comfort here. Rooms are a bit small and usually furnished with twin beds. Bathrooms, with shower stalls, are also small but well maintained.

2 Chesham St., London SW1X 8DT. © 020/7235-1544. Fax 020/7259-6153. www.btinternet.com/~diplomat. hotel. 26 units. £125–£170 ($231–$315) double. Rates include English buffet breakfast. AE, DC, MC, V. Tube: Sloane Sq. or Knightsbridge. **Amenities:** Snack bar; nearby health club; business services; babysitting; laundry service; same-day dry cleaning; rooms for those w/limited mobility. *In room:* TV, dataport, coffeemaker, hair dryer, safe (in some), trouser press.

## CHELSEA
### EXPENSIVE

**The Sloane Hotel** ★★    This "toff" (dandy) address, a redbrick Victorian-era town house that has been tastefully renovated in recent years, is located in Chelsea near Sloane Square. It combines valuable 19th-century antiques with modern comforts. Our favorite spot here is the rooftop terrace; with views opening onto Chelsea, it's ideal for a relaxing breakfast or drink. Bedrooms come in varying sizes, ranging from small to spacious, but all are opulently furnished with flouncy draperies, tasteful fabrics, and sumptuous beds. Many rooms have draped four-poster or canopied beds and, of course, antiques. The deluxe bathrooms have shower/tub combinations, with chrome power showers, wall-width mirrors (in most rooms), and luxurious toiletries.

29 Draycott Place, London SW3 2SH. © 800/324-9960 in the U.S., or 020/7581-5757. Fax 020/7584-1348. www.sloanehotel.com. 22 units. £215–£250 ($398–$463) double; from £250 ($463) suite. AE, DC, MC, V. Tube: Sloane Sq. **Amenities:** Airport transportation (with prior arrangement); business services; 24-hr. room service; babysitting; laundry service; same-day dry cleaning. *In room:* A/C, TV/VCR w/pay movies, dataport, hair dryer.

### MODERATE

**Willett Hotel** ★ *Value*    On a tree-lined street leading off Sloane Square, this dignified Victorian town house lies in the heart of Chelsea. Named for the famous London architect William Willett, its stained glass and chandeliers reflect the opulence of the days when Prince Edward was on the throne. Under a mansard roof with bay windows, the hotel is a 5-minute walk from the shopping mecca of King's Road and close to such stores as Peter Jones, Harrods, and Harvey Nichols. Individually decorated bedrooms come in a wide range of sizes. All rooms have well-kept bathrooms, equipped with shower/tub combinations. Some rooms are first class, with swagged draperies, matching armchairs, and canopied beds. But a few of the twins are best left for Lilliputians.

32 Sloane Gardens, London SW1 8DJ. © 020/7824-8415. Fax 020/7730-4830. www.eeh.co.uk. 19 units. £100–£170 ($185–$315) double. Rates include English breakfast. AE, DC, MC, V. Tube: Sloane Sq. **Amenities:** Concierge;

limited room service; babysitting; laundry service; same-day dry cleaning; nonsmoking rooms. *In room:* A/C in most rooms, TV/VCR, dataport, fridge (in some), coffeemaker, hair dryer, iron, safe.

# SOUTH KENSINGTON
## VERY EXPENSIVE

**Blake's Hotel** ★★★    Actress Anouska Hempel's opulent and highly individual creation is one of London's best small hotels. No expense was spared in converting this former row of Victorian town houses into one of the city's most original hotels. It offers an Arabian Nights atmosphere down in old Kensington: The richly appointed lobby boasts British Raj–era furniture from India, and individually decorated, elaborately appointed rooms contain such treasures and touches as Venetian glassware, cloth-covered walls, swagged draperies, and even Empress Josephine's daybed. Live out your fantasy: Choose an ancient Egyptian funeral barge or a 16th-century Venetian boudoir. Rooms in the older section have the least space and aren't air-conditioned, but are chic nevertheless. Beds are deluxe, and the marble bathrooms are richly outfitted with a combo tub and shower and robes.

33 Roland Gardens, London SW7 3PF. ℂ **800/926-3173** in the U.S., or 020/7370-6701. Fax 020/7373-0442. www.blakeshotels.com. 48 units. £170–£345 ($315–$638) double; from £545 ($1,008) suite. AE, MC, V. Parking £2.50 ($4.60) per hour. Tube: Gloucester Rd. **Amenities:** Restaurant; access to nearby health club; concierge; tour desk; secretarial services; 24-hr. room service; massage; babysitting; laundry service; same-day dry cleaning; nonsmoking rooms. *In room:* TV/VCR, CD player, dataport, minibar, hair dryer, safe.

## EXPENSIVE

**Number Sixteen** ★    This luxurious pension is composed of four early-Victorian town houses linked together. The scrupulously maintained front and rear gardens make this one of the most idyllic spots on the street. The rooms are decorated with an eclectic mix of English antiques and modern paintings, although some of the decor looks a little faded. Accommodations range from small to spacious and have themes such as tartan or maritime. The beds are comfortable, and bathrooms are tiled and outfitted with vanity mirrors, heated towel racks, and hand-held showers over small tubs. There's an honor-system bar in the library. On chilly days, a fire roars in the fireplace of the flowery drawing room, although some prefer the more masculine library. Breakfast can be served in your bedroom, in the conservatory, or if the weather's good, in the garden, with its bubbling fountain and fishpond.

16 Sumner Place, London SW7 3EG. ℂ **800/592-5387** in the U.S., or 020/7589-5232. Fax 020/7584-8615. www.numbersixteenhotel.co.uk. 42 units. £170–£195 ($315–$361) double; £250 ($463) suite. Rates include continental breakfast. AE, DC, MC, V. Parking £25 ($46). Tube: South Kensington. **Amenities:** Access to nearby health club; 24-hr. room service; babysitting; laundry service; same-day dry cleaning; nonsmoking rooms. *In room:* TV/VCR, dataport, minibar, hair dryer, safe.

## MODERATE

**Avonmore Hotel** ★ *Finds*    The recently refurbished Avonmore is easily accessible to West End theaters and shops, yet it's located in a quiet neighborhood, only 2 minutes from the West Kensington stop on the District Line. This privately owned place—a former National Award winner as the best private hotel in London—boasts wall-to-wall carpeting and radio alarms in each tastefully decorated room. All rooms have small shower-only bathrooms. The owner, Margaret McKenzie, provides lots of personal service. An English breakfast is served in a cheerful room and a wide range of drinks is available in the cozy bar.

66 Avonmore Rd., London W14 8RS. ℂ **020/7603-4296.** Fax 020/7603-4035. www.avonmorehotel.co.uk. 9 units. £105 ($194) double; £120 ($222) triple. Rates include English breakfast. AE, MC, V. Tube: West Kensington. **Amenities:** Bar; room service (7am–midnight); babysitting; laundry service; same-day dry cleaning; nonsmoking rooms. *In room:* TV, dataport, minibar, coffeemaker, hair dryer.

**The Gallery** *Finds* This is the place to go if you want to stay in an exclusive little town-house hotel but don't want to pay £300 ($555) a night for the privilege. Two splendid Georgian residences have been restored and converted into this remarkable hotel, which remains relatively unknown. The location is ideal, near the Victoria and Albert Museum, Royal Albert Hall, Harrods, Knightsbridge, and King's Road. Bedrooms are individually designed and decorated in Laura Ashley style, with half-canopied beds and marble-tiled bathrooms with brass fittings and shower/tub combos. The junior suites have private roof terraces, minibars, Jacuzzis, and air-conditioning. A team of butlers takes care of everything. The lounge, with its mahogany paneling, moldings, and deep colors, has the ambience of a private club. The drawing room beckons you to relax and read in a quiet corner. The Gallery Room displays works by known and unknown artists for sale.

8–10 Queensberry Place, London SW7 2EA. © **800/270-9206** in the U.S., or 020/7915-0000. Fax 020/7915-4400. www.eeh.co.uk. 36 units. £130–£160 ($241–$296) double; from £250 ($463) junior suite. Rates include buffet English breakfast. AE, DC, MC, V. Tube: South Kensington. **Amenities:** Bar; access to nearby health club; courtesy car; business center; 24-hr. room service; babysitting; laundry service; same-day dry cleaning; 24-hr. butler service; nonsmoking rooms. *In room:* A/C (in most rooms), TV, dataport, coffeemaker, hair dryer, safe.

## INEXPENSIVE

**The Vicarage Hotel** *Kids* Owners Eileen and Martin Diviney enjoy a host of admirers on all continents. Their much-improved hotel is tops for old-fashioned English charm, affordable prices, and hospitality. On a residential garden square close to Kensington High Street, not far from Portobello Road Market, this Victorian town house retains many original features. Individually furnished in country-house style, the bedrooms can accommodate up to four, making it a great place for families. If you want a little nest to hide away in, opt for the very private top-floor aerie (no. 19). Guests find the corridor shower-only bathrooms adequate and well maintained. Guests meet in a cozy sitting room for conversation and to watch the telly. As a thoughtful extra, hot drinks are available 24 hours a day. In the morning, a hearty English breakfast awaits.

10 Vicarage Gate, London W8 4AG. © **020/7229-4030.** Fax 020/7792-5989. www.londonvicaragehotel.com. 17 units, 8 with bathroom. £46 ($85) single without bathroom; £102 ($189) double with bathroom, £78 ($144) double without bathroom; £95 ($176) triple without bathroom; £102 ($189) family room for 4 without bathroom. Rates include English breakfast. No credit cards. Tube: High St. Kensington or Notting Hill Gate. *In room:* TV, hair dryer, beverage maker, no phone.

## EARL'S COURT
### MODERATE

**Henley House** *Value* This newly refurbished B&B stands out from the pack around Earl's Court—and it's a better value that most. The redbrick Victorian row house is on a communal fenced-in garden that you can enter by borrowing a key from the reception desk. The staff takes a keen interest in the welfare of its guests and is happy to take bewildered newcomers under their wing, so this is an ideal place for London first-timers. A ground-floor sitting room overlooks a rear courtyard. The decor is bright and contemporary; a typical room has warmly patterned Anna French wallpaper, chintz fabrics, and solid-brass lighting fixtures. Each room is fitted with a well-maintained shower-only bathroom. Breakfast is a cheerful event, served in a room decorated with terra-cotta accents and pots of dried flowers. For those who prefer to stay in rather than hitting the area's hot spots (mostly gay bars), there's a shelf of books you're welcome to borrow.

30 Barkston Gardens, London SW5 0EN. © **020/7370-4111.** Fax 020/7370-0026. www.henleyhousehotel. com. 21 units. £89 ($165) double. Rates include continental breakfast. AE, DC, MC, V. Tube: Earl's Court. **Amenities:** Nonsmoking rooms. *In room:* TV, coffeemaker, hair dryer.

**Mayflower Hotel** Originally a private Victorian town house, this family-run hotel extends a warm welcome. This hotel stands out among the many B&B disasters along this street by offering clean, comfortable, and inviting (if unremarkable) accommodations. The queen of England doesn't send overflow guests here, but frugal travelers delight in the prices. The area is young and vibrant, and is experiencing gentrification. Expect comfort rather than frills. Each room has good linens on comfortable beds, and neat, shower-only bathrooms. An elevator carries guests to every floor, and there are luggage-storage facilities if you want to venture into the countryside with a lighter load than you brought to (or acquired in) London.

26–28 Trebovir Rd., London SW5 9NJ. © 020/7370-0991. Fax 020/7370-0994. www.mayflower-group. co.uk. 48 units. £80 ($148) double; £120 ($222) triple; £145 ($268) suite. Rates include continental breakfast. AE, MC, V. Parking £20 ($37). Tube: Earl's Court. **Amenities:** Business services; laundry service; same-day dry cleaning; nonsmoking rooms. *In room:* TV/VCR, dataport, coffeemaker, hair dryer (on request), iron (on request).

## INEXPENSIVE

**Philbeach Hotel** One of Europe's largest gay hotels, the Philbeach is a Victorian row house on a wide crescent behind the Earl's Court Exhibition Centre. Open to both men and women, it offers standard budget-hotel rooms. The showers are tiny, but the private and shared baths are clean. Room no. 8A, a double with bathroom, has a balcony overlooking the small back garden.

30–31 Philbeach Gardens, London SW5 9EB. © 020/7373-1244. Fax 020/7244-0149. www.philbeachhotel. freeserve.co.uk. 40 units, 16 with bathroom. £35 ($65) single without bathroom, £65 ($120) single with bathroom; £70 ($130) double without bathroom, £90 ($167) double with bathroom. Rates include continental breakfast. AE, DC, MC, V. Tube: Earl's Court. **Amenities:** Restaurant (Thai cuisine); gay bar (Jimmies); laundry service; same-day dry cleaning. *In room:* TV.

**Rushmore Hotel** Although it became quite run-down in the early 1970s, this Victorian row house (behind a brick-faced Italianate facade) received a complete overhaul in 1987 and has since undergone periodic renewals. Today, it's one of the most pleasing hotels in this low-budget neighborhood. The hotel stands on the former site of the Manor House of Earl's Court Farm, where manorial courts were held until the mid-1850s. As long as you don't require atriums and mini-bars, the Rushmore proves that it's still possible to get good service and a fine room in London at an affordable price. The multilingual staff works hard to make your visit rewarding. The rooms are individually decorated in a variety of period schemes, and each has a comfortable feel. Rooms with shower bathrooms have such touches as marble tiling and brass fittings. The breakfast room is outfitted with French limestone floors, Murano glass wall- and floor-lighting created by Missoni, wrought-iron furniture from Tuscany, and antique terra-cotta urns holding exotic cacti.

11 Trebovir Rd., London SW5 9LS. © 020/7370-3839. Fax 020/7370-0274. www.rushmorehotel.co.uk. 22 units. £65–£79 ($120–$146) double; £82–£89 ($152–$165) triple; £89–£99 ($165–$183) family room for 4 or 5. Rates include continental breakfast. AE, DC, MC, V. Tube: Earl's Court. **Amenities:** Laundry service; same-day dry cleaning; nonsmoking rooms. *In room:* TV, coffeemaker, hair dryer.

## 5 Hotels from Marylebone to Holland Park

### MARYLEBONE
### VERY EXPENSIVE

**The Langham Hilton** ★★★ After it was bombed in World War II, this well-located hotel languished as dusty office space for the BBC until the early 1990s, when Hilton International took it over and painstakingly restored it. Today, it's Hilton's European flagship. The Langham's public rooms reflect the power and majesty of the British Empire at its apex. Guest rooms are somewhat less opulent but are still attractively furnished and comfortable, featuring French provincial furniture and red oak trim. Major refurbishment was carried out in 1999. All bathrooms are well kept and contain full shower/tub combinations. Ask for one of the rooms in the "52" series, as they are much grander and more spacious than the others. The hotel is within easy reach of Mayfair and Soho restaurants and theaters, and Oxford and Regent streets shopping. Plus, Regent's Park is just blocks away.

1C Portland Place, London W1B 1JA. © **800/774-1500** in the U.S., or 020/7636-1000. Fax 020/7323-2340. www.langham.hilton.com. 429 units. £199–£279 ($368–$516) double; £279 ($516) executive room; from £559 ($1,034) suite. AE, DC, MC, V. Tube: Oxford Circus. **Amenities:** 2 restaurants; Edwardian-style palm court; bar; indoor pool; health club; spa; sauna; concierge; tour desk; courtesy car; business center; salon; 24-hr. room service; massage; babysitting; laundry service; same-day dry cleaning; nonsmoking rooms; rooms for those w/limited mobility. *In room:* A/C, TV/VCR w/pay movies, dataport, minibar, hair dryer, iron, safe.

## EXPENSIVE

**Dorset Square Hotel** ★★★   Just steps away from Regent's Park, this is one of London's best and most stylish "house hotels," overlooking Thomas Lord's (the man who set up London's first private cricket club) first cricket pitch. Hot hoteliers Tim and Kit Kemp have furnished the interior of these two Georgian town houses with a comfy mix of antiques, reproductions, and chintz that makes you feel as if you're in an elegant private home. All of the impressive bedrooms are decorated in a personal, beautiful style—the Kemps are interior decorators known for their bold and daring taste. About half of the rooms are air-conditioned and some have balconies. Eight rooms feature crown-canopied beds, but all appointments are of a very high standard. The full marble bathrooms are exquisite, with robes, deluxe toiletries, and shower/tub combinations.

39–40 Dorset Sq., London NW1 6QN. © **020/7723-7874.** Fax 020/7724-3328. www.dorsetsquare.co.uk. 38 units. £200–£240 ($370–$444) double; from £300 ($555) suite. AE, MC, V. Parking £32 ($59) daily, free on weekends. Tube: Baker St. or Marylebone. **Amenities:** Restaurant; bar; 24-hr. room service; massage; babysitting; laundry service; same-day dry cleaning; nonsmoking rooms. *In room:* A/C, TV/VCR w/pay movies, dataport, minibar, hair dryer, iron/ironing board, safe.

**Durrants Hotel** ★   This historic hotel off Manchester Square (established in 1789) with its Georgian-detailed facade is snug, cozy, and traditional—almost like a poor man's Brown's (p. 103). We find it to be one of the most quintessentially English of all London hotels. You could invite the queen to Durrants for tea. Over the 100 years that they have owned the hotel, the Miller family has incorporated several neighboring houses into the original structure. A walk through the pine-and-mahogany-paneled public rooms is like stepping back in time: You'll even find an 18th-century letter-writing room. The rooms are rather bland but for elaborate cove moldings and comfortable furnishings, including good beds. Some are air-conditioned, and some are, alas, small. Bathrooms are tiny, with shower/tub combinations but little room to maneuver.

26–32 George St., London W1H 6BJ. © **020/7935-8131.** Fax 020/7487-3510. www.durrantshotel.co.uk. 92 units. £145–£165 ($268–$305) double; £180 ($333) family room for 3; from £285 ($527) suite. AE, MC, V. Tube: Bond St. or Baker St. **Amenities:** Restaurant; pub; concierge; 24-hr. room service; babysitting; laundry service; same-day dry cleaning; rooms for those w/limited mobility. *In room:* A/C, TV, dataport, hair dryer, safe.

## MODERATE

**Hallam Hotel**   This heavily ornamented stone-and-brick Victorian—one of the few on the street to escape the Blitz—is just a 5-minute stroll from Oxford Circus. It's the property of brothers Grant and David Baker, who maintain it

# Where to Stay from Marylebone to Holland Park

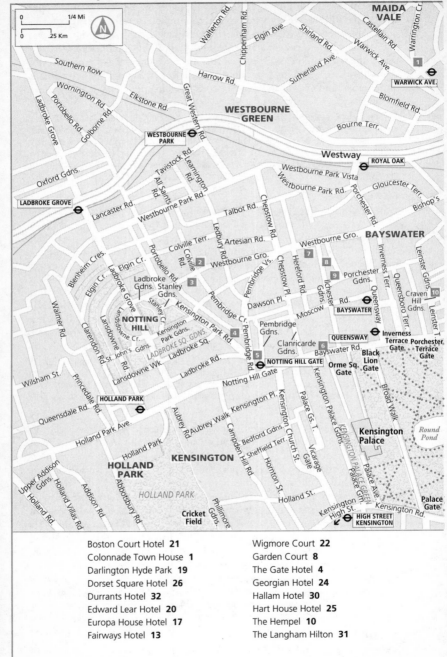

| | |
|---|---|
| Boston Court Hotel **21** | Wigmore Court **22** |
| Colonnade Town House **1** | Garden Court **8** |
| Darlington Hyde Park **19** | The Gate Hotel **4** |
| Dorset Square Hotel **26** | Georgian Hotel **24** |
| Durrants Hotel **32** | Hallam Hotel **30** |
| Edward Lear Hotel **20** | Hart House Hotel **25** |
| Europa House Hotel **17** | The Hempel **10** |
| Fairways Hotel **13** | The Langham Hilton **31** |

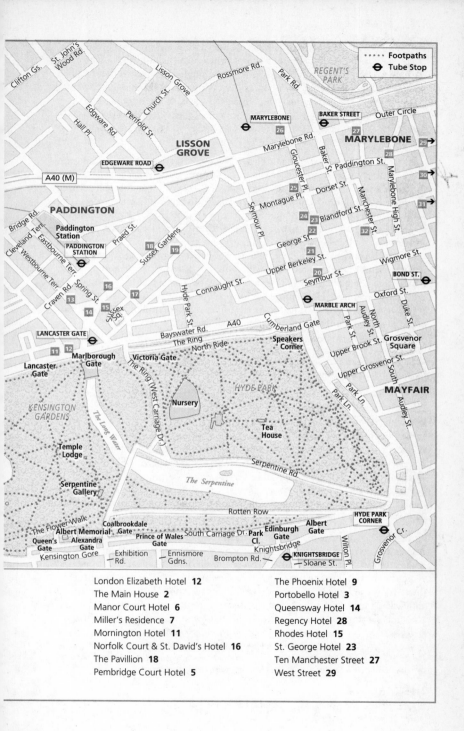

London Elizabeth Hotel **12**
The Main House **2**
Manor Court Hotel **6**
Miller's Residence **7**
Mornington Hotel **11**
Norfolk Court & St. David's Hotel **16**
The Pavillion **18**
Pembridge Court Hotel **5**

The Phoenix Hotel **9**
Portobello Hotel **3**
Queensway Hotel **14**
Regency Hotel **28**
Rhodes Hotel **15**
St. George Hotel **23**
Ten Manchester Street **27**
West Street **29**

well. The hotel is warm and friendly, and the central location that you get for these prices can't be beat. The guest rooms, which were redone in 1991, are comfortably furnished with good beds. Some of the singles are so small they're called "cabinettes." Several of the twin-bedded rooms are quite spacious and have adequate closet space. Bathrooms, which have shower stalls, are a bit cramped.

12 Hallam St., Portland Place, London W1N 5LJ. ℂ 020/7580-1166. Fax 020/7323-4527. www.hallamhotel. com. 25 units. £90 ($167) single; £100 ($185) double. Rates include English breakfast. AE, DC, MC, V. Tube: Oxford Circus. **Amenities:** Bar. *In room:* TV, minibar, coffeemaker, hair dryer.

**Hart House Hotel** *Kids*    Hart House is a long-enduring favorite with Frommer's readers. In the heart of the West End, this well-preserved historic building (one of a group of Georgian mansions occupied by exiled French nobles during the French Revolution) lies within easy walking distance of many theaters. The rooms—done in a combination of furnishings, ranging from Portobello antique to modern—are spic-and-span, each one with a different character. Favorites include no. 7, a triple with a big bathroom and shower. Ask for no. 11, on the top floor, if you'd like a brightly lit aerie. Housekeeping rates high marks here, and the bedrooms are comfortably appointed with chairs, an armoire, a desk, and a large chest of drawers. The shower-only bathrooms, although small, are efficiently organized. Hart House has long been known as a good, safe place for traveling families. Many of its rooms are triples. Larger families can avail themselves of special family accommodations with connecting rooms.

51 Gloucester Place, Portman Sq., London W1U 8JF. ℂ 020/7935-2288. Fax 020/7935-8516. www.harthouse. co.uk. 15 units. £105 ($194) double; £130 ($241) triple; £150 ($278) quad. Rates include English breakfast. AE, MC, V. Tube: Marble Arch or Baker St. **Amenities:** Babysitting; laundry service/dry cleaning; all nonsmoking rooms; rooms for those w/limited mobility. *In room:* TV, dataport, coffeemaker, hair dryer.

**St. George Hotel** *Value*    A short walk from Oxford and Baker streets, this centrally located, restored hotel is a winning, affordable choice. The hotel has been refurbished to a high quality and offers plenty of comfort in its well-furnished bedrooms, along with personal service. Some of the modern amenities include a key-card door and electronic built-in room safes. Both the business traveler and the leisure visitor are catered to here, and rooms on the ground floor offer easy access to the main entrance for those not wanting to climb stairs.

49 Gloucester Place, London W1U 8JE. ℂ 020/7486-8586. Fax 020/7486-6567. www.stgeorge-hotel.net. 19 units. £125 ($231) double; £140 ($259) triple. Rates include English breakfast. AE, MC, V. Tube: Marylebone Rd. **Amenities:** Breakfast room. *In room:* TV, dataport, minibar, hair dryer, safe, beverage maker.

**Ten Manchester Street** *Value*    Constructed in 1919 as a residence hall for nurses, this terraced redbrick building is now a smart town-house hotel. We like its location in Marylebone, close to those top shopping destinations, Bond and Regent streets, and near chic boutiques and numerous cafes and restaurants. The guest rooms are small but well designed, and are furnished with comfort in mind. Each room has a well-organized bathroom with tub and shower. There is the aura of a private home here, due to the inviting atmosphere and helpful staff.

10 Manchester St., London W1M 5PG. ℂ 020/7486-6669. Fax 020/7224-0348. 46 units. www.10manchester street.com. £120–£150 ($222–$278) double; £150–£195 ($278–$361) suite. Rates include continental breakfast. AE, DC, MC, V. Tube: Baker Street or Bond Street. **Amenities:** Same-day dry cleaning; nonsmoking rooms. *In room:* TV, dataport, fridge, coffeemaker, hair dryer, iron/ironing board, trouser press.

## INEXPENSIVE

**Boston Court Hotel**    Upper Berkeley is a classic street of B&Bs; in days of yore, it was home to Elizabeth Montagu (1720–1800), "queen of the bluestockings," who defended Shakespeare against attacks by Voltaire. Today, it's a good, safe, respectable retreat at an affordable price. This unfrilly hotel offers accommodations in a centrally located Victorian-era building within walking distance of Oxford Street shopping and Hyde Park. The small, basic rooms have been refurbished and redecorated with a no-nonsense decor and have well-kept bathrooms with private showers.

26 Upper Berkeley St., Marble Arch, London W1H 7PF. © 020/7723-1445. Fax 020/7262-8823. www. bostoncourthotel.co.uk. 15 units (7 with shower only). £69 ($128) double with shower only; £75–£79 ($139–$146) double with bathroom; £85–£89 ($157–$165) triple with bathroom. Rates include continental breakfast. MC, V. Tube: Marble Arch. **Amenities:** Laundry service; nonsmoking rooms. *In room:* TV w/pay movies, dataport, fridge, coffeemaker, hair dryer.

**Edward Lear Hotel**    This popular hotel, situated 1 block from Marble Arch, is made all the more desirable by the bouquets of fresh flowers in its public rooms. It occupies a pair of brick town houses dating from 1780. The western house was the London home of 19th-century artist and poet Edward Lear, famous for his nonsense verse, and his illustrated limericks adorn the walls of one of the sitting rooms. Steep stairs lead up to cozy rooms which range from spacious to broom-closet size. Many bedrooms have been redecorated but still look a bit drab. Few can complain, as this is an area of £400 ($740) a-night mammoths. If you're looking for classiness, know that the bacon on your plate came from the same butcher used by the queen. One major drawback to the hotel: This is a very noisy part of town. Rear rooms are quieter. Bathrooms are well maintained, most with a shower and tub.

28–30 Seymour St., London W1H 5WD. © 020/7402-5401. Fax 020/7706-3766. www.edlear.com. 31 units, 12 with bathroom. £67 ($124) double without bathroom; £74 ($137) double with bathroom; £79 ($146) suite. Rates include English breakfast. MC, V. Tube: Marble Arch. *In room:* TV w/pay movies, dataport, coffeemaker.

**Georgian Hotel**    Central London, which is filled with luxury hotels, suffers an acute lack of small, personally run places, but the Georgian fills this gap. It lies near Sherlock Holmes's Baker Street and is within walking distance of Oxford Street and Regent's Park. Run by the same family since 1973, the Georgian has a dedicated staff and management intent on improving the hotel. We especially like the top-quality English breakfast served here, and the way that original architectural features were retained even as modern comforts were added. Rooms have private bathrooms, and there's an elevator to all floors. Bedrooms are neutral in style and the ground-floor rooms are the least preferred. Don't expect views from some of the back rooms, which open onto a wall.

87 Gloucester Place (Baker St.), London W1H 3PG. © 020/7935-2211. Fax 020/7486-7535. www.london centralhotel.com. 19 units. £90 ($167) double; £100 ($185) triple; £130 ($241) family room. Rates include English breakfast. AE, MC, V. Tube: Baker St. *In room:* TV, coffeemaker.

**Regency Hotel**    This building is from the 1800s, and there has been a hotel of some kind here since the Blitz. In 1991, the building was gutted and renovated into its present form. One of the better hotels on the street, it offers simple, conservatively decorated modern bedrooms scattered over four floors, and a breakfast room set in what used to be the cellar. Bathrooms, although small, are well kept, and come mostly with shower/tub combinations. The neighborhood is protected as a historic district, and Marble Arch, Regent's Park, and Baker Street all lie within a 15-minute walk.

19 Nottingham Place, London W1U 5LQ. © 020/7486-5347. Fax 020/7224-6057. www.regencyhotelwestend. co.uk. 20 units. £89 ($165) double; £125 ($231) family room. Rates include English breakfast. AE, DC, MC, V. Parking £17–£20 ($31–$37) nearby. Tube: Baker St. or Regent's Park. *In room:* TV, minibar on request, coffeemaker, hair dryer, iron/ironing board.

**Wigmore Court** *(Value)*   A convenient family hotel, this inn lies near the street made famous as the fictional address of Sherlock Holmes—Baker Street. It is close to Marble Arch, Oxford Street, and Madame Tussaud's. A somber Georgian structure, it has been converted into a fine B&B suitable only for serious stair climbers as there is no elevator. There's traffic noise outside, so request a room in the rear. Bedrooms, many quite spacious, are comfortably furnished. Most units contain double or twin beds, plus a small bathroom. About half of the bathrooms have shower/tub combinations.

23 Gloucester Place, London W1H 3PB. ℂ **020/7935-0928.** Fax 020/7487-4254. www.wigmore-court-hotel. co.uk. 19 units. £75 ($139) double; £90 ($167) triple. MC, V. Tube: Marble Arch. **Amenities:** Guest kitchen; coin-op washers and dryers. *In room:* TV, dataport, coffeemaker.

## PADDINGTON & BAYSWATER
### VERY EXPENSIVE

**The Hempel** *(★★★)*   Set in a trio of nearly identical 19th-century row houses, this hotel is the statement of flamboyant interior designer and actress Anouska Hempel. Don't expect the swags, tassels, and elegance of her better-established hotel, Blake's (p. 122)—the feeling here is radically different. The Hempel manages to combine a grand Italian sense of proportion with Asian Zen-like simplicity. Soothing monochromatic tones prevail. Symmetrical fireplaces flank the deliberately sparse lobby, and carefully positioned mementos from Asia show up throughout the hotel, including Thai bullock carts that double as coffee tables.

Bedrooms continue the minimalist theme, except for their carefully concealed battery of electronic accessories, which includes a VCR, satellite TV, CD player, DVD player, twin phone lines, and a modem hookup. Bathrooms have cut-stone walls, countertops, and bathtubs. The hotel mostly caters to business travelers from around the world, who appreciate its tactful service and undeniably snobbish overtones.

31–35 Craven Hill Garden Sq., London W2 3EA. ℂ **020/7298-9000.** Fax 020/7402-4666. www.the-hempel. co.uk. 46 units. £275–£295 ($509–$546) double; from £440 ($814) suite. AE, DC, DISC, MC, V. Tube: Lancaster Gate or Queensway. **Amenities:** Restaurant; bar; access to health club; concierge; tour desk; business services; 24-hr. room service; massage; babysitting; laundry service; same-day dry cleaning; rooms for those w/limited mobility; nonsmoking rooms. *In room:* A/C, TV/VCR w/pay movies, dataport, minibar, coffeemaker, hair dryer, safe.

**West Street** *(★★★)* *(Finds)*   This is the hotel oddity of central London, evoking the coaching inns of yesterday but aimed at the cool Britannia crowd of today. It's got only three rooms, each sitting atop the glass-fronted restaurant and champagne bar. The hotel is located near the mother of all celebrity haunts, The Ivy, and the West Street Hotel's first floor restaurant has been hailed as "the poor man's Ivy" (that's a compliment). The London press is calling the mammoth bedrooms upstairs the city's most exclusive guest rooms—and so they are. Instead of a front desk, guests check into the *über*-trendy ground-floor restaurant before heading upstairs to claim one of the rooms in this five-floor restored structure. The Stone Room offers a private roof garden; the White Room is coated in Carrara marble; and the most spacious of them all, The Loft, is a penthouse draped in black leather and emerald-green slate. The Loft also boasts stained oak floors and vaulted ceilings, and spans the entire top of the building. Additionally, there is a pizzeria downstairs on the ground floor.

13–15 West St., London WC2H 9NE. ℂ **020/7010-8700.** 3 units. £293–£529 ($542–$979) double. AE, DC, MC, V. Tube: Leicester Sq. **Amenities:** Restaurant; bar; laundry service; same-day dry cleaning. *In room:* TV w/pay movies, dataport, minibar, hair dryer, safe.

## EXPENSIVE

**Darlington Hyde Park** ⸙    Although it's not flashy and it lacks a full range of services, the Darlington Hyde Park is a winning choice for central London. Renovated and well-maintained rooms are decorated in an updated Victorian style: tasteful and neat, albeit a bit short on flair. They range from small to medium, and each is fitted with a tiny but adequate bathroom with a shower/tub combination. There is a happy blend of businesspeople and vacationers. The in-room amenities are superior to those at other hotels along this street. Five bedrooms are nonsmoking. There is no bar, but guests are invited to BYOB and drink in the lounge. A number of neighboring restaurants cater room service for the hotel; they are listed in a restaurant book found in each room.

111–117 Sussex Gardens, London W2 2RU. ℂ 020/7460-8800. Fax 020/7460-8828. www.darlingtonhotel. co.uk. 40 units. £140 ($259) double; £155 ($287) family room; £160 ($296) suite. Rates include continental breakfast. AE, DC, MC, V. Tube: Paddington or Lancaster Gate. **Amenities:** Nearby health club; laundry service; same-day dry cleaning; all nonsmoking rooms. *In room:* TV, dataport, fridge, hair dryer, safe.

**London Elizabeth Hotel** ⸙    This elegant Victorian town house is ideally situated, overlooking Hyde Park. Amid the buzz and excitement of central London, the hotel's atmosphere is an oasis of charm and refinement. Even before the hotel's recent £3 million ($5.6 million) restoration, it oozed character. Individually decorated rooms range from executive to deluxe and remind us of staying in an English country house. Deluxe rooms are fully air-conditioned, and some contain four-poster beds. Executive units usually contain one double or twin bed. Some rooms have special features such as Victorian antique fireplaces, and all contain first-rate bathrooms with showers and tubs. Suites are pictures of grand comfort and luxury—the Conservatory Suite boasts its own veranda, part of the house's original 1850 conservatory.

Lancaster Terrace, Hyde Park, London W2 3PF. ℂ 020/7402-6641. Fax 020/7224-8900. www.londonelizabeth hotel.co.uk. 49 units. £115–£150 ($213–$278) double; £180–£250 ($333–$463) suite. AE, DC, MC, V. Parking £10 ($19). Tube: Lancaster Gate or Paddington. **Amenities:** Restaurant; bar; 24-hr. room service; laundry service; same-day dry cleaning; nonsmoking rooms. *In room:* A/C, TV, dataport, hair dryer, iron.

**Miller's Residence** ⸙⸙ (Finds)    Staying here is like spending a night in Charles Dickens' Old Curiosity Shop. Others say that the little hotel looks like the set of *La Traviata.* Miller's calls itself an 18th-century rooming house, and there's nothing quite like it in London. A roaring log fire blazes in the large book-lined drawing room in winter. The individually designed rooms are named after romantic poets. They vary in shape and size, but all are luxuriously furnished with antiques, prints, and tasteful curios. Each room contains a small bathroom with a shower and tub. In addition to its double rooms, Miller's offers two sumptuous suites with multiple bedrooms, a drawing room, and a fully equipped kitchen.

111A Westbourne Grove, London W2 4UW. ℂ 020/7243-1024. Fax 020/7243-1064. www.millersuk.com. 6 units. £150 ($278) double; £230 ($426) suite. Rates include continental breakfast. AE, DISC, MC, V. Tube: Bayswater or Notting Hill Gate. **Amenities:** Limited business services; babysitting; laundry service; same-day dry cleaning. *In room:* TV/VCR, dataport, kitchen in suites.

## MODERATE

**Mornington Hotel** ⸙    Affiliated with Best Western, the Mornington brings a touch of northern European hospitality to the center of London. Just north of Hyde Park and Kensington Gardens, the hotel has a Victorian exterior and a Scandinavian-inspired decor. The area isn't London's most fashionable, but it's close to Hyde Park and convenient to Marble Arch, Oxford Street shopping, and the ethnic restaurants of Queensway. Recently renovated guest rooms are tasteful and comfortable, all with pay movies. Bathrooms are small but tidy, with showers and tubs. Every year we get our annual Christmas card from "the gang," as we refer to the hotel staff—and what a helpful crew they are.

12 Lancaster Gate, London W2 3LG. (C) **800/528-1234** in the U.S., or 020/7262-7361. Fax 020/7706-1028. www.mornington.com. 66 units. £135–£160 ($250–$296) double; £145 ($268) triple. Rates include Scandinavian and English cooked breakfast. AE, DC, MC, V. Tube: Lancaster Gate. **Amenities:** Bar; courtesy car; business center; laundry service; same-day dry cleaning. *In room:* TV w/pay movies, coffeemaker.

**The Pavilion** *(finds* Until the early 1990s, this was a rather ordinary-looking B&B. Then a team of entrepreneurs with ties to the fashion industry took over and redecorated the rooms with sometimes wacky themes, turning it into an idiosyncratic little hotel. The result is a theatrical and often outrageous decor that's appreciated by the many fashion models and music-industry folks who regularly make this their temporary home in London. Rooms are, regrettably, rather small, but each has a distinctive style. Examples include a kitschy 1970s room ("Honky-Tonk Afro"), an Oriental bordello–themed room ("Enter the Dragon"), and even rooms with 19th-century ancestral themes. One Edwardian-style room, a gem of emerald brocade and velvet, is called "Green with Envy." Each contains tea-making facilities and small bathrooms with excellent showers.

34–36 Sussex Gardens, London W2 1UL. (C) **020/7262-0905.** Fax 020/7262-1324. 29 units. £100 ($185) double; £120 ($222) triple. Rates include continental breakfast. AE, DC, MC, V. Parking £5 ($9.25). Tube: Edgeware Rd. **Amenities:** Laundry service; same-day dry cleaning;. *In room:* TV, dataport, beverage maker.

**The Phoenix Hotel** This hotel, a member of the Best Western chain, occupies the entire south side of Kensington Gardens Square, one of the most famous garden squares in Europe. Well situated in an ethnically mixed neighborhood, The Phoenix is composed of a series of 1854 town houses. The atmosphere is welcoming. Well-furnished bedrooms keep to a smart international standard, with a palette of muted tones. Everything is designed for comfort and ease, including the luggage racks. Bathrooms, most of which contain shower/tub combinations, are a bit small but well kept. The bar is a good place to unwind, and moderately priced meals are served in the downstairs cafe. Our biggest complaint? The public areas are too small for a hotel of this size.

1–8 Kensington Gardens Sq., London W2 4BH. (C) **800/528-1234** in the U.S., or 020/7229-2494. Fax 020/7727-1419. www.phoenixhotel.co.uk. 125 units. £130 ($241) double; £179 ($331) suite; £198 ($366) family room. Rates include buffet breakfast. AE, DC, MC, V. Tube: Bayswater Station. **Amenities:** Cafe; bar; limited business services; 24-hr. room service; laundry services; same-day dry cleaning; nonsmoking rooms. *In room:* TV, dataport, hair dryer.

## INEXPENSIVE

**Europa House Hotel** This family-run hotel attracts visitors who want a room with a private bathroom, but at shared-bathroom prices. Like most hotels along Sussex Gardens, the bedrooms are a bit cramped, but they're well maintained. Each room has color-coordinated decor, and most have been recently refurbished. Some units are custom built for groups, with three, four, or five beds per unit. Some of the multiple rooms have rather thin mattresses, but most are firm and comfortable. A hearty English breakfast awaits you in the bright dining room every morning.

151 Sussex Gardens, London W2 2RY. (C) **020/7723-7343.** Fax 020/7224-9331. www.europahousehotel.com. 20 units. £60 ($111) double; from £90 ($167) family room. Rates include English breakfast. AE, DC, MC, V. Free parking. Tube: Paddington. **Amenities:** Nonsmoking rooms. *In room:* TV, dataport, coffeemaker, hair dryer.

**Fairways Hotel** A small hotel near Hyde Park, and a favorite of bargain hunters, this welcoming, well-run B&B is the domain of Jenny and Steve

Adams. The black-and-white town house is easily recognizable: Just look for its colonnaded front entrance with a wrought-iron balustrade stretching across the second floor. Scorning the modern, the Adamses opt for traditional charm and character. They call their breakfast room "homely" (Americans might say homey)—it's decorated with photos of the family and a collection of china. Bedrooms are attractive and comfortably furnished, with hot and cold running water and intercoms. Bathrooms are small but tidy, and some have showers and tubs. Those who share the corridor bathrooms will find them clean and well maintained. The home-cooked breakfast is plenty of fortification for a full day of sightseeing.

186 Sussex Gardens, London W2 1TU. (*C*) and fax **020/7723-4871**. www.fairways-hotel.co.uk. 18 units, 10 with bathroom. £60 ($111) double without bathroom, £70 ($130) double with bathroom. Rates include English breakfast. MC, V. Tube: Paddington or Lancaster Gate. *In room:* TV, coffeemaker, hair dryer (on request), safe.

**Garden Court**    You'll find this hotel on a tranquil Victorian garden square in the heart of the city. Two private houses (dating from 1870) were combined to form one efficiently run hotel, located near such attractions as Kensington Palace, Hyde Park, and the Portobello Antiques Market. Each year, rooms are redecorated and refurbished, although an overall renovation plan seems to be lacking. Most accommodations are spacious, with good lighting, generous shelf and closet space, and comfortable furnishings. If you're in a room without a bathroom, you'll generally have to share with the occupants of only one other room. There are many homelike touches throughout the hotel, including ancestral portraits and silky flowers. Each room is individually decorated and "comfy"; it's like visiting your great-aunt. Rooms open onto the square in front or the gardens in the rear. Shower-and-tub bathrooms are installed in areas never intended for plumbing, so they tend to be very cramped.

30–31 Kensington Gardens Sq., London W2 4BG. (*C*) **020/7229-2553**. Fax 020/7727-2749. www.garden courthotel.co.uk. 34 units, 16 with bathroom. £58 ($107) double without bathroom, £88 ($163) double with bathroom; £72 ($133) triple without bathroom, £99 ($183) triple with bathroom. Rates include English breakfast. MC, V. Tube: Bayswater. **Amenities:** Coin-op washers and dryers. *In room:* TV, dataport, hair dryer.

**Norfolk Court & St. David's Hotel**    George and Foula Neokledos, two of the most welcoming hosts in this highly concentrated B&B area, run these two properties with a certain friendly, personalized style. Only a 2-minute walk from Paddington Station, these small, friendly hotels were built when Norfolk Square knew a grander age. The bluebloods are long gone, but the area is still safe and recommendable. The refurbished bedrooms are well maintained and furnished comfortably, and you can't beat the price. In the rooms that do have showers, a cubicle shower does the job, though it's not the best spot for lingering. We are big fans of the large breakfast.

14–20 Norfolk Sq., London W2 1RS. (*C*) **020/7723-4963**. Fax 020/7402-9061. www.stdavidshotels.com. 75 units (70 with bathroom). £59 ($109) double without bathroom; £69 ($128) double with bathroom or shower; £80 ($148) triple with shower; £90 ($167) quad with shower. Rates include English breakfast. MC, V. Tube: Paddington. **Amenities:** Laundry service; same-day dry cleaning. *In room:* TV, dataport.

**Queensway Hotel**    On a tree-lined road close to Hyde Park and Marble Arch, this hotel, composed of two Victorian houses, is ideal for shopping along Oxford Street, Bond Street, and Knightsbridge. Personal service and hospitality have long characterized this place, which received much refurbishment during the mid-1990s. The hotel is one of the most immaculate along Sussex Gardens. Bedrooms are moderately spacious and comfortably furnished, with sleek shower-and-tub bathrooms. A reception room has its original mantelpiece and deep-cove moldings, evoking the hotel's former life as a private residence for a "family of character." The dining room is elegantly decorated with lavender tablecloths and wall art, and it serves a generous breakfast.

147–149 Sussex Gardens, London W2 2RY. ℂ 020/7723-7749. Fax 020/7262-5707. 43 units. £83 ($154) double. Rates include continental breakfast. AE, MC, V. Tube: Paddington. *In room:* TV, coffeemaker, hair dryer, iron.

**Rhodes Hotel** This elegant late-Georgian house, just a short stroll from Hyde Park, is decorated with a certain theatrical flair. The owners, Chris and Maria Crias, have poured many pounds into their hotel to give it a cozy charm, with a Victorian curtained lounge, Greek murals, lacquered walls, and *trompe l'oeil* bambini on puffy clouds. Creature comforts weren't ignored, either. You'll find air-conditioning—a bit of a rarity in the neighborhood, especially at these prices—plus new rugs and clean bathrooms with shower/tub combinations in all of the bedrooms. The best room, number 220, has access to a little roof terrace, where you can sit out and enjoy a drink if you BYOB. There's an excellent bunkroom for families. Good coffee and lively conversation make breakfast here an event.

195 Sussex Gardens, London W2 2RJ. ℂ 020/7262-0537. Fax 020/7723-4054. www.rhodeshotel.co.uk. 36 units. £75–£80 ($139–$148) double; £85–£95 ($157–$176) triple. Rates include continental buffet breakfast. MC, V. Tube: Paddington or Lancaster Gate. **Amenities:** Nonsmoking rooms. *In room:* A/C, TV, dataport, fridge, coffeemaker, hair dryer.

# NOTTING HILL GATE
## EXPENSIVE

**Pembridge Court Hotel** ★ This hotel, featuring an elegant cream-colored neoclassical facade, is located in the increasingly fashionable Notting Hill Gate residential neighborhood. Avid antiques hunters will like its proximity to Portobello Road. Most guest rooms contain at least one antique, as well as 19th-century engravings and plenty of warm-toned floral fabrics. Bathrooms are tiled in Italian marble and feature shower/tub combinations. Three air-conditioned deluxe rooms, all with VCRs, overlook Portobello Road. The Spencer and Churchill Rooms are decorated in blues and yellows, and the Windsor Room has a contrasting array of tartans.

34 Pembridge Gardens, London W2 4DX. ℂ 020/7229-9977. Fax 020/7727-4982. www.pemct.co.uk. 20 units. £160–£195 ($296–$361) double. Rates include English breakfast. AE, DC, MC, V. Tube: Notting Hill Gate. **Amenities:** Access to nearby health club w/sauna and massage; business services; 24-hr. room service; babysitting; laundry service; same-day dry cleaning. *In room:* A/C, TV, dataport, fridge, hair dryer, safe, trouser press.

**The Portobello Hotel** ★ On an elegant Victorian terrace near Portobello Road, two 1850s-era town houses have been combined to form a quirky property that has its devotees. We remember these rooms when they looked better, but they still have plenty of character. Who knows what will show up in what nook? Perhaps a Chippendale, a claw-foot tub, or a round bed tucked under a gauze canopy. Try for no. 16, with a full-tester bed facing the garden. Some of the cheaper rooms are so tiny that they're basically garrets, but others have been combined into large doubles. Most of the small bathrooms have showers but no tubs. An elevator goes to the third floor; after that, it's the stairs. Since windows are not double-glazed, request a room in the quiet rear. Some rooms are air-conditioned. Service is erratic at best, but this is still a good choice.

22 Stanley Gardens, London W11 2NG. ℂ 020/7727-2777. Fax 020/7792-9641. www.portobello-hotel. co.uk. 24 units. £160–£180 ($296–$333) double; £200–£275 ($370–$509) suite. Rates include continental breakfast. AE, MC, V. Tube: Notting Hill Gate or Holland Park. **Amenities:** 24-hr. bar and restaurant in basement; business services; 24-hr. room service; laundry service; same-day dry cleaning; nearby gym. *In room:* A/C (some rooms), TV/VCR, dataport, minibar, hair dryer, beverage maker.

## MODERATE

**The Gate Hotel**   This antiques-hunters' favorite is the only hotel along the length of Portobello Road—and because of rigid zoning restrictions, it will probably remain the only one for years to come. It was built in the 1820s as housing for farmhands at the now-defunct Portobello Farms and has functioned as a hotel since 1932. It has two cramped but cozy bedrooms on each of its three floors. Be prepared for some *very* steep English stairs. Rooms are color-coordinated, with a bit of style, and have such extras as full-length mirrors and built-in wardrobes. Bathrooms are small, with tiled shower stalls (there is a shower/tub combo in one room). Housekeeping is excellent. Especially intriguing are the wall paintings that show what the Portobello Market used to look like: Every character looks like it is straight from a Dickens novel. The on-site manager can direct you to the attractions of Notting Hill Gate and nearby Kensington Gardens, both within a 5-minute walk.

6 Portobello Rd., London W11 3DG. ℂ 020/7221-0707. Fax 020/7221-9128. www.gatehotel.com. 7 units. £75–£99 ($139–$183) double. Rates include continental breakfast. AE, MC, V. Tube: Notting Hill Gate. **Amenities:** 24-hr. room service; laundry service; rooms for those w/limited mobility. *In room:* TV, dataport, fridge, hair dryer, iron, beverage maker.

**The Main House** 🌟🌟 *Finds*   Each beautifully appointed room takes up a whole floor of this Victorian town house in Notting Hill, close to Portobello Road, the antiques markets, art galleries, and designer shops. Such attractions as Kensington Palace and Albert Hall are within walking distance. Russian princesses, Japanese pop stars, and Los Angeles film producers have already discovered this spot. Owner and creator Caroline Main is a former African explorer, Mayfair nightclub owner, and DJ. To furnish the house, she shopped "quirky" on Portobello Road, picking up gilded mirrors, watercolors of elegantly dressed 1930s women, and similar antiques. The ceilings are dramatically high, and the gleaming wood floors are swathed in animal skins. All rooms have freshly renewed private bathrooms with showers.

6 Colville Rd., London W11 2BP. ℂ 020/7221-9691. www.themainhouse.co.uk. 4 suites. £130 ($241) suite. MC, V. Tube: Notting Hill Gate. Parking: £4 ($7.40). Bus: 23, 27, 52, 94, or 328. **Amenities:** Reduced rate at nearby health club and spa; bike rental; courtesy car to and from point of arrival; limited room service (breakfast only); laundry service; same-day dry cleaning. *In room:* TV, dataport, hair dryer, safe.

## INEXPENSIVE

**Manor Court Hotel**   This B&B lies on a cul-de-sac at the edge of Kensington Gardens. Still slightly run-down, the neighborhood is improving, and real-estate prices are soaring as young professionals seek town houses here. A Victorian home, Manor Court lies only a 15-minute stroll from antiques mecca Portobello Road. A family favorite, it offers simple decor with basic—not stylish—furnishings, comfortable beds, and generous space. If you look carefully, you'll see elements that need restoration, but the comfort level is high and the housekeeping is immaculate. Bedrooms come in a variety of shapes and sizes, with the smaller units on the top floors. Those units that have a private bathroom come with shower stalls.

7 Clanricarde Gardens, London W2 4JJ. ℂ 020/7792-3361. Fax 020/7229-2875. 20 units, 16 with bathroom. £50–£55 ($93–$102) double with bathroom; £65 ($120) triple with bathroom; £75 ($139) family room with bathroom. 10% discount for any stay over 4 nights. Rates include continental breakfast. AE, MC, V. Tube: Notting Hill Gate. *In room:* TV, hair dryer.

## IN NEARBY MAIDA VALE
## MODERATE

**The Colonnade Town House** 🌟 *Kids*   Tired of large chain hotels? Head for this boutique charmer in the canal-laced "Little Venice" (an appellation bestowed by Lord Byron) area of London. A handsome Victorian edifice, the hotel was built in 1886 as two different structures, one of which was a hospital. An unusually shaped elevator, which was used to transport stretchers, still remains. Before he purchased his own place in Hampstead, Sigmund Freud stayed here in 1938. Each midsize bedroom is individually decorated, and many feature four-poster beds and small terraces. Tasteful fabrics and antiques evoke town-house living. The least desirable units are two small basement bedrooms. They are impeccably furnished, but subject to rumblings from the Underground. Families might want to opt for the spacious two-level JFK suite. All units have well-maintained bathrooms with shower/tub combinations, and half of the rooms are for nonsmokers. Thoughtful extras abound, including Penhaligon's toilet articles, Frette Egyptian-cotton bed linens, complimentary fresh fruit, and dual-line phones with voice mail.

2 Warrington Crescent, London W9 1ER. ⓒ **020/7286-1052.** Fax 020/7286-1057. www.theetongroup.com. 43 units. £147–£179 ($272–$331) double; £230–£245 ($426–$453) suite. AE, DC, MC, V. Tube: Warwick Ave. **Amenities:** 24-hr. room service; laundry service; same-day dry cleaning. *In room:* A/C, TV, CD player, dataport, minibar, coffeemaker, hair dryer, iron/ironing board, safe.

## 6 The South Bank

### NEAR LONDON BRIDGE
#### EXPENSIVE

**London Bridge Hotel** ⭐   Many guests to London today prefer to stay in a hotel on the emerging South Bank, near many sightseeing and cultural attractions. If you're among them, you can't do much better than lodging at this independently owned, government-rated four-star hotel. A former telephone exchange building, this 1915 structure was successfully recycled into a bastion of comfort and charm. Bedrooms are completely up-to-date and offer homelike comfort and plenty of amenities. Rooms in the front have double-glazing on windows to cut down on the noise. The best luxuries are found on the executive floor, in the deluxe rooms, and in the executive kings and suites. Dining and drinking facilities are first class, including a new restaurant, Georgetown, which evokes colonial days with a mixture of Malaysian, Chinese, and Indian flavors. A state-of-the-art gymnasium is in an adjacent building with direct access from the hotel.

8–18 London Bridge St., London SE1 9SG. ⓒ **020/7855-2200.** Fax 020/7855-2233. www.London-bridge-hotel.co.uk. 138 units. £190–£225 ($352–$416) double; £475 ($879) suite. Children under 12 stay free when sharing parent's room. AE, DC, MC, V. Tube: London Bridge. **Amenities:** Restaurant; bar; free access to nearby health club; 24-hr. room service; babysitting; laundry service; dry cleaning; rooms for those w/limited mobility; nonsmoking rooms. *In room:* A/C, TV w/pay movies, dataport, minibar, coffeemaker, hair dryer, iron/ironing board, safe, trouser press.

## 7 Near the Airports

### NEAR HEATHROW

The reason for staying at one of the hotels below is obvious: You either want to catch an early plane or are arriving too late to search for a hotel in central London. Unless you like plane-spotting, there isn't much reason to hang out. The hotels below provide transportation to and from the airport.

#### VERY EXPENSIVE

**Radisson Edwardian Heathrow** ⭐   The poshest digs at Heathrow, this deluxe hotel lies just south of the M4 about 5 minutes east of the long tunnel that leads to Terminals 1, 2, and 3. Since 1991 it has housed tired air travelers from all over the world. The grand spa has a swimming pool and two whirlpools. You'll enter the hotel through a courtyard with potted trees. Persian rugs, brass-railed staircases, and chandeliers live up to the "Edwardian" in the hotel's name. Rooms are medium in size but adorned with hand-painted hardwood furnishings. The bathrooms are in tile and marble, with robes, a shower, and a tub. All in-room televisions have a channel reserved to broadcast flight information.

140 Bath Rd., Hayes, Middlesex UB3 5AW. (C) **800/333-3333** in the U.S., or 020/8759-6311. Fax 020/8759-4559. www.radissonedwardian.com. 459 units. £135–£165 ($250–$305) double; from £235 ($435) suite. Rates include breakfast. AE, DC, MC, V. Parking £8 ($15). Hotel Hoppa bus service. **Amenities:** 2 restaurants; bar; indoor plunge heated pool; health club; spa; sauna; 24-hr. room service; massage; laundry service; same-day dry cleaning; rooms for those w/limited mobility; nonsmoking rooms. *In room:* A/C, TV w/pay movies, dataport, minibar, hair dryer, safe.

## EXPENSIVE

**Hilton London Heathrow Airport** ✿    This first-class hotel, with a five-story atrium that evokes a hangar, is linked to Heathrow's Terminal 4 by a covered walkway. A glass wall faces the runways, so you can see planes land and take off. You can take buses to Terminals 1, 2, or 3. Medium-size bedrooms are standard, decorated with built-in wood furniture and comfortable sofas. Bathrooms are tiled and trimmed in marble, and each contains a phone, tub, and shower. The best accommodations are on the fifth floor because they offer better extras (bathrobes, and so forth) as well as a private lounge with airport vistas.

Terminal 4, Hounslow TW6 3AF. (C) **800/774-1500** in the U.S., or 020/8759-7755. Fax 020/8759-7579. www.hilton.com. 395 units. £185–£235 ($342–$435) double; £450 ($833) suite. AE, DC, MC, V. Parking from £7.20 ($13). Tube: Heathrow Terminal 4. **Amenities:** 3 restaurants; 2 bars; indoor heated pool; health club; sauna; business services and center; car rental desk; tour desk; salon; 24-hr. room service; babysitting; laundry service; same-day dry cleaning; TV with flight information; rooms for those w/limited mobility; nonsmoking rooms. *In room:* A/C, TV (w/pay movies), dataport, minibar, coffeemaker, hair dryer, trouser press.

## MODERATE

**Holiday Inn London—Heathrow**    This is your best bet in the moderate range at London's major airport. The decor is bland, but not unpleasant. The Holiday Inn has been massively upgraded—ask for one of the millennium rooms. Rooms are midsize, with immaculate bathrooms containing shower stalls.

118 Bath Rd., Hayes, Middlesex UB3 SAJ. (C) **800/225-5843** in the U.S., or 208/990-0000 in the U.K. Fax 020/8564-7744. www.london-heathrow.holiday-inn.com. 186 units. Mon–Thurs £125–£185 ($231–$342) double; Fri–Sun £65–£90 ($120–$167) double. AE, DC, MC, V. Parking £20 ($37). Tube: Heathrow Terminals 1, 2, 3. **Amenities:** Restaurant; bar; exercise room; business center; 24-hr. room service; babysitting; laundry service; same-day dry cleaning; rooms for those w/limited mobility; nonsmoking rooms. *In room:* A/C, TV w/pay movies, dataport, minibar, coffeemaker, hair dryer, iron/ironing board.

## INEXPENSIVE

**The Swan**    Dating from the days of diarist Samuel Pepys, the Swan is on the south bank of the Thames, beside Staines Bridge and within a 15-minute drive of Heathrow. Bedrooms were refurbished in 1999. The shower-only bathrooms are small, but the corridor bathroom is adequate. The attractive inn has a reputation for good food ranging from bar snacks to traditional English fare. Food is served in a gazebo-style dining room. Staines was an important Roman settlement, and many buildings in the area date from the 17th century.

The Hythe, Staines, Middlesex TW18 3JB. (C) **0178/445-2494.** Fax 0178/446-1593. 11 units, 10 with bathroom. £85–£105 ($157–$194) double with bathroom; £105–£125 ($194–$231) suite. Rates include English breakfast. AE, DC, MC, V. Tube: Heathrow (you must take a taxi from there). **Amenities:** Restaurant; laundry; dry cleaning; nonsmoking rooms. *In room:* TV, dataport, coffeemaker, hair dryer, iron.

## NEAR GATWICK
### EXPENSIVE

**Hilton London Gatwick Airport** ⭐   This deluxe five-floor hotel—Gatwick's most convenient—is linked to the airport terminal by a covered walkway; an electric buggy service transports people between the hotel and the airport. The most impressive part of the hotel is the first-floor lobby. Its glass-covered portico rises four floors and contains a scale replica of the de Havilland Gypsy Moth airplane *Jason,* used by Amy Johnson on her solo flight from England to Australia in 1930. The reception area has a lobby bar and lots of greenery. The well-furnished, soundproof rooms have triple-glazed windows and tidily kept bathrooms equipped with a tub and shower. Rooms were recently refurbished, including the executive floor and all the junior suites.

South Terminal, Gatwick Airport, West Sussex RH6 0LL. ℂ **800/774-1500** in the U.S., or 01293/518-080. Fax 01293/528-980. www.hilton.com. 565 units. £145–£230 ($268–$426) double; from £280 ($518) suite. AE, MC, V. Parking £16 ($30). **Amenities:** 3 restaurants; 2 bars; health club; indoor heated pool; tour desk; car-rental desk; business center; salon; 24-hr. room service; babysitting; laundry service; same-day dry cleaning; rooms for those w/limited mobility; nonsmoking rooms. *In room:* A/C, TV w/pay movies, dataport, minibar in most rooms, hair dryer, iron/ironing board.

### INEXPENSIVE

**The Manor House**   Owners Steve and Jo Jeffries include transportation from Gatwick as part of the price. Their home is a sprawling neo-Tudor affair on .8 hectares (2 acres) of land, amid fields that surround it on all sides. It was built in 1894 as a supplemental home for the lord of Ifield, who occupied a larger house nearby and never actually moved in. Two of the rooms share a bathroom; the others have bathrooms with showers. Each accommodation has flowered wallpaper and simple, traditional accessories. Breakfast is the only meal served.

Bonnetts Lane, Ifield, Crawley, Sussex RH11 0NY. ℂ **01293/510-000.** Fax 01293/518-046. www.manorhouse-gatwick.co.uk. 6 units, 4 (doubles) with private bathroom. £49 ($91) double; £65 ($120) family unit. Rates include English breakfast. MC, V. Free parking. **Amenities:** All nonsmoking rooms. *In room:* TV, dataport, coffeemaker, no phone.

# Where to Dine

George Mikes, Britain's famous Hungarian-born humorist, wrote about the cuisine of his adopted country: "The Continentals have good food. The English have good table manners."

Quite a lot has happened since.

London has emerged as one of the great food capitals of the world. Both its veteran and upstart chefs have fanned out around the globe for culinary inspiration and returned with innovative dishes, flavors, and ideas that London diners have never seen before. These chefs are pioneering a style called "Modern British," which is forever changing and innovative, yet familiar in many ways.

Traditional British cooking has made a comeback, too. The dishes that British mums have been forever feeding their families are fashionable again. Yes, we're talking British soul food: bangers and mash, Norfolk dumplings, nursery puddings, cottage pie. This may be a rebellion against the minimalism of the nouvelle cuisine of the 1980s, but maybe it's just plain nostalgia. Pig's nose with parsley-and-onion sauce may not be your idea of cutting-edge cuisine, but Simpson's-in-the-Strand is serving it for breakfast.

These days, many famous chefs spend more time writing cookbooks and on TV than in their own kitchens. That chef you've read about in *Condé Nast Traveler* or *Travel & Leisure* may not be in the kitchen when you get here. But don't worry: The cuisine isn't suffering. An up-and-coming new chef, perhaps even better than the one you heard about, has probably taken over the kitchen.

If you want a lavish meal, London is the place: Gourmet havens such as Le Gavroche and a half-dozen others are reviewed in the following pages. We've also included many affordable restaurants where you can dine well and still pay off your mortgage. You'll find that London's food revolution has infiltrated every level of the dining scene—even the lowly pub has entered the culinary sweepstakes. Believe the unthinkable: At certain pubs, you can now dine better than in many restaurants. In some, standard pub grub has given way to Modern British and Mediterranean-style fare; in others, oyster bars have taken hold.

## SOME DINING NOTES

**HOURS** Restaurants in London keep varied hours, but in general, lunch is offered from noon to 2pm and dinner from 7:30 to 9:30pm, although more restaurants are staying open later. Sunday is the usual closing day for restaurants, but there are exceptions. (Many also close for a few days around Christmas, so call ahead during the holidays.) We've listed serving hours in the descriptions below.

**RESERVATIONS** Nearly all places, except pubs, cafeterias, and fast-food joints, prefer or require reservations. Almost invariably, you get a better table if you book in advance. For a few of the famous places, you might need to reserve weeks in advance, even before leaving home. (Reservations should always be confirmed when you get to London.) However, if you haven't made reservations, even at a "reservations required" restaurant, it's worth trying to walk into the restaurant if you are in the area. If they do have room, you won't be turned down.

**TAXES & TIPPING** All restaurants and cafes are required to display the prices of their food and drink in a place visible from outside. Charges for service, as well as any minimums or cover charges, must also be made clear. The prices shown must include 17.5% VAT. Most restaurants add a 10% to 15% service charge to your bill, but check to make sure. If nothing has been added, leave a 10% to 15% tip. It is not considered rude to tip, so feel free to leave something extra if service was good.

**A NOTE ABOUT PRICES** When restaurants are classified as Moderate or Inexpensive, most main courses are at the lower end of the price scale. That doesn't mean that the chefs don't prepare some expensive dishes. Often they do, especially if they offer shellfish. But if you avoid the highest-priced dishes, you can dine moderately or inexpensively in our selections.

## 1 Restaurants by Cuisine

**AFTERNOON TEA**

The Blue Room, Soho (p. 202, $)
Brown's Hotel, Mayfair ⋆ (p. 200, $$$)
Claridge's, Mayfair ⋆ (p. 200, $$$)
The Garden Café, Notting Hill (p. 203, $)
The Georgian Restaurant, Knightsbridge (p. 201, $$$)
The Lanesborough, Knightsbridge (p. 201, $$$)
The Orangery, Kensington ⋆ (p. 202, $)
The Palm Court, Mayfair (p. 200, $$$)
Richoux, Knightsbridge (p. 202, $$)
Ritz Palm Court, St. James's ⋆⋆⋆ (p. 200, $$$)
St. James Restaurant & The Fountain Restaurant, St. James's (p. 200, $$$)
The Tearoom at the Chelsea Physic Garden, Chelsea (p. 202, $)

**AMERICAN**

Ed's Easy Diner, Soho (p. 170, $)
Hard Rock Cafe, Mayfair (p. 175, $$)
Spoon+, Soho ⋆ (p. 164, $$$$)

**ASIAN**

(See also Cantonese, Chinese, Japanese, Szechuan, and Thai)
E&O, Ladbroke Grove (p. 197, $$)
Mezzo, Soho (p. 168, $$)
Oxo Tower Restaurant, South Bank ⋆ (p. 154, $$$)

**BELGIAN**

Belgo Centraal, Covent Garden & the Strand (p. 160, $$)

**BRITISH—MODERN**

Admiral Codrington, Kensington & South Kensington ⋆ (p. 190, $)
Alastair Little, Soho ⋆ (p. 165, $$$)
Allium, Westminster/Victoria ⋆ (p. 179, $$$)
Atlantic Bar & Grill, Soho ⋆⋆ (p. 166, $$)
Balans, Soho (p. 170, $)
The Bridge, the City ⋆⋆ (p. 146, $$)
Bush Bar & Grill, Marylebone ⋆ (p. 191, $$)
Circus, St. James's (p. 178, $$)
Clarke's, Kensington & South Kensington ⋆ (p. 187, $$$)
The Collection, Knightsbridge ⋆ (p. 184, $$$)

Key to Abbreviations: $$$$ = Very Expensive   $$$ = Expensive   $$ = Moderate   $ = Inexpensive

The Cow, Notting Hill Gate ✶
(p. 196, $$)

The Criterion Brasserie, Soho ✶
(p. 167, $$)

Fifteen, Shoreditch ✶✶
(p. 151, $$$)

The Ivy, Piccadilly Circus &
Leicester Square ✶✶
(p. 162, $$)

Joe's, Kensington & South Kens-
ington ✶ (p. 188, $$)

Launceston Place, Kensington &
South Kensington ✶
(p. 188, $$$)

Lindsay House, Soho ✶✶
(p. 165, $$$)

Menu, Mayfair ✶✶✶ (p. 173,
$$$$)

The Portrait Restaurant, Trafalgar
Square ✶ (p. 171, $$)

Prism, the City ✶✶ (p. 146, $$$)

Savoy Restaurant, Covent Garden
& the Strand ✶✶ (p. 158,
$$$$)

Simpson's-in-the-Strand, Covent
Garden & the Strand ✶✶
(p. 159, $$$)

Sketch, Mayfair ✶✶ (p. 173, $$$$)

St. John, Clerkenwell ✶✶
(p. 150, $$)

Tate Gallery Restaurant, Westmin-
ster & Victoria ✶✶ (p. 180, $$)

## BRITISH—TRADITIONAL

Brown's, Piccadilly Circus &
Leicester Square (p. 163, $)

Butler's Wharf Chop House,
Docklands ✶ (p. 152, $$$)

English Garden, Chelsea ✶
(p. 186, $$)

The Enterprise, Kensington &
South Kensington (p. 188, $$)

Fox and Anchor, the City ✶
(p. 149, $)

The George, Covent Garden &
the Strand (p. 161, $)

The George & Vulture, the City
(p. 149, $)

The Granary, Mayfair (p. 177, $)

Greens Restaurant & Oyster Bar,
St. James's (p. 178, $$)

Langan's Bistro, Marylebone
(p. 194, $$)

Langan's Brasserie, Mayfair
(p. 176, $$)

Porter's English Restaurant, Covent
Garden & the Strand ✶✶
(p. 160, $$)

Rules, Covent Garden & the
Strand ✶ (p. 159, $$$)

Shepherd's, Westminster & Victoria
(p. 179, $$$)

Simpson's-in-the-Strand, Covent
Garden & the Strand ✶✶
(p. 159, $$$)

The Stockpot, Piccadilly Circus &
Leicester Square (p. 164, $)

Veronica's, Paddington & Bays-
water ✶✶ (p. 196, $$)

Ye Olde Cheshire Cheese, the City
(p. 150, $)

## CANTONESE

Fung Shing, Piccadilly Circus &
Leicester Square ✶✶ (p. 161,
$$$)

Jenny Lo's Teahouse, Westminster
& Victoria (p. 180, $)

Royal China, Paddington &
Bayswater ✶ (p. 195, $$$)

Zen Central, Mayfair (p. 177, $$)

## CHINESE

(See also Cantonese and Szechuan)

Chuen Cheng Ku, Soho ✶
(p. 167, $$)

Dumpling Inn, Piccadilly Circus
& Leicester Square (p. 162, $$)

Hakkasan, Soho ✶ (p. 168, $$)

Poons in the City, the City ✶
(p. 149, $$)

## CONTINENTAL

Admiral Codrington, Kensington
& South Kensington ✶
(p. 190, $)

Alastair Little, Soho ✶ (p. 165,
$$$)

Brown's, Piccadilly Circus &
Leicester Square (p. 163, $)

Cantina Vinopolis, South Bank ✶
(p. 155, $$)

# Guide to London Restaurant Maps

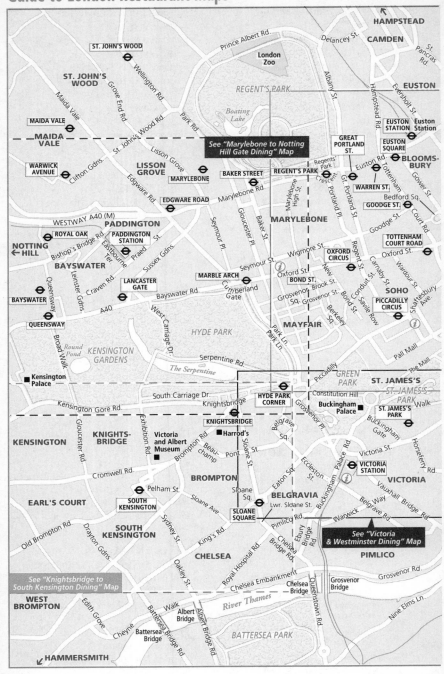

ST. JOHN'S WOOD

Prince Albert Rd.

Delancey St.

HAMPSTEAD

CAMDEN

St. Pancras Rd.

London Zoo

REGENT'S PARK

EUSTON

St. John's Wood Rd.

Albany St.

Hampstead Rd.

Eversholt St.

Boating Lake

ST. JOHN'S WOOD

Maida Vale

Wellington Rd.

Grove End Rd.

Park Rd.

Lisson Grove

MAIDA VALE

Clifton Gdns.

MAIDA VALE

See "Marylebone to Notting Hill Gate Dining" Map

GREAT PORTLAND ST.

Regents' Park Crescent

Euston Rd.

Tottenham Court Rd.

Gower St.

EUSTON STATION Euston Station

EUSTON SQUARE

BLOOMS-BURY

WARWICK AVENUE

LISSON GROVE

MARYLEBONE

BAKER STREET

REGENT'S PARK

Marylebone High St.

Gt. Portland St.

WARREN ST.

Bedford Sq.

GOODGE ST.

EDGWARE ROAD

Marylebone Rd.

Baker St.

Portland Pl.

Regent St.

Goodge St.

Court Rd.

TOTTENHAM COURT ROAD

WESTWAY A40 (M)

PADDINGTON

Bishop's Bridge Rd.

Eastbourne Ter.

Praed St.

Sussex Gdns.

Seymour Pl.

Gloucester Pl.

MARYLEBONE

Wigmore St.

OXFORD CIRCUS

New Bond St.

Carnaby St.

Wardour St.

SOHO

Shaftesbury Ave.

ROYAL OAK

PADDINGTON STATION

NOTTING HILL

BAYSWATER

Leinster Gdns.

Craven Rd.

LANCASTER GATE

A40

Bayswater Rd.

West Carriage Dr.

MARBLE ARCH

Cumberland Gate

Seymour St.

Oxford St.

BOND ST.

Grosvenor Sq.

Brook St.

Grosvenor St.

Bond St.

Savile Row

Conduit St.

PICCADILLY CIRCUS

BAYSWATER

Queensway

QUEENSWAY

Broad Walk

Round Pond

KENSINGTON GARDENS

HYDE PARK

Serpentine Rd.

The Serpentine

Berkeley Sq.

MAYFAIR

Park Ln.

Park Ln.

Piccadilly

GREEN PARK

Pall Mall

The Mall

ST. JAMES'S

ST. JAMES'S PARK

Kensington Palace

South Carriage Dr.

Kensington Gore Rd.

Knightsbridge

HYDE PARK CORNER

Constitution Hill

Buckingham Palace

ST-JAMES'S Walk

Buckingham Gate

ST. JAMES'S PARK

KENSINGTON

Gloucester Rd.

Exhibition Rd.

KNIGHTS-BRIDGE

KNIGHTSBRIDGE

Victoria and Albert Museum

Harrod's

Brompton Rd.

Beau-champ Pl.

Sloane St.

Pont St.

Belgrave Sq.

Grosvenor Pl.

Horseferry Rd.

Cromwell Rd.

Pelham St.

Sloane Ave.

Eaton Sq.

Eccleston St.

Buckingham Palace Rd.

Victoria St.

VICTORIA STATION

VICTORIA

EARL'S COURT

SOUTH KENSINGTON

Sydney St.

BROMPTON

Sloane Sq.

BELGRAVIA

Lwr. Sloane St.

Vauxhall Bridge Rd.

SOUTH KENSINGTON

Old Brompton Rd.

Drayton Gdns.

King's Rd.

SLOANE SQUARE

Pimlico Rd.

Ebury Bridge Rd.

Chelsea Bridge Rd.

Warwick Way

Belgrave Rd.

PIMLICO

See "Victoria & Westminster Dining" Map

CHELSEA

Royal Hospital Rd.

Grosvenor Rd.

See "Knightsbridge to South Kensington Dining" Map

WEST BROMPTON

Edith Grove

Oakley St.

Chelsea Embankment

Chelsea Bridge

Queenstown Rd.

Grosvenor Bridge

Nine Elms Ln.

HAMMERSMITH

Cheyne Walk

Battersea Bridge

Albert Bridge

Albert Bridge Rd.

Battersea Bridge Rd.

River Thames

BATTERSEA PARK

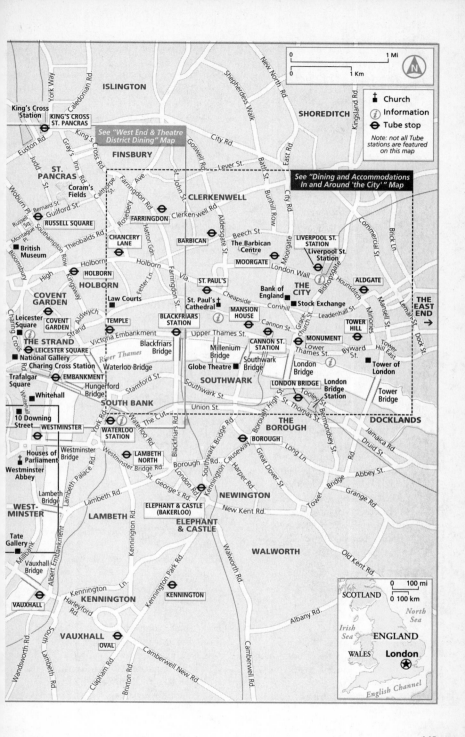

The Court Restaurant, Bloomsbury ✶ (p. 158, $)

Drones, Knightsbridge ✶
(p. 185, $$)

Mash, Marylebone ✶ (p. 194, $$)

Noble Rot, Mayfair ✶
(p. 176, $$$)

Quaglino's, St. James's ✶
(p. 179, $$)

Shampers, Soho (p. 169, $$)

Sketch, Mayfair ✶✶
(p. 173, $$$$)

The Stockpot, Piccadilly Circus &
Leicester Square (p. 164, $)

Union Cafe, Marylebone
(p. 195, $$)

Vertigo 42, the City ✶ (p. 149, $)

Villandry, Marylebone ✶
(p. 195, $$)

## CYPRIOT

Halepi, Paddington & Bayswater ✶
(p. 196, $$)

Sarastro, Covent Garden & the
Strand ✶ (p. 161, $)

## EUROPEAN

Allium, Westminister/Victoria ✶
(p. 179, $$$)

The Engineer, Camden Town ✶
(p. 198, $$)

The Enterprise, Kensington &
South Kensington (p. 188, $$)

Gordon Ramsay at Claridge's,
Mayfair ✶✶✶ (p. 172, $$$$)

Greenhouse, Mayfair (p. 175, $$)

Kensington Place, Kensington &
South Kensington (p. 189, $$)

Mezzo, Soho (p. 168, $$)

## FRENCH

Archipelago, Bloomsbury ✶✶
(p. 155, $$$)

Aubergine, Chelsea ✶✶
(p. 185, $$$$)

Bam-Bou, Soho ✶ (p. 166, $$)

Bibendum/The Oyster Bar, Kensington & South Kensington ✶
(p. 187, $$$)

Bush Bar & Grill, Marylebone ✶
(p. 191, $$)

Club Gascon, the City ✶✶
(p. 148, $$)

The Criterion Brasserie, Soho ✶
(p. 167, $$)

Deca, Soho ✶✶ (p. 167, $$)

Gordon Ramsay, Chelsea ✶✶✶
(p. 185, $$$$)

Langan's Bistro, Marylebone
(p. 194, $$)

Langan's Brasserie, Mayfair
(p. 176, $$)

Le Gavroche, Mayfair ✶✶✶
(p. 172, $$$$)

Les Trois Garçons, Shoreditch ✶✶
(p. 151, $$$)

L'Oranger, St. James's ✶
(p. 178, $$$)

Mirabelle, Mayfair ✶
(p. 175, $$$)

Orrey, Marylebone ✶✶
(p. 191, $$$)

Petrus, Knightsbridge ✶✶
(p. 180, $$$$)

Pied-à-Terre, Bloomsbury ✶
(p. 155, $$$$)

The Square, Mayfair ✶✶✶
(p. 174, $$$$)

## GREEK

Halepi, Paddington & Bayswater ✶
(p. 196, $$)

## HUNGARIAN

The Gay Hussar, Soho ✶
(p. 167, $$)

## INDIAN

The Bengal Clipper, Docklands ✶
(p. 153, $$)

Café Spice Namaste, the City ✶✶
(p. 147, $$)

Mela, Soho ✶ (p. 168, $$)

Rasa Samundra, Soho ✶
(p. 169, $$)

Soho Spice, Soho (p. 170, $$)

Tamarind, Mayfair ✶ (p. 177, $$)

Veeraswamy, Soho (p. 171, $)

Zaika, Kensington & South Kens-
ington ✶✶ (p. 190, $$)

Zen Central, Mayfair (p. 177, $$)

## INTERNATIONAL

The Bridge, the City ★★
(p. 146, $$)

Chelsea Kitchen, Chelsea
(p. 187, $)

Circus, St. James's (p. 178, $$)

The Collection, Knightsbridge ★
(p. 184, $$$)

Cork & Bottle Wine Bar, Piccadilly
Circus & Leicester Square ★★
(p. 163, $)

Greens Restaurant & Oyster Bar,
St. James's (p. 178, $$)

The Ivy, Piccadilly Circus & Leices-
ter Square ★★ (p. 162, $$)

Le Metro, Knightsbridge
(p. 185, $)

Le Pont de la Tour, Docklands ★
(p. 152, $$$)

Odin's, Marylebone ★
(p. 191, $$$)

Orrey, Marylebone ★★
(p. 191, $$$)

Oxo Tower Restaurant, South
Bank ★ (p. 154, $$$)

Prince Bonaparte, Notting Hill
Gate (p. 197, $)

Villandry, Marylebone ★
(p. 195, $$)

## ITALIAN

Assaggi, Marylebone ★★
(p. 190, $$$)

Caldesi, Marylebone (p. 194, $$)

Crivelli's Garden, Trafalgar
Square ★ (p. 171, $$)

Floriana, Knightsbridge ★
(p. 184, $$$)

Locanda Locatelli, Marylebone ★★
(p. 190, $$$)

Neal Street Restaurant, Covent
Garden & the Strand ★
(p. 159, $$$)

Quod Restaurant & Bar, Piccadilly
Circus & Leicester Square
(p. 164, $)

Quo Vadis, Soho ★ (p. 165, $$$)

The River Café, Hammersmith ★★
(p. 198, $$$$)

Zafferano, Knightsbridge ★★
(p. 184, $$$$)

## JAPANESE

Nobu, Mayfair ★★ (p. 173, $$$$)

Satsuma, Soho (p. 169, $$)

Wagamama, Bloomsbury
(p. 158, $)

## LEBANESE

Phoenicia, Kensington & South
Kensington (p. 189, $$)

## MEDITERRANEAN

Bibendum/The Oyster Bar, Kens-
ington & South Kensington ★
(p. 187, $$$)

Blue Bird, Chelsea ★ (p. 186, $$$)

Menu, Mayfair ★★★
(p. 173, $$$$)

## MOROCCAN

Momo, Mayfair (p. 176, $$)

Pasha, Kensington & South
Kensington (p. 189, $$)

## NORTH AFRICAN

Momo, Mayfair (p. 176, $$)

Moro, Clerkenwell ★★
(p. 150, $$)

## PACIFIC RIM

Pacific Oriental, the City
(p. 148, $$)

The Sugar Club, Soho ★
(p. 166, $$$)

Suze, Mayfair (p. 177, $)

## PORTUGUESE

Eyre Brothers, Shoreditch ★
(p. 152, $$)

## SEAFOOD

Back to Basics, Bloomsbury ★★
(p. 158, $$)

Greens Restaurant & Oyster Bar,
St. James's (p. 178, $$)

J. Sheekey, Piccadilly Circus &
Leicester Square ★ (p. 162,
$$$)

Livebait's Cafe Fish, Piccadilly
Circus & Leicester Square ★
(p. 162, $$)

Randall & Aubin, Piccadilly Circus
& Leicester Square ⭐
(p. 163, $$)
Vertigo 42, the City ⭐ (p. 149, $)

## SPANISH
Moro, Clerkenwell ⭐⭐ (p. 150, $$)

## STEAK
Notting Grill, Ladbroke Grove ⭐
(p. 197, $$)

## SZECHUAN
Jenny Lo's Teahouse, Westminster
& Victoria (p. 180, $)
Royal China, Paddington &
Bayswater ⭐ (p. 195, $$$)
Zen Central, Mayfair
(p. 177, $$)

## TAPAS
Vertigo 42, the City ⭐ (p. 149, $)

## THAI
Archipelago, Bloomsbury ⭐⭐
(p. 155, $$$)
Blue Elephant, Kensington &
South Kensington ⭐
(p. 188, $$)
The Engineer, Camden Town ⭐
(p. 198, $$)
Front Page, Chelsea (p. 187, $)
Nahm, Mayfair ⭐⭐ (p. 175, $$$)
Sri Nam, Canary Wharf ⭐
(p. 153, $$)

## TURKISH
Sarastro, Covent Garden & the
Strand ⭐ (p. 161, $)

## VEGETARIAN
Mildreds, Soho ⭐ (p. 170, $)

## VIETNAMESE
Bam-Bou, Soho ⭐ (p. 166, $$)

## 2 In & Around the City

### THE CITY
#### EXPENSIVE

**Prism** ⭐⭐ MODERN BRITISH   In the financial district, called the City, this restaurant attracts London's movers and shakers, at least those with demanding palates. In the former Bank of New York, Harvey Nichols—known for his chic department store in Knightsbridge—took this 1920s neo-Grecian hall and installed Mies van der Rohe chairs in chrome and lipstick-red leather. In this setting, traditional English dishes from the north are given a light touch—try the tempura of Whitby cod, or cream of Jerusalem artichoke soup with roasted scallops and truffle oil. For a first course, you may opt for a small, seared calves' liver with a mushroom risotto, or try a salad composed of flecks of Parmesan cheese seasoning a savoy cabbage salad and Parma ham. The menu reveals the chef has traveled a bit—note such dishes as Moroccan spiced chicken livers, lemon and parsley couscous, and a zesty chile sauce.

147 Leadenhall St., EC3. ✆ **020/7256-3888.** Reservations required. Main courses £16–£25 ($30–$46). AE, DC, DISC, MC, V. Mon–Fri noon–3pm and 6–10pm. Tube: Bank or Monument.

#### MODERATE

**The Bridge** ⭐⭐ INTERNATIONAL/MODERN BRITISH   As far as restaurants go, the most panoramic view of the new riverside architecture is from the terrace of this glass-walled restaurant next to the Millennium Bridge. It looks out across the Thames to Shakespeare's Globe Theatre and the Tate Modern. Peter Gladwin, the executive chef, roams the world for inspiration—perhaps a velvety smooth gazpacho from Spain. For appetizers, try such delights as the tiger prawns with red grapefruit, avocado, and ginger; the smoked trout; the delectable French onion soup. For something really English, opt for the thinly sliced and quickly seared calves' liver, served with smoky bacon and mashed potatoes laced with sage. If you want to drop in for a drink and a look at that

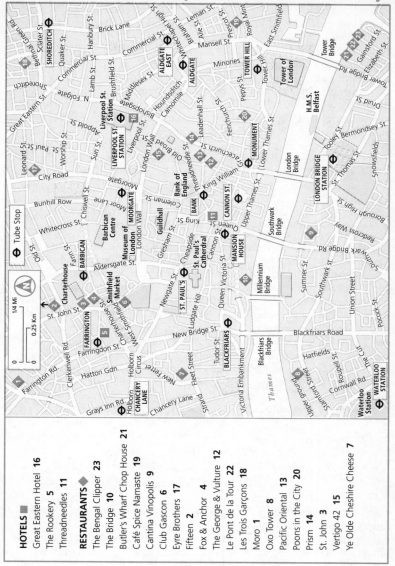

**HOTELS** ■
Great Eastern Hotel **16**
The Rookery **5**
Threadneedles **11**

**RESTAURANTS** ◆
The Bengal Clipper **23**
The Bridge **10**
Butler's Wharf Chop House **21**
Café Spice Namaste **19**
Cantina Vinopolis **9**
Club Gascon **6**
Eyre Brothers **17**
Fifteen **2**
Fox & Anchor **4**
The George & Vulture **12**
Le Pont de la Tour **22**
Les Trois Garçons **18**
Moro **1**
Oxo Tower **8**
Pacific Oriental **13**
Poons in the City **20**
Prism **14**
St. John **3**
Vertigo 42 **15**
Ye Olde Cheshire Cheese **7**

view, you can order dim sum at the bar. The house wine, Nutbourne Sussex Reserve, comes from Gladwin's own Sussex vineyard, and has won several awards. Desserts feature the chef's own homemade ice cream and iced lemon vodka parfait.

1 Paul's Walk, EC4. ℂ **020/7236-0000**. Reservations required. Main courses £12–£14 ($22–$26). AE, MC, V. Mon–Fri 11am–10pm. Tube: St. Paul's.

**Café Spice Namaste** ⋆⋆ INDIAN   This is our favorite Indian restaurant in London, where the competition is stiff. It's cheerfully housed in a landmark

Victorian hall near Tower Bridge, just east of the Tower of London. The Parsi chef, Cyrus Todiwala, is a former resident of Goa (a Portuguese territory absorbed by India long ago), where he learned many of his culinary secrets. He concentrates on southern and northern Indian dishes, with a strong Portuguese influence. Chicken and lamb are prepared a number of ways, from mild to spicy-hot. As a novelty, Todiwala occasionally even offers a menu of emu dishes; when marinated, the meat is rich and spicy and evocative of lamb. Emu is not the only dining oddity here. Ever have ostrich gizzard kebab, alligator tikka, or minced moose, bison, or blue boar? Many patrons journey here just for the complex chicken curry known as *xacutti*. Lambs' livers and kidneys are also cooked in the tandoor. A weekly specialty menu complements the long list of regional dishes. The homemade chutneys alone are worth the trip; our favorite is made with kiwi. All dishes come with fresh vegetables and Indian bread. With its exotic ingredients, often time-consuming preparation, impeccable service, warm hospitality, and spicy but subtle flavors, this is no Indian dive.

16 Prescot St., E1. © 020/7488-9242. Reservations required. Main courses £12–£16 ($22–$30). AE, DC, MC, V. Mon–Fri noon–3pm and 6:15–10:30pm; Sat 6:30–10:15pm. Tube: Tower Hill.

**Club Gascon** ★★ *Finds* FRENCH This slice of southwestern France serves such tasty treats as foie gras, Armagnac, and duck confit. Chef Pascal Aussignac is all the rage in London, ever since he opened his bistro next to the meat market in Smithfield. He dedicates his bistro to his favorite ingredient: foie gras. Foie gras appears in at least nine different incarnations on the menu, and most of the first-class ingredients are imported from France. His menu is uniquely divided into these categories—"The Salt Route," "Ocean," and "Kitchen Garden." The best way to dine here is to arrive in a party of four or five and share the small dishes, each harmoniously balanced and full of flavor. Each dish is accompanied by a carefully selected glass of wine. After a foie gras pig-out, proceed to such main courses as a heavenly quail served with pear and rosemary honey. A cassoulet of morels and truffles transforms a plain but perfectly cooked steak. To finish an absolutely elegant repast—dare we call it too rich—there is a selection of "puds," as the British say, ranging from strawberries with basil sorbet to a confit of rhubarb and sherry vinegar. If those don't interest you, opt for a moist almond tart with a biting shot of Granny Smith juice.

57 West Smithfield, EC1. © 020/7796-0600. Reservations required. Fixed-price 5-course menu £38 ($70). Main courses £7–£16 ($13–$30). AE, MC, V. Mon–Fri noon–2pm; Mon–Thurs 7–10pm; Sat 7–10:30pm. Tube: Barbican.

**Pacific Oriental** PACIFIC RIM Only a 10-minute walk from Liverpool Street, this is a fashionable brasserie, bar, and brewery, with a light, airy atmosphere enhanced by vibrant colors. The main part of the restaurant, Mezzanine, offers innovative Asian dishes with certain European overtones. Downstairs is a brasserie with slightly more exotic flavors. Both places serve market-fresh produce. At the traditional copper-clad brew house, beer is dispensed from tanks. The beers of choice here are Pacific Pilsner and Pacific Bishops. This place is ideal for a good lunch when you're touring the City. Start with such tantalizing appetizers as clam and spring onion broth with Thai asparagus, or tartare of halibut with a tomato and lime sorbet. Delightful main courses feature roasted black cod with oysters, mushrooms, Japanese artichokes, and Asian pesto, or else specialties from the grill, perhaps filet of ostrich with a chili-lime dressing.

1 Bishops Gate, EC2. © 020/7621-9988. Reservations required at lunch. Main courses £12–£20 ($22–$37). AE, DC, DISC, MC, V. Mon–Fri noon–3pm and 6–9pm. Tube: Bank Station.

**Poons in the City** ✸ CHINESE   Since 1992, Poons has operated this branch in the City, less than a 5-minute walk from the Tower of London. The restaurant is modeled on the Luk Yew Tree House in Hong Kong. Main courses feature crispy aromatic duck, prawns with cashew nuts, and barbecued pork. Poons's famous *lap yuk soom* (like Cantonese tacos) includes finely chopped wind-dried bacon. Special dishes can be ordered on 24 hours' notice. At the end of the L-shaped restaurant is an 80-seat fast-food area and takeout counter that's accessible from Mark Lane. The menu changes every 2 weeks.

2 Minster Pavement, Minster Court, Mincing Lane, EC3. ✆ 020/7626-0126. Reservations recommended for lunch. Fixed-price lunch and dinner £15–£31 ($28–$57); a la carte main courses £6–£10 ($11–$19); fast-food main dishes £5.50–£7 ($10–$13). AE, DC, MC, V. Mon–Fri noon–10:30pm. Tube: Tower Hill or Monument.

## INEXPENSIVE

**Fox and Anchor** ✸ *Finds* TRADITIONAL BRITISH   For British breakfast at its best, try this place, which has been serving traders from the nearby Smithfield meat market since 1898. Breakfasts are gargantuan, especially if you order the "Full House"—a plate with at least eight items, including sausage, bacon, kidneys, eggs, beans, black pudding, and fried bread, along with unlimited tea or coffee, toast, and jam. Add a Black Velvet (champagne with Guinness), or the more fashionable Bucks Fizz (orange juice and champagne, known in the U.S. as a mimosa). The Fox and Anchor is noted for its fine English ales, which are all available at breakfast. Butchers from the market, spotted with blood, still appear, as do nurses getting off their shifts, and clerks and City tycoons who've been making millions all night.

115 Charterhouse St., EC1. ✆ 020/7253-5075. Reservations recommended. "Full house" breakfast £7.50 ($14). Main courses £7.50–£15 ($14–$28). AE, MC, V. Mon–Fri from 7am, closing time varies from 8–10pm. Tube: Barbican or Farringdon.

**The George & Vulture** TRADITIONAL BRITISH   Dickens enthusiasts seek out this Pickwickian place. Founded in 1660, it claims that it's "probably" the world's oldest tavern, referring to an inn that operated on this spot in 1175. While they no longer put up overnight guests here, The George & Vulture does serve English lunches (but no dinners) in a warren of small dining rooms scattered over the tavern's three floors. Besides the daily specials, the menu includes a mixed grill, a loin chop, a lamb-based hot pot, and a grilled Dover-sole filet with tartar sauce. Potatoes and buttered cabbage are the standard vegetables, and the apple tart is always reliable. The system is to arrive and give your name, then retire to any of the three different pubs on the same narrow street for a drink (Simpson's Bar, the Cross Key's Pub, or the Jamaican pub across the way); you're "fetched" when your table is ready. After, be sure to explore the mazes of pubs, shops, wine houses, and other old buildings near the tavern. The Pickwick Club, a private literary group, meets here four times a year for reunion dinners. Cedric Dickens, the octogenarian great-great-grandson of Charles Dickens, heads the literary club.

3 Castle Court, Cornhill, EC3. ✆ 020/7626-9710. Reservations accepted before 12:45pm. Main courses £8–£15 ($15–$28). AE, DC, MC, V. Mon–Fri noon–2:45pm. Tube: Bank.

**Vertigo 42** ✸ *Finds* CONTINENTAL/SEAFOOD/TAPAS   This is a relatively unknown little spot, on the 42nd floor of Tower 42 in the heart of the City, that offers one of London's most spectacular views. After securing a special security pass downstairs, you're taken to Vertigo 42 in a high-speed elevator. Dining here is like being on top of the world, as you take in the views of London that eagles enjoy, from the Canada Tower to the Law Courts. We prefer to come here as the sun sets on London and the city lights begin to twinkle. Blue binoculars are provided if you want a more intimate view of the cityscape. Six champagnes are served by the glass, and there's an array of well-presented, very tasty food, ranging from lobster to Iranian fresh caviar to excellent sushi. The organic smoked salmon in salsa verde is a delight, and the fresh Cornish crab arrives from the West Country of England. You must be 18 to patronize this restaurant.

Tower 42, Old Broad St., EC2. ℂ 020/7877-7842. Reservations required. Main courses £9.50–£17 ($18–$31); tapas £7.50–£12 ($14–$22); fixed-price lunch menu £15 ($28). AE, DC, MC, V. Mon–Fri 11:45am–3pm and 5–10pm. Closed weekends. Tube: Liverpool St.

**Ye Olde Cheshire Cheese** *Kids* TRADITIONAL BRITISH   The foundation of this carefully preserved building was laid in the 13th century, and it holds the most famous of the old City chophouses and pubs. Established in 1667, it claims to be the spot where Dr. Samuel Johnson (who lived nearby) entertained admirers with his acerbic wit. Charles Dickens and other literary lions also patronized the place. Later, many of the ink-stained journalists and scandal-mongers of 19th- and early-20th-century Fleet Street made it their watering hole. You'll find five bars and two dining rooms here. The house specialties include "Ye Famous Pudding" (steak, kidney, mushrooms, and game) and Scottish roast beef with Yorkshire pudding and horseradish sauce. Sandwiches, salads, and standby favorites such as steak and kidney pie are also available, as are dishes such as Dover sole. The Cheshire is the best and safest venue to introduce your children to a British pub.

Wine Office Court, 145 Fleet St., EC4. ℂ 020/7353-6170. Main courses £7.50–£10 ($14–$19). AE, DC, MC, V. Meals: Mon–Fri noon–9:30pm; Sat noon–2:30pm and 6–9:30pm; Sun noon–2:30pm. Drinks and bar snacks: Mon–Fri 11:30am–11pm. Tube: St. Paul's or Blackfriars.

# CLERKENWELL
## MODERATE

**Moro** *★★* NORTH AFRICAN/SPANISH   If you've been hearing about all the trendy restaurants in Clerkenwell and want to try one, make it Moro. With its streamlined interior and its kitchen in open view, it attracts the chic and fashionable. The aroma of delicious meats on the charcoal grill will attract carnivores, but vegetarian meals are also available. At the long zinc bar, you can fill up on some of the city's best tapas, or a Maghreb-inspired dinner of impeccable quality. The restaurant's recipes were inspired by the epoch when Arab culture met European culture in southern Spain (8th–15th c.). From the charcoal grill emerges a delectable veal chop with spicy chorizo and cabbage, and the leg of lamb is tantalizingly prepared with okra and coriander. The quail on flatbread makes the angels weep. Begin with the lusty white-bean soup. Extra-fresh products go into the creation of these dishes, and no seasoning or flavor overpowers.

34–36 Exmouth Market, EC1. ℂ 020/7833-8336. Reservations recommended. Main courses £14–£18 ($26–$32). AE, DC, MC, V. Mon–Fri noon–3pm; Mon–Sat 7–10:30pm. Tube: Farringdon.

**St. John** *★★* MODERN BRITISH   Located in a former smokehouse just north of Smithfield Market, this air-conditioned, canteenlike dining room is the restaurant of choice for carnivores. It is a showcase for the talents of owner/chef Fergus Henderson, a leader in the offal movement, which advocates the use of all animal parts in cuisine. In true British tradition, he uses the entire animal—we're talking neck, trotters, tail, liver, heart, the works. It's called nose-to-tail cookery.

Don't think you'll be served warmed-over haggis: The food is excellent and flavor-packed. There's an earthiness and simplicity to this cuisine that's unequaled in London. The grilled lamb chops, garnished with sliced pig's tongue, bacon, salsify, and dandelion, are matchless. Roast bone marrow appears with a parsley salad, and pork chops are called pig chops. It's hard these days to find an eel, bacon, and clam stew, but you'll discover one here. French wines wash it all down. Desserts run to puddings such as vanilla-rice or dates and walnuts with butterscotch. Dessert oddity? Where else can you get a good goat curd, marc (the product of grapes and their seeds after pressing), and rhubarb concoction these days? The breads served here can also be purchased in an on-site bakery.

26 St. John St., EC1. © **020/7251-0848**. Reservations required. Main courses £15–£19 ($27–$35). AE, DC, DISC, MC, V. Mon–Fri noon–3pm; Mon–Sat 6pm–midnight. Tube: Farringdon.

## SHOREDITCH
### EXPENSIVE

**Fifteen** ★★ MODERN BRITISH    When James Oliver, author of *The Naked Chef,* opened this restaurant, it created a media blitz. Oliver chronicled his trials and tribulations on a six-part TV show on the Food Network called "Jamie's Kitchen." Oliver takes "disadvantaged" young people and trains them from scratch in just 4 months before turning them loose as your chef for the day, with all the profits going to charity. In a redbrick Victorian building, convenient for touring the trendy Hoxton Square art galleries, the decor is contemporary and clean cut, not unduly gussied up.

What to expect in the way of food? Although a bit hyped in the media, it's quite sumptuous, and has won the praise of London's battle-toughened food critics such as Fay Maschier on *The Evening Standard,* who felt that Jamie should be "knighted" for his efforts. She claimed that Fifteen serves some of the best dishes she's sampled in a long time. Even Michelin-starred chefs have shown up here, raving about the dishes, especially the succulent pastas. Our party recently delighted in such dishes as scallop crudo with Japanese yuzu lime, pomegranates, crispy ginger, fresh coconut, and herb shoots. The filet of McDuff beef poached in a Barossa Merlot is one of the most gorgeous filets you are likely to encounter in London. You can even drop in for breakfast, which is about the only time you're guaranteed a seat; dinner reservations must be made well in advance.

15 Westland Place, N1. © **020/7251-1515**. Main courses £11–£32 ($20–$59). Breakfast £2–£10 ($4–$19). Mon–Sat 8–10:30am, noon–2:15pm, and 6:30–9:30pm; bar Mon–Sat 11am–11pm. AE, MC, V. Tube: Old Street.

**Les Trois Garçons** ★★ *Finds* FRENCH    As trendy London moves east, and once-seedy districts like Shoreditch (north of the City) become cutting-edge, eye-popping restaurants like Les Trois Garçons are bound to follow. The three "garçons" of the restaurant's name are Hassan Abdullah, Michel Lassere, and Stefan Karlson. They took this pub, which opened early in Victoria's reign, and turned it into one of the hottest reservations for London's young, fashionable set. This fun, campy restaurant lies among a row of garages and secondhand shops. You can't miss the flaming torches guarding the entrance. Inside, stuffed animals, including a British bulldog, are adorned with glittering tiaras. That's Quentin the crocodile balanced on top of the baby grand. In such a setting, the cuisine could be second to the entertainment. But, happily, the restaurant serves an excellent and modern French menu, beautifully prepared and making full use of first-rate ingredients. The fish soup with *rouille* (a creamy garlic-and-red-pepper sauce) is an excellent starter, as are the sautéed tiger prawns with crushed herbs, Jersey potatoes, and tomato and garlic sauce with a hint of coconut. For main courses, we've enjoyed roasted wild sea bass filet with baby clams, cherry tomatoes, and baby spinach; grilled Dover sole, globe artichokes, button onions, baby turnips, tomato concasse, and saffron sauce; and oven-roasted free-range chicken wrapped in Bayonne ham, celeriac mash, zucchini flowers, baby carrots, and Dijon mustard sauce. For dessert, try one of the freshly made tarts of the day.

1 Club Row, E1. ℂ 020/7613-1924. Reservations essential. Main courses £18–£23 ($32–$43). AE, MC, V. Mon–Sat 7–10:30pm. Tube: Liverpool St.

## MODERATE

**Eyre Brothers** ⊛ *Finds* PORTUGUESE   At night more and more of trendy London is flocking to Shoreditch. Their goal is often this restaurant, inaugurated by David Eyre, who virtually revolutionized pub grub in London at the dawn of the millennium, but in another location. Today this setting in Shoreditch is more elegant and refined than his old quarters, containing mahogany paneling and elegantly appointed tables. The chef is often inspired by visits to Portugal. Sometimes dishes are inspired by former colonies such as Mozambique. A typical example of that would be tiger prawns piri-piri (in a hot chili marinade). Succulent T-bones are grilled on the open fire here as in the style of Lisbon. The fresh catch of the day, perhaps yellowfin tuna, is also grilled to one's request. The house specialty is a marvelous banquet of roast suckling pig flavored to perfection. For starters, we'd recommend the chicken and rice soup given added zest by lemon and fresh mint. A conceit—but a delicious one—is the basil and mascarpone ice cream.

70 Leonard St., EC16. ℂ 020/7613-5346. Reservations required. Main courses £13–£19 ($24–$35). AE, DC, MC, V. Mon–Fri noon–3pm and 6:30–11pm; Sat 7–11pm. Tube: Old Street.

## DOCKLANDS
### EXPENSIVE

**Butler's Wharf Chop House** ⊛ TRADITIONAL BRITISH   Of the four restaurants housed in Butler's Wharf (other Butler's Wharf restaurants are listed in this chapter), this one is the closest to Tower Bridge. It maintains its commitment to moderate prices. The Chop House was modeled after a large boathouse, with banquettes, lots of exposed wood, flowers, candles, and windows overlooking Tower Bridge and the Thames. Lunchtime crowds include workers from the city's financial district; evening crowds are made up of friends dining together leisurely.

Dishes are largely adaptations of British recipes: fish and chips with mushy peas; steak-and-kidney-pudding with oysters; roast rump of lamb with garlic mash and rosemary; and grilled pork filet with apples, chestnuts, and cider sauce. After, there might be a chocolate and caramel tart. The bar offers such choices as Theakston's best bitter, several English wines, and a half-dozen French clarets by the jug.

36E Shad Thames, SE1. ℂ 020/7403-3403. Reservations recommended. Fixed-price 2-course lunch £20 ($37); fixed-price 3-course lunch £24 ($44); dinner main courses £13–£25 ($23–$46). AE, DC, MC, V. Mon–Sun noon–3pm; Mon–Sat 6–11pm. Tube: Tower Hill or London Bridge.

**Le Pont de la Tour** ⊛ INTERNATIONAL   At the edge of the Thames near Tower Bridge, the Butler's Wharf complex holds condos, rental apartments, offices, and an assortment of food and wine shops collectively known as the Gastrodome. Built in the mid–19th century as a warehouse, it's now another Terence Conran playland. From its windows, diners and shoppers enjoy sweeping views of some of the densest river traffic in Europe.

The **Bar and Grill's** live piano music (on evenings and weekends) together with a wide choice of wines and cocktails creates one of the most convivial atmospheres in the area. Although such dishes as ham and foie gras terrine, and langoustines mayonnaise are featured, the culinary star is a heaping platter of fresh shellfish—perfect when shared with a friend, accompanied by a bottle of wine.

In bold contrast is the large, more formal room known simply as **The Restaurant.** Filled with burr oak furniture and decorated with framed lithographs of early-20th-century Parisian cafe society, it offers excellent food and a polite but undeniable English reserve. The menu may list such temptations as roast rabbit wrapped in herbs with pancetta and a mustard vinaigrette, or whole roast-buttered lobster with herbs. One especially winning selection is best end of lamb, with a black olive and herb crust in a red-pepper sauce. All the fish is excellent, but none better than the Dover sole, which can be ordered grilled or meunière.

36D Shad Thames, Butler's Wharf, SE1. ✆ 020/7403-8403. Reservations highly recommended in the Bar and Grill; recommended in The Restaurant. Bar and Grill main courses £14–£20 ($26–$37); The Restaurant main courses £42–£45 ($77–$83). AE, DC, MC, V. The Restaurant: daily noon–3pm, Mon–Sat 6–11pm; Bar and Grill: daily noon–3pm and 6–11pm. Tube: Tower Hill or London Bridge.

## MODERATE

**The Bengal Clipper** ⭐ INDIAN   This former spice warehouse by the Thames serves what it calls "India's most remarkable dishes." The likable and often animated restaurant is outfitted with cream-colored walls, tall columns, and modern artwork inspired by the Moghul Dynasty's depictions of royal figures, soaring trees, and well-trained elephants. Seven windows afford sweeping views over the industrialized Thames-side neighborhood, and live piano music plays in the background. The cuisine includes many vegetarian choices derived from the former Portuguese colony of Goa and the once-English colony of Bengal. There is a zestiness and spice to the cuisine, but it's never overpowering. The chefs keep the menu fairly short so that all ingredients can be purchased fresh every day.

A tasty specialty is stuffed *murgh masala,* a tender breast of chicken with potatoes, onions, apricots, and almonds, cooked with yogurt and served with a delectable curry sauce. The perfectly cooked duckling (off the bone) comes in a tangy sauce with a citrus bite. One of the finest dishes we tasted in North India is served here and has lost nothing in the transfer: marinated lamb simmered in cream with cashew nuts, seasoned with fresh ginger. One of the best offerings from the Goan repertoire is the *karkra chop,* a spicy patty of minced crab blended with mashed potatoes and peppered with Goan spices.

Shad Thames, Butler's Wharf, SE1. ✆ 020/7357-9001. Reservations recommended. Main courses £10–£25 ($19–$46); set menu from £10 ($19); Sunday buffet £7.75 ($14). AE, DC, MC, V. Daily noon–2:30pm and 6–11:30pm. Tube: Tower Hill.

## CANARY WHARF
### MODERATE

**Sri Nam** ⭐ *Finds* THAI   Celebrity chef Ken Hom is the chief exponent of Thai cookery in London, and even the Thai community agrees that he's the best. Some of his culinary secrets are revealed in his book, *Foolproof Thai Cookery.* At Canary Wharf, Sri Nam brings an authentic and very spicy (read: hot) cuisine to foodies who like to dine on the Thames. There's a buzz-filled cafe-bar on the ground floor and a more formal restaurant upstairs. The Thai cuisine served here is a fusion of modern with traditional, the latter in theory the type served to the "King of Siam." The Asian bar on the ground floor serves drinks from the Far East, plus beers and wines. The ground-floor bar also caters to those seeking speedy lunches or an early supper.

Climb the sweeping staircase for more serious dishes served against a backdrop of rich, dark woods, lush silks, and bright lanterns. The classic star of the menu is *pad thai,* a delightful stir-fry of noodles with eggs, vegetables, and bean sprouts, garnished with ground peanuts and fresh coriander. Served here (and rarely seen on other London menus) is lamb masaman, a curry from south Thailand, featuring lamb flavored with peanuts and potatoes. The signature dish—and is it ever good—is Bangkok's hot green curry with chiles, coconut milk, bamboo shoots, baby eggplant, and lime leaves.

N. Colonnade, 10 Cabot Sq., Canary Wharf, E14. 𝄞 020/7715-9515. Reservations required. Main courses £8–£18 ($15–$33). AE, DC, MC, V. Mon–Sat 11:30am–3pm and 6–10pm; Sat noon–9pm. Tube: Canary Wharf.

## SOUTH BANK
### EXPENSIVE

Oxo Tower Restaurant ✦ ASIAN/INTERNATIONAL    In the South Bank complex, on the eighth floor of the Art Deco Oxo Tower Wharf, you'll find this dining sensation. It's operated by the department store Harvey Nichols. Down the street from the newly rebuilt Globe Theatre this 140-seat restaurant could be visited for its view alone, but the cuisine is also stellar. You'll enjoy a sweeping view of St. Paul's Cathedral and the City, all the way to the Houses of Parliament. The decor is chic 1930s style.

The cuisine, under chef David Sharland, is rich and prepared with finesse. Menu items change based on the season and the market. Count on a modern interpretation of British cookery, as well as the English classics. The fish is incredibly fresh here. The whole sea bass for two is delectable, as is the roast rump of lamb with split pea, mint purée, and balsamic vinegar sauce. Recently, we were impressed with the roast filet of plaice with olive oil, and truffle cabbage cream, and the roast squab with buttered cabbage and a foie-gras sauce.

Barge House St., South Bank, SE1. 𝄞 020/7803-3888. Main courses £10–£18 ($19–$33); fixed-price lunch £20 ($37). AE, DC, MC, V. Mon–Fri noon–3pm; Mon–Sat 6–11:30pm; Sat–Sun noon–2:30pm; Sun 6–10:30pm. Tube: Blackfriars or Waterloo.

---

### ⟨Kids⟩  Family-Friendly Restaurants

**Hard Rock Cafe** (Mayfair; p. 175)    This is a great place for kids old enough to busy themselves with rock-and-roll memorabilia as they wait for their familiar burgers, fries, and salads with Thousand Island dressing.

**Porter's English Restaurant** (Covent Garden & the Strand; p. 160)    This restaurant serves traditional English meals that most kids love—especially the pies, stews, and steamed "spuds." They'll get a kick out of ordering the wonderfully named bubble-and-squeak and mushy peas.

**Royal China** (Paddington & Bayswater; p. 195)    If there's a dim sum lover in your family, head for this eatery. We saw a young brother and sister devouring a dish of seafood golden cups—stir-fried scallops, prawns, water chestnuts, and mushrooms in crispy puff pastry.

**Simpson's-in-the-Strand** (Covent Garden & the Strand; p. 159)    If your offspring is an aspiring Henry VIII, take him here for the best roasts in London, including tender roast sirloin of beef. For dessert, he might be introduced to such English favorites as treacle rolls.

**Ye Olde Cheshire Cheese** (the City; p. 150)    Fleet Street's famous chophouse, established in 1667, is an eternal favorite. If "ye famous pudding" turns your kids off, sandwiches and roasts will tempt them.

## MODERATE

**Cantina Vinopolis** *(Finds)* CONTINENTAL    Not far from the re-created Globe Theatre of Shakespeare's heyday, this place has been called a "Walk-Through Wine Atlas." In the revitalized Bankside area, south of the Thames near Southwark Cathedral, this bricked, walled, and high-vaulted brasserie was converted from long-abandoned Victorian railway arches. Inside you can visit both the Vinopolis Wine Gallery and the Cantina Restaurant. Although many come here just to drink the wine, the food is prepared with quality ingredients (very fresh), and the menu is sensibly priced. Start with a bit of heaven like the pea and ham soup. Dishes are full of flavor and never overcooked. Pan-fried snapper, with crushed new potatoes and salsa verde, won us over. A rump of lamb was tender and perfectly flavored and served with a polenta cake. Many of the dishes have the good country taste of a trattoria you'd find in the country-side of southern Italy. Naturally, the wine list is the biggest in the U.K.

1 Bank End, London Bridge, SE1. *(C)* 020/7940-8333. Reservations required. Main courses £14–£16 ($26–$30). AE, DC, MC, V. Mon–Sat noon–3pm and 6–10:45pm; Sun noon–3:45pm. Tube: London Bridge.

## 3 The West End

## BLOOMSBURY
### VERY EXPENSIVE

**Pied-à-Terre** *(R)* FRENCH    This foodie heaven understates its decor in favor of an intense focus on its subtle, sophisticated cuisine. You'll dine in a strictly mini-malist room, where gray-and pale-pink walls complement metal furniture and focused lighting that reveals a collection of modern art. France is the inspiration for the impressive wine list and some of the cuisine. The menu changes with the sea-sons but might include halibut filets with queen scallops and caramelized endive; roasted partridge with pear; and the house specialty, a ballotine (stuffed and rolled into a bundle) of duck confit. If you're not dining with a vegetarian, braised pigs' head is another specialty. Our favorite item on the menu? Sea bass with vichyssoise (a thick soup of potatoes, leeks, and cream) and caviar sauce. The food is beauti-fully presented on hand-painted plates with lush patterns. Prix-fixe menus only.

34 Charlotte St., W1. *(C)* 020/7636-1178. Reservations recommended. Fixed-price 3-course lunch £22–£35 ($40–$65), 3-course dinner £45–£60 ($83–$111); 8-course tasting menu £65 ($120). AE, MC, V. Tues–Fri noon–2:30pm (last order); Mon–Sat 7–11pm. Closed last week of Dec and 1st week of Jan. Tube: Goodge St.

### EXPENSIVE

**Archipelago** *(RR)* FRENCH/THAI    This cozy restaurant is a celebrity favorite, attracting the likes of Madonna and Hugh Hefner when they are in town. Archipelago is definitely on the see-and-be-seen circuit. Media darling Michael Von Hruschka has decorated the restaurant in a whimsical style, with everything from birdcages to a Buddha serving as props. There are precious touches, such as the drink list written on delicate paper and inserted in an ostrich eggshell. Everything is presented in exquisite boxes, and even the bill comes in a "book." Amazingly, with all the attention paid to the environment, the cuisine does not suffer in ingredients or preparation. Launch your repast with a coconut-and-lemon-grass soup or the most delectable small-carrot spring rolls. Vegetable couscous and fish-and-banana risotto are delectable, and tiramisu is given an original touch with the addition of ginger wine.

110 Whitfield St., W1. *(C)* 020/7383-3346. Reservations required as far in advance as possible. Main courses £13–£20 ($24–$37). Fixed-price 3-course lunch menu £50 ($93). MC, V. Mon–Fri noon–2:30pm; Mon–Sat 6–10:30pm. Tube: Goodge St.

# Where to Dine in the West End & Theatre District

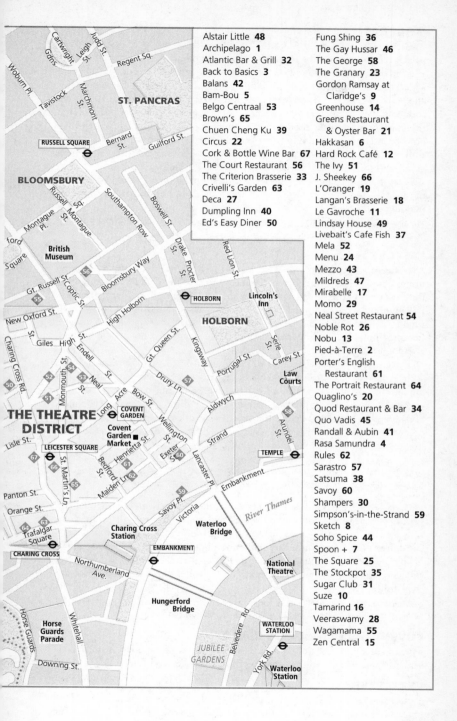

## MODERATE

**Back to Basics** ★★ SEAFOOD    Ursula Higgs's bistro draws discerning palates seeking some of the freshest seafood in London. When the weather's fair, you can dine outside. Otherwise, retreat inside to a vaguely Parisian setting with a blackboard menu and checked tablecloths. The fish is served in large portions, and you can safely forgo an appetizer unless you're ravenous. More than a dozen seafood dishes are offered; the fish can be broiled, grilled, baked, or poached, but frying is not permitted. In other words, this is no fish and chippie. Start with a bowl of tasty, plump mussels or sea bass flavored with fresh basil and chili oil. Brill appears with green peppercorn butter, and plaice is jazzed up with fresh ginger and soy sauce. For the meat eater, there is a T-bone steak or roast chicken. Also try the pastas and the vegetarian dishes. Freshly made salads accompany most meals, and an excellent fish soup is offered daily. For dessert, try the bread pudding or the freshly made apple pie.

21A Foley St., W1. ✆ 020/7436-2181. Reservations recommended. Main courses £10–£16 ($19–$30). AE, DC, MC, V. Daily noon–3pm and 6–10pm. Tube: Oxford Circus or Goodge St.

## INEXPENSIVE

**The Court Restaurant** ★ *Value* CONTINENTAL    Nothing in London brings culture and cuisine together quite as much as this gem of a restaurant on the sixth floor of the British Museum, with views opening onto Norman Fester's millennium development, the Great Court. The restaurant overlooks the famous round Reading Room and nestles close to the spectacular glass-and-steel roof. For museum buffs, it's the perfect venue for morning coffee, hot or cold lunches, afternoon tea, or a dinner.

The chef, Mandula Sachdev, turns out a succulent menu of familiar favorites such as coq au vin (chicken casserole in red wine), sesame-seed-coated Scottish salmon, or savory lamb and mint sausages with a "mash" of parsnips. You can watch the cooks as they prepare the market-fresh dishes for the day. The most blissful ending to a meal here is the chocolate truffle cake, which is really pure cocoa. The museum even serves its own beer, and it can compete with the product of any brewery.

The British Museum, Great Russell St., WC1. ✆ 020/7323-8978. Reservations required. Main courses £9.50–£13 ($18–$24). Fixed-price 2-course menu £11–£12 ($19–$21). AE, MC, V. Mon–Wed 11am–5pm; Thurs–Sat 11am–9pm; Sun 11am–5pm. Tube: Holborn, Tottenham Court Rd., or Russell Sq.

**Wagamama** JAPANESE    This noodle joint, in a basement just off New Oxford Street, is noisy and overcrowded, and you'll have to wait in line for a table. It calls itself a "non-destination food station" and caters to some 1,200 customers a day. Many dishes are built around ramen noodles with your choice of chicken, beef, or salmon. Try the tasty gyoza, light dumplings filled with vegetables or chicken. Vegetarian dishes are available, but skip the so-called Korean-style dishes.

4 Streatham St., WC1. ✆ 020/7323-9223. Reservations not accepted. Main courses £5.50–£11 ($10–$20). AE, MC, V. Mon–Sat noon–11pm; Sun 12:30–10pm. Tube: Tottenham Court Rd.

## COVENT GARDEN & THE STRAND

The restaurants in and around Covent Garden and the Strand are the most convenient choices when you're attending theaters in the West End.

## VERY EXPENSIVE

**Savoy Restaurant** ★★ MODERN BRITISH    Dinner at the Savoy Grill has long been a London tradition, attracting celebrities visiting the West End. But the room had gone stale. Under one of the country's premier chefs, Marcus Wareing, the old glory of the Grill has come back. Wareing has created a vibrant new restaurant while preserving tradition. The old carving trolley of English roasts has been done away with and an updated menu now rests in your hand. Even the decor has been brightened. Intensity of flavor and market-fresh ingredients characterize the new menu. For starters, go daring by ordering the caramelized calves' sweetbreads on pancetta with onion marmalade, or else the roasted hand-dived scallops with a fresh pea purée and a tomato confit. Gourmets along the Strand praise—and we concur—the crispy pavé of salmon with crushed new potatoes and lobster, or the pan-fried filet of John Dory with sautéed romaine lettuce and a parsnip purée. Meat and poultry dishes are still a strong point with the chefs, especially the braised Wiltshire pork belly with sautéed Jerusalem artichokes and the rump of Cornish lamb with cherry tomatoes and black olives.

The Strand, WC2. (℃ 020/7592-1600. Reservations required. Set lunch £30 ($56); pre-theater menu £30 ($56); prestige tasting menu £60 ($111); a la carte, a selection of 3 courses £50 ($93). AE, DC, MC, V. Mon–Fri noon–2:45pm and 5:45–11pm; Sat–Sun noon–3:30pm and 6–10:30pm. Tube: Charing Cross or Covent Garden.

## EXPENSIVE

**Neal Street Restaurant** ⋆ ITALIAN   This stylish restaurant offers an extravagant variety of mushrooms, truffles, and other fungi. It's operated by Turin-born Antonio Carluccio, an authority on the use of mushrooms from around the world. The brick walls of a turn-of-the-20th-century warehouse are hung with the works of such modern masters as Frank Stella and David Hockney. The restaurant operates an aperitif bar in the cellar, where prospective diners sometimes wait for a table. Between 10 and 20 of the world's most exotic mushrooms are available at any time, including an assortment of truffles. Imported seasonally from China, Tibet, Japan, France, and California, they pop up in such recipes as foie gras with balsamic sauce, wild-mushroom soup, pheasant consommé with morels and port, and tagliolini with truffle sauce. Equally appealing—but less expensive—is the venison ravioli with butter and sage, the pappardelle pasta with mixed funghi, the truffled egg tagliolini, and the black angel-hair pasta with seafood and bottarga (dried tuna roe). Service is attentive and polite and the ambience agreeable. The tiramisu is justifiably popular.

26 Neal St., WC2. (℃ 020/7836-8368. Reservations recommended. Main courses £15–£22 ($27–$40). Fixed-price lunch and pre-theater menu £21–£25 ($39–$46). AE, DC, MC, V. Mon–Sat noon–2:30pm and 6–11pm. Tube: Covent Garden.

**Rules** ⋆ TRADITIONAL BRITISH   If you're looking for London's most quintessentially British restaurant, eat here. London's oldest restaurant was established in 1798 as an oyster bar; today, the antler-filled Edwardian dining rooms exude nostalgia. You can order such classic dishes as Irish or Scottish oysters, jugged hare, and mussels. Game dishes are offered from mid-August to February or March, including wild Scottish salmon; wild sea trout; wild Highland red deer; and game birds like grouse, snipe, partridge, pheasant, and woodcock. As a finale, the "great puddings" continue to impress.

35 Maiden Lane, WC2. (℃ 020/7836-5314. Reservations recommended. Main courses £15–£21 ($28–$39). AE, DC, MC, V. Daily noon–11:30pm. Tube: Covent Garden.

**Simpson's-in-the-Strand** ⋆⋆ _Kids_ TRADITIONAL AND MODERN BRITISH   Simpson's is more of an institution than a restaurant. Long a family favorite with lots of large tables, it has been in business since 1828, and as a result of a recent £2 million ($3.7 million) renovation, it's now better than ever with its Adam paneling, crystal, and an army of grandly formal waiters (to whom nouvelle cuisine means anything after Henry VIII) serving traditional British fare.

Most diners agree that Simpson's serves the best roasts in London, an array that includes roast sirloin of beef, roast saddle of mutton with red-currant jelly, roast Aylesbury duckling, and steak, kidney, and mushroom pie. (Remember to tip the tailcoated carver.) For a pudding, you might order the treacle roll and custard or Stilton with vintage port. Simpson's also serves traditional breakfasts. The most popular one is "The Ten Deadly Sins": a plate of sausage; fried egg; streaky and back bacon; black pudding; lambs' kidneys; bubble-and-squeak; baked beans; lambs' liver; and fried bread, mushrooms, and tomatoes. That will certainly fortify you for the day.

100 the Strand (next to the Savoy Hotel), WC2. ℂ 020/7836-9112. Reservations required. Main courses £15–£25 ($28–$46); fixed-price pre-theater dinner £17–£21 ($31–$39); breakfast from £16 ($30). AE, DC, MC, V. Mon–Fri 7:15–10:30am; Mon–Sat 12:15–2:30pm and 5:30–10:45pm; Sun 6–8:30pm. Tube: Charing Cross or Embankment.

## MODERATE

**Belgo Centraal** BELGIAN   Chaos reigns supreme in this cavernous basement, where mussels marinières with frites, plus 100 Belgian beers, are the raison d'être. Take a freight elevator past the busy kitchen and into a converted cellar, divided into two large eating areas. One section is a beer hall seating about 250; the menu here is the same as in the restaurant, but you don't need reservations. The restaurant side has three nightly seatings: 5:30, 7:30, and 10pm. Between 5:30 and 8pm you can choose one of three fixed-price menus. Although heaps of fresh mussels are the big attraction, you can opt for fresh Scottish salmon, roast chicken, a perfectly done steak, or one of the vegetarian specialties. Gargantuan plates of wild boar sausages arrive with *stoemp*, Belgian mashed spuds and cabbage. Belgian stews, called *waterzooï*, are also served. With waiters in maroon monk's habits and black aprons barking orders into headset microphones, it's all a bit bizarre.

50 Earlham St., WC2. ℂ 020/7813-2233. Reservations required for the restaurant. Main courses £9–£12 ($17–$22); fixed-price menus £21–£26 ($38–$47). AE, DC, MC, V. Mon–Thurs noon–11pm; Fri–Sat noon–11:30pm; Sun noon–10:30pm. Closed Christmas. Tube: Covent Garden.

**Porter's English Restaurant** ★★ Kids TRADITIONAL BRITISH   The seventh earl of Bradford serves "real English food at affordable prices." He succeeds notably—and not just because Lady Bradford turned over her carefully guarded recipe for banana-and-ginger steamed pudding. This comfortable, two-storied restaurant is family friendly, informal, and lively. Porter's specializes in classic English pies, including Old English fish pie; lamb and apricot; and, of course, bangers and mash. Main courses are so generous—and accompanied by vegetables and side dishes—that you hardly need appetizers. They have also added grilled English fare to the menu, with sirloin and lamb steaks and marinated chicken. The puddings, including bread-and-butter pudding or steamed syrup sponge, are served hot or cold, with whipped cream or custard. The bar does quite a few exotic cocktails, as well as beers, wine, or English mead. A traditional English tea is also served from 2:30 to 5:30pm for £4.75 ($8.80) per person. Who knows? You may even bump into his Lordship.

17 Henrietta St., WC2. ℂ 020/7836-6466. Reservations recommended. Main courses £8.95–£13 ($17–$24); fixed-price menu £20 ($37). AE, DC, MC, V. Mon–Sat noon–11:30pm; Sun noon–10:30pm. Tube: Covent Garden or Leicester Sq.

## INEXPENSIVE

**The George** TRADITIONAL BRITISH   Go here for the atmosphere of old England. Although its half-timbered facade would make you believe it's older than it is, this pub has *only* been around since 1723, when it was built as a coffeehouse. Set on the Strand, at the lower end of Fleet Street opposite the Royal Courts of Justice, The George is a favorite of barristers, their clients, and the handful of journalists who haven't moved to other parts of London. The pub's illustrious history saw Samuel Johnson having his mail delivered here and Oliver Goldsmith enjoying many tankards of what eventually became draught Bass. Today, the setting seems only slightly changed, as much of the original architecture is still intact. Hot and cold platters, including bangers and mash, fish and chips, steak-and-kidney pie, and lasagna, are served from a food counter at the back of the pub. Additional seating is available in the basement, where a headless cavalier is said to haunt the same premises where he enjoyed his liquor in an earlier (and less headless) day.

213 the Strand, WC2. ℂ **020/7427-0941**. Main courses £5.50–£8 ($10–$15). AE, MC, V. Mon–Fri 11am–11pm; Sat noon–3pm. Tube: Temple.

**Sarastro** ★ CYPRIOT/TURKISH   The setting here makes you feel like you're in the prop room of an opera house. As the manager says, "We're the show after the show." The decor is sort of neo-Ottoman, and the cuisine celebrates the bounty of the Mediterranean, especially Turkey and Cyprus. In a Victorian building behind the Theatre Royal, the restaurant is decorated with battered urns, old lamps, fading lampshades, and knickknacks—an old Turkish curiosity-shop look. Ten opera boxes adorn three sides of the restaurant; the royal box is the most desired. The restaurant takes its name from a character in Mozart's *The Magic Flute*. Live opera performances are staged from time to time. Launch your meal with delights like asparagus in red-wine sauce or fresh grilled sardines. Fresh fish is the way to go for your main course, especially river trout or grilled halibut. A zesty favorite is lamb Anatolian style with carrots, zucchini, and shallots. We're also fond of the well-seasoned lamb meatballs. A good-tasting specialty is chicken Sarastro, made with walnuts and raisins.

126 Drury Lane, WC2. ℂ **020/7836-0101**. Reservations required. Main courses £8.50–£15 ($16–$28). Fixed-price menu £18–£24 ($32–$43); pre-theater menu £10 ($19). AE, DC, MC, V. Daily noon–midnight. Tube: Covent Garden.

## PICCADILLY CIRCUS & LEICESTER SQUARE

Piccadilly Circus and Leicester Square lie at the doorstep of the West End theaters. All the choices below (along with those in the "Covent Garden & the Strand" and "Soho" sections) are good candidates for dining before or after a show.

### EXPENSIVE

**Fung Shing** ★★ CANTONESE   In a city where the competition is stiff, Fung Shing emerges as London's finest Cantonese restaurant. Firmly established as a culinary landmark, it dazzles with classic and nouvelle Cantonese dishes. Look for the seasonal specials. Some of the dishes may be a bit experimental, notably stir-fried fresh milk with scrambled egg white, but you'll feel right at home with the soft-shell crab sautéed in a light batter and served with tiny rings of red-hot chile and deep-fried garlic. Chinese gourmets come here for the fried intestines; you may prefer the hotpot of stewed duck with yam. The spicy sea bass and the stir-fried crispy chicken are worthy choices. There are more than 150 dishes from which to choose and most are moderate in price.

15 Lisle St., WC2. ℂ **020/7437-1539**. Reservations required. Main courses £10–£26 ($19–$48); fixed-price menus £17–£34 ($31–$63). AE, DC, MC, V. Daily noon–11:30pm. Tube: Leicester Sq.

**J. Sheekey** ★ SEAFOOD  British culinary tradition lives on at this fish joint, long a favorite of West End actors. The jellied eels that delighted Laurence Olivier and Vivien Leigh are still here, along with an array of fresh oysters from the coasts of Ireland and Brittany, plus that Victorian favorite, fried whitebait. Sheekey's fish pie is still on the menu, as is Dover sole. The old "mushy" peas still appear, but the chefs also offer the likes of steamed organic sea beet. Opt for the traditional dishes or specials based on the fresh catch of the day. The double chocolate pudding soufflé is a delight, and many favorite puddings remain.

28–32 St. Martin's Court, WC2. ℂ **020/7240-2565.** Reservations recommended. Main courses £10–£31 ($19–$57). AE, DC, MC, V. Mon–Sat noon–3pm and 5:30pm–midnight; Sun noon–3:30pm and 6pm–midnight. Tube: Leicester Sq.

## MODERATE

**Dumpling Inn** CHINESE  Despite its cutesy name, this cool, elegant restaurant serves a delectable style of Peking Mandarin cuisine that dates back almost 3,000 years. The cooking owes some of its piquancy to various Mongolian ingredients, which are well represented in the restaurant's savory stew, called "hotpot." Regulars come for the shark-fin soup; the beef in oyster sauce; the seaweed; the sesame-seed prawns on toast; the duck with chile and black-bean sauce; and the fried, sliced fish. The specialty is dumplings, and you can make a meal from the dim sum list. Portions aren't large, so order as many dishes as you'd like to sample. Chinese tea is extra. Service is leisurely, so don't dine here before a theater date.

15a Gerrard St., W1. ℂ **020/7437-2567.** Reservations recommended. Main courses £8–£18 ($15–$33); fixed-price lunch or dinner £15–£30 ($28–$56). AE, MC, V. Sun–Thurs noon–11:30pm; Fri–Sat 11:30am–10:30pm. Tube: Leicester Sq.

**The Ivy** ★★ MODERN BRITISH/INTERNATIONAL  Effervescent and sophisticated, The Ivy is the dining choice of visiting theatrical luminaries and has been intimately associated with the theater district ever since it opened in 1911. With its ersatz 1930s look and tiny bar near the entrance, this place is fun, and hums with the energy of London's glamour scene. The kitchen has a solid appreciation for fresh ingredients and a talent for preparation. Favorite dishes include white asparagus with sea kale and truffle butter; seared scallops with spinach, sorrel, and bacon; and salmon fish cakes. You'll also find such English desserts as sticky toffee (sponge cake soaked in a thick caramelized syrup) and caramelized bread-and-butter pudding. Meals are served quite late to accommodate the post-theater crowd.

1 West St., WC2. ℂ **020/7836-4751.** Reservations required. Main courses £9–£35 ($17–$65); Sat–Sun fixed-price 3-course lunch £20 ($36). AE, DC, MC, V. Mon–Sat noon–3pm; daily 5:30pm–midnight (last order); Sun noon–3:30pm. Tube: Leicester Sq.

**Livebait's Café Fish** ★ SEAFOOD  Don't you love the name? The catch of the day can be chargrilled or pan-fried as you desire. We know of no better place in London to sample seafood favorites enjoyed by Brits back in the days of Sir Winston Churchill—we're talking smoked haddock kedgeree (a mixture of fish, rice, and hard-boiled eggs), cockles, steamed mussels, smoky grilled sardines, and the like. We like to go when the Dover sole is brought in. This eclectic menu includes fish flown all the way from the U.S. Unlike some of the soggy chips (fries) at nearby dives, the ones here are crisp and fluffy. Our moist-fleshed sea bream, served with a crisp skin, made us want to "hasten ye back" to the restaurant the next night. From grandma's pantry comes Bailey's cheesecake or sticky toffee pudding to finish off the meal.

36–40 Rupert St., W1. © 020/7287-8989. Reservations required. Main courses £10–£18 ($19–$33); set dinner £10 ($19). AE, MC, V. Mon–Sat noon–11pm; Sun noon–9pm. Tube: Piccadilly Circus.

**Randall & Aubin** *(Finds* SEAFOOD    Past the sex boutiques of Soho you stumble upon this real discovery, whose consultant is TV chef Ed Baines, an ex-Armani model who turned this butcher shop into a cool, hip champagne-and-oyster bar. It's an ideal place to take a lover for a *Sex in the City* type of meal and some champagne or a bottle of wine. You're never rushed here. The impressive shellfish display of the night's goodies is the "bait" used to lure you inside. Chances are you won't be disappointed. Loch Fyne oysters, lobster with chips, pan-fried fresh scallops—the parade of seafood we've sampled here has in each case been genuinely excellent. The *soupe de poisson* (fish soup) is the best in Soho, or else you might want one of the hors d'oeuvres such as delightful Japanese-style fish cakes or fresh Cornish crab. Yes, they still have Sevruga caviar for lotto winners. For the rare meat-only eater, there is a limited array of dishes such as a perfectly roasted chicken on the spit that has been flavored with fresh herbs. The lemon tart with crème fraîche rounds off a perfect meal.

16 Brewer St., W1. © 020/7287-4447. Reservations not accepted. Main courses £11–£19 ($19–$34). AE, DC, MC, V. Mon–Sat noon–11pm; Sun 4–10:30pm. Tube: Piccadilly Circus.

## INEXPENSIVE

**Brown's** CONTINENTAL/TRADITIONAL BRITISH    The decor of this popular restaurant is reminiscent of an Edwardian brasserie, with mirrors, dark-wood trim, and cream-colored walls. The staff is attentive, hysterically busy, and high spirited. The most amazing thing about the restaurant is its size. It's a cavernous labyrinth of tables complemented by a bar whose (often single) clients tend to be good-looking, happy-go-lucky, and usually up for a chat. Expect well-prepared cuisine here, hauled out through the stand-up crowds to battered tables and bentwood chairs by an army of well-intentioned European staff. Menu items include traditional British favorites (salmon and fish cakes; or steak, mushroom, and Guinness pies); as well as continental dishes like confit of duck on a bed of lentils with pancetta, or chicken filet in red pesto served with linguine and rocket (arugula). The site of the restaurant was originally conceived in 1787 as a magistrate's court. Today, the somber overtones of the court are gone, as the restaurant is usually awash with bubbly theatergoers either headed to or coming from a West End play.

82–94 St. Martins Lane, WC2. © 020/7497-5050. Reservations recommended. 2-course fixed-price menu £11 ($20), available noon–6:30pm Mon–Sat. Main courses £10–£16 ($19–$29). AE, DC, MC, V. Daily noon–11:30pm. Tube: Leicester Sq. or Covent Garden.

**Cork & Bottle Wine Bar** *(Value* INTERNATIONAL    Don Hewitson, a connoisseur of fine wines for more than 30 years, presides over this trove of blissful fermentation. The ever-changing wine list features an excellent selection of Beaujolais Crus from Alsace, 30 selections from Australia, 30 champagnes, and a good selection of California labels. If you want something to wash down, the most successful dish is a raised cheese-and-ham pie, with a cream cheese–like filling and crisp well-buttered pastry—not your typical quiche. There's also chicken and apple salad, black pudding, Mediterranean prawns with garlic and asparagus, lamb in ale, and tandoori chicken.

44–46 Cranbourn St., WC2. © 020/7734-7807. Reservations not accepted after 6:30pm. Main courses £6.50–£12 ($12–$22); glass of wine from £3.50 ($6.50). AE, DC, MC, V. Mon–Sat 11am–11pm; Sun noon–11pm. Tube: Leicester Sq.

**Quod Restaurant & Bar** *Value* ITALIAN   It's difficult to find a good, afford-able, nontouristy restaurant in the heavily trodden Haymarket area. But the-atergoers are welcoming this class act, which offers good value, first-rate ingredients, and an informal but stylish setting. The Italian-inspired menu appeals to a wide range of appetites and tastes. One of the creators of the menu is Alberto Brunelli, who once worked at the fabled Harry's Bar along the Grand Canal in Venice. Starters include grilled goat's cheese with baby spinach, sun-dried tomatoes, and toasted walnuts, and mixed chargrilled vegetables mari-nated in fresh herbs and garlic. Other delights are the fresh crab salad marinated in olive oil, sweet chili peppers, and fresh marjoram and thyme. Pastas and piz-zas are favorites here, and the best of the main courses include a slow-roasted lamb shank with Tuscan vegetables, or else a duck confit with mashed celeriac, bacon, spring onions, and cherry tomatoes. The chocolate marble brownie with vanilla ice cream will put you in a good mood for the rest of the day.

57 Haymarket, SW1. ✆ 020/7925-1234. Reservations rarely needed. Pizza and pasta £7.95–£9.95 ($15–$18); main courses £9–£18 ($17–$33); fixed-price pre- and post-theater 2-course menu £11 ($20). 4–7pm and 10pm–midnight. Children's menu £3.95 ($7.30). AE, DC, MC, V. Mon–Sat noon–midnight; Sun noon–9pm. Tube: Piccadilly Circus.

**The Stockpot** *Value* CONTINENTAL/TRADITIONAL BRITISH   Pound for pound (British pounds, that is), we'd hazard a guess that this cozy little restaurant offers one of the best dining bargains in London. Meals might include a bowl of minestrone, spaghetti Bolognese, a plate of braised lamb, and apple crumble (or another dessert), among other items. At these prices, the food is hardly refined, but it's filling and satisfying nonetheless. During peak hours, The Stockpot has a share-the-table policy in its two-level dining room.

38 Panton St. (off Haymarket, opposite the Comedy Theatre), SW1. ✆ 020/7839-5142. Reservations accepted for dinner. Main courses £2.70–£6.10 ($5–$11); fixed-price 2-course lunch £3.90 ($7.20); fixed-price 3-course dinner £6.40 ($12). No credit cards. Mon–Sat 7am–11pm; Sun 7am–10pm. Tube: Piccadilly Circus or Leicester Sq.

## SOHO

The restaurants of Soho are conveniently located for those rushing to have din-ner and then an evening at one of the West End theaters.

### VERY EXPENSIVE

**Spoon+** *⚡* AMERICAN   In Ian Schrager's hot new Sanderson Hotel, this is a branch of the Spoon+ that master chef Alain Ducasse lures *tout Paris* to. Like its Parisian namesake, this is Monsieur Ducasse's take on "American fusion" cuisine. This is the only place you can go in London to eat a Frenchman's take on that American favorite—macaroni and cheese. Although some menu items seem designed more to shock, much of what is offered here is really good, especially the crab ceviche (crab marinated in lime juice) or the iced tomato soup (great choice) offered at the beginning. Spoon+'s chefs allow you to compose your own meal or at least pair up ingredients—perhaps a beautiful sole with a crushed lemon confit, or do you prefer it with satay sauce? You make the choices. You choose from a trio of columns: main course, sauce, and accompanying side dish. On our last visit, we found the restaurant ridiculously overpriced but then reconsidered when the entertainment of the evening arrived. Our fellow diners turned out to be none other than Madonna and her husband, Guy Ritchie.

50 Berners St., W1. ✆ 020/7300-1400. Reservations imperative. Main courses £21–£30 ($39–$56). AE, DC, MC, V. Daily noon–3pm; Mon–Sat 6–11:30pm; Sun 6–10:30pm.

## EXPENSIVE

**Alastair Little** ★ CONTINENTAL/MODERN BRITISH    In an 1830 brick-fronted town house (which supposedly housed John Constable's art studio for a brief period), this informal, cozy restaurant is a pleasant place to enjoy a well-prepared lunch or dinner. Some critics claim that Alastair Little is the best chef in London, but lately he's been buried under the avalanche of new talent. Actually, Little is not often here; he spends a good deal of time at other enterprises. The talented James Rix is usually in charge. Style is modern European with a slant toward Italian. The menu changes daily. Starters might include a salad of winter leaves with crispy pork, or chicken livers in Vin Santo (a sweet wine), flavored with fresh tomatoes and basil. The terrine of wild duck and foie gras is a surefire pleaser, as are such main-course delights as risotto with both flap and field mushrooms,and salted cod with spicy chickpeas and greens. For dessert, you can select an array of British cheeses or order such classics as a pear-and-red-wine tart. Ever have olive-oil cake? It's served here with a winter-fruit compote.

49 Frith St., W1. ℂ 020/7734-5183. Reservations recommended. Fixed-price 3-course dinner £38 ($70); fixed-price 3-course lunch £29 ($54). AE, DC, MC, V. Mon–Fri noon–3pm; Mon–Sat 6–11pm. Tube: Leicester Sq. or Tottenham Court Rd.

**Lindsay House** ★★ MODERN BRITISH    Irish-born chef Richard Corrigan is one of our all-time favorites in London. As in an old-fashioned speakeasy, you ring the doorbell for admittance to a Regency town house deep in Soho. Unfolding before you are gilded mirrors and bare wooden floors. The staircase delivers you to one of two floors. Corrigan is one of the most inventive chefs in London, with creative offerings changing daily based on market availability. What inspires Corrigan at the market is what will end up on your plate at night. You might start with a cured foie gras rolled in spicy gingerbread, or else ravioli of rabbit in its own consommé. For your main choice, expect such delightful courses as pan-roasted filet of red mullet, or squab served with fried cabbage and bacon. An excellent poached rump of veal might also rest on your plate. Desserts are a delight—always unexpected, always a delightful surprise, such as marinated pumpkin with pistachio and chocolate sorbet.

21 Romilly St., W1. ℂ 020/7439-0450. Reservations recommended. Lunch £20–£25 ($37–$46); fixed-price 3-course dinner £48 ($89). AE, DC, MC, V. Mon–Fri noon–2:30pm; Mon–Sat 6–11pm. Tube: Leicester Sq.

**Quo Vadis** ★ ITALIAN    This hyper-trendy restaurant occupies the former apartment house of Communist patriarch Karl Marx, who would never recognize it. It was an Italian restaurant (also called Quo Vadis) from 1926 until the mid-1990s, when its interior was ripped apart and reconfigured into the stylish, postmodern place you'll find today. The stark street-level dining room is a museum-style showcase for dozens of modern paintings by the controversial Damien Hirst and other contemporary artists. But many bypass the restaurant altogether for the upstairs bar, where Hirst has put a severed cow head and a severed bull's head on display in separate aquariums. Why? They're catalysts to conversation and satirical odes to the destructive effects of Mad Cow Disease.

Quo Vadis is associated with Marco Pierre White, but don't expect to see the temperamental culinary superstar; as executive chef, he only functions as a consultant. Also, don't expect that the harassed and overburdened staff will have the time to pamper you. And the food? It's appealingly presented and very good, but not nearly as artful or innovative as the setting might lead you to believe. You might begin with one of the fresh pastas created daily, our favorite being ricotta-filled agnolotti with sage. The grilled sea bass with herb flavoring is always a delight, as are the tender and well-flavored lamb dishes. Enticing new additions are always cropping up on the chef's repertoire depending on what's good and fresh in any season.

26–29 Dean St., W1. ✆ 020/7437-9585. Reservations required. Main courses £14–£19 ($26–$35). AE, DC, MC, V. Mon–Fri noon–2:30pm; Mon–Sat 5:30–10:30pm. Tube: Leicester Sq. or Tottenham Court Rd.

**The Sugar Club** ✸ PACIFIC RIM   This restaurant, with its adventurous menu, comes from the land Down Under. The chef attracts homesick Aussies with a kangaroo salad. The elegant and spacious setting is inviting, with soft textures, pale cream colors, and wooden floors. The restaurant offers a bar waiting area for diners and an open kitchen. Every area is nonsmoking except for the bar.

The flavors are often stunning—a good example is the amazingly fresh sashimi of Iki Jimi yellowtail with a black-bean-and-ginger salsa. Throughout the menu, flavors surprise the palate in the most exciting ways. You might dig into the duck leg braised in tamarind and star anise, with coconut rice, or try the pan-fried turbot with spinach, sweet potato, and red curry sauce. Many of the starters are vegetarian and can be upgraded to a main course. For dessert, the blood orange–curd sorbet is devastatingly delicious.

21 Warwick St., W1. ✆ 020/7437-7776. Reservations recommended. Main courses £14–£23 ($26–$43). AE, DC, MC, V. Daily noon–3pm; Mon–Sat 5:30–11pm; Sun 6–10:30pm. Tube: Piccadilly Circus or Oxford Circus.

## MODERATE

**Atlantic Bar & Grill** ✸✸ MODERN BRITISH   A Titanic restaurant in a former Art Deco ballroom off Piccadilly Circus, this 160-seat locale draws a trendy crowd to London's heart. The restaurant is cosmopolitan, and it's one of the best choices for the after-theater crowd because it closes at 3am most nights. It doesn't attract celebrities as it did back in 1994, but it's still going strong. The chef turns out a new menu every 2 months, with emphasis on organic and homegrown produce, seafood, and meats. Many dishes are quite complicated and taste as good as they sound: swordfish dumplings with a salsa of plum tomatoes, fresh cilantro, sautéed shiitake, soy-infused ginger, and fresh wilted spinach.

For a starter, we recommend the smoked-chicken Caesar club salad. Also memorable is the loin of yellowfin tuna served with a wild-parsley-and-eggplant relish and a roasted red-bell-pepper pesto. The desserts are purposefully unsophisticated: Rice pudding or poached pears are standards. If you're rushed, you can drop into Dick's Bar for a quick bite. The offerings at Dick's include everything from lamb burgers sparked with yogurt and fresh mint to Cashel blue cheese and pumpkin seeds on ciabatta bread. Most dishes are at the low end of the price scale.

20 Glasshouse St., W1. ✆ 020/7734-4888. Reservations required. Main courses £11–£18 ($19–$32); fixed-price 3-course lunch £17 ($31). AE, DC, MC, V. Mon–Fri noon–3pm; Mon–Sat 6pm–3am. Tube: Piccadilly Circus.

**Bam-Bou** ✸ FRENCH/VIETNAMESE   London's best Vietnamese-inspired eatery is spread over a series of dining rooms, alcoves, and bars in a town house with tattered French colonial decor. A favorite of young London, the restaurant is so popular that you may have to wait for 30 minutes to an hour for a table. The smell of lime and lemon grass lures you to the table—this combination is married perfectly in the chicken in lemon grass dish. Equally worthy is the caramelized ginger chicken. Also try such delights as tempura of soft-shell crab, or crispy beef with papaya and crabmeat flavored with a lime dressing. Rock lobster and spring chicken hot pot is an eternal favorite, as are the flavorful prawns with green herbs and coconut. Our favorite starter is spicy raw beef with aromatic basil, lime, and chile, or fried marinated squid. A winner for dessert is the dish of sweet banana rolls with chocolate sauce.

1 Percy St., W1. © 020/7323-9130. Reservations required. Main courses £9–£14 ($17–$25). AE, DC, MC, V. Mon–Fri noon–3pm; Mon–Sat 6–11:30pm. Tube: Tottenham Court Rd.

**Chuen Cheng Ku** ⭐ CHINESE    This is one of the finest places in Soho's New China. Taking up several floors, Chuen Cheng Ku has the longest, most interesting Cantonese menu in town. Specialties of the house are paper-wrapped prawns, rice in lotus leaves, steamed spareribs in black-bean sauce, and shredded pork with cashew nuts—all served in generous portions. Other featured dishes include lobster with ginger and spring onion, sliced duck in chile and black-bean sauce, and Singapore noodles (thin, rich noodles, sometimes mixed with curry and pork, and sometimes with shrimp and red and green pepper). Dim sum is served from 11am to 5:30pm. We note, however, that the standard of service has slipped over the years.

17 Wardour St., W1. © 020/7734-3281. Reservations recommended on weekend afternoons. Main courses £6–£16 ($11–$30); fixed-price menus £8.50–£25 ($16–$46). AE, DC, MC, V. Daily 11am–11:45pm. Closed Dec 24–25. Tube: Piccadilly Circus or Leicester Sq.

**The Criterion Brasserie** ⭐ FRENCH/MODERN BRITISH    Designed by Thomas Verity in the 1870s, this palatial neo-Byzantine mirrored marble hall is a glamorous backdrop for a superb cuisine, served under a golden ceiling, with theatrical peacock-blue draperies. The menu is wide ranging, offering everything from Paris brasserie food to "nouvelle-classical," a combination of classic French cooking techniques with some of the lighter, more experimental leanings of modern French cuisine. The food is excellent but falls short of sublime. Still, roast skate wing with deep-fried snails is delectable, as is roast saddle of lamb stuffed with mushrooms and spinach.

224 Piccadilly, W1. © 020/7930-0488. Main courses £14–£23 ($26–$42); fixed-price 2-course lunch £15 ($28), 3-course lunch £18 ($33). AE, MC, V. Daily noon–2:30pm and 5:30–11pm. Tube: Piccadilly Circus.

**Deca** ⭐⭐ *Finds* FRENCH    At this brasserie-style restaurant, chef Jeremy Brown works his culinary magic, adding several innovative twists as well. His cooking is based upon sound French techniques and the lavish use of market-fresh ingredients. Tastes and textures come together in pleasing combinations, as characterized by the tender breast of chicken with wild mushrooms, and the breast of duck with honey and peppercorns. Freshness is the key to many dishes. The oysters are brought down from Loch Fyne in Scotland. The veal sweetbreads Pojarski have found many admirers.

23 Conduit St., W1. © 020/7493-7070. Reservations required. Main courses £12–£20 ($22–$37); fixed-price lunch £13 ($23). AE, DC, MC, V. Mon–Sat noon–3pm and 5:30–11pm. Tube: Oxford Circus.

**The Gay Hussar** ⭐ HUNGARIAN    Is it still the best Hungarian restaurant in the world? That's what some say. We can't agree until we've sampled every Hungarian restaurant in the world, but we're certain Gay Hussar would be near the top. Since 1953, it's been an intimate place with authentic cuisine, a loyal clientele of politicians, and a large international following, especially among visiting Hungarians. You can begin with a chilled wild-cherry soup or mixed Hungarian salami. Gutsy main courses might include cabbage stuffed with minced veal and rice, half a perfectly done chicken in mild paprika sauce with cucumber salad and noodles, roast duck with red cabbage and Hungarian-style caraway potatoes, and, of course, veal goulash with egg dumplings. Expect gigantic portions. For dessert, go with either the poppy-seed strudel or the walnut pancakes.

2 Greek St., W1. ℂ 020/7437-0973. Reservations recommended. Main courses £10–£17 ($19–$31); fixed-price 2-course lunch £16 ($29), 3-course lunch £19 ($34). AE, DC, MC, V. Mon–Sat 12:15–2:30pm and 5:30–10:45pm. Tube: Tottenham Court Rd.

**Hakkasan** *Finds* CHINESE   Asian mystique and pastiche are found in this offbeat restaurant, lying in a seedy alley off Tottenham Court Road. This is another London venture created by Alan Yau, who became a city-wide dining legend because of his Wagamama noodle bars. Designer Christian Liaigre created a dining room encapsulated in a lattice wood "cage" evocative of antique Chinese doors. The leather sofas are emblazoned with dragons, and a bar runs the length of the restaurant. Come here for great dim sum and tantalizing cocktails. Feast on such dishes as *har gau* (steamed prawn dumplings) and strips of tender barbecued pork. The spring roll is refreshing with the addition of fried mango and a delicate prawn-and-scallop filling. Steamed scallop shumai (dumplings) with tobiko caviar are fresh and meltingly soft. You may want to sample such delights as steamed asparagus with bamboo pith and dried shiitake, or fried taro croquettes. Desserts in most of London's Chinese restaurants are hardly memorable, but the offerings here are an exception to that rule, especially the layered banana sponge with chocolate cream.

8 Hanway Place. ℂ 020/7907-1888. Reservations recommended. Main courses £8.50–£28 ($16–$52). AE, MC, V. Daily noon–3pm and 6–11pm. Tube: Tottenham Court Rd.

**Mela** *Value* INDIAN   Serious foodies know that you'll likely be served some of London's finest Indian cuisine at this address. Both Carlton Television and the *London Evening Standard* named this the best Indian restaurant in Britain in 2001. Expect robust aromas and earthy flavors. Our spiced duck flavored with spring onions, ginger, and coriander evoked some of the best country dining in India. Eggplant came stuffed with a spicy lamb mince, and was superb, as was the whole fresh fish of the day in a spicy marinade flavored with saffron and cooked whole in a charcoal oven. Some of the best curries in the city are served here. Tawa cookery (which in India is street cookery on a hot plate) is a specialty. At Mela, the fresh meats and other ingredients are cooked straight on a hot plate. Look for the chef's special Tawa dish of the day, perhaps queen prawns cooked with onions and fresh tomatoes. Save room for one of their special desserts.

152–156 Shaftesbury Ave., WC2. ℂ 020/7836-8635. Reservations required. Main courses £4.95–£7.95 ($9–$15); prix-fixe lunch £11 ($20), dinner (5:30–7pm) £15 ($28). AE, MC, V. Daily noon–2:30pm and 5:30pm–midnight. Tube: Tottenham Court Rd. or Leicester Sq.

**Mezzo** ASIAN/EUROPEAN   This 750-seat, blockbuster Soho spot—the creation of Sir Terence Conran—is the biggest restaurant in London. The mammoth space is the former site of rock's legendary Marquee club. Mezzo is actually composed of several restaurants: **Mezzonine** upstairs, serving Thai/Asian cuisine with a European flair (deep-fried salt-and-pepper squid flavored with garlic and coriander; and roast duck with Thai red curry and fragrant rice are some examples); swankier **Mezzo** downstairs, offering modern European cuisine in a 1930s Hollywood atmosphere; and **Mezzo Cafe,** where you can stop in for a simple sandwich and a drink.

The food is at its most ambitious downstairs at Mezzo, where 100 chefs work behind glass to feed up to 400 diners at a time. This is dinner-as-theater. Not surprisingly for a restaurant of this size, the cuisine tends to be uneven. We suggest the rotisserie rib of beef with red wine and creamed horseradish, or the roast cod, which is crisp-skinned and cooked to perfection. For dessert, you can't beat the butterscotch ice cream with a pitcher of hot fudge. A live jazz band entertains after 10pm from Wednesday to Saturday, and the world of Marlene Dietrich and Noel Coward comes alive again.

100 Wardour St., W1. ✆ 020/7314-4000. Reservations recommended. Mezzo 3-course fixed-price dinner £17 ($31); Mezzonine 3-course dinner £15 ($27); Mezzo Cafe main courses £5–£10 ($9.25–$19). AE, DC, MC, V. Mezzo: Wed–Fri noon–3pm; Mon–Wed 5:30pm–1am; Thurs–Sat 5:30pm–3am. Mezzonine: Mon–Fri noon–3pm; Sat noon–4pm; Mon–Thurs 5:30pm–1am; Fri–Sat 5:30pm–3am. Mezzo Cafe: Mon–Sat 8am–11pm, Sun 4–10:30pm. Tube: Piccadilly Circus.

**Rasa Samundra** ★ *Value* INDIAN   This outpost offers the best southern Indian cuisine in town. While most of London's Indian restaurants specialize in the cuisine of the north, Rasa Samundra features cookery of the southern state of Kerala, focusing on specialties from the sea. Owner Das Sreedharan's mother has trained all the chefs and the results are delectable. Try *malslam pattichathu* (kingfish cooked in fresh spices, with green chile and coconut paste), *para konju nirachathu* (lobster cooked with black pepper, garlic, and Indian shallots, and served with whole-lemon and beet-root curry), *masala dosa* (paper-thin rice and black-grain pancakes filled with potato and ginger masala), and *moru kachlathu* (green bananas and mangoes cooked in a yogurt sauce with turmeric and onions). Rasa also offers a range of appetizers, side orders, breads, rice, and desserts. Most dishes are at the lower end of the price scale.

5 Charlotte St., W1. ✆ 020/7637-0222. Reservations required. Main courses £10–£30 ($19–$56); fixed-price lunch £23 ($42), dinner £30 ($56). AE, DC, MC, V. Daily noon–midnight. Tube: Tottenham Court Rd.

**Satsuma** JAPANESE   This funky Japanese canteen is all the rage in London. The clean lines, stark white walls, and long wooden tables might suggest an upmarket youth hostel. But patrons come for good food at reasonable prices. The restaurant is ideal for a pre-theater visit. Your meal comes in a lacquered bento box on a matching tray. Try the chicken teriyaki or fresh chunks of tuna and salmon. The dumplings are excellent, as is the miso soup. A specialty is the large bowl of seafood ramen, with noodles swimming in a well-seasoned broth studded with mussels, scallops, and prawns. Tofu steaks are a delight, as are udon noodles with wok-fried chicken and fresh vegetables. You can finish with deep-fried tempura ice cream.

56 Wardour St., W1. ✆ 020/7437-8338. Reservations not accepted. Main courses £6–£16 ($11–$30). AE, MC, V. Mon–Tues noon–11pm; Wed–Thurs noon–11:30pm; Fri–Sat noon–midnight; Sun noon–10:30pm. Tube: Piccadilly Circus.

**Shampers** CONTINENTAL   This is a favorite of West End wine bar aficionados. In addition to the street-level wine bar serving snacks, there's a more formal basement-level restaurant. In either venue, you can order such main dishes as grilled calves' liver with bacon, chips, and salad; pan-fried large prawns with ginger, garlic, and chili; and platters of cheeses. Salads are popular, including grilled eggplant salad with tomato, avocado, buffalo mozzarella, and pesto; and spicy chicken salad. The platter of Irish mussels cooked in a cream-and-tarragon sauce is everybody's favorite. The restaurant is closed in the evening, but the wine bar serves an extensive menu, offering such dishes as fresh squid, tuna steak, pan-fried tiger prawns, free-range chicken, and a variety of other tasty specialties. There is also a special daily menu.

4 Kingly St. (between Carnaby and Regent sts.), W1. ✆ 020/7437-1692. Reservations recommended. Main courses £8.75–£15 ($16–$27). AE, DC, MC, V. Restaurant: Mon–Sat noon–10pm; wine bar: Mon–Sat noon–11pm. Closed Dec 24–Jan 2. Tube: Oxford Circus or Piccadilly Circus.

Soho Spice INDIAN   This is one of central London's most stylish Indian restaurants, combining a hip atmosphere with the flavors and scents of southern India. You might opt for a drink at the cellar bar before heading to the street-level dining room, decorated in saffron, cardamom, bay, and pepper hues. A staff member dressed in similarly vivid apparel will propose a wide array of choices, including slow-cooked Indian tandoori specials that feature lamb, chicken, fish, or vegetables with combinations of spices. The a la carte menu offers a variety of courses, including *Jhinga Hara Pyaz,* spicy queen prawns with fresh spring onions, and *Paneer Pasanda,* cottage cheese slices stuffed with spinach and served with almond sauce. The cuisine will satisfy traditionalists but also has a modern flair.

124–126 Wardour St., W1. 📞 020/7434-0808. Reservations recommended. Main courses £9.95–£15 ($18–$28); set dinner £20 ($37). AE, V. Mon–Thurs 11:30am–12:30am; Fri–Sat 11:30am–3am; Sun 12:30–10:30pm. Tube: Tottenham Court Rd.

## INEXPENSIVE

Balans MODERN BRITISH   Located on one of the gayest streets in London, Old Compton Street, Balans is the best-known gay restaurant in London, and has been since its inauguration in 1993. Some of its diehard fans take all their meals here. Its extensive hours of service are almost without equal in London. Although the food is deemed "British," it is an eclectic cuisine, borrowing freely from whatever kitchen the chef chooses, from the Far East to America. You can fill up on one of the succulent pastas, such as linguine with crab, parsley, garlic and chili; tagliolini with wild mushrooms, fire-roasted sweet peppers, roast garlic, and truffle oil; or ricotta and spinach ravioli with Gorgonzola cream sauce. Grilled dishes delight the mostly male patrons, especially the tuna teriyaki or the charred roast chicken. Balans has a party pub atmosphere and is a good place to meet people.

60 Old Compton St., W1. 📞 020/7437-5212. Reservations recommended. Main courses £8–£17 ($15–$31). AE, MC, V. Mon–Sat 8am–5am; Sun 8am–2am. Tube: Piccadilly Circus or Leicester Sq.

Ed's Easy Diner AMERICAN   This is one of four branches of this popular retro American diner. It's the kind of place Michael J. Fox might have walked into in *Back to the Future.* Featuring 1950s and 1960s rock 'n' roll on the jukebox, a horseshoe-shaped counter with the kitchen in the middle, and a staff that fits the theme, the restaurant not only offers good diner staples such as burgers, onion rings, waffles, corned-beef hash, and cheesecake, but also good people-watching, with a broad cross-section of fashion trends on parade around the counter.

12 Moor St., W1. 📞 020/7439-1955. Reservations not accepted. Main courses £7–£12 ($13–$22). Daily 11am–11:30pm. Closed Christmas. Tube: Leicester Sq. or Tottenham Court Rd.

Mildreds 🌟 *Finds* VEGETARIAN   Mildreds may sound like a 1940s Joan Crawford movie, but it's one of London's most enduring vegetarian and vegan dining spots. It was vegetarian long before such restaurants became trendy. Jane Muir and Diane Thomas worked in various restaurants together before opening their own place. Today they run a busy, bustling diner with casual, friendly service. Sometimes it's a bit crowded and tables are shared. They do a mean series of delectable stir-fries. The ingredients in their dishes are naturally grown, and they strongly emphasize the best seasonal produce. The menu changes daily, but always features an array of homemade soups, casseroles, and salads. Organic wines are served, and portions are very large. Save room for the desserts, especially the nutmeg-and-mascarpone ice cream or the chocolate, rum, and amaretto pudding.

45 Lexington St., W1. 📞 020/7494-1634. Reservations not accepted. Main courses £6.50–£8 ($12–$15). No credit cards. Mon–Sat noon–11pm. Tube: Tottenham Court Rd.

---

> ### *Tips* Après-Theater Dining
>
> For years, lower-priced menus and a lack of late-night eateries convinced most theatergoers to dine before the show. But the city now accommodates those who prefer dining after the theater. **Quaglino's** (p. 179) is a vast establishment that stays open until 11:30pm or midnight. If a hamburger or steak will do, head for the **Hard Rock Cafe** (p. 175).
>
> At the heart of Piccadilly Circus, the **Atlantic Bar & Grill** (p. 166) offers its modern British cuisine until 3am. Nearby, you can make it to **Circus** (p. 178) before the last orders go in at midnight, or order from the bar menu until 1:30am. **Balans** (p. 170), which caters to a gay crowd, serves until the wee hours. In Soho, **Mezzo** (p. 168) seats 750, so you're guaranteed a table. It's open until 1am or 3am, depending on the day.

---

**Veeraswamy** *Value* INDIAN   The oldest Indian restaurant in England, originally established in the 1920s, Veeraswamy has been restyled and rejuvenated and is looking better than ever. Its menu has been redone, and today it serves some of the most affordable fixed-price menus in Central London, the heart of the city. Shunning the standard fare offered in most London-based Indian restaurants, Veeraswamy features authentic, freshly prepared dishes—the kind that would be served in a private Indian home. Try almost anything: spicy oysters, brochette of monkfish, chicken curry with almonds, succulent tandoori chicken, or tender and flavorful lamb curry. One of our favorite dishes is lamb with turnips from Kashmir, flavored with large black cardamoms, powdered fennel, and a red chile powder, giving the dish a savory flavor and a vivid red color.

Victory House, 99 Regent St., W1. ✆ 020/7734-1401. Reservations recommended. Lunch and pre-/post-theater menu £13–£15 ($23–$28). Sun 3-course menu £15 ($28). Lunch and dinner main courses £13–£22 ($24–$41). AE, DC, MC, V. Mon–Fri noon–2:30pm; Sat–Sun 12:30–3pm; daily 5:30–11pm. Tube: Piccadilly Circus.

## TRAFALGAR SQUARE
### MODERATE

**Crivelli's Garden** ✹ ITALIAN   In the National Gallery, this hot new dining choice lies over the foyer of the Sainsbury Wing, providing a panoramic view of fabled Trafalgar Square. The view's a bonus—it's the cuisine that attracts visitors. The restaurant is named for a striking mural by Paulo Rego that is painted on one side of a wall. The chefs are at home with Italian dishes, offering choices such as grilled skewered squid with eggplant and sun-dried tomato salad. The steamed salmon with leeks, cilantro, and ginger is an excellent dish, as is the red pepper ravioli in a chive sauce. There is a cafe offshoot of Crivelli's Garden in the basement of the main building, which is a good choice for sandwiches, pastas, soups, and pastries.

In the National Gallery, Trafalgar Sq., WC2. ✆ 020/7747-2869. Reservations required. Fixed-price lunch and Wed dinner £16–£20 ($30–$37). AE, DC, MC, V. Daily 10am–5:30pm; Wed 6–8:30pm. Tube: Charing Cross.

**The Portrait Restaurant** ✹ MODERN BRITISH   This rooftop restaurant is a sought-after dining ticket on the fifth floor of the National Portrait Gallery's Ondaatje Wing. Along with the view (Nelson's Column, the London Eye, Big Ben, and the like), you get superb meals. Patrons usually go for lunch, not knowing that the chefs also cook on Thursday and Friday nights. In spring, there's nothing finer than the green English asparagus. All the main courses are filled with flavor. The high quality of the produce really shines through in such dishes as the whole plaice cooked in shrimp butter, and the roasted organic chicken. For your "pudding," nothing is finer than the chocolate and pecan tart with espresso ice cream. Chefs aren't afraid of simple preparations mainly because they are assured of the excellence of their products. The wine list features some organic choices.

In the National Portrait Gallery, Trafalgar Sq., WC2. ℂ **020/7313-2490**. Reservations recommended. Main courses £11–£19 ($20–$35). AE, MC, V. Sat–Wed 10am–5pm; Thurs–Fri 5:30–8:30pm. Tube: Leicester Sq. or Charing Cross.

## MAYFAIR
### VERY EXPENSIVE

**Gordon Ramsay at Claridge's** ★★★ EUROPEAN    Gordon Ramsay is the hottest chef in London today, also going strong at his Chelsea restaurant, called Gordon Ramsay (p. 185). He now rules at the staid, traditional hotel of Claridge's, legendary since 1860 when Queen Victoria stopped by for tea with the Empress Eugenie. The famed Art Deco dining room still retains many of its original architectural features, but the cuisine is hardly the same. Most definitely Victoria wasn't served an *amuse-bouche* of pumpkin soup dribbled with truffle oil and studded with truffles. On a recent lunchtime visit, we were dazzled by a fixed-price menu (the only type served here) that wasn't outrageously priced.

Although the menu changes frequently, a memorable culinary highlight began with filets of baby red mullet on a juniper-flavored sauerkraut, and went on to include a breast and confit leg of guinea fowl with vegetables and foie gras, finishing off with rum-baba with glazed oranges and crème fraîche. A three-course dinner was even more spectacular, featuring such delights as filet of sea bass wrapped in fresh basil leaves and served with a caviar sauce, and roast Scottish baby lobster cooked slowly in lime butter and served with tomato couscous. The desserts are among our favorite in London, including the likes of a bread-and-butter brioche pudding with clotted-cream ice cream, or a prune-and-Armagnac vanilla tart with *fromage blanc* in cream.

Brook St., W1. ℂ **020/7499-0099**. Reservations required as far in advance as possible. Fixed-price lunch £30 ($56); a la carte menu £55 ($102); 6-course fixed-price dinner £65 ($120). Early-bird fixed-price menu (5:45–6:30pm) £30 ($56). AE, DC, MC, V. Daily noon–3pm; Mon–Sat 5:45–11pm; Sun 5:45–10:30pm. Tube: Bond St.

**Le Gavroche** ★★★ FRENCH    Although challengers come and go, this luxurious dining room remains the number-one choice in London for classical French cuisine. It may have fallen off briefly in the early 1990s, but it's fighting its way back to stellar ranks. There's always something special coming out of the kitchen of Burgundy-born Michel Roux; the service is faultless, and the ambience formally chic without being stuffy. The menu changes constantly, depending on the fresh produce that's available and the current inspiration of the chef. But it always remains classically French, though not of the "essentially old-fashioned bourgeois repertoire" that some critics suggest. Signature dishes have been honed over years

---

**⌐Fun Fact**  **Chefs on Chefs**

England's leading restaurateur, Sir Terence Conran, on Gordon Ramsay's cuisine: "Heinz baby food is as good." Ramsay's response: "I'd rather eat in the cafeteria of my daughter's school than in one of his restaurants."

of unswerving practice, including the soufflé Suissesse, papillote of smoked salmon (salmon cooked in a greased paper wrapper), or whole Bresse chicken with truffles and a Madeira cream sauce. Game is often served, depending on availability. New menu options include cassoulet of snails with frog thighs, seasoned with herbs; mousseline of lobster in champagne sauce; and filet of red snapper with caviar and oyster-stuffed tortellini.

43 Upper Brook St., W1. ℂ 020/7408-0881. Fax 020/7491-4387. Reservations required as far in advance as possible. Main courses £24–£45 ($44–$83); fixed-price lunch £42 ($78); menu exceptional £82 ($152) per person. AE, MC, V. Mon–Fri noon–2pm and 7–11pm; Sat 7–11pm. Tube: Marble Arch.

**Menu** ★★★ MEDITERRANEAN/MODERN BRITISH   The dining room at the regal Connaught used to be stodgily traditional with sumptuous roasts hauled out on their shiny carving trolley. A bevy of old school waiters served old school boys, and British tradition seemed eternal. Out with the old and in with the new in the form of Angela Hartnett, who learned her way around the pots and pans as a protégé to Gordon Ramsay, arguably London's most outstanding chef. Hartnett has breathed new life into this grand bastion of cuisine. Even the decor, under designer Nina Campbell, has been lightened and brightened with plush colors, contemporary art, and soft lighting, with crispy white tablecloths placed over black tulip-and-olive skirts.

For starters, the combinations are memorable—carpaccio of Gresshingham duck with grilled asparagus and shavings of Parmesan, or else a white onion velouté with deep-fried frogs' legs and a salsa verde. Your palate will be charmed by the fish dishes, especially the braised filet of halibut with caramelized orange chicory and an herb vinaigrette. The meat dishes are pure ambrosia, especially the oven-roasted lamb with an eggplant parmigiana and a fresh rosemary *jus*. As for the smoked pork belly with caramelized root vegetables, it doesn't get much better than this.

The Connaught, 16 Carlos Place, W1. ℂ 020/7592-1222. Reservations essential. 3-course fixed-price menu £25–£50 ($46–$93). Prestige menu £60 ($111). AE, DC, DISC, MC, V. Mon–Fri noon–3pm; Sat–Sun noon–3:30pm; Mon–Sat 5:45–11pm; Sun 6–10:30pm. Tube: Green Park.

**Nobu** ★★ JAPANESE   London's innovative Japanese restaurant owes much to its founders, actor Robert de Niro and chef Nobu Matsuhisa. The kitchen staff is brilliant and as finely tuned as their New York counterparts. The sushi chefs create gastronomic pyrotechnics. Those on the see-and-be-seen circuit don't seem to mind the high prices that go with these incredibly fresh dishes. Elaborate preparations lead to perfectly balanced flavors. Where else can you find an excellent sea urchin tempura? Salmon tartare with caviar is a brilliant appetizer. Follow with a perfectly done filet of sea bass in a sour bean paste or soft-shell crab rolls. The squid pasta is sublime, as is sukiyaki; the latter dish is incredibly popular and with good reason. Cold sake arrives in a green bamboo pitcher.

In the Metropolitan Hotel, 19 Old Park Lane, W1. ℂ 020/7447-4747. Reservations required. Main courses £16–£35 ($30–$65); sushi and sashimi £4–£6 ($7–$11) per piece; fixed-price menu £70 ($130). AE, DC, MC, V. Mon–Fri noon–2:15pm; Mon–Thurs 6–10:15pm; Fri–Sat 6–11pm; Sun 6–9:30pm. Tube: Hyde Park Corner.

**Sketch** ★★ CONTINENTAL/MODERN BRITISH   Inaugurated in 2003, this restaurant, tearoom, art gallery, bar, and patisserie became an overnight sensation. Food, art, and music are artfully harmonized. In a converted 18th-century building in Mayfair, Mourad ("Momo") Mazouz, along with a team of chefs and designers, masterminded this fashionable creation. The British press hailed Sketch as a "camp wonderland."

---

**Finds** **The Best Charcuterie in Mayfair**

Born-to-shop aficionados who spend hours trawling Oxford Street, Bond Street, and South Moulton often retreat to **Truc Vert,** 42 North Audley St., W1 (© **020/7491-9988**), for a refreshing respite. This is a combined grocery store and dining room with rush-seated chairs and tables draped in paper. In an elegantly casual atmosphere, it offers an array of some of the finest charcuterie products in Mayfair, along with cheese and wines. Extremely tasty sandwiches are served, including a popular favorite—bresaola, tomato, and arugula, on artisanal bread. Homemade salads are very fresh, and the day's quiche is always a feature—perhaps one made with blue cheese, sweet red peppers, and zucchini. The soup of the day might be a clam and bacon chowder. You can also secure the makings of a picnic here. Make sure to stock up on those orange-flavored chocolate brownies. You can also order main platters, such as chargrilled lamb, costing from £12 to £15 ($22–$28). Open daily noon to 3pm and Monday to Friday 7:30 to 9:30pm. American Express, MasterCard, and Visa are accepted. Tube: Bond Street.

---

You can come here to dine elegantly but also to bar hop, as there are a number of venues which, to confuse matters, change their venues as the day progresses. The laser-lit West Bar is a cafe by day, an exclusive bar at night. Whimsical and informal, the Parlour is for light lunches and delectable teas. In the Lecture Room and Library, each dish represents different sensations. The Art Gallery becomes a restaurant and bar at night.

The menu showcases a cuisine that is both bold and imaginative—and also delicious. For starters, you get not only fresh Gillardeau oysters, which are lightly poached, but they come with avocado purée, aquavit, and cucumber jelly. The fresh corn and lemon grass soup is always invigorating. Well-flavored, tender lamb is served with a beetroot cake, prunes, and hazelnuts, and the roasted and caramelized baby tuna comes with steamed zucchini, red pepper, and celery leaves, and toasted sesame seeds.

9 Conduit St., W1. © **0870/777-4488.** Reservations essential for dining. Main courses £14–£22 ($26–$40). West Bar: 2-course fixed-price lunch £19 ($35), 3-course fixed-price lunch £24 ($44). Lecture Room and Library: 3-course fixed-price dinner £65 ($120), 5-course fixed-price dinner £80 ($148). Art Gallery: Daily 7pm–midnight; Lecture Room and Library Tues–Sat 7–10:30pm; Parlour Mon–Fri 8am–7pm, Sat 10am–7pm; West Bar daily noon–2am. AE, MC, V. Tube: Oxford Circus.

**The Square** ✸✸✸ FRENCH Hip, chic, casual, sleek, and modern, The Square still doesn't scare Le Gavroche as a competitor for first place on London's dining circuit, but it is certainly a restaurant to visit on a serious London gastronomic tour. Chef Philip Howard delivers the goods at this excellent restaurant. You get immaculate food in a cosseting atmosphere with abstract modern art on the walls. The chef has a magic touch, with such concoctions as apple soup with grouse sausage. We urge you to savor the crusted saddle of lamb flavored with a shallot purée and fresh rosemary. Surprise dishes await in every corner of the menu—for example, loin of monkfish with pearl barley. Roast foie gras is a dazzling appetizer. Fish is stunningly fresh, and the Bresse pigeon is as good as it is in its hometown in France. If you're a vegetarian, stay clear of this place, as many dishes are aimed at the true carnivore. For dessert, try the lemon and lime soufflé with coconut ice cream.

6–10 Bruton St., W1. ✆ 020/7495-7100. Reservations required. Fixed-price lunch £25–£30 ($46–$56), dinner £55–£75 ($102–$139). AE, DC, MC, V. Mon–Fri noon–3pm; Mon–Sat 6:30–11pm; Sun 6:30–10pm. Tube: Bond St. or Green Park.

## EXPENSIVE

**Mirabelle** ✸ FRENCH   From Marlene Dietrich and Noel Coward to Princess Margaret and Aristotle Onassis to Johnny Depp and the tabloid stars of today, Mirabelle, located in the heart of Mayfair, attracts the rich and famous and the paparazzi who follow them. The interior is Art Deco, with a sexy red-leather floor and a little English garden. On the menu, the chefs remain French classicists. For a starter, foie gras terrine appears with wine-and-herb-flavored aspic. For a main dish, expect to find delight in such offerings as grilled lobster with herbs and garlic, an escalope of tuna with eggplant "caviar," or chicken in a delectable white-wine sauce. The boneless oxtail, topped by a filigree potato galette, is the finest we've sampled. Save room for dessert, especially the bitter-chocolate tart with ice cream.

56 Curzon St., W1. ✆ 020/7499-4636. Reservations required. Main courses £15–£29 ($27–$53); set lunch £17–£20 ($31–$36). AE, MC, V. Mon–Sat noon–2:30pm and 6–11:30pm; Sun noon–3pm and 6–10:30pm. Tube: Green Park.

**Nahm** ✸✸ THAI   The cookery here is extraordinary, and we like that the chef makes few, if any, concessions to Western palates. David Thompson even purchases rare books on Thai cookery and re-creates dishes that may have been lost for centuries. Take, for example, the salmon roe and fresh seafood mixed with spices and served in a fresh betel leaf, all of it garnished with watermelon. It sounds off-putting but is actually a taste sensation. The chef is against the "fusion fad," even though he's a Westerner himself (Australian), and is instead dedicated to the tenets of Thai cuisine. He's considered such an expert that even some of the citadels of haute Thai cuisine in Thailand seek his advice. Try the aromatic curry of beef with cucumber relish. For dessert, sample the addictive white sticky rice with mango topped with a coconut cream sauce.

In the Halkin Hotel, Halkin St., SW1. ✆ 020/7333-1234. Reservations recommended. Main courses £13–£21 ($23–$39); fixed-price 4-course lunch £26 ($48), 5-course dinner £47 ($87). AE, DC, MC, V. Mon–Fri noon–2:30pm and 7–11pm; Sat–Sun 7–11pm. Tube: Hyde Park Corner.

## MODERATE

**Greenhouse** EUROPEAN   Head chef Paul Merrett is quite inspired by modern European food. Dishes from the heart of England include a roast breast of pheasant that Henry VIII would have loved. The produce is first-class and dishes are beautifully prepared, without ever destroying the natural flavor of the ingredients. Fine examples included pan-fried sea bass and breast of guinea fowl. The chef deftly handles essential flavors without interfering with them, as is the case with his filet of Scottish beef. To make this dish more interesting, though, he adds such wake-up-the-taste-buds sides as sautéed foie gras and red-onion jam. The menu is backed up by a very large wine list with some 500 selections. Some of the delightfully sticky desserts, including a moist bread-and-butter pudding and a baked ginger loaf with orange marmalade, would please a Midlands granny. Most dishes are at the lower end of the price scale.

27A Hays Mews, W1. ✆ 020/7499-3331. Reservations required. Main courses £15–£30 ($28–$56). AE, DC, DISC, MC, V. Mon–Fri noon–2:30pm and 5:30–11pm; Sat 6:30–11pm. Closed Christmas and bank holidays. Tube: Green Park.

**Hard Rock Cafe** *Kids* AMERICAN   This is the original Hard Rock. Since it was established in 1971, more than 12 million people have eaten here. Just like every other Hard Rock Cafe, there's usually a line (or in this case, a queue) of people waiting to get in, plus an equally long line of people buying T-shirts. You'll find better-than-average burgers and a good selection of beers here. The collection of rock memorabilia at the original is a far sight better than the collections at later facsimiles. The restaurant also accepts U.S. dollars.

150 Old Park Lane, W1. ✆ 020/7629-0382. Reservations not accepted. Main courses £7–£12 ($13–$22). AE, DC, MC, V. Mon–Thurs and Sun 11:30am–12:30am; Fri–Sat 11:30am–1am. Closed Dec 25–26. Tube: Green Park or Hyde Park Corner.

**Langan's Brasserie** FRENCH/TRADITIONAL BRITISH   In its heyday in the early 1980s, this was one of the hippest restaurants in London, and the upscale brasserie still welcomes an average of 700 diners a day. The 1976 brainchild of actor Michael Caine and chef Richard Shepherd, Langan's sprawls over two noisy floors filled with potted plants and ceiling fans that create a 1930s feel. The menu is "mostly English with a French influence," and includes spinach soufflé with anchovy sauce, quail eggs in a pastry case served with a sautéed hash of mushrooms and hollandaise sauce, and roast crispy duck with applesauce and sage-lemon stuffing. There's always a selection of English pub fare, including bangers and mash, and fish and chips. The dessert menu is a journey into nostalgia: bread-and-butter pudding, treacle tart with custard, apple pie with clotted cream . . . wait, how did mango sorbet slip in here?

Stratton St., W1. ✆ 020/7491-8822. Reservations recommended. Main courses £14–£19 ($26–$34). AE, DC, MC, V. Mon–Fri 12:15pm–11:45pm; Sat 7pm–midnight. Tube: Green Park.

**Momo** MOROCCAN/NORTH AFRICAN   You'll be greeted at this restaurant by a friendly, casual staff member clad in a colorful T-shirt and black pants. The setting is like Marrakech, with stucco walls, a wood-and-stone floor, patterned wood window shades, burning candles, and banquettes. You can fill up on the freshly baked bread along with appetizers such as garlicky marinated olives and pickled carrots spiced with pepper and cumin. These starters are a gift from the chef. Other appetizers are also tantalizing, especially the *briouat:* paper-thin and very crisp triangular packets of puffed pastry filled with saffron-flavored chicken and other treats. One of the chef's specialties is *pastilla au pigeon,* a traditional poultry pie with almonds. Many diners visit for the *couscous maison,* among the best in London. Served in a decorative pot, this aromatic dish of raisins, meats (including merguez sausage), chicken, lamb, and chickpeas is given added flavor with *marissa,* a powerful hot sauce from the Middle East.

25 Heddon St., W1. ✆ 020/7434-4040. Reservations required. Main courses £15–£32 ($27–$59); fixed-price 2-course lunch £20 ($37). AE, DC, MC, V. Mon–Sat noon–2:30pm and 7–11:30pm; Sun 7–11pm. Tube: Piccadilly Circus or Oxford Circus.

**Noble Rot** ★ CONTINENTAL   Danish-born Soren Jessen strikes again with this modern European venue. Ladies-who-lunch and shoppers drop in during the day, but at night the lighting is lowered and the atmosphere turns romantic. Some of the best regional specialties of the Continent are prepared in light variations here, with imaginative culinary twists. You might begin a meal with roast pumpkin soup and Pecorino cheese, or else foie gras with a hazelnut dressing. Main dishes are concise, focused, and delicious, especially the supreme of guinea fowl on a bed of spinach purée and truffle *jus,* and especially the poached truffled chicken breast with fresh morels in a Riesling sauce.

3–5 Mill St., W1. ✆ 020/7629-8877. Reservations required. Main courses £17–£23 ($31–$42); fixed-price lunch £16–£20 ($30–$37). AE, MC, V. Mon–Fri noon–3pm; Mon–Sat 6–11pm. Tube: Oxford Circus.

**Tamarind** ⭐ INDIAN   In favor with critics as well as the lunchtime business crowd, Tamarind is the most popular Indian restaurant in Mayfair. The basement dining room has gold pillars and a tandoor window so that you can watch the chefs pull their flavorful dishes from the ovens. Chef Alfred Prasad leads a culinary brigade from Delhi that maintains the style of cooking they knew at home. The team selects the best, freshest ingredients in the markets each day. The kitchen prides itself on nouvelle dishes, but also excels at traditional Indian fare. The monkfish marinated in saffron and yogurt is delectable, and the mixed kebab platter, with all the kebabs cooked in a charcoal-fired tandoor, is extraordinary—these chefs are the kings of kebabs. Your best bet for a curry? Opt for the prawns in a five-spice mixture. Vegetarians will find refuge here, especially if they go for the *Dal Bukhari*, a black-lentil specialty of northwest India.

20 Queen St., W1. ℂ **020/7629-3561**. Reservations required. Main courses £11–£28 ($19–$52); 3-course set dinner menu £34–£56 ($63–$104); fixed-price 3-course lunch £17 ($31). AE, DC, DISC, MC, V. Mon–Fri noon–2:45pm; Mon–Sat 6–11:15pm; Sun noon–2:15pm and 6–10:15pm. Tube: Green Park.

**Zen Central** CANTONESE/INDIAN/SZECHUAN   Movie stars always seem to have an advance scouting party informing them of the best places to dine in a foreign city. So when we heard that Eddie Murphy and Tom Cruise were heading here, we followed. We didn't spot any stars, but we found a designer-chic Mayfair restaurant with a cool, dignified decor in black and white. Mirrors cover much of the interior (maybe that's why movie stars like it?).

Served by a competent staff, the cuisine is first-rate. Start with the soft-shell crabs cooked in a crust of salt. The steamed sea bass is perfectly cooked and, for extra flavor, served with a black bean sauce. Pork chops with lemon grass have a Thai flavor, and the baked lobster with crushed roast garlic and slivers of tangerine peel is worth a trip from anywhere. Vegetarian meals are also available. The chef's braised fish cheeks, sharks' fins, and bird's nest soup serve up flavors enjoyed in China. There is little catering to conventional Western palates, so most dishes taste the same as they would in their homeland. Most dishes are at the lower end of the price scale.

20–22 Queen St., W1. ℂ **020/7629-8103**. Reservations recommended. Main courses £10–£35 ($19–$65). AE, DC, MC, V. Mon–Sat 12:15–2:45pm and 6:15–11:15pm; Sun 12:15–2:30pm and 6:15–11pm. Tube: Green Park.

## INEXPENSIVE

**The Granary** /*Value* TRADITIONAL BRITISH   This family-operated country-style restaurant serves a simple flavor-filled array of home-cooked dishes listed daily on a blackboard. These might include lamb casserole with mint and lemon; pan-fried cod; or avocado stuffed with prawns, spinach, and cheese. Vegetarian meals include mushrooms stuffed with mixed vegetables, stuffed eggplant with curry sauce, and vegetarian lasagna. Tempting desserts are bread-and-butter pudding and apple brown betty (both served hot). The large portions guarantee you won't go hungry. The cooking is standard, but quite good for the price.

39 Albemarle St., W1. ℂ **020/7493-2978**. Main courses £8.90–£9.90 ($16–$18). MC, V. Mon–Fri 11:30am–7pm; Sat 11:30am–3pm. Tube: Green Park.

**Suze** PACIFIC RIM   This interesting wine bar lies between Upper Brook Street and Oxford Street. The owners attach equal importance to their food and to their impressive wine list (some wines are sold by the glass). On the ground floor, you can enjoy fine wines along with a well-chosen selection of bar food. Upon arrival, a basket of homemade bread, along with olives, goat cheese, salami, and roasted peppers, is placed before you. The menu has been upgraded and made more sophisticated and appealing. Begin perhaps with the zesty tandoori prawns, and follow with such delights as New Zealand rack of lamb or duck breast served on parsnip mash with a tamarillo (a type of chile pepper) sauce.

41 N. Audley St., W1. ℂ 020/7491-3237. Reservations recommended. Main courses £10–£14 ($19–$26). AE, DC, MC, V. Mon–Sat noon–11pm. Tube: Bond St.

## ST. JAMES'S
### EXPENSIVE

**L'Oranger** ✴ FRENCH   This bistro-cum-brasserie occupies a high-ceilinged space in an affluent neighborhood near the bottom of St. James's Street. Amid paneling, burnt-orange and forest-green paint, patterned carpeting, immaculate linens, flowers, and a uniformed waitstaff, you'll appreciate the choreographed set of fixed-price menus created by executive chef Michel Laurent. The clientele, whom pundits frequently refer to as "people who have made it," have praised the chef's arrangement of flavors. Depending on the chef's inspiration, the set menu may include filet of beef with "condiments" that include mashed potatoes and a croustillant of bone marrow in the Provençal style; leek and potato cappuccino garnished with flaked, garden-poached codfish; a salad of winter vegetables with black truffles and caviar; Dover sole with curried seasonal fruits and *fumet* dressing; and filet of wild sea bass with artichokes, pink radishes, and vanilla-flavored olive oil. Only fixed-price menus are served here.

5 St. James's St., SW1A. ℂ 020/7839-3774. Reservations recommended. Fixed-price lunches £24–£28 ($44–$52), dinner £12–£32 ($22–$60). AE, DC, MC, V. Mon–Fri noon–2pm; Mon–Sat 6:30–10:30pm. Tube: Green Park.

### MODERATE

**Circus** *Value*   INTERNATIONAL/MODERN BRITISH   This place buzzes during pre- and post-theater times with London foodies anxious to sample the wares of chef Richard Lee. A minimalist haven for power design and eating in the very heart of London, this restaurant took over the ground floor and basement of what used to be the Granada Television building at the corner of Golden Square and Beak Street. The place evokes a London version of a Left Bank Parisian brasserie. You may want to taste the divine skate wing with "crushed" new potatoes accompanied by a thick pestolike medley of rocket blended with black olives. Or else try the tasty sautéed chili-flavored squid with bok choy, made even more heavenly with a tamarind dressing. The sorbets are a nice finish to a meal, especially the delectable mango and pink grapefruit version. Of course, if you're ravenous, there's always the velvety smooth amaretto cheesecake with a coffee sauce. Service is a delight.

1 Upper James St., W1. ℂ 020/7534-4000. Reservations required. Main courses £13–£19 ($24–$34); fixed-price menus £13–£15 ($23–$28) 5:45–7:15pm and 10:30pm–midnight. AE, DC, MC, V. Daily noon–2:30pm, Mon–Sat 6pm–midnight; bar menu daily noon–3am. Tube: Piccadilly Circus.

**Greens Restaurant & Oyster Bar**   INTERNATIONAL/SEAFOOD/TRADITIONAL BRITISH   Critics say it's a triumph of tradition over taste, but as far as seafood in London goes, this is a tried-and-true favorite, thanks to an excellent menu with moderately priced dishes, a central location, and a charming staff. This place has a cluttered entrance leading to a crowded bar where you can sip fine wines and, from September to April, enjoy oysters. In the faux-Dickensian dining room, you can choose from a long menu of fresh seafood dishes, which changes monthly depending on what is in season. The standard menu ranges from fish cakes with leaf spinach to whole Scottish lobster. For zesty starters, opt for the smoked haddock. Other recommendable food items include seared sea bass with baby onions, celeriac, and coriander *jus*, as well as salmon fish cakes with a champagne sauce. The filet of beef appears with fresh greens and roasted artichokes. Desserts include bread-and-butter pudding. (Note that London has two different Duke streets. Greens is on the one in St. James's.)

36 Duke St., St. James's, SW1. ℂ 020/7930-4566. Reservations recommended. Main courses £11–£38 ($20–$69); most dishes are moderately priced. AE, DC, MC, V. Restaurant daily 11:30am–3pm, Mon–Sat 5:30–11pm; Oyster Bar Mon–Sat 11:30am–3pm and 5:30–11pm, Sun noon–3pm and 5:30–9pm. Tube: Green Park.

**Quaglino's** ⚑ CONTINENTAL   Come here for fun, not culinary subtlety and finesse. In 1993, noted restaurateur and designer Sir Terence Conran brought this restaurant—first established in 1929 by Giovanni Quaglino—into the postmodern age with a vital new decor. Menu items have been criticized for their quick preparation and standard format; but considering that on some nights up to 800 people might show up, the marvel is that this place functions as well as it does. That's not to say there isn't an occasional delay. The menu changes often, but your choices may include goat cheese and caramelized onion tart; seared salmon with potato pancakes; crab tartlet with saffron; and roasted cod and ox cheek with chargrilled vegetables. The prawns and oysters are the most ordered items. *Note:* A mezzanine with bar features live jazz every Friday and Saturday night and live piano music the rest of the week.

16 Bury St., SW1. ℂ 020/7930-6767. Reservations recommended. Main courses £13–£20 ($23–$36); fixed-price menu (available only for lunch and predinner theater from 5:30–6:30pm) 2 courses £17 ($31); 3 courses £19 ($34). AE, DC, MC, V. Daily noon–2:30pm; Mon–Thurs 5:30–11:30pm; Fri–Sat 5:30pm–12:30am; Sun 5:30–10:30pm. Tube: Green Park.

## 4 Westminster & Victoria

### EXPENSIVE

**Allium** ⚑ *Finds* EUROPEAN/MODERN BRITISH   In this discreet residential district, chef Anton Elderman is winning the discerning palates of the area with his take on fine dining. In the dining room's sophisticated Art Deco setting, you can partake of the chef's excellent blend of flavors and his passion for new combinations. For starters, the ravioli here is not only stuffed with butternut squash but served with a pumpkin purée and a foie gras velouté (sauce). Rosemary-scented figs come baked with goat cheese. Well-prepared main dishes based on quality ingredients include a rump of lamb with black olives and rosemary *jus,* or roasted partridge with glazed chestnuts. The steamed filet of sea bass is our favorite, served with caviar, baby spinach, and a red wine *jus.* For dessert, you've arrived in heaven if you order the apricot and chocolate soufflé in its own sorbet.

Dolphin Sq., Chichester St., SW1. ℂ 020/7798-6767. Reservations required. Main courses £10–£24 ($19–$44). AE, DC, MC, V. Tues–Fri noon–2:30pm; Tues–Sat 6–10:30; Sun noon–2:30pm. Tube: Pimlico.

**Shepherd's** TRADITIONAL BRITISH   Some observers claim that many of the inner workings of the British government operate from the precincts of this conservative, likable restaurant. Set in the shadow of Big Ben, it enjoys a regular clientele of barristers, members of Parliament, and their constituents from far-flung districts. Don't imagine that the intrigue occurs only at lunchtime; evenings seem just as ripe an hour for negotiations, particularly over the restaurant's roast rib of Scottish beef served with (what else?) Yorkshire pudding. So synchronized is this place to the goings-on at Parliament that a Division Bell rings in the dining room, calling MPs back to the House of Commons when it's time to vote. Even the decor is designed to make them feel at home, with leather banquettes, sober 19th-century accessories, and a worthy collection of European portraits and landscapes.

The menu reflects years of British culinary tradition, and dishes are prepared intelligently, with fresh ingredients. In addition to the classic roast, dishes include a cream-based mussel stew; hot salmon and potato salad with dill dressing; salmon and prawn fishcakes in spinach sauce; roast leg of lamb with mint sauce; wild rabbit; marinated venison with braised red cabbage in juniper sauce; and the English version of crème brûlée, known as "burnt Cambridge cream."

Marsham Court, Marsham St., at the corner of Page St., SW1. ℂ 020/7834-9552. Reservations recommended. Fixed-price menu 2 courses £26 ($48), 3 courses £29 ($54). AE, DC, MC, V. Mon–Fri 12:30–3pm and 6:30–11pm (last order at 11pm). Tube: Pimlico or St. James.

## MODERATE

**Tate Gallery Restaurant** *★★ Value* MODERN BRITISH   This restaurant is particularly attractive to wine fanciers. It offers what may be the best bargains for superior wines anywhere in Britain. Bordeaux and burgundies are in abundance, and the management keeps the markup between 40% and 65%, rather than the 100% to 200% added in most restaurants. In fact, the prices here are lower than they are in most wine shops. Wine begins at £15 ($28) per bottle, or £3.95 ($7.30) per glass. Oenophiles frequently come for lunch. The restaurant offers an English menu that changes about every month. Dishes might include pheasant casserole, pan-fried skate with black butter and capers, and a selection of vegetarian dishes. One critic found the staff and diners as traditional "as a Gainsborough landscape." Access to the restaurant is through the museum's main entrance on Millbank.

Millbank, SW1. ℂ 020/7887-8825. Reservations recommended. Main courses £11–£18 ($19–$33); fixed-price lunch 2 courses £18 ($32), 3 courses £21 ($38). AE, DC, MC, V. Mon–Sat noon–3pm; Sun noon–4pm. Tube: Pimlico. Bus: 77 or 88.

## INEXPENSIVE

**Jenny Lo's Teahouse** CANTONESE/SZECHUAN   London's noodle dives don't get much better than this. Before its decline, Ken Lo's Memories of China offered the best Chinese dining in London. The late Ken Lo, whose grandfather was the Chinese ambassador to the Court of St. James, made his reputation as a cookbook author. Jenny Lo is Ken's daughter, and her father taught her many of his culinary secrets. Belgravia matrons and young professionals come here for perfectly prepared, reasonably priced fare. Ken Lo cookbooks contribute to the dining room decor of black refectory tables set with paper napkins and chopsticks. Opt for such fare as a vermicelli rice noodle dish (a large plate of noodles topped with grilled chicken breast and Chinese mushrooms) or white noodles with minced pork. Rounding out the menu are stuffed Peking dumplings, chili-garnished spicy prawns, and wonton soup with slithery dumplings. The black-bean-seafood noodle dish is a delight, as is the chili beef soup.

14 Eccleston St., SW1 9LT. ℂ 020/7259-0399. Reservations not accepted. Main courses £5.75–£8 ($11–$15). No credit cards. Mon–Fri 11:30am–3pm; Sat noon–3pm; Mon–Sat 6–10pm. Tube: Victoria Station.

## 5 Knightsbridge to South Kensington

### KNIGHTSBRIDGE
#### VERY EXPENSIVE

**Petrus** *★★* FRENCH   Clubby and not at all stuffy, this is the domain of chef Marcus Wareing, a former boxer from Lancashire. The restaurant serves nouvelle French food in the grand tradition of Wareing's mentor and London's hottest chef, Gordon Ramsay. You'll find reasonably priced food prepared with technical

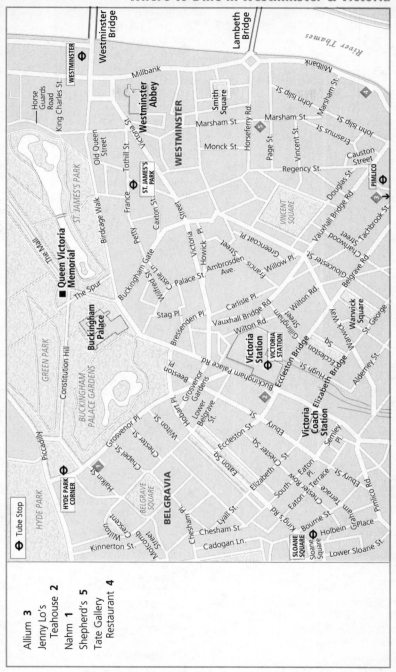

Allium **3**

Jenny Lo's Teahouse **2**

Nahm **1**

Shepherd's **5**

Tate Gallery Restaurant **4**

# Where to Dine from Knightsbridge to South Kensington

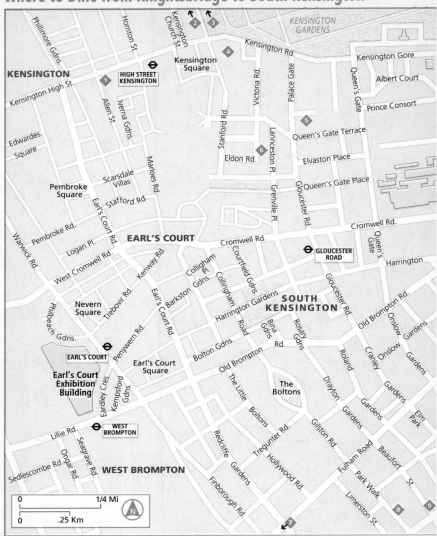

KENSINGTON GARDENS

Kensington Rd.

Kensington Gore

Kensington Square

Kensington Gore

Albert Court

Prince Consort

HIGH STREET KENSINGTON

KENSINGTON

Phillimore Gdns.

Hornton St.

Kensington Church St.

Kensington Rd.

Kensington High St.

Kensington Square

Victoria Rd.

Palace Gate

Queen's Gate

Allen St.

Iverna Gdns.

Stanford Rd.

Queen's Gate Terrace

Edwardes Square

Eldon Rd.

Lanceston Pl.

Elvaston Place

Scarsdale Villas

Marloes Rd.

Grenville Pl.

Queen's Gate Place

Pembroke Square

Earl's Court Rd.

Stafford Rd.

Gloucester Rd.

Cromwell Rd.

Queen's Gate

Pembroke Rd.

EARL'S COURT

Cromwell Rd.

GLOUCESTER ROAD

Harrington

Logan Pl.

Warwick Rd.

West Cromwell Rd.

Kenway Rd.

Collingham Pl.

Courtfield Gdns.

Gloucester Rd.

Old Brompton Rd.

Onslow Gardens

Nevern Square

Trebovir Rd.

Barkston Gdns.

Collingham Gdns.

Harrington Gardens

SOUTH KENSINGTON

Roland Gardens

Cranley Gardens

Onslow Gardens

Philbeach Gdns.

Penywern Rd.

Earl's Court Rd.

Bolton Gdns.

Bina Gdns.

Rd.

Rosary Gdns.

Drayton Gardens

Elm Park

EARL'S COURT

Eardley Cres.

Kempsford Gdns.

Earl's Court Square

Old Brompton Rd.

The Boltons

Gardens

Earl's Court Exhibition Building

WEST BROMPTON

The Little Boltons

The Boltons

Gilston Rd.

Fulham Road

Beaufort

Lillie Rd.

Seagrave Rd.

Ongar Rd.

Redcliffe Gardens

Tregunter Rd.

Hollywood Rd.

Park Walk

St.

Sedlescombe Rd.

WEST BROMPTON

Finborough Rd.

Limerston St.

0      1/4 Mi

0      .25 Km

N

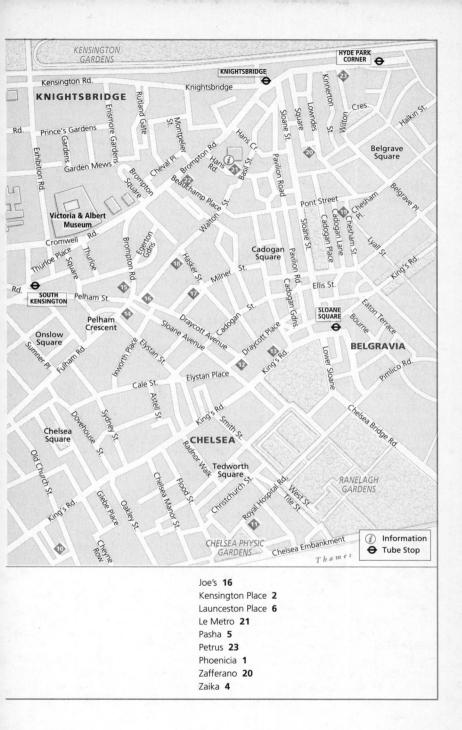

KENSINGTON GARDENS

HYDE PARK CORNER ⊖

KNIGHTSBRIDGE ⊖

Kensington Rd.

Knightsbridge

KNIGHTSBRIDGE

Kinnerton St.
Lowndes St.
Wilton Cres.
Halkin St.
Sloane St.
Lowndes Square

23

Rd.

Prince's Gardens

Ennismore Gardens

Rutland Gate

Montpelier St.

Brompton Rd.

Hans Rd.

Hans Cr.

Pavilion Road

Belgrave Square

Exhibition Rd.

Gardens

Garden Mews

Cheval Pl.

Brompton Square

Beauchamp Place

22

Hans Rd.

Basil St.

ⓘ

21

Pont Street

Belgrave Pl.

Victoria & Albert Museum

Cromwell Rd.

Walton St.

Sloane St.

Chesham Pl.

19 Chesham St.

Cadogan Place

Cadogan Lane

Lyall St.

King's Rd.

Thurloe Place

Thurloe Square

Brompton Rd.

Egerton Gdns

Hasker St.

18

Milner St.

Cadogan Square

Pavilion Rd.

Cadogan St.

SOUTH KENSINGTON ⊖

Pelham St.

15

16

17

Draycott Avenue

Cadogan St.

Draycott Place

Cadogan Gdns

Ellis St.

SLOANE SQUARE ⊖

Eaton Terrace

Bourne St.

BELGRAVIA

Onslow Square

Summer Pl.

Pelham Crescent

Fulham Rd.

14

Ixworth Place

Elystan St.

Sloane Avenue

12

Elystan Place

23

King's Rd.

Lower Sloane St.

Pimlico Rd.

Cale St.

Astell St.

King's Rd.

Smith St.

Chelsea Bridge Rd.

Chelsea Square

Dovehouse St.

Sydney St.

Chelsea Manor St.

Flood St.

Radnor Walk

CHELSEA

Tedworth Square

Christchurch St.

Royal Hospital Rd.

West St.

Tite St.

RANELAGH GARDENS

Old Church St.

King's Rd.

Glebe Place

Oakley St.

Cheyne Row

10

11

CHELSEA PHYSIC GARDENS

Chelsea Embankment

Thames

ⓘ Information
⊖ Tube Stop

precision and a touch of whimsy, served in a sleek, opulent setting. It's best to order the chef's six-course tasting menu to appreciate Wareing's culinary ambitiousness. You'll be dazzled with everything from marinated foie gras to an apple-and-artichoke salad, from Bresse pigeon in a truffle confit to a Valhrona chocolate fondant. We've delighted in all the dishes we've sampled here, from the eggplant caviar to the slow-baked sea bass with shallots braised in red wine and port, sautéed green beans, and parsnip purée.

The Berkeley Hotel, Wilton Place, Knightsbridge, SW1. © 020/7235-1200. Reservations required. Fixed-price menu 3 courses £30–£60 ($56–$111); 6-course tasting menu £70 ($130). AE, DC, MC, V. Mon–Fri noon–2:30pm; Mon–Sat 6:45–10:45pm. Tube: Hyde Park Corner or Knightsbridge.

**Zafferano** ✶✶ ITALIAN There's something honest and satisfying about this restaurant, where decor consists of little more than ochre-colored walls, immaculate linens, and a bevy of diligent staff members. A quick review of past clients includes Margaret Thatcher, Richard Gere, Princess Margaret, and Eric Clapton. The modernized interpretation of Italian cuisine features such dishes as ravioli of pheasant with black truffles, wild pigeon with garlic purée, sea bream with spinach and balsamic vinegar, and monkfish with almonds. Joan Collins claimed that the chefs produce culinary fireworks, but found the bright lighting far too harsh. The owners pride themselves on one of the most esoteric and well-rounded collections of Italian wine in London: You'll find as many as 20 different vintages each of Brunello and Barolos and about a dozen vintages of Sassecaia.

15 Lowndes St., SW1. © 020/7235-5800. Reservations required. Set menus £30–£42 ($55–$77). AE, MC, V. Daily noon–2:30pm and 7–11pm (until 10:30pm on Sun). Tube: Knightsbridge.

## EXPENSIVE

**The Collection** ✶ INTERNATIONAL/MODERN BRITISH This is a temple to voyeurism and the vanities, catering to the aesthetics and preoccupations of the fashion industry. It occupies an echoing warehouse; the only access is by a 9m (30-ft.) catwalk that feels like it should have couture models striding along it. Don't worry about a snobbish chill: Manager Julian Shaw is one of the most adept and humorous in London, a celebrity in his own right because of his skill at dealing with big-ticket, big-ego fashion moguls. Yummy menu items include such appetizers as scallops with a green-mango salad, and such main courses as seared yellowfin tuna with eggplant, cumin, and caperberries. For a change of pace, perhaps you'll opt for the grilled bison with mushrooms and a green peppercorn sauce. Don't overlook this place as a stop on your after-dark bar hop.

264 Brompton Rd., SW3. © 020/7225-1212. Reservations recommended. Main courses £11–£25 ($20–$46); fixed-price menu £35–£40 ($65–$74). AE, DC, MC, V. Mon–Fri 6:30–midnight; Sat noon–4pm and 6:30–11:30pm; Sun noon–4:30pm and 6–11pm. Tube: South Kensington.

**Floriana** ✶ ITALIAN Shoppers along Knightsbridge Street flock to this dining room, where Princess Di used to go for her Italian meal fix. The decor is smart and modern, with marble, mirrors, and an atrium roof. Chef Luca Dal Bosco prepares his food with love. He knows the classics but can be inventive. We are especially devoted to his pumpkin, chestnut, and mushroom soup. Some of his Italian dishes are as good as any we've tasted in *luxe* restaurants in Milan. Among these winners is the roast cod with Italian bacon, red onions, and Gorgonzola; and the roast filet of pork flavored with garlic and served with lemon sauce and perfectly cooked broccoli. Also especially delectable is the chef's version of ravioli, stuffed with Scottish lobster, artichoke hearts, and sage.

15 Beauchamp Place, SW3. © **020/7838-1500.** Reservations required. Main courses £15–£20 ($28–$37). Fixed-price 2-course lunch £15 ($28), 3-course lunch £20 ($36). AE, DC, MC, V. Mon–Sat 12:30–3pm and 7–11pm. Tube: Knightsbridge.

## MODERATE

**Drones** ✪ CONTINENTAL   Britain's wonder chef, Marco Pierre White, took this once-famous but stale restaurant and has once again turned it into a chic dining venue, decorated with black-and-white photographs of the famous people lining the wall. Redesigned by David Collins, it is now referred to as "the Ivy of Belgravia." The food and Art Deco ambience is delightful, as is the staff. Food is fresh and delicately prepared, including such favorites as cauliflower cream soup with truffles and sea scallops, or smoked haddock and rice pudding. All the delectable meat and fish dishes are prepared with consummate care and served with a certain finesse. Always expect some unusual flavor combination, such as oxtail *en daube* with a rutabaga purée and a bourguignon garnish. For dessert, a summer specialty is *gelée* of red fruits with a raspberry syrup drizzle.

1 Pont St. SW1© **020/7235-9555.** Reservations required. Main courses £9.50–£22 ($18–$41). Mon–Fri noon–2:30pm and 6–11pm; Sat 6–11pm; Sun noon–3:30pm. Tube: Knightsbridge.

## INEXPENSIVE

**Le Metro** INTERNATIONAL   Located just around the corner from Harrods, Le Metro draws a fashionable crowd to its basement precincts. The place serves good, solid, reliable food prepared with flair. The menu changes frequently, but try the chargrilled salmon with pesto, or the chicken and asparagus pie. You can order special wines by the glass.

28 Basil St., SW3. © **020/7589-6286.** Main courses £7–£11 ($13–$20). AE, DC, MC, V. Mon–Sat 7:30am–11pm. Tube: Knightsbridge.

## CHELSEA
## VERY EXPENSIVE

**Aubergine** ✪✪ FRENCH   "Eggplant" is luring savvy diners down to the lower reaches of Chelsea where new chef William Drabble takes over from where the renowned Gordon Ramsay left off. Drabble, who earned his first Michelin star in 1998, has remained true to the style and ambience of this famous establishment. Although popular with celebrities, the restaurant remains unpretentious and refuses to pander to the whims of the rich and famous. (Madonna was once refused a late-night booking!)

Every dish is satisfyingly flavorsome, from warm salad of truffled vegetables with asparagus purée, to roasted monkfish served with crushed new potatoes, roasted leeks, and red-wine sauce. Starters continue to charm and delight palates, ranging from ravioli of crab with mussels, chili, ginger, and coriander nage, to terrine of foie gras with confit of duck and pears poached in port. Also resting on your Villeroy & Boch aubergine plate might be mallard with a celeriac fondant, or assiette of lamb with a thyme-scented jus. Another stunning main course is a tranche of sea bass with bouillabaisse potatoes. A new dish likely to catch your eye is roasted veal sweetbreads with caramelized onion purée and a casserole of flap mushrooms. There are only 14 tables, so bookings are imperative.

11 Park Walk, SW10. © **020/7352-3449.** Reservations required and accepted up to 4 weeks in advance. 3-course lunch £32 ($59); fixed-price 3-course dinner £50 ($93); menu gourmand £72 ($133). AE, DC, MC, V. Mon–Fri noon–2:30pm; Mon–Sat 7–10:30pm. Tube: South Kensington.

**Gordon Ramsay** ✪✪✪ *Finds* FRENCH   One of the city's most innovative and talented chefs is Gordon Ramsay. All of London is rushing to sample Mr. Ramsay's wares, and he has had to turn away some big names. The queen hasn't been denied a table yet, but that's only because she hasn't called.

Every dish from this kitchen is gratifying, reflecting subtlety and delicacy without any sacrifice to the food's natural essence. Try, for example, Ramsay's celebrated cappuccino of white beans with grated truffles. His appetizers are likely to dazzle: salad of crispy pigs' trotters with calves' sweetbreads, fried quail eggs and a cream vinaigrette, or foie gras three ways: sautéed with quince, *mi-cuit* with an Earl Grey consommé, or pressed with truffle peelings. From here, you can grandly proceed to filet of brill poached in red wine, grilled filet of red mullet on a bed of caramelized endives, or else caramelized Challandaise duck cooked with dates. Desserts are equally stunning, especially the pistachio soufflé with chocolate sorbet or the passion fruit and chocolate parfait.

68 Royal Hospital Rd., SW3. ℂ 020/7352-4441. Reservations essential (1 month in advance). Fixed-price lunch 3 courses £35 ($65); dinner 3 courses £65 ($120) or 7 courses £80 ($148). AE, DC, MC, V. Mon–Fri noon–2:30pm and 6:30–10:30pm. Tube: Sloane Sq.

## EXPENSIVE

**Blue Bird** ✿ MEDITERRANEAN   This enormous space resounds with clinking silverware and peals of laughter from a loyal clientele. Locals and staff alike refer to it as a *restaurant de gare*—a railway-station restaurant. Downstairs is a cafe, upscale deli, and housewares store under separate management. But most of the business occurs upstairs at this restaurant, which can hold 220 diners at a time. You'll find a color scheme of red-and-blue canvas cutouts in the shape of birds in flight. Tables are close together, but the scale of the place makes dining private and intimate. The massive menu emphasizes savory, precisely cooked cuisine, some emerging from a wood-burning stove used to roast everything from lobster to game. An immense shellfish bar stocks every crustacean you can think of, and the liquor bar does a thriving business with the Sloane Square subculture. Perennial favorites include the pan-fried halibut with mussels and baby leeks, as well as pasta and fresh fish. We're also fond of the chef's smoked haddock chowder. Most recently, we followed the chowder with deliciously seared scallops with an artichoke purée, and the filet of beef with pancetta and braised onions.

Oh, the name: Before it was a restaurant, the site was a garage that repaired the legendary Bluebird, an English sports car that is, alas, no longer produced.

350 King's Rd., SW3. ℂ 020/7559-1000. Reservations recommended. Main courses £8–£47 ($15–$87); fixed-price menu £15–£20 ($28–$37). AE, DC, MC, V. Mon–Fri 12:30–3pm and 6–11:30pm; Sat noon–3:30pm and 6–11:30pm; Sun noon–3:30pm and 6–10:30pm. Tube: Sloane Sq.

**English Garden** ✿ TRADITIONAL BRITISH   This is a metropolitan restaurant par excellence. The decor in this historic town house is pretty and lighthearted: The Garden Room is whitewashed brick with a domed conservatory roof; vivid florals, rattan chairs, banks of plants, and candy-pink linens complete the scene. Every component of the meal is carried out perfectly. Some of the dishes sound as if they were copied directly from an English cookbook of the Middle Ages—and are they ever good. For a main course, opt for such delights as roast baron of rabbit with oven-dried tomato, prunes, and olive-oil mash; or saddle of venison with potted cabbage. Desserts, especially the rhubarb-and-cinnamon ice cream, and the candied-orange tart with orange syrup, would've pleased Miss Marple. Only fixed-price menus are served.

10 Lincoln St., SW3. ℂ 020/7584-7272. Reservations required. Fixed-price lunch £24 ($43), 3-course dinner £29 ($54). AE, DC, MC, V. Mon–Sat noon–3pm and 6:30–10:30pm. Tube: Sloane Sq.

## INEXPENSIVE

**Chelsea Kitchen** INTERNATIONAL    This simple restaurant feeds large numbers of Chelsea residents in a setting that's changed little since 1961. The food and the clientele move fast, almost guaranteeing that the entire inventory of ingredients is sold out at the end of each day. Menu items usually include leek-and-potato soup, chicken Kiev, chicken parmigiana, steaks, sandwiches, and burgers. The clientele includes a broad cross-section of Londoners—all having a good and cost-conscious time.

98 King's Rd., SW3. ℭ 020/7589-1330. Reservations recommended. Main courses £4–£6 ($7.40–$11); fixed-price menu £6.40 ($12). MC, V. Daily 7am–11:45pm. Tube: Sloane Sq.

**Front Page** THAI    Front Page is favored by young professionals who like the atmosphere of wood paneling, wooden tables, and pews and benches. On cold nights, an open fire burns. The pub stands in a residential section of Chelsea and is a good place to go for a drink and some Thai pub grub. Check the chalkboard for the daily specials, which might include hot chicken salad and fish cakes.

35 Old Church St., SW3. ℭ 020/7352-2908. Main courses £7.50–£12 ($14–$22). AE, DC, DISC, MC, V. Restaurant Mon–Fri noon–2:30pm, Sat–Sun 12:30–3pm, Mon–Sat 7–11pm, Sun 7–10:30pm; pub Mon–Sat 11am–11pm, Sun noon–10:30pm. Tube: Sloane Sq.

# KENSINGTON & SOUTH KENSINGTON
## EXPENSIVE

**Bibendum/The Oyster Bar** ✪ FRENCH/MEDITERRANEAN    In trendy Brompton Cross, this still-fashionable restaurant occupies two floors of a garage that's now an Art Deco masterpiece. Though its heyday came in the early 1990s, the white-tiled room with stained-glass windows, lots of sunlight, and a chic clientele, is still an extremely pleasant place. The eclectic cuisine, known for its freshness and simplicity, is based on what's available seasonally. Dishes might include roast pigeon with celeriac purée and apple sauté, rabbit with artichoke and parsley sauce, or grilled lamb cutlets with a delicate sauce. Some of the best dishes are for splitting between two people, including Bresse chicken flavored with fresh tarragon, and grilled veal chops with truffle butter.

Simpler meals and cocktails are available in the **Oyster Bar** on the building's street level. The bar-style menu stresses fresh shellfish presented in the traditional French style, on ice-covered platters adorned with strands of seaweed. It's a crustacean-lover's dream.

81 Fulham Rd., SW3. ℭ 020/7581-5817. Reservations required in Bibendum; not accepted in Oyster Bar. Main courses £16–£24 ($30–$44); fixed-price 3-course lunch £29 ($53); cold seafood platter in Oyster Bar £48 ($89) for 2. AE, DC, MC, V. Bibendum: Mon–Fri noon–2:30pm and 7–11pm, Sat–Sun 12:30–3pm and 7–11pm; Oyster Bar: Mon–Sat noon–10:30pm, Sun noon–3pm and 7–10:30pm. Tube: South Kensington.

**Clarke's** ✪ MODERN BRITISH    Sally Clarke is one of the finest chefs in London, and this is one of the hottest restaurants around. *Still.* She opened it in the Thatcher era, and it's still going strong. In this excellent restaurant, everything is bright and modern, with wood floors, discreet lighting, and additional space in the basement where tables are more spacious and private. Some people are put off by the fact that there is only a fixed-price menu, but the food is so well prepared that diners rarely object to what ends up in front of them. The menu, which changes daily, emphasizes chargrilled foods with herbs and seasonal veggies. You might begin with an appetizer salad of blood orange with red onions, watercress, and black olive–anchovy toast, then follow with roasted breast of chicken with black truffle, crisp polenta, and arugula. Desserts are likely to include a warm pear-and-raisin puff pastry with maple syrup ice cream. Just put yourself in Clarke's hands—you'll be glad you did.

124 Kensington Church St., W8. © 020/7221-9225. Reservations recommended. Fixed-price lunch £15–£17 ($27–$31), 4-course dinner £50 ($92); Sat brunch £7.50–£11 ($14–$20). AE, DC, MC, V. Mon 12:30–2pm, Tues–Fri 12:30–2pm and 7–10pm; Saturday brunch 11am–2pm and dinner 7–10pm. Tube: High St. Kensington or Notting Hill Gate.

**Launceston Place** ★ MODERN BRITISH  Launceston Place is in an almost villagelike neighborhood where many Londoners would like to live, if only they could afford it. This stylish restaurant lies within a series of uncluttered Victorian parlors, the largest of which is illuminated by a skylight. Each room contains a collection of Victorian-era oils and watercolors, as well as contemporary paintings. The restaurant has been known for its new British cuisine since 1986. The menu changes every 6 weeks, but you're likely to be served such appetizers as smoked salmon with horseradish crème fraîche, goat-cheese soufflé, or seared foie gras with lentils and vanilla dressing. For a main dish, perhaps it'll be roast partridge with bacon, onions, and parsnip mash, or grilled sea bass with tomato-and-basil cream.

1A Launceston Place, W8. © 020/7937-6912. Reservations required. Main courses £14–£18 ($26–$33); fixed-price 2-course menu for lunch and early dinner until 8pm £16 ($29), 3 courses £19 ($34). AE, DC, MC, V. Mon–Fri and Sun 12:30–2:30pm; Mon–Sat 7–11:30pm; Sun 7–10pm. Tube: Gloucester Rd. or High St. Kensington.

## MODERATE

**Blue Elephant** ★ THAI  This is the counterpart of the famous L'Éléphant Bleu restaurant in Brussels. In a converted factory building in West Brompton, the Blue Elephant has been all the rage since 1986. It remains the leading Thai restaurant in London, where the competition seems to grow daily. In an almost magical garden setting of tropical foliage, diners are treated to an array of MSG-free Thai dishes. You can begin with a "Floating Market" (shellfish in clear broth, flavored with chile paste and lemon grass), then go on to a splendid selection of main courses, for which many of the ingredients have been flown in from Thailand. We recommend the roasted-duck curry served in a clay cooking pot.

4–6 Fulham Broadway, SW6. © 020/7385-6595. Reservations required. Main courses £10–£18 ($19–$33); Royal Thai banquet £35–£39 ($65–$72); Sun buffet £22 ($41). AE, DC, MC, V. Mon–Fri and Sun noon–2:30pm; daily 7pm–midnight. Tube: Fulham Broadway.

**The Enterprise** EUROPEAN/TRADITIONAL BRITISH  The Enterprise's proximity to Harrods attracts both regulars and out-of-town shoppers. Although the joint swarms with singles at night, during the day it attracts the ladies who lunch. With banquettes, white linen, and fresh flowers, you won't mistake it for a lowly boozer. The kitchen serves respectable traditional English fare as well as European favorites, all prepared with fresh ingredients. Featured dishes include fried salmon cakes with butter spinach, golden calamari, and grilled steak with fries and salad. The juicy, properly aged, flavorful, and thin entrecôte slice of beef is about the best you can find in London.

35 Walton St., SW3. © 020/7584-3148. Reservations accepted for lunch only Mon–Fri. Main courses £8–£13 ($15–$24). AE, MC, V. Mon–Fri 12:30–2:30pm; Sat–Sun 12:30–3:30pm; daily 6–10pm (the bar is open all day). Tube: South Kensington or Knightsbridge.

**Joe's** ★ *Finds* MODERN BRITISH  One of three London restaurants established by fashion designer Joseph Ettedgui, it's often filled at breakfast and lunch with well-known names from the British fashion, music, and entertainment industries, thanks to its sense of glamour and fun. You can enjoy such dishes as spiced venison strips and vegetables, fresh fish of the day, or pasta of the day.

Also very popular is Joe's Burger, the chargrilled vegetables, or the grilled chicken on a bed of steamed vegetables. It's all safe, but a bit unexciting. No one will mind if your meal is composed exclusively of appetizers. There's a bar near the entrance, a cluster of tables for quick meals near the door, and more leisurely (and gossipy) dining available in an area a few steps up. The atmosphere remains laid-back and unstuffy, just like trendsetters in South Ken prefer it. With a name like Joe's, what else could it be?

126 Draycott Ave., SW3. ℂ 020/7225-2217. Reservations required on weekdays, not accepted on weekends. Main courses £10–£15 ($19–$28). AE, MC, V. Daily 9:30am–6pm. Tube: South Kensington.

**Kensington Place** EUROPEAN    Rowley Leigh, the chef here, has attracted a devoted following of regulars. But word of his delicious cuisine is spreading, and now more and more visitors are rushing here to sample some of his signature dishes, such as griddled foie gras on a sweet-corn pancake, and scallops with pea purée and mint vinaigrette. His slow-braised lamb shank is one of the best dishes of its kind. Also look for Leigh's innovative seasonal dishes. The chef has a marvelous way with grouse, venison, roast partridge, and sea bass. He grills scallops to golden perfection, and goat-cheese mousse and olives enhance even the simplest chicken dish. Everybody from pop stars to Kensington dowagers flock to this animated, noisy bistro. The set lunch is one of the best values in the area. Save room for the steamed chocolate pudding with custard. Harking back to olde England, the chef still serves rhubarb fool or a summer trifle flavored with red fruits and liqueur.

201 Kensington Church St., W8. ℂ 020/7727-3184. Reservations required. Main courses £13–£27 ($23–$49); fixed-price lunch £17 ($31) Mon–Sat, £19 ($34) Sun. AE, DC, MC, V. Mon–Sat noon–3:30pm and 6:30–11:45pm; Sun noon–3:30pm and 6:30–10:15pm. Tube: Notting Hill Gate.

**Pasha** MOROCCAN    You'll find virtually every kind of ethnic restaurant within London, but few boast the zest and stylishness of this re-creation of a palace within the medina at Marrakech. Each of the two dining rooms is outfitted with Bedouin colors, rich upholsteries, flickering candles, and belly-dancing music. You'll enjoy regional specialties that were once sampled only by cherished royal-family guests. Examples include a crispy lamb salad with pomegranate and mint, grilled sea bass with warm hummus and parsley salad, chicken *merguez* (spicy sausage) with a coriander tagine, and chargrilled skewered chicken with green-chile salsa. And if you have a fondness for couscous, you'll have at least three different kinds to choose from.

1 Gloucester Rd., SW7. ℂ 020/7589-7969. Reservations recommended. Main courses £9.75–£17 ($18–$31). AE, DC, MC, V. Mon–Sat noon–3pm and 6–11pm; Sun 7–10:30pm. Tube: Gloucester Rd.

**Phoenicia** *Value* LEBANESE    Phoenicia is highly regarded for its Lebanese cuisine—outstanding in presentation and freshness—and for its moderate prices. For the best value, go for lunch on Saturday or Sunday and enjoy a buffet of more than two dozen *meze* (appetizers) in little pottery dishes. Try the chef's chicken in garlic sauce or stuffed lamb with vegetables. Many Lebanese patrons begin their meals with the *aperitif arak,* a liqueur that some compare to the Greek anise-flavored liqueur *ouzo.* To start, select from such classic Middle Eastern dishes as hummus or stuffed vine leaves. The chefs bake fresh bread and two types of pizza daily. Minced lamb, spicy and well flavored, is an eternal favorite. Charcoal-grilled dishes are also offered.

11–13 Abingdon Rd., W8. ℂ 020/7937-0120. Reservations required. Main courses £11–£15 ($20–$28); buffet lunch £13–£15 ($24–$28); fixed-price dinner £17–£25 ($31–$46). AE, DC, MC, V. Daily noon–midnight; buffet lunch daily 12:15–3:30pm. Tube: High St. Kensington.

**Zaika** ★★ INDIAN   Although a dish might miss here and there, this restaurant nonetheless continues to receive accolades as one of the most accomplished of its type in Britain. In a former bank building in Kensington, the restaurant serves one innovative dish after another in flavors and combinations that may be new to you. Zaika lives up to its name, which, translated, means "sophisticated flavors." Of course, you can also order traditional dishes such as lamb and lentil patties stuffed with egg and onion. For starters, launch your repast with such delights as a platter of minced duck rolls or else morsels of tandoori chicken breast in green herbs. Main courses feature some sublime harmonies of flavor such as pan-fried and spicy sea bass with Indian couscous, raw mango, and a turmeric sauce, or else—one of our favorites—"butter chicken," a classic tandoori chicken breast, with a buttery tomato sauce flavored with fenugreek, with saffron rice and stir-fried spinach. For a true feast, order the tasting menu, *Jugalbandi.*

1 Kensington High St., W8. ✆ **020/7795-6533**. Reservations required. Main courses £13–£22 ($23–$40), 5-course *Jugalbandi* menu £34 ($62) excluding wine. AE, MC, V. Mon–Fri noon–2:30pm; Mon–Sat 6:30–10:45pm; Sun noon–2:45pm and 6:30–10pm. Tube: High St. Kensington.

## INEXPENSIVE

**Admiral Codrington** ★ *Finds* CONTINENTAL/MODERN BRITISH Once a lowly pub, this stylish bar and restaurant is now all the rage. The exterior has been maintained, but the old "Cod," as it is affectionately known, has emerged to offer plush dining with a revitalized decor by Nina Campbell and a glass roof that rolls back on sunny days. The bartenders still offer a traditional pint, but the sophisticated menu features such delectable fare as grilled calves' liver and crispy bacon, or pan-fried rib-eye with a truffled horseradish cream. Opt for the charbroiled tuna with eggplant caviar and a red-pepper vinaigrette.

17 Mossop St., SW3. ✆ **020/7581-0005**. Reservations recommended. Main courses £10–£15 ($19–$28). AE, MC, V. Mon–Sat 11:30am–midnight; Sun noon–10:30pm. Tube: South Kensington.

## 6 Marylebone to Notting Hill Gate

## MARYLEBONE
### EXPENSIVE

**Assaggi** ★★ *Finds* ITALIAN   Some of London's finest Italian cuisine is served in this room above a pub. This place is a real discovery, and completely unpretentious. The relatively simple menu highlights the creative, outstanding cookery. All the ingredients are fresh and deftly handled by a skilled kitchen staff. Simplicity and flavor reign throughout. The appetizers, such as smoked swordfish salad or beef carpaccio, are so truly sublime that you'll want to make a meal entirely of them. At least three freshly made pastas are featured nightly. The tortellini (pocket-shaped noodles filled with cheese) with pork and a zesty tomato sauce is especially delicious. For a main course, opt for such delights as the thick, juicy, tender grilled veal, flavored with fresh rosemary; or the grilled sea bass with braised fennel. Another savory choice is a plate of lamb cutlets (without any fat) with eggplant and a raisin salad. The flourless chocolate cake is the finest you'll find this side of northern Italy.

39 Chepstow Place, W2. ✆ **020/7792-5501**. Reservations required (as far in advance as possible). Main courses £16–£20 ($30–$37). DC, MC, V. Mon–Fri 12:30–2:30pm and 7:30–11pm; Sat 1–2:30pm and 7:30–11pm. Closed 2 weeks at Christmas. Tube: Notting Hill Gate.

**Locanda Locatelli** ★★ ITALIAN   Inside InterContinental's Churchill Hotel, this Italian restaurant is the success of the moment, attracting the likes of everybody from Tony Blair to Madonna (but not together). Its charismatic owner, Giorgio Locatelli, is something of a celebrity himself these days. In a sleek, modern dining room with etched glass panels and leather banquettes, you are served some of London's finest Italian fare. Beginning with the appetizers, dishes burst with flavor. We are especially fond of the artichoke and ham hock salad, and the pan-fried scallops with saffron, both served as starters. The food is superbly cooked and beautifully presented, especially the succulent home-made pastas, such as ravioli filled with lemon cream and a pork ragout, or the chargrilled fresh tuna with wild rocket and cherry tomatoes. We give high praise to the roast rabbit with Parma ham and polenta, and the rolled pork stuffed with herbs and fried zucchini. For dessert? Heaven sent is the dark-red, spiced-wine polenta with a licorice mousse and poached pears, or else a feathery mascarpone mousse with frangipane *tuiles*.

8 Seymour St., W1. © 020/7935-9088. Reservations required. Main courses £16–£27 ($30–$50). AE, DISC, MC, V. Mon–Fri noon–3pm and 7–11pm; Sat 7–11:30pm. Tube: Marble Arch.

**Odin's** ⭐ INTERNATIONAL    This elegant restaurant is one of at least four in London owned by chef Richard Shepherd and actor Michael Caine. Set adjacent to its slightly less expensive twin, Langan's Bistro, it features ample space between tables and an eclectic decor that includes evocative paintings and Art Deco accessories. As other restaurants nearby have come and gone, the cookery here remains solid and reliable. The standard of fresh ingredients and well-prepared dishes is always maintained. The menu changes with the seasons: Typical fare may include forest mushrooms in brioche, braised leeks glazed with mustard and tomato sauce, roast duck with applesauce and sage and onion stuffing, or roast filet of sea bass with a juniper cream sauce.

27 Devonshire St., W1. © 020/7935-7296. Reservations required. Fixed-price 2-course lunch or dinner £26 ($48), 3 courses £29 ($54). AE, DC, MC, V. Mon–Fri 12:30–2:30pm and 6:30–11pm. Tube: Regent's Park.

**Orrey** ⭐⭐ FRENCH/INTERNATIONAL    With ingredients imported from France, this is one of London's classic French restaurants. Sea bass from the shores of Montpellier, olive oil from Maussane-les-Alpilles, mushrooms from the fields of Calais, and poultry from Bresse—they all turn up on a highly refined menu, the creation of chef Andre Garret. On the second floor of The Conran Shop in Marylebone, Orrey changes its menu seasonally to take advantage of the best produce. Garret is a purist in terms of ingredients. Our favorites among his first-rate dishes are Bresse pigeon with savoy cabbage and mushroom ravioli, or duckling with an endive tatin and *cepe* (flap mushrooms) sauce. Everything has a brilliant often-whimsical touch, as evoked by the sautéed leeks in pumpkin oil. Skipping the blueberry soufflé, we ended with a cheese plate featuring a Banton goat cheese from Provence so fresh that it oozed onto the plate. Enjoy lazy summer evenings on a fourth-floor terrace while drinking and ordering light fare from the bar menu.

55 Marylebone High St., W1. © 020/7616-8000. Reservations required. Main courses £17–£30 ($31–$56); fixed-price 3-course lunch £24 ($43), 6-course dinner £55 ($102). AE, DC, MC, V. Daily noon–3pm; Mon–Sat 7–11pm; Sun 7–10:30pm. Tube: Baker St.

## MODERATE

**Bush Bar & Grill** ⭐ *Finds* FRENCH/MODERN BRITISH    Hip, light-hearted, and sought after by the quasi-celebrities of London's world of media and entertainment, this bar and brasserie was established in 2000 by the owners of two of the city's most desirable private clubs, Woody's and The Groucho Club. Both of these are membership-only venues in other parts of town. At the tables near you at this spin-off restaurant (not a members-only spot), you're

# Where to Dine from Marylebone to Notting Hill Gate

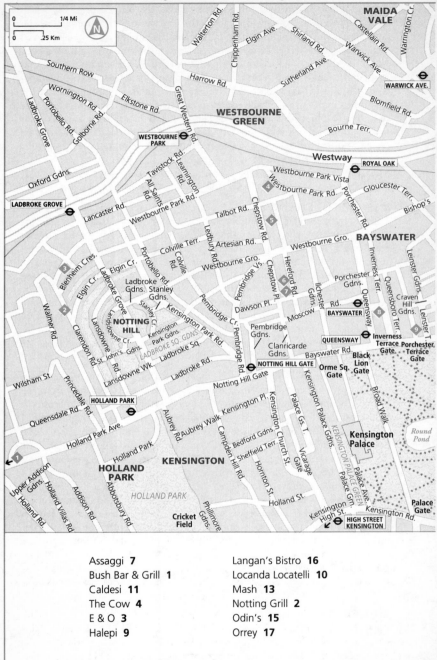

Assaggi **7**

Bush Bar & Grill **1**

Caldesi **11**

The Cow **4**

E & O **3**

Halepi **9**

Langan's Bistro **16**

Locanda Locatelli **10**

Mash **13**

Notting Grill **2**

Odin's **15**

Orrey **17**

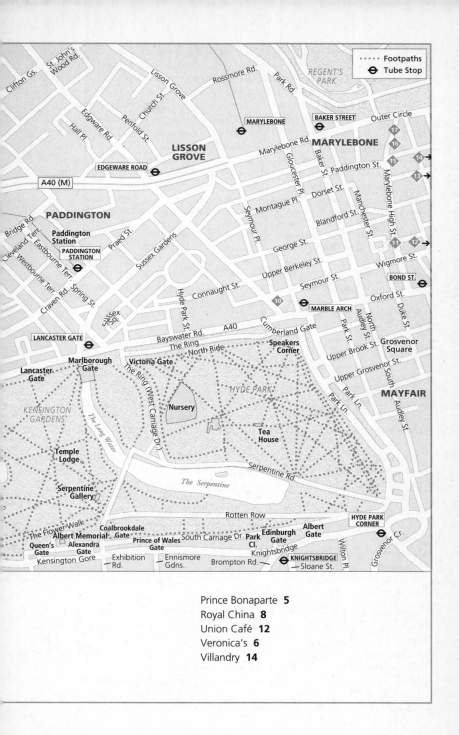

Prince Bonaparte **5**
Royal China **8**
Union Café **12**
Veronica's **6**
Villandry **14**

likely to see members of those clubs plus celebs like Jerry Hall, Kate Moss, cookbook author Nigella Lawson, pop singer Kylie Minogue, and writers from such publications as *British Vogue* and *Tatler*. The setting was originally conceived as a milk-bottling plant, but since a team of decorators revamped it, it evokes an arts-conscious Manhattan bistro with a neo-industrial decor, exposed air ducts, and a busy kitchen that's open to view. Chefs here place an emphasis on organic produce, preparing dishes that include French onion soup, marinated mussels, rémoulade of celeriac, roasted rib of beef served with béarnaise and french fries (made only for two diners sharing the meal), and roasted duck with mashed potatoes and black-peppercorn sauce.

45 Goldhawk Rd. ℂ 020/8746-2111. Reservations required. Main courses £9.75–£17 ($18–$31); fixed-price menus served at lunch (daily) and dinner (Mon–Sat) until 7:30pm £13–£15 ($23–$28). AE, MC, V. Mon–Sat noon–3pm and 5:30–11:30pm; Sun noon–4pm and 5:30–10:30pm. Tube: Goldhawk Rd.

**Caldesi** ITALIAN    Good food, reasonable prices, fresh ingredients, and authentic Tuscan family recipes attract a never-ending stream of patrons to this eatery founded by owner and head chef Giancarlo Caldesi. The extensive menu includes a wide array of pasta, fish, and meat dishes. Start with the excellent *insalata Caldesi*, made with tomatoes slow-roasted in garlic and rosemary oil, and served with mozzarella flown in from Tuscany. Pasta dishes include an especially flavor-filled homemade tortellini stuffed with salmon. Monkfish and prawns are flavored with wild fennel and fresh basil, or you might sample the tender duck breast à l'orange, steeped in white wine, honey, thyme, and rosemary.

15–17 Marylebone Lane, W1. ℂ 020/7935-9226. Reservations required. Main courses £9–£20 ($17–$37). AE, MC, V. Mon–Fri noon–2:30pm; Mon–Sat 6–11pm. Tube: Bond St.

**Langan's Bistro** FRENCH/TRADITIONAL BRITISH    This unpretentious bistro is still around—although perhaps it's not quite the happening scene it was when Michael Caine founded it back in the 1960s. Of the restaurants in this chain (see Langan's Brasserie, earlier in this chapter, and Odin's, above), it's the least expensive, but the most visually appealing. Set behind a brightly colored storefront, the dining room is decorated with clusters of Japanese parasols, mirrors, surrealistic paintings, and old photographs. The menu is "mostly English with a French influence." Dishes change with the seasons but might include such specialties as confit of duck with stir-fried vegetables. Longtime brasserie favorites like mussels marinara, barbecued spareribs, and baked salmon in pastry are reassuringly familiar and as good as they ever were. Check out the dish of the day. Chocoholics should finish off with the extravaganza known as "Mrs. Langan's Chocolate Pudding." Only fixed-price menus are served here.

26 Devonshire St., W1. ℂ 020/7935-4531. Reservations recommended. Fixed-price 2-course lunch or dinner £19 ($34), 3 courses £21 ($39). AE, DC, MC, V. Mon–Fri 12:30–2:30pm; Mon–Sat 6:30–11pm. Tube: Regent's Park or Baker St.

**Mash** ⟨ *Finds* CONTINENTAL    What is it, you ask? A bar? A deli? A microbrewery? Actually, it's all of the above, plus a restaurant. Breakfast and weekend brunch are the highlights, but don't ignore dinner. The owners of the hot Atlantic Bar & Grill have opened this "sunken chill-out zone" created by leading designer John Currin. The atmosphere is trendy, hip, breezy, and arty. The novelty decor includes curvy sci-fi lines that might remind you of a *Star Trek* set, and lizard-eye lighting fixtures, but ultimately the food is the attraction.

Suckling pig with spring cannellini stew made us forget all about the trendy mirrored bathrooms. So did the terrific pizzas emerging from the wood-fired oven. On another occasion, we returned for sea bass freshly grilled over wood and presented enticingly with grilled artichoke. Also try the chargrilled tuna with sautéed new potatoes, wilted spinach, and puttanesca dressing.

19–21 Great Portland St., W1. © 020/7637-5555. Reservations required. Main courses £9–£15 ($17–$28); fixed-price 2-course lunch £12 ($22), 3 courses £15 ($28). AE, DC, MC, V. Mon–Sat 7–11am, noon–3pm, and 6–11pm. Tube: Oxford Circus.

**Union Cafe** CONTINENTAL   After shopping along Oxford Street, restore your spirits with the exceptional food served at this sleek spot. The mainly female chefs use the finest-quality ingredients in every season. Everything from farmhouse English cheeses to free-range meat will tempt you. Rarely is any item oversauced, so natural, fresh flavors come to the fore. In most cases, the fresh fish and meat are chargrilled to perfection. The pepper tuna steaks, served rare, are an exceptional taste sensation, as is the oak-smoked salmon with fresh horserad-ish sauce, and the wild-boar-and-apple sausage. The wild-mushroom risotto is also especially good. If you don't want wine, you can choose some homemade drinks that might have delighted Dickens, including, for example, elderflower cordial. Desserts include that nursery-room favorite so beloved of the English: sticky toffee pudding with butterscotch sauce.

96 Marylebone Lane, W1. © 020/7486-4860. Reservations recommended. Main courses £12–£19 ($21–$34). AE, MC, V. Mon–Sat noon–3pm and 6:30–11pm. Tube: Bond St.

**Villandry** ✪ CONTINENTAL/INTERNATIONAL   Food lovers and gour-mands flock to this food store, delicatessen, and restaurant, where racks of the finest meats, cheese, and produce in the world are displayed and changed virtually every hour. The best of the merchandise is whimsically transformed into the restaurant's menu choices. The setting is an oversize Edwardian-style storefront north of Oxford Circus. The inside is a kind of minimalist temple dedicated to the glories of fresh produce and esoteric foodstuffs. Ingredients here change so frequently that the menu is rewritten twice a day—during our latest visit, it proposed such perfectly crafted dishes as breast of duck with fresh spinach and a gratin of baby onions; and pan-fried turbot with deep-fried celery, artichoke hearts, and hollandaise sauce.

170 Great Portland St., W1. © 020/7631-3131. Reservations recommended. Main courses £16–£21 ($30–$39). AE, DC, MC, V. Restaurant: Mon–Sat noon–3pm and 6–10:30pm; food store: Mon–Sat 8am–10pm, Sun 11am–4pm. Tube: Great Portland St.

## PADDINGTON & BAYSWATER
### EXPENSIVE

**Royal China** ✪ *Kids* CANTONESE/SZECHUAN   Unexpectedly delightful Szechuan and Cantonese specialties are available at this popular eatery, a family favorite. Come here for the best dim sum in London. Forget the garish decor and concentrate on what's on your plate—you'd probably have to go to Hong Kong to find Chinese cooking as authentic as this. The eight-page menu is over-whelming in its choices, and many of the classic dishes are only known to true students of Chinese cuisine. We were delighted by the Shanghai dumplings, steamed on one side and sautéed on the other. Various whole ducks and chick-ens are prepared with skill passed down through centuries. We noticed a table of London Chinese raving about the jellyfish with sesame oil, although we opted for the steamed eel with black-bean sauce.

13 Queensway, W2. © 020/7221-2535. Reservations recommended. Main courses £6–£18 ($11–$33); fixed-price dinner £28–£36 ($52–$67). AE, DC, MC, V. Mon–Sat noon–11pm; Sun noon–11:30pm. Tube: Bayswater or Queensway.

## MODERATE

**Halepi** ⭐ *Finds* CYPRIOT/GREEK    Run by the Kazolides family since 1966, this establishment is hailed by the *Automobile Association of America Guide* as the best Greek restaurant in the world. Despite its reputation, the atmosphere is informal, with rows of brightly clothed tables, *bouzouki* background music, and a large native Greek clientele.

Portions are generous. Menu items rely heavily on lamb and include kebabs, *klefticon* (baby lamb prepared with aromatic spices), moussaka (minced lamb and eggplant with béchamel sauce), and *dolmades* (vine leaves stuffed with lamb and rice). Other main courses include scallops; sea bass; Scottish halibut; huge Indonesian shrimp with lemon juice, olive oil, garlic, and spring-onion sauce; and *afelia* (filet of pork cooked with wine and spices, served with potatoes and rice). The homemade baklava is recommended for dessert. The wine list features numerous selections from Greece and Cyprus. Most dishes are moderate in price.

18 Leinster Terrace, W2. ℂ 020/7262-1070. Reservations required. Main courses £10–£26 ($19–$48); set-price menu £18–£29 ($33–$53). AE, DC, MC, V. Daily noon–1am. Closed Dec 25–26. Tube: Queensway.

**Veronica's** ⭐⭐ *Finds* TRADITIONAL BRITISH    Called the "market leader in cafe salons," Veronica's offers traditional—and historical—fare at prices you won't mind paying. It's a celebration of British cuisine over a 2,000-year period, with dishes based on medieval, Tudor, and even Roman-age recipes. The chef gives these traditional dishes imaginative, modern twists. One month she'll focus on Scotland; another month she'll concentrate on Victorian foods; during yet another she'll feature dishes from Wales; the next she'll offer an all-Irish menu; and so on. Your appetizer might be a salad called *salmagundy*, made with crunchy pickled vegetables, that Elizabeth I enjoyed in her day. Another concoction might be "Tweed Kettle," a 19th-century salmon stew recipe. Many dishes are vegetarian, and everything tastes even better when followed with a British farmhouse cheese or a pudding. The restaurant offers a moderated menu to help keep cholesterol down. The interior is brightly and attractively decorated, and the service is warm and ingratiating.

3 Hereford Rd., W2. ℂ 020/7229-5079. Reservations required. Main courses £12–£18 ($22–$32); fixed-price meals £15–£19 ($28–$35). AE, MC, V. Mon–Sat 6pm–midnight; Sun 6–10pm. Tube: Bayswater.

## NOTTING HILL GATE
## MODERATE

**The Cow** ⭐ *Finds* MODERN BRITISH    You don't have to be a young fashion victim to enjoy the superb cuisine served here (although many of the diners are). Tom Conran (son of entrepreneur Sir Terence Conran) holds forth in this increasingly hip Notting Hill watering hole. It looks like an Irish pub, but the accents you'll hear are trustafarian rather than street-smart Dublin. With a pint of Fuller's or London Pride, you can linger over the modern European menu, which changes daily but is likely to include ox tongue poached in milk; mussels in curry and cream; or a mixed grill of lamb chops, calves' liver, and sweetbreads. The seafood selections are delectable. "The Cow Special"—a half-dozen Irish rock oysters with a pint of Guinness or a glass of wine for £7 ($13)—is the star of the show. A raw bar downstairs serves other fresh seafood choices. To finish, skip the filtered coffee served upstairs (it's wretched), and opt for an espresso downstairs.

89 Westbourne Park Rd., W2. ℂ 020/7221-0021. Reservations required. Main courses £14–£20 ($26–$37). MC, V. Mon–Sat 6–11pm, Sun 12:30–4pm (brunch) and 6:30–10pm; bar daily noon–4pm and 6pm–midnight. Tube: Westbourne Grove.

## INEXPENSIVE

**Prince Bonaparte** INTERNATIONAL   This offbeat restaurant serves great pub grub in what used to be a grungy boozer before Notting Hill Gate became fashionable. Now pretty young things show up, spilling onto the sidewalk when the evenings are warm. The pub is filled with mismatched furniture from schools and churches; and CDs of jazz and lazy blues fill the air, competing with the babble. It may seem at first that the staff doesn't have its act together, but once the food arrives, you won't care—the dishes served here are very good. The menu roams the world for inspiration: Moroccan chicken with couscous is as good or better than any you'll find in Marrakech, and the seafood risotto is delicious. Roast lamb, tender and juicy, appears on the traditional Sunday menu. We recommend the London Pride or Grolsch to wash it all down.

80 Chepstow Rd., W2. ℂ 020/7313-9491. Reservations required. Main courses £9.50–£15 ($18–$28). AE, MC, V. Mon–Sat noon–11pm; Sun noon–10:30pm. Tube: Notting Hill Gate or Westbourne Park.

## LADBROKE GROVE
### MODERATE

**E&O** ASIAN   Nicole Kidman comes here to nibble on the succulent pumpkin and litchi curry, Kate Moss to devour prawn-and-chive dumplings without fear of weight gain, and Richard Branson to feast on the barbecue roasts. In an offbeat, out-of-the-way location, E&O is hailed as the "new Ivy," a reference to the most famous restaurant in the West End theater district, also a celeb favorite (after all these years). Melburnian restaurant guru Will Ricker is known for having created several hot east London dining spots. With its tiny windows, this restaurant reminds some patrons of a dance club.

We recently sampled the crispy fried fish and pronounce it a winner, as is the crispy-skin chicken and the *char siu* pork—baby pork spareribs crusted with sesame seeds and served with a garlic-and-ginger sauce. Succulent sushi and sashimi appear on the menu. One London reviewer found the patrons "comically trendy," although we'd call them more fashionable instead. At least they were insiderish enough to book a table at this place.

14 Blenheim Crescent, W11. ℂ 020/7229-5454. Reservations required. Main courses £9.50–£20 ($18–$37). AE, DC, MC, V. Mon–Fri 12:15–3pm and 6:15–10:30pm; Sat 12:15–4pm and 6:15–10:30pm; Sun 1–4pm and 6:15–10pm. Tube: Ladbroke Grove or Notting Hill Gate.

**Notting Grill** ⭐ *Finds* STEAK   Notting Grill owner Anthony Worrall-Thompson looks for well-bred, well-fed animals in his search for "the Holy Grail of British meats." His dream of creating the best grill house in London, using the *crème de la crème* of beef and fish, is more or less coming true in this out-of-the-way, offbeat rendezvous for serious foodies. Since Britain is known for its great breeds of beef cattle, Worrall-Thompson features a different purebread steak each month, ranging from Welsh Black to Aberdeen Angus, from Hereford to Ruby Red. He also searches Britain for the best of lamb and pork, and regardless of food scares, he serves only British-raised meat. With little fuss or bother, he also offers succulent scallops, "Big Daddy" prawns, organic sausages, and calf's liver. He has even brought back Sir Winston's favorite, the mixed grill. Celebs, media types, and the arty crowd show up here. If they're not chowing down on the steaks, they're likely to be seen dining on the rare-breed Middle White pork or organic chicken with hand-cut chips. Middle White suckling pig and the 24-ounce T-bone steak are the chef's specialties.

123A Clarendon Rd., W11. (C) **020/7229-1500.** Reservations required. Main courses £15–£25 ($27–$46). AE, MC, V. Mon–Thurs 6:30–10:30pm; Fri 6:30–11:30pm; Sat noon–11:30pm; Sun noon–10pm. Tube: Ladbroke Grove (a bit of a hike from the station).

## 7 A Bit Farther Afield

## HAMMERSMITH

To see where Hammersmith lies in relation to central London, refer to the map "Greater London Area" (p. 74).

### VERY EXPENSIVE

**The River Café** ★★ ITALIAN  For the best Italian cuisine in London, head to this Thames-side bistro operated by Ruth Rogers and Rose Gray. The charmingly contemporary establishment, with a polished steel bar, was designed by Ruth's husband, Richard, who also designed the Pompidou Centre in Paris. The cafe attracts a trendy crowd that comes to eat fabulous food and to see and be seen. The menu changes regularly. The owners' goal was to re-create the kind of cuisine they'd enjoyed in private homes in the Italian countryside, and they've succeeded. Some of London's chefs can be seen shopping in local markets—but not The River Café's chefs. The market comes to them: first-spring asparagus harvested in Andalusia and arriving in London within the day; live scallops and langoustines taken by divers in the icy North Sea; and a daily shipment of the finest harvest of Italy, ranging from radicchio to artichokes. Even tiny bulbs of fennel are zipped across the Channel from France. Britain's own rich bounty appears on the menu as well—in the form of pheasant and wild salmon. The best dishes are either slowly roasted or quickly seared.

Thames Wharf, Rainville Rd., W6. (C) **020/7386-4200.** Reservations required. Main courses £25–£30 ($46–$56). AE, DC, MC, V. Mon–Sat 12:30–2:30pm and 7–11pm; Sun 12:30–2:30pm. Tube: Hammersmith.

## CAMDEN TOWN
### MODERATE

**The Engineer** ★ *Finds* EUROPEAN/THAI  This temple to north London chic is another one of our favorites. The stylishly converted pub is owned by Abigail Osborne and Tamsin Olivier, daughter of Lord Laurence Olivier (or "Larry's Daughter," as she's called locally), and is named for Victorian bridge, tunnel, and railway builder Isambard Kingdom Brunel. It sits beside Regent's

---

*Finds* **The Brew House**

Unknown to most visitors, there's a charming little place in North London for breakfast, afternoon tea, and lunches at one of Hampstead Heath's most alluring attractions. It's **The Brew House,** in Kenwood House (p. 259), Hampstead Lane, NW3 ((C) **020/8341-4384**), open in summer daily from 9am to 6pm. Off-season hours are daily 9am to 4pm. In between gazing upon that Vermeer or Rembrandt, you can enjoy one of the most idyllic breakfasts in North London or else come back for lunch. There is always a freshly made soup of the day and at least one vegetarian dish. Main courses are likely to include free-range sausages or else fresh Scottish salmon, and even free-range chicken. You can partake of the breakfast buffet for £5.75 ($11); at lunch main courses cost £4 to £9 ($7.40–$17). American Express and Visa are accepted. Tube: Northern line to Golders Green, then bus. no. 210.

Canal, one of Brunel's creations. The pub is divided into a bar, a dining room, and a garden area for warm days. The decor is light and modern. The cuisine is modern European with a Thai influence and relies on seasonal produce and organic meat and eggs. For an appetizer, try steamed mussels in a Thai-inspired spicy coconut broth, or hummus with warm flatbread. The most delightful main courses are pan-fried filet of snapper with a minted orange and date couscous, or else the chicken breast stuffed with wild mushrooms and served with an almond and parsley pesto. Desserts change nightly and might include an orange-and-cardamom pudding.

65 Gloucester Ave., NW1. ✆ 020/7722-0950. Reservations recommended. Main courses £11–£17 ($20–$31). MC, V. Daily 9am–midnight (the bar closes at 11pm). Tube: Chalk Farm or Camden Town.

## 8 Teatime

Everyone should indulge in a formal afternoon tea at least once while in London. It's a relaxing, drawn-out, civilized affair that usually consists of three courses, all elegantly served on delicate china: first, dainty finger sandwiches (with the crusts cut off, of course), then fresh-baked scones served with jam and deliciously decadent clotted cream (Devonshire cream), and then an array of bite-size sweets. All the while, an indulgent server keeps the pot of tea of your choice fresh at hand. Sometimes ports and aperitifs are on offer to accompany your final course. High tea, popular with the before-theater crowd, includes an extra serving or two, including a sandwich, making it, in essence, a light supper. Having tea is a quintessentially British experience, and we've listed our favorite tea venues below. Note that for the most popular hotels (especially The Ritz), you should make reservations as far in advance as possible. If you go to a place that doesn't take reservations, show up at least half an hour early, especially between April and October. Jacket and tie are often required for gentlemen, and jeans and sneakers are usually frowned upon.

The British Empire no longer comes to a grinding halt at 4pm with all of England rushing for their cuppa. The English still like a cup of tea in the afternoon, but in workaday London that tea is often consumed at desks piled high with papers. A proper sit-down tea is reserved mainly for those ladies-who-lunch who like to follow lunch with fattening but delectable pastries in the late afternoon. Visitors also are fond of participating in this ritual.

London is awash in coffee-bar chains, and many have abandoned the time-honored custom of afternoon tea altogether, but not all of them have. Some Londoners are returning to this quaint custom and the city is experiencing a revival of tea-drinking.

There are variations in tea-drinking, as today's London is a rainbow-hued city. Take **Mô** at 23 Heddon St. (✆ 020/7434-4040). At this offshoot of a North African restaurant, you'll think you're in Morocco as you're served mint tea in gold-encrusted glasses against a backdrop of hanging lanterns and embroidered cushions. Quite different from the traditional afternoon tea that Queen Victoria enjoyed!

If drinking tea with your pinky extended just isn't your style, we've also included a handful of less formal (and less expensive) alternatives. A full high tea costs more than £21 ($39) at the finest hotels.

Be careful when you make reservations that you are reserving at the right "Palm Court," as there are several of them.

# HIGH TEA
## MAYFAIR

Brown's Hotel ★   Along with The Ritz, Brown's ranks as one of the most chic venues for tea in London. Tea is served in the drawing room, which is decorated with English antiques, oil paintings, and floral chintz—much like the drawing room of a country estate. Give your name to the concierge upon arrival; he'll seat you at one of the sofas and settees or at a low table. There's a choice of 12 teas, plus sandwiches, scones, and pastries (all made in the hotel kitchens) rolled around on a trolley for your selection.

29–34 Albemarle St., W1. ✆ 020/7518-4108. Reservations recommended. Afternoon tea £25 ($46). AE, DC, MC, V. Daily 2–5:30pm. Tube: Green Park.

Claridge's ★   Claridge's teatime rituals have managed to persevere through the years with as much pomp and circumstance as the British Empire itself. The experience is never stuffy, though; you'll feel very welcome. Tea is served in the Reading Room. A portrait of Lady Claridge gazes from above as your choice from 17 kinds of tea is served ever so politely. The courses are served consecutively, including finger sandwiches with cheese savories, apple-and-raisin scones, and yummy pastries.

Brook St., W1. ✆ 020/7629-8860. Reservations recommended. Jacket and tie required for men after 6pm. High tea Mon–Fri £26 ($48); Sat–Sun £35 ($65) including champagne. AE, DC, MC, V. Daily 3–5:30pm. Tube: Bond St.

The Palm Court   This is one of the great London favorites for tea. Restored to its former charm, the lounge has an atmosphere straight from 1927, with a domed yellow-and-white glass ceiling, *torchères,* and palms in Compton stoneware *jardinières.* A delightful afternoon repast that includes a long list of different teas is served daily against the background of live harp music.

In the Sheraton Park Lane Hotel, Piccadilly, W1. ✆ 020/7290-7328. Reservations recommended. Afternoon tea £19 ($35); with a glass of Park Lane champagne £25 ($46). AE, DC, MC, V. Daily 3–6pm. Tube: Hyde Park Corner or Green Park.

## ST. JAMES'S

Ritz Palm Court ★★★   This is the most fashionable place in London to order afternoon tea—and the hardest to get into without reserving way in advance. The spectacular setting is straight out of *The Great Gatsby,* complete with marble steps and columns, and a baroque fountain. You can choose from a long list of teas served with delectable sandwiches and luscious pastries.

In The Ritz Hotel, Piccadilly, W1. ✆ 020/7493-8181. Reservations required at least 8 weeks in advance. Jeans and sneakers not accepted. Jacket and tie required for men. Afternoon tea £32 ($59). AE, DC, MC, V. 3 seatings daily at 1:30, 3:30, and 5:30pm. Tube: Green Park.

St. James Restaurant & The Fountain Restaurant   This pair of tea salons functions as a culinary showplace for London's most prestigious grocery store, Fortnum & Mason. The more formal of the two, the St. James, on the store's fourth floor, is a pale green-and-beige homage to formal Edwardian taste. More rapid and less formal is The Fountain Restaurant, on the street level, where a sense of tradition and manners is very much a part of the dining experience, but in a less opulent setting. There is no longer an "official" afternoon tea at The Fountain, but you can order pots of tea plus food from an a la carte menu that includes sandwiches, scones, and the like (£4.50–£12/$8.30–$22).

In Fortnum & Mason, 181 Piccadilly, W1. ✆ 020/7734-8040. St. James afternoon tea £19 ($34); high tea £21 ($38). The Fountain: A la carte menu £4.50–£12 ($8.30–$22). AE, DC, MC, V. St. James: Mon–Sat 3–5:30pm. The Fountain: Mon–Sat 3–6pm. Tube: Piccadilly Circus.

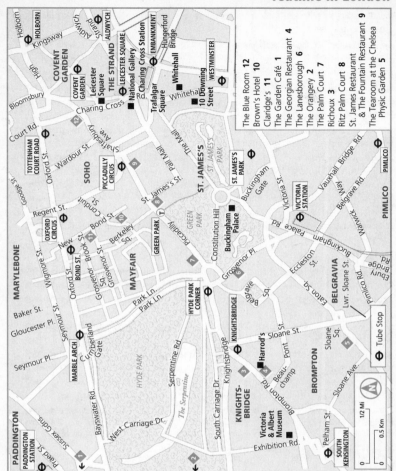

The Blue Room **12**
Brown's Hotel **10**
Claridge's **11**
The Garden Café **1**
The Georgian Restaurant **4**
The Lanesborough **6**
The Orangery **2**
The Palm Court **7**
Richoux **3**
Ritz Palm Court **8**
St. James Restaurant
& The Fountain Restaurant **9**
The Tearoom at the Chelsea
Physic Garden **5**

## KNIGHTSBRIDGE

**The Georgian Restaurant**   For as long as anyone can remember, tea at Harrods has been a distinctive feature of Europe's most famous department store. A flood of visitors is gracefully herded into a high-volume but elegant room. Many come here for the ritual of the tea service, as staff members haul silver pots and trolleys laden with pastries and sandwiches through the cavernous dining hall. Most exotic is Betigala tea, a rare blend from China, similar to Lapsang souchong.

On the 4th floor of Harrods, 87–135 Brompton Rd., SW1. © **020/7225-6800**. High tea £19 ($34) or £26 ($47) with Harrods champagne, per person. AE, DC, MC, V. Mon–Sat 3:15–5:30pm (last order). Tube: Knightsbridge.

**The Lanesborough**   You'll suspect that many of the folks sipping exotic teas here have dropped in to inspect the public areas of one of London's most expensive hotels. The staff offers a selection of seven teas that include the Lanesborough special blend, and herbal esoterica like Rose Cayou. The focal point for this ritual is the Conservatory, a glass-roofed Edwardian fantasy filled with potted plants and a sense of the long-gone majesty of empire. The finger sandwiches, scones, and sweets are all appropriately lavish and endlessly correct. Live piano music is played during afternoon tea.

Hyde Park Corner, SW1 (in the Lanesborough Hotel). © 020/7259-5599. Reservations required. High tea £25 ($45); high tea with strawberries and champagne £30 ($55); pot of tea £4.20 ($7.80). Min. charge £9.50 ($18) per person. AE, DC, MC, V. Mon–Sat 3:30–6pm and Sun 4–6pm. Tube: Hyde Park Corner.

**Richoux** There's an old-fashioned atmosphere at Richoux, established in the 1920s. You can order four hot scones with strawberry jam and whipped cream or choose from a selection of pastries. Of course, tea is obligatory; always specify lemon or cream, one lump or two. A full menu, with fresh salads, sandwiches, and burgers, is served all day. There are three other locations, open Monday through Saturday from 8am to 11pm, Sunday from 9am to 10:30pm. There's a branch at the bottom of Bond Street, 172 Piccadilly (© 020/7493-2204; Tube: Piccadilly Circus or Green Park); one at 41A S. Audley St. (© 020/7629-5228; Tube: Green Park or Hyde Park Corner); and one at 3 Circus Rd. (© 020/7483-4001; Tube: St. John's Wood).

86 Brompton Rd. (opposite Harrods), Knightsbridge, SW3. © 020/7584-8300. Full tea £13 ($25). AE, MC, V. Mon–Sat 8am–8pm; Sun 9am–8pm. Tube: Knightsbridge.

## KENSINGTON

**The Orangery** ⭐ *Finds* In its way, the Orangery is the most amazing place for afternoon tea in the world. Set 50 yards north of Kensington Palace, it occupies a long narrow garden pavilion built in 1704 by Queen Anne. In homage to her original intentions, rows of potted orange trees bask in sunlight from soaring windows, and tea is served amid Corinthian columns, ruddy-colored bricks, and a pair of Grinling Gibbons woodcarvings. There are even some urns and statuary that the royal family imported from Windsor Castle. The menu includes soups and sandwiches, with a salad and a portion of upscale potato chips known as kettle chips. The array of different teas is served with high style, accompanied by fresh scones with clotted cream and jam, and Belgian chocolate cake.

In the gardens of Kensington Palace, W8. © 020/7376-0239. Reservations not accepted. Pot of tea only £1.75–£1.95 ($3.25–$3.60); summer cakes and puddings £2.95–£3.95 ($5.45–$7.30); sandwiches £5.95–£8.95 ($11–$17). MC, V. Daily 10am–6pm. Tea 3–5pm. Tube: High St. Kensington or Queensway.

## CASUAL TEAROOMS
### SOHO

**The Blue Room** Nothing about this place will remind you of the grand tearooms above, where tea-drinking is an intricate and elaborate social ritual. What you'll find here is a cozy, eccentric enclave lined with the artworks of some of the regular patrons, battered sofas that might have come out of a college dormitory, and a gathering of likable urban hipsters to whom very little is sacred. You can enjoy dozens of varieties of tea, including herbals, served in steaming mugs. Lots of arty types gather here during the late afternoon, emulating some of the rituals of old-fashioned tea service with absolutely none of the hauteur.

3 Bateman St., W1. © 020/7437-4827. Reservations recommended. Cup of tea £1.50 ($2.80); cakes and pastries £1.50–£3.80 ($2.80–$7); sandwiches £2.70–£4.50 ($5–$8). No credit cards. Mon–Fri 8am–10:30pm; Sat 10am–10:30pm; Sun noon–10pm. Tube: Leicester Sq.

### CHELSEA

**The Tearoom at the Chelsea Physic Garden** The garden encompasses a small area, crisscrossed with gravel paths and ringed with a high brick wall that shuts out the roaring traffic of Royal Hospital Road. These few spectacular acres revere the memory of industries that were spawned from seeds developed and tested within the garden's walls. Founded in 1673 as a botanical education center, the Chelsea Physic Garden's list of successes includes the exportation of rubber from South America to Malaysia and tea from China to India.

On the 2 days a week that it's open, the tearoom is likely to be filled with botanical enthusiasts sipping cups of tea as fortification for their garden treks. The setting is a banal-looking Edwardian building. Since the tearoom is second to the garden itself, don't expect the lavish pomp of some other teatime venues. But you can carry your cakes and cups of tea out into a garden that, despite meticulous care, always looks a bit unkempt. (Herbaceous plants within its hallowed precincts are left untrimmed to encourage bird life and seed production.) Botanists and flower lovers in general find the place fascinating.

66 Royal Hospital Rd., SW3. ✆ 020/7352-5646. Tea with cake £3.50 ($6.50). MC, V (in shop only). Wed noon–5pm; Sun 2–6pm. Closed Nov–Mar. Tube: Sloane Sq.

## NOTTING HILL

**The Garden Café**    This is the most unusual of the places we recommend, and one of the most worthwhile. The Garden Café is in The Lighthouse, the largest center in Europe for people with HIV and AIDS. Princess Diana made the organization one of her projects. The cafeteria is open to the public and is less institutional looking than you might expect; French doors open onto a garden with fountains and summertime tables. Tea is available throughout the day, although midafternoon, between 3:30 and 5:30pm, seems to be the most convivial time. The Notting Hill location is a short walk from Portobello Road.

London Lighthouse, 111–117 Lancaster Rd., W11. ✆ 020/7792-1200. Cup of tea 40p (75¢); platter of food £3–£5 ($5.55–$9.25). No credit cards. Mon–Fri 9am–9pm; Sat 11am–4pm. Tube: Ladbroke Grove.

# 7

# Exploring London

Dr. Samuel Johnson said, "When a man is tired of London, he is tired of life, for there is in London all that life can afford." It would take a lifetime to explore every alley, court, street, and square in this city, and volumes to discuss them. Since you don't have a lifetime to spend, we've chosen the best that London has to offer.

For the first-time visitor, the question is never what to do, but what to do first. The "Suggested Itineraries" and "The Top Attractions" should help.

*A note about admission and open hours:* In the listings below, children's prices generally apply to those 16 and under. To qualify for a senior discount, you must be 60 or older. Students must present a student ID to get discounts, where available. In addition to closing on bank holidays, many attractions close around Christmas and New Year's (and, in some cases, early in May), so always call ahead if you're visiting in those seasons. All museums are closed Good Friday, Dec. 24 through 26, and New Year's Day.

## SUGGESTED ITINERARIES

### If You Have 1 Day

No first-time visitor should leave London without a visit to **Westminster Abbey,** with its Poet's Corner (where Browning, Dickens, and Chaucer, among others, are buried) and royal tombs. Also see the **Changing of the Guard** at Buckingham Palace if it's on, and walk to **10 Downing Street,** home of the prime minister. After lunch, see **Big Ben** and the **Houses of Parliament.** Dine at one of the little restaurants in **Covent Garden** such as **Porter's,** owned by the earl of Bradford (p. 160). Try one of their classic English pies (maybe lamb and apricot). For a pre-theater drink, head over to the ultimate Victorian pub, the Red Lion in Mayfair; it's the kind of place Oscar Wilde might have chosen for a brandy. If you're so inclined, head for a play, musical, or drama in the West End. London has the best English-language theater in the world, and the offerings are even greater than those of New York (see chapter 9, "London After Dark," for details on the theater scene).

### If You Have 2 Days

**Day 1** Spend Day 1 as above.

**Day 2** Devote a good part of the day to exploring the **British Museum,** one of the world's best museums. In the afternoon, visit the **Tower of London** and see the **Crown Jewels** (expect slow-moving lines). Later, go to a local place for dinner, such as **Shepherd's** in Westminster (p. 179), where you can dine alongside MPs from the House of Commons. Perhaps you'll catch another play this evening or head for one of London's nightclubs to dance the night away.

### If You Have 3 Days

**Days 1–2** Spend Days 1 and 2 as above.

**Day 3** In the morning, take in the masterworks at the **National Gallery.** For a change of pace in the afternoon, head to **Madame Tussaud's** waxworks if you have kids in tow. In the evening, take in a **West End** play or a performance at the **National Theatre** or at Queen Elizabeth Hall at South Bank Centre.

### If You Have 4 or 5 Days

**Days 1–3** Spend Days 1, 2, and 3 as above.

**Day 4** In the morning, head for the **City,** London's financial district. Your major sightseeing here will be Sir Christopher Wren's **St. Paul's Cathedral.** In the afternoon, head for **King's Road** in Chelsea for boutique hopping and to dine at one of Chelsea's restaurants. Later, take in a show at a **Soho** nightclub, such as Ronnie Scott's (p. 303), which features some of the city's best jazz.

**Day 5** Explore the **Victoria and Albert Museum** in the morning. Then go to the **Tate Britain Gallery** for a look at some of its masterpieces, and have lunch at its restaurant, which offers some of the best values on wine in Britain. For a glimpse of the dark days of World War II, visit the **Cabinet War Rooms** at Clive Steps, where Churchill directed British operations in the war against the Nazis. Spend the evening at the theater, or take a themed walking tour.

## 1 Sights & Attractions by Neighborhood

### BELGRAVIA
Apsley House, The Wellington Museum ✦ (p. 239)

### BLOOMSBURY
British Library ✦✦ (p. 240)
British Museum ✦✦✦ (p. 207)
Dickens House (p. 238)
Percival David Foundation of Chinese Art ✦ (p. 249)
St. Pancras Station (p. 237)

### CAMDEN TOWN
Jewish Museum (p. 246)

### CHELSEA
Carlyle's House (p. 237)
Chelsea Physic Garden (p. 254)
Chelsea Royal Hospital ✦✦ (p. 234)
National Army Museum ✦ (p. 248)

### THE CITY
All Hallows Barking-by-the-Tower (p. 223)
Guildhall Art Gallery ✦ (p. 244)
London Bridge (p. 255)
Museum of London ✦✦ (p. 248)
Old Bailey (p. 236)

Samuel Johnson's House ✦✦ (p. 239)
St. Bride's ✦ (p. 224)
St. Giles Cripplegate ✦ (p. 228)
St. Mary-le-Bow ✦✦ (p. 232)
St. Paul's Cathedral ✦✦✦ (p. 216)
Temple Church ✦✦ (p. 232)
Tower Bridge ✦✦ (p. 218)
Tower of London ✦✦✦ (p. 219)

### CLERKENWELL
St. Etheldreda's (p. 228)
Wesley's Chapel, House & Museum of Methodism (p. 233)

### COVENT GARDEN & THE STRAND
Courtauld Gallery (p. 241)
Gilbert Collection ✦✦✦ (p. 243)
Hermitage Rooms at Somerset House ✦✦✦ (p. 244)
London's Transport Museum ✦ (p. 247)
St. Paul's Church (the Actors' Church) ✦ (p. 232)
Theatre Museum (p. 252)

### DOCKLANDS
Butler's Wharf (p. 257)
Canary Wharf (p. 256)

Royal Mews ★★ (p. 250)
Spencer House ★★ (p. 236)
St. James's Church ★ (p. 228)
St. James's Park ★ (p. 253)

**TRAFALGAR SQUARE**
National Gallery ★★★ (p. 213)
National Portrait Gallery ★★
    (p. 215)
St. Martin-in-the-Fields (and
    The London Brass Rubbing
    Centre) ★ (p. 229)

**WESTMINSTER**
Banqueting House ★★ (p. 233)
Cabinet War Rooms ★ (p. 234)
Horse Guards ★ (p. 235)
Houses of Parliament & Big
    Ben ★★ (p. 211)
Jewel Tower ★ (p. 212)
Tate Britain ★★★ (p. 216)
Westminster Abbey ★★★
    (p. 222)
Westminster Cathedral ★ (p. 233)

## 2 The Top Attractions

**British Museum** ★★★    Set in scholarly Bloomsbury, this immense museum grew out of a private collection of manuscripts purchased in 1753 with the proceeds of a lottery. It grew and grew, fed by legacies, discoveries, and purchases, until it became one of the most comprehensive collections of art and artifacts in the world. It's impossible to take in this museum in a day.

The overall storehouse splits basically into the national collections of antiquities; prints and drawings; coins, medals, and banknotes; and ethnography. Even on a cursory first visit, be sure to see the Asian collections (the finest assembly of Islamic pottery outside the Islamic world), the Chinese porcelain, the Indian sculpture, and the Prehistoric and Romano-British collections. Special treasures you might want to seek out on your first visit include the **Rosetta Stone,** in the Egyptian Room, whose discovery led to the deciphering of hieroglyphics; the **Elgin Marbles,** a series of pediments, metopes, and friezes from the Parthenon in Athens, in the Duveen Gallery; and the legendary **Black Obelisk,** dating from around 860 B.C., in the Nimrud Gallery. Other treasures include the contents of Egyptian royal tombs (including mummies); fabulous arrays of 2,000-year-old jewelry, cosmetics, weapons, furniture, and tools; Babylonian astronomical instruments; and winged lion statues (in the Assyrian Transept) that guarded Ashurnasirpal's palace at Nimrud. The exhibits change throughout the year, so if your heart is set on seeing a specific treasure, call to make sure it's on display.

*Insider's Tip:* If you're a first-time visitor, you will, of course, want to concentrate on some of the fabled treasures previewed above. But what we do is duck into the British Museum several times on our visits to London, even if we have only an hour or two, to see the less heralded but equally fascinating

### *Tips* Timesaver

With 4km (2½ miles) of galleries, the British Museum is overwhelming. To get a handle on it, we recommend taking a 1½-hour overview tour for £8 ($15), £5 ($9.25) for seniors, students and children under 16. Daily at 10:30am, 1pm, or 3pm. Afterwards, you can return to the galleries that most interest you. If you have limited time to spend on the museum, concentrate on the Greek and Roman rooms (nos. 1–15), which hold the golden hoard of booty both bought and stolen from the Empire's once far-flung colonies. For information on the British Library, see p. 240.

# The Top Attractions

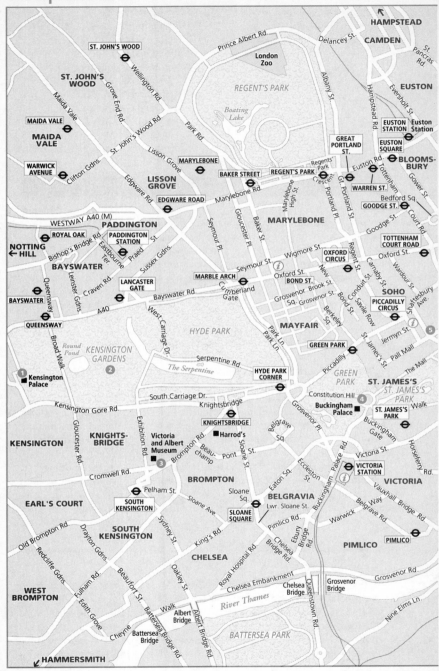

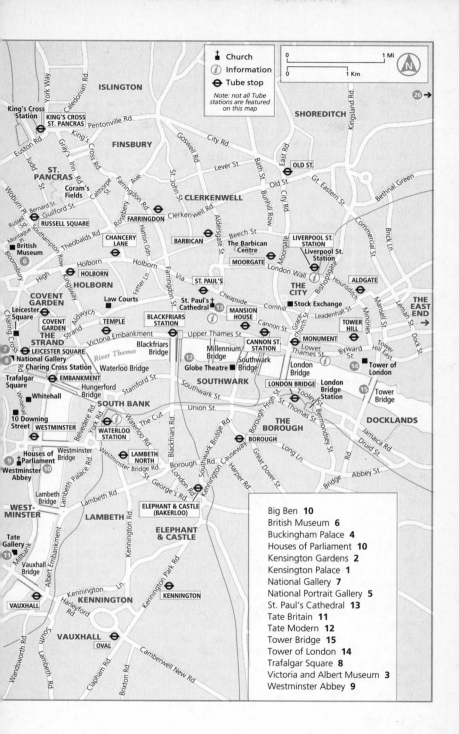

ISLINGTON

SHOREDITCH

0        1 Mi
0        1 Km

N

26 →

King's Cross
Station
KING'S CROSS
ST. PANCRAS

York Way
Caledonian Rd.
Pentonville Rd.
Euston Rd.
Judd
Grays' Inn Rd.
King's Cross Rd.
Woburn Pl.

FINSBURY

City Rd.
Goswell Rd.
Lever St.
Bath St.
City Rd.
East Rd.
OLD ST.
Old St.
Gt. Eastern St.
Kingsland Rd.
Bethnal Green

ST.
PANCRAS

Coram's
Fields
Russell
Sq.
Bernard St.
Guilford St.
Montague Pl.
Southampton Row
Theobalds Rd.
Bloomsbury

RUSSELL SQUARE

British
Museum 6

CLERKENWELL

FARRINGDON

Clerkenwell Rd.
Farringdon Rd.
Rosebery Ave.
Calthorpe
St. John St.
Aldersgate St.
Beech St.
Moorgate
Bunhill Row
London Wall
Moorgate
Commercial St.
Brick Ln.

CHANCERY
LANE

Hatton Gdn.

BARBICAN

The Barbican
Centre

MOORGATE

LIVERPOOL ST.
STATION
Liverpool St.
Station

ALDGATE

HOLBORN
HOLBORN
Holborn
High
Kingsway
Drury Ln.
Fetter Ln.

ST. PAUL'S

THE
CITY

Bishopsgate
Houndsditch
Mansell St.
Leman St.
Commercial Rd.

THE
EAST
END →

COVENT
GARDEN
Leicester
Square
COVENT
GARDEN
THE
STRAND
Charing Cross
Aldwych

Law Courts

TEMPLE

St. Paul's ✝
Cathedral 13
MANSION
HOUSE

Cheapside
Cornhill
Stock Exchange
Grace... St.
Leadenhall St.

TOWER
HILL

BLACKFRIARS
STATION

CANNON ST.
STATION

MONUMENT
Lower
Thames St.
By Ward
St.

Tower
Hill East

Tower of
London 14

7 ⊖ LEICESTER SQUARE
8 ⊖
National Gallery
Charing Cross Station
EMBANKMENT
Trafalgar
Square
Whitehall
10 Downing
Street
WESTMINSTER

River Thames
Victoria Embankment
Blackfriars
Bridge
Waterloo Bridge
Hungerford
Bridge
Stamford St.

Upper Thames St.
Millennium
Bridge
Globe Theatre ■ 12
Southwark
Bridge

SOUTHWARK

Southwark St.

Union St.

CANNON ST.
London
Bridge

LONDON BRIDGE
London
Bridge
Station
Tooley St.
St. Thomas St.
Bermondsey St.

Tower
Bridge 15

DOCKLANDS

SOUTH BANK
York Rd.
Belvedere Rd.
Waterloo Rd.
The Cut

WATERLOO
STATION

Borough High St.
Borough Rd.
Long Ln.
Great Dover St.

THE
BOROUGH

BOROUGH

Jamaica Rd.
Druid St.
Abbey St.

9 ✝
Houses of
Parliament
Westminster
Abbey 10

Westminster
Bridge
Lambeth Palace Rd.
LAMBETH
NORTH
Westminster Bridge Rd.

London Rd.
St. George's Rd.
Blackfriars Rd.
Borough Rd.
Kennington Rd.
Southwark Bridge Rd.
Kennington Causeway
Harper Rd.

Bridge
Rd.

WEST-
MINSTER

Lambeth
Bridge
Lambeth Rd.

LAMBETH

ELEPHANT & CASTLE
(BAKERLOO)

ELEPHANT
& CASTLE

Tate
Gallery
11 ⊖
Millbank
Vauxhall
Bridge
Albert Embankment

Kennington Park Rd.
Kennington Rd.

KENNINGTON

⊖ VAUXHALL
Kennington Ln.
Harleyford
Rd.

KENNINGTON

VAUXHALL ⊖
OVAL
Camberwell New Rd.

Wandsworth Rd.
South Lambeth Rd.
Clapham Rd.
Brixton Rd.

Big Ben **10**
British Museum **6**
Buckingham Palace **4**
Houses of Parliament **10**
Kensington Gardens **2**
Kensington Palace **1**
National Gallery **7**
National Portrait Gallery **5**
St. Paul's Cathedral **13**
Tate Britain **11**
Tate Modern **12**
Tower Bridge **15**
Tower of London **14**
Trafalgar Square **8**
Victoria and Albert Museum **3**
Westminster Abbey **9**

exhibits. We recommend wandering rooms 33 and 34, and 91 to 94, to take in the glory of the Orient, covering Taoism, Confucianism, and Buddhism. The Chinese collection is particularly strong. Sculpture from India is as fine as anything at the Victoria and Albert. The ethnography collection is increasingly beefed up, especially the Mexican Gallery in room 33C, which traces that country's art from the 2nd millennium B.C. to the 16th century A.D. A gallery for the North American collection is also open nearby. Another section of the museum is devoted to the **Sainsbury African Galleries** (🎯), one of the finest collections of African art and artifacts in the world, featuring changing displays selected from more than 200,000 objects. Finally, the museum has opened a new Money Gallery in room 68, tracing the story of money. You'll learn that around 2000 B.C. in Mesopotamia, money was grain, and that printed money came into being in the 10th century in China.

The museum's inner courtyard is now canopied by a lightweight, transparent roof, transforming the area into a covered square that houses a Centre for Education, exhibition space, bookshops, and restaurants. The center of the Great Court features the Round Reading Room, which is famous as the place where Karl Marx hung out while writing *Das Kapital.*

For information on the British Library, see p. 240.

Great Russell St., WC1. (📞) **020/7323-8299** or 020/7636-1555 for recorded information. www.thebritishmuseum. ac.uk. Free admission. Sat–Wed 10am–5:30pm; Thurs–Fri 10am–8:30pm. Tube: Holborn, Tottenham Court Rd., Goodge St., or Russell Sq.

**Buckingham Palace** ★★ *Kids*   This massive, graceful building is the official residence of the queen. The redbrick palace was built as a country house for the notoriously rakish duke of Buckingham. In 1762, King George III, who needed room for his 15 children, bought it. It didn't become the official royal residence, though, until Queen Victoria took the throne; she preferred it to St. James's Palace. From George III's time, the building was continuously expanded and remodeled, faced with Portland stone, and twice bombed (during the Blitz). Located in a 40-acre garden, it's 108m (354 ft.) long and contains 600 rooms. You can tell whether the queen is at home by checking to see if the Royal Standard is flying from the mast outside. For most of the year, you can't visit the palace without an official invitation. Since 1993, though, much of it has been open for tours during an 8-week period in August and September, when the royal family is usually vacationing outside London. Elizabeth II agreed to allow visitors to tour the State Room, the Grand Staircase, the Throne Room, and other areas designed by John Nash for George IV, as well as the Picture Gallery, which displays masterpieces by Van Dyck, Rembrandt, Rubens, and others. The admission charges help pay for repairs to Windsor Castle, damaged by fire in 1992. You have to buy a timed-entrance ticket the same day you tour the palace. Tickets go on sale at 9am, but rather than lining up at sunrise with all the other tourists—this is one of London's most popular attractions—book by phone with a credit card and give yourself a few more hours of sleep.

During the 8 weeks of summer, visitors are also allowed to stroll through the royal family's garden, along a 4,455m (14,612-ft.) walk on the south side of the grounds, with views of a lake and the usually off-limits west side of the palace. The garden is home to 30 types of birds, including the great crested grebe, plus 350 types of wildflowers.

Buckingham Palace's most famous spectacle is the vastly overrated **Changing of the Guard** (daily Apr–July and on alternating days for the rest of the year). The new guard, marching behind a band, comes from either the Wellington or

> ## *Tips*  The Guard Doesn't Change Every Day
>
> The schedule for the Changing of the Guard ceremony is variable at best. In theory, at least, the guard is changed daily from some time in April to mid-July, at which time it goes on its "winter" schedule—that is, alternating days. Always check locally with the tourist office to see if it's likely to be staged at the time of your visit. The ceremony has been cut at the last minute, leaving thousands of tourists feeling that they have missed out on a London must-see.

Chelsea barracks and takes over from the old guard in the forecourt of the palace. The ceremony begins at 11:30am, although it's frequently canceled due to bad weather, state events, and other harder-to-fathom reasons. We like the changing of the guard at Horse Guards better (p. 235) because you can actually see the men marching and you don't have to battle such tourist hordes. However, few first-time visitors can resist the Buckingham Place Changing of the Guard. If that's you, arrive as early as 10:30am and claim territorial rights to a space in front of the palace. If you're not firmly anchored here, you'll miss much of the ceremony.

***Insider's Tip:*** You can avoid the long queues for Buckingham Palace tours by purchasing tickets before you go through **Global Tickets,** 234 W. 44th St., Suite 1000, New York, NY 10034 (© **800/223-6108**). You'll have to pick the exact date on which you'd like to go. Visitors with disabilities can reserve tickets directly through the palace by calling © **020/7930-5526.**

At end of The Mall (on the road running from Trafalgar Sq.). © 020/7839-1377 or 020/7321-2233. www.royal.gov.uk. Palace tours £13 ($23) adults, £11 ($19) seniors, £6.50 ($12) children under 17. Changing of the Guard free. Palace open for tours Aug 6–Sept 28 daily 9:30am–4:30pm. Changing of the guard daily from Apr–July at 11:30am, and alternating days for the rest of the year at 11am. Tube: St. James's Park, Green Park, or Victoria.

**Clarence House** ★★    From 1953 until her death in 2002, the Queen Mother lived at Clarence House in a wing of St. James's Palace. It was constructed between 1825 and 1927 to the designs of John Nash. Today it is the official residence of the Prince of Wales, and is open to the public only during a specified period of the year (see below). The present Queen Elizabeth and the duke of Edinburgh lived here following their marriage in 1947.

After the death of the Queen Mother, the house was refurbished and redecorated, with antiques and art added from the royal collection. Visitors are taken on a guided tour of five of the staterooms, where much of the Queen's collection of works of art and furniture is on display, along with pieces added by Prince Charles. The Queen Mother had an impressive collection of 20th-century British art, including works by John Piper, Augustus John, and Graham Sutherland. She also was known for her superb collection of Fabergé and English porcelain and silver, especially pieces from her family collection (the Bowes-Lyon family).

Stable Yard Gate, SW1. © 020/7766-7303. www.royal.gov.uk. Admission £5.50 ($10) adults, £3 ($5.55) ages 5–17. Free for 4 and under. Aug 4–Oct 17 (dates subject to change—call first); daily 9:30am–6pm. Tube: Green Park or St. James's Park.

**Houses of Parliament & Big Ben** ★★    The Houses of Parliament, along with their trademark clock tower, Big Ben, are the ultimate symbols of London. They're the strongholds of Britain's democracy, the assemblies that effectively trimmed the sails of royal power. Both the House of Commons and the House of Lords are in the former royal Palace of Westminster, which was the king's residence until Henry VIII moved to Whitehall. The current Gothic Revival buildings date from 1840 and were designed by Charles Barry. (The earlier buildings were destroyed by fire in 1834.) Assisting Barry was Augustus Welby Pugin, who designed the paneled ceilings, tiled floors, stained glass, clocks, fireplaces, umbrella stands, and even the inkwells. There are more than 1,000 rooms and 3km (2 miles) of corridors. The clock tower at the eastern end houses the world's most famous timepiece. **"Big Ben"** refers not to the clock tower itself, but to the largest bell in the chime, which weighs close to 14 tons and is named for the first commissioner of works, Sir Benjamin Hall.

You may observe debates for free from the **Stranger's Galleries** in both houses. Sessions usually begin in mid-October and run to the end of July, with recesses at Christmas and Easter. The chances of getting into the House of Lords when it's in session are generally better than for the more popular House of Commons. Although we can't promise you the oratory of a Charles James Fox or a William Pitt the Elder, the debates in the House of Commons are often lively and controversial (seats are at a premium during crises).

For years, London tabloids have portrayed members of the House of Lords as a bunch of "Monty Pythonesque upper-class twits," with one foreign secretary calling the House of Lords "medieval lumber." Today, under Tony Blair's Labour government, the House of Lords is being shaken up as lords lose their inherited posts. Panels are studying what to do with this largely useless house, its members often descendants of royal mistresses and ancient landowners.

Those who'd like to book a tour can do so, but it takes a bit of work. Both houses are open to the general public for guided tours only for a limited season in July and August. The palace is open Monday, Tuesday, Friday, and Saturday from 9:15am to 4:30pm during those times. All tour tickets cost £7 ($13) adult, £5 ($9.25) for seniors, students, and children under 16. Under 4 years old may enter free. For advance tickets call © **087/0906-3773.**

If you arrive just to attend a session, these are free. You line up at Stephen's Gate, heading to your left for the entrance into the Commons or to the right for the Lords. The London daily newspapers announce sessions of Parliament.

*Insider's Tip:* The hottest ticket and the most exciting time to visit is during "Prime Minister's Question Time" on Wednesdays, which is only from 3 to 3:30pm, but which must seem like hours to Tony Blair, who is on the hot seat. It's not quite as thrilling as it was back when Margaret Thatcher exchanged barbs with the MPs (members of Parliament), but Blair holds his own admirably against any and all who try to embarrass him and his government. He is given no mercy from these MPs, especially those who oppose his policies.

Across the street is the **Jewel Tower** 🪧, Abingdon Street (© **020/7222-2219**), one of only two surviving buildings from the medieval Palace of Westminster. It was constructed in 1365 as a place where Edward III could stash his treasure trove. The tower hosts an exhibition on the history of Parliament and makes for a great introduction to the inner workings of the British government. The video presentation on the top floor is especially informative. A touch-screen computer allows visitors to take a virtual tour of both houses of Parliament. The tower is open daily from 10am to 6pm April to September; 10am to 5pm in October; and 10am to 4pm November to March. Admission is £2.20 ($4.05) for adults, £1.70 ($3.15) for students and seniors, and £1.10 ($2.05) for children.

Westminster Palace, Old Palace Yard, SW1. House of Commons ☏ **020/7219-4272.** House of Lords ☏ **020/7219-3107.** www.parliament.uk. Free admission. House of Lords open mid-Oct to Aug Mon–Wed from 2:30pm, Thurs from 11am, and sometimes Fri (check by phone). House of Commons mid-Oct to Aug Mon 2:30–10:30pm, Tues–Wed 11:30am–7:30pm, Thurs 11:30am–6pm, Fri not always open—call ahead. Both houses are open for tours (see above). Join line at St. Stephen's entrance. Tube: Westminster.

**Kensington Palace** *(★ Kids)*    Once the residence of British monarchs, Kensington Palace hasn't been the official home of reigning kings since George II. William III and Mary II acquired it in 1689 as an escape from the damp royal rooms along the Thames. Since the end of the 18th century, the palace has housed various members of the royal family, and the State Apartments are open for tours.

It was here in 1837 that a young Victoria was awakened with the news that her uncle, William IV, had died and she was now the queen of England. You can view a collection of Victoriana, including some of her memorabilia. In the apartments of Queen Mary II is a striking 17th-century writing cabinet inlaid with tortoiseshell. Paintings from the Royal Collection line the walls. A rare 1750 lady's court dress and splendid examples of male court dress from the 18th century are on display in rooms adjacent to the State Apartments, as part of the Royal Ceremonial Dress Collection, which features royal costumes dating as far back as 200 years.

Kensington Palace was the London home of the late Princess Margaret, and is the current home of the duke and duchess of Kent. The palace was also the home of Diana, Princess of Wales, and her two sons. (Harry and William now live with their father at St. James's Palace.) The palace is probably best known for the millions of flowers placed in front of it during the days following Diana's death. The former apartment of the late Princess Margaret has opened to the public as an education center and an exhibition space for royal ceremonial dress.

*Warning:* You don't get to see the apartments where Princess Di lived or where both Di and Charles lived until they separated. Many visitors think they'll get to peek at these rooms and are disappointed. Charles and Di lived on the west side of the palace, still occupied today by minor royals.

The **Kensington Gardens** are open to the public for leisurely strolls through the manicured grounds and around the Round Pond. One of the most famous sights is the controversial Albert Memorial, a lasting tribute not only to Victoria's consort, but also to the questionable artistic taste of the Victorian era. There's a wonderful afternoon tea offered in The Orangery (p. 263).

The Broad Walk, Kensington Gardens, W8. ☏ **020/0751-5170.** www.kensington-palace.org.uk. Admission £11 ($19) adults, £7 ($13) seniors/students, £6.50 ($12) children, £31 ($57) family. Mar–Oct daily 10am–7pm; Nov–Feb daily 10am–6pm. Tube: Queensway or Notting Hill Gate; High St. Kensington on south side.

**National Gallery** *(★★★)*    This stately neoclassical building contains an unrivaled collection of Western art spanning 7 centuries—from the late 13th to the early 20th—and covering every great European school. For sheer skill of display and arrangement, it surpasses its counterparts in Paris, New York, Madrid, and Amsterdam.

The largest part of the collection is devoted to the Italians, including the Sienese, Venetian, and Florentine masters. They're now housed in the Sainsbury Wing, which was designed by noted Philadelphia architects Robert Venturi and Denise Scott Brown and opened by Queen Elizabeth II in 1991. On display are such works as Leonardo's *Virgin of the Rocks;* Titian's *Bacchus and Ariadne;* Giorgione's *Adoration of the Magi;* and unforgettable canvases by Bellini, Veronese, Botticelli, and Tintoretto. Botticelli's *Venus and Mars* is eternally enchanting. The Sainsbury Wing is also used for large temporary exhibits.

---

*Fun Fact* **Trafalgar: London's Most Famous Square**

London is a city full of landmark squares. Without a doubt, the best-known is **Trafalgar Square** 🟊🟊 (Tube: Charing Cross), which honors one of England's great military heroes, Horatio Viscount Nelson (1758–1805). Although he suffered from seasickness, he went to sea at the age of 12 and was an admiral by age 39. Nelson was a hero of the Battle of Calvi in 1794, where he lost an eye; the Battle of Santa Cruz in 1797, where he lost an arm; and the Battle of Trafalgar in 1805, where he lost his life. He is also famous for his affair with Lady Hamilton, the subject of books and films (including *That Hamilton Woman*, with Laurence Olivier and Vivien Leigh).

The square is dominated by the 44m (144-ft.) granite *Nelson's Column*, built by E. H. Baily in 1843. The column looks down Whitehall toward the Old Admiralty, where Lord Nelson's body lay in state. The figure of the naval hero towers 5m (16 ft.) high—not bad for a man who stood 5'4" in real life. The capital is of bronze, cast from cannons recovered from the wreck of the *Royal George*, which sank in 1782. Queen Victoria's favorite animal painter, Sir Edward Landseer, added the four lions at the base of the column in 1868. The pools and fountains weren't added until 1939; they were the last work of Sir Edwin Lutyens.

Political demonstrations take place in the square and around the column, which has the most aggressive pigeons in London. Much of the world focuses on the square via TV cameras on New Year's Eve, watching revelers jumping into the chilly waters of the fountains. The Christmas tree that's installed here every December is a gift from Norway to the British people, in appreciation of Britain's sheltering the Norwegian royal family during World War II. The tree is surrounded by carolers most December evenings. Year-round, street performers (now officially licensed) will entertain you in hopes of receiving a token of appreciation for their efforts.

To the southeast of the square, at 36 Craven St., stands a house that was occupied by Benjamin Franklin from 1757 to 1774. On the north side of the square rises the National Gallery, constructed in the 1830s. In front of the building is a copy of a statue of George Washington by J. A. Houdon.

To the left of St. Martin's Place is the National Portrait Gallery, a collection of portraits of famous Brits—from Chaucer and Shakespeare to Nell Gwynne, Margaret Thatcher, and Lady Diana. Also on the square is the steeple of St. Martin–in–the–Fields, the final resting place of Sir Joshua Reynolds, William Hogarth, and Thomas Chippendale.

---

Of the early Gothic works, the Wilton Diptych (French or English school, late 14th c.) is the rarest treasure; it depicts Richard II being introduced to the Madonna and Child by John the Baptist and the Saxon kings, Edmund and Edward the Confessor. Then there are the Spanish giants: El Greco's *Agony in the Garden* and portraits by Goya and Velázquez. The Flemish-Dutch school is represented by Brueghel, Jan van Eyck, Vermeer, Rubens, and de Hooch; the

Rembrandts include two of his immortal self-portraits. None of van Eyck's art creates quite the stir that the **Arnolfini Portrait** does. You probably studied this painting from 1434 in your Art History 101 class. The stunning work depicts Giovanni di Nicolao Arnolfini and his wife (who is not pregnant as is often thought; she is merely holding up her full-skirted dress in the contemporary fashion). There's also an immense French Impressionist and post-Impressionist collection that includes works by Manet, Monet, Degas, Renoir, and Cézanne. Particularly charming is the peep-show cabinet by Hoogstraten in one of the Dutch rooms: It's like spying through a keyhole.

British and modern art are the specialties of the Tate Gallery (see listings below), but the National Gallery does have some fine 18th-century British masterpieces, including works by Hogarth, Gainsborough, Reynolds, Constable, and Turner.

Guided tours of the National Gallery are offered daily at 11:30am and 2:30pm, with an extra tour at 6:30pm on Wednesday. A Gallery Guide Soundtrack is also available. A portable CD player provides audio information on paintings of your choice with the mere push of a button. Although this service is free, contributions are appreciated.

*Insider's Tip:* The National Gallery has a computer information center where you can design your own personal tour map for free. The computer room, located in the Micro Gallery, includes a dozen hands-on workstations. The online system lists 2,200 paintings and has background notes for each work. Using a touch-screen computer, you can design your own personalized tour by selecting a maximum of 10 paintings you would like to view. Once you have made your choices, you print a personal tour map with your selections.

N. side of Trafalgar Sq., WC2. ℂ 020/7747-2885. www.nationalgallery.org.uk. Free admission. Thurs–Tues 10am–6pm; Wed 10am–9pm. Tube: Charing Cross or Leicester Sq.

**National Portrait Gallery** ★★    In a gallery of remarkable and unremarkable portraits (they're collected for their subjects rather than their artistic quality), a few paintings tower over the rest, including Sir Joshua Reynolds's first portrait of Samuel Johnson ("a man of most dreadful appearance"), Nicholas Hilliard's miniature of handsome Sir Walter Raleigh, a full-length of Elizabeth I, and a Holbein cartoon of Henry VIII. There's also a portrait of William Shakespeare (with a gold earring) by an unknown artist that bears the claim of being the "most authentic contemporary likeness" of its subject. One of the most famous pictures in the gallery is the group portrait of the Brontë sisters (Charlotte, Emily, and Anne) by their brother, Bramwell. An idealized portrait of Lord Byron by Thomas Phillips is also on display.

The galleries of Victorian and early-20th-century portraits were radically redesigned recently. The later 20th-century portraiture includes major works by such artists as Warhol and Hambling. Some of the more flamboyant personalities of the past 2 centuries are on show: T. S. Eliot; Disraeli; Macmillan; Sir Richard Burton (the explorer, not the actor); Elizabeth Taylor; and our two favorites, G. F. Watts's famous portrait of his great actress wife, Ellen Terry, and Vanessa Bell's portrait of her sister, Virginia Woolf. A portrait of the late Princess Diana is on the Royal Landing, and this painting seems to attract the most viewers.

In 2000, Queen Elizabeth opened the Ondaatje Wing of the gallery, increasing the gallery's exhibition space by over 50%. The most intriguing new space is the splendid Tudor Gallery, featuring portraits of Richard III and Henry II, Richard's conqueror in the Battle of Bosworth in 1485. There's also a portrait of

Shakespeare that the gallery acquired in 1856. Rooms lead through centuries of English monarchs, with literary and artistic figures thrown in. A Balcony Gallery taps into the cult of celebrity, displaying more recent figures whose fame has lasted longer than Warhol's 15 minutes. These include everybody from Mick Jagger to Joan Collins, and of course, the Baroness Thatcher.

The Gallery operates a cafe and art bookshop.

St. Martin's Place, WC2. © 020/7306-0055. www.npg.org.uk. Free admission; fee charged for certain temporary exhibitions. Mon–Wed 10am–6pm; Thurs–Fri 10am–9pm; Sat–Sun 10am–6pm. Tube: Charing Cross or Leicester Sq.

**St. Paul's Cathedral** ★★★   During World War II, newsreel footage reaching America showed St. Paul's Cathedral standing virtually alone among the rubble of the City, its dome lit by fires caused by bombings all around it. That the cathedral survived at all is a miracle, since it was badly hit twice during the early years of the bombardment of London during World War II. But St. Paul's is accustomed to calamity, having been burned down three times and destroyed by invading Norsemen. It was during the Great Fire of 1666 that the old St. Paul's was razed, making way for a new structure designed by Sir Christopher Wren and built between 1675 and 1710. The cathedral is architectural genius Wren's ultimate masterpiece.

---

**⌒ Moments   Roses Are Red**

One of the most enjoyable activities of a spring visit to London is a stroll through the gardens of St. Paul's when the roses are in bloom.

---

The classical dome of St. Paul's dominates the City's square mile. The golden cross surmounting it is 110m (361 ft.) above the ground; the golden ball on which the cross rests measures 2m (6½ ft.) in diameter, though it looks like a marble from below. In the interior of the dome is the Whispering Gallery, an acoustic marvel in which the faintest whisper can be heard clearly on the opposite side. Sit on one side, have your traveling companions sit on the opposite side, and whisper away. You can climb to the top of the dome for a 360-degree view of London. From the Whispering Gallery a second steep climb leads to the **Stone Gallery,** opening onto a panoramic view of London. Another 153 steps take you to the **Inner Golden Gallery,** situated at the top of the inner dome. Here an even more panoramic view of London unfolds.

St. Paul's Churchyard, EC4. © 020/7236-4128. www.stpauls.co.uk. Cathedral and galleries £6 ($11) adults, £3 ($5.55) children 6–16. Guided tours £2.50 ($4.65) adults, £2 ($3.70) students and seniors, £1 ($1.85) children; recorded tours £3.50 ($6.50). Free for children 5 and under. Cathedral (excluding galleries) Mon–Sat 8:30am–4pm; galleries Mon–Sat 9:30am–4pm. No sightseeing Sun (services only). Tube: St. Paul's.

**Tate Britain** ★★★   Fronting the Thames near Vauxhall Bridge in Pimlico, the Tate looks like a smaller and more graceful relation of the British Museum. The most prestigious gallery in Britain, it houses the national collections, covering British art from the 16th century to the present day, as well as an array of international works. In the spring of 2000, the Tate moved its collection of 20th- and 21st-century art to the **Tate Modern** (see below). This split helped to open more display space at the Tate Britain, but the collection here is still much too large to be displayed all at once; so the works on view change from time to time.

The older works include some of the best of Gainsborough, Reynolds, Stubbs, Blake, and Constable. William Hogarth is well represented, particularly by his satirical *O the Roast Beef of Old England* (known as *The Gate of Calais*). You'll find the illustrations of William Blake, the incomparable mystical poet,

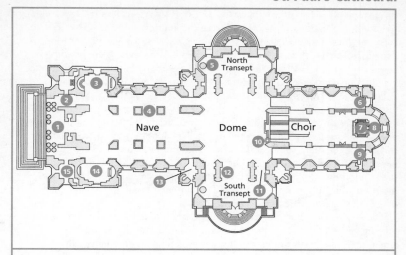

| | |
|---|---|
| All Souls' Chapel **2** | High Altar **7** |
| American Memorial Chapter **8** | Lady Chapel **9** |
| Anglican Martyr's Chapel **6** | Nelson Monument **12** |
| Chapel of St. Michael | Pulpit **10** |
|   & St. George **14** | St. Dunstan's Chapel **3** |
| Dean's Staircase **15** | Staircase to Library, |
| Entrance to Crypt |   Whispering Gallery & Dome **13** |
|   (Wren's grave) **11** | Wellington Monument **4** |
| Font **5** | West Doorway **1** |

including such works as *The Book of Job, The Divine Comedy,* and *Paradise Lost.* The collection of works by J. M. W. Turner is the Tate's largest collection of works by a single artist—Turner himself willed most of his paintings and watercolors to the nation.

Also on display are the works of many major 19th- and 20th-century painters, including Paul Nash, Matisse, Dalí, Modigliani, Munch, Bonnard, and Picasso. Truly remarkable are the several enormous abstract canvases by Mark Rothko, the group of paintings and sculptures by Giacometti, and the paintings by one of England's best-known modern artists, Francis Bacon. Sculptures by Henry Moore and Barbara Hepworth are also occasionally displayed.

***Insider's Tip:*** After you've seen the grand art, don't hasten away. Drop in to the Tate Gallery Shop for some of the best art books and postcards in London. The gallery sells whimsical T-shirts with art masterpieces on them. Those ubiquitous Tate Gallery canvas bags seen all over London are sold here, as are the town's best art posters (all make great souvenirs). Invite your friends for tea at the Coffee Shop with its excellent cakes and pastries, or lunch at the Tate Gallery Restaurant (p. 180). You'll get to enjoy good food, Rex Whistler art, and the best and most reasonably priced wine list in London.

Millbank, SW1. ℭ 020/7887-8000. www.tate.org.uk. Free admission; special exhibitions sometimes incur a charge varying from £3–£8.50 ($5.55–$16). Daily 10:30am–5:40pm. Tube: Pimlico.

**Tate Modern** ✦✦✦　In a transformed Bankside Power Station in Southwark, this museum, which opened in 2000, draws some 2 million visitors a year to see the greatest collection of international 20th-century art in Britain. How would we rate the collection? At the same level of the Pompidou in Paris, with a slight edge over New York's Guggenheim. Of course, New York's Museum of Modern Art remains in a class of its own. Tate Modern is also viewer-friendly, with eye-level hangings. All the big painting stars are here, a whole galaxy ranging from Dalí to Duchamp, from Giacometti to Matisse and Mondrian, from Picasso and Pollock to Rothko and Warhol. The Modern is also a gallery of 21st-century art, displaying new and exciting art recently created.

You can cross the Millennium Bridge, a pedestrian-only walk from the steps of St. Paul's, over the Thames to the new gallery. Or else you can take the **Tate to Tate** boat (© **020/7887-8888**), which takes art lovers on an 18-minute journey across the Thames from the Tate Britain to the Tate Modern, with a stop at the London Eye and the Saatchi Gallery. A day pass costs £4.50 ($8.35). Leaving from Millbank Pier, this catamaran is decorated by the trademark colorful dots of that *enfant terrible* artist, Damien Hirst.

The Tate Modern makes extensive use of glass for both its exterior and interior, offering panoramic views. Galleries are arranged over three levels and provide different kinds of space for display. Instead of exhibiting art chronologically and by school, the Tate Modern, in a radical break from tradition, takes a thematic approach. This allows displays to cut across movements.

Bankside, SE1. © 020/7887-8008. www.tate.org.uk. Free admission. Sun–Thurs 10am–6pm; Fri–Sat 10am–10pm. Tube: Southwark.

**Tower Bridge** ★★   This is one of the world's most celebrated landmarks, and possibly the most photographed and painted bridge on earth. (Presumably, this is the one the Arizona businessman thought he was getting, instead of the London Bridge.) Despite its medieval appearance, Tower Bridge was built in 1894.

In 1993, an exhibition opened inside the bridge to commemorate its century-old history; it takes you up the north tower to high-level walkways between the two towers with spectacular views of St. Paul's, the Tower of London, and the Houses of Parliament. You're then led down the south tower and into the bridge's original engine room, containing the Victorian boilers and steam engines that used to raise and lower the bridge for ships to pass. Exhibits in the bridge's towers use animatronic characters, video, and computers to illustrate the history of the bridge.

## The Wren Style

One of the great geniuses of his age, Sir Christopher Wren (1632–1723) was a professor of astronomy at Oxford before becoming an architect. After the Great Fire of London in 1666, Wren was chosen to rebuild the devastated city and its many churches, including St. Paul's, on which work began in 1675. His designs had great originality, and he became known for his spatial effects and his impressive fusion of classical and baroque. He believed in classical stability and repose, yet he liked to enliven his churches with baroque whimsy and fantasy.

Nothing better represents the Wren style than the facade of St. Paul's, for which he combined classical columns, reminiscent of Greek temples, with baroque decorations and adornments. In our view, his crowning glory is the dome over St. Paul's, which is celebrated for the beauty of its proportions.

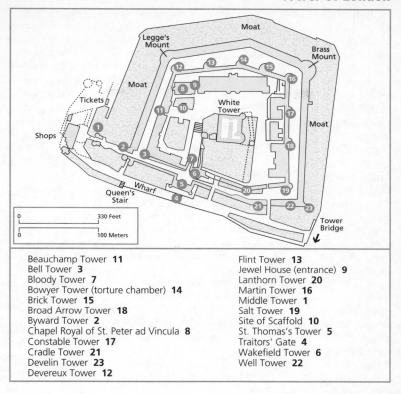

Beauchamp Tower **11**
Bell Tower **3**
Bloody Tower **7**
Bowyer Tower (torture chamber) **14**
Brick Tower **15**
Broad Arrow Tower **18**
Byward Tower **2**
Chapel Royal of St. Peter ad Vincula **8**
Constable Tower **17**
Cradle Tower **21**
Develin Tower **23**
Devereux Tower **12**

Flint Tower **13**
Jewel House (entrance) **9**
Lanthorn Tower **20**
Martin Tower **16**
Middle Tower **1**
Salt Tower **19**
Site of Scaffold **10**
St. Thomas's Tower **5**
Traitors' Gate **4**
Wakefield Tower **6**
Well Tower **22**

At Tower Bridge, SE1. 🕐 **020/7403-3761.** www.towerbridge.org.uk. Tower Bridge Experience £5.50 ($10) adults; £3.30 ($6.10) children 5–15, students, and seniors; free for children 4 and under. Tower Bridge Experience open daily 9:30am–6pm (last entrance 5pm). Closed Christmas Eve and Christmas Day. Tube: Tower Hill or London Bridge.

**Tower of London** ★★★ *Kids*   This ancient fortress continues to pack in the crowds with its macabre associations with the legendary figures imprisoned and/or executed here. There are more spooks here per square foot than in any other building in the whole of haunted Britain. Headless bodies, bodiless heads, phantom soldiers, icy blasts, clanking chains—you name them, the Tower's got them. Centuries after the last head rolled on Tower Hill, a shivery atmosphere of impending doom still lingers over the Tower's mighty walls. Plan on spending a lot of time here.

The Tower is actually an intricately patterned compound of structures built throughout the ages for varying purposes, mostly as expressions of royal power. The oldest is the **White Tower,** begun by William the Conqueror in 1078 to keep London's native Saxon population in check. Later rulers added other towers, more walls, and fortified gates, until the buildings became like a small town within a city. Until the reign of James I (beginning in 1603), the Tower was also one of the royal residences. But above all, it was a prison for distinguished captives.

Every stone of the Tower tells a story—usually a gory one. In the **Bloody Tower,** according to Shakespeare, Richard III's henchmen murdered the two little princes (the sons of Edward IV). Richard knew that his position as king could not be secure as long as his nephews were alive. There seems no reasonable doubt that the little princes were murdered in the Tower on orders of their uncle. Attempts have been made by some historians to clear his name, but Richard remains the chief suspect, and his deed caused him to lose the "hearts of the people," according to the *Chronicles of London* at the time.

Sir Walter Raleigh spent 13 years in the Bloody Tower before his date with the executioner. On the walls of the **Beauchamp Tower,** you can still read the last messages scratched by despairing prisoners. Through **Traitors' Gate** passed such ill-fated, romantic figures as Robert Devereux, the second earl of Essex and a favorite of Elizabeth I. A plaque marks the eerie place at **Tower Green** where two wives of Henry VIII, Anne Boleyn and Catherine Howard, plus Sir Thomas More, and the 4-day queen, Lady Jane Grey, all lost their lives.

The Tower, besides being a royal palace, a fortress, and a prison, was also an armory, a treasury, a menagerie, and in 1675, an astronomical observatory. Reopened in 1999, the White Tower holds the **Armouries,** which date from the reign of Henry VIII, as well as a display of instruments of torture and execution that recall some of the most ghastly moments in the Tower's history. In the Jewel House, you'll find the tower's greatest attraction, the **Crown Jewels.** Here, some of the world's most precious stones are set into robes, swords, scepters, and crowns. The Imperial State Crown is the most famous crown on earth; made for Victoria in 1837, it's worn today by Queen Elizabeth II when she opens Parliament. Studded with some 3,000 jewels (principally diamonds), it includes the Black Prince's Ruby, worn by Henry V at Agincourt. The 530-carat Star of Africa, a cut diamond on the Royal Sceptre with Cross, would make Harry Winston turn over in his grave. You'll have to stand in long lines to catch just a glimpse of the jewels as you and hundreds of others scroll by on moving sidewalks, but the wait is worth it.

In the latest development here, the presumed prison cell of Sir Thomas More opened to the public in 2000. More left this cell in 1535 to face his executioner after he'd fallen out with King Henry VIII over the monarch's desire to divorce Catherine of Aragon, the first of his six wives. More is believed to have lived in the lower part of the Bell Tower, here in this whitewashed cell, during the last 14 months of his life, although some historians doubt this claim.

A **palace** inhabited by King Edward I in the late 1200s stands above Traitors' Gate. It's the only surviving medieval palace in Britain. Guides at the palace are dressed in period costumes, and reproductions of furniture and fittings, including Edward's throne, evoke the era, along with burning incense and candles.

Oh, yes—don't forget to look for the ravens. Six of them (plus two spares) are all registered as official Tower residents. According to a legend, the Tower of London will stand as long as those black, ominous birds remain, so to be on the safe side, one of the wings of each raven is clipped.

A 21st-century addition to the Tower complex is the New Armories restaurant, offering a range of snacks and meals, including the traditional cuppa for people about to lose their heads from too many attractions and not enough to eat.

**One-hour guided tours** of the entire compound are given by the Yeoman Warders (also known as "Beefeaters") every half-hour, starting at 9:30am, from the Middle Tower near the main entrance. The last guided walk starts about 3:30pm in summer, 2:30pm in winter—weather permitting, of course.

You can attend the nightly **Ceremony of the Keys,** the ceremonial locking-up of the Tower by the Yeoman Warders. For free tickets, write to the Ceremony of the Keys, Waterloo Block, Tower of London, London EC3N 4AB, and request a specific date, but also list alternate dates. At least 6 weeks' notice is

---

*Tips* **Tower Tips**

You can spend the shortest time possible in the Tower's long lines if you buy your ticket in a kiosk at any Tube station before emerging above ground. Even so, choose a day other than Sunday—crowds are at their worst then—and arrive as early as you can in the morning.

---

required. Accompany all requests with a stamped, self-addressed envelope (British stamps only) or two International Reply Coupons. With ticket in hand, a Yeoman Warder will admit you at 9:35pm. Frankly, we think it's not worth the trouble you go through to see this rather cheesy ceremony, but we know some who disagree with us.

Tower Hill, EC3. © 087/756-6060. www.tower-of-london.com. Admission £14 ($25) adults, £11 ($19) students and seniors, £9 ($17) children, free for children under 5, £38 ($69) family ticket for 5 (but no more than 2 adults). Mar–Oct Mon–Sat 9am–6pm, Sun 10am–6pm; Nov–Feb Tues–Sat 9am–5pm, Sun–Mon 10am–5pm. Tube: Tower Hill.

**Victoria and Albert Museum** ★★★   The Victoria and Albert is the greatest decorative-arts museum in the world. It's also one of the liveliest and most imaginative museums in London—where else would you find the quintessential "little black dress" in the permanent collection?

The medieval holdings include such treasures as the early-English Gloucester Candlestick; the Byzantine Veroli Casket, with its ivory panels based on Greek plays; and the Syon Cope, a unique embroidery made in England in the early 14th century. An area devoted to Islamic art houses the Ardabil Carpet from 16th-century Persia.

The V&A boasts the largest collection of Renaissance sculpture outside Italy. A highlight of the 16th-century collection is the marble group *Neptune with Triton* by Bernini. The cartoons by Raphael, which were conceived as designs for tapestries for the Sistine Chapel, are owned by the queen and are on display here. A most unusual, huge, and impressive exhibit is the Cast Courts, life-size plaster models of ancient and medieval statuary and architecture.

The museum has the greatest collection of Indian art outside India, plus Chinese and Japanese galleries. In complete contrast are suites of English furniture, metalwork, and ceramics, and a superb collection of portrait miniatures, including the one Hans Holbein the Younger made of Anne of Cleves for the benefit of Henry VIII, who was again casting around for a suitable wife. The Dress Collection includes a collection of corsets through the ages that's sure to make you wince. There's also a remarkable collection of musical instruments.

V&A has recently opened 15 new galleries—the **British Galleries** ★★★— telling the story of British design from 1500 to 1900. No other museum in the world houses such a diverse collection of British design and decorative art. From Chippendale to Morris, all of the top British designers are featured in some 3,000 exhibits, ranging from the 5m (16-ft.) high Melville Bed (1697) with its luxurious wild-silk damask and red-velvet hangings, to 19th-century classics such as furniture by Charles Rennie Mackintosh. One of the most prized possessions is the "Great Bed of Ware," mentioned in Shakespeare's *Twelfth Night.* Also on exhibit is the wedding suite of James II. And don't miss the V&A's most bizarre gallery, Fakes and Forgeries. The impostors here are amazingly authentic—in fact, we'd judge some of them as better than the old masters themselves. The interactive displays hold special interest. Learning about heraldry is far more interesting when you're designing your own coat of arms.

*Insider's Tip:* In the winter of 2004, V&A opened a suite of five renovated painting galleries that were originally built in 1850. A trio of these galleries focus on British landscapes as seen through the eyes of Turner, Constable, and others. Constable's oil sketches were donated by his daughter, Isabel, in 1888. Another gallery showcases the bequest of Constantine Ionides, a Victorian collector, with masters such as Botticelli, Delacroix, Degas, Tintoretto, and Ingres. There's even a piano here designed by the famous Edward Burne-Jones, which once belonged to Ionides's brother.

Cromwell Rd., SW7. © 020/7942-2000. www.vam.ac.uk. Free admission. Daily 10am–5:45pm (Wed until 10pm). Tube: S. Kensington.

**Westminster Abbey** ★★★   With its identical square towers and superb archways, this early-English Gothic abbey is one of the greatest examples of ecclesiastical architecture on earth. But it's far more than that: It's the shrine of a nation, the symbol of everything Britain has stood for and stands for, and the place in which most of its rulers were crowned and where many lie buried.

Nearly every figure in English history has left his or her mark on Westminster Abbey. Edward the Confessor founded the Benedictine abbey in 1065 on this spot overlooking Parliament Square. The first English king crowned in the Abbey may have been Harold, in January 1066. The man who defeated him at the Battle of Hastings later that year, William the Conqueror, had the first recorded coronation in the Abbey on Christmas Day in that year. The coronation tradition has continued to the present day. The essentially early-English Gothic structure existing today owes more to Henry III's plans than to those of any other sovereign, although many architects, including Wren, have contributed to the Abbey.

Built on the site of the ancient Lady Chapel in the early 16th century, the **Henry VII Chapel** is one of the loveliest in Europe, with its fan vaulting, Knights of Bath banners, and Torrigiani-designed tomb for the king himself, near which hangs a 15th-century Vivarini painting, *Madonna and Child.* Also here, ironically buried in the same tomb, are Catholic Mary I and Protestant Elizabeth I (whose archrival, Mary Queen of Scots, is entombed on the other side of the Henry VII Chapel). In one end of the chapel, you can stand on Cromwell's memorial stone and view the **Royal Air Force Chapel** and its Battle of Britain memorial window, unveiled in 1947 to honor the Royal Air Force.

You can also visit the most hallowed spot in the abbey, the **shrine of Edward the Confessor** (canonized in the 12th c.). Near the tomb of Henry V is the Coronation Chair, made at the command of Edward I in 1300 to display the mystical Stone of Scone (which some think is the sacred stone mentioned in Genesis and known as Jacob's Pillar). Scottish kings were once crowned on the stone (it has since been returned to Scotland).

When you see a statue of the Bard, with one arm resting on a stack of books, you've arrived at **Poets' Corner.** Shakespeare himself is buried at Stratford-upon-Avon, but resting here are Chaucer, Samuel Johnson, Tennyson, Browning, Dickens, and many others have memorials; There's even an American, Henry Wadsworth Longfellow, as well as monuments to just about everybody: Milton, Keats, Shelley, Henry James, T. S. Eliot, George Eliot, and others. The most stylized monument is Sir Jacob Epstein's sculptured bust of William Blake. More recent tablets commemorate poet Dylan Thomas and Lord Laurence Olivier.

Statesmen and men of science—Disraeli, Newton, Charles Darwin—are also interred in the abbey or honored by monuments. Near the west door is the 1965 memorial to Sir Winston Churchill. In the vicinity of this memorial is the tomb of the **Unknown Warrior,** commemorating the British dead of World War I.

Although most of the Abbey's statuary commemorates notable figures of the past, 10 new statues were unveiled in July 1998. Placed in the Gothic niches above the West Front door, these statues honor 10 modern-day martyrs drawn from every continent and religious denomination. Designed by Tim Crawley and carved under his general direction from French Richemont limestone, the sculptures include Elizabeth of Russia, Janani Luwum, and Martin Luther King Jr., representatives of those who have sacrificed their lives for their beliefs.

Off the Cloisters, the **College Garden** is the oldest garden in England, under cultivation for more than 900 years. Established in the 11th century as the abbey's first infirmary garden, this was once a magnificent source of fruits, vegetables, and medicinal herbs. Five of the trees in the garden were planted in 1850 and they continue to thrive today. Surrounded by high walls, flowering trees dot the lawns, and park benches provide comfort where you can hardly hear the roar of passing traffic. The garden is only open Tuesday through Thursday, April through September from 10am to 6pm, and October through March from 10am to 4pm.

***Insider's Tip:*** Far removed from the pomp and glory is the **Abbey Treasure Museum,** which displays a real bag of oddities in the undercroft—or crypt—part of the monastic buildings erected between 1066 and 1100. You'll find royal effigies that were used instead of the real corpses for lying-in-state ceremonies because they smelled better. You'll see the almost lifelike effigy of Admiral Nelson (his mistress arranged his hair) and even that of Edward III, his lip warped by the cerebral hemorrhage that felled him. Other oddities include Henry V's funeral armour, an unique corset from Elizabeth I's effigy and the Essex Ring that Elizabeth I gave to her favorite (Robert Devereux, the earl of Essex) when she was feeling good about him.

On Sundays, the Abbey is not open to visitors; the rest of the church is open unless a service is being conducted. For times of services, phone the **Chapter Office** (© **020/7222-5152**).

Broad Sanctuary, SW1. © **020/7654-4900.** www.westminster-abbey.org. Admission £7.50 ($14) adults; £5 ($9.25) for students, seniors, and children 11–18; free for children under 11; family ticket £15 ($28). Mon–Tues and Thurs–Fri 9:30am–3:45pm; Wed 9:30am–7pm, Sat 9am–1:45pm. Tube: Westminster or St. James's Park.

## 3 More Central London Attractions

See the "Sights & Attractions by Neighborhood" list on p. 205 for more information on which attraction is in which neighborhood.

### CHURCHES & CATHEDRALS

Many of London's churches offer free lunchtime concerts; a full list is available from the London Tourist Board. It's customary to leave a small donation.

**All Hallows Barking-by-the-Tower** This fascinating church, which houses a brass-rubbing center, is located next door to the Tower. It features a crypt museum, Roman remains, and traces of early London, including a Saxon arch predating the Tower. Samuel Pepys, the famed diarist, climbed the spire of the church to watch the raging fire of London in 1666. In 1644, William Penn was baptized here, and in 1797, John Quincy Adams was married here. Bombs

---

### Finds  Drake's Long Voyage

As you're strolling along the riverside, you come upon the old dock of St. Mary Overie, SE1. Here to your delight is an exact replica of the *Golden Hinde,* in which Sir Francis Drake circumnavigated the globe. It's amazingly tiny for such an around-the-world voyage. But this actual ship has sailed around the world some two dozen times, exploring both oceans and the American coast. Visits are daily from 10am to 5pm, Guided tours cost £3 ($5.55) for adults, £2.60 ($4.80) for students and seniors, and £2.25 ($4.20) for children. For information, call © 020/7403-0123.

---

destroyed the church in 1940, leaving only the tower and walls standing. The church was rebuilt from 1949 to 1958. See "'The City' Attractions" map.

Byward St., EC3. © 020/7481-2928. www.allhallowsbythetower.org.uk. Free admission; crypt museum tour £2.50 ($4.65). Museum Mon–Fri 11am–4pm, Sat 10am–4pm, Sun 1–4:30pm; church Mon–Fri 9am–6pm, Sat–Sun 10am–5pm. Tube: Tower Hill.

**Southwark Cathedral** ★★  There's been a church on this site, in the heart of London's first theater district, for more than a thousand years. The present one dates from the 15th century, and was partly rebuilt in 1890. The previous one was the first Gothic church to be constructed in London (in 1106). A wooden effigy of a knight dates from 1275. Shakespeare and Chaucer worshipped here; a Shakespeare birthday service is held annually, and inside is a memorial to the playwright. In 1424, James I of Scotland married Mary Beaufort here. During the reign of Mary Tudor, Stephen Gardiner, the Bishop of Winchester, held a consistory court in the retro choir that condemned seven Protestants—the Marian martyrs—to death. Later, from 1540 to 1671, the same retro choir was rented to a baker and used to house pigs. Lunchtime concerts are regularly given on Monday and Tuesday; call for exact times and schedules. See "'The City' Attractions" map.

Montague Close, London Bridge, SE1. © 020/7367-6734. Free admission; suggested donation £4 ($7.40). Cathedral exhibition £3 ($5.55) adults, £2.50 ($4.65) students and seniors, and £1.50 ($2.80) children. Mon–Fri 8:30am–5:30pm. Tube: London Bridge.

**St. Bride's** ★  Known as the "the church of the press," thanks to its location at the end of Fleet Street, St. Bride's is a remarkable landmark. The current church is the eighth one that has stood here. After it was bombed in 1940, an archaeologist excavated the crypts and was able to confirm much of the site's legendary history: A Roman house was discovered, and it was established that in the 6th century, St. Brigit of Ireland had founded the first Christian church that was built here. In addition, a crypt with evidence of six subsequent churches was discovered. Among the famous parishioners have been writers John Dryden, John Milton, Richard Lovelace, and John Evelyn. Diarist Samuel Pepys was baptized here, and novelist Samuel Richardson and his family are buried here. After the Great Fire destroyed it, Christopher Wren rebuilt the church with a spire that's been described as a "madrigal in stone." The crypt was a burial chamber and charnel house for centuries; today, it's a museum. Choral concerts are given on Tuesday and Friday, though they are often suspended during Lent and Christmas. See "'The City' Attractions" map.

Fleet St., EC4. © 020/7427-0133. Free admission. Mon–Fri 8am–4:45pm; Sat 10am–3pm; Sun 11am–12:30pm and 5:30–7:30pm. Choral concerts at 1:15pm Tues and Fri. Tube: Blackfriars.

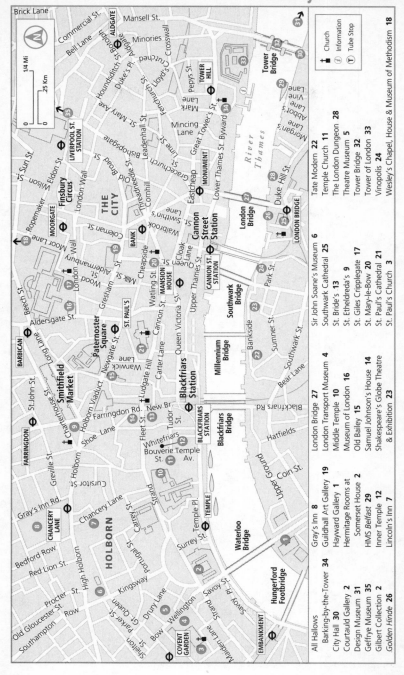

# "The City" Attractions

Church
Information
T  Tube Stop

Tate Modern **22**
Temple Church **11**
The London Dungeon **28**
Theatre Museum **5**
Tower Bridge **32**
Tower of London **33**
Vinopolis **24**
Wesley's Chapel, House & Museum of Methodism **18**

Sir John Soane's Museum **6**
Southwark Cathedral **25**
St. Bride's **13**
St. Etheldreda's **9**
St. Giles Cripplegate **17**
St. Mary-le-Bow **20**
St. Paul's Cathedral **21**
St. Paul's Church **3**

London Bridge **27**
London Transport Museum **4**
Middle Temple **10**
Museum of London **16**
Old Bailey **15**
Samuel Johnson's House **14**
Shakespeare's Globe Theatre
  & Exhibition **23**

Gray's Inn **8**
Guildhall Art Gallery **19**
Hayward Gallery **1**
Hermitage Rooms at
  Somerset House **2**
HMS *Belfast* **29**
Inner Temple **12**
Lincoln's Inn **7**

All Hallows
Barking-by-the-Tower **34**
City Hall **30**
Courtauld Gallery **2**
Design Museum **31**
Geffrye Museum **35**
Gilbert Collection **2**
*Golden Hinde* **26**

225

# West End Attractions

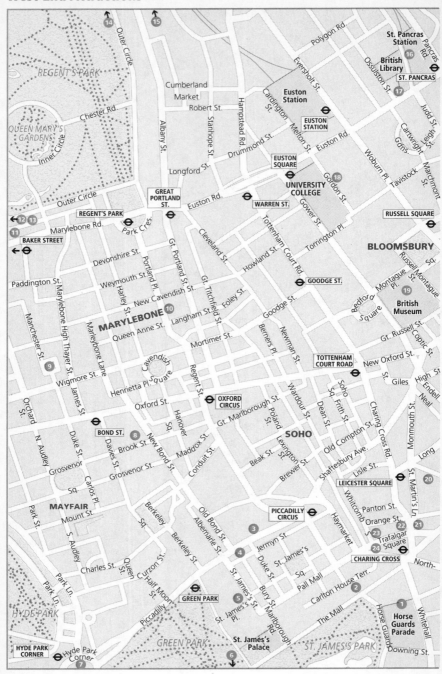

REGENT'S PARK

QUEEN MARY'S GARDENS

Outer Circle

Chester Rd.

Inner Circle

Outer Circle

14

15

Cumberland Market

Robert St.

Albany St.

Stanhope St.

Hampstead Rd.

Polygon Rd.

Eversholt St.

St. Pancras Station

British Library

16

St. Pancras Rd.

ST. PANCRAS

17

Judd St.

Cartwright Gdns.

Leigh St.

Euston Station

Cardington St.

Melton St.

EUSTON STATION

Drummond St.

Longford St.

Euston Square

EUSTON SQUARE

UNIVERSITY COLLEGE

Gordon St.

18

Woburn Pl.

Tavistock

Marchmont

REGENT'S PARK

11

12 13

BAKER STREET

Marylebone Rd.

Park Cres.

Euston Rd.

WARREN ST.

Euston Rd.

Gower St.

Torrington Pl.

RUSSELL SQUARE

BLOOMSBURY

Russell Sq.

Montague Pl.

Bedford Square

19

British Museum

Devonshire St.

Paddington St.

Weymouth St.

Harley St.

New Cavendish St.

Portland Pl.

Gt. Portland St.

Gt. Titchfield St.

Cleveland St.

Howland St.

Tottenham Court Rd.

GOODGE ST.

Goodge St.

Foley St.

Langham St.

MARYLEBONE

10

Queen Anne St.

Mortimer St.

Berners Pl.

Newman St.

Montague St.

Gt. Russell St.

Coptic St.

New Oxford St.

St. Giles High St.

Endell

Neal

Manchester St.

Thayer St.

Marylebone High St.

Marylebone Lane

Wigmore St.

9

Cavendish Square

Henrietta Pl.

Regent St.

Oxford St.

OXFORD CIRCUS

Gt. Marlborough St.

Poland St.

Wardour St.

Dean St.

Frith St.

Soho Sq.

TOTTENHAM COURT ROAD

Charing Cross Rd.

Monmouth St.

Long

Orchard St.

James St.

BOND ST.

8

Davies St.

Brook St.

New Bond St.

Hanover Sq.

Maddox St.

Conduit St.

Lexington St.

Beak St.

Brewer St.

Old Compton St.

SOHO

Shaftesbury Ave.

LEICESTER SQUARE

Lisle St.

St. Martin's Ln.

20

N. Audley

Duke St.

MAYFAIR

Grosvenor Sq.

Grosvenor St.

Old Bond St.

Albemarle St.

Carlos Pl.

Mount St.

Berkeley Sq.

Berkeley St.

Whitcomb St.

Panton St.

Orange St.

21

PICCADILLY CIRCUS

3

Jermyn St.

Duke St.

Haymarket

23

Trafalgar Square

CHARING CROSS

24

North-

Park St.

S. Audley

Charles St.

Queen St.

Curzon St.

Half Moon St.

Piccadilly

GREEN PARK

5

St. James's Pl.

St. James's St.

Bury St.

Marlborough Rd.

St. James's Sq.

Pall Mall

Carlton House Terr.

2

The Mall

Horse Guards

1

Horse Guards Parade

Whitehall

Downing St.

HYDE PARK

HYDE PARK CORNER

Hyde Park Corner

7

GREEN PARK

St. James's Palace

6

ST. JAMES'S PARK

226

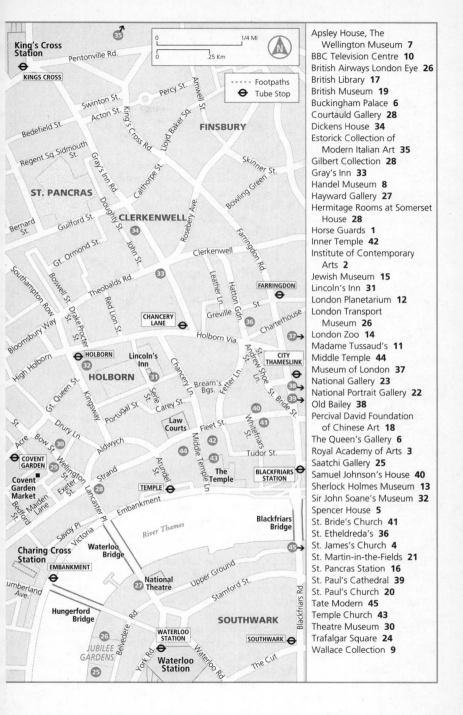

---

*Fun Fact* **American Woman**

The parents of Virginia Dare, the first English child born in America (at Roanoke in 1587) were married in St. Bride's. An effigy of Virginia can be seen over the baptismal font.

---

**St. Etheldreda's**    The oldest Roman Catholic church in London, St. Etheldreda's stands on Ely Place, off Charterhouse Street, at Holborn Circus. Built in 1251, it was mentioned by the Bard in both Richard II and Richard III. A survivor of the Great Fire of 1666, the church and the area surrounding it were the property of the diocese of the city of Ely, in the days when many bishops had episcopal houses in London, as well as in the cathedral cities in which they held their sees. The property still has a private road, with impressive iron gates and a lodge for the gatekeeper. Six elected commissioners manage the church and area.

St. Etheldreda, whose name is sometimes shortened to St. Audrey, was a 7th-century king's daughter who left her husband and established an abbey on the Isle of Ely. St. Etheldreda's has a distinguished musical tradition, with the 11am mass on Sunday sung in Latin. Other masses are on Sunday at 9am, Monday through Friday at 8am and 1pm, and Saturday at 9:30am. Lunch, with a varied choice of hot and cold dishes, is served Monday through Friday from 11:30am to 2pm in the Pantry. See "'The City' Attractions" map.

Ely Place, Holborn Circus, EC1. © **020/7405-1061.** Free admission. Daily 7:30am–6:30pm; Sat mass 9:30am, Sun masses 9 and 11am, weekday masses Mon–Fri 8am and 1pm. Tube: Farringdon or Chancery Lane.

**St. Giles Cripplegate** ⊛    Named for the patron saint of cripples, St. Giles was founded in the 11th century. The church survived the Great Fire, but the Blitz left only the tower and walls standing. In 1620, English revolutionary Oliver Cromwell was betrothed to Elizabeth Bourchier here, and in 1674, John Milton, author of *Paradise Lost,* was buried here. More than a century later, someone opened the poet's grave, knocked out his teeth, stole a rib bone, and tore hair from his skull. Guided tours are available on most Tuesday afternoons. Call to confirm. See "'The City' Attractions" map.

At Fore and Wood sts., London Wall, EC2. © **020/7638-1997.** www.stgilescripplegate.com. Free admission. Mon–Fri 11am–4pm; Sat–Sun 9am–noon for services. Tours on Tues afternoon. Tube: Moorgate or St. Paul's.

**St. James's Church** ⊛    When the aristocratic area known as St. James's was developed in the late 17th century, Sir Christopher Wren was commissioned to build its parish church. Diarist John Evelyn wrote of the interior, "There is no altar anywhere in England, nor has there been any abroad, more handsomely adorned." Wren's master carver Grinling Gibbons created the reredos (a screen decorated with religious icons and placed behind the altar), organ case, and font. As might be expected, this church has rich historical associations: The poet William Blake was baptized here, as was William Pitt, the first earl of Chatham, who became England's youngest prime minister at age 24. Caricaturist James Gillray, auctioneer James Christie, and coffeehouse founder Francis White are all buried here. One of the more colorful marriages celebrated here was that of explorer Sir Samuel Baker and the woman he had bought at a slave auction in a Turkish bazaar. St. James's Church is a radical, inclusive Anglican church. It's also the Centre for Health and Healing and holds seminars on New Age and Creation Spirituality. There's a Bible Garden and a crafts market in the courtyard. The Wren Cafe is open daily, and lunchtime and evening concerts are presented.

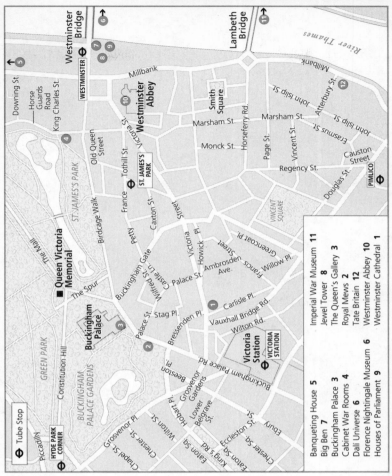

Banqueting House **5**
Big Ben **7**
Buckingham Palace **3**
Cabinet War Rooms **4**
Dali Universe **6**
Florence Nightingale Museum **6**
Houses of Parliament **9**
Imperial War Museum **11**
Jewel Tower **8**
The Queen's Gallery **3**
Royal Mews **2**
Tate Britain **12**
Westminster Abbey **10**
Westminster Cathedral **1**

There is an antiques market at St. James's on Tuesday from 10am to 6pm, and a crafts market Wednesday through Saturday from 10am to 6pm.

197 Piccadilly, W1. ℭ 020/7734-4511. Free admission. Lunchtime concerts are held on Mon, Wed, and Fri at 1:10pm. Evening concerts are on an irregular schedule; check at the church for a poster listing the current slate of evening concerts. Tube: Piccadilly Circus or Green Park.

**St. Martin-in-the-Fields** ⚘   Designed by James Gibbs, a disciple of Christopher Wren, and completed in 1726, this classical church stands at the northeast corner of Trafalgar Square, opposite the National Gallery. Its spire, added in 1824, towers 56m (184 ft.) higher than Nelson's Column, which also rises on the square. The steeple became the model for many churches in colonial America. Since the first year of World War I (1914), the homeless have sought "soup and shelter" at St. Martin, a tradition that continues.

At one time, the crypt held the remains of Charles II (he's in Westminster Abbey now), who was christened here, giving St. Martin a claim as a royal parish church. His mistress, Nell Gwynne, and the highwayman Jack Sheppard are

# Knightsbridge to Kensington Attractions

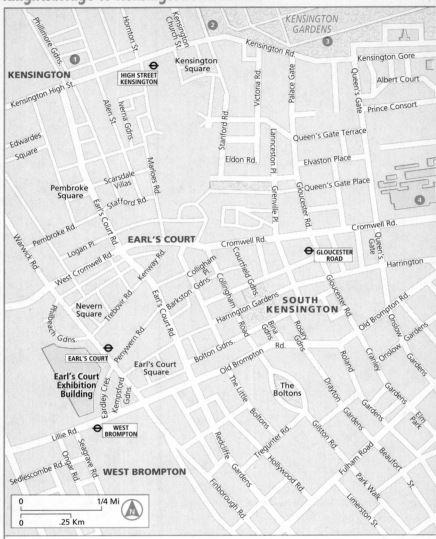

Apsley House, The Wellington Museum **7**
Carlyle's House **11**
Chelsea Physic Garden **10**
Chelsea Royal Hospital **8**
Kensington Gardens **3**
Kensington Palace **2**

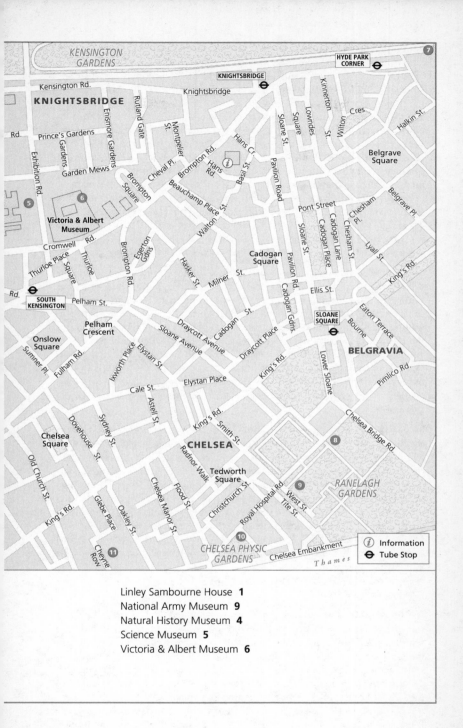

KENSINGTON GARDENS

Kensington Rd.

**KNIGHTSBRIDGE**

KNIGHTSBRIDGE

Knightsbridge

HYDE PARK CORNER

Prince's Gardens

Rd.

Exhibition Rd.

Ensmore Gardens

Gardens

Rutland Gate

Garden Mews

Montpelier St.

Cheval Pl.

Brompton Square

Brompton Rd.

Hans Rd.

Hans Cr.

Basil St.

Beauchamp Place

Lowndes Square

Sloane St.

Kinnerton St.

Wilton Cres.

Halkin St.

Belgrave Square

Belgrave Pl.

⑤ ⑥

**Victoria & Albert Museum**

Cromwell Rd.

Thurloe Place

Thurloe Square

Thurloe

Brompton Rd.

Egerton Gdns

Hasker St.

Walton

Milner St.

Pont Street

Cadogan Square

Pavilion Road

Sloane St.

Cadogan Lane

Cadogan Place

Chesham St.

Chesham Pl.

Lyall St.

King's Rd.

**SOUTH KENSINGTON**

Rd.

Pelham St.

Pelham Crescent

Draycott Avenue

Cadogan St.

Pavilion Rd.

Cadogan Gdns.

Ellis St.

Draycott Place

Eaton Terrace

**SLOANE SQUARE**

Bourne

**BELGRAVIA**

Onslow Square

Sumner Pl.

Fulham Rd.

Ixworth Place

Elystan St.

Sloane Avenue

Cale St.

Elystan Place

King's Rd.

Lower Sloane

Pimlico Rd.

Astell St.

Sydney St.

Dovehouse St.

King's Rd.

Smith St.

Chelsea Bridge Rd.

**CHELSEA**

⑧

Chelsea Square

Old Church St.

King's Rd.

Glebe Place

Oakley St.

Chelsea Manor St.

Flood St.

Radnor Walk

Tedworth Square

Christchurch St.

Royal Hospital Rd.

West St.

Tite St.

⑨

RANELAGH GARDENS

Cheyne Row

⑪

⑩

CHELSEA PHYSIC GARDENS

Chelsea Embankment

Thames

*(i)* Information
**⊖** Tube Stop

Linley Sambourne House **1**
National Army Museum **9**
Natural History Museum **4**
Science Museum **5**
Victoria & Albert Museum **6**

231

both interred here. The floors of the crypt are actually gravestones, and the walls date from the 1500s. The little restaurant, **Café in the Crypt,** is still called "Field's" by its devotees. Also in the crypt is **The London Brass Rubbing Centre** (© **020/7930-9306**) with 88 exact copies of bronze portraits ready for use. Paper, rubbing materials, and instructions on how to begin are furnished, and there's classical music for you to enjoy as you proceed. Fees to make the rubbings range from £3 to £16 ($5.55–$30), the latter price for the largest—a life-size Crusader knight. There's also a gift shop with brass-rubbing kits for children, budget-priced ready-made rubbings, Celtic jewelry, miniature brasses, and model knights. The center is open Monday through Saturday from 10am to 6pm and Sunday from noon to 6pm. See the "'West End Attractions" map.

*Insider's Tip:* In back of the church is a crafts market. Also, lunchtime and evening concerts are staged Monday, Tuesday, and Friday at 1:05pm, and Thursday through Saturday at 7:30pm. Tickets cost £6.50 to £16 ($12 to $29).

Trafalgar Sq., WC2. © **020/7766-1100.** Mon–Fri 7:45am–6pm; Sat–Sun 8:45am–7:30pm as long as no service is taking place. Concerts Mon, Tues, Fri 1pm and Thurs–Sat 7:30pm. Tube: Charing Cross.

### St. Mary-le-Bow ★★
It's said that a true Cockney must be born within the sound of this church's famous Bow bells. The church has a sometimes-gruesome history. In 1091, its roof was ripped off in a storm; in 1271, the church tower collapsed and 20 people were killed; in 1331, Queen Philippa and her ladies-in-waiting fell to the ground when a balcony collapsed during a joust celebrating the birth of the Black Prince. Wren rebuilt the church after the Great Fire of 1666 engulfed it. The original "Cockney" Bow bells were destroyed in the Blitz, but have been replaced. The church was rededicated in 1964 after extensive restoration work. See "'The City' Attractions" map.

Cheapside, EC2. © **020/7248-5139.** Free admission. Mon–Thurs 7:30am–6pm; Fri 7:30am–4pm. Tube: St. Paul's or Bank.

### St. Paul's Church (the Actors' Church) ★
With the Drury Lane Theatre, the Royal Opera House, and many other theaters within its parish, St. Paul's has long been associated with the theatrical arts. Inside you'll find scores of memorial plaques dedicated to such luminaries as Vivien Leigh, Boris Karloff, Margaret Rutherford, and Noel Coward, to name only a few. Designed by Inigo Jones in 1631, this church has been substantially altered over the years, but has retained a quiet garden-piazza in the rear. Among the famous people buried here are woodcarver Grinling Gibbons, writer Samuel Butler, and actress Ellen Terry. Landscape painter J. M. W. Turner and librettist W. S. Gilbert were both baptized here. The church still draws members of the entertainment world. See "'The City' Attractions" map.

Bedford St., Covent Garden, WC2. © **020/7836-5221.** Free admission. Tues–Fri 9:30am–4:30pm; Sun service 11am. Tube: Covent Garden.

### Temple Church ★★
One of three Norman "round churches" left in England, this one was first completed in the 12th century. Not surprisingly, it has been restored. Look for the knightly effigies and the Norman door, and take note of the circle of grotesque portrait heads, including a goat in a mortarboard. On Inner Temple Lane, about where the Strand becomes Fleet Street going east, you'll see the memorial pillar called **Temple Bar,** which marks the boundary of the City of London. See "'The City' Attractions" map.

The Temple (within the Inner Temple), King's Bench Walk, EC4. © **020/7353-3470.** Free admission. Wed 1–4pm; Thurs and Sat 11am–noon and 1–4pm; Fri 11am–noon and 1–3:30pm; Sun 1–4pm. Tube: Temple.

*Fun Fact* **The Case of the Wobbling Bridge**

The first major new crossing over the Thames in a century, and the first ever dedicated to pedestrians, the $26 million ($48 million) **Millennium Bridge** had to be closed 3 days after it opened in the summer of 2000. Under certain conditions, the bridge designed by Sir Norman Foster wobbled. Nearly 100 dampers and shock absorbers were installed beneath the 315m (1,033-ft.) span, and independent consultants have pronounced the bridge stable for pedestrians. The bridge links Tate Modern on the South Bank of the river to St. Paul's Cathedral on the northern side.

**Wesley's Chapel, House & Museum of Methodism**    John Wesley, the founder of Methodism, established this church in 1778 as his London base. Wesley, who rode on horseback throughout the English countryside and preached in the open air, lived at no. 47, next door to the chapel. He's buried in a grave behind the chapel. The house contains many of Wesley's belongings, including his "electrical machine" (a contraption that he claimed was successful in treating melancholy) and his study chair. While it survived the Blitz, the church later fell into disrepair; major restoration was completed in the 1970s. In the crypt, a museum traces the history of Methodism to present times.

Across the road in Bunhill Fields is the **Dissenters Graveyard,** where Daniel Defoe, William Blake, and John Bunyan are buried. See "'The City' Attractions" map.

49 City Rd., EC1. © 020/7253-2262. Chapel free. House and museum are also free, but donation of £2 ($3.70) per person is expected. House and museum Mon–Sat 10am–4pm, Sun noon–2pm. Tube: Old St. or Moorgate.

**Westminster Cathedral** ★    This spectacular brick-and-stone church (1903) is the headquarters of the Roman Catholic Church in Britain. Adorned in early-Byzantine style, it's massive: 108m (354 ft.) long and 47m (154 ft.) wide. One hundred different marbles compose the richly decorated interior, and eight marble columns support the nave. Eight yellow-marble columns hold up the huge canopy over the high altar. Mosaics emblazon the chapels and the vaulting of the sanctuary. If you take the elevator to the top of the 82m (269-ft.) campanile, you'll be rewarded with sweeping views that take in Buckingham Palace, Westminster Abbey, and St. Paul's Cathedral. There is a cafe serving light snacks and soft drinks from 9am to 5pm and a gift shop open from 9:30am to 5:15pm. See "Westminster & Victoria Attractions" map.

Ashley Place, SW1. © 020/7798-9055. www.westminstercathedral.org.uk. Cathedral free. Audio tours £2.50 ($4.65). Tower £3 ($5.55). Cathedral services Mon–Fri 7am–7pm; Sat 8am–6pm; Sun 8am–7pm. Tower May–Nov daily 9am–12:30pm and 1–5pm; Dec–Apr Thurs–Sun 9am–5pm. Tube: Victoria.

## HISTORIC BUILDINGS

**Banqueting House** ★★    The feasting chamber in Whitehall Palace is probably the most sumptuous dining hall on earth. (Unfortunately, you can't dine here unless you're a visiting head of state.) Designed by Inigo Jones and decorated with, among other things, original ceiling paintings by Rubens, the hall is dazzling enough to make you forget food altogether. Among the historic events that took place here were the beheading of King Charles I, who stepped through a window onto the scaffold outside, and the restoration ceremony of Charles II, marking the return of monarchy after Cromwell's brief Puritan Commonwealth. See "Westminter & Victoria Attractions" map.

Whitehall Palace, Horse Guards Ave., SW1. ℂ 0870/7515-178. www.hrp.org.uk. Admission £4 ($7.40) adults, £3 ($5.55) seniors and students, £2.60 ($4.85) children. Mon–Sat 10am–5pm (last admission 4:30pm). Tube: Westminster or Embankment.

**Cabinet War Rooms** ⭐    Visitors today can see the **Cabinet War Rooms,** the bombproof bunker suite of rooms, just as they were when abandoned by Winston Churchill and the British government at the end of World War II. You can see the Map Room with its huge wall maps, the Atlantic map a mass of pinholes (each hole represents at least one convoy). Next door is Churchill's bedroom-cum-office, which has a bed and a desk with two BBC microphones on it for his famous speech broadcasts that stirred the nation. In 2003, nine more underground Cabinet War Rooms were restored and opened to the public, including the Chiefs of Staff map room, Churchill's kitchen and dining room, Sir Winston's private detectives' room, and Mrs. Churchill's bedroom. There's everything here from a pencil cartoon of Hitler to a mousetrap in the kitchen to the original chamber pots under the beds (they had no flush toilets).

The **Transatlantic Telephone Room,** its full title, is little more than a broom closet, but it housed the Bell Telephone Company's special scrambler phone, called *Sigsaly,* and it was where Churchill conferred with Roosevelt. Visitors are provided with a step-by-step personal sound guide, providing a detailed account of each room's function and history.

Clive Steps, at end of King Charles St. (off Whitehall near Big Ben), SW1. ℂ 020/7930-6961. www.iwm. org.uk. Admission £7.50 ($14) adults, £6 ($11) seniors and students, free for children 16 and under. Apr–Sept daily 9:30am–6pm (last admission at 5:15pm); Oct–Mar daily 10am–6pm. Tube: Westminster or St. James's.

**Chelsea Royal Hospital** ⭐⭐    This dignified institution, founded by Charles II in 1682 as a home for veterans, was designed and completed by Sir Christopher Wren in 1692. It consists of a main block containing the hall and the chapel, flanked by east and west wings. There's been little change to Wren's design, except for minor work done by Robert Adam in the 18th century and the addition of stables by Sir John Soane in 1814. The Duke of Wellington lay in state here from November 10 to 17, 1852. So many people thronged to see

---

*Finds*  **A City of Wine**

At **Vinopolis,** 1 Bank End, Park St., SE1 (ℂ 0870/4444-777; www.vinopolis. co.uk), you can partake of London's largest selection of wine sold by the glass. On the South Bank, this "city of wine" lies under cavernous railway arches created in Victoria's era. The bacchanalian attraction was created in a multimedia format, at the cost of £23 million ($43 million). You can journey virtually through some of the earth's most prestigious wine regions, driving a Vespa through the Tuscan countryside or taking a "flight" over the vineyards of Australia. The price of entrance includes free tastings of five premium wines, and an on-site shop sells almost any item related to the grape. The site also boasts a good restaurant (see "Cantina Vinopolis," p. 155). Admission is £13 ($23) for adults, free for ages 5 to 14, and £12 ($21) for seniors. Open Tuesday to Thursday and Sunday noon to 6pm. See "'The City' Attractions" map.

him that two were crushed to death. Today, the hospital is home to bachelor pensioners who fought in World War II or other conflicts.

If you want a tour, apply in writing to Adjutant, Royal Hospital Chelsea, London, SW3 4SR. Guided tours are free, but donations are gratefully accepted. Otherwise, you are welcome to explore on your own. See "Knightsbridge to Kensington Attractions" map.

Royal Hospital Rd., SW3. ℂ 020/7881-5244. Free admission. Mon–Sat 10am–noon and 2–4pm; Sun 2–4pm. Museum and shop closed Sun Oct–Mar. Tube: Sloane Sq.

**City Hall**   On the South Bank of the Thames, adjacent to Tower Bridge, this is the new home of the mayor of London and the London Assembly. Her Majesty dedicated the gleaming, egg-shaped building—a 10-story steel-and-glass structure—in July 2002. Foster and Partners, one of Britain's leading architectural firms, designed the building. The new home of the city government has become London's latest—and some say, most controversial—landmark. Half of City Hall is open to the public. The views from the rooftop gallery are worth the trek over to the South Bank. An exhibition space displays changing cultural exhibits, and there is a cafe on site. See "'The City' Attractions" map.

The Queen's Walk, SE1. ℂ 020/7983-4100. www.london.gov.uk. Free admission. Visitors Center daily 9:30am–5pm; cafe daily 8am–8pm. Tube: London Bridge.

**Gray's Inn** ⭐   Gray's Inn is one of four ancient Inns of Court still in operation. As you enter, you'll see a late-Georgian terrace lined with buildings that serve as both residences and offices. Gray's was restored after suffering heavy damage in World War II. It contains a rebuilt Tudor Hall, but its greatest attraction is the tree-shaded lawn and handsome gardens. A 17th-century atmosphere exists today in the square. Scientist-philosopher Francis Bacon (1561–1626) was the inn's most eminent tenant. See "'The City' Attractions" map.

Gray's Inn Rd. (north of High Holborn; entrance on Theobald's Rd.), 8 South Sq., WC1. ℂ 020/7458-7800. www.graysinn.org.uk. Free admission to squares and gardens. Gardens Mon–Fri noon–2:30pm; squares Mon–Fri 6:30am–midnight. Tube: Chancery Lane.

**Horse Guards** ⭐   North of Downing Street, on the west side of Whitehall, is the building of the Horse Guards, which is the headquarters of the British Army. The building was designed by William Kent, chief architect to George II. The real draw here is the Horse Guards themselves: the Household Cavalry Mounted Regiment, a combination of the oldest and most senior regiments in the British Army—the Life Guards and the Blues and Royals. In theory, their duty is to protect the sovereign. Life Guards wear red tunics and white plumes, and Blues and Royals are attired in blue tunics with red plumes. Two much-photographed mounted members of the Household Cavalry keep watch daily from 10am to 4pm. The mounted sentries change duty every hour as a benefit to the horses. Foot sentries change every 2 hours. The chief guard rather grandly inspects the troops here daily at 4pm. The guard, with flair and fanfare, dismounts at 5pm.

We prefer the **changing of the guards** here to the more famous ceremony at Buckingham Palace. Beginning around 11am Monday through Saturday and 10am on Sunday, a new guard leaves the Hyde Park Barracks on horseback, rides down Pall Mall, and arrives at the Horse Guards building, all in about 30 minutes. The old guard then returns to the barracks.

If you pass through the arch at Horse Guards, you'll find yourself at the **Horse Guards Parade,** which opens onto St. James's Park. This spacious court provides the best view of the various architectural styles that make up Whitehall. Regrettably, the parade ground itself is now a parking lot.

The military pageant—the most famous in Britain—known as **Trooping the Colour,** celebrating the queen's birthday, takes place in June at the Horse Guards Parade (see "London Calendar of Events," in chapter 3). The "Colour" refers to the flag of the regiment. For devotees of pomp and circumstance, "Beating the Retreat" is staged here 3 or 4 evenings a week during the first 2 weeks of June. It's only a dress rehearsal, though, for Trooping the Colour. See "West End Attractions" map.

Whitehall, SW1. ℂ 020/7414-2479. www.army.mod.uk. Free admission. Tube: Charing Cross, Westminster, or Embankment.

**Lincoln's Inn** ★★    Lincoln's Inn is the oldest of the four Inns of Court (see the box "Legal London" on p. 237). Between the City and the West End, Lincoln's Inn comprises 4.4 hectares (11 acres), including lawns, squares, gardens, a 17th-century chapel (open Mon–Fri noon–2pm), a library, and two halls. One of these, Old Hall, dates from 1490 and has remained almost unaltered, with its linenfold paneling, stained glass, and wooden screen by Inigo Jones. It was once the home of Sir Thomas More, and it was where barristers met, ate, and debated 150 years before the *Mayflower* sailed on its epic voyage. Old Hall is the scene for the opening chapter of Charles Dickens's *Bleak House.* The other hall, Great Hall, remains one of the finest Tudor Revival buildings in London and was opened by Queen Victoria in 1843. It's now the center of the inn and is used for the formal ceremony of calling students to the bar. See "'The City' Attractions" map.

Lincoln's Inn Fields, WC2. ℂ 020/7405-1393. www.lincolnsinn.org.uk. Free admission to grounds. Mon–Fri 10am–4pm. Tube: Holborn or Chancery Lane.

**Old Bailey**    This courthouse replaced the infamous Newgate Prison, once the scene of hangings and other forms of "public entertainment." It's affectionately known as the "Old Bailey" after a street that runs nearby. It's fascinating to watch the bewigged barristers presenting their cases to the high-court judges. Entry is strictly on a first-arrival basis, and guests line up outside; security will then direct you to one of the rooms where cases are being tried. It's impossible to predict how long a line you might face. If there's a London equivalent of the O. J. Simpson trial, forget about it—you'll never get in. On a day with trials attracting little attention, you can often enter after only 15 minutes or so. You never know until you show up. The best time to line up is 10am. You enter courts 1 to 4, 17, and 18 from Newgate Street, and the others from Old Bailey Street. See "'The City' Attractions" map.

Newgate St., EC4. To get here from the Temple, travel east on Fleet St., which becomes Ludgate Hill; cross Ludgate Circus and turn left at the Old Bailey, a domed structure with the figure of *Justice* atop it. ℂ 020/ 7248-3277. Free admission. Court in session Mon–Fri 10:30am–1pm and 2–4pm. Children under 14 not admitted; those 14–16 must be accompanied by a responsible adult. No cameras, tape recorders, or cellphones (and there are no coat-checking facilities). Tube: St. Paul's.

**Spencer House** ★★    This is one of the city's most beautiful buildings. It was constructed in 1766 for the first Earl Spencer, who intended it as a shrine to Georgiana Poyntz, his childhood sweetheart whom he had secretly married the year before. It hasn't been a private residence since 1927, and had something of a checkered history until it was restored and opened as a museum in 1990. Rooms are filled with period furniture and art, some even loaned by the queen herself. The most spectacular salon is the Palm Room, all in white, gold, and green. See the "West End Attractions" map.

27 St. James's Place, SW1. ℂ 020/7499-8620. www.spencerhouse.co.uk. Admission £6 ($11) adults, £5 ($9.25) children 10–16; children under 10 not allowed. Open only on Sun 10:30am–5:45pm (last admission 4:45pm). Closed Jan and Aug. Tube: Green Park.

## Legal London

The smallest borough in London, bustling **Holborn** (*ho*-burn) is often referred to as "Legal London." It's home to the majority of the city's barristers, solicitors, and law clerks, as well as the ancient **Inns of Court** (Tube: Holborn or Chancery Lane), the beautiful complexes where barristers have their chambers and law students perform their apprenticeships. All barristers (litigators) must belong to one of these institutions: **Gray's Inn, Lincoln's Inn** (the best preserved), the **Middle Temple,** or the **Inner Temple** (both just over the line inside the City). Many barristers also work from one of these dignified ancient buildings. The area was severely damaged during World War II, and some razed buildings were replaced with modern offices, but the borough still retains pockets of architecture of former days. See "'The City' Attractions" map.

**St. Pancras Station**    The London terminus for the Midland Railway, St. Pancras Station (built from 1863–67) is a masterpiece of Victorian engineering. Designed by W. H. Barlow, the 207m (679-ft.) long glass-and-iron train station spans 72m (236 ft.) in width and rises to a peak of 30m (98 ft.) above the rails. The platforms were raised 6m (20 ft.) above the ground because the tracks ran over the Regent's Canal before entering the station. The pièce de résistance, though, is Sir George Gilbert Scott's fanciful Midland Grand Hotel. Done in high Gothic style, the Hotel is graced with pinnacles, towers, and gables; it now functions as office space. The facade runs 170m (558 ft.) and is flanked by a clock tower and a west tower. See the "West End Attractions" map.

Euston Rd., NW1. Tube: King's Cross/St. Pancras.

## LITERARY & MUSICAL LANDMARKS

Besides the homes of the authors and composers listed below, you can also visit the abodes of other celebrated Londoners (detailed in other sections of this chapter), including Apsley House, the former mansion of the Duke of Wellington (p. 239). The homes of John Keats and Sigmund Freud are also open to the public; both are north of London in Hampstead (p. 258). Finally, the fascinating home of legendary architect Sir John Soane (p. 252) is open to the public and now houses a museum about Soane.

**Carlyle's House**    From 1834 to 1881, Thomas Carlyle, author of *The French Revolution,* and Jane Baillie Welsh Carlyle, his noted letter-writing wife, resided in this modest 1708 terraced house. Furnished essentially as it was in Carlyle's day, the house is located about half a block from the Thames, near the Chelsea Embankment, along King's Road. It was described by his wife as being "of most antique physiognomy, quite to our humour; all wainscoted, carved, and queer-looking, roomy, substantial, commodious, with closets to satisfy any Bluebeard." The second floor contains Mrs. Carlyle's drawing room, but the most interesting chamber is the not-so-soundproof "soundproof" study in the skylit attic. Filled with Carlyle memorabilia—his books, a letter from Disraeli, personal effects, a writing chair, even his death mask—this is where the author did his work. See the "Knightsbridge to Kensington Attractions" map.

24 Cheyne Row, SW3. (C) **020/7352-7087.** Admission £3.80 ($7) adults, £1.80 ($3.33) children 5–16, free for children 4 and under. Apr–Oct Wed–Sun 11am–5pm. Closed Nov–Mar. Tube: Sloane Sq.

**Dickens House**   Here in Bloomsbury stands the simple abode in which Charles Dickens wrote *Oliver Twist* and finished *The Pickwick Papers* (his American readers actually waited at the dock for the ship that brought in each new installment). The place is almost a shrine: It contains his study, manuscripts, and personal relics, as well as reconstructed interiors. During Christmas week (including Christmas Day), the museum is decorated in the style of Dickens's first Christmas there. During Christmas, the raised admission prices of £10 ($19) for adults and £5 ($9.25) for children include hot mince pies and a few glasses of "Smoking Bishop," Dickens's favorite hot punch, as well as a copy of the museum's guidebooks. See the "West End Attractions" map.

48 Doughty St., WC1. © 020/7405-2127. www.dickensmuseum.com. Admission £5 ($9.25) adults, £4 ($7.40) students, £1 ($1.85) children, £14 ($26) families. Mon–Sat 10am–5pm; Sun 11am–5pm. Tube: Russell Sq.

**Handel Museum**   This is the first composer museum to open in London. George Frederic Handel lived in this town house until his death in 1759, and it was here that he composed *Messiah*. Most of his organ concerts were written here, as well as "Israel in Egypt" and "Coronation Anthems." Handel settled in

## A Neighborhood of One's Own: The Homes of Virginia Woolf

Born in London in 1882, author and essayist Virginia Woolf used the city as the setting for many of her novels, including *Jacob's Room* (1922). The daughter of Sir Leslie Stephen and his wife, Julia Duckworth, Virginia spent her formative years at **22 Hyde Park Gate,** off Kensington Road, west of Royal Albert Hall. Her mother died in 1895 and her father in 1904.

After the death of their father, Virginia and her sister Vanessa left Kensington for Bloomsbury, settling near the British Museum. It was an interesting move, as Bloomsbury was a neighborhood that upper-class Victorians didn't view as "respectable." But Virginia was to make it her own, and in the process, make the district world-famous as the hub of literary London. From 1905, the Stephens lived at **46 Gordon Sq.,** east of Gower Street and University College. It was here that the celebrated literary and artistic circle known as the "Bloomsbury Group" came into being. In time, the group would embrace art critic Clive Bell and author Leonard Woolf, future husbands of Vanessa and Virginia, respectively. Later, Virginia went to live at **29 Fitzroy Sq.,** west of Tottenham Court Road, in a house once occupied by Bernard Shaw.

During the next 2 decades, Virginia resided at several more Bloomsbury addresses, including **Brunswick Square, Tavistock Square,** and **Mecklenburg Square.** These homes have disappeared or been altered beyond recognition. During this time, the Bloomsbury Group reached out to include the artists Roger Fry and Duncan Grant, and Virginia became a friend of economist John Maynard Keynes and author E. M. Forster (*A Passage to India*). At Tavistock Square (1924–39) and at Mecklenburg Square (1939–40), she operated the Hogarth Press with Leonard. She published her own early work here, as well as T. S. Eliot's *The Waste Land.*

London in 1710 but didn't move to this Georgian house until 1723. The house has been restored to its original 18th-century styling, with furniture and fabrics accurate to the time Handel lived here (not the originals, though). The museum is hung with portraits and prints of Handel, his colleagues, and his patrons.

On display are two harpsichords, which are played frequently by professionals and harpsichord students when the museum is open. Precious objects include Mozart's handwritten arrangement of a Handel fugue, and furnishings such as a canopied bedroom from 1720 on loan from the Victoria and Albert Museum. See the "West End Attractions" map.

25 Brook St., W1. © 020/7495-1685. www.handelhouse.org. Admission £4.50 ($8.35) adults, £3.50 ($6.50) students, £2 ($3.70) children 12 and under. Tues–Sat 10am–6pm (until 8pm Thurs), Sun noon–6pm. Tube: Bond St.

**Samuel Johnson's House** ✦✦   Dr. Johnson and his copyists compiled his famous dictionary in this Queen Anne house, where the lexicographer, poet, essayist, and fiction writer lived from 1748 to 1759. Although Johnson also lived at Staple Inn in Holborn and at a number of other places, the Gough Square house is the only one of his residences remaining in modern London. The 17th-century building has been painstakingly restored, and it's well worth a visit.

After you're done touring the house, you might want to stop in at **Ye Olde Cheshire Cheese,** Wine Office Court, 145 Fleet St. (© **020/7353-6170**), Johnson's favorite locale. He must have had some lean nights at the pub because by the time he had compiled his dictionary, he'd already spent his advance of 1,500 guineas. G. K. Chesterton, author of *What's Wrong with the World* (1910) and *The Superstition of Divorce* (1920), was also a familiar patron at the pub. See "'The City' Attractions" map.

17 Gough Sq., EC4. Walk up New Bridge St. and turn left onto Fleet; Gough Sq. is tiny and hidden, north of Fleet St. © 020/7353-3745. www.drjh.dircon.co.uk. Admission £4 ($7.40) adults, £3 ($5.55) students and seniors, £1 ($1.85) children, free for children 10 and under. Oct–Apr Mon–Sat 11am–4:45pm; May–Sept Mon–Sat 11am–5:30pm. Tube: Blackfriars or Chancery Lane.

## MUSEUMS & GALLERIES

**Apsley House, The Wellington Museum** ✦   This was the mansion of the Duke of Wellington, the "Iron Duke," one of Britain's greatest generals, who defeated Napoleon at Waterloo. Later, for a short period while he was prime minister, the duke had to have iron shutters fitted to his windows to protect him from a mob outraged by his autocratic opposition to reform. (His unpopularity soon passed, however.)

The house is crammed with art treasures, including three original Velázquez paintings, and military mementos that include the duke's medals and battlefield orders. Apsley House also holds some of the finest silver and porcelain pieces in Europe, displayed in the Plate and China Room. Grateful to Wellington for saving their thrones, European monarchs showered him with treasures. The collection includes a Sèvres Egyptian service that was intended as a divorce present from Napoleon to Josephine (but she refused it); Louis XVIII eventually presented it to Wellington. Another treasure, the Portuguese Silver Service, created between 1812 and 1816, has been hailed as the single greatest artifact of Portuguese neoclassical silver. See the "West End Attractions" map.

149 Piccadilly, Hyde Park Corner, SW1. © 020/7499-5676. www.apsleyhouse.org.uk. Admission £4.50 ($8.35) adults, £3 ($5.55) seniors, free for children under 18. Tues–Sun 11am–5pm. Tube: Hyde Park Corner.

## *Value*  A Money-Saving Pass

The **London Pass** provides admission to 60 attractions in and around London, £5 ($9.25) worth of phone calls, "timed" admission at some attractions (bypassing the queues), plus free travel on public transport (buses, Tubes, and trains) and a pocket guidebook. It costs £23 ($43) for 1 day, £44 ($81) for 3 days, or £72 ($133) for 6 days (children pay £15/$28, £29/$54, or £41/$76), and includes admission to St. Paul's Cathedral, HMS *Belfast,* the Jewish Museum, and the Thames Barrier Visitor Centre—and many other attractions. Visit the website at **www. londonpass.com**. Purchase the pass before you go because passes purchased in London do not include free transportation.

**BBC Television Centre**   Have you ever wanted to go backstage to take a look at one of the most famous television studios in the world? The behind-the-scenes tours of this news center include visits to the weather center, the prop storehouse, and the production galleries. Because this is a working studio, no tours are exactly the same. Those looking for souvenirs, books, or videos will find an on-site shop. There is also a lunch cafe. You must book in advance, and visitors must be 10 years of age or over. *Tip:* Because this is such a popular attraction, make reservations 2 to 3 days in advance. See the "West End Attractions" map.

Television Centre, Wood Lane, W12. ℂ **0870/603-0304.** www.bbc.co.uk/tours. Admission £7.95 ($15) adults, £6.95 ($13) seniors, £5.95 ($11) students and children, £22 ($41) family ticket. Mon–Sat tours are at 10am, 10:20am, 1:15pm, 1:30pm, 3:30pm, and 3:45pm. Tube: White City.

**British Library** ★★   In December 1996, one of the world's great libraries began moving its collection of some 12 million books, manuscripts, and other items from the British Museum to its very own home in St. Pancras. In the new building, you get modernistic beauty rather than the fading glamour and the ghosts of Karl Marx, Thackeray, and Virginia Woolf of the old library at the British Museum. You are also likely to get the book you want within an hour instead of 3 days. Academics, students, writers, and bookworms from the world over come here. On a recent visit, we sat next to a student researching the history of pubs.

The bright, roomy interior is far more inviting than the rather dull redbrick exterior suggests (the writer Alain de Botton likened the exterior to a supermarket). Still, Colin St. John Wilson, the architect, says he has been delighted by the positive response to his building. The most spectacular room is the Humanities Reading Room, constructed on three levels with daylight filtered through the ceiling.

The fascinating collection includes such items of historic and literary interest as two of the four surviving copies of the *Magna Carta* (1215), a Gutenberg Bible, Nelson's last letter to Lady Hamilton, and the journals of Captain Cook. Almost every major author—Dickens, Jane Austen, Charlotte Brontë, Keats, and hundreds of others—is represented in the section devoted to English literature. Beneath Roubiliac's 1758 statue of Shakespeare stands a case of documents relating to the Bard, including a mortgage bearing his signature and a copy of the First Folio of 1623. There's also an unrivaled collection of stamps and stamp-related items.

Visitors can view the *Diamond Sutra,* dating from 868 and said to be the oldest surviving printed book. Using headphones set around the room, you can hear thrilling audio snippets such as James Joyce reading a passage from *Finnegans Wake.* Curiosities include the earliest known tape of a birdcall, dating from 1889. Particularly intriguing is an exhibition called "Turning the Pages," where you can, for example, electronically read a complete Leonardo da Vinci notebook by putting your hands on a special computer screen that flips from one page to another. There is a copy of *The Canterbury Tales* from 1410, and even manuscripts from *Beowulf* (ca. 1000). Illuminated texts from some of the oldest known Biblical displays include the *Codex Sinaitticus* and *Codex Alexandrius,* 3rd-century Greek gospels. In the Historical Documents section are letters by everybody from Henry VIII to Napoleon, from Elizabeth I to Churchill. In the music displays, you can seek out original sheet music by Beethoven, Handel, Stravinsky, and Lennon and McCartney. An entire day spent here will only scratch the surface.

Walking tours of the library cost £6 ($11) for adults and £4.50 ($8.35) for seniors, students, and children. They are conducted Monday, Wednesday, and Friday at 3pm, and Saturday at 10:30am and 3pm. Library tours that include a visit to one of the reading rooms take place on Sundays and bank holidays at 11:30am and 3pm; £7 ($13) adults, £5.50 ($10) for seniors and students. Reservations can be made up to 2 weeks in advance. See the "West End Attractions" map.

96 Euston Rd., NW1. © 020/7412-7000. www.bl.uk. Free admission. Mon, Wed, Thurs, Fri 9:30am–6pm; Tues 9:30am–8pm; Sat 9:30am–5pm; Sun and bank holidays 11am–5pm. Tube: King's Cross/St. Pancras, or Euston.

**Courtauld Gallery**   The nucleus of this collection was acquired by Samuel Courtauld, who died in 1947 leaving his collection to the University of London. Today it houses the biggest collection of Impressionist and post-Impressionist paintings in Britain, with masterpieces by Monet, Manet, Degas, Renoir, Cézanne, van Gogh, and Gauguin. The gallery also has a superb collection of old-master paintings and drawings, including works by Rubens and Michelangelo; early-Italian paintings, ivories, and majolica; the Lee collection of old masters; and early-20th-century English, French, and British paintings.

The new galleries on the second floor display a series of paintings and sculptures, some 100 pieces of art from the late 19th and 20th centuries, including an outstanding grouping of Fauve paintings along with art by everybody from Matisse to Dufy, along with a remarkable series of paintings and drawings by Kandinsky. We come here at least once every season to revisit one work in particular: Manet's exquisite *A Bar at the Folies-Bergère* ⚘. Many of the paintings are displayed without glass, giving the gallery a more intimate feeling than most. This gallery is but one of three major attractions at Somerset House. For information about the other attractions, such as the Gilbert Collection and the Hermitage Rooms, see below.

Somerset House, The Strand, WC2. © 020/7848-2777. www.courtauld.ac.uk. Admission £5 ($9.25) adults, £4 ($7.40) seniors and students, free for children under 18. Free admission Mon 10am–2pm. Daily 10am–6pm; last admission 5:15pm. Tube: Temple, Covent Garden, Charing Cross, or Holborn.

**Dalí Universe** ⚘ *Finds*   Next to the "London Eye," this exhibition is devoted to the remarkable Spanish artist Salvador Dalí (1904–89), and is one of London's newest attractions. Featuring more than 500 works of art, including the Mae West Lips sofa, the exhibitions are divided into a trio of themed areas: Sensuality and Femininity, Religion and Mythology, and Dreams and Fantasy. Showcased are important Dalí sculptures, rare graphics, watercolors, and even furnishings and jewelry. You can feast on such surreal works as Dalí's monumental oil painting for the Hitchcock movie *Spellbound,* or view a series of original watercolors and collages including the mystical *Tarot Cards.* You can also see the world's largest collection of rare Dalí graphics, illustrating themes from literature. See the "Westminster & Victoria Attractions" map.

County Hall, Riverside Bldg., South Bank, SE1. ⓒ 020/7620-2720. www.daliuniverse.com. Admission £8.50 ($16) adults, £7 ($13) students and seniors, £5.50 ($10) ages 5–16, and £23 ($43) family ticket. Daily 10am–5:30pm. Tube: Waterloo.

**Design Museum**    The Design Museum is a showcase of modern design— kind of like Pottery Barn without the price tags. It's the only museum in Europe that explains why and how mass-produced objects work and look the way they do, and how design contributes to the quality of our lives. The collection of objects includes cars, furniture, domestic appliances, graphics, and ceramics, as well as changing displays of new products and prototypes from around the world. The cafe offers panoramic views of Tower Bridge and the Thames. See "'The City' Attractions" map.

28 Shad Thames, SE1. ⓒ 0870/833-9955. www.designmuseum.org. Admission £6 ($11) adults, £4 ($7.40) children, £16 ($30) family ticket. Daily 10am–5:45pm. Tube: Tower Bridge or London Bridge.

**Dulwich Picture Gallery** ⭐ *Finds*    Just 12 minutes by train from Victoria Station, this rarely visited museum houses one of the world's most significant collections of European old masters from the 17th and 18th centuries. In a purpose-built gallery designed by Sir John Soane in 1811, the collection is one of the oldest in Britain, having been assembled in the 1790s. Many of the paintings were collected by Stanislaus Augustus of Poland for shipment to his homeland. Before that happened, his kingdom had been partitioned out of existence, and the paintings remained in London. You can view works by such old masters as Rembrandt, Rubens, Canaletto, Gainsborough, Watteau, Pousin, and others. The *Sunday Telegraph* has hailed Dulwich as "the most beautiful small art gallery in the world."

Gallery Road, Dulwich Village, SE21. ⓒ 020/8693-5254. Admission £4 ($7.40) adults, £3 ($5.55) seniors, free students and children. Tues–Fri 10am–5pm; Sat–Sun 11am–5pm. Tube: West Dulwich Station.

**Estorick Collection of Modern Italian Art**    Long dismissed as "unfashionable," early-20th-century Italian art is given a showcase in London. Eric Estorick (1913–93) was an American political scientist and writer who was a passionate collector. The year he died, he established a foundation to display his collection and to stage temporary-loan exhibitions. His collection has been hailed as one of the finest early-20th-century Italian art collections anywhere in the world. Estorick had a remarkable eye and prophetic judgment in art when he began his collection, although his treasure trove was dismissed by the art snobs of his day. Powerful images by the main protagonists of the early-20th-century Italian avant-garde Futurist movement, including Balla, Boccioni, Carrá, Serverini, and Russolo, are on permanent view. The collection includes works by figurative artists like Modigliani, Sironi, and Campigli, plus works by the metaphysical painter de Chirico. See the "West End Attractions" map.

39A Canonbury Sq., N1. ⓒ 020/7704-9522. www.estorickcollection.com. Admission £3.50 ($6.50) adults, £2.50 ($4.65) seniors and children. Wed–Sat 11am–6pm; Sun noon–5pm. Tube: Victoria Line to Highbury and Islington.

**Fashion & Textile Museum**    Fashion museums are all the rage on the Continent, and London weighs in with this Bermondsey (south of the Thames) new museum. It was designed by Mexican architect Ricardo Legorreta from a converted warehouse. The concept was the inspiration of eccentric fashion designer Zandra Rhodes, known for her vibrant dresses—half punk, half posh. The museum is the first in the United Kingdom devoted to textiles and contemporary fashion. The museum showcases British designers such as Mary Quant, who startled the fashion world of London's "Swinging Sixties." In addition, the exhibit showcases the personal favorite dresses of 70 of the most respected designers of the 20th and 21st centuries. FTM aims to hold two to three major exhibitions per year.

83 Bermondsey St., SE1. ℂ **020/7403-0222.** Admission £6 ($11) adults, £4 ($7.40) students and senior citizens, and £16 ($30) family ticket. Tues–Sun 11am–5:45pm. Tube: London Bridge.

**Florence Nightingale Museum**  The life and work of one of England's most influential women of the 1800s is celebrated here. You'll learn that her most famous accomplishment—nursing soldiers during the Crimean War—was only part of a career spanning half a century. Nightingale did everything from raising the image of the British soldier (from a brawling lowlife to a heroic working man) to making nursing a respectable profession. Before the "Lady with the Lamp," nursing was seen as a job fit only for prostitutes.

In 1896, Nightingale "retired to her bed," but didn't slow down. She continued to write on public health. Much of her advice is still valid today. When she died in 1910 at the age of 90, she had become so reclusive that the general public assumed she was already dead. See the "Westminster & Victoria" map.

St. Thomas' Hospital, 2 Lambeth Palace Rd., SE1. ℂ **020/7620-0374.** www.florence-nightingale.co.uk. Admission £5.80 ($11) adults, £4.20 ($7.80) seniors, children, and persons with disabilities. Mon–Fri 10am–5pm; Sat–Sun 10am–4:30pm. Tube: Westminster or Waterloo.

**Geffrye Museum** ★  If you'd like an overview of British interiors and lifestyles of the past 4 centuries, head to this museum, housed in a series of restored 18th-century almshouses that escaped Hitler's Blitz. Period rooms are arranged chronologically, allowing you to follow changing tastes in the days of the Empire. You'll see the development of furnishings and *objets d'art* in English middle-class homes. The collection is rich in Jacobean and Georgian interiors and strongest in the Victorian period. In the 20th-century rooms, you'll see the richness of the Art Deco style and the bleakness of the utilitarian designs that followed in the aftermath of World War II. Newer galleries showcase the decor of the later 20th century.

Originally, in 1715, these almshouses belonged to the Ironmongers' Company. Their architecture alone is worth a visit. Gardens in front attract much attention, especially the herb garden. There is a design center, which showcases changing exhibitions of the latest works from contemporary British designers. There is also a cafe/restaurant. See "'The City' Attractions" map.

136 Kingsland Rd., Shoreditch, E2. ℂ **020/7739-9893.** www.geffrye-museum.org.uk. Free admission. Tues–Sat 10am–5pm; Sun and bank holidays noon–5pm. Closed Good Friday, Dec 24–26, New Year's Day. Gardens open Apr–Oct. Tube: Liverpool St. then bus 149 or 242, or Old St. Tube then bus 243.

**Gilbert Collection** ★★★ *Finds*  In 2000, Somerset House became the permanent home for the Gilbert Collection of decorative arts, one of the most important bequests ever made to England. Sir Arthur Gilbert made his gift of gold, silver, mosaics, and gold snuffboxes to the nation in 1996, at which time the value was estimated at £75 million ($139 million). The collection of some 800 objects in three fields (gold and silver, mosaics, and gold snuffboxes) is among the most distinguished in the world. The silver collection here is arguably better than the one at the V&A. The array of mosaics is among the most comprehensive ever gathered, with Roman and Florentine examples dating from the 16th to the 19th centuries. The gold and silver collection has exceptional breadth, ranging from the 15th to the 19th centuries, spanning India to South America. It is strong in masterpieces of great 18th-century silversmiths, such as Paul de Lamerie. Such exhibits as the Maharajah pieces, the "Gold Crown," and Catherine the Great's Royal Gates are fabulous. The gallery also displays one of the most representative collections of gold snuffboxes in the world, with some 200 examples. Some of the snuffboxes were owned by Louis XV, Frederick the Great, and Napoleon. The Gilbert Collection is only one of three major museums and galleries at Somerset House. For recommendations of the other two, see Courtauld Gallery (see above) or the Hermitage Rooms (see below).

Somerset House, the Strand WC2. © **020/7240-9400.** www.gilbert-collection.org.uk. Admission £5 ($9.25) adults, free for full-time students under 18. Daily 10am–6pm. Tube: Temple, Covent Garden, Charing Cross, or Embankment.

### Guildhall Art Gallery ★
In 1999, Queen Elizabeth opened a new £70 million ($130 million) gallery in the City, a continuation of an original gallery that was launched in 1886 but burned down in a severe air raid in May 1941. Many famous and much-loved pictures, which for years were known only through temporary exhibitions and reproductions, are again available for the public to see in a permanent setting. The new gallery can display only 250 of the 4,000 treasures it owns. The art ranges from classical to modern. A curiosity is the huge double-height wall built to accommodate Britain's largest independent oil painting, John Singleton Copley's *The Defeat of the Floating Batteries at Gibraltar, September 1782.* The Corporation of London in the City owns these works and has been collecting them since the 17th century. The most popular art is in the Victorian collection, including such well-known favorites as Millais's *My First Sermon* and *My Second Sermon,* and Landseer's *The First Leap.* There is also a landscape of Salisbury Cathedral by John Constable. Since World War II, all paintings acquired by the gallery concentrate on London subjects. See "'The City' Attractions" map.

Guildhall Yard, EC2 2P2EJ. © **020/7332-3700.** www.guildhall-art-gallery.org.uk. Admission £2.50 ($4.65) adults, £1 ($1.85) seniors and students. Free for children under 16. Free Fri and after 3:30pm on every other day. Mon–Sat 10am–5pm; Sun noon–4pm. Tube: Bank, St. Paul's, Mansion House, or Moorgate.

### Hayward Gallery
Opened by Elizabeth II in 1968, this gallery presents a changing program of major contemporary and historical exhibits. It's managed by the South Bank Board, which also includes Royal Festival Hall, Queen Elizabeth Hall, and the Purcell Room. Every exhibition is accompanied by a variety of educational activities, including tours, workshops, lectures, and publications. The gallery closes between exhibitions, so call before crossing the Thames.

Belvedere Rd., South Bank, SE1. © **020/7960-5226.** www.hayward.org.uk. Admission varies but usually £8 ($15) adults, £5.50 ($10) students and seniors, free for children under 12. Hours subject to change, depending on the exhibit: Thurs, Sat, Sun, Mon 11am–7pm, Fri 11am–9pm, Tues–Wed 11am–8pm. Tube: Waterloo.

### Hermitage Rooms at Somerset House ★★★
This is a virtual branch of St. Petersburg's State Hermitage Museum, which owns a great deal of the treasure trove left over from the Czars, including possessions of art-collecting Catherine the Great. Now you don't have to go to Russia to see some of Europe's great treasures.

The rotating exhibitions will change, but you'll get to see such Czarist treasures as medals, jewelry, portraits, porcelain, clocks, and furniture. A rotating "visiting masterpiece" overshadows all the other collections. Some items that amused us on our first visit (and you are likely to see similar novelties) were a wig made entirely out of silver thread for Catherine the Great; a Wedgwood "Green Frog" table service; and two very rare Chinese silver filigree toilet sets. The rooms themselves have been designed in the style of the Winter Palace at St. Petersburg. *Note:* Because this exhibit attracts so much interest, tickets should be purchased in advance. Tickets are available from Ticketmaster at © **020/7413-3398** (24 hr.). You can book online at **www.ticketmaster.co.uk**. The other two museums at Somerset House, the Courtauld Gallery and the Gilbert Collection, were previewed above.

Somerset House, the Strand, WC2. © 020/7845-4600. www.hermitagerooms.com. Admission £5 ($9.25) adults, £4 ($7.40), free for students under 16 and seniors. Daily 10am–6pm. Tube: Temple, Covent Garden, Charing Cross, or Holborn.

**Imperial War Museum** ⭐    One of the few major sights south of the Thames, this museum occupies 1 city block the size of an army barracks, greeting you with 38cm (15-in.) guns from the battleships *Resolution* and *Ramillies*. The large domed building, constructed in 1815, was the former Bethlehem Royal Hospital for the insane, known as "Bedlam."

A wide range of weapons and equipment is on display, along with models, decorations, uniforms, posters, photographs, and paintings. You can see a Mark V tank, a Battle of Britain Spitfire, and a German one-man submarine, as well as a rifle carried by Lawrence of Arabia. In the Documents Room, you can view the self-styled "political testament" that Hitler dictated in the chancellery bunker in the closing days of World War II, witnessed by henchmen Joseph Goebbels and Martin Bormann, as well as the famous "peace in our time" agreement that Neville Chamberlain brought back from Munich in 1938. (Of his signing the agreement, Hitler later said, "[Chamberlain] was a nice old man, so I decided to give him my autograph.") It's a world of espionage and clandestine warfare in the major permanent exhibit known as the "Secret War Exhibition," where you can discover the truth behind the image of James Bond—and find out why the real secret war is even stranger and more fascinating than fiction. Displays include many items never before seen in public: coded messages, forged documents, secret wirelesses, and equipment used by spies from World War I to the present day.

Public film shows take place on weekends at 4pm and on certain weekdays during school holidays and on public holidays.

Supported by a £12.6 million ($23.3 million) grant from the Heritage Lottery Fund, a permanent Holocaust exhibition now occupies two floors. Through original artifacts, documents, film, and photographs, some lent to the museum by former concentration camps in Germany and Poland, the display poignantly relates the story of Nazi Germany and the persecution of the Jews. In addition, the exhibition brings attention to the persecution of other groups under Hitler's regime, including Poles, Soviet prisoners of war, people with disabilities, and homosexuals. Among the items on display are a funeral cart used in the Warsaw Ghetto, a section of railcar from Belgium, a sign from the extermination camp at Belzec, and the letters of an 8-year-old French Jewish boy who hid in an orphanage before being sent to Auschwitz.

Another new exhibition, called "Crimes Against Humanity," explores the theme of genocide. See the "Westminster & Victoria" map.

Lambeth Rd., SE1. © **020/7416-5000** or 020/7416-5320 (info line). www.iwm.org.uk. Free admission. Daily 10am–6pm. Closed Dec 24–26. Tube: Baker Line to Lambeth North or Elephant and Castle.

**Institute of Contemporary Arts**    London's liveliest cultural program takes place in this temple to the avant-garde, launched in 1947. It keeps Londoners and others up-to-date on the latest in the worlds of cinema, theater, photography, painting, sculpture, and other visual and performing arts. Foreign or experimental movies are shown, and special tributes—perhaps a retrospective of the films of Rainer Werner Fassbinder—are often the order of the day. Classics and cult favorites are frequently dusted off here. On Saturday and Sunday at 3pm, the cinema offers screenings for kids. Sometimes well-known writers and artists speak here, which makes the low cost of membership even more enticing. Experimental plays are also presented. Sun Microsystems, the American Internet pioneer, donated £2 million ($3.7 million) to build a state-of-the-art New Media Centre in 1998. The photo galleries, showing the latest from British and foreign photographers, probably wouldn't win the approval of the people who set up "decency" panels for the arts. See the "West End Attractions" map.

The Mall, SW1. ⓒ 020/7930-3647. www.ica.org.uk. Admission £1.50 ($2.80) Mon–Fri, £2.50 ($4.65) Sat–Sun. Galleries daily noon–7:30pm; bookstore daily noon–9pm. Film screenings daily. Tube: Piccadilly Circus or Charing Cross.

**Jewish Museum**    This museum tells the story of Jewish life in Britain. Arriving at the time of the Norman Conquest, Jews survived in England until King Edward I forced them out in 1290. From that time, no Jews (or at least no known Jews) lived in Britain until a small community returned in 1656 during the reign of Elizabeth I. The museum has recently been awarded designated status by the Museums and Galleries Commission for its outstanding collection of Jewish ceremonial art. On display are silver Torah bells made in London, and two loving cups presented by the Spanish and Portuguese Synagogue to the lord mayor in the 18th century. The museum's Ceremonial Art Gallery contains a beautiful 16th-century Venetian ark, one of the oldest preserved in the world. An old English lord bought it from a furniture dealer without knowing what it was, and for years his maid used it as a wardrobe until someone discovered its true identity. The museum also sponsors **walking tours of Jewish London.**

The Jewish Museum has another location in Finchley, which focuses attention on Jewish immigration and settlement in London. On display there are reconstructions of East End tailoring and furniture workshops. Holocaust education is also a fundamental feature of this museum. The Finchley branch is open Monday through Thursday 10:30am to 5pm, and Sunday from 10:30am to 4:30pm; admission is £2 ($3.70) adults, £1 ($1.85) seniors and students. Children are admitted free. For further information, call ⓒ **020/8349-1143.** See the "West End Attractions" map.

129–131 Albert St., Camden Town, NW1. ⓒ 020/7284-1997. www.jewishmuseum.org.uk. Main branch admission £3.50 ($6.50) adults, £2.50 ($4.65) seniors, £1.50 ($2.80) children. Main branch: Sun 10am–5pm; Mon–Thurs 10am–4pm. Closed Fri, Sat, bank holidays, and Jewish festivals. Tube: Camden Town.

**Linley Sambourne House** ★ (Finds)    You'll step back into the days of Queen Victoria when you visit this house, which has remained unchanged for more than a century. Part of a terrace built in the late 1860s, this five-story Suffolk brick structure was the home of Linley Sambourne, a legendary cartoonist for *Punch.* In the entrance hall, you'll see the mixture of styles and clutter that typifies Victorian decor, with a plush portière, a fireplace valance, stained glass, and a large set of antlers vying for attention. The drawing room alone contains an incredible number of Victorian items. An actor in period costume leads tours.

You should budget about 1½ hours for your visit. *Insider's Tip:* It's best to pre-book your tour by phone. See the "Knightsbridge to Kensington" map.

18 Stafford Terrace, W8. © 020/7602-3316. www.rbkc.gov.uk/linleysambournehouse. Admission £6 ($11) adults, £4 ($7.40) senior citizens, £1 ($1.85) children 18 and under. Sat–Sun 10am–3:30pm; Sat and Sun guided tours only (10am, 11:15am, 1pm, 2:15pm, and 3:30pm). Closed mid-Mar to mid-June. Tube: High St. Kensington.

## London's Transport Museum ★ (Kids)

A collection of nearly 2 centuries of historic vehicles is displayed in a splendid Victorian building that formerly housed the Flower Market at Covent Garden. The museum shows how London's transport system evolved, and a representative collection of road vehicles includes a reconstruction of George Shillibeer's Omnibus of 1829. A steam locomotive that ran on the world's first underground railway, a knifeboard horse bus, London's first trolleybus, and a Feltham tram are also of particular interest.

Originally an operational Tube depot, the Depot at Acton Town is now a branch of the main museum, containing 370,000 items not currently on display at the Covent Garden site, ranging from station signs and posters to transportation memorabilia. Highlights include the first Routemaster bus and a spiral escalator from 1906. The Depot is open to the public on a limited basis through guided tours. Call © **020/7379-6344** to find out when the Depot is open, and to book a tour. The Depot is located at Gunnersbury Road, Acton Town. The Tube stop is Acton Town. See the "West End Attractions" map.

Covent Garden Piazza, WC2. © **020/7379-6344**, or 020/7565-7299 for recorded info. www.ltmuseum.co.uk. Admission £5.95 ($11) adults, £4.50 ($8.35) students and seniors, free for children under 16 accompanied by an adult. Sat–Thurs 10am–6pm; Fri 11am–6pm (last entrance at 5:15pm). Tube: Covent Garden, Leicester Sq., Holborn, or Charing Cross.

## Madame Tussaud's (Overrated) (Kids)

Madame Tussaud's is not so much a wax museum as an enclosed amusement park. A weird, moving, sometimes terrifying (to children) collage of exhibitions, panoramas, and stage settings, it manages to be most things to most people, most of the time.

Madame Tussaud attended the court of Versailles and learned her craft in France. She personally took the death masks from the guillotined heads of Louis XVI and Marie Antoinette (which you'll find among the exhibits). She moved her original museum from Paris to England in 1802. Her exhibition has been imitated in every part of the world, but never with the realism and imagination on hand here. Madame herself molded the features of Benjamin Franklin, whom she met in Paris. All the rest—from George Washington to John F. Kennedy, Mary Queen of Scots to Sylvester Stallone—have been subjects for the same painstaking (and often breathtaking) replication.

In the well-known Chamber of Horrors—a kind of underground dungeon—are all kinds of instruments of death, along with figures of their victims. The shadowy presence of Jack the Ripper lurks in the gloom as you walk through a Victorian London street. Present-day criminals are portrayed within the confines of prison. The latest attraction to open here is "The Spirit of London," a musical ride that depicts 400 years of London's history, using special effects that include audio-animatronic figures that move and speak. Visitors take "time-taxis" that allow them to see and hear "Shakespeare" as he writes and speaks lines, be received by "Queen Elizabeth I," and feel and smell the Great Fire of 1666 that destroyed London.

We've seen these changing exhibitions so many times over the years that we feel they're a bit cheesy, but we still remember the first time we were taken here as a kid. We thought it fascinating back then.

*Insider's Tip:* To avoid the long lines, sometimes more than an hour in summer, call the waxworks in advance and reserve a ticket for fast pickup at the entrance. If you don't want to bother with that, be aggressive and form a group of nine people waiting in the queue. A group of nine or more can go in almost at once through the "group door." Otherwise, go when the gallery first opens or late in the afternoon when crowds have thinned.

Marylebone Rd., NW1. © **0870/400-3000.** www.madame-tussauds.com. Admission £18 ($33) adults, £15 ($28) seniors, £14 ($26) children under 16. *Note:* Admission prices can go higher at certain peak periods Sat–Sun. Mon–Fri 9:30am–5:30pm; Sat–Sun 9am–6pm. Tube: Baker St.

**Museum of London** ★★ In London's Barbican district, near St. Paul's Cathedral and overlooking the city's Roman and medieval walls, this museum traces the history of London from prehistoric times to the 20th century through archaeological finds; paintings and prints; social, industrial, and historic artifacts; and costumes, maps, and models. Exhibits are arranged so that you can begin and end your chronological stroll through 250,000 years at the main entrance to the museum. The museum's pièce de résistance is the Lord Mayor's Coach, a gilt-and-scarlet fairy-tale coach built in 1757 and weighing in at 3 tons. You can also see the Great Fire of London in living color and sound in an audiovisual presentation; the death mask of Oliver Cromwell; cell doors from Newgate Prison, made famous by Charles Dickens; and most amazing of all, a shop counter showing pre–World War II prices. Early in 2002, the museum unveiled its latest permanent gallery, occupying an entire floor. Called the World City Gallery, the exhibit examines life in London between 1789 and 1914, the beginning of World War I. Some 2,000 objects are on view. See the "West End Attractions" map.

150 London Wall, EC2. © **020/7600-3699.** www.museumoflondon.org.uk. Free admission. Mon–Sat 10am–5:50pm; Sun noon–5:50pm. Tube: St. Paul's or Barbican.

**National Army Museum** ★ *Kids* The National Army Museum occupies a building adjoining the Royal Hospital, a home for retired soldiers. Whereas the Imperial War Museum is concerned with wars of the 20th century, the National Army Museum tells the colorful story of British armies from 1485 on. Here you'll find uniforms worn by British soldiers in every corner of the world, plus weapons and other gear, flags, and medals. Even the skeleton of Napoleon's favorite charger is here. Also on display are Florence Nightingale's jewelry, the telephone switchboard from Hitler's headquarters (captured in 1945), and Orders and Medals of HRH the Duke of Windsor. A more recent gallery, "The Rise of the Redcoats," contains exhibitions detailing the life of the British soldier from 1485 to 1793. Included in the exhibit are displays on the English Civil War and the American War of Independence. See the "Knightsbridge to Kensington Attractions" map.

Royal Hospital Rd., SW3. © **020/7730-0717.** www.national-army-museum.ac.uk. Free admission. Daily 10am–5:30pm. Closed Good Friday, 1st Mon in May, and Dec 24–26. Tube: Sloane Sq.

**Natural History Museum** ★★ *Kids* This is the home of the national collections of living and fossil plants, animals, and minerals, with many magnificent specimens on display. The zoological displays are quite wonderful—not up to the level of the Smithsonian in Washington, D.C., but still definitely worthwhile. Exciting exhibits designed to encourage people of all ages to learn about natural history include "Human Biology—An Exhibition of Ourselves," "Our Place in Evolution," "Origin of the Species," "Creepy Crawlies," and "Discovering

Mammals." The Mineral Gallery displays marvelous examples of crystals and gemstones. Visit the Meteorite Pavilion, which exhibits fragments of rocks that have crashed into the earth, some from the farthest reaches of the galaxy. What attracts the most attention is the dinosaur exhibit, displaying 14 complete skeletons. The center of the show depicts a trio of full-size robotic Deinonychus enjoying a freshly killed Tenontosaurus. "Earth Galleries" is an exhibition outlining humankind's relationship with planet Earth. Here, in the exhibition "Earth Today and Tomorrow," visitors are invited to explore the planet's dramatic history from the big bang to its inevitable death. The latest development here is the new Darwin Centre, with final completion scheduled for 2007, although there is much on view now. Dedicated to the great naturalist Charles Darwin, the center reveals the museum's scientific research and outreach facilities and activities. You're given an insider look at the storage facilities—including 22 million preserved specimens—and the laboratories of the museum. Fourteen behind-the-scenes free tours (ages 10 and up only) are given daily; you should book immediately upon entering the museum if you're interested. See the "Knightsbridge to Kensington Attractions" map.

Cromwell Rd., SW7. © 020/7942-5000. www.nhm.ac.uk. Free admission. Mon–Sat 10am–5:50pm; Sun 11am–5:50pm. Tube: S. Kensington.

### Percival David Foundation of Chinese Art ☆

This foundation displays the greatest collection of Chinese ceramics outside China. Approximately 1,700 ceramic objects reflect Chinese court taste from the 10th to 18th centuries and include many pieces of exceptional beauty. An extraordinary collection of stoneware from the Song (960–1279) and Yuan (1279–1368) dynasties includes examples of rare Ru and Guan wares. Among the justifiably famous blue-and-white porcelains are two unique temple vases, dated by inscription to A.D. 1351. A wide variety of polychrome wares is also represented; they include examples of the delicate doucai wares from the Chenghua period (1465–87), as well as a remarkable group of 18th-century porcelains.

53 Gordon Sq., WC1. © 020/7387-3909. www.pdfmuseum.org.uk. Free admission; donations encouraged. £4 ($7.40) per person for a guided tour of 10–20 people. Admission to the library must be arranged with the curator ahead of time. There is a charge for use of the library. Mon–Fri 10:30am–5pm. Tube: Russell Sq. or Euston Sq.

### The Queen's Gallery ☆☆

The refurbished gallery at Buckingham Palace reopened to the public in 2002 in time for the Golden Jubilee celebration of Queen Elizabeth II. Visitors going through the Doric portico entrance will find three times as much space as before. A chapel for Queen Victoria in 1843, the 1831 building by John Nash was destroyed in an air raid in 1940. The gallery is dedicated to changing exhibitions of the wide-ranging treasure trove that forms the Royal Collection. Anticipate special exhibitions of paintings, prints, drawings, watercolors, furniture, porcelain, miniatures, enamels, jewelry, and other works of art. At any given time, expect to see such artistic peaks as Van Dyck's equestrian portrait of Charles I, the world-famous *Lady at the Virginal* by Vermeer, a dazzling array of gold snuffboxes, paintings by Monet from the collection of the late Queen Mother, personal jewelry, studies by Leonardo da Vinci, and even the recent and very controversial portrait of the present queen by Lucian Freud.

Buckingham Palace, SW1. © 020/7321-2233. www.royalgov.uk. Admission £4.50 ($8.35) adults, £3.50 ($6.50) students and seniors, £2 ($3.70) children 5–16, free for children 4 and under. Daily 10am–5:30pm. Tube: Hyde Park Corner, Green Park, or Victoria.

**Royal Academy of Arts**    Established in 1768, this organization included Sir Joshua Reynolds, Thomas Gainsborough, and Benjamin West among its founding members. Since its beginning, each member has had to donate a work of art, and so, over the years, the academy has built up a sizable collection. The outstanding treasure is Michelangelo's beautiful relief of *Madonna and Child.* The annual Summer Exhibition has been held for more than 200 years; see the "London Calendar of Events" in chapter 3 for details. See the "West End Attractions" map.

Burlington House, Piccadilly, W1. © 020/7300-8000. www.royalacademy.org.uk. Admission varies, depending on the exhibition. Sat–Thurs 10am–6pm (last admission 5:30pm); Fri 10am–10pm (last admission 9:30pm). Tube: Piccadilly Circus or Green Park.

**Royal Mews** ✸✸    This is where you can get a close look at Her Majesty's State Coach, built in 1761 to the designs of Sir William Chambers and decorated with paintings by Cipriani. Traditionally drawn by eight gray horses, it was used by sovereigns when they traveled to open Parliament and on other state occasions; Queen Elizabeth traveled in it to her 1953 coronation and in 1977 for her Silver Jubilee Procession. There are other state coaches to see here. You can also pay a visit to the queen's carriage horses, which are housed here. See the "Westminster & Victoria Attractions" map.

Buckingham Palace, Buckingham Palace Rd., SW1. © 020/7766-7302. www.royal.gov.uk. Admission £5.50 ($10) adults, seniors and students £4.50 ($8.35), children 5–17, free for children under 5. Mon–Thurs and Sat–Sun 11am–3:15pm; summer hours daily 10am–5pm (last entrance at 4:15pm). Tube: Green Park or Victoria.

**Saatchi Gallery** ✸✸✸    Art lovers either define the controversial collector, Charles Saatchi, as the vision of the 21st century—or else they demand he be jailed at once and the key thrown away. If you're not among the faint-of-heart, you can make your way to this river-bordering Edwardian pile on the South Bank, a one-time seat of city government until Margaret Thatcher did away with the local council. Saatchi's taste for cocksure spectacle and his outrageous showcases defined modern British art in the 1990s. This former ad man has been called everything from a "modern day Medici" to "a Machiavellian mogul." He could even outrage part of New York City with his Chris Ofili's glittery Madonna with elephant dung, which went on show in Brooklyn (it now rests peacefully in this gallery).

It's all here, ranging from Sarah Lucas's photographs of herself with cash stuffed between her legs or fried eggs on her breasts, to Damien Hirst's pickled shark. Hirst's sliced-up cow appears butchered in separate glass containers that evoke Donald Judd boxes. Take delight—or horror—at Richard Wilson's famous *"20:50"*, a surrealistic chest-high lake of smelly sump oil. And, of course,

---

### Treaure Trove of Modern Art Goes Up in Flames

On May 26, 2004, a fire swept through a warehouse in East London, destroying millions of pounds worth of work done by some of the leading British contemporary artists of today. Art Collector Charles Saatchi suffered the greatest loss, as many of the painters he championed since the early 90s lost art that went up in flames. Even though the works lost are considered irreplaceable by leading British art critis, it will no affect visitors to the Saatchi gallery in 2005. They will be treated to a vast array of some of Saatchi's greatest treasures. The warehouse touched by the fire held art works that were going to be displayed at his gallery on a rotating basis or lent to other leading galleries in Britain or abroad.

you can't leave the gallery without checking out Marc Quinn's frozen "head," cast from nine pints of blood plasma extracted from the artist over a period of several months, or Marcus Harvey's *Myra,* a portrait of the child murderer, Myra Hindley.

County Hall, Southbank, SE1. (C) 020/7823-2363. Admission £8.50 ($16) adults, £6.50 ($12) seniors and students, £25 ($46) family ticket. Sun–Thurs 10am–8pm; Fri–Sat 10am–10pm. Tube: Waterloo.

**Science Museum** ★★★ *Kids*    This museum traces the development of science and industry and their influence on everyday life. These scientific collections are among the largest, most comprehensive, and most significant anywhere. On display is Stephenson's original rocket and the tiny prototype railroad engine; you can also see Whittle's original jet engine and the *Apollo 10* space module. The King George III Collection of scientific instruments is the highlight of a gallery on science in the 18th century. Health Matters is a permanent gallery on modern medicine. The museum has two hands-on galleries, as well as working models and video displays.

The museum also presents a behind-the-scenes look at the science and technology that went into making the film trilogy, *The Lord of the Rings.* Exhibitions showcase the artifacts and animatronics, costumes, and characters from the fable. The exhibition also offers a number of interactive displays—for example, you are given the chance to be shrunk to the size of a hobbit.

*Insider's Tip:* A large addition to this museum explores such topics as genetics, digital technology, and artificial intelligence. Four floors of a new Welcome Wing shelter half a dozen exhibition areas and a 450-seat IMAX theater. One exhibition explores everything from drug use in sports to how engineers observe sea life with robotic submarines. On an upper floor, visitors can learn how DNA was used to identify living relatives of the Bleadon Man, a 2,000-year-old Iron Age Man. On the third floor is the computer that Tim Berners-Lee used to design the World Wide Web outside Geneva, writing the first software for it in 1990.

Note also the marvelous interactive consoles placed strategically in locations throughout the museum. These display special itineraries, including directions for getting to the various galleries for families, teens, adults, and those with special interests.

Exhibition Rd., SW7. (C) 0870/870-4868. www.sciencemuseum.org.uk. Free admission. Daily 10am–6pm. Closed Dec 24–26. Tube: S. Kensington.

**Shakespeare's Globe Theatre & Exhibition** ★    This is a recent re-creation of what was probably the most important public theater ever built, Shakespeare's Globe, on the exact site where many of Shakespeare's plays opened. The late American filmmaker Sam Wanamaker worked for some 20 years to raise funds to re-create the theater as it existed in Elizabethan times, thatched roof and all. A fascinating exhibit tells the story of the Globe's construction, using the material (including goat hair in the plaster), techniques, and craftsmanship of 400 years ago. The new Globe isn't an exact replica: It seats 1,500 patrons, not the 3,000 who regularly squeezed in during the early 1600s, and this thatched roof has been specially treated with a fire retardant. Guided tours of the facility are offered throughout the day. See "'The City' Attractions" map.

See "The Play's the Thing: London's Theater Scene" in chapter 9 for details on attending a play here.

21 New Globe Walk, Southwark, SE1. (C) 020/7902-1400. www.shakespeares-globe.org. Admission £8 ($15) adults, £5.50 ($10) children 15 and under, £6.50 ($12) seniors and students. Oct–Apr daily 10am–5pm; May–Sept daily 9am–noon and 12:30–5pm. Tube: Mansion House or London Bridge.

**Sherlock Holmes Museum** *Overrated*   Where but on Baker Street would there be a museum displaying mementos of this famed fictional detective? Museum officials call it "the world's most famous address" (although 10 Downing Street is a rival for the title). It was here that mystery writer Sir Arthur Conan Doyle created a residence for Sherlock Holmes and his faithful Dr. Watson. These sleuths "lived" here from 1881 to 1904. In Victorian rooms, you can examine a range of exhibits, including published Holmes adventures and letters written to Holmes. This is a very commercial and artificial museum, and strikes us as a tourist trap. Holmes fans might be better off just visiting the gift shop downstairs and buying a postcard or a deerstalker. Some of the merchandise is interesting, though no Persian slippers—for shame. See the "West End Attractions" map.

221B Baker St., NW1. ℂ 020/7935-8866. www.sherlock-holmes.co.uk. Admission £6 ($11) adults, £4 ($7.40) children, free for children under 7. Daily 9:30am–6pm. Tube: Baker St.

**Sir John Soane's Museum** ★   This is the former home of Sir John Soane (1753–1837), an architect who rebuilt the Bank of England (although not the present structure). With his multiple levels, fool-the-eye mirrors, flying arches, and domes, Soane was a master of perspective and a genius of interior space (his picture gallery, for example, is filled with three times the number of paintings that a room of similar dimensions would be likely to hold). One prize of the collection is William Hogarth's satirical series *The Rake's Progress*, which includes his much-reproduced *Orgy and The Election*, a satire on mid-18th-century politics. Soane also filled his house with classical sculpture: The sarcophagus of Pharaoh Seti I, found in a burial chamber in the Valley of the Kings, is here. Also on display are architectural drawings from Soane's collection of 30,000. See the "West End Attractions" map.

13 Lincoln's Inn Fields, WC2. ℂ 020/7405-2107. www.soane.org. Free admission (donations invited). Tues–Sat 10am–5pm; 1st Tues of each month 6–9pm. Tours given Sat at 2:30pm; £3 ($6) tickets distributed at 2pm, first-come, first-served (group tours by appointment only). Tube: Holborn.

**Theatre Museum**   This branch of the Victoria and Albert Museum contains the national collections of the performing arts, encompassing theater, ballet, opera, music hall, pantomime, puppets, circus, and rock and pop music. Daily makeup demonstrations and costume workshops use costumes from the Royal Shakespeare Company and the Royal National Theatre. The museum also has a major Diaghilev archive. See the "West End Attractions" map.

Russell St., WC2. ℂ 0207/943-4700. www.theatremuseum.org. Free admission. Tues–Sun 10am–6pm. Tube: Covent Garden, Leicester Sq. or Waterloo.

**Wallace Collection** ★★ *Finds*   Located in a palatial setting (the modestly described "town house" of the late Lady Wallace), this collection is a contrasting array of art and armaments. The collection is evocative of the Frick Museum in New York and the Musée d'Jacque André in Paris. The art collection (mostly French) includes works by Watteau, Boucher, Fragonard, and Greuze, as well as such classics as Frans Hals's *Laughing Cavalier* and Rembrandt's portrait of his son Titus. The paintings of the Dutch, English, Spanish, and Italian schools are outstanding. The collection also contains important 18th-century French decorative art, including furniture from a number of royal palaces, Sèvres porcelain, and gold boxes. The European and Asian armaments, on the ground floor, are works of art in their own right: superb inlaid suits of armor, some obviously for parade rather than battle, with more businesslike swords, halberds, and magnificent Persian scimitars.

Manchester Sq., W1. ℂ 020/7563-9500. www.the-wallace-collection.org.uk. Free admission. Mon–Sat 10am–5pm; Sun noon–5pm. Tube: Bond St. or Baker St.

## PARKS & GARDENS

London's parks are the most advanced system of "green lungs" in any large city on the globe. Although not as rigidly maintained as those of Paris (Britons traditionally prefer a more natural look), they're cared for with a loving and lavishly artistic hand that puts their American counterparts to shame.

The largest of the central London parks is **Hyde Park** ★★ (Tube: Marble Arch, Hyde Park Corner, or Lancaster Gate), once a favorite deer-hunting ground of Henry VIII. With the adjoining Kensington Gardens (see below), it covers 246 hectares (608 acres) of central London with velvety lawns interspersed with ponds, flowerbeds, and trees. Running through its width is a 16.5-hectare (41-acre) lake known as the **Serpentine,** where you can row, sail model boats, or swim (provided you don't mind sub-Florida water temperatures). **Rotten Row,** a 2.5km (1½-mile) sand riding track, attracts some skilled equestrians on Sunday. You can rent a paddleboat or a rowboat from the boathouse (open Mar–Oct) on the north side of **Hyde Park's Serpentine** (© 020/7262-1330).

At the northeastern tip, near Marble Arch, is **Speakers Corner** (www. speakerscorner.net). Since 1855 (before the legal right to assembly was guaranteed), people have been getting on their soapboxes about any and every subject under the sky. In the past you might have heard Karl Marx, Frederick Engels, or Lenin, certainly William Morris and George Orwell. The corpse of Oliver Cromwell was hung here in a cage for the public to gape at or throw rotten eggs at. The king wanted to warn others against what might happen to them if they wished to abolish the monarchy. Hecklers, often aggressive, are part of the fun. Anyone can speak; just don't blaspheme, use obscene language, or start a riot.

Blending with Hyde Park and bordering the grounds of Kensington Palace, well-manicured **Kensington Gardens** (Tube: High St. Kensington or Queensway) contains the famous statue of Peter Pan, with bronze rabbits that toddlers are always trying to kidnap. The park is also home to that Victorian extravaganza, the Albert Memorial. The Orangery is an ideal place to take afternoon tea (p. 263).

East of Hyde Park, across Piccadilly, stretch **Green Park** ★ (Tube: Green Park) and **St. James's Park** ★ (Tube: St. James's Park), forming an almost unbroken chain of landscaped beauty. These parks are ideal for picnics; you'll find it hard to believe that this was once a swamp near a leper hospital. There's a romantic lake stocked with ducks and some surprising pelicans, descendants of the pair that the Russian ambassador presented to Charles II in 1662.

**Regent's Park** ★★★ (Tube: Regent's Park or Baker St.) covers most of the district of that name, north of Baker Street and Marylebone Road. Designed by the 18th-century genius John Nash to surround a palace for the prince regent (the palace never materialized), this is the most classically beautiful of London's parks. Its core is a rose garden planted around a small lake alive with waterfowl

---

### *Tips* Where to In-Line Skate

London's parks are great places to skate. Rental skates are available at **Slick Willies,** 41 Kensington High St., W8 (© 020/7225-0004; Tube: High St. Kensington), costing £10 ($19) for skates and wrist guards. A £100 ($185) deposit is required, which can be imprinted on a credit card. Hours are Monday through Saturday from 10am to 6:30pm, Sunday from noon to 5pm.

and spanned by Japanese bridges; in early summer, the rose perfume in the air is as heady as wine. The park is home to the **Open-Air Theatre** (p. 296) and the **London Zoo** (see "Especially for Kids," later in this chapter). As at all the local parks, hundreds of chairs are scattered around the lawns, waiting for sunbathers. The deck-chair attendants, who rent the chairs for a small fee, are mostly college students on break. Rowboats and sailing dinghies are available in **Regent's Park** (© 020/7486-7905). Sailing and canoeing cost around £6 ($11) for 1½ hours.

**Chelsea Physic Garden,** 66 Royal Hospital Rd., SW3 (© 020/7352-5646; www.chelseaphysicgarden.co.uk; Tube: Sloane Sq.), founded in 1673 by the Worshipful Society of Apothecaries, is the second-oldest surviving botanical garden in England. Sir Hans Sloane, doctor to George II, required the apothecaries of the empire to develop 50 plant species a year for presentation to the Royal Society. The objective was to grow plants for medicinal study. Plant specimens and even trees arrived at the gardens by barge, many to grow in English soil for the first time. Cottonseed from this garden launched an industry in the new colony of Georgia. Some 7,000 plants still grow here, everything from the pomegranate to the willow pattern tree; there's even exotic cork oak, as well as England's earliest rock garden. The garden is open April through October, Wednesday from noon to 5pm and Sunday from 2 to 6pm. Admission is £5 ($9.25) for adults, £3 ($5.55) for children 5 to 15 and students. The garden is a perfect setting for a well-recommended afternoon tea—you can carry your cuppa on promenades through the garden (p. 202).

**Battersea Park,** SW11 (© 020/8871-7530; Tube: Sloane Sq.), is a vast patch of woodland, lakes, and lawns on the south bank of the Thames, opposite Chelsea Embankment, between Albert Bridge and Chelsea Bridge. Formerly known as Battersea Fields, the park was laid out between 1852 and 1858 on an old dueling ground. (The most famous duel was between Lord Winchelsea and the Duke of Wellington in 1829.) There's a lake for boating, a deer field with fenced-in deer and wild birds, and tennis and soccer areas. There's also a children's zoo, open from Easter to late September, daily from 10am to 5pm, and weekends only in winter, from 1 to 3pm. The park's architectural highlight is the Peace Pagoda, built by Japanese craftspeople in cooperation with British architects. The stone-and-wood pagoda was dedicated in 1986 to the now-defunct Council of Greater London by an order of Japanese monks. The park is open from dawn to dusk. From the Sloane Square Tube stop, it's a brisk 15-minute walk to the park, or you can pick up bus no. 137 (get off at the first stop after the bus crosses the Thames).

The hub of England's—and perhaps the world's—horticulture is in Surrey, at the **Royal Botanic Gardens at Kew** (also known as Kew Gardens). See "Attractions on the Outskirts," below.

## 4 Exploring London by Boat

All of London's history and development is linked with the River Thames: This winding ribbon of water connects the city with the sea, from which London first drew its wealth and power. The Thames was London's chief commercial thoroughfare and royal highway. Every royal procession was undertaken on gorgeously painted and gilded barges (which you can still see at the National Maritime Museum in Greenwich). Important state prisoners were delivered to the Tower of London by water, eliminating the chance of an ambush in one of the narrow, crooked alleys surrounding the fortress. Much commercial traffic on the water disappeared when London's streets were widened enough for horse-drawn coaches to maintain a decent pace.

## RIVER CRUISES ALONG THE THAMES

A trip up or down the river will give you an entirely different view of London than the one you get from land. You'll see how the city grew along and around the Thames and how many of its landmarks turn their faces toward the water. Several companies operate motor launches from the Westminster piers (Tube: Westminster), offering panoramic views of one of Europe's most historic water-ways en route.

**Westminster-Greenwich Thames Passenger Boat Service,** Westminster Pier, Victoria Embankment, SW1 (© **020/7930-4097;** www.westminsterpier.co.uk), concerns itself only with downriver traffic from Westminster Pier to such destinations as Greenwich. The most popular excursion departs for Greenwich (a 50-min. ride) at half-hour intervals between 10am and 4pm in April, May, September, and October, and between 10:30am and 5pm from June to August; from November to March, boats depart from Westminster Pier at 40-minute intervals daily from 10:40am to 3:20pm. One-way fares are £6.50 ($12) for adults, £3.25 ($6) for children under 16, £5.25 ($9.75) for seniors. Round-trip fares are £8 ($15) for adults, £4 ($7.40) for children, £6.50 ($12) for seniors. A family ticket for two adults and up to three children under 15 costs £18 ($32) one-way, £22 ($40) round-trip.

**Westminster Passenger Association (Upriver) Ltd.,** Westminster Pier, Victoria Embankment, SW1 (© **020/7930-2062** or 020/7930-4721; www. wpsa.co.uk), offers the only riverboat service upstream from Westminster Bridge to Kew, Richmond, and Hampton Court, with regular daily sailings from the Monday before Easter until the end of October on traditional riverboats, all with licensed bars. Trip time, one-way, can be as little as 1½ hours to Kew and between 2½ to 4 hours to Hampton Court, depending on the tide. Cruises from Westminster Pier to Hampton Court via Kew Gardens leave daily at 10:30, 11:15am, and noon. Round-trip tickets are £18 ($33) for adults, £12 ($22) for seniors, and £9 ($17) for children ages 4 to 14; one child under 4 accompanied by an adult goes free.

## THAMES-SIDE SIGHTS
### THE BRIDGES

Some of the Thames bridges are household names. **London Bridge,** contrary to the nursery rhyme, never fell down, but it has been replaced a number of times and is vastly different from the original London Bridge, which was lined with houses and shops. The one that you see now is the ugliest of the versions; the previous incarnation was dismantled and shipped to Lake Havasu, Arizona, in the 1960s.

Also on the Thames, you can visit London's newest park, **Thames Barrier Park,** SE1, which is the city's first riverside park in years. It lies on the north bank of the Thames alongside the Thames Barrier, a steel-and-concrete movable flood barrier inaugurated in 1982. The park is spread across 8.8 hectares (22 acres), and has fountains that flow into a channel in the 390m (1,279-ft.) sunken landscaped garden. There's also a riverside promenade and a children's playground here. The park is open daily from sunrise to sunset (reached via the no. 69 bus from the Canning Town Tube station).

## Hanging "Around" in London

The world's largest observation wheel, the **British Airways London Eye** 👁️, Millennium Jubilee Gardens (📞 0870/5000-600; www.londoneye.com), opened in February 2000. It is the fourth-tallest structure in London, offering panoramic views that extend for some 40km (25 miles) if the weather's clear. Passengers are carried in 32 "pods" that make a complete revolution every half-hour. Along the way you'll see some of London's most famous landmarks from a bird's-eye view.

Built out of steel by a European consortium, it was conceived and designed by London architects Julia Barfield and David Marks, who claim inspiration from the Statue of Liberty in New York and the Eiffel Tower in Paris. Some 2 million visitors are expected to ride the Eye every year.

The Eye lies close to Westminster Bridge (you can hardly miss it). Tickets for the ride are £12 ($21) for adults, £9 ($17) for seniors and students, £5.75 ($11) for children 5 to 15. In May and September hours are Monday to Thursday 9:30am to 8pm, Friday to Sunday 9:30am to 10pm; June Monday to Thursday 9:30am to 9pm; Friday and Sunday 9:30am to 10pm; July and August daily 9:30am to 10pm; February to April daily 9:30am to 8pm. Tube: Westminster or Waterloo.

## HMS *BELFAST*

An 11,500-ton cruiser, the **HMS *Belfast,*** Morgan's Lane, Tooley Street, SE1 (📞 020/7940-6300; www.iwm.org.uk; Tube: Tower Hill or London Bridge), is a World War II ship preserved as a floating museum. It's moored opposite the Tower of London, between Tower Bridge and London Bridge. During the Russian convoy period and on D-day, the *Belfast* saw distinguished service, and in the Korean War it was known as "that straight-shootin' ship." You can explore all its decks, right down to the engine room; exhibits above and below show how sailors lived and fought over the past 50 years. It's open daily from 10am with last boarding at 6pm in summer, 5pm in winter. Admission is £6 ($11) adults, children under 16 free; seniors and students pay £4.40 ($8.15).

## DOCKLANDS 👁️

What was a dilapidated wasteland surrounded by water—some 89km (55 miles) of waterfront acreage within a sailor's cry of London's major attractions—has been reclaimed, restored, and rejuvenated. **London Docklands** is coming into its own as a leisure, residential, and commercial lure.

Next to the Tower of London, **St. Katharine's Dock** was the first of the docks to be given an entirely new role. Originally built from 1827 to 1828, this was for many years a leading dock, with the advantage of being closest to the City. Today, as a residential center and yacht marina, St. Katharine's again profits from its proximity to the City. The modern World Trade Centre looks down on the brick-brown sails of barges and gleaming hulls of moored luxury yachts. Blocks of fashionable Manhattan-style loft apartments sit between the docks and the river.

**Canary Wharf,** on the Isle of Dogs, is the heart of Docklands. This huge site is dominated by a 240m (787-ft.) tower, the tallest building in the United Kingdom, designed by Cesar Pelli. The **Piazza** is lined with shops and restaurants. A visit to the **Exhibition Centre** gives you an overview of the Docklands—past, present, and future. Already, the area has provided welcome space for the overflow from the City of London's square mile, and its development is more than promising.

On the south side of the river at Surrey Docks, the Victorian warehouses of **Butler's Wharf** have been converted into offices, houses, shops, and restaurants; this area is home to the **Design Museum** (p. 242).

Docklands can be reached via the **Docklands Light Railway,** which links the Isle of Dogs to the London Underground's Tower Hill station. To see the whole complex, take the railway at Tower Gateway near Tower Bridge for a short journey through Wapping and the Isle of Dogs. You can get off at Island Gardens and then cross through the 100-year-old Greenwich Tunnel under the Thames to see the attractions at Greenwich (see "Attractions on the Outskirts," below).

## EXPLORING LONDON'S CANALS BY BOAT

Boat trips on London's canals, especially Regent's Canal in London's canal-laced "Little Venice," are becoming an increasingly popular way of seeing the city. Bus no. 214 takes you to Little Venice, where you can board one of several boats for a tour along the canals. You can return either by boat or by Tube from the nearby Underground station at the end of a one-way trip.

Since the Festival of Britain in 1951, some of the traditional painted canal boats have been resurrected for Venetian-style trips through the waterways. One of them is *Jason,* which takes you on a 90-minute trip from Bloomfield Road in Little Venice through the long Maida Hill tunnel under Edgware Road, through Regent's Park, past the Mosque, the London Zoo, Lord Snowdon's Aviary, and the Pirate's Castle, to Camden Lock, and finally back to Little Venice. Passengers making the 45-minute one-way journey disembark at Camden Lock.

The season runs from April through October, with daily trips at 10:30am, and 12:30 and 2:30pm. In June, July, and August, an additional trip on weekends and bank holidays leaves at 4:30pm. A canalside seafood specialty restaurant/ cafe at Jason's mooring offers lunches, dinners, and teas, all freshly made. Advance notice must be made for lunch service on the boat. The round-trip fare is £6.95 ($13) for adults and £5.50 ($10) for children and seniors. One-way fares are £5.95 ($11) for adults and £4.75 ($8.80) for children and seniors. Family tickets cost £20 to £22 ($37–$41). For reservations, contact **Jason's Trip,** Jason's Wharf, opposite 60 Bloomfield Rd., Little Venice, London W9 (© **020/ 7286-3428;** Tube: Warwick Avenue).

### 5 Attractions on the Outskirts

These sights are perfect for a morning or afternoon jaunt and are easily accessible by Tube, train, boat, or bus.

## HAMPSTEAD ⚐

About 6.5km (4 miles) north of the center of London lies the lovely village of Hampstead (Tube: Northern Line to Hampstead) and scenic Hampstead Heath.

The 320-hectare (790-acre) expanse of high heath known as **Hampstead Heath** is a chain of formal parkland, woodland, heath, meadowland, and ponds. On a clear day, you can see St. Paul's Cathedral and even the hills of Kent. Londoners would certainly mount the barricades if Hampstead Heath were imperiled; for years, they've come here to sun worship, fly kites, fish the ponds, swim, picnic, and jog. In good weather, it's also the site of big 1-day fairs. At the shore of Kenwood Lake, in the northern section, is a concert platform devoted to symphony performances on summer evenings. In the northeast corner, in Waterlow Park, ballets, operas, and comedies are staged at the Grass Theatre in June and July.

Once the Underground came to **Hampstead Village** in 1907, writers, artists, architects, musicians, and scientists were among those who decamped for the leafy village. Keats, D. H. Lawrence, Shelley, Robert Louis Stevenson, and Kingsley Amis all once lived here, and John Le Carré still does.

The Regency and Georgian houses of the village and the rolling greens of the heath are just 20 minutes by Tube from Piccadilly Circus. The village has a quirky mix of historic pubs, toy shops, and chic boutiques along **Flask Walk,** a pedestrian mall. The original village, on the side of a hill, still has old alleys, steps, courts, and groves ideal for strolling.

**Burgh House**    This Queen Anne home (1703), in the center of the village, was the residence of the daughter and son-in-law of Rudyard Kipling, who often visited here. It's now used for local art exhibits, concerts, recitals, talks, and public meetings on many subjects. The house is the headquarters of several local societies, including the Hampstead Music Club and the Hampstead Scientific Society. **Hampstead Museum,** in Burgh House, illustrates the local history of the area. It has a room devoted to reproductions of works by the great artist John Constable, who lived nearby for many years and is buried in the local parish church. There's also a licensed **buttery** (© **020/7431-2516**) that's popular for lunch or tea, with lunches for just £5 ($9.25) during the week (Sat £5.35/$9.90 and Sun £5.95/$11). In pricey Hampstead, it's a real bargain.

New End Sq., NW3. © 020/7431-0144 or 020/7431-2516 for buttery reservations. www.burghhouse.org.uk. Free admission. House and museum Wed–Sun noon–5pm, Sat by appt.; buttery Wed–Sun 11am–5:30pm. Tube: Northern Line to Hampstead.

**Fenton House**    This National Trust property is on the west side of Hampstead Grove, just north of Hampstead Village. Built in 1693, its paneled rooms contain furniture and pictures; 18th-century English, German, and French porcelain; and an outstanding collection of early keyboard musical instruments.

Windmill Hill, NW3. © 020/7435-3471. Admission £4.50 ($8.35) adults, £2.25 ($4.20) children, £12 ($21) family ticket. Mar Sat–Sun 2–5pm; Apr–Oct Sat–Sun 11am–5pm, Wed–Fri 2–5pm. Closed Nov–Feb. Tube: Northern Line to Hampstead.

**Freud Museum**    After he and his family left Nazi-occupied Vienna as refugees, Sigmund Freud lived, worked, and died in this spacious three-story house in northern London. In view are rooms with original furniture, letters, photographs, paintings, and the personal effects of Freud and his daughter, Anna. In the study and library, you can see the famous couch and Freud's large collection of Egyptian, Roman, and Asian antiquities.

20 Maresfield Gardens, NW3. © 020/7435-2002. www.freud.org.uk. Admission £5 ($9.25) adults, £2 ($3.70) full-time students, free for children under 12. Wed–Sun noon–5pm. Tube: Jubilee Line to Finchley Rd.

**Keats House** ★★    The poet lived here for only 2 years, but that was approximately two-fifths of his creative life; he died of tuberculosis in Rome at the age of 25 (in 1821). In Hampstead, Keats wrote some of his most celebrated odes, including "Ode on a Grecian Urn" and "Ode to a Nightingale." His Regency house possesses the manuscripts of his last sonnet ("Bright star, would I were steadfast as thou art") and a portrait of him on his deathbed in a house on the Spanish Steps in Rome.

Wentworth Place, Keats Grove, NW3. © 020/7435-2062. www.cityoflondon.gov.uk/keats. Admission £3 ($5.55) adults, £1.50 ($2.80) students and seniors, free for children under 16. Apr–Oct Tues–Sun noon–5pm; Nov–Mar call for hours. Tube: Northern Line to Hampstead or Belsize Park.

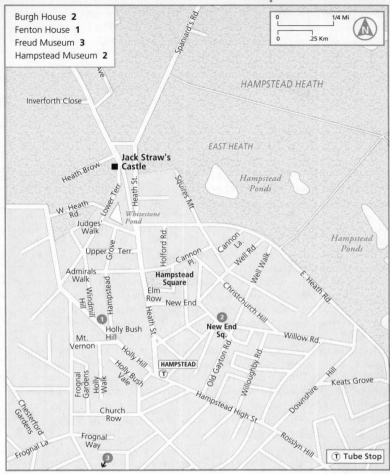

Burgh House **2**
Fenton House **1**
Freud Museum **3**
Hampstead Museum **2**

0           1/4 Mi
0          .25 Km

HAMPSTEAD HEATH

Inverforth Close

EAST HEATH

Jack Straw's Castle

Hampstead Ponds

Heath Brow

W. Heath Rd.

Judges' Walk

Whitestone Pond

Hampstead Ponds

Upper Terr.

Admirals Walk

Holford Rd.

Cannon Pl.

Cannon La.

Well Rd.

Well Walk

E. Heath Rd.

Windmill Hill

Hampstead Square

Elm Row

New End

Christchurch Hill

Holly Bush Hill

New End Sq.

Willow Rd.

Mt. Vernon

Heath St.

HAMPSTEAD

Old Gayton Rd.

Willoughby Rd.

Downshire Hill

Keats Grove

Holly Hill

Holly Bush Vale

Frognal Gardens

Holly Walk

Church Row

Hampstead High St.

Rosslyn Hill

Chesterford Gardens

Frognal La.

Frognal Way

T Tube Stop

Kenwood House ★★   Kenwood House was built as a gentleman's country home and was later enlarged and decorated by the famous Scottish architect Robert Adam, starting in 1764. The house contains period furniture and paintings by Turner, Frans Hals, Gainsborough, Reynolds, and more.

Hampstead Lane, NW3. ℂ **020/8348-1286**. www.English-heritage.org.uk. Free admission. Apr–Oct daily 10am–5:30pm; Nov–Mar daily 10am–4pm. Tube: Northern Line to Golders Green, then bus no. 210.

## IN NEARBY HIGHGATE

Highgate Cemetery   A stone's throw east of Hampstead Heath, Highgate Village has a number of 16th- and 17th-century mansions and small cottages, lining three sides of the now-pondless Pond Square. Its most outstanding feature, however, is this beautiful cemetery, laid out around a huge, 300-year-old cedar tree and laced with serpentine pathways. The cemetery was so popular and fashionable in the Victorian era that it was extended on the other side of Swain's Lane in 1857. The most famous grave is that of Karl Marx, who died in Hampstead in 1883; his grave, marked by a gargantuan bust, is in the eastern cemetery. In the old western cemetery—accessible only by guided tour, given hourly in summer—are scientist Michael Faraday and poet Christina Rossetti.

Swain's Lane, N6. ℭ 020/8340-1834. http://highgate-cemetery.org. Western Cemetery guided tour £3 ($5.55). Eastern Cemetery £2 ($3.70) admission, £1 ($1.85) camera pass charge (no video cameras; hand-held still cameras only). Western Cemetery, Mar–Oct guided tours only Mon–Fri at 2 and 4pm, and Sat–Sun hourly 11am–4pm; Nov–Feb, tours Sat–Sun hourly 11am–3pm; Eastern Cemetery, Apr–Oct Mon–Fri 10am–4:30pm, Sat–Sun 11am–4:30pm, Nov–Mar Mon–Fri 10am–3:30pm, Sat–Sun 11am–3:30pm. Both cemeteries closed at Christmas and during funerals. Tube: Northern Line to Archway, then walk or take bus no. 143, 210, or 271.

## GREENWICH ★★★

When London overwhelms you and you'd like to escape for a beautiful, sunny afternoon on the city's outskirts, make Greenwich your destination.

Greenwich Mean Time is the basis of standard time throughout most of the world, and Greenwich has been the zero point used in the reckoning of terrestrial longitudes since 1884. But this lovely village—the center of British seafaring when Britain ruled the seas—is also the home of the Royal Naval College, the National Maritime Museum, and the Old Royal Observatory. In dry dock at Greenwich Pier is the clipper ship *Cutty Sark*. Greenwich also has some wonderful shopping, including a famous weekend market (see the "GST: Greenwich Shopping Time" box on p. 275).

Greenwich was the site of Britain's Millennium Dome, a multimedia extravaganza mixing education and entertainment. Most of the project's cost, estimated at more than $1.3 billion ($2.4 billion), came from a national lottery. Then, the much-heralded Dome bombed with audiences. The project became a national joke, and finally closed. Prince Charles ridiculing it as a monstrous *blanc mange,* that unattractive milky gelatin dessert, didn't help it along. Now, the much-maligned **Millennium Dome** will be transformed into a 20,000-seat sports and music venue. The Dome is expected to become the "Madison Square Garden of Europe." See "Greater London Area" map on p. 74 to see Greenwich's location in relation to central London.

**GETTING THERE**    The fastest way to get to Greenwich is to take the Tube in Central London to Waterloo Station, where you can take a fast train to Greenwich Station.

The Tube is for speed, taking only 15 minutes, but if you'd like to travel the 6.5km (4 miles) to Greenwich the way Henry VIII did, you still can. In fact, getting to Greenwich is still half the fun. The most appealing way involves boarding any of the frequent ferryboats that cruise along the Thames at intervals that vary from every half-hour (in summer) to every 45 minutes (in winter). Boats that leave from Charing Cross Pier (Tube: Embankment) and Tower Pier (Tube: Tower Hill) are run by **Catamaran Cruises, Ltd. (ℭ 020/7987-1185).** Depending on the tides and the carrier you select, travel time varies from 50 to 75 minutes each way. Passage is £6 to £10 ($11–$19) round-trip for adults, £4 to £6 ($7.40–$11) round-trip for children 5 to 12; it's free for those under 5.

**VISITOR INFORMATION**    The **Greenwich Tourist Information Centre** is at 2 Cutty Sark Gardens (ℭ **0870/608-2000**); open daily from 10am to 5pm. The Tourist Information Centre conducts **walking tours** of Greenwich's major sights. Tours cost £4 ($7.40) for adults and £3 ($5.55) for students, seniors, and children, and depart daily at 12:15 and 2:15pm, and last 1½ to 2 hours. Advance reservations aren't required, but you may want to phone in advance to find out any last-minute schedule changes.

## SEEING THE SIGHTS

The **National Maritime Museum,** the **Old Royal Observatory,** and **Queen's House** stand together in a beautiful royal park, high on a hill overlooking the Thames. All three attractions are free to get into and open daily from 10am to 5pm. For more information, call ℭ **020/8312-6608** or visit **www.nmm.ac.uk**.

From the days of early seafarers to 20th-century sea power, the **National Maritime Museum** 😽😽 illustrates the glory that was Britain at sea. The cannon, relics, ship models, and paintings tell the story of a thousand naval battles and a thousand victories, as well as the price of those battles. Look for some oddities here—everything from the dreaded cat-o'-nine-tails used to flog sailors until 1879 to Nelson's Trafalgar coat, with the fatal bullet hole in the left shoulder clearly visible. In time for the millennium, the museum spent £20 million ($37 million) in a massive expansion that added 16 new galleries devoted to British maritime history and improved visitor facilities.

**Old Royal Observatory** 😽 is the original home of Greenwich Mean Time. It has the largest refracting telescope in the United Kingdom and a collection of historic timekeepers and astronomical instruments. You can stand astride the meridian and set your watch precisely by the falling time-ball. Sir Christopher Wren designed the Octagon Room. Here the first royal astronomer, Flamsteed, made his 30,000 observations that formed the basis of his *Historia Coelestis Britannica*. Edmond Halley, he of the eponymous Halley's Comet, succeeded him. In 1833, the ball on the tower was hung to enable shipmasters to set their chronometers accurately.

Designed by Inigo Jones, **Queen's House** 😽😽 (1616) is a fine example of this architect's innovative style. It's most famous for the cantilevered tulip staircase, the first of its kind. Carefully restored, the house contains a collection of royal and marine paintings and other objets d'art.

**The Wernher Collection at Ranger's House** 😽😽, Chesterfield Walk (ℭ **020/8853-0035;** www.English-heritage.org.uk), is a real find and one of the finest and most unusual 19th-century mixed-art collections in the world. Acquired by

### The Last of the Great Clipper Ships

Nearly 6.5km (4 miles) east of London, at Greenwich Pier, now in permanent dry dock, lies the last and ultimate word in sail power: the *Cutty Sark* 😽😽, King William Walk, Greenwich, SE10 (ℭ **020/8858-3445;** www.cuttysark.org.uk; bus no. 177, 180, 188, or 199). Named after the witch in Robert Burns's poem "Tam O'Shanter," it was the greatest of the clipper ships that carried tea from China and wool from Australia in the most exciting ocean races ever sailed. The *Cutty Sark*'s record stood at a then unsurpassed 584km (362 miles) in 24 hours. Launched in Scotland in 1869, the sleek black three-master represented the final fighting run of canvas against steam. Although the age of the clippers was brief, they outpaced the steamers as long as wind filled their billowing mountain of sails. On board the *Cutty Sark* is a museum devoted to clipper lore. Admission is £4.25 ($7.90) for adults and £2.95 ($5.50) for children over 5, £3.25 ($6) students and seniors. A family ticket costs £11 ($19). It's open daily from 10am to 5pm, with last admission at 4:30pm.

a German diamond dealer, Sir Julius Wernher, the collection contains some 650 exhibits, some dating as far back as 3 B.C. It's an eclectic mix of everything, including jewelry, bronzes, ivory, antiques, tapestries, porcelain pieces, and classic paintings. Hanging on the walls of the gallery are rare works by such old masters as Hans Memling and Filippino Lippi, along with portraits by such English painters as Reynolds and Romney. One salon is devoted to the biggest collection of Renaissance jewelry in Britain. Look also for the carved medieval, Byzantine, and Renaissance ivories, along with Limoges enamels and Sèvres porcelain. The most unusual items are enameled skulls and a miniature coffin complete with 3-D skeleton. Don't expect everything to be beautiful—Wernher's taste was often bizarre. Admission is £4.50 ($8.35) adults, £3.50 ($6.50) seniors and students, £2.50 ($4.65) children, free for children under 5. *Note:* The museum is closed from December 23 to March 4.

Nearby is the **Royal Naval College** ★★, King William Walk, off Romney Road (© **020/8269-4747;** www.greenwichfoundation.org.uk). Designed by Sir Christopher Wren in 1696, it occupies 4 blocks named after King Charles, Queen Anne, King William, and Queen Mary. Formerly, Greenwich Palace stood here from 1422 to 1640. It's worth stopping in to see the magnificent Painted Hall by Thornhill, where the body of Nelson lay in state in 1805, and the Georgian chapel of St. Peter and St. Paul. Open daily from 10am to 5pm; admission is free.

## KEW ★★★

About 15km (9 miles) southwest of central London, Kew is home to one of the best-known botanical gardens in Europe. It's also the site of **Kew Palace** ★★, former residence of George III and Queen Charlotte. A dark redbrick structure, it is characterized by its Dutch gables. The house was constructed in 1631, and at its rear is the Queen's Garden in a very formal design and filled with plants thought to have grown here in the 17th century. The interior is very much an elegant country house of the time, fit for a king, but not as regal as Buckingham Palace. You get the feeling that someone could have actually lived here as you wander through the dining room, the breakfast room, and go upstairs to the queen's drawing room, where musical evenings were staged. The rooms are wall-papered with designs actually used at the time. Perhaps the most intriguing exhibits are little possessions once owned by royal occupants here—everything from snuffboxes to Prince Frederick's gambling debts. The most convenient way to get to Kew is to take the **District Line** Tube to the Kew Gardens stop, on the south bank of the Thames. Allow about 30 minutes.

**Royal Botanic Gardens, Kew** ★★★   These world-famous gardens offer thousands of varieties of plants. But Kew Gardens, as it's known, is no mere pleasure garden—it's essentially a vast scientific research center that happens to be beautiful. The gardens, on a 120-hectare (296-acre) site, encompass lakes, greenhouses, walks, pavilions, and museums, along with examples of the archi-tecture of Sir William Chambers. Among the 50,000 plants are notable collec-tions of ferns, orchids, aquatic plants, cacti, mountain plants, palms, and tropical water lilies.

No matter what season you visit, Kew always has something to see, from the first spring flowers through to winter. Gigantic hothouses grow species of shrubs, blooms, and trees from every part of the globe, from the Arctic Circle to tropical rainforests. Attractions include a newly restored Japanese gateway in traditional landscaping, as well as exhibitions that vary with the season. The newest greenhouse, the Princess of Wales Conservatory (beyond the rock garden), encompasses 10 climatic zones, from arid to tropical; it has London's most thrilling collection of miniature orchids. The Marianne North Gallery (1882) is an absolute gem, paneled with 246 different types of wood that the intrepid Victorian artist collected on her world journeys; she also collected 832 paintings of exotic and tropical flora, all displayed on the walls. The Visitor Centre at Victoria Gate houses an exhibit telling the story of Kew, as well as a bookshop.

Kew. © 020/8940-1171. www.rbgkew.org.uk. Admission £8.50 ($16) adults, £6 ($11) students and seniors, free for children 16 and under. Daily: Feb 9–Mar 26 9:30am–5:30pm; Mar 27–Sept 5 Mon–Fri 9:30am–6:30pm, Sat–Sun 9:30am–7:30pm; Sept 6–Oct 30 9:30am–6pm; Oct 31–Feb 8 9:30am–4:15pm. Tube: District Line to Kew Gardens.

## KEW FOR TEA

Visitors are flocking to the newly reopened and historic **Orangery** at Kew Gardens. The Orangery, built for Princess Augusta by Sir William Chambers in 1761, is a venue for top-quality refreshments, morning coffees, lunches, and afternoon snacks. For us, the highlight is the very traditional English tea offered here on the new outdoor terrace constructed of York and Portland stone, opening onto panoramic views of some of the world's most beautiful gardens.

Across the street from the Royal Botanic Gardens is one of the finest tearooms in the area, the **Original Maids of Honour Tearooms,** 288 Kew Rd. (© 020/8940-2752). Oak paneling and old leaded-glass windows give the place a cozy warmth. The homemade cakes are delectable, as are the delightfully light scones. The Maids of Honour (flavored with jam, cottage cheese, golden raisins, almond extract, and almonds) is their pastry specialty, originally baked for Henry VIII, who liked it so much that its secret recipe has been passed along through the centuries. Afternoon tea is £5.55 to £8 ($10–$15). The tearoom is open Monday from 9:30am to 1pm and Tuesday through Saturday from 9:30am to 6pm, and tea is served from 2:30 to 5:30pm.

## HAMPTON COURT

Hampton Court, on the north side of the Thames, 21km (13 miles) west of London in East Molesey, Surrey, is easily accessible, and is one of the great palaces of England. But if you have very limited time, we'd save it for a future visit. If you're going to be in London for perhaps a week, then we'd recommend a visit, but only after you've spent a day at Windsor. Frequent **trains** (© 08457/484-950 in the U.K. or 01603/764-776) run from Waterloo Station (Network Southeast) to Hampton Court Station. **London Transport** (© 020/7730-3466) bus nos. 111, 131, 216, 267, and 461 make the trip from Victoria Coach Station on Buckingham Palace Road (just southwest of Victoria Station). Boat service is offered to and from Kingston, Richmond, and Westminster (see "River Cruises Along the Thames," earlier in this chapter). If you're **driving** from London, take A308 to the junction with A309 on the north side of Kingston Bridge over the Thames. See the "Side Trips from London" map on p. 321 to find Hampton Court in relation to London.

**Hampton Court Palace** ★★★    The 16th-century palace of Cardinal Wolsey can teach us a lesson: Don't try to outdo your boss, particularly if he happens to be Henry VIII. The rich cardinal did just that, and he eventually lost his fortune, power, prestige, and ended up giving his lavish palace to the Tudor monarch. Henry took over, even outdoing the Wolsey embellishments. The Tudor additions included the Anne Boleyn gateway, with its 16th-century astronomical clock that even tells the high-water mark at London Bridge. From Clock Court,

---

**Finds   Live Like a King**

The **Landmark Trust,** Shootesbrooke, Maidenhead, Berkshire SL6 3SW
(© **01628/825925;** www.landmarktrust.co.uk), an architectural preservation charity, oversees two palace buildings that offer modest rental facilities on the grounds of Hampton Palace. The first, Fish Court, sleeps six
and originally housed the palace pastry chefs. Four-day bookings cost
£585 to £873 ($1,082–$1,615), with weekly bookings costing £1,056 to
£1,850 ($1,954–$3,423). Sleeping eight guests, the Georgian House is a
former palace kitchen, with private garden. It accepts 4-night bookings
for £666 to £1,044 ($1,232–$1,931), or weekly bookings for £1,176 to
£2,269 ($2,176–$4,198). You're not in the palace proper but on its grounds;
you have the run of the place at night and can explore the gardens.

---

you can see one of Henry's major contributions, the aptly named Great Hall,
with its hammer-beam ceiling. Also added by Henry were the tiltyard (where
jousting competitions were held), a tennis court, and a kitchen.

To judge from the movie *A Man for All Seasons,* Hampton Court had quite a
retinue to feed. Cooking was done in the Great Kitchen. Henry cavorted
through the various apartments with his wife of the moment—from Anne
Boleyn to Catherine Parr (the latter reversed things and lived to bury her erst-
while spouse). Charles I was imprisoned here and managed to temporarily
escape his jailers.

Although the palace enjoyed prestige and pomp in Elizabethan days, it owes
much of its present look to William and Mary—or rather to Sir Christopher
Wren, who designed and had built the Northern or Lion Gates, intended to be
the main entrance to the new parts of the palace. The fine wrought-iron screen
at the south end of the south gardens was made by Jean Tijou around 1694 for
William and Mary. You can parade through the apartments today, filled as they
were with porcelain, furniture, paintings, and tapestries. The King's Dressing
Room is graced with some of the best art, mainly paintings by old masters on
loan from Queen Elizabeth II. Finally, be sure to inspect the royal chapel
(Wolsey wouldn't recognize it). To confound yourself totally, you may want to
get lost in the serpentine shrubbery maze in the garden, also the work of Wren.
More and more attention is focusing on improving and upgrading the famous
gardens here—the formal gardens are among the last surviving examples of garden methods and designs from several important periods of history.

The 24-hectare (60-acre) gardens—including the Great Vine, King's Privy
Garden, Great Fountain Gardens, Tudor and Elizabethan Knot Gardens, Board
Walk, Tiltyard, and Wilderness—are open daily year-round from 7am until dusk
(but not later than 9pm), and can be visited free except for the Privy Garden. A
garden cafe and restaurant is located in the Tiltyard Gardens.

Hampton Court, on the north side of the Thames and 21km (13 miles) west
of London, is easily accessible. Frequent trains run from Waterloo Station (Network Southeast) to Hampton Court Station (© **0845/748-4950** or 01603/
764776). Victoria Station (© **020/7730-3466**) buses numbered 216, 411, 451,
461, 513, 726, and R68 make the trip from Victoria Coach Station on Buckingham Palace Road (just southwest of Victoria Station). If you're driving from
London, take the A308 to the junction with the A309 on the north side of
Kingston Bridge over the Thames.

© **0870/752-7777.** www.hrp.org.uk. Admission £12 ($21) adults, £8.50 ($16) students and seniors, £7.50 ($14) children 5–15, free for children under 5, family ticket £34 ($63). Gardens open year-round daily 7am–dusk (no later than 9pm); free admission to all except Privy Garden (admission £3/$5.55 adults, £2/$3.70 child) without palace ticket during summer months. Cloisters, courtyards, state apartments, great kitchen, cellars, and Hampton Court exhibition open Mar 28–Oct 25 Mon 10:15am–6pm, Tues–Sun 9:30am–6pm, last entry 5:15pm; Oct 26–Mar 27 Mon 10:15am–4:30pm, Tues–Sun 9:30am–4:30pm, last entry 3:45pm.

## 6 Especially for Kids

London has fun places for kids of all ages. In addition to the attractions listed below, kids love to explore **Buckingham Palace, Kensington Palace,** the **London's Transport Museum, Madame Tussaud's,** the **National Army Museum,** the **National Maritime Museum** (in Greenwich), the **Natural History Museum,** the **Science Museum,** and the **Tower of London,** all discussed above.

**Bethnal Green Museum of Childhood** *Kids*   This branch of the Victoria and Albert specializes in toys. The variety of dolls alone is staggering; some have such elaborate period costumes that you don't even want to think of the price tags they would carry today. With the dolls come dollhouses, from simple cottages to miniature mansions, complete with fireplaces, grand pianos, kitchen utensils, and carriages. You'll also find optical toys, marionettes, puppets, a considerable exhibit of soldiers and war toys from both World War eras, trains and aircraft, and a display of clothing and furniture relating to the social history of childhood.

Cambridge Heath Rd., E2. © **020/8983-5200.** www.museumofchildhood.org.uk. Free admission. Sat–Thurs 10am–5:50pm. Tube: Central Line to Bethnal Green.

**Horniman Museum** *Kids*   This century-old museum set in 6.4 hectares (16 acres) of landscaped gardens is quirky, funky, and fun. The collection was accumulated by Frederick Horniman, a Victorian tea trader. A full range of events and activities takes place here, including storytelling and arts-and-crafts sessions for kids, along with workshops for adults. The museum owns some 350,000 objects ranging from a gigantic, overstuffed walrus to such oddities as oversize model insects. There are also displays of live insects and a small aquarium constructed in waterfall-like tiers. The torture chair thought to have been an original used at the Spanish Inquisition was proven to be a fake, although the instruments are genuine.

100 London Rd., Forest Hill, SE23. © **020/9699-1872.** www.horniman.ac.uk. Free admission except for temporary exhibitions. Daily 10:30am–5:30pm. Tube: Forest Hill.

**Little Angel Theatre** *Kids*   Puppetry in all its forms is presented at this charming small theater in Islington, north of the city. There are homegrown shows that tour nationally and internationally, as well as performances by a variety of visiting companies. The range of puppetry is wide, from marionettes (string puppets) to rod-and-glove puppets. Most of the work is targeted at children; age limits are stated for every show presented (for example, "no under-3s allowed"); grown-ups will enjoy them, too. There's a coffee bar and an adjacent workshop where the puppets, sets, and costumes are made. Call for information. The theater is accessible to people with disabilities.

14 Dagmar Passage, N1. © **020/7226-1787** or 020/7359-8581. Admission £8.50 ($16) adults, £6 ($11) children. Show times Sat–Sun 11am and 2pm; some weekdays. Tube: Northern Line to Angel or Victoria Line to Highbury and Islington.

# Especially for Kids

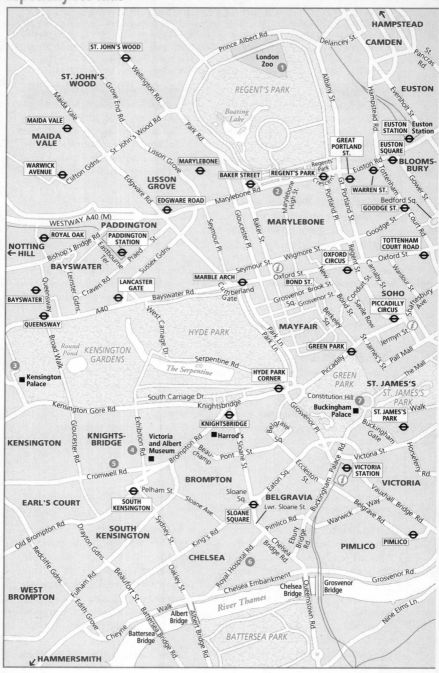

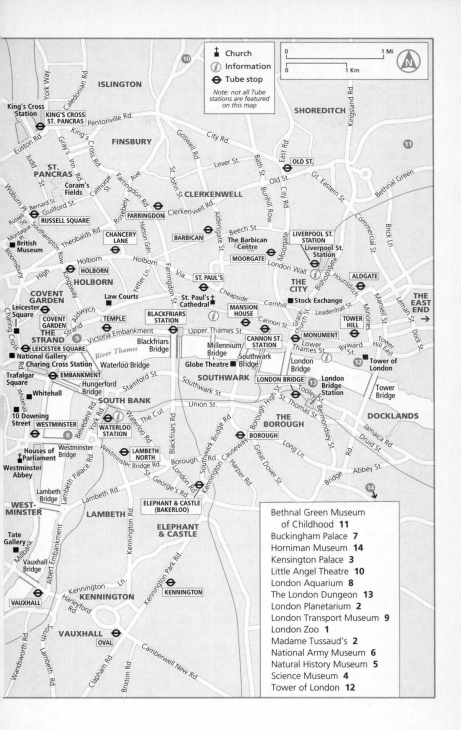

**Church** †
**Information** (i)
**Tube stop** ⊖
Note: not all Tube stations are featured on this map

ISLINGTON

SHOREDITCH

King's Cross Station
KING'S CROSS ST. PANCRAS
Pentonville Rd.

York Way
Caledonian Rd.
Gray's Inn Rd.
King's Cross Rd.

Euston Rd.
Judd St.
St. Pancras
Woburn Pl.
Russell St.
Bernard St.
Guilford St.
Coram's Fields

FINSBURY
Goswell Rd.
City Rd.
Lever St.
Bath St.
East Rd.
OLD ST.
Old St.
Gt. Eastern St.
Bethnal Green
Kingsland Rd.
Commercial St.
Brick Ln.

CLERKENWELL
St. John St.
Farringdon Rd.
Rosebery Ave.
Clerkenwell Rd.
Aldersgate St.
Beech St.
Bunhill Row

FARRINGDON
Hatton Gdn.

RUSSELL SQUARE
Montague Pl.
Southampton Row
Theobalds Rd.
Bloomsbury
British Museum
High Holborn
Kingsway

CHANCERY LANE
Holborn
Fetter Ln.

BARBICAN
The Barbican Centre
MOORGATE
Moorgate
London Wall
LIVERPOOL ST. STATION
Liverpool St. Station
Bishopsgate
Hounsditch
ALDGATE
Leman St.
Mansell St.
THE EAST END →

HOLBORN
HOLBORN
Via.
Farringdon St.

ST. PAUL'S
St. Paul's † Cathedral
Cheapside
Cornhill
THE CITY
Stock Exchange
Gracechurch St.
Leadenhall St.
Minories
Tower Hill East

COVENT GARDEN
Leicester Square
COVENT GARDEN
THE STRAND
Aldwych
Strand
TEMPLE

Law Courts
BLACKFRIARS STATION
MANSION HOUSE
Cannon St.
CANNON ST. STATION
Lower Thames St.
MONUMENT
TOWER HILL
By Ward St.
Tower of London 12
Tower Bridge

Charing Cross
Leicester Square
National Gallery
Charing Cross Station
Trafalgar Square
EMBANKMENT
Whitehall
Whitehall
10 Downing Street
WESTMINSTER
Houses of Parliament
Westminster Abbey

LEICESTER SQUARE
Victoria Embankment
Upper Thames St.
Millennium Bridge
Globe Theatre ■
Blackfriars Bridge
Waterloo Bridge
Hungerford Bridge
Stamford St.
River Thames
Southwark Bridge
SOUTHWARK
Southwark St.
Union St.
London Bridge
LONDON BRIDGE
London Bridge Station
Tooley St.
St. Thomas St.
Bermondsey St.
THE BOROUGH
Long Ln.
DOCKLANDS
Jamaica Rd.
Druid St.
Abbey St.

SOUTH BANK
WATERLOO STATION
The Cut
WESTMINSTER
Westminster Bridge
Westminster Bridge Rd.
LAMBETH NORTH
York Rd.
Belvedere Rd.
Waterloo Rd.
Blackfriars Rd.
Borough Rd.
St. George's Rd.
Southwark Bridge Rd.
London Rd.
Kennington Rd.
BOROUGH
Borough High St.
Kennington Causeway
Harper Rd.
Great Dover St.
Bridge Rd.

WEST-MINSTER
Lambeth Bridge
Lambeth Rd.
Lambeth Palace Rd.
LAMBETH
ELEPHANT & CASTLE (BAKERLOO)
ELEPHANT & CASTLE
Albert Embankment

Tate Gallery
Millbank
Vauxhall Bridge
VAUXHALL
Kennington Ln.
Harleyford Rd.
KENNINGTON
Kennington Park Rd.
KENNINGTON
South Lambeth Rd.
Wandsworth Rd.
VAUXHALL
OVAL
Clapham Rd.
Brixton Rd.
Camberwell New Rd.

10
11
14
13

1 Mi
1 Km
N

**London Aquarium** ★ *Kids*  One of the largest aquariums in Europe, this South Bank attraction boasts 350 species of fish, everything from British freshwater species to sharks that once patrolled the Pacific. Observe the bountiful riches of the coral reefs of the Indian Ocean, and what lurks in the murky depths of the Atlantic and Pacific oceans, including an array of eels, sharks, piranhas, rays, jellyfish, and other denizens of the deep. You ford a freshwater stream into a mangrove swamp to reach a tropical rainforest. The seawater, incidentally, is just normal Thames water mixed with 8 tons of salt at a time.

County Hall, Westminister Bridge Rd., SE1. ℂ 020/7967-8000. www.londonaquarium.co.uk. Admission £8.75 ($16) adults, £6.50 ($12) students and seniors, £5.25 ($9.75) ages 3–14, family ticket £25 ($46). Daily 10am–6pm. Tube: Waterloo.

**The London Dungeon**  This ghoulish place was designed to chill the blood while reproducing the conditions of the Middle Ages. Set under the arches of London Bridge Station, the dungeon is a series of tableaux more grisly than those at Madame Tussaud's. The rumble of trains overhead adds to the atmosphere, and tolling bells bring a constant note of melancholy; dripping water and caged rats make for even more atmosphere. Naturally, it offers a burning at the stake as well as a torture chamber with racking, branding, and fingernail extraction, and a spine-chilling "Jack the Ripper Experience." The special effects were originally conceived for major film and TV productions. They've recently added a new show called "Judgment Day." You're sentenced to death (by actors, of course) and taken on a boat ride to meet your fate. If you survive, a Pizza Hut is on site, and a souvenir shop sells certificates that testify you made it through the works.

28–34 Tooley St., SE1. ℂ 020/7403-7221. www.thedungeons.com. Admission £13 ($24) adults, £11 ($21) students and seniors, £8.95 ($17) children under 15. Admission includes Judgment Day boat ride. Sept–July daily 10:30am–5pm; Aug daily 10am–7:30pm. Tube: London Bridge.

**London Planetarium** *Kids*  Located next to Madame Tussaud's, the planetarium explores the mysteries of the stars and the night sky. The most recent show starts with a spaceship of travelers forced to leave their planet when a neighboring star explodes. Accompanying them on their journey, the audience travels through the solar system, visiting its major landmarks and witnessing spectacular cosmic activity. There are also several hands-on exhibits that relate to planets and space. For example, you can see what shape or weight you'd be on other planets, and you can hear a recorded Stephen Hawking talk about mysterious black holes.

Marylebone Rd., NW1. ℂ 0870/4003-000. www.london-planetarium.com. Admission £3 ($5.55) adults, £2 ($3.70) seniors and children 5–17. Daily from 10am, with shows beginning at 12:20pm (10:30am on Sat–Sun), and last show at 5pm. Tube: Baker St.

**London Zoo** ★ *Kids*  One of the greatest zoos in the world, the London Zoo is more than 1½ centuries old. This 14-hectare (35-acre) garden houses about 8,000 animals, including some of the rarest species on earth. There's an insect house (incredible bird-eating spiders); a reptile house (huge dragonlike monitor lizards); and others, such as the Sobell Pavilion for Apes and Monkeys and the Lion Terraces. In the Moonlight World, special lighting simulates night for the nocturnal beasties while rendering them visible to onlookers, so you can see all the night rovers in action.

In 1999, the Millennium Conservation Centre opened, combining animals, visuals, and displays to demonstrate the nature of life on this planet. Many families budget almost an entire day here, watching the penguins being fed, enjoying an animal ride in summer, and meeting elephants on their walks around the zoo.

Regent's Park, NW1. (C) 020/7722-3333. www.londonzoo.co.uk. Admission £13 ($24) adults, £9.75 ($18) children and students 3–15, £41 ($76) family ticket (2 adults and 2 children or 1 adult and 3 children). Daily 10am–4:30pm. Tube: Regent's Park or Camden Town, or Bus: C2 or 274.

## 7 Organized Tours

### BUS TOURS

For the first-timer, the quickest and most economical way to bring the big city into focus is to take a bus tour. One of the most popular is **The Original London Sightseeing Tour,** which passes by all the major sights in just about 1½ hours. The tour, which uses a traditional double-decker bus with live commentary by a guide, costs £15 ($28) for adults, £10 ($19) for children under 16, free for those under 5. The tour allows you to hop on or off the bus at any point in the tour at no extra charge. The tour plus admission to Madame Tussaud's is £28 ($52) for adults, £20 ($37) for children.

Departures are from convenient points within the city; you can choose your departure point when you buy your ticket. Tickets can be purchased on the bus or at a discount from any London Transport or London Tourist Board Information Centre. Most hotel concierges also sell tickets. For information or phone purchases, call (C) **020/8877-1722.** It's also possible to book online at **www. theoriginaltour.com**.

**Big Bus Company Ltd.,** Waterside Way, London SW17 ((C) **020/8944-7810** or 0800/169-1365; www.bigbus.co.uk), operates a 2-hour tour in summer, departing frequently between 8:30am and 4:30pm daily from Marble Arch by Speakers Corner, Green Park by the Ritz Hotel, and Victoria Station (Buckingham Palace Rd. by the Royal Westminster Hotel). Tours cover the highlights— 18 in all—ranging from the Houses of Parliament and Westminster Abbey to the Tower of London and Buckingham Palace (exterior looks only), accompanied by live commentary. The cost is £17 ($31) for adults, £8 ($15) for children. A 1-hour tour follows the same route but covers only 13 sights. Tickets are valid all day; you can hop on and off the bus as you wish.

### WALKING TOURS

**The Original London Walks,** 87 Messina Ave., P.O. Box 1708, London NW6 4LW ((C) **020/7624-3978**), the oldest established walking-tour company in London, is run by an Anglo-American journalist/actor couple, David and Mary Tucker. Their hallmarks are variety, reliability, reasonably sized groups, and— above all—superb guides. The renowned crime historian Donald Rumbelow, the leading authority on Jack the Ripper and author of the classic guidebook *London Walks,* is a regular guide, as are several prominent actors (including classical actor Edward Petherbridge). Walks are regularly scheduled daily and cost £5 ($9.25) for adults, £4 ($7.40) for students and seniors; children under 15 go free. Call for schedule; no reservations needed.

**Discovery Walks,** 67 Chancery Lane, London WC2 ((C) **020/8530-8443;** www.Jack-the-Ripper-Walk.co.uk), are themed walks, led by Richard Jones, author of *Frommer's Memorable Walks in London.*

## 8 Spectator Sports

**CRICKET**   In summer, attention turns to cricket, played either at **Lord's,** St. John's Wood Road, NW8 ((C) **020/7289-1611;** www.lords.org; Tube: Jubilee Line to St. John's Wood), in north London, or at the somewhat less prestigious **Oval Cricket Ground,** The Oval, Kennington, London SE11

(© **020/7582-6660;** Tube: Northern Line to The Oval or Vauxhall), in south London. During the international test matches between Britain and Australia, the West Indies, India, or New Zealand (as important as the World Series in the United States), Britons go into a collective trance, with everyone glued to the nearest radio or TV.

**FOOTBALL (SOCCER)**    The season runs from August to April and attracts fiercely loyal fans. Games usually start at 3pm and are great to watch, but the stands can get very rowdy, so think about reserving seats. Centrally located first-division football clubs include **Arsenal,** Arsenal Stadium, Avenell Road, N5 (© **020/7704-4000,** box office 020/7704-4040; Tube: Piccadilly Line to Arsenal); **Tottenham Hotspur,** 748 High Rd., N17 (© **020/8365-5000,** box office 087/420-5000; Tube: Victoria Line to Seven Sisters); and **Chelsea,** Stamford Bridge, Fulham Road, SW6 (© **020/7915-2951,** box office 0870/300-2322; Tube: District Line to Fulham Broadway). Tickets cost £31 to £67 ($57–$124). The country's most visible site of world-class soccer matches is **Wembley Stadium,** Wembley, Middlesex (© **020/8902-8833;** Tube: Metropolitan Line to Wembley Park), about 9.5km (6 miles) north of London's center.

**HORSE RACING**    Within reach of central London are horse-racing tracks at Kempton Park, Sandown Park, and the most famous, Epsom, where the Derby is the main event of early June. Contact **United Racecourses Ltd.** (© **01372/ 470047**) for information on the next races at one of these tracks.

**TENNIS**    Fans from around the world focus on **Wimbledon** (Tube: District Line to Wimbledon). At Wimbledon's All England Lawn Tennis & Croquet Club, you'll see some of the world's best tennis players. The famous annual championship spans roughly the last week in June to the first week in July, with matches lasting from about 2pm until dark. (The gates open at 10:30am.) Tickets usually range in price from £15 to £75 ($28–$139). Coveted center-court seats are sold by lottery. A limited number of tickets for the outside courts are available at the gate. For recorded ticket information, call © **020/8946-2244,** or send a self-addressed stamped envelope (Aug–Dec) to the **All England Lawn Tennis & Croquet Club,** P.O. Box 98, Church Road, Wimbledon, SW19 5AE.

# 8

# Shopping

When Prussian Field Marshal Blücher, Wellington's stout ally at Waterloo, first laid eyes on London, he allegedly slapped his thigh and exclaimed, "Herr Gott, what a city to plunder!" He was gazing at what, for the early 19th century, was a phenomenal mass of shops and stores. Since those days, other cities may have equaled London as a shopping mecca, but none have surpassed it.

## 1 Shopping London

Although London is one of the world's best shopping cities, it often seems made for wealthy visitors. To find real values, do what most Londoners do: Wait for sales or search out discount stores.

American-style shopping has taken Britain by storm, in concept—warehouse stores and outlet malls—and in actual name: One block from Hamleys, you'll find the Disney Store. The Gap is everywhere, and Tiffany sells more wedding gifts than Asprey these days. Your best bet is to concentrate on British goods. You can also do well with French products; values are almost as good as in Paris.

**TAXES & SHIPPING** Value-added tax (VAT) is the British version of sales tax. VAT is a whopping 17.5% on most goods, but it's included in the price, so the number you see on the price tag is exactly what you'll pay at the register. Non-EU residents can get back much of the tax by applying for a VAT refund (see "How to Get Your VAT Refund," above).

In Britain, the minimum expenditure needed to qualify for a refund on value-added tax is £50 ($93). Not every single store honors this minimum, but it's far easier to qualify for a tax refund in Britain than almost any other country in the European Union.

Vendors at flea markets might not be equipped to provide the paperwork for a refund, so if you're contemplating a major purchase and are counting on a refund, ask before you buy. Be suspicious of any dealer who tells you there's no VAT on antiques. This was once true, but things have changed—the European Union has made the British add VAT to antiques, and pricing should reflect this. So ask if it's included—before you bargain. Get to the price you're comfortable with first, then ask for the VAT refund.

VAT is not charged on goods shipped out of the country, whether you spend £50 ($93) or not. Many London shops will help you beat the VAT by shipping for you. But watch out: Shipping may be even more expensive than the VAT, and you might also have to pay U.S. duties when the goods get to you at home.

You can ship your purchases on your flight home by paying for excess baggage (rates vary by airline) or have your packages shipped independently, which is generally less expensive than shipping it through the airlines. To ship independently, try **Burns International Facilities,** at Heathrow Airport Terminal 1 (© **020/8745-5301**) and Terminal 4 (© **020/8745-6460**). You can avoid the

## Tips   How to Get Your VAT Refund

You *must* get your VAT refund form from the retailer. Several readers have reported that merchants have told them they can get refund forms at the airport as they leave the country. *This is not true.* Don't leave the store without a form—it must be completed by the retailer on the spot. After you have asked if the store does VAT refunds and determined their minimum, request the paperwork.

Global Refund (www.taxfree.se) is your best bet for getting VAT refunds at the airport. Shop where you see the Global Refund Tax-Free Shopping sign, and ask for a Global Refund Tax-Free check when you purchase your items.

Fill out your form and then present it—with the goods, receipts, and passports—at the Customs office in the airport. Allow a half-hour to stand in line. Remember: You're required to show the goods, so put them in your carry-on.

Once the paperwork has been stamped, you have two choices: You can mail the papers (remember to bring a stamp) and receive your refund as a British check (no!) or a credit-card refund (yes!), or go to the Cash VAT Refund desk at the airport and get your refund in cash. Know that if you accept cash other than British pounds, you will lose money on the conversion.

Many stores charge a fee for processing your refund, so £3 to £5 ($5.55–$9.25) may be deducted from the total you receive. But since the VAT in Britain is 17.5%, it's worth the trouble to get the money back.

*Note:* If you're heading to other countries in the European Union, you should file all of your VAT refunds at once at your final EU destination.

VAT upfront *only* if you have the store ship directly for you. If you ship via excess baggage or an independent shipping company, you still have to pay the VAT upfront and apply for a refund.

**HOURS**   London keeps fairly uniform store hours, mostly shorter than American equivalents. The norm is a 10am opening and 5:30pm closing Monday through Saturday, with a late Wednesday or Thursday night until 7pm, maybe 8pm. Some stores in districts such as Chelsea and Covent Garden tend to keep slightly later hours.

Sunday shopping is now legal. Stores are allowed to be open for 6 hours; usually they choose 11am to 5pm. Stores in designated tourist areas and flea markets are exempt from this law and may stay open all day on Sunday. Therefore, Covent Garden, Greenwich, and Hampstead are big Sunday destinations for shoppers.

**SALES**   Traditionally, stores in Britain held only two sale periods: January and July. Now, whenever they need cash they have a sale, although January and July sales are still prevalent. July sales begin in June—or earlier—and promotions are commonplace. The January sale is still the big event of the year. Boxing Day in England (Dec 26), following the Christmas shopping spree, marks the end of the year-end clearance sales, which often run through January. On Boxing Day itself, many merchants take an additional 10% off merchandise that has already been marked down. Though some stores start their after-Christmas sales on December 26, most usually start after the first week in January, when round-trip airfares are in the low range, and savings on sale items might earn your travel money back if you find enough bargains.

Discounts can range from 25% to 50% at leading department stores. Depending on their inventories and their sense of timing, Harrods produces some very visible sales events, spending large amounts on promotions and publicity. Depending on the sale, extra discounts might apply to souvenirs with Harrods logos, furniture and gift items, English china (seconds are trucked in from factories in Stoke-on-Trent), and English designer brands like Jaeger. But while the Harrods sale is the most famous in London, it's not the only game in town. Just about every other store—except Boots—also has big sales in January and June. Beware, though: There's a huge difference in the quality of the finds at genuine sales, when stores are actually clearing the shelves, and the goods bought at "produced" sales, when special merchandise has been hauled in just for the sale.

**DUTY-FREE AIRPORT SHOPPING**    Shopping at airports is big business. Terminal 4 at Heathrow is a virtual shopping mall, and each of the other terminals at Heathrow has a wide range of shopping outlets, with not a lot of crossover between brands. Prices at the airport for items like souvenirs and candy bars are, of course, higher than on the streets of London, but duty-free prices on luxury goods are usually fair. There are often promotions and coupons that allow for pounds off at the time of the purchase. Most of the sales at these airport shops are made for passengers waiting for flights to other destinations, usually home. Most passengers, by the end of their stay in London, have at least some grasp of what items are available in London shops and at what prices, and therefore have some basis of comparison to prices of equivalent goods outside the airports.

## 2 Central London Shopping

Thankfully for those pressed for time, several key streets offer some (or even all) of London's best retail stores, compactly located in a niche or neighborhood so you can just stroll and shop.

**THE WEST END**    As a neighborhood, the West End includes Mayfair and is home to the core of London's big-name shopping. Most of the department stores, designer shops, and multiples (chain stores) have their flagships in this area.

The key streets are **Oxford Street** (in either direction) for affordable shopping (start at Marble Arch Tube station if you're ambitious, or Bond St. station if you only care to see some of it), and **Regent Street,** which intersects Oxford Street at Oxford Circus (Tube: Oxford Circus). The Oxford Street flagship (at Marble Arch) of the private-label department store Marks & Spencer ("Marks & Sparks" in the local parlance) is worth visiting for quality goods. Regent Street, which leads all the way to Piccadilly, has more upscale department stores (including the famed Liberty of London), chains (Laura Ashley), and specialty dealers.

Parallel to Regent Street, **Bond Street** (Tube: Bond St.) connects Piccadilly with Oxford Street and is synonymous with the luxury trade. Divided into New and Old, it has experienced a recent revival and is the hot address for international designers—Donna Karan has two shops here. A slew of international hot-shots, from Chanel to Ferragamo to Versace, have digs nearby.

**Burlington Arcade** (Tube: Piccadilly Circus), the famous glass-roofed, Regency-style passage leading off Piccadilly, looks like a period exhibition and is lined with intriguing shops and boutiques. Lit by wrought-iron lamps and dec-orated with clusters of ferns and flowers, its small, smart stores specialize in fash-ion, jewelry, Irish linen, cashmere, and more. If you linger there until 5:30pm, you can watch the beadles (the last London representatives of Britain's oldest police force), in their black-and-yellow livery and top hats, ceremoniously place the iron grills that block off the arcade until 9am, at which time they just as ceremoniously remove them to start a new business day. (There are only three beadles remaining.) Also at 5:30pm, a hand bell called the Burlington Bell is sounded, signaling the end of trading.

For a total contrast, check out **Jermyn Street** (Tube: Piccadilly Circus), on the far side of Piccadilly, a tiny 2-block-long street devoted to high-end men's hab-erdashers and toiletries shops; many have been doing business for centuries. Sev-eral hold royal warrants, including Turnbull & Asser, where HRH Prince Charles has his pj's made. A bit to the northwest, Savile Row (between Regent St. and New Bond St.) is synonymous with the finest in men's tailoring.

The West End theater district borders two more shopping areas: the still-not-ready-for-prime-time **Soho** (Tube: Tottenham Court Rd.), where the sex shops are slowly converting into cutting-edge designer shops, and **Covent Garden** (Tube: Covent Garden), a shopping masterpiece full of fashion, food, books, and everything else. The original Covent Garden marketplace has overflowed its boundaries and eaten up the surrounding neighborhood; it's fun to wander the narrow streets and shop. Covent Garden is mobbed on Sundays.

Just a stone's throw from Covent Garden, **Monmouth Street** is somewhat of a London shopping secret: Londoners know they can find a wide array of stores in a space of only 2 blocks. Many shops here are outlets for British designers, such as Alexander Campbell, who specializes in outfits made of wispy materials. Some shops along this street sell both used and new clothing. Besides clothing, stores specialize in everything from musical instruments from the Far East to palm and crystal-ball readings.

**KNIGHTSBRIDGE & CHELSEA**    Knightsbridge (Tube: Knightsbridge), the home of Harrods, is the second-most-famous London retail district. (Oxford St. edges it out.) Nearby Sloane Street is chock-a-block with designer shops.

Walk southwest on **Brompton Road** (toward the Victoria and Albert Museum) and you'll find **Cheval Place,** lined with designer resale shops, and Beauchamp (*Bee*-cham) Place. It's only a block long, but it's very "Sloane Ranger" or "Sloanie" (as the Brits would say), featuring the kinds of shops where young British aristocrats buy their clothing for the "season."

If you walk farther along Brompton Road, you'll connect to **Brompton Cross,** another hip area for designer shops made popular when Michelin House was rehabbed by Sir Terence Conran, becoming the Conran Shop. Seek out **Walton Street,** a tiny snake of a street running from Brompton Cross back toward the museums. Most of the shops along this street specialize in nonessen-tial luxury products, the kind a severe and judgmental Victorian moralist might dismiss as vanities and fripperies. This is where you'll find aromatherapy from Jo Malone, needlepoint, and costume jewelry. **King's Road** (Tube: Sloane Sq.), the main street of Chelsea, will forever remain a symbol of the Swinging '60s. It's still popular with the young crowd, but there are fewer mohawk haircuts, Bovver boots, and Edwardian ball gowns than before. More and more, King's Road is a lineup of markets and "multi-stores," conglomerations of indoor stands, stalls, and booths within one building or enclosure. About a third of King's Road is

*Tips* **GST: Greenwich Shopping Time**

Though many London shops are now open on Sundays, the best Sunday shopping is in the stalls of the flea and craft markets in the royal city of Greenwich.

The best way to enjoy the trip is to float downstream on a boat from Charing Cross or Westminster Pier (service begins at 10:30am on Sun; see "River Cruises Along the Thames," under "Exploring London by Boat," in chapter 7). The trip takes about a half-hour, and you'll get a knowledgeable commentary on the Docklands development and the history of the river. You'll also be able to view the Tower and much of London from the water along the way.

The boat leaves you in the heart of Greenwich, minutes from the craft market held on Saturday and Sunday. Follow the signs—or the crowd. After you're done, follow the crowd again to Greenwich's several antiques markets. First is **Canopy Market,** which isn't under a canopy at all, but sprawls through several parking lots where junk and old books abound, and then onto **High Street,** where the fancier flea market is held. It's possible that there will be yet another antiques market at **Town Hall,** across the street, but these shows usually charge an admission fee.

You're only a half block from the Greenwich BritRail station now, which is on Greenwich High Road; and there's a train back to London every half-hour until about 11:30pm.

devoted to "multi-store" antiques markets; another third houses design-trade showrooms and stores of household wares; and the remaining third is faithful to the area's teenybopper roots.

Finally, don't forget all those museums in nearby **South Kensington**—they all have great gift shops.

**KENSINGTON, NOTTING HILL & BAYSWATER  Kensington High Street** (Tube: High St. Kensington) is the hangout of the classier breed of teen, one who has graduated from Carnaby Street and is ready for street chic. While there are a few staples of basic British fashion here, most of the stores feature items that stretch; are very, very short; very, very tight; and very, very black.

From Kensington High Street, you can walk up **Kensington Church Street,** which, like Portobello Road, is one of the city's main shopping avenues for antiques, selling everything from antique furniture to Impressionist paintings.

Kensington Church Street dead-ends at the Notting Hill Gate Tube station, jumping-off point for Portobello Road, whose antiques dealers and weekend market are 2 blocks beyond.

Not far from Notting Hill Gate is **Whiteleys of Bayswater,** Queensway, W2 (© **020/7229-8844;** Tube: Bayswater or Queensway), an Edwardian mall whose chief tenant is Marks & Spencer. Whiteleys also contains 75 to 85 other shops, mostly specialty outlets, plus restaurants, cafes, bars, and an eight-screen movie theater.

## 3 The Department Stores

Contrary to popular belief, Harrods is not the only department store in London. The British invented the department store, and they have lots of them, mostly in Mayfair, and each has its own customer profile.

**DAKS**    Opened in 1936 as the home of DAKS clothing, DAKS has been going strong ever since. It's known for menswear—its basement-level men's shoe department is a model of the way quality shoes should be fitted and sold—as well as women's fashions, perfume, jewelry, and lingerie. Many of the clothes are lighthearted, carefully made, and casually elegant. Solid, reliable, and dependable, this is a well-established store whose core market is male and female clients ages 30 to 50. Clothes aren't particularly cutting edge (and indeed, many of the regular clients here aren't necessarily looking for that), except for the clothing from the recently inaugurated youth line, "Daks E1." 10 Old Bond St., W1. © 020/ 7409-4000. Tube: Green Park.

**Fenwick of Bond Street**    Fenwick (the "w" is silent), dating from 1891, is a stylish fashion store that offers an excellent collection of designer womenswear, ranging from moderately priced ready-to-wear items to more expensive designer fashions. An extensive selection of lingerie in all price ranges is also sold. 63 New Bond St., W1. © 020/7629-9161. Tube: Bond St.

**Fortnum & Mason** ★★★    Catering to well-heeled clients as a full-service department store since 1707, Fortnum & Mason recently spent £14 million ($26 million) on an overhaul of its premises and inventories. Offerings include one of the most comprehensive delicatessens and food markets in London, as well as stationery, gift items, porcelain and crystal, and lots and lots of clothing for men, women, and children. 181 Piccadilly, W1. © 020/7734-8040. Tube: Piccadilly Circus.

**Harrods**    Harrods remains an institution, but in the last decade or so it has grown increasingly dowdy and is not nearly as cutting edge as it used to be. For the latest trends, shop elsewhere. However, we always stop here during our visits to London. As entrenched in English life as Buckingham Palace and the Ascot Races, it's still an elaborate emporium. Goods are spread across 300 departments, and the range, variety, and quality will still dazzle the visiting out-of-towner.

The whole fifth floor is devoted to sports and leisure, with a wide range of equipment and attire. Toy Kingdom is on the fourth floor, along with children's wear. The Egyptian Hall, on the ground floor, sells crystal from Lalique and Baccarat, plus porcelain.

There's also a barber, a jewelry department, and a fashion department for younger customers. You'll have a choice of 18 restaurants and bars. Best of all are the **Food Halls,** with a huge variety of foods and several cafes. Harrods began as a grocer in 1849, and food and drinks are still at the heart of the business. The motto remains, "If you can eat or drink it, you'll find it at Harrods." 87–135 Brompton Rd., Knightsbridge, SW1. © 020/7730-1234. Tube: Knightsbridge.

**Harvey Nichols**    Locals call it "Harvey Nicks." Once a favorite of the late Princess Di, this store is large, but it doesn't compete directly with Harrods because it has a more upmarket, fashionable image. Harvey Nicks has its own gourmet food hall and fancy restaurant, **The Fifth Floor,** and is crammed with the best in designer home furnishings, gifts, and fashions for all, although women's clothing is the largest segment of its business. The store carries many

American designer brands; avoid them, as they're more expensive in London than they are in the U.S. 109–125 Knightsbridge, SW1. © 020/7235-5000. Tube: Knightsbridge.

**John Lewis**    This department store remains one of the most tried-and-true, traditional outlets in London. Their motto is that they are never knowingly undersold, and they mean it. We've always found great bargains at this store, most recently in a clearance sale of fine earthenware by Royal Stafford. Whatever you're looking for, ranging from mauve Egyptian towels to clothing and jewelry, it's likely to be for sale here. 278–306 Oxford St., W1. © 020/7629-7711. Tube: Oxford St.

**Liberty** ★★    This department store is celebrated for its Liberty Prints: top-echelon fabrics, often in floral patterns, prized by decorators for the way they add a sense of English tradition to a room. The front part of the Regent Street store isn't particularly distinctive, but don't be fooled: Other parts of the place have been restored to Tudor-style splendor that includes half-timbering and interior paneling. There are six floors of fashion, china, and home furnishings, including the famous Liberty Print fashion fabrics, upholstery fabrics, scarves, ties, luggage, gifts, and more. 214–220 Regent St., W1. © 020/7734-1234. Tube: Oxford Circus.

**Peter Jones**    Founded in 1877 and rebuilt in 1936, Peter Jones is known for household goods, household fabrics and trims, china, glass, upholstered furniture, and linens. The linen department is one of the best in London. Sloane Sq., SW1. © 020/7730-3434. Tube: Sloane Sq.

## 4 Goods A to Z
## ANTIQUES

Also check out the description of **Portobello Market** on p. 293.

**Alfie's Antique Market**    This is the biggest (and one of the best-stocked) conglomerate of antiques dealers in London, crammed into the premises of a 19th-century store. It has more than 370 stalls, showrooms, and workshops in over 35,000 square feet of floor space. You'll find the biggest Susie Cooper (a well-known designer of tableware and ceramics for Wedgwood) collection in Europe here. A whole antiques district has grown up around Alfie's along Church Street. 13–25 Church St., NW8. © 020/7723-6066. Fax 020/7724-0999. Tube: Marylebone or Edgware Rd.

**Antiquarius**    The recently redecorated Antiquarius echoes the artistic diversity of King's Road. More than 120 dealers offer specialized merchandise, usually of the small, domestic variety, such as antique and period jewelry, porcelain, silver, first-edition books, boxes, clocks, prints, and paintings, with an occasional piece of antique furniture. You'll find a lot of items from the 1950s. 131–141 King's Rd., SW3. © 020/7969-1500. Tube: Sloane Sq. or S. Kensington.

**Bond Street Antiques Centre** ★★    This place, in the heart of London's finest shopping district, enjoys a reputation for being London's preeminent center for antique jewelry, silver, watches, porcelain, glass, and Asian antiques and paintings. 124 New Bond St., W1. © 020/7351-5353 or 020/7493-1854. Tube: Bond St. or Green Park.

**Grays Antiques and Grays Mews**    These markets have been converted into walk-in stands with independent dealers. The term "antiques" covers items from oil paintings to, say, the 1894 edition of the *Encyclopedia Britannica*. Also sold are antique jewelry; silver; gold; maps and prints; bronzes and ivories; arms and armor; Victorian and Edwardian toys; furniture; Art Nouveau and Art Deco items; antique lace; scientific instruments; craft tools; and Asian, Persian, and Islamic pottery, porcelain, miniatures, and antiquities. There's a cafe in each building. Check out the 1950s-style **Victory Cafe** on Davies Street for their homemade cakes. 58 Davies St. and 1–7 Davies Mews, W1. ℭ 020/7629-7034. Tube: Bond St.

**The Mall at Camden Passage**    The Mall contains one of Britain's greatest concentrations of antiques dealers. In individual shops, you'll find some 35 dealers offering fine furniture, porcelain, and silver. The area expands into a street market on Wednesday and Saturday. Islington, N1. ℭ 020/7351-5353. Tube: Northern Line to Angel.

## ARCHITECTURAL SALVAGE

**LASSCO (London Architectural Salvage & Supply Co.)**  ⚡  Established in 1978, this company controls the largest inventories of architectural remnants in the U.K., with warehouses chock-full of mantelpieces, stained-glass windows, antique doors, statuary, ecclesiastical accessories (including, among others, assorted pews from Victorian-era churches), and garden ornaments. Each piece was rescued during the renovation or demolition of buildings throughout Greater London. Many of them originated within unheralded private homes; others come from public buildings that have included the Palace of Westminster and the Royal Opera House. The company's headquarters and most impressive showroom occupy a deconsecrated Victorian church.

A particularly interesting annex of this outfit (same phone, same Tube stop) lies within a 5-minute walk at Britannia Walk, N1. It specializes in antique doors, a resource that building contractors and architects usually find fascinating. Small, easy-to-transport antique items are also available, including some charming 19th-century woodworking tools. Any of the large objects available here can be crated and shipped. Headquarters at St. Michael and All Angels, on Mark St., off Paul St., EC2. ℭ 020/7749-9944. Tube: Old St.

## ART & CRAFTS

**ACAVA** *(Finds*    This London-based visual-arts organization provides studios and other services for professional artists, and represents about 250 artists working in spaces around London. Call for individual open-studio schedules, as well as dates for the annual Open Studios weekend. ℭ 020/8960-5015.

**Cecilia Colman Gallery**    One of London's most established crafts galleries, Cecilia Colman features decorative ceramics, studio glass, jewelry, and metalwork. Among the offerings are glass sculptures by Lucien Simon, jewelry by Caroline Taylor, and pottery by Simon Rich. Exhibitions of contemporary original works in ceramic, glass, and metal are featured. There's also a large selection of mirrors and original-design perfume bottles. 67 St. John's Wood High St., NW8. ℭ 020/7722-0686. Tube: Jubilee Line to St. John's Wood.

**Contemporary Applied Arts**  ⚡  This association encourages traditional and progressive contemporary artwork. Many of Britain's best-established craftspeople, as well as promising talents, are represented within this contemporary-looking space. The gallery houses a diverse display of glass, ceramics, textiles, wood, furniture, jewelry, and metalwork—all by contemporary artisans. A program of special exhibitions, including solo and small-group shows, focuses on innovations in craftwork. There are new exhibitions every 6 weeks. 2 Percy St., W1. ℭ 020/7436-2344. Tube: Tottenham Court Rd.

**Crafts Council Gallery**  ⚡⚡  This gallery is run by the Crafts Council, the national body promoting contemporary crafts. You'll discover some of today's most creative work here. There's a shop specializing in craft objects and publications, and a reference library. The gallery is closed on Mondays. 44A Pentonville Rd., Islington, N1. © 020/7278-7700. Tube: Northern Line to Angel.

**England & Co.**    Under the guidance of Jane England, this gallery specializes in Outsider Art and Art in Boxes (that is, art which incorporates a box structure into the composition or frame of a three-dimensional work). The gallery focuses attention on neglected postwar British artists such as Tony Stubbings and Ralph Romney. One-person and group shows are mounted frequently, and many young artists get early exposure here. 216 Westbourne Grove, W11. © 020/7221-0417. Tube: Notting Hill Gate.

**Gabriel's Wharf**    This is a South Bank complex of shops, restaurants, and bars open Tuesday to Sunday 11am to 6pm (dining and drinking establishments are open later). Lying 2 minutes by foot from Oxo Tower Wharf, it is filled with some of London's most skilled craftspeople, turning out original pieces of sculpture, jewelry, ceramics, art, and fashion. Food, fashion, art, and crafts await you here, making this place a lot of fun to poke around. 56 Upper Ground, SE1. © 020/ 7401-2255. Tube: Blackfriars, Southwark, Waterloo, or Embankment.

**Gong**    One of the best selections of offbeat crafts and jewelry in England awaits you here. The merchandise is the work of both Asian and other international artisans. 142 Portobello Rd., W11 © 020/7565-4162. Tube: Notting Hill Gate.

**Grosvenor Prints**    London's largest stock of antique prints, ranging from the 17th up to the 20th century, is on sale here. Obviously, views of London are the biggest-selling items. Some prints depict significant moments in the city's

---

**Finds  Go East, Art Lover**

The East End neighborhood of Hoxton used to be a tawdry backwater until artists starting flocking here and opening studios, cleaning up the discarded mattresses and rejuvenating abandoned buildings.

Success was assured with the opening of **White Cube 2,** 48 Hoxton Sq., EC2 (© 020/7930-5373), owned by Jay Jopling, the leading dealer in modern English art, whose artists include Britain's most contentious, Damien Hirst. The other hot gallery is **Victoria Miro Gallery,** 16 Wharf Rd., EC2 (© 020/7336-8109). Some of London's most controversial art appears here. Miro represents Chris Ofili, whose "Madonna and Dung" painting enraged former New York mayor and art critic Rudolph Giuliani.

These art dealers and the artists themselves (that is, those who've sold a painting recently) can be found dining at **Cantaloupe, 35–42** Charlotte Rd., EC2 (© 020/7729-5566), which serves Mediterranean cuisine and great tapas. This informal bar/restaurant, with its wooden tables and industrial fittings, prepares such superb dishes as chargrilled Aberdeen Angus steak with rosemary butter or fried *halloumi* (a white cheese from Cyprus) with olive salsa. Open Monday through Friday from noon to 3pm, and Monday through Saturday from 7 to 11pm. Main courses cost from £8.50 to £15 ($16–$28).

Take the Tube to Old Street to arrive near the doorsteps of all of these establishments.

history, including the Great Fire. Of course, the British are great animal lovers, so expect plenty of prints of dogs and horses. 28 Shelton St., WC2. © **020/7836-1979.** Tube: Covent Garden.

**Kelly Hoppen** The British press has labeled interior designer Kelly Hoppen as its own minimalist Martha Stewart (pre-scandal). Hoppen's designer emporium on Fulham Road opened to great fanfare, and even Hoppen herself has been pleased with the "stock just flying out." Expect a little bit of everything here, including her own charming medley of ceramics (some designed for Wedgwood), furniture, and original accessories such as giant horn buttons or pony-skin bags from Argentina. 175–177 Fulham Rd., SW3. © **020/7351-1910.** Tube: S. Kensington.

**Whitechapel Art Gallery** ★ Ever since this East End gallery opened its Art Nouveau doors in 1901, collectors have been heading here to find out what's hot. The gallery maintains its cutting edge; to some, it's the incubation chamber for some of the most talented of east London's artists. The collections are fun, hip, often sexy, and in your face. 80–81 Whitechapel High St., E1. © **020/7522-7888** or 020/7522-7878 (recorded). Tube: District or Hammersmith & City Lines to Aldgate E.

## BATH & BODY

**The Body Shop** There's a branch of The Body Shop in every shopping area and tourist zone in London. Some are bigger than others, but all are filled with politically and environmentally friendly beauty, bath, and aromatherapy products. Prices are much lower in the U.K. than they are in the U.S. There's an entire children's line, a men's line, and lots of travel sizes and travel products. 374 Oxford St., W1. © **020/7409-7868.** Tube: Bond St. Other locations throughout London.

**Boots the Chemist** This store has branches all over Britain. The house brands of beauty products are usually the best, including original Boots products (try the cucumber facial mask), Boots' versions of The Body Shop (two lines, Global and Naturalistic), and Boots' versions of Chanel makeup (called No. 7). They also sell film, pantyhose (called tights), sandwiches, and all of life's other little necessities. 490 Oxford St., W1G. © **020/7491-8546.** Tube: Marble Arch. Other locations throughout London.

**Culpeper the Herbalist** ★ This store has another branch in Mayfair, at 21 Bruton St., W1 (© **020/7629-4559**), but the hours are better at the Covent Garden location. You'll have to put up with a cramped space to check out all the food, bath, and aromatherapy products, but it's worth it. Stock up on essential oils, or go for the dream pillows, candles, sachets, and many a shopper's fave— the aromatherapy fan, for home and the car. 8 The Piazza, Covent Garden, WC2. © **020/7379-6698.** Tube: Covent Garden.

**Floris** ★★ A variety of toilet articles and fragrances fill Floris's floor-to-ceiling mahogany cabinets, which are architectural curiosities in their own right. They were installed relatively late in the establishment's history—that is, 1851—long after the shop had received its royal warrants as suppliers of toilet articles to the king and queen. 89 Jermyn St., SW1. © **020/7930-2885.** Tube: Piccadilly Circus.

**Lush** In our view, the handmade soaps and cosmetics sold here are the most intriguing in London. The store is always launching something new, such as its latest soap, "Rock Star," looking very pink and smelling like candy. Among the extensive selection is "Tam O'Santa," an allspice, sandalwood, and frankincense bubble bath, and "Banana Moon," a creamy banana soap. The products are made with fresh fruit and vegetables, the finest essential oils, and safe synthetics—no animal ingredients. 11 The Piazza, Covent Garden. © 020/7240-4570. Tube: Covent Garden. Other locations throughout London.

**Neal's Yard Remedies**    Noted the world over for their cobalt-blue bottles, these chic bath, beauty, and aromatherapy products are must-haves for those who pooh-pooh The Body Shop as too common. Prices are higher in the United States, so stock up here. 15 Neal's Yard, WC2. © 020/7379-7222. Tube: Covent Garden.

**Penhaligon's** ★★★    This Victorian perfumery, established in 1870, holds royal warrants to HRH Duke of Edinburgh and HRH Prince of Wales. All items sold are exclusive to Penhaligon's. The store offers a large selection of perfume, aftershave, soap, and bath oils for women and men. Gifts include antique-silver scent bottles, grooming accessories, and leather traveling goods. Penhaligon's is now in more than 20 Saks Fifth Avenue stores across the United States. 41 Wellington St., WC2. © 020/7836-2150. Tube: Covent Garden.

## BOOKS, MAPS & ENGRAVINGS

In addition to the bookstores below, you'll find well-stocked branches of the **Dillon's** chain around town, including one at 82 Gower St. (Tube: Euston Sq.).

**Children's Book Centre**    With thousands of titles, this is the best place to go for children's books. Fiction is arranged according to age, up to 16. There are also videos and toys for kids. 237 Kensington High St., W8. © 020/7937-7497. Tube: Kensington.

**Foyle's Bookshop**    Claiming to be the world's largest bookstore, Foyle's has an impressive array of hardcovers and paperbacks, as well as travel maps, new records, CDs, videotapes, and sheet music. 113–119 Charing Cross Rd., WC2. © 020/7437-5660. Tube: Tottenham Court Rd. or Leicester Sq.

**Gay's the Word**    Britain's leading gay and lesbian bookstore offers a large selection of books, as well as magazines, cards, and guides. There's also a used-books section. 66 Marchmont St., WC1. © 020/7278-7654. Tube: Russell Sq.

**Hatchards**    On the south side of Piccadilly, Hatchards offers a wide range of books on all subjects and is particularly renowned in the areas of fiction, biography, travel, cookery, gardening, art, history, and finance. In addition, Hatchards is second to none in its range of books on royalty. 187 Piccadilly, W1. © 020/7439-9921. Tube: Piccadilly Circus or Green Park.

**The Map House of London**    An ideal place to find an offbeat souvenir. The Map House sells antique maps and engravings, plus a vast selection of old prints of London and England, both original and reproduction. The cost of a century-old original engraving begins at £20 ($37). 54 Beauchamp Place, SW3. © 020/7589-4325. Tube: Knightsbridge.

**Murder One** *Finds*    Maxim Jakubowski's bookshop is dedicated to the genres of crime, romance, science fiction, and horror. Crime and science fiction magazines, some of them obscure, are also available. 71–73 Charing Cross Rd., WC2. © 020/7734-3483. Tube: Leicester Sq.

**Stanfords**    Established in 1852, Stanfords is the world's largest map shop. Many maps, including worldwide touring and survey maps, are unavailable elsewhere. It's also London's best travel bookstore (with a complete selection of Frommer's guides!). 12–14 Long Acre, WC2. © 020/7836-1321. Tube: Covent Garden.

## CASHMERE & WOOLENS

**Belinda Robertson**    Some of the most beautiful and most chic cashmeres, in lovely colors, are sold at this centrally located outlet at Knightsbridge. Bold colors are a hallmark of Ms. Robertson's designs, ranging from carnival red to canary yellow. She designs for women, men, and children. 4 West Halkin St., SW1. ℂ 020/7235-0519. Tube: Knightsbridge.

**Berk**   This store boasts one of the largest collections of cashmere sweaters in London—at least the top brands. The outlet also carries capes, stoles, scarves, and camelhair sweaters. 46 Burlington Arcade, Piccadilly, W1. ℂ 020/7493-0028. Tube: Piccadilly Circus or Green Park.

## CHINA, GLASS & SILVER

**London Silver Vaults** ★ *Finds*   Don't let the out-of-the-way location or the facade's lack of charm slow you down. Downstairs, you'll enter vaults—40 in all—that are filled with tons of silver and silverplate, plus collections of jewelry. It's a staggering selection of old and new, with excellent prices and friendly dealers. Chancery House, 53–64 Chancery Lane, WC2. ℂ 020/7242-3844. Tube: Chancery Lane.

**Reject China Shop** *Value*   Don't expect too many rejects or too many bargains, despite the name. This shop sells seconds (sometimes) along with first-quality pieces of china with such names as Royal Doulton, Spode, and Wedgwood. You can also find a variety of crystal, glassware, and flatware. If you'd like to have your purchases shipped home for you, the shop can do it for a fee. 183 Brompton Rd., SW3. ℂ 020/7581-0739. Tube: Knightsbridge. Other locations throughout London.

**Royal Doulton** ★★★   Founded in the 1930s, this store has one of the largest inventories of china in Britain. A wide range of English bone china, as well as crystal and giftware, is sold. The firm specializes, of course, in Royal Doulton (plus Minton and Royal Crown Derby) china, Lladró figures, Border Fine Arts, and other famous names. The January and June sales are excellent. 167 Piccadilly, W1. ℂ 020/7493-9121. Tube: Piccadilly Circus or Green Park.

**Thomas Goode** ★★   This is one of the most famous emporiums in Britain; it's worth visiting for its architectural interest and nostalgic allure alone. Originally built in 1876, Goode's has 14 rooms loaded with porcelain, gifts, candles, silver, tableware, and even a private museum. There's also a tearoom-cum-restaurant tucked into the corner. 19 S. Audley St., W1. ℂ 020/7499-2823. Tube: Bond St., Green Park, Marble Arch, or Hyde Park.

## CHOCOLATES

**Godiva Chocolates** ★   This world-famous chocolate maker has invaded Covent Garden with the tastiest sweets in town. The store offers London's finest selection of chocolates, with some seasonal products. In addition to handcrafted chocolates, the salespeople here also hawk the chocolate jam. 17 Russell St., WC2. ℂ 020/7836-5706. Tube: Covent Garden.

## FASHION

We have divided this category into "Classic," "Cutting Edge," and "Vintage & Secondhand," below.

### CLASSIC

While every internationally known designer worth his or her weight in Shantung silk has a boutique in London, the best buys are on the sturdy English styles that last forever. See also the separate sections on "Cashmere & Woolens," "Handbags," "Jewelry," "Lingerie," and "Shoes."

**Austin Reed**   Austin Reed has long stood for superior-quality clothing and excellent tailoring. Chester Barrie's off-the-rack suits, for example, are said to fit like tailor-made. The polite employees are unusually honest about telling you what looks good. The store always has a wide variety of top-notch jackets and suits, and men can outfit themselves from dressing gowns to overcoats. For women, there are carefully selected suits, separates, coats, shirts, knitwear, and accessories. 103–113 Regent St., W1. ℂ 020/7534-7779. Tube: Piccadilly Circus.

**Beau Monde**   This outlet earns its fame selling chic but affordable "nouvelle couture" for women—fitted and adjusted to your body. All designs are by the locally famous London designer Sylvia Young. Her design philosophy is that a busy woman should be conscious of fashion, but not a victim of its whims, and that clothes should work for her—not against her. Her women's wear is comfortable to wear and fashionable, but not stuffy. 43 Lexington St., W1. ℂ 020/7734-6563. Tube: Piccadilly Circus.

**Burberry** ★★★   The name has been synonymous with raincoats ever since Edward VII ordered his valet to "bring my Burberry" when the skies threatened. An impeccably trained staff sells the famous raincoats, plus excellent men's shirts, sportswear, knitwear, and accessories. Raincoats are available in women's sizes and styles as well. Prices are high, but you get quality and prestige. 18–22 Haymarket, SW1. ℂ 020/7930-3343. Tube: Piccadilly Circus.

**Designer Sale UK** *Value*   Amazingly, you can sometimes get 90% off designer clothing for both men and women at this outlet. Of course, you've got to sift through 140 rails of clothing and accessories, much of which had a good reason for not selling in the first place. The shop claims it caters to both the discerning label lover and the devoted bargain hunter. Yes, those rails carry Armani, Vivienne Westwood, Alexander McQueen, and a lot of the lesser lights in designer fashion. £2 ($3.70) is charged to attend the sale. Atlantis Gallery, Old Truman Brewery, 146 Brick Lane, E1. ℂ 01273/470-880. Tube: Aldgate E. or Liverpool St.

**Emmett** ★   Some of the finest men's shirts in London are sold at this Chelsea outlet. Shirt styles are sold in limited editions of about two dozen each, so chances are you'll never run into another man wearing the same garb as you. Complementary patterns line collars and cuffs, and the look is very British, very Prince Charles sophisticated. Beautiful woven silk ties are also featured. 380 King's Rd., SW3. ℂ 020/7351-7529. Tube: Sloane Sq.

**Gieves & Hawkes** ★★★   This men's clothing store has a prestigious address and a list of clients that includes the Prince of Wales, yet its prices aren't as lethal as others on this street. They're high, but you get good quality. Cotton shirts, silk ties, Shetland sweaters, and exceptional ready-to-wear and tailor-made ("bespoke") suits are sold. 1 Savile Row, W1. ℂ 020/7434-2001. Tube: Piccadilly Circus or Green Park.

**Hilditch & Key** ★★   The finest name in men's shirts, Hilditch & Key has been in business since 1899. The two shops on this street both offer men's clothing (including a custom-made shirt service) and women's ready-made shirts. There's also an outstanding tie collection. Shirts go for half price during the twice-yearly sales (in Jan and June); men fly in from all over the world for them. 37 and 73 Jermyn St., SW1. ℂ 020/7734-4707. Tube: Piccadilly Circus or Green Park.

**Jigsaw**   Branches of this fashion chain are numerous, but the Long Acre branch features trendy, middle-market womenswear and children's clothing. Around the corner, the Floral Street shop carries menswear, including a wide range of colored moleskin items. 21 Long Acre, WC2. ℂ 020/7240-3855. Tube: Covent Garden.

**Laura Ashley**   This is the flagship store of the company whose design ethos embodies the flowery English country look. The store carries a wide choice of women's clothing, plus home furnishings. Prices are lower than in the United States. 256–258 Regent St., W1. (© 020/7437-9760. Tube: Oxford Circus. Other locations around London.

**Next**   This chain of "affordable fashion" stores saw its heyday in the 1980s, when it was celebrated for its success in marketing avant-garde fashion ideas to a wide spectrum of the British public. No longer at its peak, it still merits a stop. The look is still very contemporary, with a Continental flair, and there are clothes for men, women, and kids. 15–17 Long Acre, WC2. (© 020/7420-8280. Tube: Covent Garden. Other locations throughout London.

**Reiss**   In a city where men's clothing often sells at exorbitant prices, Reiss is a haven of reasonable sporty and casual wear. Take your pick from everything from pullovers to rugged cargo pants. 114 King's Rd., SW3. (© 020/7225-4910. Tube: Sloane Sq.

**Thomas Pink** ★★★   This Jermyn Street shirt-maker, named after an 18th-century Mayfair tailor, gave the world the phrase "in the pink." It has a prestigious reputation for well-made cotton shirts for both men and women. The shirts are created from the finest two-fold Egyptian and Sea Island pure-cotton poplin. Some patterns are classic, others new and unusual. All are generously cut with long tails and finished with a choice of double cuffs or single-button cuffs. A small pink square in the tail tells all. 85 Jermyn St., SW1. (© 020/7930-6364. Tube: Green Park or Piccadilly Circus.

**Turnbull & Asser** ★★   Over the years, everyone from David Bowie to Ronald Reagan has been seen in custom-made shirts from Turnbull & Asser. Excellent craftsmanship and simple lines—plus bold colors—distinguish these shirts. The outlet also sells shirts and blouses to women, a clientele that has ranged from Jacqueline Bisset to Candice Bergen. Note that T&A shirts come in only one sleeve length and are then altered to fit, a ritual that takes only a few days, and costs £8 ($15). If you want custom shirts created from scratch, the made-to-measure service takes 10 to 12 weeks, and you must order at least a half dozen. Of course, the monograms are included. 71–72 Jermyn St., SW1. (© 020/7808-3000. Tube: Piccadilly Circus or Green Park.

## CUTTING EDGE

Currently, the most cutting-edge shopping area in London is on **Conduit Street,** W1, in Mayfair (Tube: Oxford Circus). Once known for its dowdy airline offices, it is now London's smartest fashion street. Trendy shops are opening between Regent Street and the "blue-chip" boutiques of New Bond Street. Current stars include **Vivienne Westwood,** 44 Conduit St., W1 (© 020/7439-1109), who has left her punk origins behind and is now the grande dame of English fashion. See below for her flagship store. **Krizia,** 24 Conduit St., W1 (© 020/7491-4987), the fashion rage of Rome since the 1950s, displays not only Krizia's clothing lines but her luxury home goods as well.

For muted fashion elegance, **Yohji Yamamoto,** 14–15 Conduit St., W1 (© 020/7491-4129), is hard to beat, and **Issey Miyake,** 52 Conduit St., W1 (© 020/7349-3300), is the Japanese master of minimalism.

**Accessorize** *Value*   This aptly named store is often packed with women who have an eye for bargains but want top-notch style. The store stays abreast of the latest fads and trends, especially in evening bags, which range from antique to

## The Comeback of Carnaby Street

What happened to Carnaby Street? A faded echo left over from the Swinging '60s? That was true for a long time. But Carnaby is rising again. A new influx of talented designers and offbeat shops are popping up not only on Carnaby but along its offshoot streets—Newburgh, Foubert's Place, Kingly Street, Marlborough Court, and Lowndes Court. Innovative boutiques seem to open each week behind small Georgian shop fronts.

Among the zillions of shops are such favorites as **Mikey,** 26 Carnaby St., W1 (✆ 020/7437-1101), London's pioneering jewelry shop, which has chosen Carnaby Street for its flagship store. **Lambretta Clothing,** 29 Carnaby St., W1 (✆ 020/7437-7078), retains the mod lifestyle philosophy and has launched a range of casual wear for men and footwear for men and women. The line has a retro feel, but uses the latest fibers and fabric finishes of today. **All Saints,** 1 Great Titchfield St., W1 (✆ 020/7323-3883), is the creation of noted designer Stuart Trevor, one of the most innovative British menswear designers.

To reach the stores above, take the Tube to Oxford Circus.

high fashion. All sorts of treasures are stocked here, everything from hologram-flecked nail polish to silk scarves. 123A Kensington High St., W8. ✆ 020/7937-1433. Tube: Kensington High St.

**Anya Hindmarch**    Although her fashionable bags are sold at Harvey Nichols, Liberty, Harrods, and throughout the U.S. and Europe, this is the only place to see the complete range of Anya Hindmarch's handbags, wallets, purses, and key holders. Smaller items start at £45 ($83), whereas handbag prices start at £200 ($370), with alligator being the most expensive. There's a limited custom-made service; bring in your fabric if you want a bag to match. 15–17 Pont St., SW3. ✆ 020/7838-9177. Tube: Sloane Sq. or Knightsbridge.

**Browns** ★★    This is the only place in London to find the designs of Alexander McQueen, head of the House of Givenchy in Paris and one of the fashion industry's stars. Producing his own cottons, silks, and plastics, McQueen creates revealing, feminine women's couture and ready-to-wear, and has started a menswear line. McQueen made his reputation creating shock-value apparel that was more photographed than worn. But recently, fashion critics have called his new outfits "consumer friendly." Browns has introduced "Browns Living," an eclectic array of lifestyle products. 23–27 S. Molton St., W1. ✆ 020/7491-7833. Tube: Bond St.

**Egg**    This shop is hot, hot, hot with fashionistas. It features imaginatively designed, contemporary clothing by Indian textile designer Asha Sarabhai and knitwear by Eskandar. Designs, created from handmade textiles at a workshop in India, range from everyday dresses to hand-embroidered silk coats. Crafts and ceramics are also available. Closed Sunday and Monday. 36 Kinnerton St., SW1. ✆ 020/7235-9315. Tube: Hyde Park Corner or Knightsbridge.

**H&M Hennes**    Here are copies of hot-off-the-catwalk fashions at affordable prices. While the quality isn't to brag about, the prices are. For disposable cutting-edge fashion, you can't beat it. 261 Regent St., W1. ✆ 020/7493-4004. Tube: Oxford Circus.

**Joseph**    Joseph Ettedgui, a fashion retailer born in Casablanca, is a maverick in the fashion world. He's known for his daring designs and his ability to attract some of the most talented designers in the business to work with him. The stretch jeans with flair ankles are the label's best-selling items.

The most complete collection of Joseph Ettedgui clothing anywhere, with clothes for both men and women (including suits, knitwear, suede, and leather clothing), is available within the two largest branches of his empire. Both carry signs that simply say "Joseph" on the front, and they're located at 23 Old Bond St., W1. ℂ **020/7629-3713.** Tube: Green Park and at 26 Sloane St., SW1X. ℂ 020/7235-1991. Tube: Knightsbridge.

Three smaller branches of Joseph lie clustered close to one another, each of them within a very short walk of the South Kensington Tube stop. They're at 315 Brompton Rd., SW3 (ℂ 020/7225-3335); and 77 Fulham Rd., SW4 (ℂ 020/7823-9500). Close by, and focusing only on menswear, is a Joseph boutique at 74 Sloane Ave., SW3 (ℂ 020/7591-0808). Newest of all is a branch in Notting Hill selling clothes for men and women at 236 Westbourne Grove, W11 (ℂ 0207/243-9920; Tube: Notting Hill Gate). See the body of this review for various store addresses, telephone numbers, and nearby Tube stops.

**The Library**    Despite its name, this is a showcase for some of the best young designers for men. It's very cutting edge without dipping into the extremes of male fashion. The Library is famous for having introduced Helmut Lang to London, and now features such designers as Fabrizio del Carlo, Kostas Murkudis, and even Alexander McQueen. 268 Brompton Rd., SW3. ℂ **020/7589-6569.** Tube: S. Kensington.

**Miss Selfridge** *Kids*    This is a hip young women's clothing and accessory store that sells its own cosmetic brand, Kiss & Make-Up. For pajama parties, there is a wide selection of sexy cotton pajamas. There is also a large array of products you can't live without, like two-toned nail polish and shimmery hair mascara. After, head for the "chill-out" zone, where patrons get comfy on sofas and listen to the latest tunes. 36–38 Great Castle St., W8. ℂ **020/7927-0214.** Tube: Charing Cross.

**Paul Smith's Westbourne House**    This shop was converted from a stately three-story Edwardian town house into a showcase for the clothing of Paul Smith, whose well-made ready-to-wear men's (and to a lesser extent, women's and children's) clothing defies the preconceptions of Savile Row tailors who believe that only custom-made garments will fit well. Preferred colors, with occasional exceptions, include grays, browns, and blacks, though there is a medley of velvet prints inspired by Carnaby Street in the 1960s. Look for women's clothes and accessories on the building's street level, men's clothes and accessories on the two floors above street level. 122 Kensington Park Rd., W11. ℂ **020/7727-3553.** Tube: Notting Hill Gate.

**Vivienne Westwood** ★★    No one in British fashion is hotter than the unstoppable Vivienne Westwood. While it's possible to purchase some Westwood pieces around the world, her U.K. shops are the best places to find her full range of fashion designs. The flagship location (on Davies St.) concentrates on her couture line, known as the Gold Label. One of the U.K.'s most watched designers, Westwood creates jackets, skirts, trousers, blouses, dresses, and evening dresses that manage to be elegant, alluring, and stylish all at the same time. Many of the fabrics and accessories for her garments are made in Britain, and at least some of them are crafted and tailored there as well. Westwood came out with her own fragrance in 1997. Westwood's World's End line of clothing focuses on casual designs for youthful bodies, including T-shirts, jeans, and sportswear. 6 Davies St., W1. ℂ 020/7629-3757. Tube: Bond St.; World's End branch: 430 King's Rd., SW3 ℂ 020/7352-6551. Tube: Sloane Sq.

## VINTAGE & SECONDHAND

Note that there's no VAT refund on used clothing.

**Annie's Vintage Costume and Textiles** *Finds*   This shop concentrates on carefully preserved dresses from the 1920s and 1930s, but also has a range of clothing and textiles from the 1880s through the 1960s. A 1920s fully beaded dress will run you about £300 ($555), but there are scarves for £15 ($28), camisoles for £30 ($56), and a range of exceptional pieces priced between £50 and £60 ($93–$111). Clothing is located on the main floor; textiles, including old lace, bed linens, and tapestries, are upstairs. 12 Camden Passage, N1. ℂ 020/ 7359-0796. Tube: Northern Line to Angel.

**Pandora** *Value*   A London institution since the 1940s, Pandora stands in fashionable Knightsbridge, a stone's throw from Harrods. Several times a week, chauffeurs drive up with bundles packed anonymously by England's gentry. One woman voted best-dressed at the Ascot Horse Races several years ago was wearing a secondhand dress acquired here. Prices are generally one-third to one-half the retail value. Chanel and Anne Klein are among the designers represented. Outfits are usually no more than two seasons old. 16–22 Cheval Place, SW7. ℂ 020/ 7589-5289. Tube: Knightsbridge.

**Pop Boutique**   For the best in original streetwear from the 1950s, 1960s, and 1970s, this clothing store is tops. Right next to the chic Covent Garden Hotel, it sells fabulous vintage wear at affordable prices: Leather jackets that would run in the hundreds in the vintage shops of downtown New York go for as little as £45 ($83) here. 6 Monmouth St., WC2. ℂ 020/7497-5262. Tube: Covent Garden.

**Steinberg & Tolkien**   London's leading dealer in vintage costume jewelry and clothing also offers some used designer clothing that's not old enough to be vintage but is prime for collectors; other pieces are merely secondhand designer thrills. 193 King's Rd., SW3. ℂ 020/7376-3660. Tube: Sloane Sq.

## FILOFAX

All major department stores sell Filofax supplies, but for the full range (and a shopping experience), check out a Filofax store. They also have good sales; calendars for the next year go on sale very early the previous year (about 10 months in advance), so you can stock up and save.

**The Filofax Centre**   Go to the Conduit Street shop if you can; it stocks the entire range of inserts and books at prices that will floor you: half what you pay in the U.S. 21 Conduit St., W1. ℂ 020/7499-0457. Tube: Oxford Circus. Also at 69 Neal St., WC2. ℂ 020/7836-1977. Tube: Covent Garden.

## FOOD

English food has come a long way, and it's worth enjoying and bringing home. Don't miss the Food Halls in Harrods. Consider the Fifth Floor at Harvey Nicks if Harrods is too crowded—it isn't the same, but it'll do. Also, check out the internationally famous Fortnum & Mason food emporium. See "The Department Stores," above for descriptions, plus other options.

**Charbonnel et Walker** ✦   Charbonnel et Walker is famous for its hot chocolate in winter (buy it by the tin) and its chocolate-covered strawberries that are available whenever strawberries are available or in season. The company will send messages of thanks or love spelled out on the chocolates themselves. Ready-made presentation boxes are also available. 1 The Royal Arcade, 28 Old Bond St., W1. © 020/7491-0939. Tube: Green Park.

**Neal's Yard Dairy** Specializing in British and Irish cheeses, this shop occupies the very photogenic premises of what was originally built as a warehouse for the food stalls at Covent Garden. Today, you'll see a staggering selection of artisan cheeses, including cloth-bound cheddars and a wide selection of mild farmer's cheeses, set in big display windows behind an antique, dark-blue Victorian facade. There are also olive oils, breads, fresh produce, and a lot of the fixings of a picnic. 17 Shorts Gardens, WC2. © 020/7240-5700. Tube: Covent Garden.

## GIFTS & SOUVENIRS
**Asprey & Garrard** This is as well-known and well-respected a name in luxury gift giving as anything you're likely to find in all of Britain, with a clientele that includes the likes of the Sultan of Brunei and Queen Elizabeth. Scattered over four floors of a dignified Victorian building, you'll find antiques, porcelain, leather goods, crystal, clocks, and enough unusual objects of dignified elegance to stock an entire English country house. 167 New Bond St., W1. © 020/7493-6767. Tube: Green Park.

**Muji** An emporium for Japanese wares, this store is known for its bargain offerings. Among its merchandise, the frugal shopper will find everything from "simple and functional chic" clothing to flatware, most of it in avant-garde, minimalist styles that are completely devoid of any traditional or baroque influences of Olde England. The bath soaps are a delight, coming in such unusual scents as grapefruit and mandarin orange. Funky umbrellas and a host of other ever-changing wares tempt shoppers. 157 Kensington High St., W8. © 020/7323-2208. Tube: High St. Kensington.

## HANDBAGS
**Bill Amberg's** Most famous for his logo-free classic handbags, Amberg has opened his own shop and expanded his line to include luggage, picture frames, and furniture. Fans of Amberg's designs include Donna Karan, Romeo Gigli, Jerry Hall, and Christy Turlington. Given those celebrity clients, fashion-conscious shoppers may consider the £40 to £400 ($74–$740) price range of most items a steal. 10 Chepstow Rd., W2. © 020/7727-3560. Tube: Notting Hill Gate.

**Lulu Guinness** This self-taught British handbag designer, who launched her business in 1989, is known as the finest such designer in London. Many of the world's greatest retail outlets, such as Neiman Marcus, sell her handbags. Her signature handbags, such as the "Florist Basket" and the "House Bag," are immortalized in the fashion collection at the Victoria and Albert Museum. Seen about London carrying Lulu Guinness handbags are such celebrities as Madonna and Elizabeth Hurley. 3 Ellis St., SW1. © 020/7823-4828. Tube: Sloane Sq.

## HOME DESIGN, FURNISHINGS & HOUSEWARES
Also see "Jewelry," and "Art & Crafts."

**The Conran Shop** You'll find Sir Terence Conran's high style at reasonable prices at this outlet. The fashion press cites Conran as "the director" of British middle-class taste since the 1960s. This place is great for gifts, home furnishings, and tabletop ware—or just for gawking. Michelin House, 81 Fulham Rd., SW3. © 020/7589-7401. Tube: S. Kensington.

**The Couverture Shop**   This is an emporium of the unexpected, with original products for both adults and children as well as the home. It's strongest on what they call "bedroom must-haves," embracing bed linen, throws, cushions, and the like. Vintage finds along with designer pieces—often handmade—are also sold. 310 King's Rd., SW3. ⓒ 020/7795-1200. Tube: Sloane Sq.

**David Linley Furniture** ★★★   This is a showcase for the remarkable furniture of Viscount Linley, son of the late Princess Margaret. He designs pieces of furniture of a complex nature. For example, one of his designs, called the Apsley House Desk, is built in French walnut with ebony and nickel-plated detailing, and contains secret drawers. The desk is rimmed with a miniature of the neoclassical Apsley House. Linley's clients include the likes of Elton John, Mick Jagger, and Nina Campbell. The director at the Victoria and Albert Museum predicts that Linley's furnishings and accessories will become "the antiques of the future." 60 Pimlico Rd., SW1. ⓒ 020/7730-7300. Tube: Sloane Sq.

**Designers Guild**   After more than 3 decades in business, creative director Tricia Guild and her young designers still lead the pack in all that's bright and whimsical. They are often copied but never outdone. There's an exclusive line of handmade furniture and accessories at the no. 267–271 location, and wallpaper and more than 2,000 fabrics at the neighboring no. 275–277 shop. The colors remain vivid forever, and the designs are always irreverent. Also available are children's accessories, toys, crockery, and cutlery. 267–271 and 275–277 King's Rd., SW3. ⓒ 020/7351-5775. Tube: Sloane Sq.

**Purves & Purves**   This store has a varied collection of modern furniture from Britain and the Continent. Many designers make individual pieces that are sold here. The light and airy store displays this eye-catching array of furniture, lighting, fabrics, rugs, and beds. 220 Tottenham Court Rd., W1. ⓒ 020/7580-8223. Tube: Goodge St. or Tottenham Court Rd.

**Summerill & Bishop**   Some of London's most sophisticated kitchenware is sold here, items that may not be available in your hometown store. The range is from Edward S. Wohl's charming bird's-eye maple breadboards to John Julian Sainsbury's black granite mortar with a stainless steel handled pestle. Some of the top designers in Britain created the unusual ware at this outlet. 100 Portland Rd., Holland Park W11. ⓒ 020/7221-4566. Tube: Holland Park.

## JEWELRY

**Asprey & Garrard**   Previously known as Garrard & Co., this recently merged jeweler specializes in both antique and modern jewelry, and silverware. The in-house designers also produce pieces to order and do repairs. You can have a pair of pearl earrings or silver cufflinks for a mere £60 ($111)—but the prices go nowhere but up from there. 167 New Bond St., W1. ⓒ 020/7493-6767. Tube: Green Park.

**Lesley Craze Gallery/Craze 2/C2 Plus**   This complex has developed a reputation as a showcase of the best contemporary British jewelry and textile design. The gallery shop focuses on precious metals and includes pieces by such renowned designers as Wendy Ramshaw. Prices start at £60 ($111). Craze 2 features costume jewelry in materials ranging from bronze to paper, with prices starting at £25 ($46). C2 Plus features contemporary textile designs, including wall hangings, scarves, and ties by artists such as Jo Barker, Dawn DuPree, and Victoria Richards. 34 Clerkenwell Green, EC1. ⓒ 020/7608-0393 (Gallery), ⓒ 020/7251-0381 (Craze 2), ⓒ 020/7251-9200 (C2 Plus). Tube: Farringdon.

**Sanford Brothers Ltd.**    In business since 1923, this family firm sells all styles of jewelry (Victorian through modern), silver, and a fine selection of clocks and watches. Old Elizabeth Houses, 3 Holborn Bars, EC1. ℂ 020/7405-2352. Tube: Chancery Lane.

## LINENS

**Irish Linen Company**    This royal-warrant boutique carries items crafted of Irish linen, including hand-embroidered handkerchiefs and bed and table linens. 35–36 Burlington Arcade, W1. ℂ 020/7493-8949. Tube: Green Park or Piccadilly Circus.

## LINGERIE

**Bradley's** ⭐    Bradley's is the best-known lingerie store in London; members of the royal family shop here. Established in the 1950s and very fashionable today, Bradley's fits all sizes in silk, cotton, lace, poly-cotton, or whatever else you might desire. 57 Knightsbridge, SW1. ℂ 020/7235-2902. Tube: Knightsbridge or Hyde Park Corner.

## LUGGAGE

**Mulberry Company**    This flagship store offers a complete line of the town's most cutting-edge designer luggage. Their signature grosgrain luggage begins at £195 ($361). Mulberry is also earning a name in fashion for its English country-style ready-to-wear clothes for men and women. It also carries fashionable furnishings and accessories for the home, including throws and cushions in chenille and damask. 11–12 Gees Court, W1. ℂ 020/7493-2546. Tube: Bond St.

## MUSEUM SHOPS

**Victoria and Albert Museum Gift Shop** ⭐⭐    This is the best museum shop in London—indeed, one of the best in the world. It sells cards, a fabulous selection of art books, and the usual items, along with reproductions from the design museum archives. Cromwell Rd., SW7. ℂ 020/7942-2696. Tube: S. Kensington.

## MUSIC

Collectors should browse **Notting Hill,** because there are a handful of good shops near the Notting Hill Gate Tube stop. Also browse **Soho** in the Wardour Street area, near the Tottenham Court Road Tube stop. Sometimes dealers show up at Covent Garden on the weekends.

In addition to the two below, the ubiquitous **Our Price** chain is worth checking out for current chart-toppers at great prices.

**Tower Records**    Attracting throngs in a neighborhood whose pedestrian traffic is almost overwhelming, this is one of the largest record and CD stores in Europe. Sprawling over four floors, it's practically a tourist attraction in its own right. In addition to a huge selection of music, you'll find everything that's on the cutting edge of music technology. 1 Piccadilly Circus, W1. ℂ 020/7439-2500. Tube: Piccadilly Circus. Other locations throughout London.

**Virgin Megastore**    If a record has just been released—and if it's worth hearing in the first place—chances are this store carries it. It's like a giant musical grocery store. You get to hear many of the new releases on headphones at listening stations before making a purchase. Even rock stars come here to pick up new releases. A large selection of classical and jazz recordings is sold, as are computer software and video games. In between selecting your favorites, you can enjoy a coffee at the cafe or purchase an airline ticket from the Virgin Atlantic office. 14–16 Oxford St., W1. ℂ 020/7631-1234. Tube: Tottenham Court Rd. Also at King's Walk Shopping Centre, King's Rd., Chelsea, SW3. ℂ 020/7591-0957. Tube: Sloane Sq.

## SHOES

Also see **DAKS** in "The Department Stores," above.

**Koko**    This is a sprawling, hip, trendy, style-conscious shop that sells footwear, and only footwear, from three different vendors, the most famous and visible being Dr. Marten's. Dr. Marten's shoes have unisex punk-rock associations and you can expect lots of British rocker types trying on shoes around you. This store has the largest inventory of Doc Marten's in London. 9 Carnaby St., W1. ✆ 020/ 7734-8890. Tube: Oxford Circus.

**Natural Shoe Store**    A range of shoes for men and women is stocked in this shop, which also does repairs. The selection includes all comfort and quality footwear, from Birkenstock to the British classics. 21 Neal St., WC2. ✆ 020/7836-5254. Tube: Covent Garden.

**Office**    In spite of its dull name, this is a most unusual store for style-setters on a budget. Its imitations of some of the world's leading shoe designers have earned it the reputation of being the "Madame Tussaud's of footwear." All the shoe designers, from Kenneth Cole to Patrick Cox, get ripped off here. 107 Queensway, W2. ✆ 020/7792-4000. Tube: Queensway.

**Shelly's**    Shelly's flagship on Oxford Circus is the largest shoe store in London, selling footwear to fashionable young things and style-conscious individuals at affordable prices. They're famous for their Dr. Marten's, but there's much more. 266–268 Regent St., W1. ✆ 020/7287-0927. Tube: Oxford Circus. Other locations throughout London.

## SPORTING GOODS

**Harrods** (see "The Department Stores," above) has a surprising collection of sporting goods, including everything you'll need for a polo match.

**Lillywhites Ltd.** ✫✫✫    Europe's biggest and most famous sports store has floor after floor of sports clothing, equipment, and footwear. It also offers collections of fashionable leisurewear for men and women. 24–36 Lower Regent St., Piccadilly Circus, SW1. ✆ 0870/3339-600. Tube: Piccadilly Circus.

## STATIONERY & PAPER GOODS

**Paperchase**    This flagship store has three floors of paper products, including handmade paper, wrapping paper, ribbons, picture frames, and a huge selection of greeting cards. It's the best of its kind in London. 213 Tottenham Court Rd., W1. ✆ 020/7467-6200. Tube: Goodge St. or Tottenham Court Rd. Other locations throughout London.

## TEA

Of course, don't forget to visit **Fortnum & Mason** for tea as well (see "The Department Stores," above).

**The Tea House**    This shop sells everything associated with tea, tea drinking, and teatime. It boasts more than 70 quality teas and tisanes, including whole-fruit blends, the best tea of China (Gunpowder, and jasmine with flowers), India (Assam leaf, and choice Darjeeling), Japan (Genmaicha green), and Sri Lanka (pure Ceylon), plus such longtime favorite English blended teas as Earl Grey. The shop also offers novelty teapots and mugs. 15A Neal St., WC2. ✆ 020/7420-7539. Tube: Covent Garden.

## TOYS

**Hamleys**    This flagship is the finest toy shop in the world—more than 35,000 toys and games on seven floors of fun and magic. The huge selection includes soft, cuddly stuffed animals as well as dolls, radio-controlled cars, train sets, model kits, board games, outdoor toys, computer games, and more. 188–196 Regent St., W1. © 0870/333-2455. Tube: Oxford Circus. Also at Covent Garden and Heathrow Airport.

## TRAVEL SERVICES

**British Airways Travel Shop**    The retail flagship of British Airways offers worldwide travel and ticketing, as well as a range of services and shops, including a clinic for immunization, a pharmacy, a *bureau de change,* a passport and visa service, and a theater-booking desk. The ground floor sells luggage, guidebooks, maps, and other goods. Passengers who are carrying only hand baggage can check in here for a BA flight. Travel insurance, hotel reservations, and car rentals can also be arranged. 156 Regent St., W1. © 020/7491-4989. Tube: Piccadilly Circus or Oxford Circus.

## 5 Street & Flea Markets

If Mayfair stores are not your cup of tea, don't worry; you'll have more fun, and find a better bargain, at any of the city's street and flea markets.

**THE WEST END    Covent Garden Market** ⚜ (© **020/7836-9136;** Tube: Covent Garden), the most famous market in all of England, offers several markets daily from 9am to 6:30pm (we think it's most fun to come on Sun). It can be a little confusing until you dive in and explore. **Apple Market** is the bustling market in the courtyard, where traders sell—well, everything. Many of the items are what the English call collectible nostalgia: a wide array of glassware and ceramics, leather goods, toys, clothes, hats, and jewelry. Some of the merchandise is truly unusual. Many items are handmade, with some of the craftspeople selling their own wares—except on Mondays, when antiques dealers take over. Some goods are new, some are very old. Out back is **Jubilee Market** (© **020/ 7836-2139**), also an antiques market on Mondays. Tuesday to Sunday, it's sort of a fancy hippie market with cheap clothes and books. Out front there are a few tents of cheap stuff, except on Monday.

The indoor market section of Covent Garden Market (in a superbly restored hall) is one of the best shopping venues in London. Specialty shops sell fashions and herbs, gifts and toys, books and dollhouses, cigars, and much more. There are bookshops and branches of famous stores (Hamleys, The Body Shop), and prices are kept moderate.

**St. Martin–in-the-Fields Market** (Tube: Charing Cross) is good for teens and hipsters who don't want to trek all the way to Camden Market (see "North London," below) and are interested in imports from India and South America, crafts, and local football souvenirs. It's located near Trafalgar Square and Covent Garden; hours are Monday through Saturday from 11am to 5pm, and Sunday from noon to 5pm.

**Berwick Street Market** (Tube: Oxford Circus or Tottenham Court Rd.) may be the only street market in the world that's flanked by two rows of strip clubs, porno stores, and adult-movie dens. Don't let that put you off. Humming 6 days a week in the scarlet heart of Soho, this array of stalls and booths sells the best and cheapest fruit and vegetables in town. It also hawks ancient records, tapes, books, and old magazines, any of which may turn out to be a collector's item one day. It's open Monday through Saturday from 9am to 5pm.

On Sunday mornings along **Bayswater Road,** artists hang their work on the railings along the edge of Hyde Park and Kensington Gardens for more than

1.5km (1 mile). If the weather's right, start at Marble Arch and walk. You'll see the same thing on the railings of Green Park along Piccadilly on Saturday afternoon.

**NOTTING HILL   Portobello Market** *★★* (Tube: Notting Hill Gate) is a magnet for collectors of virtually anything. It's mainly a Saturday event, from 6am to 5pm. You needn't be here at the crack of dawn; 9am is fine. Once known mainly for fruit and vegetables (still sold throughout the week), in the past decades Portobello has become synonymous with antiques. But don't take the stallholder's word for it that the fiddle he's holding is a genuine Stradivarius left to him in the will of his Italian great-uncle; it might have been "nicked" from an East End pawnshop.

The market is divided into three major sections. The most crowded is the antiques section, running between Colville Road and Chepstow Villas to the south. (*Warning:* Be careful of pickpockets in this area.) The second section (and the oldest part) is the fruit and veg market, lying between Westway and Colville Road. In the third and final section, there's a flea market where Londoners sell bric-a-brac and lots of secondhand goods they didn't really want in the first place, but poking around this section still makes for interesting fun.

The serious collector can pick up a copy of a helpful official guide, *Saturday Antique Market: Portobello Road & Westbourne Grove,* published by the Portobello Antique Dealers Association. It lists where to find what, be it music boxes, lace, or 19th-century photographs.

*Note:* Some 90 antiques and art shops along Portobello Road are open during the week when the street market is closed. This is actually a better time for the serious collector to shop because you'll get more attention from dealers and you won't be distracted by the organ grinder.

**SOUTH BANK**   Open on Fridays only, New Caledonian Market is known as the **Bermondsey Market** because of its location on the corner of Long Lane and Bermondsey Street (Tube: London Bridge, then bus 78, or walk down Bermondsey St.). The market is at the east end, beginning at Tower Bridge Road. Only the most hopelessly addicted shopping junkies will go here. We have sadly watched this market decline year by year. Instead of a true antiques market, its vendors often sell newly manufactured stuff. If chipped crockery, dented tea kettles, and cheap glass are your thing, then head here. Otherwise, we'd recommend that you skip it. Many dealers come into London from the countryside. Prices are generally lower here than at Portobello and other markets. It gets under way at 5am—with the bargains gone by 9am—and closes at noon. Bring a "torch" (flashlight) if you go in the wee hours.

**NORTH LONDON**   If it's Wednesday or Saturday, it's time for **Camden Passage** (© 020/7359-0190; Tube: Northern Line to Angel) in Islington, where there's a very upscale antiques market. It starts in Camden Passage and sprawls into the streets behind. It's on Wednesday from 7am to 2pm, and Saturday from 8am to 4pm.

Don't confuse Camden Passage with Camden Market (very downtown). **Camden Market** (Tube: Camden Town) is for teens and others into body piercings, blue hair, and vintage clothing. Serious collectors of vintage may want to explore during the week, when the teen scene isn't quite so overwhelming. Market hours are from 9:30am to 5:30pm daily, with some parts opening at 10am.

# London After Dark

London's pulsating nightlife scene is the most vibrant in Europe. Although pubs still close at 11pm, the city is staying up later, and more and more clubs have extended partying into the wee hours.

London is on a real high right now, especially in terms of music and dance—much of the currently popular techno and electronica originated in London clubs. Youth culture prevails here, as downtown denizens flock to the clubs where pop-culture superstars are routinely spotted.

London nightlife is always in a state of flux. What's hot today probably just opened, and many clubs have the lifespan of fruit flies. At the time of this writing, **Groucho,** at 45 Dean St., W1 (© **020/7439-4685**), is still the *in* club, although it is members only. A few perennials, like Ronnie Scott's, are still favorites.

But London nightlife is not just about music and dance clubs. The city abounds with the world's best theater (sorry, New York!), loads of classical music, pubs oozing historic charm, and tons of other options for a night out.

## 1 The Play's the Thing: London's Theater Scene

Even more than New York, London is the theater capital of the world. Few things in London are as entertaining and rewarding as the theater. The number and variety of productions, and the standards of acting and directing, are unrivaled. The London stage accommodates both the traditional and the avant-garde and is, for the most part, accessible and reasonably affordable. The new Globe Theatre is an exciting addition to the theater scene. Because the Globe is also a sightseeing attraction, it's previewed in chapter 7, "Exploring London."

To find out what's on stage before you leave home, check www.officiallondon theatre.co.uk.

**TICKET AGENCIES**  If your heart is set on seeing a specific show, particularly a big hit, reserve way in advance through one of London's ticket agencies. You can check www.officiallondontheatre.co.uk to find out what will be on stage when you're in London. For tickets and information before you go, try **Global Tickets,** 234 W. 44th St., Suite 1000, New York, NY 10036 (© **800/223-6108** or 212/398-1468; www.keithprowse.com). Their London office (which operates under the name of both Global Tickets and First Call Tickets) is at the British Visitors Center, 1 Regent St., W1 V1PJ (© **020/7014-8550**), or at the Harrods ticket desk, 87–135 Brompton Rd. (© **020/7589-9109**), opposite the British Airways desk. They'll mail your tickets, fax a confirmation, or leave your tickets at the appropriate production's box office. Instant confirmations are immediately available for most shows. A booking and handling fee of up to 20% is added to the price of all tickets.

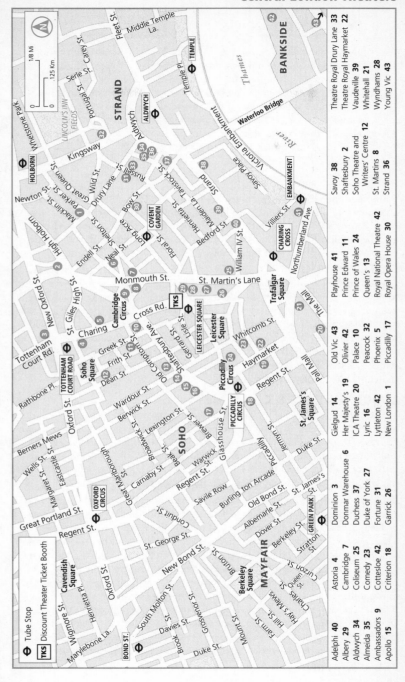

Theatre Royal Drury Lane **33**
Theatre Royal Haymarket **22**
Vaudeville **39**
Whitehall **21**
Wyndhams **28**
Young Vic **43**

Savoy **38**
Shaftesbury **2**
Soho Theatre and
Writers' Centre **12**
St. Martins **8**
Strand **36**

Playhouse **41**
Prince Edward **11**
Prince of Wales **24**
Queen's **13**
Royal National Theatre **42**
Royal Opera House **30**

Old Vic **43**
Olivier **42**
Palace **10**
Peacock **32**
Phoenix **5**
Piccadilly **17**

Gielgud **14**
Her Majesty's **19**
ICA Theatre **20**
Lyric **16**
Lyttleton **42**
New London **1**

Dominion **3**
Donmar Warehouse **6**
Duchess **37**
Duke of York **27**
Fortune **31**
Garrick **26**

Astoria **4**
Cambridge **7**
Coliseum **25**
Comedy **23**
Cottesloe **9**
Criterion **18**

Adelphi **40**
Albery **29**
Aldwych **34**
Almeida **35**
Ambassadors **9**
Apollo **15**

Ⓟ Tube Stop
TKS Discount Theater Ticket Booth

> ## Tips   Curtain Going Up!
>
> Prices for shows vary from £18 to £70 ($33–$130), depending on the theater and the seat. Matinees, performed Tuesday through Saturday, are cheaper than evening performances. Evening performances begin between 7:30 and 8:30pm, midweek matinees at 2:30 or 3pm, and Saturday matinees at 5:45pm. West End theaters are closed Sundays.
>
> Many theaters accept telephone bookings at regular prices with a credit card. They'll hold your tickets for you at the box office, where you pick them up at show time with a credit card.

Another option is **Theatre Direct International (TDI)** (✆ **800/334-8457,** U.S. only). TDI specializes in providing London fringe theater tickets, but also has tickets to major productions, including those at the Royal National Theatre and the Barbican. The service allows you to arrive in London with your tickets or have them held for you at the box office.

**GALLERY & DISCOUNT TICKETS**   Sometimes gallery seats (the cheapest) are sold on the day of the performance. Head to the box office early in the day to purchase these tickets and, since these are not reserved seats, return an hour before the performance to grab good seats. Many theaters offer reduced-price tickets to students on a standby basis. When available, these tickets are sold 30 minutes before curtain. Line up early for popular shows, as standby tickets get snapped up quickly. Call the theater directly to find out if gallery, discount, or standby tickets are offered for a particular show. Of course, you'll need a valid student ID for student discounts.

## MAJOR THEATERS & COMPANIES

We have listed some of the most popular theaters and companies below. To find out what's on currently in all of the major and fringe theaters, pick up *Time Out London, Where,* a London daily newspaper, or "The Official London Theatre Guide" pamphlet (online at www.officiallondontheatre.co.uk), available at ticket brokers and all West End theaters.

**Barbican Theatre—Royal Shakespeare Company**   The Barbican is the London home of the Royal Shakespeare Company, one of the world's finest theater companies. The core of its repertoire remains, of course, the plays of William Shakespeare. It also presents a wide-ranging program in its two theaters. Three productions are in repertory each week in the Barbican Theatre—a 2,000-seat main auditorium with excellent sight lines throughout, thanks to a raked orchestra. The Pit, a small studio space, is where the company's new writing is presented. The Royal Shakespeare Company performs both here and at Stratford-upon-Avon. It is in residence in London during the winter months; in the summer, it tours in England and abroad. For more information on the company and its current productions, check **www.rsc.org.uk.** In the Barbican Centre, Silk St., Barbican, EC2Y. ✆ **0870/609-1110.** Barbican Theatre £5–£40 ($9.25–$74). The Pit £7–£24 ($13–$44) matinees and evening performances. Box office daily 9am–8pm. Tube: Barbican or Moorgate.

**Open-Air Theatre**   This outdoor theater is in Regent's Park; the setting is idyllic, and both seating and acoustics are excellent. Presentations are mainly of Shakespeare, usually in period costume. Its theater bar, the longest in London, serves both drink and food. In the case of a rained-out performance, tickets are given for another date. The season runs from June to mid-September, Monday through Saturday at 8pm, plus Wednesday, Thursday, and Saturday matinees at 2:30pm. Inner Circle, Regent's Park, NW1. ℂ 08700/601811. Tickets £8.50–£25 ($16–$46). Tube: Baker St.

**Royal Court Theatre**    This theater has always been a leader in producing provocative, cutting-edge, new drama. In the 1950s, it staged the plays of the angry young men, notably John Osborne's then-sensational *Look Back in Anger;* earlier it debuted the plays of George Bernard Shaw. A recent work was *The Beauty Queen of Leenane,* which won a Tony on Broadway. The theater is home to the English Stage Company, formed to promote serious stage writing. Sloane Sq., SW1. ℂ 020/7565-5000. www.royalcourttheatre.com. Tickets £7.50–£28 ($14–$51); call for the latest information. Box office 10am–6pm. Tube: Sloane Sq.

**Royal National Theatre**    Home to one of the world's greatest stage companies, the Royal National Theatre is not one but three theaters—the Olivier, reminiscent of a Greek amphitheater with its open stage; the more traditional Lyttelton; and the Cottesloe, with its flexible stage and seating. The National presents the finest in world theater, from classic drama to award-winning new plays, including comedies, musicals, and shows for young people. A choice of at least six plays is offered at any one time. It's also a full-time theater center, with an amazing selection of bars, cafes, restaurants, free foyer music and exhibitions, short early-evening performances, bookshops, backstage tours, riverside walks, and terraces. You can have a three-course meal in Mezzanine, the National's restaurant; enjoy a light meal in the brasserie-style Terrace cafe; or have a snack in one of the coffee bars. South Bank, SE1. ℂ 020/7452-3000. www.nt-online.org. Tickets £11–£40 ($20–$74); midweek matinees, Sat matinees, and previews cost less. Tube: Waterloo, Embankment, or Charing Cross.

**Shakespeare's Globe Theatre**    In May 1997, the new Globe Theatre—a replica of the Elizabethan original, thatched roof and all—staged its first slate of

---

*Value*  **Ticket Bargains**

The **Society of London Theatre** (ℂ 020/7557-6700) operates the tkts booth in Leicester Square (see the "Central London Theaters" map on p. 295 for the location), where same-day tickets for many shows are available at half price or 25% off, plus a £2.50 ($4.65) service charge. tkts also sells full-price same-day tickets for shows that are not offering half-price or 25%-off tickets. In addition, the booth often offers a limited number of seats for shows that are usually sold out. Tickets are available for any of 55 theaters, including the English National Opera and the Royal Opera House. All major credit and debit cards are accepted. Tickets (limited to four per person) are sold only on the day of performance. You cannot return tickets. Hours are Monday through Friday from 10am to 6pm. We prefer this ticket agency to the others that populate Leicester Square. Some of the other agencies might offer you a legitimate discount, but over the years readers have lodged dozens of complaints that their so-called discount tickets turned out to be more expensive than tickets sold at the theater box office. Exercise caution when purchasing tickets at other booths.

plays (*Henry V* and *A Winter's Tale*) yards away from the site of the 16th-century theater where the Bard originally staged his work.

Productions vary in style and setting; not all are performed in Elizabethan costume. In keeping with the historic setting, no lighting is focused just on the stage, but floodlighting is used during evening performances to replicate daylight in the theater—Elizabethan performances took place in the afternoon. Theater-goers sit on wooden benches of yore—in thatch-roofed galleries, no less—but these days you can rent a cushion to make yourself more comfortable. About 500 "groundlings" can stand in the uncovered yard around the stage, just as they did when the Bard was here. Mark Rylance, the artistic director of the Globe, wanted the theatergoing experience to be as authentic as possible—he told the press he'd be delighted if the audience threw fruit at the actors, as they did in Shakespeare's time.

From May to September, the company intends to hold performances Tuesday through Saturday at 2 and 7pm. There will be a limited winter schedule. In any season, the schedule may be affected by weather because this is an outdoor theater. Performances last 2½ to 4 hours, depending on the play.

For details on the exhibition that tells the story of the painstaking re-creation of the Globe, as well as guided tours of the theater, see p. 251. New Globe Walk, Bankside, SE1. ℂ **020/7902-1400**. Box office: ℂ 020/7902-1401. http://shakespeares-globe.org. Tickets £5 ($9.25) for groundlings, £11–£29 ($20–$54) for gallery seats. Exhibition tickets £8 ($15) adults, £6.50 ($12) seniors and students, £5 ($9.25) ages 5–15. Tube: Mansion House or Blackfriars.

**Theatre Royal Drury Lane**    Drury Lane is one of London's oldest and most prestigious theaters, crammed with tradition—not all of it respectable. This, the fourth theater on this site, dates from 1812; the first was built in 1663. Nell Gwynne, the rough-tongued cockney lass who became Charles II's mistress, used to sell oranges under the long colonnade in front. Nearly every star of London theater has taken the stage here at some time. It has a wide-open repertoire but leans toward musicals, especially long-running hits. Guided tours of the backstage area and the front of the house are given most days at 2:15 and 4:45pm. Call ℂ **020/7494-5091** for more information. Catherine St., Covent Garden, WC2. ℂ **020/7494-5000**. Tickets £9–£58 ($17–$107). Box office Mon–Sat 10am–8pm. Evening performances Mon–Sat 8pm; matinees Wed and Sat 3pm. Tube: Covent Garden.

## FRINGE THEATER

Some of the best theater in London is performed on the "fringe"—at the dozens of theaters devoted to alternative plays, revivals, contemporary dramas, and musicals. These shows are usually more adventurous than established West End productions; they are also consistently lower in price. Expect to pay from £10 to £30 ($19–$56). Most offer discounted seats to students and seniors.

Fringe theaters are scattered around London. Check the weekly listings in *Time Out* for schedules and show times. Some of the more popular and centrally located theaters are listed below; call for details on current productions. Also check www.officiallondontheatre.co.uk and www.londontheatre.co.uk for current fringe show schedules and descriptions.

**Almeida Theatre**    The Almeida is known for its adventurous stagings of new and classic plays. The theater's legendary status is validated by consistently good productions at lower-than-average prices. Among the recent celebrated productions have been *Hamlet* with Ralph Fiennes and *Medea* with Dame Diana Rigg. Performances are usually held Monday through Saturday. The Almeida is also home to the Festival of Contemporary Music (also called the Almeida Opera) from mid-June to mid-July, featuring everything from atonal jazz to 12-tone chamber orchestra pieces. Almeida St., N1. ✆ 020/7359-4404. Tickets £15–£27 ($28–$50). Box office Mon–Sat 10am–6pm. Tube: Northern Line to Angel or Victoria Line to Highbury & Islington.

**The Gate**    This tiny room above a Notting Hill pub is one of the best alternative stages in London. Popular with local cognoscenti, the theater specializes in translated works by foreign playwrights. Performances are held Monday through Saturday at 7:30pm. Call for shows and times. In the Prince Albert Pub, 11 Pembridge Rd., Notting Hill, W11. ✆ 020/7229-0706. Tickets £7–£14 ($13–$26). Box office Mon–Fri 10am–6pm. Tube: Notting Hill Gate.

**ICA Theatre**    In addition to a cinema, cafe, bar, bookshop, and galleries, the Institute of Contemporary Arts (ICA) boasts one of London's top experimental theaters. The government-subsidized productions are usually of high quality. Bar hours are Tuesday through Saturday from noon to 1am, Sunday and Monday from noon to 11pm. Galleries are open daily from noon to 7:30pm. The Mall, SW1. ✆ 020/7930-3647. Tickets £6.50–£15 ($12–$28). Box office daily noon–9:30pm. Tube: Charing Cross or Piccadilly Circus.

**The King's Head**    London's most famous fringe locale, the King's Head is also the city's oldest pub-theater. Despite its tiny stage, the theater is heavy on musicals; several have gone on to become successful West End productions. Matinees are held on Saturday and Sunday at 3:30pm. Evening performances are held Tuesday through Saturday at 8pm. 115 Upper St., N1. ✆ 020/7226-1916. Tickets £13–£18 ($23–$32). Box office Mon–Fri 10am–8pm; Sat 10:30am–8pm; Sun 11am–6pm. Tube: Northern Line to Angel.

**Young Vic** *Kids*    In two showrooms, the Young Vic presents classical and modern plays in the round for theatergoers of all ages and backgrounds, but primarily caters to young adults. Recent productions have included Shakespeare, Ibsen, Arthur Miller, and specially commissioned plays for children. Performances are usually Monday through Saturday at 7:30pm, with a Saturday matinee at 2 or 2:30pm, but call for specific times as the schedule has been known to change. 66 The Cut, Waterloo, SE1. ✆ 020/7928-6363. Tickets £20–£25 ($37–$46) adults, £15–£20 ($28–$37) seniors, £10 ($19) students and children. Box office Mon–Sat 10am–8pm. Tube: Waterloo or Southwark.

## 2 Classical Music, Dance & Opera

Currently, London supports five major orchestras—the London Symphony Orchestra (www.lso.co.uk), the Royal Philharmonic (www.rpo.co.uk), the London Philharmonic Orchestra (www.lpo.co.uk), the BBC Symphony (www.bbc.co.uk/orchestras/so), and the BBC Philharmonic (www.bbc.co.uk/orchestras/philharmonic)—plus several choirs and operas, and many smaller chamber groups and historic-instrument ensembles. In addition to the big stars listed above, also look for the London Sinfonietta (www.londonsinfonietta.org.uk), a contemporary-music ensemble; the English Chamber Orchestra (www.englishchamberorchestra.co.uk); and the Academy of St. Martin-in-the-Fields (www.academysmif.co.uk). Concerts for many of the groups mentioned above are presented, with exceptions, in the South Bank Arts Centre or the Barbican. For smaller recitals, venues include Wigmore Hall and St. John's Smith Square. Check the websites to find out where and when the orchestras and ensembles listed here are performing.

**Barbican Centre (home of the London Symphony Orchestra & more)**
The largest art and exhibition center in Western Europe, the roomy and comfortable Barbican complex is the perfect setting for enjoying music and theater. Barbican Hall is the permanent home address of the London Symphony Orchestra, as well as host to visiting orchestras and performers of all styles, from classical to jazz, folk, and world music.

In addition to its hall and two theaters, Barbican Centre encompasses the Barbican Art Gallery, the Concourse Gallery, and foyer exhibition spaces; Cinemas One and Two, which show recently released mainstream films and film series; the Barbican Library, a general lending library that places a strong emphasis on the arts; the Conservatory, one of London's largest greenhouses; and restaurants, cafes, and bars. Silk St., the City, EC2. (C) 020/7638-8891. www.barbican.org.uk. Tickets £8–£42 ($15–$78). Box office daily 9am–8pm. Tube: Barbican or Moorgate.

**Kenwood Lakeside Concerts**    These band and orchestral concerts on the north side of Hampstead Heath have been a British tradition for some 50 years. In recent years, laser shows and fireworks have been added to a repertoire that includes everything from rousing versions of the *1812 Overture* to jazz to operas such as *Carmen*. The final concert of the season always features some of the "Pomp and Circumstance" marches of Sir Edward Elgar. Music drifts across the lake to serenade wine-and-cheese parties on the grass. Concerts take place from July to early September, Saturday at 7:30pm. Kenwood, Hampstead Lane, Hampstead Heath, London NW3 7JR. (C) 020/7413-1443. Tickets for adults £11 ($20) for seats on the grass lawn, £13–£18 ($24–$33) for reserved deck chairs. Reductions of 12.5% for students and persons over 60. Box office Mon–Sat 9:30am–6:30pm. Tube: Northern Line to Golders Green or Archway, then bus no. 210.

**London Coliseum (home of the English National Opera)**    Built in 1904 as a variety theater and converted into an opera house in 1968, the London Coliseum is the city's largest theater. One of two national opera companies, the English National Opera performs a range of works here, from classics to Gilbert and Sullivan to new experimental works. All performances are in English. The Opera presents a repertory of 18 to 20 productions 5 or 6 nights a week for 10 months of the year (the theater is dark mid-July to mid-September). The theater also hosts touring companies. Although balcony seats are cheaper, many visitors seem to prefer the upper circle or dress circle. London Coliseum, St. Martin's Lane, WC2. (C) 020/7632-8300. Tickets £5–£12 ($9.25–$22) balcony, £20–£70 ($37–$130) upper or dress circle or stalls; about 100 discount balcony tickets sold on the day of performance from 10am. Box office Mon–Sat 10am–8pm. Tube: Charing Cross or Leicester Sq.

**Royal Albert Hall**    Opened in 1871 and dedicated to the memory of Victoria's consort, Prince Albert, this circular building holds one of the world's most famous auditoriums. With a seating capacity of 5,200, it's a popular place to hear music by stars. Occasional sporting events (especially boxing) figure strongly here, too.

Since 1941, the hall has hosted the BBC Henry Wood Promenade Concerts, known as "The Proms," an annual series that lasts for 8 weeks between mid-July and mid-September. The Proms, incorporating a medley of rousing, mostly British orchestral music, have been a British tradition since 1895. Although most of the audience occupies reserved seats, true aficionados usually opt for standing room in the orchestra pit, with close-up views of the musicians on stage. Newly commissioned works are often premiered here. The final evening is the most traditional; the rousing favorites "Jerusalem" or "Land of Hope and Glory" echo through the hall. Recently, the hall has seen performances by Liza Minnelli, an avant-garde production of Bizet's *Carmen,* orchestral and symphonic works from orchestras visiting from other cities, lots of British and European pop, and the London production of *Cirque du Soleil.* Kensington Gore, SW7 2AP. © 020/7589-8212. Tickets £18–£52 ($33–$96), depending on the event. Box office daily 9am–9pm. Tube: S. Kensington.

**Royal Festival Hall** Three of the most acoustically perfect concert halls in the world were erected here between 1951 and 1964: the Royal Festival Hall, the Queen Elizabeth Hall, and the Purcell Room, all located in this complex. Together, the halls present more than 1,200 performances a year, including classical music, ballet, jazz, popular music, and contemporary dance. Also here is the internationally renowned Hayward Gallery (p. 244).

Royal Festival Hall, which opens daily at 10am, offers an extensive array of things to see and do, including free exhibitions in the foyers and free lunchtime music at 12:30pm. On Friday, Commuter Jazz in the foyer from 5:15 to 6:45pm is free. The Poetry Library is open Tuesday through Sunday from 11am to 8pm, and shops display a selection of books, records, and crafts. The Festival Buffet has food at reasonable prices, and bars dot the foyers. The People's Palace offers lunch and dinner with a panoramic view of the River Thames; making reservations by calling © **020/7928-9999** is recommended. On the South Bank, SE1. © **020/7960-4242.** www.rfh.org.uk. Tickets £6–£55 ($11–$102). Box office daily 9am–8pm. Tube: Waterloo or Embankment.

**The Royal Opera House (home of the Royal Ballet & the Royal Opera)** The Royal Ballet and the Royal Opera are at home again in this magnificently restored theater. Opera and ballet aficionados hardly recognize the renovated place, with its spectacular new public spaces, including the Vilar Floral Hall (a chamber-music venue), a rooftop restaurant, and bars and shops. The entire northeast corner of one of London's most famous public squares has been transformed, finally realizing Inigo Jones's original vision for this colonnaded plaza. Regular backstage tours are offered daily at 10:30am, and 12:30 and 2:30pm (not on Sun or matinee days).

Performances of the Royal Opera are usually sung in the original language, but supertitles are projected. The Royal Ballet, which ranks with top companies such as the Kirov and the Paris Opera Ballet, performs a repertory with a tilt toward the classics, including works by its earlier choreographer-directors Sir Frederick Ashton and Sir Kenneth MacMillan. Bow St., Covent Garden, WC2. © 020/7304-4000. www.royalopera.org. Tickets £15–£170 ($28–$315). Box office Mon–Sat 10am–8pm. Tube: Covent Garden.

**Sadler's Wells Theatre** This is a premier venue for dance and opera. It occupies the site of a series of theaters, the first built in 1683. In the early 1990s, the turn-of-the-century theater was mostly demolished, and construction began on an innovative new design completed at the end of 1998. The turn-of-the-century facade has been retained, but the interior has been completely revamped with a stylish cutting-edge theater design. The new theater offers classical ballet, modern dance of all degrees of "avant-garde-ness," and children's theatrical productions, including a Christmas ballet. Performances are usually at 8pm. Rosebery Ave., EC1. © 0870/7333-9000. www.sadlers-wells.com. Tickets £11–£50 ($19–$92). Box office Mon–Sat 9am–8:30pm. Tube: Northern Line to Angel.

**Wigmore Hall** An intimate auditorium, Wigmore Hall offers an excellent series of voice recitals, piano and chamber music, early and baroque music, and jazz. A cafe-bar and restaurant are on the premises; a cold supper can be preordered if you are attending a concert. Performances are held nightly in addition to the Sunday Morning Coffee Concerts and Sunday concerts at 11:30am or 4pm. 36 Wigmore St., W1. ℂ 020/7935-2141. www.wigmore-hall.org.uk. Tickets £10–£35 ($19–$65). Box office Mon–Sat 10am–8pm; Sun 10:30am–5pm. Tube: Bond St. or Oxford Circus.

## 3 Live Rock, Jazz, Blues, Folk & More

In addition to the venues listed below, see Bar Rumba, Cargo, The Cross, Cuba, Electric Ballroom, The End, Equinox, Fabric, Notting Hill Art Club, Salsa, and Smollensky's on the Strand (all are dance clubs with live music) in section 4, "Dance Clubs"; and American Bar and The Phoenix Artist Club in section 6, "Bars & Cocktail Lounges."

## ROCK & POP

**The Bull & Gate**   Outside central London, and smaller, cheaper, and often more animated and less touristy than many of its competitors, The Bull & Gate is the unofficial headquarters of London's pub rock scene. Indie and relatively unknown rock bands are served up in back-to-back handfuls at this somewhat battered Victorian pub. The place attracts a young crowd mainly in their 20s. If you like spilled beer, this is off-the-beaten-track London at its most authentic. Bands that have played here and later ascended to fame on Europe's club scene have included Madness, Blur, and Pulp. There's music nightly from 9pm to midnight. 389 Kentish Town Rd., NW5. ℂ 020/8806-8062. Cover £5 ($9.25). Tube: Northern Line to Kentish Town.

**Shepherd's Bush Empire**   Located in an old BBC television theater with great acoustics, this is a major venue for big-name pop and rock stars. Announcements appear in the local press. There's a seating capacity of 2,000. The spot mostly attracts fans in their 20s. Shepherd's Bush Green, W12. ℂ 020/8354-3300. Ticket prices vary according to show. Box office hours: Mon–Fri noon–5pm. Tube: Hammersmith & City Line to Shepherd's Bush or Goldhawk Rd.

**Sound**   In the heart of London, this 700-seat venue books the big acts, everybody from Sinead O'Connor to Puff Daddy to the Spice Girls. Sound functions as a restaurant and bar every night, with limited live music and a DJ until 11pm; after 11pm, the mood changes, the menu is simplified to include only bar snacks, and the site focuses much more heavily on live music and dancing. The music program is forever changing; call to see what's on at the time of your visit and to reserve tickets. Crowds and age levels can vary here depending on what act is featured. Reservations are recommended for dinner, but reservations after 11pm are not accepted. Swiss Centre at 10 Wardour St., Leicester Sq., W1. ℂ 020/7287-1010. Tickets £8–£12 ($15–$22). Box office Mon–Sat 10am–8pm. Tube: Leicester Sq.

## JAZZ

**100 Club**   Although less plush and expensive than some jazz clubs, 100 Club is a serious contender on the music front, with presentations of some remarkably good jazz. Its cavalcade of bands includes the best British jazz musicians and some of their Yankee brethren. Rock, R&B, and blues are also on tap. Serious devotees of jazz from 20 to 45 show up here. Open Monday through Thursday and Sunday from 7:30 to 11:30pm; Friday from noon to 3pm, and 8:30pm to 2am; and Saturday from 7:30pm to 1am. 100 Oxford St., W1. ℂ 020/7636-0933. Cover Fri £7–£12 ($13–$22). Club members get a £1 ($1.85) discount on Sat nights. Tube: Tottenham Court Rd. or Oxford Circus.

**606 Club**    Located in a discreet basement in Chelsea, the 606, a jazz supper club in the boondocks of Fulham, presents live music nightly. Predominantly a venue for modern jazz, styles range from traditional to contemporary. Local musicians and some very big names play here, whether at planned gigs or informal jam sessions after they finish shows elsewhere in town. Because of license requirements, patrons can order alcohol only with food. Locals show up here along with a trendy crowd from more posh neighborhoods in London. Open Monday through Wednesday from 7:30pm to 1am; Thursday from 8pm to 1:30am; Friday and Saturday from 10pm to 2am; Sunday from 8:30 to 11:30pm. 90 Lots Rd., SW10. ℭ 020/7352-5953. Cover Mon–Thurs £7 ($13), Fri–Sat £9 ($17), Sun £6–£8 ($11–$15). Bus: 11, 19, 22, 31, 39, or C3. Tube: Earl's Court.

**Bull's Head**    This club has showcased live modern jazz every night of the week for more than 30 years. One of the oldest hostelries in the area, it was a 19th-century staging post where travelers on their way to Hampton Court could rest while coach horses were changed. Today, the bar features jazz by musicians from all over the world. Since it's way off the tourist trail, it attracts mainly locals in a wide age group, all of whom appreciate good music. Live jazz plays on Sunday from 2 to 4pm and 8 to 10:30pm; Monday through Saturday, from 8:30 to 11pm. You can order lunch at the Carvery in the Saloon Bar or dinner in the 17th-century Stable Restaurant. The club is open Monday through Saturday from 11am to 11pm, and Sunday from noon to 10:30pm. 373 Lonsdale Rd., Barnes, SW13. ℭ 020/8876-5241. Cover £5–£10 ($9.25–$19). Tube: Hammersmith, then bus 219 to Barnes Bridge, then retrace the path of the bus for some 100 yd. on foot; or take Hounslow Look train from Waterloo Station and get off at Barnes Bridge Station, then walk 5 min. to the club.

**Jazz Café**    Afro-Latin jazz fans know that this club hosts great combos from around the globe. Weekends, described by a patron as "bumpy jazzy-funk nights," are the best time to decide what that means. To fit in here, be young or dress the part. Call ahead for listings, cover, and table reservations (often necessary); opening times can vary. 5 Parkway, NW1. ℭ 020/7916-6060. Reservations recommended. Cover £8–£20 ($15–$37). Tube: Camden Town.

**Pizza Express**    Don't let the name fool you: This restaurant/bar serves up some of the best jazz in London by mainstream artists, along with thin-crust Italian pizza. You'll find local bands or visiting groups, often from the United States. The place draws an equal mix of Londoners and visitors in the 20s-to-40s age bracket. Although the club has been enlarged, it's still important to reserve ahead of time. The restaurant is open daily from noon to midnight; there is jazz from 9pm to midnight. 10 Dean St., W1. ℭ 020/7437-9595. Cover £11–£20 ($20–$37). Tube: Tottenham Court Rd.

**Ronnie Scott's Jazz Club**    Inquire about jazz in London and people immediately think of Ronnie Scott's, the European vanguard for modern jazz. Only the best English and American combos, often fronted by top-notch vocalists, are booked here. The programs make for an entire evening of cool jazz. In the heart of Soho, Ronnie Scott's is a 10-minute walk from Piccadilly Circus along Shaftesbury Avenue. In the Main Room, you can watch the show from the bar or sit at a table, at which you can order dinner. The Downstairs Bar is more intimate; among the regulars at your elbow may be some of the world's most talented musicians. This place is so well known that all visiting musicians show up here along with the diehard music fans. On weekends, the separate Upstairs Room has a disco called Club Latino. The club is open Monday through Saturday from 8:30pm to 3am. Reservations are recommended. 47 Frith St., W1. ℭ 020/7439-0747.

Cover £15–£25 ($28–$46) for nonmembers, £5 ($9.25) for members, Fri and Sat £10 ($19). Tube: Leicester Sq. or Piccadilly Circus.

## BLUES

**Ain't Nothing But Blues Bar**   This club, which bills itself as the only true blues venue in town, features local acts and occasional touring American bands. On weekends, prepare to wait in line for a while. Open Monday through Thursday from 6pm to 1am, Friday and Saturday from 6pm to 2am, and Sunday from 7:30pm to midnight. 20 Kingly St., W1. ℂ **020/7287-0514.** Cover Thurs £3 ($5.55); Fri–Sat £5 ($9.25); free before 8:30pm. Tube: Oxford Circus or Piccadilly Circus. From the Oxford Circus Tube stop, walk south on Regent St., turn left on Great Marlborough St., and then make a quick right on Kingly St.

## FOLK

**Cecil Sharpe House**   CSH was the focal point of the folk revival in the 1960s, and it continues to treasure and nurture folk music and dance. You'll find a whole range of traditional music and dance here, with different evenings devoted to, among others, Irish set dances, English barn dances (similar to American square dances), dances from Louisiana's Cajun country, even re-enactments of 18th-century quadrilles. Although many of the regular patrons of this bar and dance club know these arcane dances by heart, they're usually charitable towards quick-learning and agile newcomers who can pick up the steps and the beat quickly. Call to see what's happening on the nights that you're in town. 2 Regent's Park Rd., NW1. ℂ **020/7485-2206.** Tickets £7–£10 ($13–$19). Box office Tues–Fri 9:30am–5:30pm. Tube: Northern Line to Camden Town.

## 4 Dance Clubs

It's the nature of dance clubs to come and go with alarming speed, or to shift violently from one trend to another. *Time Out* (available on newsstands in the U.S. and in London) is the best way to keep up.

Nearly all the clubs below cater to a crowd in its 20s and early 30s, with an almost equal mixture of locals and visitors. These clubs hit their groove around 1 to 2am.

In addition to those clubs listed here, check out Cecil Sharpe House (for folk dancing), Sound, and Ronnie's Scott's Jazz Club under section 3, "Live Rock, Jazz, Blues, Folk & More"; and The Edge, G.A.Y., and Heaven under section 8, "The Gay & Lesbian Scene".

**Bar Rumba**   Despite its location on Shaftesbury Avenue, this Latin bar and music club could be featured in a book of "Underground London." A hush-hush address, it leans toward radical jazz-fusion on some nights, and phat funk on other occasions. It boasts two full bars and a different musical theme every night. Tuesday and Wednesday are the only nights you probably won't have to queue at the door. Monday's "That's How It Is" showcase features jazz, hip-hop, and drum and bass; Friday provides R&B and swing; and Saturday's "Garage City" buzzes with house and garage. All the music here is live. On weeknights you have to be 18 or older; on Saturday and Sunday, nobody under 21 is allowed in. Open Monday through Thursday from 6pm to 3:30am, Friday from 6pm to 4am, Saturday from 7pm to 6am, and Sunday from 8pm to 1:30am. 36 Shaftesbury Ave., W1. ℂ **020/7287-6933.** Cover £3–£12 ($5.55–$22). Tube: Piccadilly Circus.

**Cargo**   Another watering hole in ultra-trendy Hoxton draws a smart urban crowd from their expensive West End flats. Its habitués assure us it's the place to go for a "wicked time" and great live bands. If there are no bands on a particular night, then great DJs dominate the club. Music and dancing starts at 6pm and the joint is jumping by 9:30 nightly. It's fun and funky, with two big arched rooms, fantastic acoustics, and a parade of videos. As for the patrons, the bartender characterized it just right: "We get the freaks and the normal people." Drinks are reasonably priced, as is the self-styled "street food." Open Monday to Thursday 6pm to 1am, Friday and Saturday 6pm to 3am, and Sunday 6pm to midnight. Kingsland Viaduct, 83 Rivington St., Shoreditch, EC2. ✆ 020/7739-3440. Cover £5–£9 ($9.25–$17) after 10pm. Tube: Liverpool St.

The Cross    In the backwaters of King's Cross, this club has been hot since 1993. Hipsters come here for private parties thrown by Rough Trade Records or Red Or Dead, or to dance in the space's industrial-looking brick-lined vaults. Music runs the gamut from acid rock to Caribbean/African fusion to Jamaican soca. This place is shadowy, sweaty, raunchy, and sometimes down and dirty. Call to find out who's performing. Open Friday and Saturday from 10pm to 6am. The Arches, King's Cross Goods Yard, York Way, N1. ✆ 020/7837-0828. Cover £8–£15 ($15–$28). Tube: King's Cross.

Cuba    This Spanish/Cuban bar-restaurant, which has a music club downstairs, features live acts from Spain, Cuba, Brazil, and the rest of Latin America. The crowd is equal parts restaurant diners, after-work drinkers, and dancers. Salsa classes are offered daily from 7:30 to 9:30pm for £4 to £7 ($7.40–$13). Happy hour is Monday through Friday from 5 to 7:30pm. Open Monday through Thursday from 5pm to 2am; Sunday from 5 to 10:30pm; Friday to Saturday noon to 2am; Sunday all-day Happy Hour. 11 Kensington High St., W8. ✆ 020/7938-4137. Cover £3–£8 ($5.55–$15). Tube: High St. Kensington.

Electric Ballroom    Though this club's been around long enough to come down a few points on the trendiness scale, the joint is still packed and jumping with a mixture of Londoners and visitors having a hot time. Two floors are set aside for gyrating to live music throughout the night; another is set up for chilling out. Many nights are '70s and '80s retro. Call to see what's happening. Thursday night is often theme night, at which time the cover varies. Perhaps it'll be an alternative night called "Full Tilt," when you'll discover a parade of pierced flesh and leather. Open 10:30pm to 3am Friday and Saturday. 184 Camden High St., NW1. ✆ 020/7485-9006. Cover varies on weekdays; £7–£10 ($13–$19) Fri–Sat. Tube: Camden Town.

The End    This club is better than ever after its recent enlargement. Now you'll find a trio of large dance floors, along with four bars and a chill-out area. Speaker walls will blast you into orbit. The End is the best club in London for live house and garage music. It draws both straight and gay Londoners. "We can't tell the difference anymore," the club owner confessed, "and who cares anyway?" From its drinking fountain to its swanky toilets, the club is alluring. Dress for glam and to be seen on the circuit. Some big names in London appear on the weekends to entertain. Open Monday through Thursday from 10pm to 3am, Friday 10pm to 5am, and Saturday from 10pm to 7am. 16A W. Central St., WC1. ✆ 020/7419-9199. Cover £4–£15 ($7.40–$28). Tube: Tottenham Court Rd.

Equinox    Built in 1992 on the site of the London Empire, a dance emporium that had witnessed the changing styles of social dancing since the 1700s, the Equinox has established itself as a perennial favorite. It contains nine bars, the largest dance floor in London, and a restaurant modeled after a 1950s American diner. With the exception of rave, virtually every kind of live dance music is featured, including dance hall, pop, rock, and Latin. The setting is illuminated with one of Europe's largest lighting rigs, and the crowd is as diverse as London itself. On Friday and Saturday nights, summer visitors can enjoy theme nights, which are geared toward entertaining a worldwide audience. Open Monday through Thursday from 9pm to 3am, and Friday and Saturday from 9pm to 4am. Leicester Sq., WC2. © 020/7437-1446. Cover £6–£12 ($11–$22) depending on the night of the week. Tube: Leicester Sq.

**Fabric**   While other competitors have come and gone, Fabric continues to draw crowds since opening in 1999. Its main allure is that it has a license for 24-hour music and dancing from Thursday to Sunday night. This is one of the most famous clubs in the increasingly trendy East London sector. It is said that when the owners power up the underfoot subwoofer, lights dim in London's East End. On some crazed nights, at least 2,500 members of young London, plus a medley of international visitors, crowd into this mammoth place. It has a trio of dance floors, bars wherever you look, unisex toilets, chill-out beds, and even a roof terrace. Live acts are presented every Friday, with DJs reigning on weekends. You'll hear house, garage, soca, reggae, and whatever else is on the cutting edge of London's underground music scene at the time. Open Thursday and Friday from 10pm to 7am, Saturday from 10:30pm to 7am, and Sunday from 10pm to 5am. 77A Charterhouse St., EC1. © 020/7336-8898. Cover £12–£15 ($22–$28). Tube: Farringdon.

**Hippodrome**   Near Leicester Square, the Hippodrome is London's granddaddy of discos, a cavernous place with DJed music, a great sound system, and lights to match. It was Lady Di's favorite in her bar-hopping days. Tacky and touristy, it's packed on weekends. Open Monday through Friday from 9pm to 3am, and Saturday from 9pm to 3:30am. Corner of Cranbourn St. and Charing Cross Rd., WC2. © 020/7437-4311. Cover £8–£11 ($15–$20). Tube: Leicester Sq.

**Limelight**   Although it opened in 1985, this dance club—located in a former Welsh chapel dating from 1754—has only recently come into its own. The dance floors and bars share space with cool Gothic nooks and crannies. DJs spin the latest house music. Open Monday through Thursday from 10pm to 3am, and Friday and Saturday from 9pm to 3:30am. 136 Shaftesbury Ave., W1. © 020/7434-0572. Cover £2–£12 ($3.70–$22). Tube: Leicester Sq.

**Ministry of Sound**   Removed from the city center, this club-of-the-hour remains hot, hot, hot. With a large bar and huge sound system, it blasts garage and house music for the energetic crowds that pack the two dance floors. If music and lights in the rest of the club have gone to your head, you can chill in the lounge. *Note:* The cover charge is stiff, and bouncers decide who is cool enough to enter, so slip into your grooviest and most glamorous club gear. Open Friday from 10:30pm to 5am, and Saturday from 11pm to 8am. 103 Gaunt St., SE1. © 020/7740-8600. Cover £12–£15 ($22–$28). Tube: Northern Line to Elephant & Castle.

**Notting Hill Art Club**   This is one of the hippest nighttime venues in London, with the action taking place in a no-frills basement in increasingly fashionable Notting Hill Gate. One habitué called it "the coolest night club on earth." Yes, that was Liam Gallagher you spotted dancing with Courtney Love. To justify the name of the club, art exhibitions are sometimes staged here. Most of the clients are under 35, and they come from a wide range of backgrounds—from Madonna to Bob Marley wannabes. The music is eclectic, varying from night to night—jazz, salsa, hip-hop, indie, and so on. Open Wednesday through Friday from 6pm to 1am, Saturday from 6pm to 2am, and Sunday from 4pm to 1am. Bands perform Wednesday through Saturday. 21 Notting Hill Gate, W11. © 020/7460-4459. Cover £3–£6 ($5.55–$11). Tube: Notting Hill Gate.

**The Office**  This is an eclectic club with a bureaucratic name—nights feature more traditional recorded pop, rock, soul, and disco. Ambience wins out over decor. During the week, a social lounge atmosphere pervades; on the weekends, this place is pure dance club. Open Monday and Tuesday from noon to 11:30pm, Wednesday through Friday from noon to 3am, and Saturday from 9:30pm to 3am. 3–5 Rathbone Place, W1. ✆ 020/7636-1598. Cover £3–£9 ($5.55–$17). Tube: Tottenham Court Rd.

**Salsa**  This lively bar/restaurant/club for Latin music aficionados mostly features bands from Central and South America. Dance lessons are available nightly starting at 7 to 7:30pm; live music starts at 9:30pm. Some of the best dancers in London strut their stuff here. Open Monday to Saturday from 5:30pm to 2am, Sunday 6pm to 12:30am. 96 Charing Cross Rd., WC2. ✆ 020/7379-3277. Cover Mon–Thurs £4 ($7.40) after 9pm; Fri–Sat £2–£8 ($3.70–$15). Tube: Leicester Sq. or Tottenham Court Rd.

**Scala**  This area of London is risky at night—so much so that the security staff at the club is happy to escort you to a taxi when you leave. But despite its sketchy surroundings, this is a hot, happening venue for young London. A former movie theater has been converted into this successful club, where DJs spin the latest music and ramped balconies offer dancing on different tiers. The gigantic screen will blow your mind with scintillating visuals. There is often some form of live entertainment, including theme nights. One of these events is a randomly scheduled bash called Popstarz, at which extroverted performers wear campy, tongue-in-cheek outfits inspired by the rock stars of the 1980s. Music runs the range from garage to R&B to salsa. Wear anything except on Saturday nights, when caps and sportswear are forbidden. Open nightly from 8pm to 2am. 275 Pentonville Rd., King's Cross, N1. ✆ 020/7833-2022. Cover £9–£15 ($17–$28). Tube: King's Cross.

**Smollensky's on the Strand**  This is an American eatery and bar where you can dance from Thursday to Saturday nights. Sunday night features a special live jazz session. Meals average £30 ($56). Open Thursday through Saturday from noon to 12:30am; Sunday from noon to 5:30pm, and 6:30 to 10:30pm; and Monday through Wednesday from noon to midnight. 105 the Strand, WC2. ✆ 020/7497-2101. Cover £6 ($11) on Sun, when they present big jazz bands. Tube: Charing Cross or Embankment.

**Trap**  This is one of the leading clubs of the West End lying in the vicinity of Oxford and Regent streets. It's a stylish rendezvous, drawing a crowd in their 20s and 30s to its plush precincts. The young Mick Jagger or aspirant Madonna of today might be seen lounging on one of the large white-covered sofas across from the sleek bar. Drinks are expensive, so be duly warned. Recorded music plays for dancing; Thursday and Friday nights are especially busy. A supper club adjoins the joint and is open for most of the night. 201 Wardour St., W1. ✆ 020/7434-3820. Cover £5–£15 ($9.25–$28). Tues–Wed 5pm–midnight; Thurs–Fri 5pm–3am; Sat 5–10pm. Tube: Tottenham Court Rd. or Oxford Circus.

**Vibe Bar**  As more and more of hip London heads east, bypassing even Clerkenwell for Hoxton, Vibe has been put on the map. The *Evening Standard* named it among the top five DJ bars in London. The paper compared it to an "expensively distressed pair of designer jeans." It's a nightspot operated by Truman Brewery. In summer the action overflows onto a courtyard. Patrons check their e-mail, lounge on comfortable couches, and listen to diverse music such as reggae, Latin, jazz, R&B, Northern Soul, African, or hip hop. 91–95 Brick Lane, E1. ✆ 020/7428-0491. Cover: Free or £1–£2 ($1.85–$3.70) sometimes assessed after 6pm. Sun–Thurs 1:30–11pm; Fri–Sat 7:30pm–1am. Tube: Liverpool St.

**Zoo Bar** The owners spent millions of pounds outfitting this club in the slickest, flashiest, and most psychedelic decor in London. If you're looking for a true Euro nightlife experience replete with gorgeous *au pairs* and trendy Europeans, this is it. Zoo Bar upstairs is a menagerie of mosaic animals beneath a glassed-in ceiling dome. Downstairs, the music is intrusive enough to make conversation futile. Clients range from 18 to 35; androgyny is the look of choice. 13–18 Bear St., WC2. ℂ 020/7839-4188. Cover £3–£7 ($5.55–$13) after 10pm. Mon–Fri 4pm–3:30am; Sat 1pm–3:30am; Sun 4pm–12:30am. Tube: Leicester Sq.

## 5 The Best of London's Pubs: The World's Greatest Pub Crawl

Dropping into the local pub for a pint of real ale or bitter is the best way to soak up the character of the different villages that make up London. You'll hear local accents and slang and see firsthand how far removed upper-crust Kensington is from blue-collar Wapping. Catch the local gossip or football talk—and, of course, enjoy some of the finest ales, stouts, ciders, and malt whiskies in the world.

**Anchor** You can follow in the footsteps of Shakespeare and Dickens by quenching your thirst at this pub. If literary heroes are not your bag, then perhaps you'll enjoy knowing that Tom Cruise had a pint or two here during the filming of *Mission Impossible*. Rebuilt in the mid–18th century to replace an earlier pub that managed to withstand the Great Fire of 1666, the rooms are worn and comfortable. You can choose from Scottish and Newcastle brews on tap. 34 Park St., Bankside, SE1. ℂ 020/7407-1577. Tube: Jubilee Line to London Bridge.

**Black Friar** The Black Friar will transport you to the Edwardian era. The wedge-shaped pub is swimming in marble and bronze Art Nouveau, featuring bas-reliefs of monks, a low-vaulted mosaic ceiling, and seating recesses carved out of gold marble. It's popular with the City's after-work crowd, and it features Adams, Wadworths 6X, Tetleys, and Brakspears on tap. 174 Queen Victoria St., EC4. ℂ 020/7236-5474. Tube: Blackfriars.

**Bow Wine Vaults** Bow Wine Vaults has existed since long before the wine-bar craze began in the 1970s. One of the most famous in London, the bar attracts cost-conscious diners and drinkers to its vaulted cellars for such traditional fare as deep-fried Camembert, lobster ravioli, and a mixed grill, along with fish. The cocktail bar is popular with City employees after work (open weekdays 11:30am–11pm). More elegant meals, served in the street-level dining room, include mussels in cider sauce, English wild mushrooms in puff pastry, beef Wellington, and steak with brown-butter sauce. Wines from around the world are available; the last time we were there the wine of the day was a Chilean chardonnay. 10 Bow Churchyard, EC4. ℂ 020/7248-1121. Tube: Mansion House, Bank, or St. Paul's.

**Churchill Arms** Stop here for a nod to the empire's end. Loaded with Churchill memorabilia, the pub hosts a week of celebration leading up to Churchill's birthday on November 30th. Show up at the right time and you may be recruited to help decorate the place—visitors are often welcomed like regulars. Decorations and festivities are featured for Halloween, Christmas, and St. Paddy's Day as well as for Churchill's birthday, helping to create the homiest village pub atmosphere you're likely to find in London. 119 Kensington Church St., W8. ℂ 020/7727-4242. Tube: Notting Hill Gate or High St. Kensington.

**Cittie of Yorke** This pub boasts the longest bar in Britain, rafters ascending to the heavens, and a row of immense wine vats, all of which give it the air of a great medieval hall—appropriate, since a pub has existed at this location since 1430. Samuel Smiths is on tap, and the bar offers novelties such as chocolate-orange-flavored vodka. 22 High Holborn, WC1. © 020/7242-7670. Tube: Holborn or Chancery Lane.

**Cutty Sark Tavern**    Retreat here for great antiquarian ambience inside a 16th-century dwelling with flagstones, barrel tables, open fires, and rough-hewn brick walls. The pub has such an Old London feel that you may find yourself seeing Dickensian riffraff after a few pints of Bass or Worthington's Best. Ballast Quay, off Lassell St., SE10. © 020/8858-3146. Train: Cutty Sark.

**Dog & Duck**    This snug little joint, a Soho landmark, is the most intimate pub in London. A former patron was the author George Orwell, who came here to celebrate his sales of *Animal Farm* in the United States. A wide mixture of ages and persuasions flock here, usually chatting amiably. Publicans here stock an interesting assortment of English beers, including Tetleys, Fuller London, and Timothy Taylor Landlord. In autumn, customers will ask for Addlestone's Cider. A lot of patrons head to Ronnie Scott's Jazz Club, which is close by, after having a few pints here. The cozy upstairs bar is also open. 18 Bateman St. (corner of Frith St.), W1. © 020/7494-0697. Tube: Tottenham Court Rd. or Leicester Sq.

**Dove**    You can relax by the Thames at the place where James Thomson composed "Rule Britannia" and part of his lesser-known "The Seasons." To toast Britannia, you can hoist a Fullers London Pride or ESB. 19 Upper Mall, W6. © 020/8748-5405. Tube: District Line to Ravenscourt Park.

**George**    The existing structure was built in 1877 to replace the original pub, which was destroyed in the Great Fire of 1666. That pub's accolades date to 1598, when it was reviewed as a "faire inn for the receipt of travelers." The present pub was built in the typical "traditional Victorian" style, with stripped oak floors, paneled walls, a curved bar counter, brass ceiling lights, and windows with etched and cut glass. Three huge mirrors decorate the walls. It's still a great place to enjoy Flowers Original, Boddingtons, and London Pride Abbot on tap. Off 77 Borough High St., SE1. © 020/7407-2056. Tube: Northern Line to London Bridge or Borough.

**Grapes**    This rustic 16th-century pub served as Dickens's inspiration for "Six Jolly Fellowship Porters" in *Our Mutual Friend.* Whistler came here, too, inspired by the view of the river. Taps include Friary Meux and Tetleys; there are several single-malt whiskies to choose from as well. 76 Narrow St., E14. © 020/7987-4396. Tube: Docks Light Railway, Westbury.

**Grenadier**    Tucked away in a mews, the Grenadier is one of London's reputedly haunted pubs, the ghost here being an 18th-century British soldier. Aside from the poltergeist, the basement houses the original bar and skittles alley used by the Duke of Wellington's officers. The scarlet front door of the one-time officers' mess is guarded by a scarlet sentry box and shaded by a vine. The bar is nearly always crowded. Lunch and dinner are offered daily—even on Sunday, when it's a tradition to drink Bloody Marys here. In the stalls along the side, you can order good-tasting fare based on seasonal ingredients. Well-prepared dishes include pork Grenadier, and a chicken-and-Stilton roulade. Snacks like fish and chips are available at the bar. 18 Wilton Row, SW1. © 020/7235-3074. Tube: Hyde Park Corner.

**Holly Bush**    The Holly Bush is the real thing: authentic Edwardian gas lamps, open fires, private booths, and a tap selection of Benskins, Eldridge Pope, and Ind Coope Burton. 22 Holly Mount, NW3. © 020/7435-2892. Tube: Northern Line to Hampstead.

# World's Greatest Pub Crawl

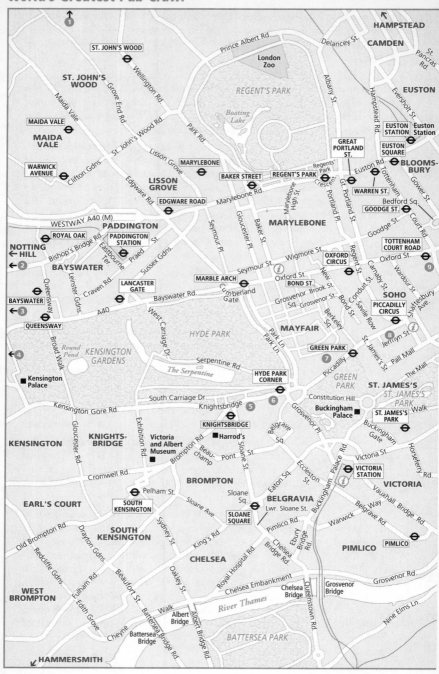

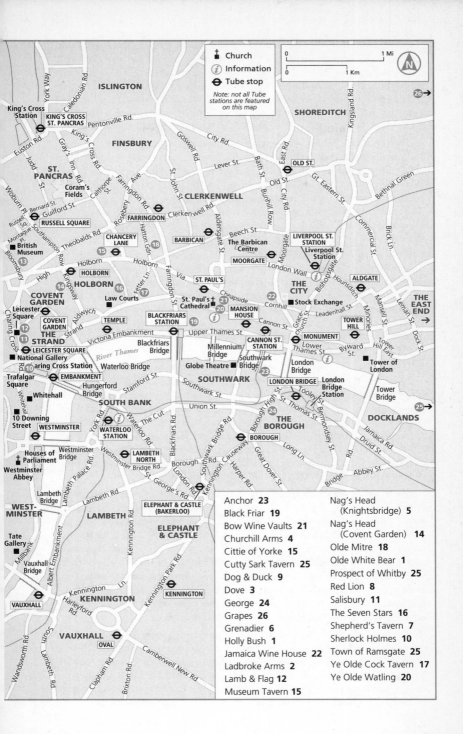

**Jamaica Wine House**   This was one of the first coffeehouses in England and, reputedly, the Western world. For years, merchants and sea captains came here to transact deals over rum and coffee. Nowadays, the two-level house dispenses coffee, beer, ale, lager, and fine wines, among them a variety of ports. The oak-paneled bar is on the street level, and attracts crowds of investment bankers. You can order standard but filling dishes such as a ploughman's lunch and toasted sandwiches. St. Michael's Alley, off Cornhill, EC3. ℂ 020/7929-6972. Tube: Bank.

**Ladbroke Arms**   Previously honored as London's "Dining Pub of the Year," Ladbroke Arms is that rare pub known for its food. A changing menu includes chicken breast stuffed with avocado, and garlic steak in pink-peppercorn sauce. With background jazz and rotating art prints, the place strays from the traditional pub environment. This place makes for a pleasant stop and a good meal. The excellent Eldridge Pope Royal is on tap, as well as John Smiths, Courage Directors, and several malt whiskies. 54 Ladbroke Rd., W11. ℂ 020/7727-6648. Tube: Notting Hill Gate.

**Lamb & Flag**   Dickens once frequented this pub, and the room has changed little from the days when he prowled the neighborhood. The pub has an amazing and scandalous history. Poet and author Dryden was almost killed by a band of thugs outside its doors in December 1679, and the pub gained the nickname the "Bucket of Blood" during the Regency era (1811–20) because of the bare-knuckled prizefights here. Tap beers include Courage Best and Directors, Old Speckled Hen, John Smiths, and Wadworths 6X. 33 Rose St., off Garrick St., WC2. ℂ 020/7497-9504. Tube: Leicester Sq.

**Museum Tavern**   Across the street from the British Museum, this pub (ca. 1703) retains most of its antique trappings: velvet, oak paneling, and cut glass. It lies right in the center of the University of London area and is popular with writers, publishers, and researchers from the museum. Supposedly, Karl Marx wrote while dining here. Traditional English food is served: shepherd's pie, sausages cooked in English cider, turkey-and-ham pie, ploughman's lunch, and salads. Several English ales, cold lagers, cider, Guinness, wines, and spirits are available. Food and coffee are served all day. The pub gets crowded at lunchtime. 49 Great Russell St., WC1. ℂ 020/7242-8987. Tube: Holborn or Tottenham Court Rd.

**Nag's Head**   This Nag's Head (not to be confused with the more renowned one at 10 James St.; see below) is on a back street a short walk from the Berkeley Hotel. Previously a jail dating from 1780, it's said to be the smallest pub in London. In 1921, it was sold for £12 ($22) and 6p(11¢) . Have a drink up front or wander to the tiny bar in the rear. For food, you might enjoy "real ale sausage" (made with pork and ale), shepherd's pie, or the quiche of the day, all served by the welcoming staff. A cosmopolitan clientele—newspaper people, musicians, and travelers—patronizes this warm, cozy pub. This pub touts itself as an "independent," or able to serve any "real ale" they choose because of their lack of affiliation. 53 Kinnerton St., SW1. ℂ 020/7235-1135. Tube: Hyde Park.

**Nag's Head**   This Nag's Head (as opposed to the one above) is one of London's most famous Edwardian pubs. In days of yore, patrons had to make their way through a fruit and flower market to drink here. Today, the pub is popular with young people. The draft Guinness is very good. Lunch (served noon–4pm) is typical pub grub: sandwiches, salads, pork cooked in cider, and garlic prawns. Snacks are available all afternoon. 10 James St., WC2. ℂ 020/7836-4678. Tube: Covent Garden.

**Olde Mitre**    Olde Mitre is the name of a working-class inn built here in 1547, when the Bishops of Ely controlled the district. It's a small pub with an odd assortment of customers. Friary Meux, Ind Coope Burton, and Tetleys are on tap. 1 Ely Place, EC1. © 020/7405-4751. Tube: Chancery Lane.

**Olde White Bear**    This is a friendly place, hosting many regulars, that's decorated with Victorian prints, cartoons, and furnishings. Tap offerings include Greene King Abbott and Youngs Bitter. Well Rd., NW31. © 020/7435-3758. Tube: Hampstead.

**Prospect of Whitby**    One of London's most historic pubs, Prospect was founded in the days of the Tudors, taking its name from a coal barge that made trips between Yorkshire and London. Come here for a tot, a noggin, or whatever it is you drink, and soak up the atmosphere. The pub has got quite a pedigree. Dickens and diarist Samuel Pepys used to drop in, and Turner came here for weeks at a time studying views of the Thames. In the 17th century, the notorious Hanging Judge Jeffreys used to get drunk here while overseeing hangings at the adjoining Execution Dock. Tables in the courtyard look out over river views. You can order a Morlands Old Speckled Hen from a hand-pump, or a malt whisky. 57 Wapping Wall, E1. © 020/7481-1095. Tube: Wapping.

**Red Lion**    This Victorian pub, with its early-1900s decorations and 150-year-old mirrors, has been compared to Manet's painting *A Bar at the Folies-Bergère* (on display at the Courtauld Gallery). You can order premade sandwiches, and on Saturday, homemade fish and chips are served. Wash down your meal with Ind Coope's fine ales or the house's special beer, Burton's, a brew made of spring water from the Midlands town of Burton-on-Trent. 2 Duke of York St. (off Jermyn St.), SW1. © 020/7321-0782. Tube: Piccadilly Circus.

**Salisbury**    Salisbury's cut-glass mirrors reflect the faces of English stage stars (and hopefuls) sitting around the curved buffet-style bar. A less prominent place to dine is the old-fashioned wall banquette with its copper-topped tables and Art Nouveau decor. The pub's specialties, home-cooked pies set out in a buffet cabinet with salads, are quite good and inexpensive. 90 St. Martin's Lane, WC2. © 020/7836-5863. Tube: Leicester Sq.

**The Seven Stars**    In 2001, its 399th year, this tranquil little pub facing the back of the Royal Courts of Justice was taken over by Roxy Beaujolais, author of the pub cookbook "Home From the Inn Contented," whose former pub was voted the Soho Society's Pub of the Year. Within the ancient charm of two narrow rooms that are listed landmarks, drinking in Queer Street (as Carey St. was called because of the bankruptcy courts) is pleasant. One can linger over pub food and real ales behind Irish-linen lace curtains, with litigants, barristers, reporters, and pit musicians from West End shows. Then, try to navigate to the lavatories up some comically narrow Elizabethan stairs. In mild weather, the law courts' stone balustrade under the trees provides customers with a long bar and beer garden. 53 Carey St., WC2. © 020/7242-8521. Tube: Chancery Lane or Temple.

**Shepherd's Tavern**    One of the focal points of the all-pedestrian shopping zone of Shepherd's Market, this pub occupies an 18th-century town house amid a warren of narrow, cobble-covered streets behind Park Lane. The street-level bar is cramped but congenial. Many of the regulars recall this tavern's popularity with the pilots of the Battle of Britain. Bar snacks include simple plates of shepherd's pie, and fish and chips. More formal dining is available upstairs in the cozy, cedar-lined Georgian-style restaurant. The classic British menu probably hasn't changed much since the 1950s, and you can always get Oxford ham or roast beef with Yorkshire pudding. 50 Hertford St., W1. © 020/7499-3017. Tube: Green Park.

**Sherlock Holmes** The Sherlock Holmes was the gathering spot for the Baker Street Irregulars, a once-mighty clan of mystery lovers who met to honor the genius of Sir Arthur Conan Doyle's famous fictional character. Upstairs, you'll find a re-creation of the living room at 221B Baker St. and such "Holmesiana" as the serpent from *The Speckled Band* and a faux beast's head from *The Hound of the Baskervilles*. In the upstairs dining room, you can order complete meals with wine. Try "Copper Beeches" (grilled chicken breasts with lemon and herbs), and then select dessert from the trolley. Downstairs is mainly for drinking, but there's a good snack bar with cold meats, salads, cheeses, and wine and ales sold by the glass. 10 Northumberland St., WC1. © 020/7930-2644. Tube: Charing Cross or Embankment.

**Town of Ramsgate** At this old-world pub, overlooking King Edward's Stairs and the Thames, you can enjoy Bass and Fullers London Pride on tap. 62 Wapping High St., E1. © 020/7481-8000. Tube: East London Line to Wapping.

**Ye Olde Cock Tavern** Dating back to 1549, this tavern boasts a long line of literary patrons: Pepys mentioned it, Dickens frequented it, and Tennyson referred to it in a poem (a copy of which is proudly displayed near the front entrance). It's one of the few buildings in London that survived the Great Fire of 1666. At street level, you can order a pint as well as snacks, steak-and-kidney pie, or a cold chicken-and-beef plate with salad. At the Carvery upstairs, a meal includes a choice of appetizers, followed by lamb, pork, beef, or turkey. 22 Fleet St., EC4. © 020/7353-8570. Tube: Temple or Chancery Lane.

**Ye Olde Watling** Ye Olde Watling was rebuilt after the Great Fire of 1666. On the ground level is a mellow pub. Upstairs is an intimate restaurant where, sitting at trestle tables under oak beams, you can dine on simple English main dishes for lunch. The menu varies daily, with such choices and reliable standbys as fish and chips, lasagna, fish cakes, and usually a vegetarian dish. All are served with two vegetables or salad, plus rice or potatoes. 29 Watling St., EC4. © 020/7653-9971. Tube: Mansion House.

## 6 Bars & Cocktail Lounges

**American Bar** The bartender in this sophisticated gathering place is known for his special concoctions, including "Savoy Affair" and "Prince of Wales," as well as what is reputedly the best martini in town. Monday through Saturday evenings, jazz piano is featured from 7 to 11pm. Located near many West End theaters, this spot is ideal for a pre- or post-theater drink. Dress is smart casual: no jeans, sneakers, or T-shirts. In The Savoy, the Strand, WC2. © 020/7836-4343. Tube: Charing Cross, Covent Garden, or Embankment.

**Beach Blanket Babylon** Go here if you're looking for a hot singles bar that attracts a crowd in their 20s and 30s. This Portobello joint is very cruisy. The decor is a bit wacky, no doubt designed by an aspiring Salvador Dalí who decided to make it a fairy-tale grotto (or was he going for a medieval dungeon look?). It's close to the Portobello Market. Saturday and Sunday nights are the hot, crowded times for bacchanalian revelry. 45 Ledbury Rd., W11. © 020/7229-2907. Tube: Notting Hill Gate.

**Cantaloupe** This bustling pub and restaurant is hailed as the bar that jump-started the increasingly fashionable Shoreditch scene. Businesspeople commuting from their jobs in the City mix with East End trendoids in the early evening at what has been called a "gastro pub/pre-club bar." Wooden tables and benches are found up front, although the Red Bar is more comfortable, as patrons lounge on Chesterfield chairs. The urban beat is courtesy of the house DJ. The restaurant and tapas menus are first rate. 35–42 Charlotte Rd., Shoreditch, EC2. ⓒ 020/7613-4411. Tube: Old St.

**The Library**    One of London's poshest drinking retreats, this deluxe bar boasts high ceilings, leather Chesterfields, respectable oil paintings, and grand windows. Its collection of ancient cognacs is unparalleled in London. In the Lanesborough Hotel, 1 Lanesborough Place, SW1. ⓒ 020/7259-5599. Tube: Hyde Park Corner.

**The Lobby Bar & The Axis Bar**    These bars are found in London's newest five-star hotel. We advise that you check out the dramatic visuals of both bars before selecting your preferred nesting place. The Lobby Bar occupies what was built in 1907 as the grand, high-ceilinged reception area for one of London's premier newspapers. If the Lobby Bar setting doesn't appeal, take a look at the travertine, hardwood, and leather-sheathed bar in the Axis restaurant. The Lobby Bar is open daily from 9am to 11pm; the Axis bar is open Monday through Saturday from 5:45 to 11pm. In the Hotel One Aldwych, 1 Aldwych, WC2. ⓒ 020/7300-1000. Tube: Covent Garden.

**The Mandarin Bar**    No other bar in London showcases the art of the cocktail as beautifully as this one. Created by design-industry superstar Adam Tihany around a geometric theme of artfully backlit glass, it provides the kind of cool, hip, confidently prosperous venue where men look attractive, women look fantastic, and cocktails are sublime. Drinks are prepared without fuss behind frosted-glass panels, in a style akin to a holy rite at a pagan temple, and are then presented with charm. There's live music every Monday to Saturday from 9pm until closing, and a leather-upholstered area off to the side, with a state-of-the-art air-filtration system, for cigar smokers and their friends. In the Mandarin Oriental Hyde Park Hotel, 66 Knightsbridge, SW1. ⓒ 020/7235-2000. Tube: Knightsbridge.

**Match EC1**    This epicenter for the fashionable 20s-to-30s set in London has put the *P* in partying in the once staid Clerkenwell district. Drinkers sit on elegant sofas or retreat to one of the cozy booths for a late snack. The bar claims to be the home of the Cosmopolitan cocktail, which swept across the drinking establishments of New York. The bartenders make some of the best drinks in London but warn you, "there is no such thing as a chocolate martini." 45–47 Clerkenwell Rd., EC1. ⓒ 020/7250-4002. Tube: Farringdon.

**The Met Bar**    Very much the place to be seen, this has become the hottest bar in London. Mix with the elite of the fashion, TV, and music world. A lot of American celebrities have been seen here sipping on a martini, from Demi Moore to Courteney Cox. Despite the caliber of the clientele, the bar has managed to maintain a relaxed and unpretentious atmosphere. In the Metropolitan Hotel, 19 Old Park Lane, W1. ⓒ 020/7447-1000. Members only and hotel guests. Tube: Hyde Park Corner.

**The Phoenix Artist Club**    What's something so old it's new again? This is where Laurence Olivier made his stage debut in 1930, although he couldn't stop giggling even though the play was a drama. Live music is featured, but it's the hearty welcome, the good beer, and the friendly patrons that make this rediscovered theater bar worth a detour. 1 Phoenix St., WC2. ⓒ 020/7836-1077. Tube: Tottenham Court Rd.

**Spring Bok Bar**    Established long ago in Dublin, this lively venue washes Ireland up on the shores of London. Featuring live music, four bars and "Lillie's Bordello" form the ultimate party place and a setting for live music. 6 Chandos Place, W1. © 020/7836-8000. Tube: Leicester Sq.

## 7 A Comedy Club

**The Comedy Store**    This is London's showcase for established and rising comic talent. Inspired by comedy clubs in the U.S., the club has given many comics their start, and today a number of them are established TV personalities. Even if their names are unfamiliar, you'll enjoy the spontaneity of live comedy before a British audience. Visitors must be 18 and older; dress is casual. Reserve through **Ticketmaster** (© 020/7344-4444); the club opens 1½ hours before each show. *Insider's Tip:* Go on Tuesday when the humor is more cutting-edge. Tuesday through Sunday doors open at 6:30pm and the show starts at 8pm; on Friday and Saturday there is an extra show that starts at midnight (doors open at 11:30pm). 1A Oxendon St., off Piccadilly Circus, SW1. © 0870/060-2340. Cover £12–£15 ($22–$28). Tube: Leicester Sq. or Piccadilly Circus.

## 8 The Gay & Lesbian Scene

The most reliable source for information on gay clubs and activities is the **Lesbian and Gay Switchboard** (© 020/7837-7324). The staff runs a 24-hour service for information on gay-friendly places and activities. *Time Out* also carries information on lesbian and gay-geared events and places. A good place for finding out what's hot and hip is **Prowler Soho,** 5–7 Brewer St., Soho, W1 (© 020/7734-4031; Tube: Piccadilly Circus), the largest gay-lifestyle store in London. You can buy anything from jewelry to CDs, books, fashion, and sex toys here. It's open until midnight on Friday and Saturday.

**Admiral Duncan**    Gay men and their friends go here to drink, to have a good time, and to make a political statement. British tabloids shocked the world in 1999 when they reported that this pub had been bombed, with three people dying in the attack. Within 6 weeks, the pub reopened its doors. We're happy to report that the bar is better than ever, now also attracting nongays who show up to show their support. 54 Old Compton St., W1. © 020/7437-5300. No cover. Tube: Piccadilly Circus.

**Barcode**    This is a very relaxed and friendly bar. Hosting everyone from skinheads to "pint-of-lager" types, it has much of a "local pub" atmosphere. The bar is fairly male-dominated, but does not object to women entering. Open daily from 1pm to 1am. 3–4 Archer St., W1. © 020/7734-3342. No cover. Tube: Piccadilly Circus.

**The Box**    Adjacent to one of Covent Garden's best-known junctions, Seven Dials, this sophisticated Mediterranean-style bar attracts all kinds of men. In the afternoon, it is primarily a restaurant, serving meal-size salads, club sandwiches, and soups. Food service ends abruptly at 5:30pm, after which the place reveals its core: a cheerful, popular rendezvous for London's gay and counter-culture crowds. The Box considers itself a "summer bar," throwing open doors and windows to a cluster of outdoor tables at the slightest hint of sunshine. The bar is open Monday through Saturday from 11am to 11pm, and Sunday from noon to 10:30pm. The cafe is open Monday to Saturday 11am to 5:30pm, and Sunday noon to 6:30pm. 32–34 Monmouth St. (at Seven Dials), WC2. © 020/7240-5828. No cover. Tube: Leicester Sq.

**Candy Bar**   This is the most popular lesbian bar in London at the moment. It has an extremely mixed clientele, ranging from butch to femme and from young to old. There is a bar and a club downstairs. Design is simple, with bright colors and lots of mirrors upstairs, and darker, more flirtatious decor downstairs. Men are welcome as long as a woman escorts them. Open Monday through Thursday from 8pm to midnight, Friday and Saturday from 8pm to 2am, and Sunday from 7 to 11pm. 4 Carlisle St., W1. ℂ 020/7494-4041. Cover £5–£7 ($9.25–$13). Tube: Tottenham Court Rd.

**The Edge**   Few bars in London can rival the tolerance, humor, and sexual sophistication found here. The first two floors are done up with decorations that, like an English garden, change with the seasons. Dance music can be found on the crowded, high-energy lower floors. Three menus are featured: a funky daytime menu, a cafe menu, and a late-night menu. Dancers hit the floors starting around 7:30pm. Clientele ranges from flamboyantly gay to hetero pub-crawlers. One downside: A reader claims the bartenders water down the drinks. Open Monday through Saturday from 11am to 1am, and Sunday from noon to 10:30pm. 11 Soho Sq., W1. ℂ 020/7439-1313. No cover. Tube: Tottenham Court Rd.

**First Out**   First Out prides itself on being London's first (est. 1986) all-gay coffee shop. Set in a 19th-century building whose wood panels have been painted the colors of the gay-liberation rainbow, the bar and cafe are not particularly cruisy. Cappuccino and whiskey are the preferred libations; and an exclusively vegetarian menu includes curry dishes, potted pies in phyllo pastries, and salads. Don't expect a raucous atmosphere—some clients come here with their grandmothers. Look for the bulletin board with leaflets and business cards of gay and gay-friendly entrepreneurs. Open Monday through Saturday from 10am to 11pm, and Sunday from 11am to 10:30pm. 52 St. Giles High St., W1. ℂ 020/7240-8042. No cover. Tube: Tottenham Court Rd.

**Friendly Society**   This is a Soho hot spot that bustles with young gay life, and there's even a rumor that Mrs. Guy Ritchie (Madonna) made a secret appearance here heavily disguised. "As what?" we asked, but no one knew. The action takes place in the basement of the building, which one patron called a "space-age lair." Perhaps the white-leather pod seating creates that aura. Come here for the drinks and the company—it's very cruisy. *Time Out London* describes the spot as a "gay, women-friendly venue with an alternative underground feel." Open daily noon to 11:30pm. In the basement of 79 Wardour St. (entrance is via a side street named Tisbury Court), W1. ℂ 020/7434-3805. No cover. Tube: Piccadilly Circus.

**G.A.Y.**   Name notwithstanding, the clientele here is mixed, and on a Saturday night this could be the most rollicking club in London. You may not find love here, but you could discover a partner for the evening. Patrons have been known to strip down to their briefs or shorts. A mammoth place, this club draws a young crowd to dance beneath its mirrored disco balls. Open Monday through Friday from 10:30am to 4am, and Saturday from 10:30pm to 5am. London Astoria, 157 Charing Cross Rd., WC2. ℂ 020/7734-9592. Cover £10–£13 ($19–$24). Tube: Tottenham Court Rd.

**Heaven**   This club, housed in the vaulted cellars of Charing Cross Railway Station, is a London landmark. Heaven is one of the biggest and best-established gay venues in Britain. Painted black and reminiscent of an air-raid shelter, the club is divided into at least four areas, connected by a labyrinth of catwalk stairs and hallways. Each room offers a different type of music, from hip-hop to rock.

Heaven also has theme nights, which are frequented at different times by gays, lesbians, or a mostly heterosexual crowd. Thursday in particular seems open to anything, but on Saturday it's gays only. Call before you go. Open Monday and Wednesday from 10:30pm to 3am, Friday from 10:30pm to 6am, and Saturday from 10:30pm to 5am. The Arches, Villiers, and Craven sts., WC2. ✆ 020/7930-2020. Cover £5–£12 ($9.25–$22). Tube: Charing Cross or Embankment.

**Ku Bar**　The Happy Hour here lasts from noon to 9pm, and the bartenders assure us that their watering hole attracts "the tastiest men in London." Those bartenders serve up some of the tastiest drinks, including peach, melon, apple, lemon, and butterscotch schnapps. Come here for a fab time, to throw a bash, and to cruise. 75 Charing Cross Rd., WC2. ✆ 020/7437-4303. No cover. Tube: Leicester Sq.

**Shadow Lounge**　This is the current fave hot spot for gay men in Soho. "Our male patrons are fresh and sexy," a seasoned bartender told us. Shadow Lounge is in the vanguard of gay life in London, which, as the millennium deepens, is showing a tendency to shift from gargantuan dance palaces like Heaven to more intimate rendezvous points. Young men, who look like the cast of the British version of "Queer as Folk," meet here at 8pm for drinks. Some return after dinner to dance to raucous house music. Open Monday through Wednesday from 10pm to 3am, and Thursday through Saturday from 9pm to 3am. 5 Brewer St., W1. ✆ 020/7287-7988. Cover £3–£10 ($5.55–$19). Tube: Piccadilly Circus.

# 10

# Side Trips from London

You could spend the best part of a year—or a lifetime—exploring London, without risking boredom or repetition. But there's much more to England than just London. We advise you to tear yourself away from Big Ben for at least a day or two to explore some of the easily accessible and wonderfully memorable spots that surround the city.

## 1 Windsor & Eton ✦

34km (21 miles) W of London

Windsor—the site of England's best-known and greatest castle and its most famous boys' school, Eton—would be a captivating Thames-side town to visit even if it was not associated with the royal Windsors.

Though a disastrous fire raged through the building in 1992, things are on the mend at Windsor Castle. But not without controversy—some of the new designs being unveiled have been called "Gothic shockers" and "ghastly." If you visit, you can decide for yourself. In summer it's overrun with tourists, which tends to obscure its charm, so plan your visit for spring or fall if possible.

### ESSENTIALS

**GETTING THERE**   The train from Waterloo or Paddington Station in London takes 30 minutes, involving a transfer at Slough to the Slough–Windsor shuttle train. There are more than a dozen trains per day; fares start at £6.10 ($11) one-way or £6.50 ($12) for a round-trip ticket. You can buy a round-trip ticket only if you are returning on the same day. If you stay over, you'll have to purchase another one-way ticket at full price. For information and schedules, call © **08457/484950.**

   **Green Line** coaches (© **0870/608-7261**), nos. 700 and 702 from Hyde Park Corner in London, take about 1½ hours. A same-day round-trip costs £8 ($15). The bus will drop you near the Town Guildhall in Windsor. From there, it's only a short walk up Castle Hill to the top sights.

   If you're traveling by car, take the M4 west from London.

**VISITOR INFORMATION**   A Tourist Information Centre is located across from Windsor Castle on High Street (© **01753/743900**). There's also an information booth in the tourist center at Windsor Coach Park. Both information centers are open Monday through Friday and Sunday from 10am to 4pm, and Saturday from 10am to 5pm.

### CASTLE HILL SIGHTS

**Windsor Castle** ★★★ *Kids*   When William the Conqueror ordered Windsor Castle to be built, he established a base for English sovereignty that has known many vicissitudes: King John cooled his heels at Windsor while waiting to put his signature on the Magna Carta at nearby Runnymede; Charles I was imprisoned here before losing his head; Queen Bess (Elizabeth I) renovated the castle; Victoria mourned her beloved Albert, who died at the castle; and the royal family rode out much of World War II behind its sheltering walls.

With 1,000 rooms, Windsor is the world's largest inhabited castle. When Queen Elizabeth II is in residence, the royal standard flies. Many works of art, porcelain, armor, furniture, three Verrio ceilings, and several 17th-century Gibbons carvings are displayed. Works by Rubens adorn the King's Drawing Room. In the relatively small King's Dressing Room are a Dürer, Rembrandt's portrait of his mother, and Van Dyck's triple portrait of Charles I. Of the apartments, the Grand Reception Room, with its Gobelin tapestries, is the most spectacular.

George IV's elegant **Semi-state Chambers** ✿✿ can only be visited from the end of September until the end of March. The king created the chambers in the 1820s as part of a series of Royal Apartments designed for his personal use. Seriously damaged in 1992, they have been returned to their former glory, with lovely antiques, paintings, and decorative objects. The Crimson Drawing Room, decorated with gilt, crimson silk damask hangings, and sumptuous art works, is a perfect example of the king's flamboyant taste.

It is recommended that you take a free guided tour of the castle grounds, including the Jubilee Garden (p. 322). Guides are very well informed and skilled at explaining the rich historical background of the castle.

In our opinion, the Windsor changing of the guard is a much more exciting experience than the London exercises. The guard marches through the town whether the court is in residence or not, stopping traffic as it wheels into the castle to the tunes of a full regimental band; when the queen is not here, a drum-and-pipe band is mustered. From April to July, the ceremony takes place Monday through Saturday at 11am. In winter, the guard is changed every 48 hours Monday through Saturday. It's best to call ✆ **020/7321-2233** for a schedule.

Castle Hill. ✆ **020/7321-2233.** www.royalresidences.com. Admission £12 ($21) adults; £6 ($11) children 16 and under; £30 ($56) family of 4. Mar–Oct daily 9:45am–5:15pm; Nov–Feb daily 9:45am–4:15pm. Last admission 1 hr. before closing. Closed for periods in Apr, June, and Dec when the royal family is in residence.

**Queen Mary's Doll's House**    A palace in perfect miniature, the Doll's House was given to Queen Mary in 1923 as a symbol of national goodwill. The house, designed by Sir Edwin Lutyens, was created on a 1-inch-to-1-foot scale. It took 3 years to complete and involved the work of 1,500 tradesmen and artists. Every item is a miniature masterpiece, each room is exquisitely furnished, and every item is made exactly to scale. Working elevators stop on every floor, all five bathrooms have running water, and electric lighting brightens the house.

Windsor Castle. ✆ **01753/831118.** Castle tickets include admission here (you cannot buy a separate admission). Open same days and hour as Windsor.

**St. George's Chapel** ✿✿✿    St. George's Chapel is built in the Perpendicular style, a late English Gothic architectural style characterized by vertical lines in the tracery of the building. Along with Westminster Abbey, this chapel shares the distinction of being a pantheon of English monarchs. The present St. George's was founded in the late 15th century by Edward IV on the site of the original Chapel of the Order of the Garter. At the chapel's center is a flat tomb containing the vault of the beheaded Charles I, along with Henry VIII and his third wife, Jane Seymour. Other monarchs entombed here include George V, George VI, and Edward IV. History's path forks at Princess Charlotte's memorial; had she

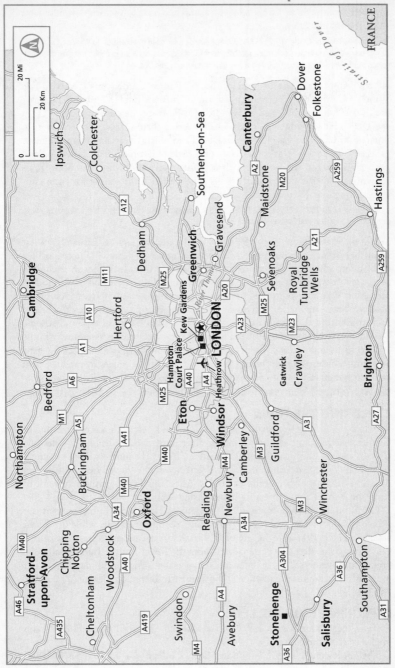

survived childbirth in 1817, she—and not her cousin Victoria—would have ruled the British Empire.

The Cloisters, Windsor Castle. © 01753/865538. Admission included in admission to Windsor Castle (you cannot buy a separate admission). Mon–Sat 9:45am–4:15pm. Sun services open to public, but closed to sight-seeing tours. Closed during services, and a few days in mid-June and Dec.

**Jubilee Garden** The .8 hectare (2-acre) Jubilee Garden was created inside Windsor Castle's main entrance to celebrate Queen Elizabeth's Jubilee. This garden was the first established at Windsor Castle since the days of George IV in the 1820s. Filled with trees, roses, and flowering shrubs, it was created by Tom Stuart-Smith, a Chelsea Flower Show gold medallist. Extending from the main gates of Windsor to St. George's Gate on Castle Hill, broad swaths of woodland perennials endow the garden with vibrant color, and white rambling roses romantically clothe the old stone walls. The garden is the setting for band concerts throughout the year.

Castle Hill. © 020/7321-2233. Castle tickets include admission here (you cannot buy a separate admission). Open same days and hour as Windsor.

**Windsor Farm Shop** *Finds* Had any of the queen's jars of jam lately? What about her homemade pork pie, or a bottle of her special brew? If not, head for this outlet, which sells produce from her estates outside Windsor, including pheasants and partridges bagged at royal shoots. This retail outlet is found in converted Victorian potting sheds on the edge of the royal estate. Much of the produce bears the seal of the Royal Farms. The cream, yogurt, ice cream, and milk come from the two Royal Dairy Farms. This latest make-a-pound scheme was devised in the brain of Prince Philip. The meat counter is awesome, with its cooked hams and massive ribs of beef. The steak-and-ale pies are especially tasty. You can stock up on the Queen's vittles and head for a picnic in the area. You can also purchase 15-year-old whisky from Balmoral Castle in Scotland.

Datchet Rd., Old Windsor. © 01753/623800. Free admission. Mon–Fri 9am–5pm; Sat 9–6pm; Sun 10am–4pm.

## EXPLORING THE TOWN

Windsor is a largely Victorian town of brick buildings, with a few remnants of Georgian architecture. Antiques shops, silversmiths, and pubs line cobblestone Church and Market streets near the castle. Charles II's mistress, Nell Gwynne, supposedly occupied a shop on Church Street, which allowed her to be within shouting distance of her beau's chambers. After lunch or tea, you may want to stroll the 3 miles along the aptly named Long Walk.

On Sundays, in Windsor Great Park and at Ham Common, you may see Prince Charles playing polo and Prince Philip serving as umpire while the queen watches. The park is also the site of Her Majesty's occasional equestrian jaunts. On Sunday she attends a little church near the Royal Lodge. Traditionally, she prefers to drive herself there, later returning to the castle for Sunday lunch. For more information on the town, call the Tourist Information Centre (© **01753/ 743900**).

## EXPLORING ETON COLLEGE

From Windsor, Eton is an easy stroll across the Thames Bridge. Follow Eton High Street to the college.

The adolescent Henry VI founded **Eton College** ✹✹ (© **01753/671000;** www.etoncollege.com) in 1440. Some of England's greatest men, notably the duke of Wellington, have played on the school's fields. Twenty prime ministers

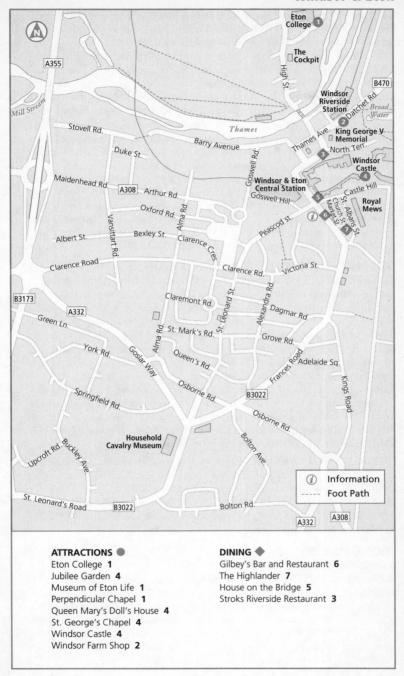

Eton College **1**

The Cockpit

High St.

A355

A308

A355

Mill Stream

Stovell Rd.

Duke St.

Maidenhead Rd.

A308

Arthur Rd.

Oxford Rd.

Alma Rd.

Vansittart Rd.

Albert St.

Bexley St.

Clarence Cres.

Clarence Road

B3173

A332

Green Ln.

Claremont Rd.

St. Mark's Rd.

St. Leonard St.

York Rd.

Gosfar Way

Alma Rd.

Queen's Rd.

Springfield Rd.

Osborne Rd.

Upcroft Rd. Buckley Ave.

**Household Cavalry Museum**

St. Leonard's Road

B3022

Barry Avenue

*Thames*

Goswell Rd.

Thames Ave.

**Windsor Riverside Station** **2**

B470

Datchet Rd.

*Broad Water*

**King George V Memorial**

North Terr.

**3**

**Windsor Castle** **4**

**Windsor & Eton Central Station**

Goswell Hill

Castle Hill

St. Albans St.

Church St.

Market St.

**Royal Mews**

**5**

Peascod St.

**6**

**7**

Clarence Rd.

Victoria St.

Alexandra Rd.

Dagmar Rd.

Grove Rd.

Frances Road

Adelaide Sq.

Kings Road

B3022

Osborne Rd.

Bolton Ave.

Bolton Rd.

A332

A308

*(i)* Information

----- Foot Path

---

**ATTRACTIONS** ●
Eton College **1**
Jubilee Garden **4**
Museum of Eton Life **1**
Perpendicular Chapel **1**
Queen Mary's Doll's House **4**
St. George's Chapel **4**
Windsor Castle **4**
Windsor Farm Shop **2**

**DINING** ◆
Gilbey's Bar and Restaurant **6**
The Highlander **7**
House on the Bridge **5**
Stroks Riverside Restaurant **3**

were educated here, in addition to such literary figures as George Orwell, Aldous Huxley, Ian Fleming, and Percy Bysshe Shelley—who, during his years at Eton (1804–10), was called Mad Shelley by his fellow pupils.

The history of Eton College since its inception is depicted in the Museum of Eton Life, located in vaulted wine cellars under College Hall. The displays include a turn-of-the-century boy's room, schoolbooks, sports trophies, canes used by senior boys to apply punishment to their juniors, and birch sticks used by masters for the same purpose. Also on display are letters written home by students describing day-to-day life at the school, as well as samples of the numerous magazines produced by students over the centuries. Old Etonians provided many of the items on display. If it's open, take a look at the Perpendicular Chapel's 15th-century paintings and reconstructed fan vaulting.

Admission to the school and museum costs £3.80 ($7.05) for adults. You can take guided tours for £4.90 ($9.10). Eton College is open from March 27 to April 20 and July 3 to September 7, daily from 10:30am to 4:30pm; from April 21 to July 2 and September 7 to October 3, daily from 2 to 4:30pm. Call in advance; Eton may close for special occasions. These dates vary every year depending on term and holiday dates. It's best to call ahead.

## ORGANIZED TOURS OF WINDSOR & ETON

**BOAT TOURS**    Tours depart from The Promenade, Barry Avenue, for a 35-minute round-trip ride to Boveney Lock. There's also a 35-minute round-trip tour from Runnymede on the *Lucy Fisher,* a replica of a Victorian paddle steamer. The boat passes Magna Carta Island (commemorating the signing of the document), among other places. Both tours cost £4.40 ($8.15) for adults and £2.20 ($4.10) for children. A 2-hour tour through the Boveney Lock and up past stately private riverside homes, the Bray Film Studios, Queens Eyot (a beautifully landscaped private island), and Monkey Island is £6.80 ($13) for adults, £3.40 ($6.30) for children. Longer tours are offered between Maidenhead and Hampton Court. The boats serve refreshments and have a well-stocked bar, and the decks are covered in case of an unexpected shower. Contact French Brothers, Ltd., Clewer Boathouse, Clewer Court Road, Windsor (𝄐 **01753/ 851900;** fax 01753/832303; www.boat-trips.co.uk).

**HORSE-DRAWN CARRIAGE RIDES**    You can take a horse-drawn carriage for a half-hour promenade up the sycamore-lined length of Windsor Castle's Long Walk. Horses with carriages and drivers should be lined up beside the castle waiting for fares, which run from £19 ($35) for up to four passengers for a 30-minute ride or £39 ($72) for a 1-hour ride. Call South Gates, 𝄐 **01784/ 435983,** for more information.

## WHERE TO DINE
### WINDSOR

**The Highlander** PUB GRUB    This Scottish-themed pub is a choice place for a pub lunch on a fair day since it boasts a beer garden opening onto a view of Windsor Castle. It lies directly south of the fortification of Windsor Castle and is patronized by household staff and security guards who work at the castle. Housed in a 1790s building, it is one of the old town's most popular pubs. Young people come here in the evening, and there is varied live music on Friday. Hot food is served during the day, along with a wide selection of British ales. Church Lane. 𝄐 **01753/864257.** Pub meals £4–£8 ($7.40–$15). AE, MC, V. Mon–Sat 11am–11pm; Sun noon–10:30pm.

**Stroks Riverside Restaurant** FRENCH/MODERN BRITISH   A 3-minute walk from the castle, this restaurant is the most elegant and charming in Windsor, with garden terraces and a conservatory. The dining room is designed a bit like a greenhouse, and a pianist entertains at dinner. Enjoy such dishes as roasted squab with goat-cheese gnocchi; rosettes of spring lamb with green beans, roasted artichokes, and Yorkshire pudding; and traditional Chateaubriand carved at your table with a vegetable medley. The chef, Phillip Wild, studied at two- and three-star Michelin restaurants in Switzerland and cooks with passion and intensity. Each dish is freshly prepared with local ingredients if possible. Lamb and beef are cooked "pink," and vegetables are served al dente.

In Sir Christopher Wren's House Hotel, Thames St. ℂ **01753/861354.** Main courses £15–£20 ($27–$37); fixed-price menu £30 ($55). AE, DC, MC, V. Daily 12:30–2:30pm and 6:30–9:30pm.

## ETON

**Gilbey's Bar and Restaurant** MODERN BRITISH   Just across the bridge from Windsor, this graceful bar is set among the antiques shops on Eton's main street. Inside are pinewood tables, old church pews, and chairs, and there's a glassed-in conservatory out back. A brigade of chefs turns out a fine array of modern British cookery. Appetizers usually include well-prepared soups and a roasted sweet-pepper tart. Main dishes include pine-nut-and-spinach risotto topped with pecorino cheese, and roast lamb filet served with *boulangère* potatoes and vegetables. For dessert, try the *tarte tatin,* a tasty and creative upside-down apple pie.

82–83 High St. ℂ **01753/854921.** Reservations recommended. Main courses £11–£17 ($19–$31). AE, DC, MC, V. Mon–Fri noon–2:30pm; Sat–Sun noon–3pm; Mon–Thurs 6–9:30pm; Fri–Sat 6–10:30pm; Sun 6–9:30pm.

**House on the Bridge** ENGLISH/INTERNATIONAL   This charming restaurant is housed in a lovely redbrick and terra-cotta Victorian building adjacent to the bridge at the edge of Eton. Near the handful of outdoor tables is a steep garden whose plants range down to the Thames. For what the British call a "good tuck-in," order the terrine of duck and foie gras or the traditional oak-smoked salmon to launch your repast. For a main course, enjoy the grilled Dover sole or the roasted filet of sea bass with caramelized scallops. Breast of magret duck appears tantalizingly in orange sauce, and a filet of veal with wild mushrooms is perfectly dressed in a Chablis sauce. Some specialties, such as roast rack of herb-flavored lamb, are served only for two. Although traditionally based, the preparations have many modern touches, and the chefs always use good, fresh ingredients. Desserts include flambés and crêpes suzette.

71 High St. ℂ **01753/860914.** Reservations recommended. Main courses £14–£22 ($26–$41); fixed-price lunch £20 ($37), dinner £30 ($56); Sun lunch £22 ($41). AE, DC, MC, V. Daily noon–3pm and 6–11pm.

## 2 Oxford, City of Dreaming Spires ✶✶✶

87km (54 miles) NW of London

A walk down the long sweep of The High Street, one of the most striking streets in England; a mug of cider in one of the old student pubs; the sound of May Day dawn when choristers sing in Latin from Magdalen Tower; the Great Tom bell from Tom Tower, whose 101 peals traditionally signal the closing of the college gates; towers and spires piercing the clouds; barges on the upper reaches of the Thames; nude swimming at Parson's Pleasure; the roar of a cannon launching the bumping races (in which each boat tries to bump the boat ahead of it and avoid being bumped by the boat behind it); a dusty bookstall where you can pick up a valuable first edition—all are found in Oxford, home of one of the greatest universities in the world.

Romantic Oxford still exists, but to get to it, you'll have to navigate the bustling and crowded city that has grown about it. A never-ending stream of polluting buses and fast-flowing pedestrian traffic can make the city core feel more like London than an ancient university town.

At any time of the year, you can enjoy a tour of the colleges, some of the loveliest in all England. The Oxford Tourist Information Centre (see "Visitor Information," below) conducts walking tours throughout the year. Just don't mention the other place (Cambridge), and you shouldn't have any trouble. The city predates the university—it emerged as a Saxon town in the 10th century. By the 12th century, Oxford was growing in reputation as a seat of learning. When the first colleges emerged in the 13th century, Oxford began to churn out powerful and distinguished alumni, among them Roger Bacon, Sir Walter Raleigh, John Donne, Sir Christopher Wren, Samuel Johnson, Edward Gibbon, William Penn, John Wesley, Lewis Carroll, T. E. Lawrence, and W. H. Auden.

## ESSENTIALS

GETTING THERE   Trains from **Paddington Station** (© 0845/748-4950) reach Oxford in 1½ hours. Five trains run every hour. A cheap, same-day round-trip ticket costs £17 ($31); a 5-day round-trip ticket is £19 ($35).

The **Oxford CityLink** departs from Victoria Station (© 08705/808080; www.nationalexpress.co.uk) for the Oxford Bus Station daily. Coaches usually leave about every 30 minutes during the day, taking 1¾ hours. A same-day round-trip ticket costs £11 ($20) for adults, £5.50 ($10) for children 3 to 15.

Or take the **Oxford Tube,** an express coach that takes you from London to Oxford in 90 minutes off-peak. Coaches leave three to six times an hour from 6am to 10:30pm, and hourly overnight. Tickets are £9 ($17) one-way and £11 ($20) for a 24-hour round-trip return. For schedules, call © 01865/772250 or visit www.stagecoach-oxford.co.uk/tube.

If you're driving, take the M40 west from London and just follow the signs. Traffic and parking are a disaster in Oxford, and not just during rush hours. However, there are four large park-and-ride parking lots on the north, south, east, and west of the city's ring road, all well marked. Parking is 60p ($1.10) per car. From 9:30am on and all day Saturday, you pay £1.40 ($2.60) or £1.80 ($3.35) for a round-trip ticket for a bus ride into the city, which drops you off at St. Aldate's, Cornmarket, or Queen Street to see the city center. The buses run every 8 to 10 minutes in each direction. There is no service on Sunday. The parking lots are on the Woodstock road near the Peartree traffic circle, on the Botley road toward Farringdon, on the Abingdon road in the southeast, and on the A40 toward London.

VISITOR INFORMATION   The **Oxford Tourist Information Centre** is at 15 to 16 Broad St. (© 01865/726871; www.visitoxford.org). The center sells a comprehensive range of maps, brochures, and souvenir items, as well as the famous Oxford University T-shirt. It provides hotel-booking services for £3 ($5.55). Open Monday through Saturday from 9:30am to 5pm and Sunday and bank holidays in summer from 10am to 3:30pm.

## EXPLORING OXFORD UNIVERSITY

Many visitors arriving at Oxford ask: "Where's the campus?" If a local chortles when answering, it's because Oxford University is made up of 35 widely dispersed

# Oxford

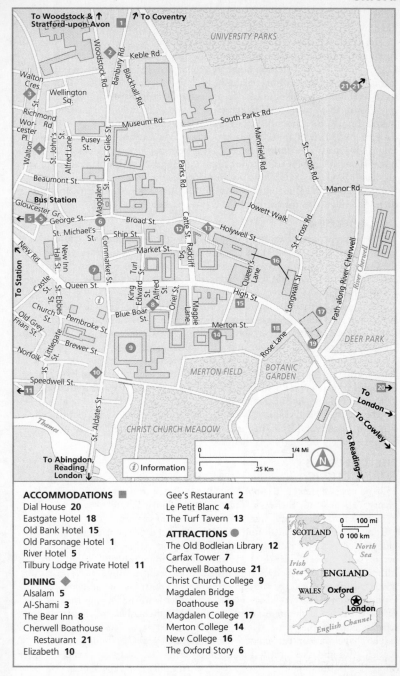

**To Woodstock & Stratford-upon-Avon** 1
**To Coventry**
UNIVERSITY PARKS
Woodstock Rd. 2
Keble Rd.
Banbury Rd.
Blackhall Rd.
Walton Cres. 3
Wellington Sq.
Richmond Rd.
Worcester Pl.
Walton 4
Museum Rd.
South Parks Rd.
Pusey St.
St. John's St.
St. Giles St.
Alfred Lane
Beaumont St.
Parks Rd.
Mansfield Rd.
St. Cross Rd.
Manor Rd.
Bus Station
Gloucester Gr.
George St. 5 5
Magdalen St.
St. Michael's St.
Broad St. 6
Jowett Walk
Path along River Cherwell
River Cherwell
New Rd.
Ship St.
Cornmarket St.
Market St.
Catte St.
Radcliffe Sq. 12
Holywell St. 13
Queen's Lane
16
Longwall St.
To Station
Castle St.
New Inn Hall St.
St. Ebbes St.
Queen St. 7
Turf St.
King Edward St.
Alfred St.
Oriel St.
High St. 15
17
DEER PARK
Church St.
Pembroke St.
Blue Boar St. 8
Magpie Lane
Merton St. 18
19
Old Grey Friars St.
Littlegate St.
Brewer St.
9
14
Rose Lane
Norfolk St.
Speedwell St. 10
MERTON FIELD
BOTANIC GARDEN
20
To London
11
St. Aldates St.
To Cowley
Thames
CHRIST CHURCH MEADOW
To Reading
To Abingdon, Reading, London
ℹ Information
0 ———— 1/4 Mi
0 ———— .25 Km
N

## ACCOMMODATIONS ■
Dial House **20**
Eastgate Hotel **18**
Old Bank Hotel **15**
Old Parsonage Hotel **1**
River Hotel **5**
Tilbury Lodge Private Hotel **11**

## DINING ◆
Alsalam **5**
Al-Shami **3**
The Bear Inn **8**
Cherwell Boathouse
  Restaurant **21**
Elizabeth **10**

Gee's Restaurant **2**
Le Petit Blanc **4**
The Turf Tavern **13**

## ATTRACTIONS ●
The Old Bodleian Library **12**
Carfax Tower **7**
Cherwell Boathouse **21**
Christ Church College **9**
Magdalen Bridge
  Boathouse **19**
Magdalen College **17**
Merton College **14**
New College **16**
The Oxford Story **6**

SCOTLAND
0 ———— 100 mi
0 ———— 100 km
North Sea
Irish Sea
ENGLAND
WALES
Oxford
★ London
English Channel

327

colleges. To tour all of these would be a formidable task. It's best to focus on a handful of the better-known colleges.

**The Oxford Story,** 6 Broad St. (© **01865/790055**), has packaged Oxford's complexities into a concise and entertaining audiovisual ride and exhibit (a la Disneyland). The presentation highlights some of the architectural and historic features that hurried visitors might miss. The ride includes a trip through a three-level former warehouse and takes you through more than 800 years of history. You're filled in on the backgrounds of the colleges and those who have passed through their portals. In July and August the audiovisual presentation is daily from 9:30am to 5pm. In July and August The Oxford Story is open daily from 9:30am to 5pm; from September to December it's open Monday to Saturday 10am to 4:30pm, and Sunday 11am to 4:30pm; and from January to June it's open Monday to Saturday 10am to 4:30pm, and Sunday 11am to 4:30pm. Admission is £7 ($13) for adults and £5.50 ($10) for seniors, students, and children. A family ticket for two adults and two children is £23 ($42).

## GUIDED TOURS

The best way to get a running commentary on the highlights of Oxford is to take a 2-hour walking tour of the city and major colleges. Tours leave daily from the Oxford Tourist Information Centre at 11am and 2pm. Tours cost £6 ($11) for adults, and £3 ($5.55) for children; they do not include New College or Christ Church.

For a good orientation, hour-long, open-top bus tours around Oxford are available from **Guide Friday,** whose office is at the railway station (tours also start from the railway station; other pickup points are: Sheldonian Theatre, Gloucester Green Bus Station, and Pembroke College—© **01865/790522**). Buses leave every 20 minutes daily; in summer, buses leave every 5 to 10 minutes. Tickets are good for the day. Tours run daily from 9:30am to 3:45pm November through January, and daily from 9:30am to 4:45pm February and March; daily 9:30am to 6:30pm April through October. The cost is £9 ($17) for adults, £7 ($13) for students and seniors, £3 ($5.55) for children 5 to 14 years old; a family ticket for 2 adults and 2 children is £19 ($35). Children under 5 get to ride free. Tickets can be purchased from the driver.

## THE COLLEGES

**CHRIST CHURCH** ★★  Begun by Cardinal Wolsey as Cardinal College in 1525, Christ Church (© **01865/276150**; www.chch.ox.ac.uk) was renamed by Henry VIII in 1546. Facing St. Aldate's Street, Christ Church—known as the House—has the largest quadrangle of any college in Oxford.

Tom Tower houses Great Tom, the 18,000-pound bell that rings nightly at 9:05pm, signaling the closing of the college gates. Its 101 peals signify the number of students in residence at the time of the founding of Christ Church. Although the student body has grown, Oxford traditions live forever. In the 16th-century great hall, you'll find several notable portraits, including works by Gainsborough and Reynolds. The walls are thick with prime ministers, since Christ Church was the training ground for 13 of them. The college also has a separate portrait gallery.

The chapel was constructed over several hundred years, beginning in the 12th century. (It's also the cathedral of the diocese of Oxford.) The chapel's most impressive features are its 15th-century Norman pillars and the vaulting of the choir.

Outside, in the center of the quadrangle, is a statue of Mercury in the middle of a fishpond. The college and cathedral can be visited between 9am and 5:30pm, though times vary (Sun 1–5:30pm). It's best to call before you visit. The entrance fee is £4 ($7.40) for adults and £3 ($5.55) for children.

*Insider's Tip:* Almost overlooked by the average visitor is an unheralded little gem known as Christ Church Picture Gallery, entered through the Canterbury Quad. Here you come across a stunning collection of old masters, mainly from the Dutch, Flemish, and Italian schools, including works by Michelangelo and Leonardo da Vinci. It's open April through September Monday through Saturday from 10:30am to 1pm and 2 to 5:30pm (closes at 4:30pm Oct–Mar). Admission is £2 ($3.70) for adults or £1 ($1.85) for seniors and students.

**MAGDALEN COLLEGE** Magdalen (*Maud*-lin) College, High Street (© **01865/276000;** www.magd.ox.ac.uk), was founded in 1458. Its alumni range from statesman Cardinal Thomas Wolsey to Oscar Wilde. Opposite the botanic garden (the oldest in England), is the bell tower, where the choristers sing in Latin at dawn on May Day (May 1). This 15th-century tower reflects mightily in the waters of the Cherwell below. Visit the equally old chapel, which feels ancient despite many of its latter-day trappings. Ask when the hall and other places of special interest are open. The grounds of Magdalen are the most extensive of any Oxford college; there's even a deer park. You can visit daily from 1pm to dusk. Admission is £3 ($5.55) adults, £2 ($3.70) children.

*Insider's Tip:* Often missed by the average visitor, the Botanic Gardens opposite Magdalen were first planted in 1621 on the location of an old Jewish graveyard from the early Middle Ages. Bounded by a curve of the Cherwell, they still stand today and are the best place in Oxford to escape the invading hordes. Open daily from 10am to 5pm (last admission 4:15pm) April to November; Monday through Friday 10am to 4:30pm December to March. Admission is £2 ($3.70).

**MERTON COLLEGE** ✦✦ Founded in 1264, Merton College (© **01865/276310**) is among the three oldest colleges at the university. It stands near Corpus Christi College on Merton Street, the sole survivor of Oxford's medieval cobbled streets. Merton College is noted for its library, built between 1371 and 1379 and said to be the oldest college library in England. One of the treasures is an astrolabe (an astronomical instrument used for measuring the altitude of the sun and stars) thought to have belonged to Chaucer. It costs £1 ($1.85) to visit the ancient library, including admission to the Max Beerbohm Room, honoring the satirical English caricaturist who died in 1956. The library and college are open Monday through Friday from 2 to 4pm and Saturday and Sunday from 10am to 4pm. Merton College is closed for 1 week at Easter and 1 week at Christmas.

*Insider's Tip:* A favorite pastime is to take Addison's Walk near here through the water meadows. The stroll is named after former alumnus Joseph Addison, an 18th-century essayist and playwright noted for his contributions to *The Spectator* and *The Tatler.*

**NEW COLLEGE** New College, Holywell Street (© **01865/279555;** www.new.ox.ac.uk), was founded in 1379. The first quadrangle, dating from before the end of the 14th century, was the first one built in Oxford and served as architectural boilerplate for many other colleges. In the antechapel are Sir Jacob Epstein's remarkable modern sculpture of Lazarus and a fine El Greco study of St. James. One of the treasures of the college is a crosier (pastoral staff of a

330 CHAPTER 10 · SIDE TRIPS FROM LONDON

bishop) belonging to the founding father, William of Wykeham. In the garden, you can stroll among the remains of the old city wall and the mound (a common decorative feature of Tudor gardens).

*Insider's Tip:* New College is known for its notorious gargoyles. Check them out on the bell tower, which is decorated with the seven virtues on one side and the seven deadly sins on the other. The virtues are just as grotesque as the deadly sins. The college (entered at New College Lane) can be visited from Easter to October, daily between 11am and 5pm; and in the off-season daily between 2 and 4pm. Admission is £1.50 to £2 ($2.80–$3.70), depending on what is open, from Easter to October, and free off-season.

**THE OLD BODLEIAN LIBRARY** ★★   This famed library on Catte Street (© **01865/277224;** www.bodley.ox.ac.uk) was launched in 1602, funded by Sir Thomas Bodley. It is home to some 50,000 manuscripts and more than 5 million books. Over the years the library has expanded from the Old Library complex to other buildings, including the Radcliffe Camera next door. The easiest way to visit is by taking a guided tour, leaving from the Divinity School across from the main entrance. In summer there are four tours every day from Monday to Friday, and two on both Saturday and Sunday; in winter, two tours leave per day. Call for specific times.

## WHERE TO STAY

**Oxford Tourist Information Centre,** Gloucester Green, opposite the bus station (© **01865/726871;** fax 01865/240261; www.oxford.gov.uk), operates a year-round room-booking service for a fee of £3 ($5.55), plus a refundable deposit. If you'd like to seek lodgings on your own, the center has a list of accommodations, plus maps and guidebooks.

### EXPENSIVE

**Eastgate Hotel** ★   Eastgate stands opposite the ancient Examination Halls, next to Magdalen Bridge and within walking distance of the city center. It offers recently refurbished facilities but retains the atmosphere of an English country house. The rooms are well worn but still cozy and comfortable. Mattresses are replaced frequently, and the small shower-tub combination bathrooms are well maintained.

23 Merton St. at High St., Oxford, Oxfordshire, OX1 4BE. © **0870/400-8201.** Fax 01865/791681. www.macdonaldhotels.co.uk. 64 units. £160 ($296) double; £180 ($333) suite. AE, DC, MC, V. Bus: 3, 4, 7, or 52. **Amenities:** Restaurant; bar; room service (noon–2:30pm and 6–9:45pm); babysitting; laundry service; dry cleaning; nonsmoking rooms. *In room:* A/C, TV, dataport, coffeemaker, hair dryer, trouser press.

**Old Bank Hotel** ★★★   Opened in 1999, this was Oxford's first new hotel in 135 years, and it immediately surpassed traditional favorite Randolph in style and luxuries. The good-size rooms are elegantly appointed and often boast views. Understated elegance prevails, and each unit comes with a state-of-the-art marble bathroom with tubs and power showers. Throughout the hotel is an array of 20th-century British art.

92–94 High St., Oxford OX1 4BN. © **01865/799599.** Fax 01865/799598. www.oxford-hotels-restaurants.co.uk. 42 units. £160–£235 ($296–$435) double; £265–£320 ($490–$592) suite. AE, DC, MC, V. Bus: 7. **Amenities:** Restaurant; bar; concierge; 24-hr. room service; babysitting; laundry service; dry cleaning; 1 room for those w/limited mobility; nonsmoking rooms. *In room:* A/C, TV, CD player, dataport, coffeemaker, hair dryer, safe.

**Old Parsonage Hotel** ★★   This extensively renovated hotel near St. Giles Church and Keble College is so old (1660) that it looks like an extension of one of the colleges. Once a 13th-century hospital, the building was restored in the early 17th century. Oscar Wilde lived here for a time; this is where he said, "Either this wallpaper goes, or I do." In the 20th century, a modern wing was added, and in 1991, the hotel was completely renovated and made into a first-rate establishment. The recently redecorated bedrooms are not large, but each room is individually decorated, often with fine antiques and original artwork. The majority of the accommodations open onto the private walled garden or the roof garden, and all have marble-clad shower-tub combination bathrooms. Rooms boast such luxuries as phones in the bathrooms.

1 Banbury Rd., Oxford OX2 6NN. ℂ **01865/310210.** Fax 01865/311262. www.oxford-hotels-restaurants.co. uk. 30 units. £135–£170 ($250–$315) double; £195 ($360) suite. AE, DC, MC, V. Bus: 7. **Amenities:** Restaurant; bar; car and limo service for hire; 24-hr. room service; laundry service; dry-cleaning service, nonsmoking rooms. *In room:* TV, dataport, hair dryer, safe, trouser press.

## MODERATE

**Dial House**   This country house, built in the 1920s, rests beside the highway to London, 3km (2 miles) east of the heart of Oxford. Graced with mock-Tudor half-timbering and a prominent blue-faced sundial, it has roomy and recently renovated bedrooms. In the conversion from private home to guesthouse, much of the original architecture was retained. The owners have done much to provide comfort in the bedrooms, and the decor reminds us of a visit to one's favorite aunt in the country. Most of the individually furnished units open onto an attractive garden. Thoughtful extras include a pack of helpful information about the area. Even special dietary requirements are heeded at breakfast if management is notified in advance. Bathrooms are small and most of them have a shower only, but a few offer a combination tub-and-shower. No smoking is permitted in the house.

25 London Rd., Headington, Oxford, Oxfordshire OX3 7RE. ℂ and fax **01865/760743.** www.oxfordcity.co.uk/ accom/dialhouse. 8 units. £65–£70 ($120–$130) double; £85 ($157) family room. AE, MC, V. Bus: 2, 2A, 7, 7A, or 22. *In room:* TV, coffeemaker, hair dryer, safe, no phone.

**River Hotel**   This hotel lies a quarter-mile west of Oxford's commercial core and charges less than many of its more central competitors. It was built around 1900 by a local craftsman whose casement windows and flower boxes are still in place. About a quarter of the accommodations are across the street in a stone-sided annex. Bedrooms have cozy furnishings, including comfortable beds, and are continually renewed. Bathrooms are small and come with showers.

17 Botley Rd., Oxford, Oxfordshire OX2 0AA. ℂ **01865/243475.** Fax 01865/724306. www.riverhotel.co.uk. 20 units. £76–£96 ($141–$178) double. Rates include English breakfast. MC, V. Bus: 4C or 52. **Amenities:** Restaurant, bar. *In room:* Coffeemaker, hair dryer from reception; no phone.

**Tilbury Lodge Private Hotel** *Value*   This small hotel lies on a quiet country lane 3km (2 miles) west of the center of Oxford, less than a mile from the railway station. Eddie and Eileen Trafford house guests in well-furnished and comfortable bedrooms. Each room is immaculately kept and furnished in traditional English style with wood furnishings, excellent beds (the most expensive room has a four-poster bed), rugs, and wall art to give each accommodation a homelike touch. Like similar accommodations at Dial House, Tilbury Lodge offers a tranquil location on a country lane right outside the bustle of town. Many use it as a base for exploring not only Oxford, but the Cotswolds, Blenheim Palace, Stratford-upon-Avon, and even Bath. Because of the ample street parking, you can leave your car here and go by bus into the city center. Rooms vary in size; most have adequate space and each comes with a tiny, well-kept bathroom with a shower. If you don't arrive by car, Eddie can pick you up at the train station; a bus also stops nearby.

5 Tilbury Lane, Eynsham Rd., Botley, Oxford, Oxfordshire OX2 9NB. © **01865/862138.** Fax 01865/863700. 9 units. £66–£75 ($122–$139) double. Rates include English breakfast. MC, V. Bus: 4A, 4B, or 100. **Amenities:** Jacuzzi. *In room:* TV, coffeemaker, hair dryer.

## WHERE TO DINE
### EXPENSIVE
**Elizabeth** ✸ CONTINENTAL/FRENCH    This stone-sided house opposite Christ Church College is named not for Elizabeth II (although her portraits hang near the entrance), but for the matriarch who founded the place in the 1930s. Today, you'll find a well-trained staff from Spain, who serve beautifully presented dishes in the French style. The larger of the two dining rooms exudes a restrained dignity; the smaller is devoted to *Alice in Wonderland* designs inspired by Lewis Carroll. Dishes are based on the use of fine ingredients prepared with a skilled culinary technique, as exemplified by the filet of salmon sautéed in butter and cooked with a white-wine sauce, or the grilled filet steak in a Madeira-flavored mushroom sauce. Breast of chicken is cooked in butter and delectably served in a creamy cognac and white-wine sauce.

82 St. Aldate's St. © 01865/242230. Reservations recommended. Main courses £14–£33 ($25–$61); lunch £16 ($30). AE, DC, MC, V. Tues–Sat 12:30–2:30pm and 6:30–11pm; Sun 7–10:30pm. Closed Easter weekend and Christmas week. Bus: 7.

### MODERATE
**Al-Shami** LEBANESE    Ideal for meals all afternoon and late into the evening, this Lebanese restaurant awakens Oxford's sleepy taste buds. Many diners don't go beyond the appetizers, with more than 35 delectable hot-and-cold selections— everything from falafel to lamb's-brain salad. Charcoal-grilled chopped lamb, chicken, and beef constitute most of the main-dish selections. In between, guests nibble on uncut raw vegetables; afterward they choose desserts from the trolley. Al-Shami also serves vegetarian meals.

25 Walton Crescent. © 01865/310066. Reservations recommended. Main courses £5.75–£12 ($11–$22); fixed-price menu £15 ($28). MC, V. Daily noon–midnight.

**Cherwell Boathouse Restaurant** FRENCH/MODERN ENGLISH    This landmark on the River Cherwell is owned by Anthony Verdin, who offers a fixed-price menu that changes every 2 weeks to take advantage of the availability of fresh vegetables, fish, and meat. The kitchen is often cited for its "sensible combinations" of ingredients, as reflected quite well by its cream of artichoke and celery soup for a starter, or its shellfish terrine with a velvety chive-flavored crème fraîche. The successful main dishes include savory treats such as a pink and juicy breast of pigeon matched with a salad of smoked bacon, on which tantalizing dribbles of raspberry dressing have been dropped. The tender and flavorful pork is perfectly married to an apple-and-prune compote. The restaurant has an exciting, reasonable wine list. In summer, dinner is served on the terrace. Before dinner, you can try punting; there's a rental agency on the other side of the boathouse.

Bardwell Rd. © 01865/552746. www.cherwellboathouse.co.uk. Reservations recommended. Fixed-price dinner from £23 ($42); Sun lunch £22 ($40); Mon–Fri lunch £20 ($36). AE, DC, MC, V. Mon–Sun 12:30pm–2pm and 6:30–9pm. Closed Dec 24–30. Bus: Banbury Rd.

**Gee's Restaurant** ✸ INTERNATIONAL/MEDITERRANEAN    This restaurant is housed in a spacious Victorian glass conservatory that was converted from what for 80 years was the leading florist of Oxford. The owners, who also own the Old Parsonage Hotel and the Old Bank Hotel (reviewed earlier in this section), have retained all of the building's original features, turning the space into one of the most nostalgic and delightful places to dine in the city. It's been around since 1984, but the skills of new chefs have made it even more popular. Clientele ranges from students to professors, and all enjoy a well-chosen menu that features everything from succulent pastas to chargrilled steaks, from fresh fish to crisp salads. The grilled halibut steak with lemon-and-thyme butter is predictable but nonetheless fine in every way. The confit of duck is a savory choice, enhanced by Savoy cabbage, smoked bacon, and herb-roasted potatoes. Count on a freshly made soup and such Mediterranean-inspired salads as roast pepper, French beans, and olives. The Scottish prime rib-eye steak with mushrooms and shoestring "chips" is always reliable.

61 Banbury Rd. (C) **01865/553540.** Reservations recommended. Fixed-price lunch £13–£17 ($24–$31); main courses £11–£20 ($20–$37). AE, MC, V. Mon–Sat noon–2:30pm and 6–11pm; Sun noon–11pm.

**Le Petit Blanc** ⭐ FRENCH/MEDITERRANEAN     This buzzing brasserie, located in a former piano shop converted into a stylish restaurant, promises something for every palate. Here you can get a taste of famous chef Raymond Blanc's creations without the high prices charged in his other restaurants. The menu is fairly straightforward, with a special emphasis on fresh ingredients, and the restaurant is conveniently located 2 blocks from the bus station.

The aim is simple—to provide the best food, service, and value for your money. The food is wholesome and delicious, based on authentic Provençal French cuisine, complemented by Mediterranean and Asian accents. The crab-and-lobster spring roll with spicy fig compote might get you going. We recently delighted in an appetizer of deep-fried goat's cheese with olive tapenade, French beans, and tomato chutney, followed by a perfectly roasted John Dory with a coriander dressing. For other mains, the braised rabbit with sweet-onion *tarte tatin* and flap mushrooms, and the Oxford sausage and parsleyed mash with Madeira and sweet-onion sauce are superb. The desserts are first-rate, especially the raspberry soufflé.

71–72 Walton St. (C) **01865/510999.** Reservations recommended. Main courses £10–£15 ($19–$28); fixed-price lunch £16 ($30). AE, DC, MC, V. Mon–Sat noon–3:30pm and 6–11pm; Sun 12:30–3pm and 6:30–10:30pm.

## INEXPENSIVE

**Alsalam** ⭐ *Value* LEBANESE     Some Oxford students think this place offers the best food value in the city. The menu depends on what's available in the marketplace, and the chef's skill is reflected in such dishes as king prawns sautéed with a garlic-and-tomato sauce, or spicy lamb with a chile-and-onion sauce. Long lines can form at the door, especially on Fridays and Saturdays.

6 Park End St. (C) **01865/245710.** Reservations recommended. Main courses £7.50–£12 ($14–$22). MC, V. Daily noon–midnight.

## PUBS

**The Bear Inn**     A short block from The High Street, overlooking the north side of Christ Church College, this village pub is an Oxford tradition. Its swinging sign depicts a bear and a ragged staff, the old insignia of the earls of Warwick, who were among its early patrons. Many famous Oxford students and residents have caroused within the pub's walls since the 13th century, earning it a well-worn place in English literature. Some past owners developed the prankish habit of clipping their guests' neckties. Around the lounge bar you'll see the remains of thousands of ties, all labeled with their owners' names.

Alfred St., at the corner of Alfred and Blue Boar. ✆ **01865/728164.** Snacks and bar meals £2.75–£7 ($5.10–$13). MC, V. Mon–Sat noon–11pm; Sun noon–10:30pm. Bus: 2A or 2B.

**The Turf Tavern** This 13th-century tavern, the oldest in Oxford, stands on a very narrow passageway near the Bodleian Library. Thomas Hardy used it as a setting in *Jude the Obscure,* and it was "the local" of Richard Burton and Liz Taylor when they were in Oxford many years ago making a film. Today's patrons include a healthy sampling of the university's students and faculty. During warm weather you can choose a table in one of the three separate gardens that radiate outward from the pub's core. For wintertime warmth, braziers are lit in the courtyard and in the gardens. A separate food counter, set behind a glass case, displays the day's fare. The pub is reached via St. Helen's Passage, which stretches between Holywell Street and New College Lane.

7 Bath Place (off Holywell St.). ✆ **01865/243235.** Main courses £5–£10 ($9.25–$19). MC, V. Mon–Sat 11am–11pm; Sun noon–10:30pm, last meal served at 7:30pm. Bus: 52.

## 3 The Pursuit of Science: Cambridge ★★★

89km (55 miles) N of London, 129km (80 miles) NE of Oxford

The university town of Cambridge is a collage of images: the Bridge of Sighs; spires and turrets; willows; dusty secondhand bookshops; the lilt of Elizabethan madrigals; lanes where Darwin, Newton, and Cromwell walked; the grassy Backs of the colleges, sweeping down to the banks of the Cam; punters; and the tattered robes of hurried upperclassmen flying in the wind.

Along with Oxford, Cambridge is one of Britain's ancient seats of knowledge. In many ways their stories are similar. However, beyond its campus, Cambridge has a thriving, high-tech industry. And while Oxford concentrates on the arts, Cambridge has embraced the sciences. Both Isaac Newton and Stephen Hawking are graduates, joined by luminaries in every field.

There is much to explore in Cambridge, so give yourself time to wander.

### ESSENTIALS
**GETTING THERE** Trains depart frequently from London's Liverpool Street and King's Cross stations, arriving an hour later. For inquiries, call ✆ **0845/ 748-4950.** A one-way ticket costs £16 ($29).

**National Express** buses leave hourly from London's Victoria Coach Station for the 2-hour trip to Drummer Street Station in Cambridge. A one-way ticket costs £9 ($17). For schedules and information, call ✆ **0870/580-8080.**

If you're driving from London, head north on the M11.

**VISITOR INFORMATION** In back of the guildhall, the **Cambridge Tourist Information Centre,** Wheeler Street (✆ 09065/862-526; www. tourismcambridge.com), has a wide range of information, including data on public transportation and sightseeing attractions. From April to October, hours are Monday to Saturday from 10am to 6pm and Sunday from 11am to 4pm. In July and August, the office is open daily from 10am to 7pm. From November to March, hours are Monday through Saturday from 10am to 5:30pm.

A tourist reception center for Cambridge and Cambridgeshire is operated by **City Sightseeing** at Cambridge Railway Station (✆ 01223/362444). The center, on the concourse of the railway station, sells brochures and maps. Also

# Cambridge

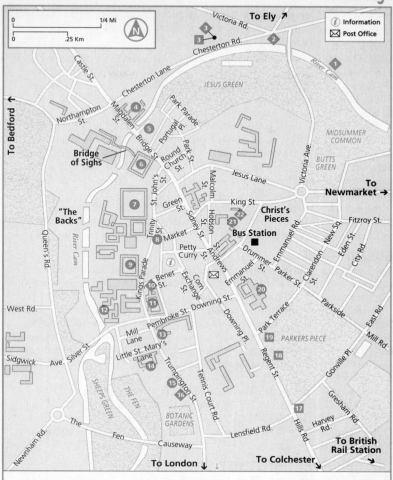

To Ely ↗

Victoria Rd.
Chesterton Rd.

ⓘ Information
✉ Post Office

Chesterton Lane
Castle St.
JESUS GREEN
River Cam

To Bedford ←
Northampton St.
Magdalene St.
Bridge St.
Park Parade
Portugal Pl.
Park St.
Round Church St.

MIDSUMMER COMMON
Victoria Ave.
BUTTS GREEN

Bridge of Sighs

"The Backs"

St. John's St.
Green St.
Malcolm St.
Sidney St.
Trinity St.
Market St.
Petty Cury
Andrews St.
Hobson St.

Jesus Lane
King St.

Christ's Pieces

Bus Station ■

To Newmarket →

Fitzroy St.
New Sq.
Eden St.
City Rd.

Queen's Rd.
River Cam
Kings Parade

West Rd.

Benet St.
Corn Exchange St.
Pembroke St.
Downing St.

Drummer St.
Emmanuel Rd.
Emmanuel St.
Parker St.
Clarendon St.

Parkside
East Rd.

Mill Lane

Downing Pl.
Park Terrace

Gonville Pl.
Mill Rd.

Sidgwick Ave.
Silver St.
Little St. Mary's Lane
Trumpington St.
Tennis Court Rd.

PARKERS PIECE

Regent St.

SHEEPS GREEN
THE FEN
BOTANIC GARDENS

The Fen
Causeway

Lensfield Rd.
Hills Rd.
Harvey Rd.
Gresham Rd.

Newnham Rd.

To London ↓

To Colchester ↘

To British Rail Station ↘

English Channel

## ATTRACTIONS ●
Christ's College **21**
Corpus Christi College **11**
Emmanuel College **20**
Fitzwilliam Museum **15**
Great St. Mary's **8**
King's College **9**
Magdalene College **4**
Pembroke College **13**
Peterhouse College **14**
Queens' College **12**
St. John's College **6**
Scudamores Boatyards **5**
Trinity College **7**

## ACCOMMODATIONS ■
Arundel House **3**
Gonville Hotel **17**
Regent Hotel **18**
University Arms Hotel **19**

## DINING ◆
Arundel House Restaurant **3**
Browns **16**
Cambridge Arms **22**
The Eagle Pub **10**
Midsummer House **1**
Twenty-Two **2**

0   100 mi
0   100 km

SCOTLAND
North Sea
Irish Sea
ENGLAND
**Cambridge**
WALES
★ **London**

available is a full range of tourist services, including accommodations booking. Open in summer daily from 8:45am to 7pm (closes at 5pm off-season). Guided tours of Cambridge leave the center daily.

**GETTING AROUND**   The center of Cambridge is made for pedestrians, so park your car at one of the car parks (they increase in price as you approach the city center) and stroll the widely dispersed colleges. Follow the courtyards through to the Backs (the college lawns) and walk through to Trinity (where Prince Charles studied) and St. John's colleges, where you'll find the Bridge of Sighs.

Another popular way of getting around is bicycling. **Station Cycles** (© 01223/ 307125; www.stationcycles.co.uk) has bicycles for rent for £6 ($11) for half-day, £8 ($15) per day, or £16 ($30) per week. A deposit of £50 ($93) is required. Call their number to reserve a bike. At that time you'll be told the address at which to pick up the cycle. Open Monday through Friday from 7am to 8pm, Saturday from 9am to 5pm, Sunday 10am to 4pm.

**Stagecoach Cambus,** 100 Cowley Rd. (© 01223/423-578), services the Cambridge area with a network of buses, with fares ranging in price from 65p to £3 ($1.20–$5.55) for a day pass. The local tourist office has bus schedules.

## GUIDED TOURS

The **Cambridge Tourist Information Centre** (see above) sponsors 2-hour walking tours, taking in the highlights of the city, costing £13 ($23) for adults or £6 ($11) for children. Call for opening times.

In addition to its visitor information services (see "Essentials," above), **City Sightseeing,** on the concourse of Cambridge Railway Station (© 01223/ 362444), offers daily guided tours of Cambridge via open-top, double-decker buses. In summer, they depart every 15 minutes from 9:30am to 4pm. Departures are curtailed off-season depending on demand. The tour can be a 1-hour ride, or you can get off at any of the many stops and rejoin the tour whenever you wish. Tickets are valid all day. The fare is £7.50 ($14) for adults, £5.50 ($10) for seniors and students, £3 ($5.55) for children 6 to 12, and free for kids 5 and under. A family ticket for £20 ($37) covers two adults and up to three children. Office hours are daily from 8:45am to 7pm in summer and from 9:30am to 5pm during the off-season.

## EXPLORING THE UNIVERSITY

Oxford University predates Cambridge, but by the early 13th century scholars began gathering here. Eventually, Cambridge won partial recognition and received funds from Henry III. After Henry III's reign, approval and funding rose and fell depending on the monarch. Cambridge consists of 31 colleges for both men and women. Colleges are closed to the public during exams from mid-April until the end of June.

The following listing is only a sample of some of the more interesting colleges. If you're planning to be in Cambridge awhile, you might also want to visit **Magdalene College,** on Magdalene Street, founded in 1542; **Pembroke College,** on Trumpington Street, founded in 1347; **Christ's College,** on St. Andrew's Street, founded in 1505; and **Corpus Christi College,** on Trumpington Street, which dates from 1352.

**EMMANUEL COLLEGE**   On St. Andrew's Street, Emmanuel (© 01223/ 334200; www.emma.cam.ac.uk) was founded in 1584 by Sir Walter Mildmay, a chancellor of the exchequer to Elizabeth I. John Harvard, of the university that bears his name in another city called Cambridge, studied here. You can stroll around Emmanuel's attractive gardens and visit the chapel designed by Sir Christopher Wren, consecrated in 1677. Both the chapel and college are open daily during sunlight hours.

*Insider's Tip:* Harvard men and women, and those who love them, can look for a memorial window in Wren's chapel dedicated to John Harvard, an alumnus of Emmanuel who lent his name to that other university.

**KING'S COLLEGE** ★★    The adolescent Henry VI founded King's College on King's Parade (℃ **01223/331100;** www.kings.cam.ac.uk) in 1441. Most of its buildings today date from the 19th century, but the construction of its crowning glory, the **Perpendicular King's College Chapel** ★★★, began in the Middle Ages. The Perpendicular King's College Chapel is one of England's irreplaceable monuments. Owing to the whims of royalty, the chapel wasn't completed until the early 16th century.

Henry James called King's College Chapel "the most beautiful in England." Its most striking features are its magnificent fan vaulting, all in stone, and its great windows, most of which were fashioned by Flemish artisans between 1517 and 1531 (the west window dates from the late Victorian period). In hues of red, blue, and amber, the long range of windows around the back of the chapel depicts the Birth of the Virgin; the Annunciation; the Birth of Christ; the Life, Ministry, and Death of Christ; the Resurrection; the Ascension; the Acts of the Apostles; and the Assumption. The upper range contains Old Testament parallels to these New Testament stories. The chapel also boasts Rubens's *Adoration of the Magi* and an ornamental screen from the early 16th century. The chapel is famous for its choir and musical concerts. You can call the college (phone number above) for concert dates and times.

*Insider's Tip:* For a classic view of the chapel, you can admire the architectural complex from the rear, which is an ideal picnic spot along the river. E. M. Forster came here to contemplate scenes for his novel *Maurice.*

The chapel is open during vacation time, Monday through Friday from 9:30am to 3:30pm, Saturday from 9:30am to 3:15pm, and Sunday from 1:15 to 2:15pm and 5 to 5:30pm. During the term, the public is welcome to attend choral services Monday through Saturday at 5:30pm and on Sunday at 10:30am and 3:30pm. During school vacations, the chapel is open to visitors Monday through Saturday from 9:30am to 4:30pm and on Sunday from 10am to 5pm; it is closed from December 23 to January 1. It may be closed at other times for recording sessions, broadcasts, and concerts.

An exhibition in the seven northern side chapels shows why and how the chapel was built. Admission to the college and chapel, including the exhibition, is £3.50 ($6.50) for adults, £2.50 ($4.65) for students and children 12 to 17, and free for children under 12.

**PETERHOUSE COLLEGE**    On Trumpington Street, Peterhouse College (℃ **01223/338200;** www.pet.cam.ac.uk) attracts visitors because it's the oldest Cambridge college, founded in 1284 by Hugh de Balsham, the bishop of Ely. Of the original buildings, only the hall remains. It was restored in the 19th century and has stained-glass windows by William Morris. The chapel, called Old Court, dates from 1632 and was renovated in 1754. Ask to enter at the porter's lodge.

*Insider's Tip:* Almost sadly neglected, the Little Church of St. Mary's next door was the college chapel until 1632. Pay it the honor of a visit.

**QUEENS' COLLEGE** 🏛 On Silver Street, Queens' College (© **01223/ 335511**; www.quns.cam.ac.uk) is the loveliest of Cambridge's colleges. Dating back to 1448, it was founded by two English queens, Margaret of Anjou, the wife of Henry VI, and Elizabeth Woodville, the wife of Edward IV. Its second cloister is the most interesting, flanked by the early 16th-century half-timbered President's Lodge.

Admission is £1.50 ($2.80), free for children under 12 accompanied by parents. A printed guide is issued. From November until March 19, hours are daily from 1:45 to 4:30pm; from March 20 to May 15, Monday through Friday from 1:45 to 4:30pm, Saturday and Sunday from 10am to 4:45pm; closed from May 17 to June 19. From June 20 to September 19, Monday through Friday from 10am to 4:30pm and Saturday and Sunday from 10am to 4:45pm; from September 20 to October 31, Monday through Friday from 1:45 to 4:30pm, Saturday and Sunday from 10am to 4:45pm. Entry and exit is by the old porter's lodge in Queens' Lane only. The old hall and chapel are usually open to the public when not in use.

*Insider's Tip:* Here's your chance to relax from a hectic day of sightseeing. Queens' College's wide lawns lead down to the "Backs" (the backs of the colleges), where you can stroll, sit, or go punting. Take in Mathematical Bridge, best viewed from the Silver Street bridge, dating from 1902. By this bridge, stop off at the old pub, the Anchor, and contemplate what life would have been like if you'd attended Cambridge.

**ST. JOHN'S COLLEGE** 🏛🏛🏛 On St. John's Street, this college (© **01223/ 338600**; www.joh.cam.ac.uk) was founded in 1511 by Lady Margaret Beaufort, mother of Henry VII, who had launched Christ's College a few years earlier. The impressive gateway bears the Tudor coat of arms, and the Second Court is a fine example of late Tudor brickwork. The college's best-known feature is the Bridge of Sighs crossing the Cam. Built in the 19th century, it was patterned after the covered bridge in Venice. It connects the older part of the college with New Court, a Gothic revival on the opposite bank, where there is an outstanding view of the famous "Backs" (the backs of the colleges). The Bridge of Sighs is closed to visitors, but can be seen from neighboring Kitchen Bridge. Wordsworth was an alumnus of this college, which is open March through October, daily from 9:30am to 5pm. The college is open from March to October daily from 9:30am to 5:30pm. Admission is £2 ($3.70) for adults and £1.50 ($2.80) for children. Visitors are welcome to attend choral services in the chapel.

*Insider's Tip:* The Bridge of Sighs links the old college with an architectural "folly" of the 19th century, the elaborate New Court, which is a crenellated neo-Gothic fantasy. It's adorned with a "riot" of pinnacles and a main cupola. Students call it "the wedding cake."

**TRINITY COLLEGE** 🏛🏛 On Trinity Street, Trinity College (not to be confused with Trinity Hall) (© **01223/338400**; www.trin.cam.ac.uk) is the largest college in Cambridge. It was founded in 1546 by Henry VIII, who consolidated a number of smaller colleges that had existed on the site. The courtyard is the most spacious in Cambridge, built when Thomas Neville was master. Sir Christopher Wren designed the library.

*Insider's Tip:* What's fun to do here is to contemplate what went on here before you arrived. Pause at Neville's Court where Isaac Newton first calculated the speed of sound. Take in the delicate fountain of the Great Court where Lord Byron used to bathe naked with his pet bear. Why a bear? The university forbade students from having dogs, but there was no proviso for bears. Years later, Vladimir Nabokov walked through that same courtyard dreaming of the young lady he would later immortalize as *Lolita*. For admission to the college, apply at the porter's lodge. There's a charge of £2 ($3.70) from March to November.

## MORE CAMBRIDGE ATTRACTIONS

**Fitzwilliam Museum** ☆☆    This is one of Britain's finest museums, founded by the bequest of the seventh viscount Fitzwilliam of Merrion to the University of Cambridge in 1816. The permanent collections contain remarkable antiquities from ancient Egypt, Greece, and Rome. Galleries display Roman and Romano-Egyptian art along with Western-Asiatic exhibits. The Fitzwilliam's Applied Arts section showcases English and European pottery and glass, as well as furniture, clocks, armor, fans, rugs and samplers, Chinese jades, and ceramics from Japan and Korea. The museum also has married a rare ancient and medieval coin collection with a host of medals created from the Renaissance onward. The Fitzwilliam is best loved for its collection of paintings, which includes masterpieces by Simone Martini, Titian, Veronese, Rubens, Van Dyck, Canaletto, Hogarth, Gainsborough, Constable, Monet, Degas, Renoir, Cézanne, and Picasso. There is also a fine collection of other 20th-century art, miniatures, drawings, watercolors, and prints. The Fitzwilliam stages occasional musical events, including evening concerts, in Gallery III. Throughout the year, it plays host to some of the best lectures in England.

Trumpington St., near Peterhouse. © 01223/332900. www.fitzmuseum.cam.ac.uk. Free admission, donations appreciated. Tues–Sat 10am–5pm; Sun 2:15–5pm. Guided tours £3 ($5.55) per person, Sun 2:45pm. Closed Jan 1, Good Friday, May Day, and Dec 24–31.

**Great St. Mary's**    Closely associated with events of the Reformation because the leaders of the movement (Erasmus, Cranmer, Latimer, and Ridley) preached here, this university church was built mostly in 1478 on the site of an 11th-century church. The cloth that covered the hearse of King Henry VII is on display in the church. There is a fine view of Cambridge from the top of the tower.

King's Parade. © 01223/741716. Admission to tower £2 ($3.70) adults, £1 ($1.85) children. Tower summer Mon–Sat 9:30am–5pm, Sun 12:30–5pm; church daily 9am–6pm.

## WHERE TO STAY
### EXPENSIVE

**De Vere University Arms Hotel** ☆    This 1834 hotel maintains much of its antique charm and many original architectural features despite modernization over the years. Near the city center and the university, it offers suitable bedrooms. Rooms range from small to midsize, each with bedside controls; the premium rooms also have slippers and robes. Many of the bedrooms have been recently refurbished; eight have four-poster beds. Rooms in front are smaller but more up-to-date and have double-glazed windows. Each room comes with a king-size or twin beds, and bathrooms have a shower-and-tub combo (except the single rooms, which have showers only). Three rooms are suitable for families.

Regent St., Cambridge, Cambridgeshire CB2 1AD. © 01223/351241. Fax 01223/273037. www.devereonline.co.uk. 118 units. £200–£250 ($370–$463) double; from £350 ($648) suite. Rates include English breakfast. AE, DC, MC, V. Parking £8 ($15). Bus: 1. **Amenities:** Restaurant; bar; room service; babysitting; laundry service; dry cleaning; nonsmoking rooms; units for those w/limited mobility. *In room:* TV, dataport, minibar, coffeemaker, hair dryer, iron/ironing board.

## MODERATE

**Gonville Hotel**    This hotel and its grounds are opposite Parker's Piece Park, only a 5-minute walk from the center of town. The Gonville has been much improved in recent years, and is better than ever, although not yet the equal of the University Arms (above). It's like an ivy-covered country house, with shade trees and a formal car entry. The recently refurbished rooms are comfortable and modern in style. Bedrooms have small but well-kept bathrooms with showers.

Gonville Place, Cambridge, Cambridgeshire CB1 1LY. ✆ 800/528-1234 in the U.S. and Canada, or 01223/366611. Fax 01223/315470. www.gonvillehotel.co.uk. 78 units. £120 ($222) double. AE, DC, MC, V. **Amenities:** Restaurant; bar; limited room service; laundry service/dry cleaning; nonsmoking rooms. *In room:* TV, coffeemaker, hair dryer, iron/ironing board.

## INEXPENSIVE

**Arundel House**    Occupying one of the most desirable sites in Cambridge, this hotel consists of six interconnected identical Victorian row houses—all fronted with dark-yellow local bricks. In 1994, after two additional houses were purchased, the hotel was enlarged, upgraded, and expanded into the well-maintained hostelry you'll see today. Though not as well appointed as the University Arms, it competes successfully with the Gonville, and has the best cuisine of the three hotels. Rooms overlooking the River Cam and Jesus Green cost more, as do those on lower floors (there's no elevator). All rooms are clean, simple, and comfortable, with upholstered chairs, carpeting, and small but efficient and tidily kept shower-only bathrooms.

53 Chesterton Rd., Cambridge, Cambridgeshire CB4 3AN. ✆ 01223/367701. Fax 01223/367721. www.arundelhousehotels.co.uk. 102 units. £95–£125 ($176–$231) double; £120–£135 ($222–$250) family bedroom. Rates include continental breakfast. AE, DC, MC, V. Bus: 1 or 3. **Amenities:** Restaurant; bar; laundry. *In room:* A/C, TV, hair dryer, coffeemaker.

**Regent Hotel**    This is one of the most desirable of Cambridge's reasonably priced small hotels. Right in the city center, overlooking Parker's Piece Park, the house was built in the 1840s as the original site of Newnham College. It became a hotel when the college outgrew its quarters. Bedrooms are on the small side, but are redecorated frequently in traditional Georgian style. Bathrooms are small, but have adequate shelf space and tubs with shower attachments.

41 Regent St., Cambridge, Cambridgeshire CB2 1AB. ✆ 01223/351470. Fax 01223/236608. www.regenthotel.co.uk. 22 units. £90 ($167) double. Rates include continental breakfast. AE, DC, MC, V. Bus: 1. **Amenities:** Bar, all nonsmoking rooms. *In room:* TV, dataport, coffeemaker, hair dryer.

## WHERE TO DINE
### EXPENSIVE

**Midsummer House** 🏵🏵 *Finds* MEDITERRANEAN    Located in an Edwardian-era cottage near the River Cam, the Midsummer House is a real find. We prefer to dine in the elegant conservatory, but you can also find a smartly laid table upstairs. The fixed-price menus are wisely limited, and quality control and high standards are much in evidence here. Daniel Clifford is the master chef, and he has created such specialties as filet of beef Rossini with braised winter vegetables and sauce Perigourdine; and roast squab pigeon, pomme Anna, *tarte tatin* of onions, caramelized endives, and jus of morels.

Midsummer Common. ✆ 01223/369299. Reservations required. 3-course fixed-price lunch £26 ($48); dinner £45 ($83). AE, MC, V. Tues–Sat noon–2pm and 7–10pm.

## MODERATE

**Arundel House Restaurant** 🏵 BRITISH/FRENCH/VEGETARIAN    One of the best and most acclaimed restaurants in Cambridge is in a hotel overlooking the

River Cam and Jesus Green, a short walk from the city center. Winner of many awards, it's noted not only for its excellence and use of fresh produce, but also for its good value. The decor is warmly inviting with Sanderson curtains, Louis XV–upholstered chairs, and spacious tables. The menu changes frequently, and you can dine both a la carte or from the set menu. Perhaps you'll begin with a homemade golden-pea-and-ham soup or a white-rum-and-passion-fruit cocktail. Fish choices include plaice or salmon; try the pork-and-pigeon casserole or the Japanese-style braised lamb.

53 Chesterton Rd. ℂ **01223/367701.** Reservations required. Main courses £10–£16 ($19–$30); fixed-price Sun lunch £16 ($30); fixed-price dinner £20 ($37). AE, DC, MC, V. Daily 12:30–2pm and 6:30–9:30pm. Bus: 3 or 5.

**Browns** ★ *Value* CONTINENTAL/ENGLISH    After wowing them at Oxford, Browns now lures Cambridge students in equal numbers. The building lies opposite the Fitzwilliam Museum and was constructed in 1914 as the outpatient department of a hospital dedicated to Edward VII; that era's grandeur is apparent in the building's neoclassical colonnade. Today, it's the most lighthearted place for dining in the city, with wicker chairs, high ceilings, pre–World War I woodwork, and a long bar covered with bottles of wine. The extensive bill of fare includes pastas, scores of fresh salads, several selections of meat and fish (from charcoal-grilled leg of lamb with rosemary to fresh fish in season), hot sandwiches, and the chef's daily specials. If you drop by in the afternoon, you can also order thick milkshakes or natural fruit juices. In fair weather, outdoor seats are prized possessions.

23 Trumpington St. (5 min. from King's College and opposite the Fitzwilliam Museum). ℂ **01223/461655.** Main courses £7–£14 ($13–$26). AE, MC, V. Mon–Thurs 11am–11pm; Fri–Sat 11am–11:30pm; Sun noon–10:30pm. Bus: 2.

**Twenty Two** ★ CONTINENTAL/ENGLISH    One of the best in Cambridge, this restaurant is located in a quiet district near Jesus Green, and is a secret jealously guarded by the locals. The homelike but elegant Victorian dining room offers an ever-changing fixed-price menu based on fresh market produce. Owners David Carter and Louise Crompton use time-tested recipes along with their own inspirations, offering creations such as white onion soup with toasted goat's cheese, or sautéed breast of chicken on braised celery with thyme jus.

22 Chesterton Rd. ℂ **01223/351880.** Reservations required. Fixed-price menu £25 ($46). AE, MC, V. Tues–Sat 7–9:30pm.

## PUBS

**Cambridge Arms**    This no-nonsense pub in the center of town, just 1 block from the train station, bustles with atmosphere and dispenses endless platters of food over the bar's countertop. The menu includes the chef's daily specials, grilled steaks, vegetarian meals, and an array of both hot and cold dishes. The pub was recently refurbished and now features a music-oriented theme. Guitars and music paraphernalia adorn the walls.

4 King St. ℂ **01223/505015.** Bar snacks £1.50–£3 ($2.80–$5.55), main courses £4–£10 ($7.40–$19). MC, V. Mon–Sat noon–3pm and 6–9pm; Sun noon–4pm. Pub Mon–Sat 11am–11pm; Sun noon–10:30pm.

**The Eagle Pub**    This pub dates back to the 1500s and was the favorite Cambridge watering hole for American and British pilots during World War II. It's still going strong, and you don't have to visit it just in the evening, as it also serves pub lunches. A former coaching inn, it offers several separate bars and a cobblestone courtyard for summer-overflow beer drinking. It is famous as the place where Nobel laureates Watson and Crick first announced their discovery of the DNA double helix. Real ales include Icebreaker and Greene King's Abbot. Place your order and raise a pint to the wonders of modern science.

Benet St. off King's Parade. (℃ **01223/505020.** Main courses £6–£8.50 ($11–$16). DC, MC, V. Mon–Sat 11am–11pm; Sun noon–10:30pm.

## 4 Shakespeare's Stratford-upon-Avon ✴✴

147km (91 miles) NW of London, 65km (40 miles) NW of Oxford

Crowds of visitors overrun this market town on the River Avon during the summer months. In fact, Stratford so aggressively hustles its Shakespeare connection that it seems at times that everybody here is trying to make a buck off the Bard. If he could return today, Shakespeare would be inundated with T-shirts bearing his likeness and china models of Anne Hathaway's cottage. He might look for a less trampled town to pen his masterpieces in.

One visitor magnet is the Royal Shakespeare Theatre, where Britain's foremost actors perform. Other than the theater, Stratford is nearly devoid of cultural life, and you may want to rush back to London after you've done the literary pilgrimage and seen a show. If you can, visit in winter, when the throngs dwindle.

## ESSENTIALS

**GETTING THERE** The journey from London's Paddington Station to Stratford-upon-Avon takes about 2 hours, and a round-trip ticket costs £23 ($43). For schedules and information, call (℃ **0845/748-4950.** The train station at Stratford is on Alcester Road. On Sundays from October to May, it is closed, so you'll have to rely on the bus.

Eight **National Express** buses a day leave from London's Victoria Station, with a trip time of 3¼ hours. A single-day round-trip ticket costs £13 ($24), except Friday when the price is £20 ($37). For schedules and information, call (℃ **0870/580-8080.**

If you're driving from London, take the M40 toward Oxford and continue to Stratford-upon-Avon on the A34.

**VISITOR INFORMATION** The **Tourist Information Centre,** Bridgefoot, Stratford-upon-Avon, Warwickshire, CV37 6GW (℃ **01789/293127;** www. shakespeare-country.co.uk), provides any details you may wish to know about the Shakespeare houses and properties, and will assist in booking rooms (see "Where to Stay," below). Call and ask for a copy of their free *Shakespeare Country Holiday* guide. They also operate an American Express currency-exchange office. It's open from April to October, Monday through Saturday from 9am to 6pm and Sunday from 10:30am to 4:30pm; from November to March, Monday through Saturday from 9am to 5pm and Sunday from 10am to 4pm.

To contact **Shakespeare Birthplace Trust,** which administers many of the attractions, call the Shakespeare Centre (℃ **01789/204016;** www.shakespeare. org.uk).

## VISITING THE SHRINES

Besides the attractions on the periphery of Stratford, many Elizabethan and Jacobean buildings are in town, a number of them administered by the **Shakespeare Birthplace Trust** (℃ **01789/204016**). One ticket—costing £13 ($24) adults, £12 ($22) for seniors and students, and £6.50 ($12) for children—lets you visit the five most important sights. You can also buy a family ticket to

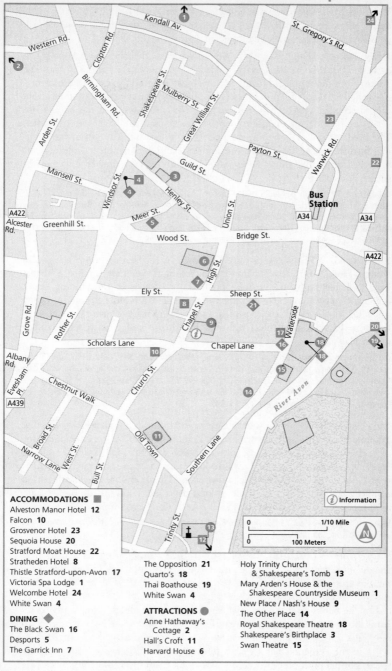

**ACCOMMODATIONS** ■
Alveston Manor Hotel **12**
Falcon **10**
Grosvenor Hotel **23**
Sequoia House **20**
Stratford Moat House **22**
Stratheden Hotel **8**
Thistle Stratford-upon-Avon **17**
Victoria Spa Lodge **1**
Welcombe Hotel **24**
White Swan **4**

**DINING** ◆
The Black Swan **16**
Desports **5**
The Garrick Inn **7**

The Opposition **21**
Quarto's **18**
Thai Boathouse **19**
White Swan **4**

**ATTRACTIONS** ●
Anne Hathaway's
  Cottage **2**
Hall's Croft **11**
Harvard House **6**

Holy Trinity Church
  & Shakespeare's Tomb **13**
Mary Arden's House & the
  Shakespeare Countryside Museum **1**
New Place / Nash's House **9**
The Other Place **14**
Royal Shakespeare Theatre **18**
Shakespeare's Birthplace **3**
Swan Theatre **15**

ⓘ Information

0 ————————— 1/10 Mile
0 ————————— 100 Meters

all five sights (good for two adults and three children) for £29 ($54)—a good deal. Pick up the ticket if you're planning to do much sightseeing (obtainable at your first stopover at any one of the Trust properties).

**Anne Hathaway's Cottage** ⭐  Before she married Shakespeare, Anne Hathaway lived in this thatched, wattle-and-daub cottage in the hamlet of Shottery, 1.6km (1 mile) from Stratford. It's the most interesting and the most photographed of the Trust properties. The Hathaways were yeoman farmers, and their descendants lived in the cottage until 1892. As a result, it was never renovated and provides a rare insight into the life of a family in Shakespearean times. The Bard was only 18 when he married Anne, who was much older. Many original furnishings, including the courting settle and various kitchen utensils, are preserved inside the house. After visiting the house, take time to linger in the garden and orchard.

Cottage Lane, Shottery. ⓒ **01789/292100.** Admission £5.20 ($9.65) adults, £2 ($3.70) children, £12 ($22) family ticket (2 adults, 3 children) for all 5 Shakespeare-related houses. Nov–Mar daily 10am–4pm; Apr–May Mon–Sat 9:30am–5pm, Sun 10am–5pm; June–Aug Mon–Sat 9am–5pm, Sun 9:30am–5pm; Sept–Oct Mon–Sat 9:30am–5pm, Sun 10am–5pm. Closed Dec 23–26. Take a bus from Bridge St. or walk via a marked pathway from Evesham Place in Stratford across the meadow to Shottery.

**Hall's Croft**  This house is on Old Town Street, not far from the parish church, Holy Trinity. It was here that Shakespeare's daughter Susanna probably lived with her husband, Dr. John Hall. Hall's Croft is an outstanding Tudor house with a walled garden, furnished in the style of a middle-class home of the time. Dr. Hall was widely respected and built up a large medical practice in the area. Fascinating exhibits illustrate the theory and practice of medicine in Dr. Hall's time.

Old Town (near Holy Trinity Church). ⓒ **01789/292107.** Admission £3.50 ($6.50) adults, £1.70 ($3.15) children, £9 ($17) family ticket (2 adults, 3 children) for all 5 Shakespeare-related houses. Nov–Mar daily 11am–4pm; Apr–May daily 11am–5pm; June–Aug Mon–Sat 9:30am–5pm, Sun 10am–5pm; Sept–Oct daily 11am–5pm. Closed Dec 23–28. To reach Hall's Croft, walk west from High St., which becomes Chapel St. and Church St. At the intersection with Old Town, go left.

**Harvard House**  The most ornate home in Stratford, Harvard House is a fine example of an Elizabethan town house. Rebuilt in 1596, it was once the home of Katherine Rogers, mother of John Harvard, who founded Harvard College. In 1909, Chicago millionaire Edward Morris purchased the house and presented it as a gift to the famous American university. The rooms are filled with period furniture, and the floors are made of local flagstone. Look for the Bible Chair, used for hiding the Bible during the days of Tudor persecution.

High St. ⓒ **01789/204507.** £2 ($3.80) adults. Free for children. May–Nov Tues–Sat and bank holiday Mon 11:30am–4:30pm, Sun 10:30am–4:30pm.

**Holy Trinity Church (Shakespeare's Tomb)**  In an attractive setting near the Avon River is the parish church where Shakespeare is buried (with the famous epitaph "And curst be he who moves my bones"). The church is one of the most beautiful parish churches in England.

On the banks of the Avon, "whit gentle murmur glides," the church dates from the 13th century. An avenue of lime trees frames the church entrance. To see Will's grave, head for the chancel, which was reconstructed from 1465 to 1491 in the Perpendicular style, its tomb lit by stained-glass windows. Shakespeare's burial position in the church was not a result of his literary prowess. He earned this stellar tomb because he was a lay rector in Stratford-upon-Avon. In 1623, Gerald Janse created a marble bust of Shakespeare on the north wall of the sanctuary over the altar steps. You'll also find the grave of Shakespeare's wife, Anne Hathaway, his daughter Susanna, and Susanna's husband, John Hall. The Parish Register displays the Bard's baptismal entry from 1564 and his burial notice from 1616.

Old Town. ℂ **01789/266316.** Church, free; Shakespeare's tomb, donation £1 ($1.85) adults, 50p (95¢) students. Apr–Oct Mon–Sat 8:30am–6pm, Sun 12:30–5pm; Mar Mon–Sat 9am–5pm, Sun 12:30–5pm; winter Mon–Sat 9am–4pm, Sun 12:30–5pm. Walk 4 min. past the Royal Shakespeare Theatre with the river on your left.

**Mary Arden's House & the Shakespeare Countryside Museum** 🏵  So what if millions of visitors over the years have been tricked into thinking that this timber-framed farmhouse, with its old stone dovecote and various out-buildings, was the girlhood home of Shakespeare's mother, Mary Arden? It's still one of the most intriguing sights outside Stratford, even if historian Dr. Nat Alcock discovered in 2000 that Arden's actual childhood home was the brick farmhouse, Glebe Farm, next door. The confusion was the result of a tour guide's ruse. In the 18th century, tour guide John Jordan decided that Glebe Farm was too unimpressive to be the home of the Bard's mother, so he told tourists that it was this farmstead instead. In actuality, the so-called Mary Arden's House wasn't constructed until the late 16th century, a little late to be the home of the Bard's mother. Visit it anyway, as it contains interesting country furniture and domestic utensils. In the barns, stable, cowshed, and farmyard you'll find an extensive collection of farming implements that give a window into life and work in the local countryside from Shakespeare's time to the present.

Wilmcote. ℂ **01789/204016.** Admission £5.70 ($11) adults, £5 ($9.25) students and seniors, £2.50 ($4.65) children, family ticket £14 ($25). Nov–Mar Mon–Sat 10am–4pm, Sun 10:30am–4pm; Apr–May Mon–Sat 10am–5pm, Sun 10:30am–5pm; June–Aug Mon–Sat 9:30am–5pm, Sun 10am–5pm; Sept–Oct Mon–Sat 10am–5pm, Sun 10:30am–5pm. Closed Dec 23–26. Take A3400 (Birmingham) for 5.5km (3½ miles).

**New Place/Nash's House**  Shakespeare retired to New Place in 1610, a pros-perous man by the standards of his day, and died here 6 years later. Regrettably, the house was torn down, so only the garden remains. A mulberry tree planted by the Bard was so popular with latter-day visitors to Stratford that the garden's cantankerous owner chopped it down. The mulberry tree that grows here today is said to have been planted from a cutting of the original tree. You enter the gardens through Nash's House (Thomas Nash married Elizabeth Hall, a grand-daughter of Shakespeare). Nash's House has 16th-century period rooms and an exhibition illustrating the history of Stratford. The lovely Knott Garden adjoins the site and represents the style of a fashionable Elizabethan garden.

Chapel St. ℂ **01789/204016.** Admission £3.50 ($6.50) adults, £3 ($5.55) seniors and students, £1.70 ($3.15) children, £9 ($17) family ticket (2 adults, 3 children) for all 5 Shakespeare-related houses. Nov–Mar daily 11am–4pm; Apr–May daily 11am–5pm; June–Aug Mon–Sat 9:30am–5pm, Sun 10am–5pm; Sept–Oct daily 11am–5pm. Closed Dec 23–26. Walk west down High St.; Chapel St. is a continuation of High St.

**Shakespeare's Birthplace** 🏵  The son of a glover and leather worker, the Bard was born on St. George's Day, April 23, 1564, and died on the same date 52 years later. Filled with Shakespeare memorabilia, this half-timbered structure dates from the first part of the 16th century. It was bought by public donors in 1847 and pre-served as a national shrine. You can visit the bedroom where Shakespeare was probably born, a fully equipped kitchen of the period (look for the "babyminder"), and the Shakespeare Museum, illustrating the Bard's life and times. Walk through the garden, planted with all of the flowers mentioned in the plays. You won't be alone: It's estimated that some 660,000 visitors pass through the house annually.

Built next door to Shakespeare's birth home to commemorate the 400th anniversary of the Bard's birth, the Shakespeare Centre serves both as the administrative headquarters of the Trust and as a library and study center. An extension houses a visitor center, which acts as a reception area for all those coming to the birthplace.

Henley St. (in the town center near the post office, close to Union St.). *C* **01789/204016**. Admission £6.50 ($12) adults, £5.50 ($10) students and seniors, £2.60 ($4.80) children, £15 ($28) family ticket (2 adults, 3 children) for all 5 Shakespeare-related houses. Nov–Mar Mon–Sat 10am–4pm, Sun 10:30am–4pm; Apr–May Mon–Sat 10am–4pm, Sun 10:30am–5pm; June–Aug Mon–Sat 9am–5pm, Sun 9:30am–5pm; Sept–Oct Mon–Sat 10am–5pm, Sun 10:30am–5pm. Closed Dec 23–26.

## GUIDED TOURS

Guided tours of Stratford-upon-Avon are conducted by **City Sightseeing,** Civic Hall, Rother Street. In summer, open-top double-decker buses depart every 15 minutes daily from 9am to 6pm. You can take a 1-hour ride without stops, or you can get off at any or all of the town's five Shakespeare properties. Though the bus stops are clearly marked along the historic route, the most logical starting point is the sidewalk in front of the Pen & Parchment Pub, at the bottom of Bridge Street. Tour tickets are valid all day so you can hop on and off the buses as many times as you want. The tours cost £8.50 ($16) for adults, £6 ($11) for seniors or students, and £3.50 ($6.50) for children under 12. A family ticket sells for £20 ($36), and children under 5 go free.

## GOING TO THE PLAYS

On the banks of the Avon, the **Royal Shakespeare Theatre,** Waterside, Stratford-upon-Avon CV37 6BB (*C* **01789/403403**), is a major showcase for the Royal Shakespeare Company and seats 1,500 patrons. The theater's season runs from November to September and typically features five Shakespearean plays. The company has some of the finest actors on the British stage.

You usually need **ticket reservations,** with two successive booking periods, each one opening about 2 months in advance. You can pick these up from a North American or English travel agent. A small number of tickets are always held for sale on the day of a performance, but it may be too late to get a good seat if you wait until you arrive in Stratford. Tickets can be booked through **Keith Prowse** (*C* **800/223-6108** in North America or 020/7014-8550 in London; www.keithprowse.com).

You can also call the **theater box office** directly (*C* **0870/6091110**) and charge your tickets. The box office is open Monday through Saturday from 9am to 8pm, although it closes at 6pm on days when there are no performances. Seat prices range from £8 to £50 ($15–$93). You can make a credit card reservation and pick up your tickets on the performance day, but you must cancel at least 1 full week in advance to get a refund.

Opened in 1986, the **Swan Theatre** is architecturally connected to the back of its older counterpart and shares the same box office, address, and phone number. It seats 425 on three sides of the stage, as in an Elizabethan playhouse, an appropriate design for plays by Shakespeare and his contemporaries. The Swan presents a repertoire of about five plays each season, with tickets ranging from £10 to £36 ($19–$67).

Within the Swan Theatre is a **painting gallery,** which has a basic collection of portraits of famous actors and scenes from Shakespeare's plays by 18th- and 19th-century artists. It also operates as a base for **guided tours,** with lively running commentary through the world-famous theaters. Guided tours are conducted

Monday through Saturday at 1:30 and 5:30pm, and four times every Sunday afternoon, production schedules permitting. Tours cost £4 ($7.40) for adults and £3 ($5.55) for students, seniors, or children. Call ahead for tour scheduling, which is subject to change.

## WHERE TO STAY

During the theater season, it's best to reserve in advance. The Tourist Information Centre (part of the national "Book-a-Bed-Ahead" service, which enables visitors to make reservations in advance) will help find accommodations in all ranges. The fee for any room reservations that the service makes is 10% of the first night's stay (bed-and-breakfast rate only), deductible from the visitor's final bill.

## VERY EXPENSIVE

**Welcombe Hotel** ✦✦✦  For a formal, historic hotel in Stratford, there's nothing better than the Welcombe. One of England's great Jacobean country houses, this hotel is a 10-minute ride from the heart of Stratford-upon-Avon. Its key feature is an 18-hole golf course. It's surrounded by 63 hectares (156 acres) of grounds and has a formal entrance on Warwick Road, a winding driveway leading to the main hall. Bedrooms are luxuriously furnished in traditional Jacobean style, with fine antiques and elegant fabrics. Most bedrooms are seemingly big enough for tennis matches, but those in the garden wing, although comfortable, are small. Some of the bedrooms are sumptuously furnished with elegant four-posters, and all of them have deluxe linens and well-kept bathrooms with shower-tub combinations.

Warwick Rd., Stratford-upon-Avon, Warwickshire CV37 0NR. ℂ 01789/295252. Fax 01789/414666. www. welcombe.co.uk. 66 units. £150–£250 ($278–$463) double; £275–£450 ($509–$833) suite. Rates include English breakfast. AE, DC, MC, V. Take A439 2km (1¼ miles) northeast of the town center. **Amenities:** Restaurant; bar; golf course; tennis court; 24-hr. room service; laundry service/dry cleaning; rooms for those w/limited mobility. *In room:* TV, hair dryer, iron/ironing board (in some).

## EXPENSIVE

**Alveston Manor Hotel** ✦✦  This Tudor manor is perfect for theatergoers—it's just a 5-minute walk from the theaters. The hotel has a wealth of chimneys and gables, and everything from an Elizabethan gazebo to Queen Anne windows. Mentioned in the *Domesday Book,* the building predates the arrival of William the Conqueror. The rooms in the manor will appeal to those who appreciate the old-world charm of slanted floors, overhead beams, and antique furnishings. Some triples or quads are available in the modern section, connected by a covered walk through the rear garden. Most rooms here have built-in walnut furniture and a color-coordinated decor; 15 are set aside for nonsmokers. All come equipped with well-maintained bathrooms with shower-tub combinations. Your opinion of this hotel will depend on your room assignment. You can live in luxury in the original rooms with their walnut furniture, or be assigned a rather routine standard twin that, though comfortable, will lack romance. Ask for an original.

Clopton Bridge (off B4066), Stratford-upon-Avon, Warwickshire CV37 7HP. ℂ 800/225-5843 in the U.S. and Canada, or 0870/400-8181. Fax 01789/414095. www.macdonald-hotels.co.uk. 113 units. £125–£160 ($231–$296) double; £195–£230 ($361–$426) suite. AE, DC, MC, V. **Amenities:** Restaurant; bar; indoor pool; gym; sauna; 24-hr. room service; babysitting; laundry service/dry cleaning; rooms for those w/limited mobility. *In room:* TV, minibar, coffeemaker, hair dryer, iron/ironing board.

**Stratford Moat House** ✦  Moat House stands on ample landscaped lawns on the banks of the River Avon near Clopton Bridge. Although it lacks the charm of the Alveston Manor, as far as amenities go, this modern hotel is on the same level as the Welcombe. It's one of the flagships of Queens Moat Houses, a British hotel chain, built in the early 1970s and renovated in 1995. Every room has a high standard of comfort, especially the bathrooms, which feature generous shelf space and shower-tub combinations.

Bridgefoot, Stratford-upon-Avon, Warwickshire CV37 6YR. ℰ **01789/279988.** Fax 01789/298589. www. moathousehotels.com. 251 units. £120 ($222) double; £200 ($370) suite. AE, DC, MC, V. **Amenities:** 2 restaurants; 2 bars; heated indoor pool; exercise room; spa; sauna; room service; laundry service. *In room:* TV, dataport, coffeemaker, hair dryer, iron/ironing board, safe, trouser press.

## MODERATE

**Falcon**  This inn blends the very old and the very new. The black-and-white timbered inn was licensed a quarter of a century after Shakespeare's death; connected to its rear by a glass passageway is a more sterile bedroom extension added in 1970. In the heart of Stratford, the inn faces the Guild Chapel and the New Place Gardens. The recently upgraded rooms in the older section have oak beams, diamond leaded-glass windows, antiques, and good reproductions. Bathrooms aren't special; some have brown linoleum floors and plastic shower-tub enclosures.

In the inn's intimate **Merlin Lounge,** you'll find an open copper-hooded fireplace where fires are stoked under beams salvaged from old ships. The **Oak Bar** is a forest of weathered beams, and on either side of the stone fireplace is paneling removed from the Bard's last home, New Place.

Chapel St., Stratford-upon-Avon, Warwickshire CV37 6HA. ℰ **01789/279953.** Fax 01789/414260. www. corushotels.com/thefalcon. 84 units. £80–£125 ($148–$231) double; from £140 ($259) suite. AE, DC, MC, V. **Amenities:** Restaurant; 3 bars; 24-hr. room service; rooms for those w/limited mobility. *In room:* TV, dataport, coffeemaker, hair dryer.

**Grosvenor Hotel**  A pair of Georgian town houses, built in 1832 and 1843, join together to form this hotel, which is one of the second-tier choices in Stratford, on equal footing with the Thistle Stratford-upon-Avon (below). In the center of town, with lawns and gardens to the rear, it is a short stroll from the intersection of Bridge Street and Waterside, allowing easy access to the Avon River, Bancroft Gardens, and the Royal Shakespeare Theatre. There is a rambling ground floor that has tremendous character—it reminds us of an elegant English country house, with small intimate lounges and open fires. **The Garden** Restaurant, with its hand-painted mural, serves a Continental and British menu. Bedrooms are midsize to spacious, each personally designed with a high standard of tasteful modern furnishings. Rooms are not overly adorned or stylish, but they're snug and cozy. All bedrooms have small bathrooms with well-maintained showers.

12–14 Warwick Rd., Stratford-upon-Avon, Warwickshire CV37 6YT. ℰ **01789/269213.** Fax 01789/266087. 67 units. £88–£114 ($163–$211) double; £164 ($303) suite. AE, MC, V. **Amenities:** Restaurant; bar; free pass to nearby recreation center; 24-hr. room service; babysitting; laundry service; nonsmoking rooms; rooms for those w/limited mobility. *In room:* TV, dataport, coffeemaker, hair dryer, iron/ironing board, safe (in some), trouser press.

**Thistle Stratford-upon-Avon** 🗶  Theatergoers flock to this Georgian-townhouse-style hotel, located across the street from the entrance to the Royal Shakespeare and Swan theatres. The hotel's redbrick main section dates from the Regency period, although over the years a handful of adjacent buildings were included in the hotel and an uninspired modern extension was added. Today, the interior has a well-upholstered lounge and bar, a covered garden terrace, and comfortable but narrow bedrooms. Though small, rooms have a sitting area with a couple of armchairs and round side tables, plus twin beds (for the most part). Sometimes a room is graced with a four-poster bed. The bathrooms are small but efficient, with a shower-and-tub combination.

44 Waterside, Stratford-upon-Avon, Warwickshire CV37 6BA. © **0870/333-9146.** Fax 0870/333-9246. www. stratfordthistle.co.uk. 63 units. £73–£179 ($135–$331) double. AE, DC, MC, V. **Amenities:** Restaurant; bar; 24-hr. room service; laundry service; dry cleaning. *In room:* TV, dataport, coffeemaker, hair dryer, iron, trouser press.

**White Swan**   This cozy, intimate hotel, housed in Stratford's oldest building, is one of the most atmospheric in Stratford. In business for more than a century before Shakespeare appeared on the scene, it competes successfully with the Falcon (above) in offering an ancient atmosphere. The gabled medieval front would present the Bard with no surprises, but the modern comforts inside would surely astonish him. Many of the rooms have been well preserved despite the addition of modern conveniences. Paintings dating from 1550 hang on the lounge walls. All bedrooms are well appointed; bathrooms are small but have tub-and-shower combinations.

Rother St., Stratford-upon-Avon, Warwickshire CV37 6NH. © **01789/297022.** Fax 01789/268773. www. e-travelguide.info/whiteswan. 41 units. £80 ($148) double. Rates include English breakfast. AE, DC, MC, V. **Amenities:** Restaurant; bar; limited room service. *In room:* TV; dataport (in some), coffeemaker, hair dryer, trouser press.

## INEXPENSIVE

**Sequoia House** *(Value*   This privately run hotel stands in its own beautiful garden across the Avon opposite the Royal Shakespeare Theatre, conveniently located for visiting the major Shakespeare sites. Renovations have vastly improved the house, which was created from two late-Victorian buildings. Bedrooms retain some Victorian features and come in various shapes and sizes. Bedrooms have fine beds and are warmly decorated and color-coordinated. Bathrooms are small, seven with a shower-and-tub combination, the others with a stall shower only.

51–53 Shipston Rd., Stratford-upon-Avon, Warwickshire CV37 7LN. © **01789/268852.** Fax 01789/414559. www.sequoiahotel.co.uk. 23 units. £79–£89 ($146–$165) double. Rates include English breakfast. MC, V. **Amenities:** Bar. *In room:* TV, coffeemaker, hair dryer.

**Stratheden Hotel**   A short walk north of the Royal Shakespeare Theatre, this hotel is tucked away on a plot of land that was first mentioned in a property deed in 1333. Built in 1673, it is the oldest remaining brick building in the town center, with a tiny rear garden and top-floor rooms with slanted, beamed ceilings. It has improved again in both decor and comfort with the addition of fresh paint, new curtains, and good beds. Units are small, but each comes with a comfortable bed and small bathroom. Three units have only a tub; the rest have showers.

5 Chapel St., Stratford-upon-Avon, Warwickshire CV37 6EP. © and fax **01789/297119.** www.ukstay.com/ warwick/stratheden. 9 units. £66–£72 ($122–$133) double. Rates include full English breakfast. AE, MC, V. **Amenities:** Breakfast room. *In room:* TV.

**Victoria Spa Lodge**   This B&B is old fashioned and atmospheric. Opened in 1837, the year Queen Victoria ascended to the throne, this was the first establishment to be given her name, and it is still going strong. This lodge was originally a spa frequented by the queen's eldest daughter, Princess Vicky. The accommodating hosts offer tastefully decorated, comfortable bedrooms. The small bathrooms are neatly organized with a shower stall. No smoking.

Bishopton Lane (2.5km/1½ miles north of the town center where A3400 intersects A46), Stratford-upon-Avon, Warwickshire CV37 9QY. © **01789/267985.** Fax 01789/204728. www.stratford-upon-avon.co.uk/victoriaspa.htm. 7 units. £65 ($120) double; £80 ($148) for 3; £100 ($185) for 5-person family suite. Rates include English breakfast. MC, V. *In room:* TV, coffeemaker, hair dryer.

## WHERE TO DINE
### EXPENSIVE

**Callands** ★★ ECLECTIC/INTERNATIONAL   At last Stratford boasts a restaurant worth writing home about. In the town center between the Shakespeare Centre and Market Place, Callands was installed in a 16th-century building. Here Callands offers good food in what had been a gastronomic wasteland in England (except for our recommendations, of course!). Extremely professional cooking, vivid use of spices, imaginative menus, and reasonable prices attract a never-ending stream of visitors and locals alike. We like experiments with Asian flavors and spices, and the chefs always get the balance right. Is this the Stratford of yore, you ask, as you taste the aromatic pumpkin and Cerny cheese tagliatelle with almond pesto, tomato, and candied eggplant? Grilled vegetables in lemon oil with rosemary chickpeas and saffron couscous are followed by cashew-nut and herb risotto with wilted rocket and shaved Parmesan. Even such English classics as bubble-and-squeak (cabbage and potatoes) are given added zest by an orange Dubonnet sauce.

13–14 Meer St. ⓒ **01789/269304.** Fixed-price lunch 2-course £19 ($35), 3-course £24 ($44). Main courses £12–£18 ($22–$33). AE, DC, MC, V. Tues–Sat noon–2pm and 5:45–10:30pm.

**Quarto's** FRENCH/ITALIAN/TRADITIONAL ENGLISH   This restaurant enjoys the best location in town—it's in the Royal Shakespeare Theatre itself—with glass walls providing an unobstructed view of the swans on the Avon. You can partake of an intermission snack of smoked salmon and champagne or dine by flickering candlelight after the performance. Many dishes, such as apple-and-parsnip soup, are definitely old English; others reflect a Continental touch, such as fried polenta with filets of pigeon and bacon. For your main course, you might select Dover sole, salami of wild boar, pheasant, or roast pork loin, among other offerings.

In the Royal Shakespeare Theatre, Waterside. ⓒ **01789/403415.** Reservations required. Matinee lunch £18 ($33); dinner £16–£22 ($30–$41). AE, MC, V. Thurs and Sat noon–2:30pm; Mon–Sat 5:30pm–midnight. Closed when theater is shut down.

### MODERATE

**Thai Boathouse** ★ THAI   The only restaurant set on the Avon, this charming choice is reached by crossing Clopton Bridge toward Oxford and Banbury. The second-floor dining room opens onto vistas of the river. This restaurant, originally established 4 decades ago in Bangkok, has brought spice and zest to Stratford's lazy restaurant scene. The decor comes from Thailand itself, with elephants, woodcarvings, and Buddhas adorning the restaurant. Seasonal specialties such as wild duck and pheasant are a special feature of the menu. Fresh produce, great skill in the kitchen, and exquisite presentations are the hallmarks of this restaurant. Sample a selection of authentic Thai appetizers before going on to such delectable main courses as fresh sea bass in lemon grass or a salmon stir-fry with curry sauce and coconut cream served over charcoal-grilled banana and lime leaves. One of our favorites is their lamb in yellow curry with potatoes, onions, and cashew nuts.

Swan's Nest Lane. ⓒ **01789/297733.** Reservations recommended. Fixed-price menus £21–£27 ($39–$50); main courses £5.50–£12 ($10–$22). MC, V. Daily noon–2:30pm and 5:30–10:30pm.

### INEXPENSIVE

**The Oppo** INTERNATIONAL   Located in the heart of Stratford within a 16th-century building, this refreshingly unpretentious restaurant serves up good bistro cooking at reasonable prices. Menu choices include breast of chicken with banana roasted in lime butter, basmati rice with a mild curry sauce, or salmon fish cakes served on a bed of spinach.

13 Sheep St. ℂ **01789/269980.** Reservations recommended. Main courses £8.50–£18 ($16–$33). MC, V. Daily noon–2pm and 5–10:30pm.

## PUBS

**The Black Swan**   Affectionately known as "The Dirty Duck," this has been a popular hangout for Stratford players since the 18th century. The wall is lined with autographed photos of famous patrons, such as Lord Olivier. The front lounge and bar crackle with intense conversation; in the spring and fall, an open fire blazes. Typical English grills are featured in the Grill Room, which has never been accused of serving the best food in Stratford. Main dishes include goose pie, roast chicken, or honey-roasted duck. In fair weather, you can have drinks in the front garden and watch the swans glide by on the Avon.

Waterside. ℂ **01789/297312.** Reservations required for dining. Main courses £8–£16 ($15–$30); bar snacks £5–£7.25 ($9.25–$13). AE, DC, MC, V (in the restaurant only). Daily 11am–11pm. No dinner Sun.

**The Garrick Inn**   Near Harvard House, this black-and-white timbered Elizabethan pub, dating from 1595, has an unpretentious charm. The front bar is decorated with tapestry-covered settles, an old oak refectory table, and an open fireplace that attracts the locals. The back bar has a circular fireplace with a copper hood and mementos of the triumphs of the English stage. Specialties are homemade pies such as steak and ale, steak and kidney, or cottage pie.

25 High St. ℂ **01789/292186.** Main courses £6.50–£13 ($12–$24). MC, V. Meals daily noon–9pm. Pub Mon–Sat 11am–11pm; Sun noon–10:30pm.

**White Swan**   Housed in the town's oldest building, this is one of the most atmospheric pubs in Stratford. As you step inside, you're drawn into a world of cushioned leather armchairs, old oak paneling, and fireplaces. You're likely to meet a worthy cross-section of amiable drinkers in a setting once enjoyed by Shakespeare himself, when it was known as the Kings Head. At lunch you can partake of the hot dishes of the day, along with fresh salads and sandwiches (all self-service). Steaks, pies, and fried fish are on the menu for dinner.

In The White Swan hotel, Rother St. ℂ **01789/297022.** Dinner reservations recommended. Bar snacks £3.95–£15 ($7.30–$28); fixed-price 3-course Sun lunch £6.95 ($13). AE, DC, MC, V. Morning coffee daily 9am–noon; self-service bar snacks daily 12:30–3pm; afternoon tea daily 2–5:30pm; hot meals noon–2:30pm and 5:30–9:30pm.

# Index

See also Accommodations, Restaurant, and Afternoon Tea indexes, below.

## AFTERNOON TEA

# Not just 4 anoraks

...but 3 duffel coats
59 gorgeous models
5 Tube simulators
4 dead man's handles
3 mucky miners
and 1 brilliant time had by all.

## ... be *moved*

kids go FREE

London's Transport Museum
Covent Garden Piazza

www.ltmuseum.co.uk

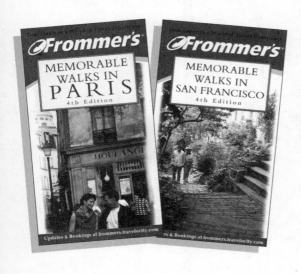

# Great Trips Like Great Days Begin with a Plan

### FranklinCovey and Frommer's Bring You *Frommer's Favorite Places®* Planner

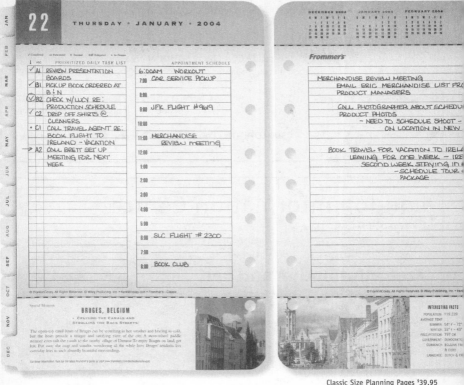

Classic Size Planning Pages $39.95

The planning experts at FranklinCovey have teamed up with the travel experts at Frommer's. The result is a full-year travel-themed planner filled with rich images and travel tips covering fifty-two of Frommer's Favorite Places.

- Each week will make you an expert about an intriguing corner of the world
- New facts and tips every day
- Beautiful, full-color photos of some of the most beautiful places on earth
- Proven planning tools from FranklinCovey for keeping track of tasks, appointments, notes, address/phone numbers, and more

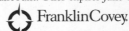

# 0800 LONDON®

## LONDON'S FREE TELEPHONE BOOKING SERVICE

You can now call **FREE** on **0800 LONDON** for London information and to book discounted rates for London hotels, theatre and sightseeing.

Advisors available every day from 8am to midnight.
From outside the UK dial **+44 800 LONDON**

**0800 LONDON - London's Free Telephone Booking Service**

---

# London Information Centre™
## LEICESTER SQUARE

## Free information and half price hotels. Every day.

Visit us in person in the centre of Leicester Square or call us on **020 729 22 333**.
From outside the UK call **+44 20 729 22 333**.

London Information Centre, Leicester Square, London
Open every day from 8am to 11pm

---

.com™

The number one internet site for London offers essential information to help organise the perfect visit to London. Guaranteed lowest rates on London's leading hotels and information on 15,000 reviewed and quality assessed London products and services.

**You can now also book over the phone on 0207 437 4370**
**From outside the UK call +44 207 437 4370**

### The #1 Internet Site for London™
*Over 30 million customers served*

## FROMMER'S® NATIONAL PARK GUIDES

Algonquin Provincial Park
Banff & Jasper
Family Vacations in the National
  Parks

Grand Canyon
National Parks of the American
  West
Rocky Mountain

Yellowstone & Grand Teton
Yosemite & Sequoia/Kings
  Canyon
Zion & Bryce Canyon

## FROMMER'S® MEMORABLE WALKS

Chicago
London

New York
Paris

San Francisco

## FROMMER'S® WITH KIDS GUIDES

Chicago
Las Vegas
New York City

Ottawa
San Francisco
Toronto

Vancouver
Walt Disney World® & Orlando
Washington, D.C.

## SUZY GERSHMAN'S BORN TO SHOP GUIDES

Born to Shop: France
Born to Shop: Hong Kong,
  Shanghai & Beijing

Born to Shop: Italy
Born to Shop: London

Born to Shop: New York
Born to Shop: Paris

## FROMMER'S® IRREVERENT GUIDES

Amsterdam
Boston
Chicago
Las Vegas
London

Los Angeles
Manhattan
New Orleans
Paris
Rome

San Francisco
Seattle & Portland
Vancouver
Walt Disney World®
Washington, D.C.

## FROMMER'S® BEST-LOVED DRIVING TOURS

Austria
Britain
California
France

Germany
Ireland
Italy
New England

Northern Italy
Scotland
Spain
Tuscany & Umbria

## THE UNOFFICIAL GUIDES®

Beyond Disney
Central Italy
Chicago
Cruises
Disneyland®
England
Florida
Florida with Kids
Inside Disney

Hawaii
Las Vegas
London
Maui
Mexico's Best Beach Resorts
Mini Las Vegas
Mini-Mickey
New Orleans
New York City

Paris
San Francisco
Skiing & Snowboarding in the
  West
Walt Disney World®
Walt Disney World® for
  Grown-ups
Walt Disney World® with Kids
Washington, D.C.

## SPECIAL-INTEREST TITLES

Athens Past & Present
Cities Ranked & Rated
Frommer's Best Day Trips from London
Frommer's Caribbean Hideaways
Frommer's China: The 50 Most Memorable Trips
Frommer's Exploring America by RV
Frommer's Gay & Lesbian Europe
Frommer's Best RV and Tent Campgrounds
  in the U.S.A.

Frommer's Road Atlas Europe
Frommer's Road Atlas France
Frommer's Road Atlas Ireland
Frommer's Wonderful Weekends from
  New York City
The New York Times' Guide to Unforgettable
  Weekends
Retirement Places Rated
Rome Past & Present

*Travel Tip:* He who finds the best hotel deal has more to spend on facials involving knobbly vegetables.

Hello, the Roaming Gnome here. I've been nabbed from the garden and taken round the world. The people who took me are so terribly clever. They find the best offerings on Travelocity. For very little cha-ching. And that means I get to be pampered and exfoliated till I'm pink as a bunny's doodah.

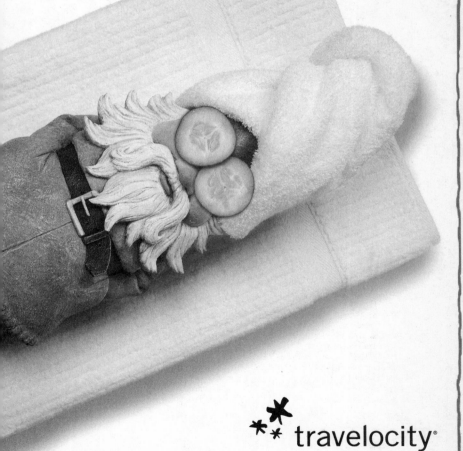

✳ travelocity®

1-888-TRAVELOCITY / travelocity.com / America Online Keyword: Travel

Travel Tip: Make sure there's customer service for any change of plans — involving friendly natives, for example.

One can plan and plan, but if you don't book with the right people you can't seize le moment and canoodle with the poodle named Pansy. I, for one, am all for fraternizing with the locals. Better yet, if I need to extend my stay and my gnome nappers are willing, it can all be arranged through the 800 number at, oh look, how convenient, the lovely company coat of arms.

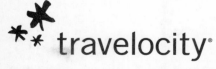

**travelocity**®

1-888-TRAVELOCITY | travelocity.com | America Online Keyword: Travel